The Pre-Raphaelites and Italy

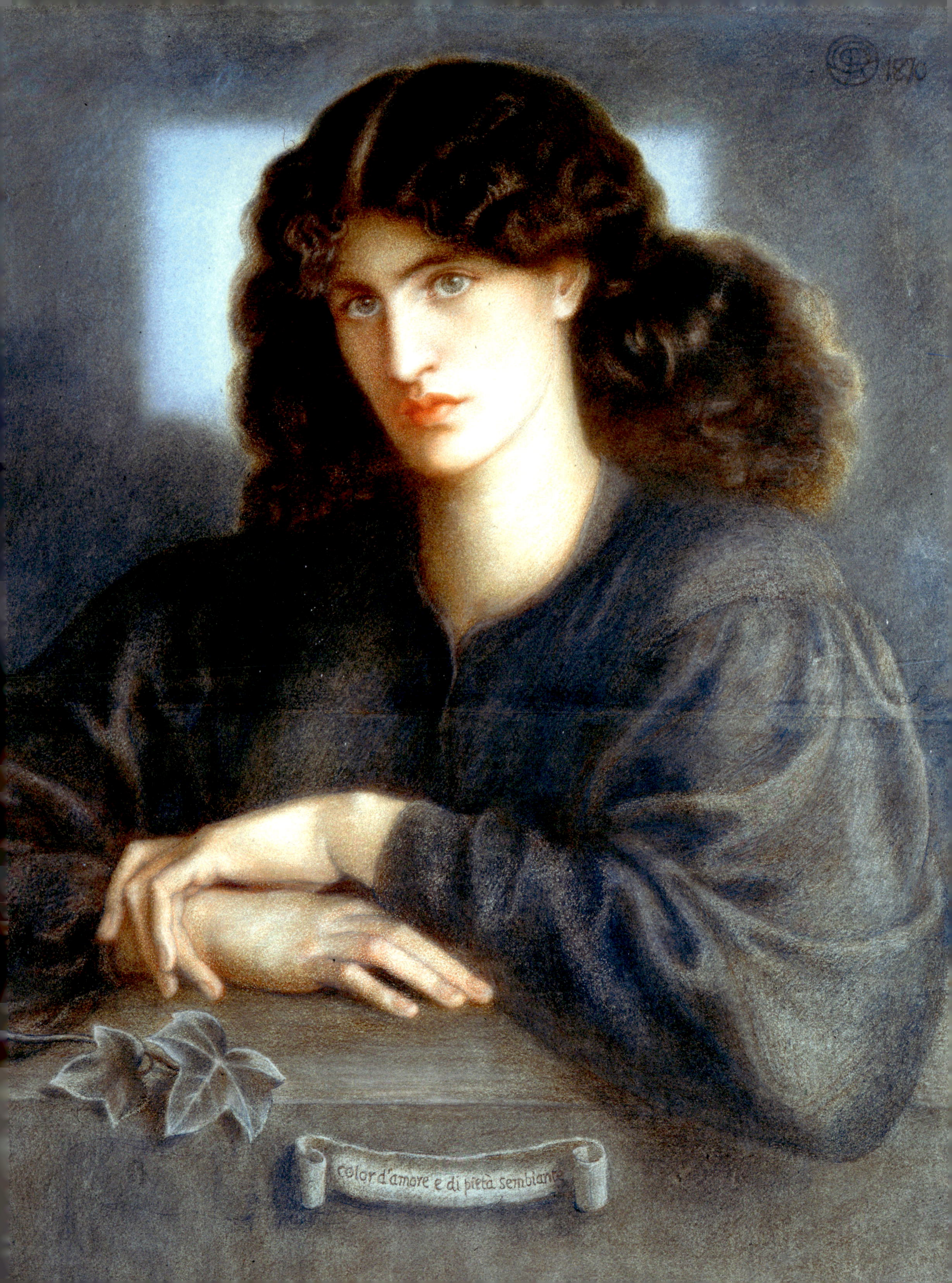
1870
Color d'amore e di pietà sembiante

The Pre-Raphaelites and Italy

Colin Harrison and Christopher Newall
with essays by Maurizio Isabella and Martin McLaughlin

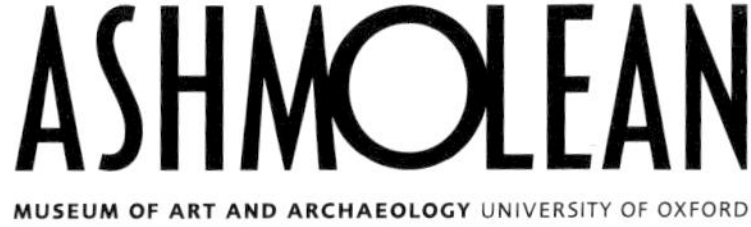

2010

The Pre-Raphaelites and Italy

Ashmolean Museum, University of Oxford
16th September 2010 to 5th December 2010
Proudly sponsored by Minoli, Coutts & Co, and the Friends of the Ashmolean Museum.

British Library Cataloguing in Publications Data

A catalogue record for this book is available from the British Library

EAN 13: 978 1 85444 250 5 (paperback edition)

Catalogue designed by Vermillion Design
Typeset in Minion Pro and ITC Galliard
Printed and bound in Belgium by Deckers Snoeck Ltd.

Front cover illustration: *Music* by Edward Burne-Jones (1833–1898) (Ashmolean Museum, University of Oxford, WA2008.15)
Half-title *verso* image: *La Donna della Finestra* by Dante Gabriel Rossetti (1828–1882), Bradford Art Galleries and Museums

For further details of Ashmolean titles please visit:
www.ashmolean.org/shop

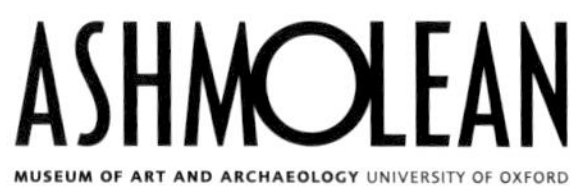

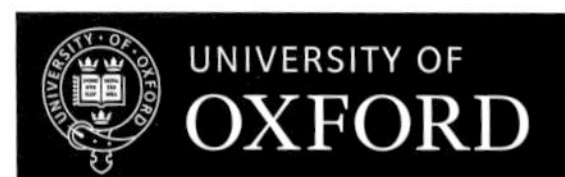

This Exhibition has been organised by the Ashmolean Museum, University of Oxford and Museo d'Arte della Città di Ravenna and would not have been possible without the generosity of the lenders.

We are grateful to the private collectors and the staff of the institutions listed below, as well as to a number of private lenders who prefer to remain anonymous:

Dr Richard Dorment
Castle Howard Collection, Yorkshire,
courtesy of the Hon. Simon Howard
Sir Stephen Oliver
Lord Lloyd-Webber

Girton College, Cambridge
Somerville College, Oxford

Aberdeen Art Gallery
Birmingham Museum & Art Gallery
Department of Prints & Drawings, British Museum
Bury Art Gallery, Museum + Archives
Cartwright Hall, Bradford Museums
Royal Institution of Cornwall, Royal Museum Of Cornwall, Truro
Fitzwilliam Museum, University of Cambridge
Government Art Collection UK
Leeds City Art Gallery
Lady Lever Gallery, National Museums Liverpool
Manchester City Galleries
St Paul's Within the Walls, Rome
Ruskin Foundation, Ruskin Library, Lancaster University
Schaeffer Collection, courtesy of Nevill Keating Pictures
National Galleries of Scotland
Museums Sheffield
Whitworth Art Gallery, University of Manchester
Tate
Victoria & Albert Museum

The Ashmolean Museum is especially grateful to Martin Beisly, Dr Judith Bronkhurst, Marion Dawson Carr, Susanna Fergusson, Robert Holden, Thomas Loyd, Sarah Miller, Gabriel Naughton, Paul Nicholls, Dr Christiana Payne, Simon Reynolds, Alison Smith, Professor Stephen Wildman and Andrew Wyld for their advice and assistance.

Exhibition Curators: Colin Harrison and Christopher Newall in consultation with Claudio Spadoni.

Exhibition Organisation: Claudia Casali, Davide Caroli, Nadia Ceroni (Ravenna) and Aisha Burtenshaw, Stella Ditschkovski, Jevon Thistlewood, Agnes Valenčak (Oxford)
Photographic Co-ordination: Ashmolean Photo Studio and Picture Library
Catalogue: Emily Jolliffe and Declan McCarthy

Contents

Preface 1

Introduction: The Pre-Raphaelites and Italy 3

The Pre-Raphaelites and Italian Art before and after Raphael 10
Colin Harrison

The Pre-Raphaelites and Italian Literature 22
Martin McLaughlin

Interlocking Patriotisms: Italy and England in the Long Nineteenth Century 36
Maurizio Isabella

Catalogue

I Themes from Italian Literature and History 43

II Ruskin and Italy 65

III Ruskin's Disciples in Italy 91

IV Other Pre-Raphaelite Travellers in Italy 131

V Giovanni Costa and The Etruscans—Painters of the Italian Landscape 155

VI Aestheticism—The Inspiration of the Renaissance 183

VII Burne-Jones's Designs for the American Church in Rome 199

Bibliography 212

Index of works 214

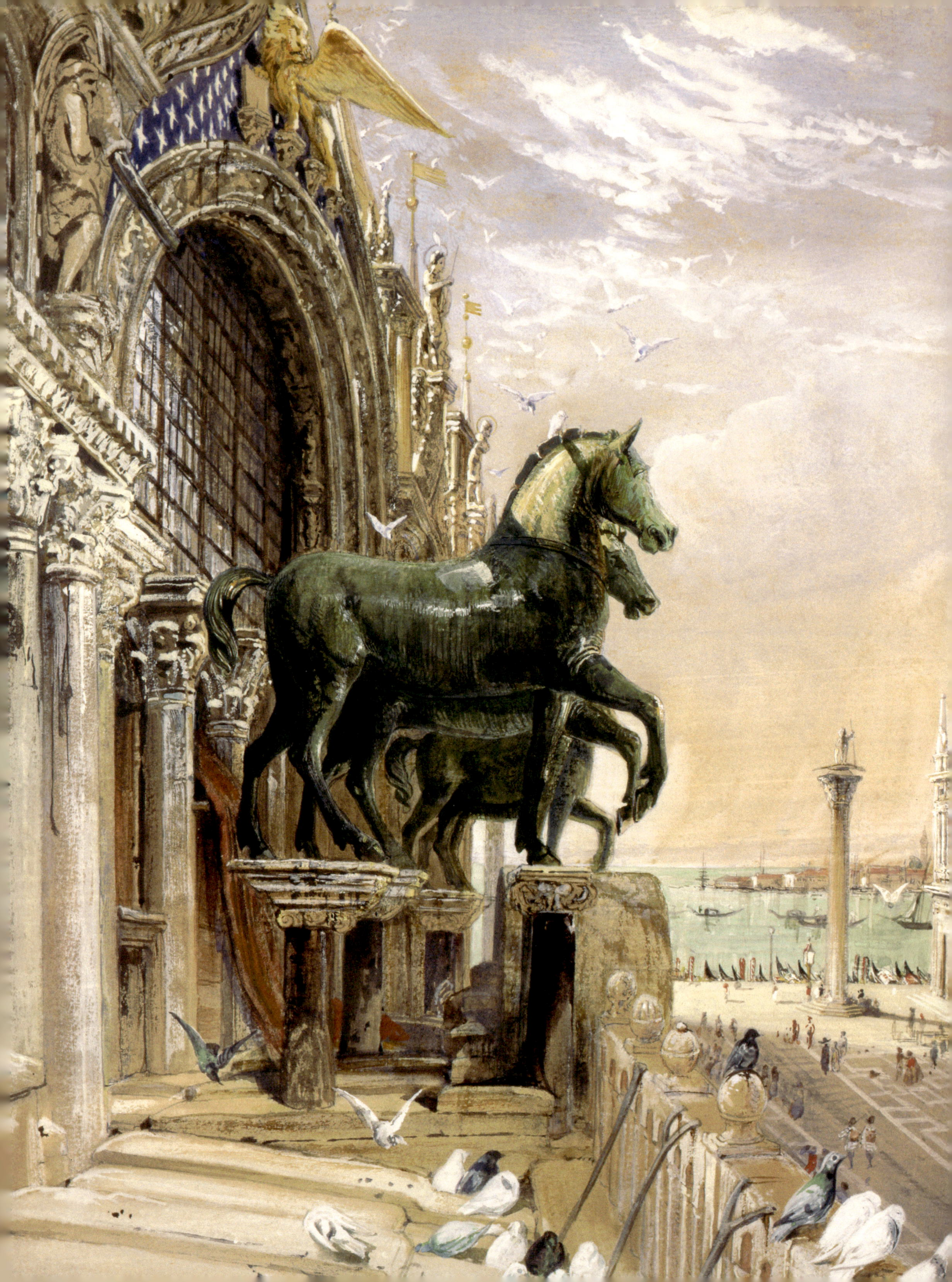

Preface

The original members of the Pre-Raphaelite Brotherhood were closely associated with Oxford, and, since the bequest of the pioneering collection of Thomas Combe in 1894, the Ashmolean Museum has housed one of the principal collections of works by the Pre-Raphaelites and their followers and associates. Although they have not always been fashionable, the Pre-Raphaelite pictures are now among the most popular in the Ashmolean. We were therefore delighted when Christopher Newall suggested that we should collaborate on an exhibition on the theme of the Pre-Raphaelites and Italy with the Museo Civico d'Arte di Ravenna: not only is the subject one that has never been comprehensively explored, but it is also central to the very meaning of the term 'Pre-Raphaelite' and its usage and dissemination, in both Great Britain and Italy. The figure of John Ruskin looms large, and, once again, we are proud to be able to underline the association of one of the most influential of nineteenth-century writers and thinkers with his university.

The Pre-Raphaelites have been the subject of several major exhibitions in recent years, with more planned in the near future. The major works are thus in considerable demand for loan. We are enormously grateful to the museums and private collectors who have generously agreed to lend to the exhibition. We are especially indebted to Tate, the Sheffield Galleries and Museums Trust, Birmingham Museums and Art Gallery, the Victoria and Albert Museum, and our sister institution in Cambridge, the Fitzwilliam Museum. Through the generosity of private lenders, in particular Lord Lloyd Webber, we are able for the first time to illustrate one of Burne-Jones's greatest projects, the decoration of the American Church in Rome.

The exhibition has been selected by Christopher Newall and my colleague Colin Harrison, who have worked closely with Claudia Casali in Ravenna and Agnes Valenčak in Oxford to ensure that the exhibition is as visually striking as possible.

This will be the first exhibition to be held in the new suite of temporary exhibition galleries in the Ashmolean. They are part of the transformation of the museum just undertaken with the support of the Heritage Lottery Fund, the Linbury Trust, and many other trusts, foundations, and private individuals. We very much look forward to welcoming the exhibition to Oxford in September 2010, and to further collaborations with our colleagues in Ravenna in the future.

Christopher Brown
Director

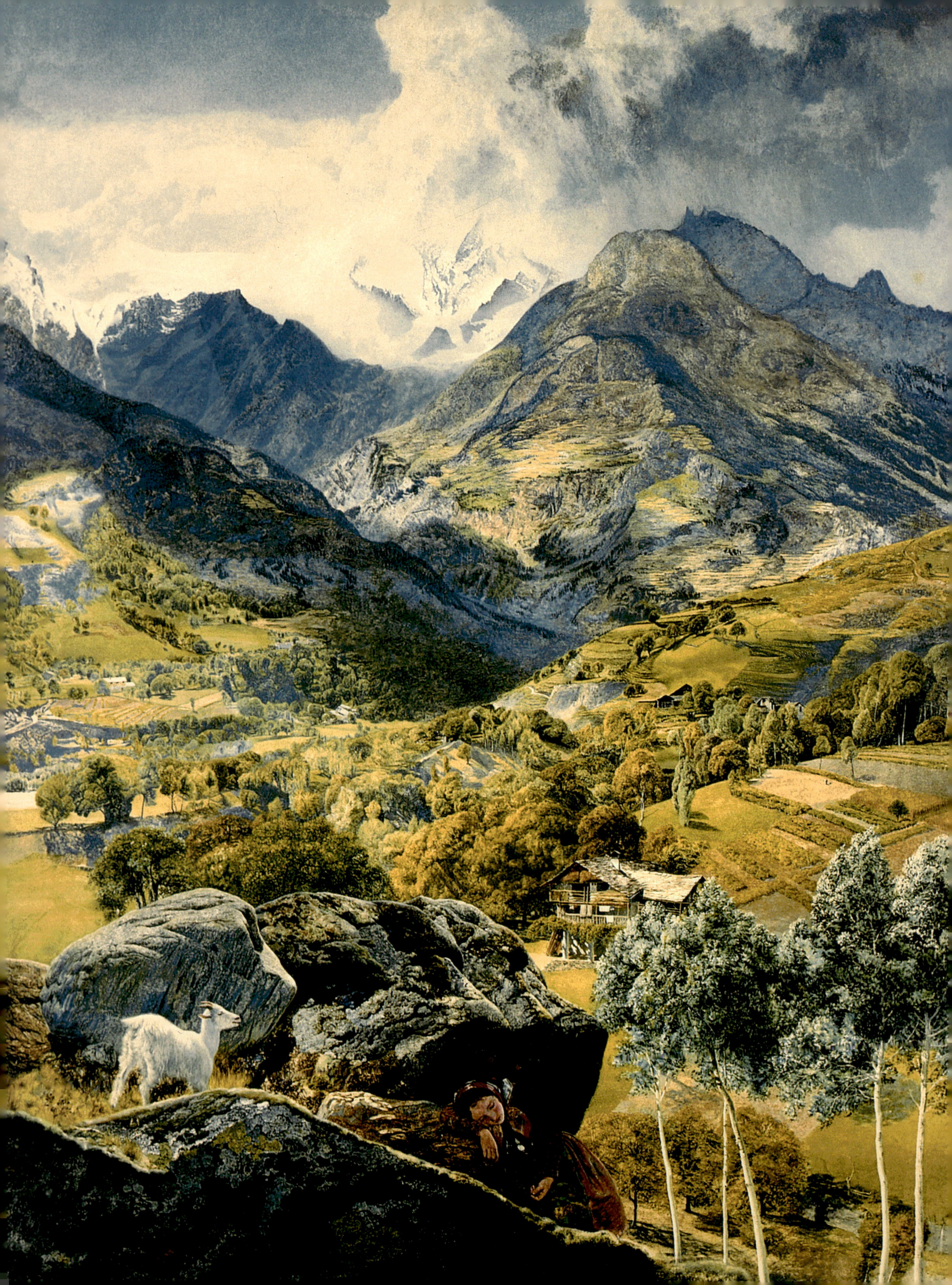

Introduction

Italy – her art, literature, history, and landscape – was one of the central sources of inspiration for the reforming movement known as Pre-Raphaelitism. The very name of the Pre-Raphaelite Brotherhood was chosen to exalt Italian art before Raphael, over the conventional academic hierarchy which put Raphael himself as the supreme classical master. However, the relationship between Italy and Pre-Raphaelitism was always complex, and changed considerably in the three decades after the formation of the Brotherhood in 1848. At the outset, the Pre-Raphaelites had little knowledge of early Italian art beyond the engravings by Carlo Lasinio of the frescoes in the Campo Santo at Pisa (**fig. 1**). Nor, surprisingly, did they have any particular interest in their ostensible models. Unlike many of their contemporaries on the Continent, the members of the Pre-Raphaelite Brotherhood did not spend prolonged periods in Italy. The Royal Academy Schools, where Rossetti, Millais, and Holman Hunt studied in the 1840s, had no 'Rome Prize' or other mechanism to send them to Rome to study. British artists of earlier generations had relied on private patronage to enable them to study and work in Italy; the Pre-Raphaelites had no such opportunities. Nor were their parents in a position to fund a Grand Tour. So, Rossetti never visited Italy; Millais and his wife went there as tourists in 1865; and if Holman Hunt spent an extended period in Florence and Naples between 1866 and 1868, it was initially because his plans to travel to the Near East had to be cancelled owing to quarantine restrictions. By contrast, John Ruskin, the great champion and mentor of the Pre-Raphaelites, travelled repeatedly in Italy, where his study of the art and architecture were fundamental to his intellectual and emotional development.

Dante Gabriel Rossetti (**fig. 2**), the most influential, if not the most representative, member of the Pre-Raphaelite Brotherhood, was the most ardently Italian of the Pre-Raphaelites. His father, Gabriele, was born at Vasto on the Adriatic coast in 1783, but, after joining the illicit Carbonaro movement, was eventually forced to flee his homeland, disguised as a British sailor aboard a Royal Navy ship. In 1830, he was appointed professor of Italian at King's College, London, and devoted himself to Dante studies and the cause of Italian liberation and unification, and became a notable figure among the Italian expatriates in London. He married Frances Polidori, herself half-Italian, and their children thus grew up in a household speaking Italian. From his early adulthood, Dante Gabriel Rossetti identified with Dante Alighieri, to the extent that, in 1849, he reorganised his baptismal names from 'Gabriel Charles Dante' to 'Dante Gabriel'. He was intimately familiar with Italian literature of the early Renaissance, and held Dante's *Vita nuova* in particular esteem. He later worked on a translation of this and other poems, which was eventually published as *Early Italian Poets from Ciullo d'Alcamo to Dante Alighieri* in 1861. In the biographical note to this volume, he proudly proclaimed his Italian ancestry. Throughout his career, from the late 1840s until his death, Rossetti found inspiration in Dante and other Italian writers. His greatest achievement in the 1850s was a series of watercolours illustrating passages from Dante; the turning point in his work, and arguably in the history of English art, came with an evocation from Boccaccio, *Bocca baciata* of 1859 (Museum of Fine Arts, Boston); and throughout the 1860s and 1870s, he arranged the sitters in his portraits in poses inspired

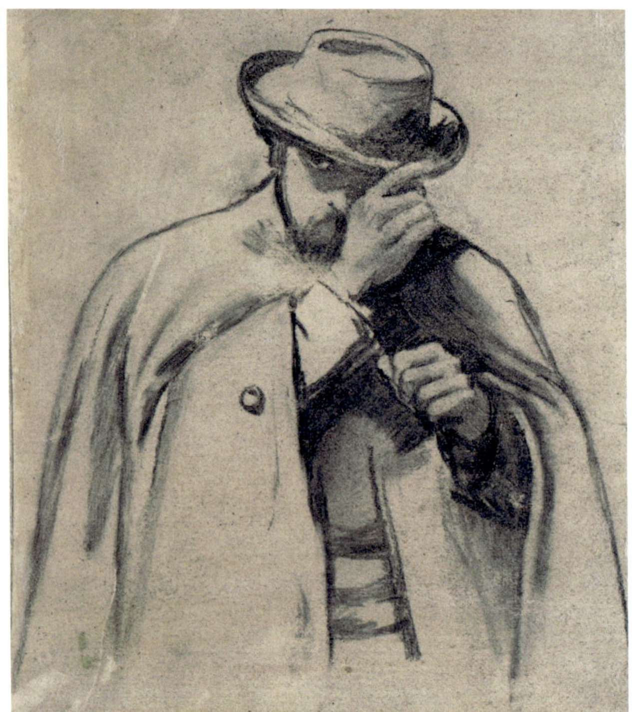

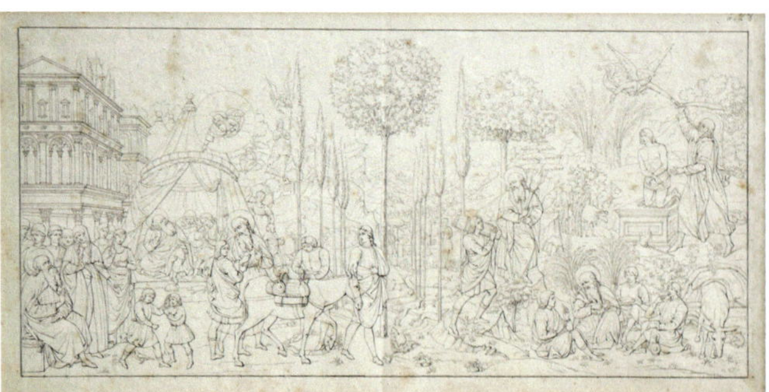

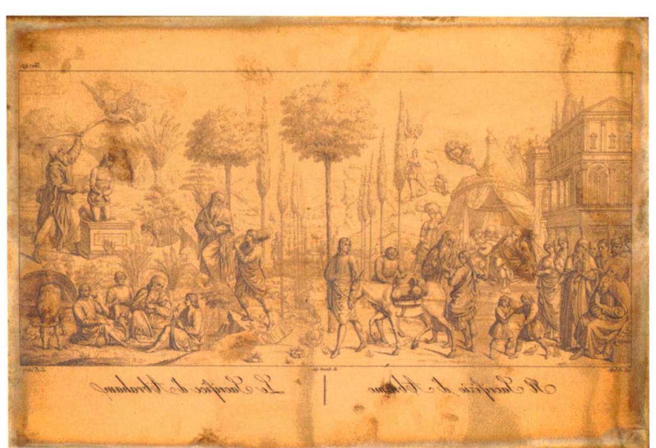

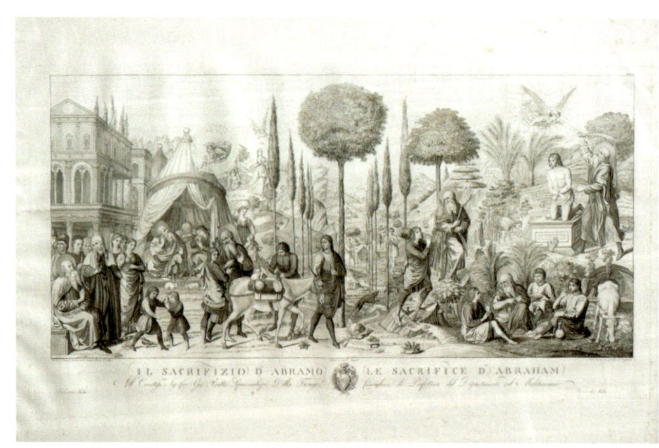

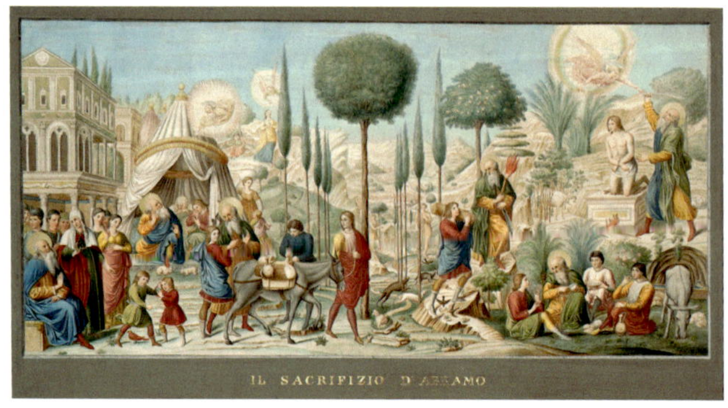

Fig. 1 (Right, top to bottom) Carlo Lasinio (1759–1838), *The Sacrifice of Abraham* (a) Etching, (b) Copper plate, (c) Etching, (d) Hand-coloured etching. Pisa, Opera Primaziale Pisana

Fig. 2 (Above) Charles Samuel Keene (1823–1891), *Portrait of Dante Gabriel Rossetti*, Charcoal on grey paper, 13.3 x 11.7 cm, Ashmolean Museum, University of Oxford, WA1950.178.311

by lines from Dante. His political opinions were never as strong as his father's, and, although he had been brought up to believe in Italy's right to national self-determination, his commitment to progressive politics later waned. Already in 1848, his poem 'A Last Confession' tells the story of the tragic love of a patriot and an orphan girl, herself a symbolical representation of Italy, who is unfaithful and is killed by her lover; it serves as a sad insight into Rossetti's incipient doubts about Italy's national will to gain her independence. Later in life, Rossetti defended his decision not to carry on his father's commitment to the cause of Italian liberation, by arguing that his only effective contribution was to expand knowledge of Italian literature in Britain. For, in spite of his ancestry, Rossetti always regarded England as home. He made several plans to visit Italy, usually with his brother, William Michael, and his close friend, William Bell Scott, but his state of health and, perhaps, a deep-rooted inhibition that the reality might not live up to the expectations of his imagination, always prevented him from setting out.

Ruskin (**fig. 3**), on the other hand, first visited Italy in 1833, when he was fourteen, and, over the next fifty years, he returned no fewer than fifteen times. Particularly momentous was his first tour unaccompanied by his parents, in 1845, when he explored Tuscany and Venice in preparation for the second volume of *Modern Painters* and discovered the art of Fra Angelico and Tintoretto, and his winters in Venice in 1849-50 and 1851-2, which led to *The Stones of Venice* (1851-3). Later in life, he was sometimes accompanied by friends and pupils, such as Edward and Georgiana Burne-Jones in 1862, or Joan and Arthur Severn and Albert Goodwin in 1873. These visits chronicle his growing appreciation of Italian art – it was not until 1862, for example, that he began his pioneering work on Leonardo's follower, Bernardino Luini; and not until 1870 that, stimulated by Burne-Jones, he allowed himself to be seduced by Carpaccio. Gradually, Italy became for Ruskin a place of inspiration, stimulating new insights and understanding of how art might reveal the spiritual, economic, and political conditions of past ages. It was also a place where he confronted his own inner turmoil and distress, notably during the agonised winter of 1876-7, where, alone in Venice, he was beset by memories and a sense of loss after the death of Rose La Touche.

Ruskin was a passionate conservationist who believed that Europe's architectural heritage was being irretrievably destroyed by the 'restoration' – meaning in most cases wholesale reconstruction – of buildings, which entailed the destruction of the past. From the mid-1840s, he drew buildings at risk. Indeed, in 1845, he realised that he must completely change his style of drawing from the picturesque manner of his master, J.D. Harding (**fig. 4**), to one that was more informative but less pleasing: 'His sketches are always pretty because he balances their parts together and considers them as pictures – mine are always ugly, for I consider my sketch as a written note of certain *facts* ... Harding's are all for impression – mine all for information.'[1] Later, Ruskin commissioned younger artists such as J.W. Bunney (**cat. 59**), Frank Randal (**cat. 69**), and Arthur Burgess (**cat. 60**) to compile a systematic record of architecture and decoration, in Italy and elsewhere, for the collections of the Guild of St George at Sheffield and the Ruskin Drawing School at Oxford. Such drawings are truly Pre-Raphaelite in their concentration on detail, invaluable as records if less appealing as works of art.

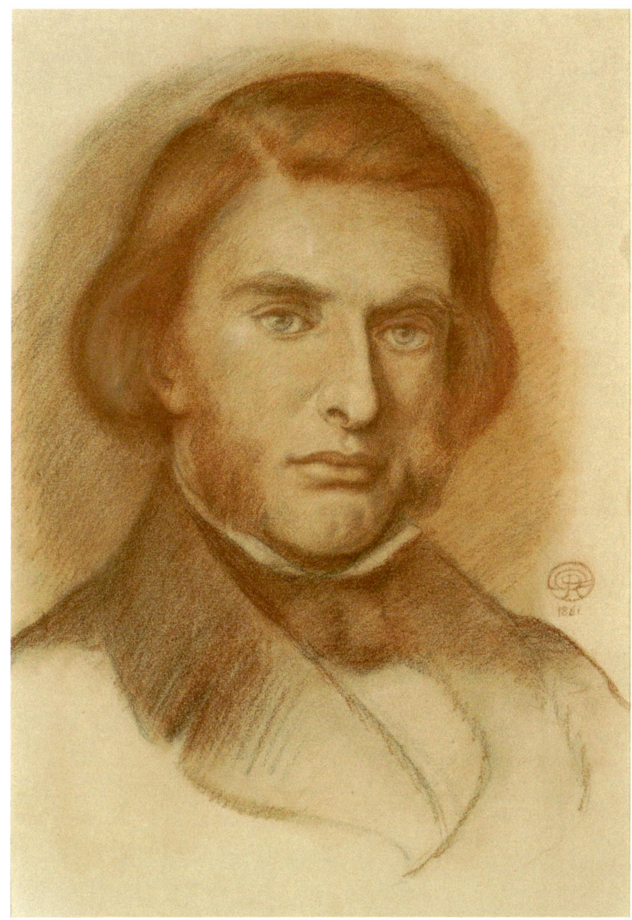

Fig. 3 Dante Gabriel Rossetti (1828–1882), *Portrait of John Ruskin*, 1861, Red and some black chalk, 48 x 33.5 cm, Ashmolean Museum, University of Oxford, WA1891.1

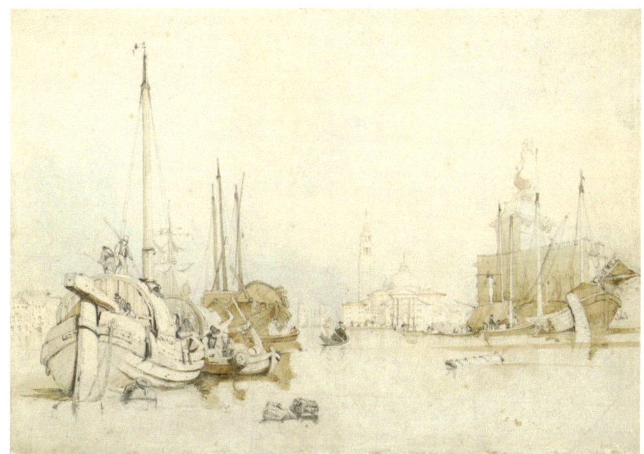

Fig. 4 James Duffield Harding (1797–1863), *View of San Giorgio from the Grand Canal*, Watercolour with graphite, 26.6 x 39.5 cm, Ashmolean Museum, University of Oxford, WA1950.178.125

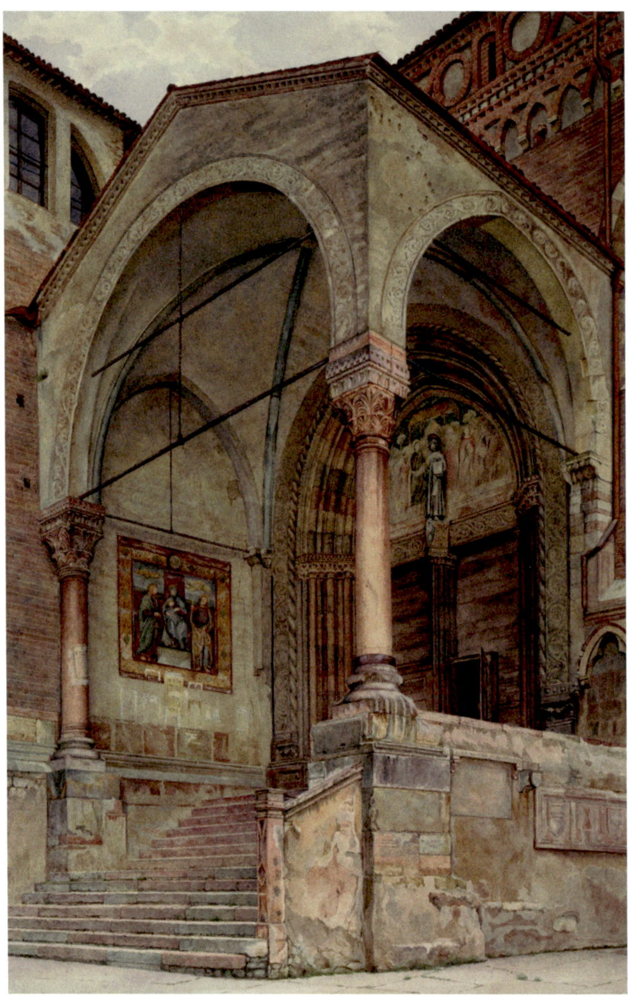

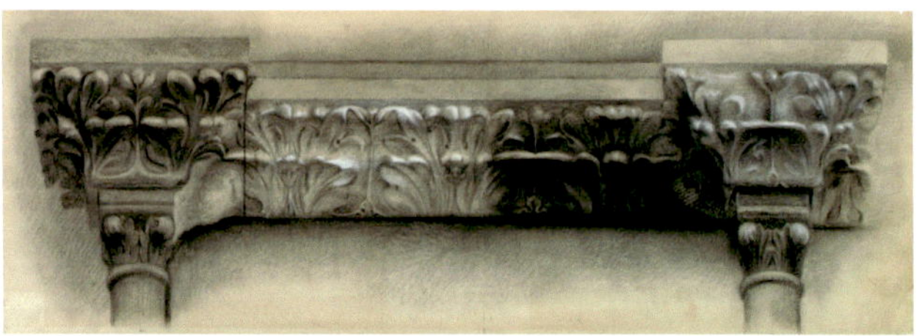

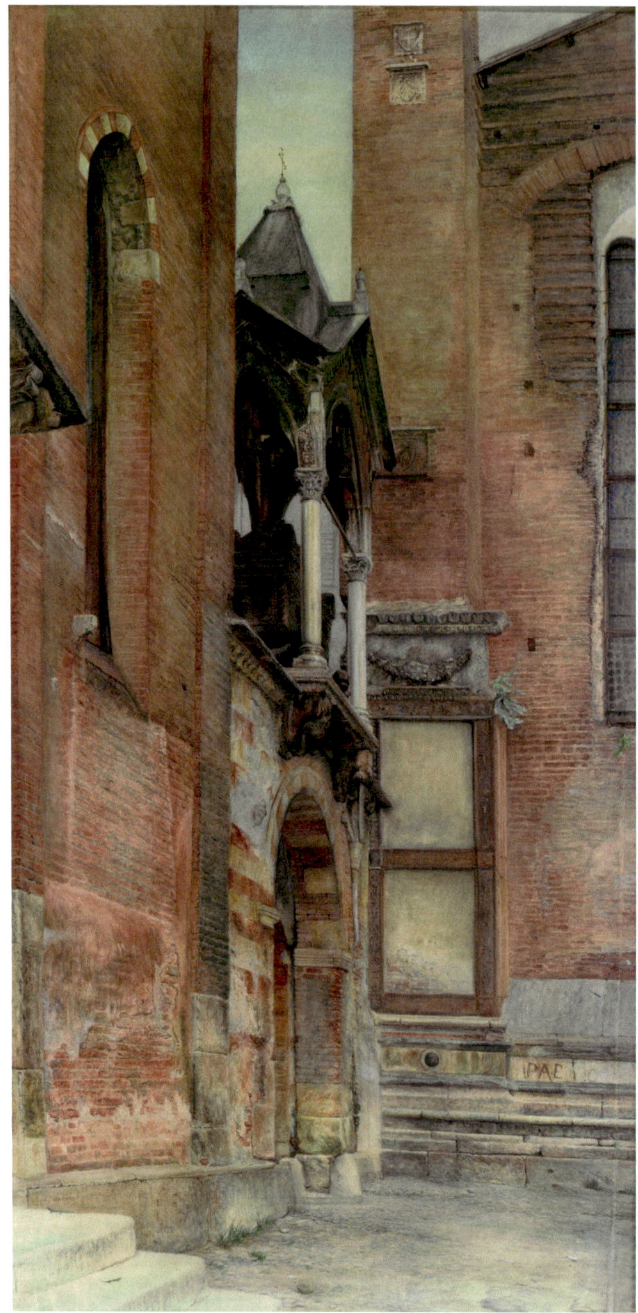

Directly and indirectly, Ruskin led the growing consciousness of the importance of protecting the very fabric of buildings and works of art. *The Stones of Venice*, in particular, was of enormous and lasting influence. Even though much of the text is given over to close analysis of the development of architectural form, some sections offer ecstatic and compelling flights of descriptive prose. The chapter on 'The Nature of Gothic' in volume II galvanised a whole generation into a new appreciation of the beauty and variety of such architectural forms. Later, Ruskin was the inspiration behind the Society for the Protection of

Cat. 59 (Above) John Wharlton Bunney (1828–1882), *Castelbarco Tomb, Verona* 1869, Watercolour and bodycolour over pencil on paper, 98 x 48 cm, Signed and dated: *Verona 1869 John Bunney*, Ashmolean Museum, University of Oxford. Ruskin School Collection (WAL 6)

Cat. 69 (Top left) Frank Randal (*c.* 1858–1910), *The North Porch of San Fermo Maggiore, Verona* 1884, Watercolour on paper, 37.9 x 25.4 cm, Ashmolean Museum, University of Oxford. Ruskin School Collection (Rud. 23bis)

Cat. 60 (Bottom left) Arthur Burgess (1843–1886), *Sculpted Moulding on Tomb of Mastino II della Scala* 1869, Charcoal heightened with white bodycolour on paper, 25.4 x 188 cm, Collection of the Guild of St George, Museums Sheffield (R 140), Ref: Morley 1984, II, pp. 47–8

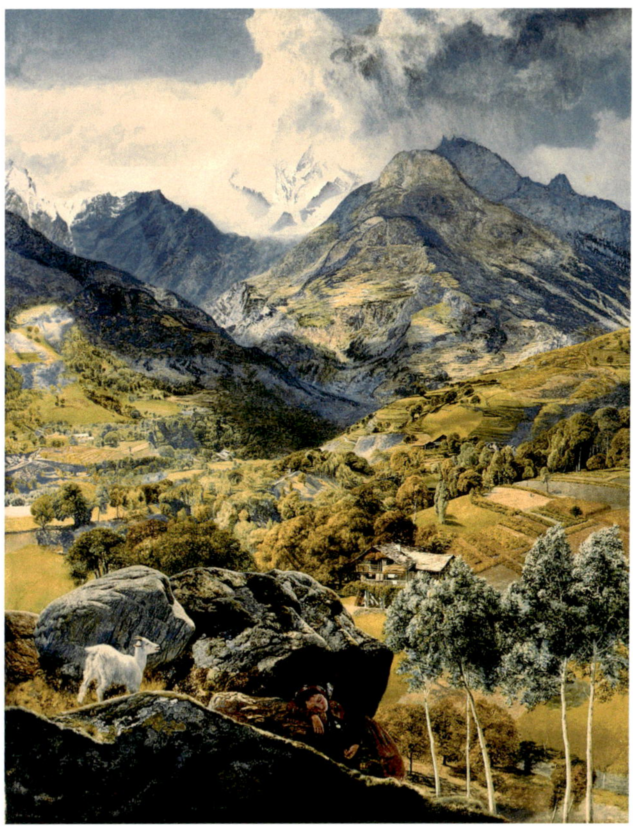

Cat. 55 John Brett (1831–1902), *Val d'Aosta* 1858, Oil on canvas, 87.6 x 68 cm, Signed and dated: John Brett 1858, Private collection of Lord Lloyd-Webber. Also on page 104.

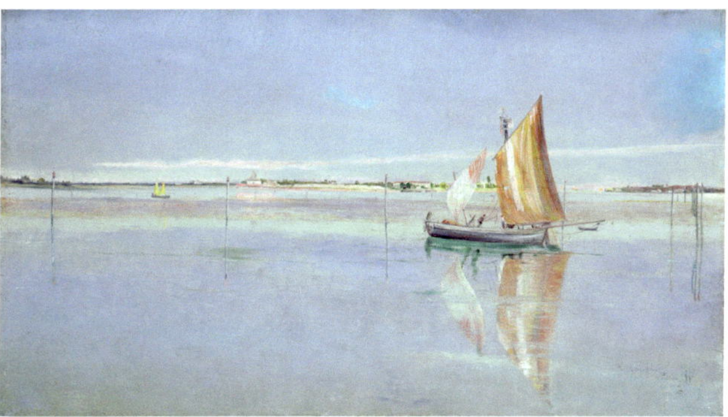

Cat. 87 John William Inchbold (1830–1888), *On the Lagoon, Venice*, Oil on canvas, 40.6 x 72.5 cm, Leeds Museums and Galleries (City Art Gallery). Also on page 143

Ancient Buildings, founded by William Morris in 1877, and led the international campaign against the proposed reconstruction of the façade of St Mark's in Venice in 1880. His sensuous descriptions also inspired an entire genre of writing about Venice, notably that of Marcel Proust.

Ruskin's principle of 'truth to nature', expounded at the end of the first volume of *Modern Painters* in 1843, coloured a whole generation of artists, whose representation of the physical world insisted on the individuality of each object, whether man-made or naturally occurring. In the 1850s and early 1860s, the Pre-Raphaelite landscape artists created many of their most original works in Italy, notably John Brett, whose *Val d'Aosta* (**cat. 55**) was hailed by Ruskin in his *Academy Notes* in 1859 as the first in a new genre:

> Yes, here we have it at last … historical landscape, properly so called – landscape painting with a meaning and a use…Here, for the first time in history, we have, by help of art, the power of visiting a place, reasoning about it, and knowing it, just as if we were there.

Ruskin's only reservation was that 'it seems to me wholly emotionless. I cannot find from it that the painter loved, or feared, anything in all that wonderful piece of work. There seems to me no awe of the mountains there – no real love of the chestnuts or the vines. Keenness of eye and fineness of hand as much as you choose; but of emotion, or of intention, nothing traceable.'[2]

Ruskin's strictures were shared by many of the artists themselves, some of whom adopted a new and more aesthetically sophisticated approach, seeking to evoke rather than to document objectively. In 1854, for example, George Price Boyce, explored alternative ways of treating Venice in watercolour, with such Ruskinian works as the view of the Basilica of St Mark contrasting with extraordinarily personal distillations of the experience of the city at night. In the early 1860s, J.W. Inchbold (**cat. 87**) painted views of Venice which are in pictorial terms close to abstraction, and far removed from the microscopic evocations of geology and vegetation that he had painted in the mid-1850s. Ruskin himself, in the drawings of his later years, understood this inversion of the principle of documentation, making views of buildings on the Grand Canal and elsewhere in the city which, while they were done directly from the motif, are impressionistic in effect and infinitely more personal than his earlier studies.

The influence of Ruskin and Rossetti was combined in perhaps the most completely Pre-Raphaelite of all the artists in the exhibition, Edward Burne-Jones. While at Oxford, Burne-Jones had read Ruskin and fallen under the spell of Rossetti's vision of the Middle Ages, and in later life, he acknowledged Rossetti as the only true Pre-Raphaelite. On the first of his four expeditions to

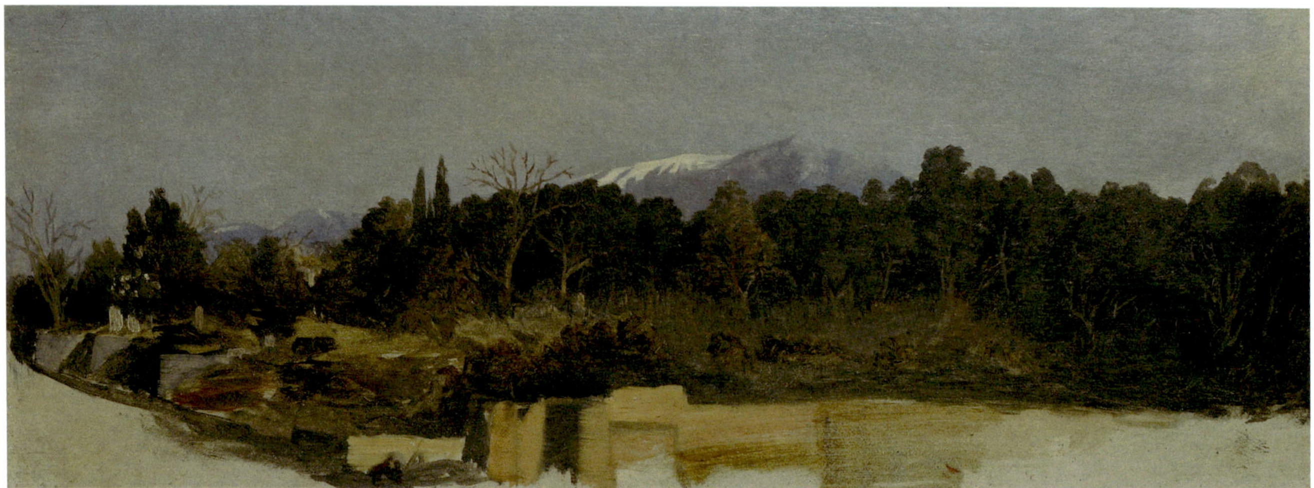

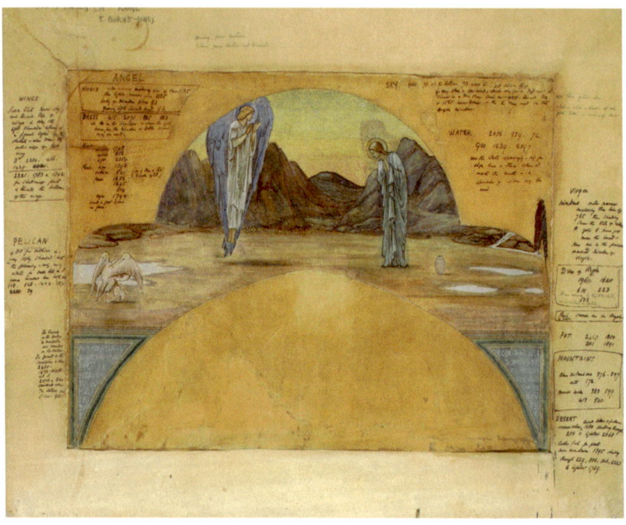

Cat. 134 Sir Edward Burne-Jones (1833–1898), Study for *'The Annunciation'*, Watercolour and body colour on brown paper, 52.1 x 74.9 cm, extensively inscribed, St Paul's within the Walls, Rome

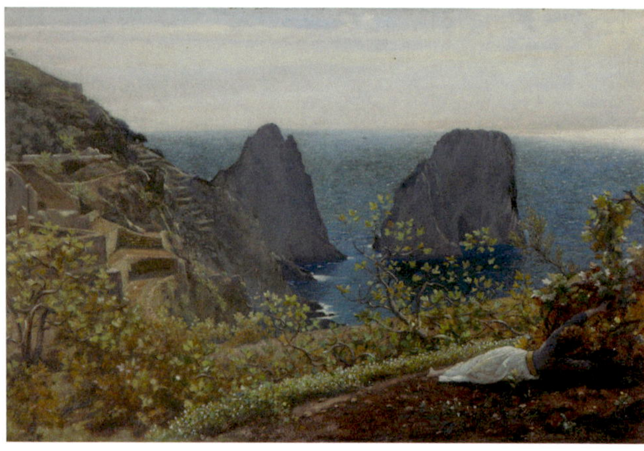

Cat. 100 (top) George Heming Mason (1818–1872), *Villa Borghese* c. 1852–3, Oil on paper mounted on board, 13.5 x 36.1 cm, The Gere Collection

Cat. 106 (bottom) Giovanni Costa (1826–1903), *The Faraglioni Rocks, Capri – An October Morning* 1875–7, Oil on canvas, 29.5 x 45.5 cm, from the Castle Howard Collection

Italy, made in the autumn of 1859 at Ruskin's expense, his travelling companion, Val Prinsep, described how in Venice, with 'Ruskin in hand, we sought out every cornice, design, or monument praised by him. We bowed before Tintoret and scoffed at Sansovino. A broken pediment was a thing of horror'.[3] In later visits, Burne-Jones no longer depended on Ruskin's teaching, but studied works by artists who remained virtually unknown in Britain, such as Carpaccio, and which he in turn recommended to Ruskin; or allowed himself to be consumed by the creative genius of artists whom Ruskin abhorred, notably Michelangelo. Burne-Jones's work was always indebted to Rossetti's love of pattern and innate sense of design, but his artistic curiosity extended far beyond, even to the Byzantine mosaics at Ravenna, which he saw in 1873 and which were then little known in England. His designs for the mosaics in the American Church in Rome **(cats. 134–143)**, which preoccupied him between 1881 and his death, gave him particular pleasure, and the mosaics themselves, which he never saw, are widely regarded as the greatest of all Pre-Raphaelite decorative schemes – the only fulfilment of the artist's dream of doing 'big things [in] vast spaces and for common people to see.'

On one of his visits, Burne-Jones described Italy as 'home'. So did his contemporary, Frederic Leighton, whose education in England and on the Continent set him apart from his contemporaries, and aligned him with artists of the previous generation, notably William Dyce and Ford Madox Brown, who had studied in Rome and knew at first hand the work of the Nazarenes. Leighton's experience of Italian painting was far wider than that of the Pre-Raphaelites, and during his years in Rome in 1852-5, he immersed himself in the cosmopolitan community of artists. He learnt the art of landscape painting from Giovanni 'Nino' Costa (**cat. 106**), an ardent patriot who had served in 1848 with the Roman Legion in the war against the Austrians in northern Italy, and had joined Garibaldi's personal guard in the following year. Costa and Leighton (**cat. 104**) were joined by George Heming Mason (**cat. 100**) on painting expeditions in the Roman Campagna. Later, Costa was introduced to Burne-Jones and his friend and patron, George Howard (later ninth Earl of Carlisle), and founded a new school of landscape painting, which came to be known as the Etruscans. Their work is characterised by panoramic views with high horizons painted in a wide format, and with a general lack of concern for foreground details. Such an approach was anathema to the early Pre-Raphaelites, but welcomed by their later followers such as William Blake Richmond and Walter Crane. Indeed, until Costa arranged the first exhibition of paintings by the Pre-Raphaelites such as Burne-Jones and Rossetti in 1890, it was the Etruscans who were seen by the Italian public as representing the Pre-Raphaelite movement in England; the small colony of Pre-Raphaelites living in Florence in the 1870s (not represented in this exhibition) still sent all their works to the London venues.

Gradually, the meaning of the term 'Pre-Raphaelite' evolved. Ruskinian 'truth to nature' came to be seen as an anachronism, and Ruskin's own taste evolved away from the spiritual fervour of the early Florentine artists, towards the sensuous richness of the Venetian masters of the High Renaissance; the final volume of *Modern Painters*, published in 1860, celebrated the art of Titian and Veronese. Progressive artists, notably Rossetti, Burne-Jones, and Leighton, moved away from the moral didacticism of the early Pre-Raphaelites to a less intellectual art of emotional and sexual suggestion. When Swinburne visited the Uffizi in 1864, he found amorality in Titian's *Venus of Urbino* and listed works by obscure Mannerist artists in preference to the acknowledged masters. He wrote of Michelangelo's works that they 'fill and exalt the mind with a strange and violent pleasure which is the highest mood of worship; reverence intensified to the last endurable degree'.[4] It is perhaps ironic that, as the opportunities for studying early Italian art increased in England, the later Pre-Raphaelites should have cared for these artists even less than the members of the Brotherhood in the 1850s.

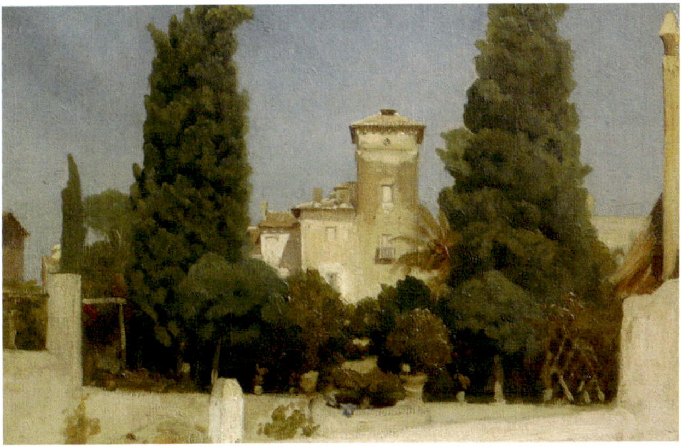

Cat. 104 Frederic Leighton (1830–1896), *The Villa Malta* 1860s ?, Oil on canvas, 27.2 x 41.5 cm, The Gere Collection, Ref: Jones 1996, no. 51; Riopelle 1999 no. 51

1 quoted in Robert Hewison, *Ruskin's Venice* (London, 2000), p. 21.

2 *The Works of John Ruskin*, ed. E.T. Cook and Alexander Wedderburn, 39 vols (London, 1903–12), XIV, pp. 234–6

3 Val Prinsep, 'An Artist's Life in Italy', *The Magazine of Art* 1904, p. 417

4 quoted in Rikky Rooksby, *A.C. Swinburne: A Poet's Life* (Aldershot, 1997), p. 92.

The Pre-Raphaelites and Italian Art before and after Raphael

Colin Harrison

The artists who founded the Pre-Raphaelite Brotherhood at a meeting at 85, Gower Street, London, one day in September 1848, saw themselves as revolutionaries. Their intention was no less than to alter the course of English art. Their host, John Everett Millais, had been the youngest ever student at the Royal Academy Schools, admitted at the age of 11 in 1840. There, he had met William Holman Hunt and Dante Gabriel Rossetti. These three young men, aged between 19 and 21, were joined by several others, all of whom intended to become artists: James Collinson, the sculptor Thomas Woolner, Rossetti's brother William Michael, and Frederick George Stephens. On an earlier occasion, they had joined Rossetti to look at 'engravings from the Campo Santo, and other somewhat archaic designs'. At the meeting in Gower Street, the assembled company examined the same engravings. Holman Hunt later remembered that, in contrast to the 'grandiose disregard for the simplicity of truth' found in Raphael, in Lasinio's engravings they 'recognised as we turned from one print to another that the Campo Santo designs were remarkable for incident derived from attentive observation of inexhaustible Nature, and dwelt on all their quaint charms of execution'.[1] The essential character of the art they admired, therefore, was its close study of nature, not its 'quaint charms of execution'; and, for as long as their Brotherhood existed, it was the paramount role of Nature that both they and their champion, John Ruskin, emphasised. Indeed, Ruskin himself later suggested that the Brotherhood fulfilled his rallying cry in volume II of *Modern Painters*, published in 1846, that artists 'should go to Nature in all singleness of heart, and walk with her laboriously and trustingly, having no other thought but how best to penetrate her meaning; rejecting nothing, selecting nothing, and scorning nothing.'[2] However, they felt that the name of the group should signal their determination to defy convention. Rossetti proposed Early Christian, a term he had learnt from his mentor Ford Madox Brown; but the others found that it was redolent of the 'German Quattro Centists', as Hunt termed the Nazarenes. Hunt therefore proposed that the movement should be known not as Pre-Raphaelism, but Pre-Raphaelitism.[3] Seldom has such a decision led to such momentous consequences, not only for contemporary critics, but for generations of art historians seeking to make sense of an apparently casual choice by naïve and inexperienced young men.

At its most immediate, the formation of the Pre-Raphaelite Brotherhood was a protest against the training of the Royal Academy, and its name was intended as a challenge to that institution. Since its foundation in 1768, the Academy had been modelled on earlier academies of art in Italy and France, and its first President, Sir Joshua Reynolds, felt obliged to glorify the supremacy of history painting, which was the most intellectual branch of art and the one that allowed its practitioners to be considered liberal artists. The training at the Academy Schools was entirely unoriginal. Although few of the Pre-Raphaelites' student works survive, those by Millais demonstrate how conventional the training was – copies after casts of antique models, and life drawing.[4] Raphael was still held up to be the ideal artist, the epitome of the classical style. Reynolds's view that 'Raphael … stands in general foremost of the first painter,'[5] was still maintained, and, during the 1840s, the decoration of the new Palace of Westminster had only served to reaffirm his status as a paragon.[6]

The Pre-Raphaelite Brotherhood never drew up a public manifesto, or fully explained what they meant by their name. This is perhaps not surprising, since the nature of their meetings was as much social as artistic, and much of what they did high-spirited and far from serious. However, they did produce a short-lived periodical to which they all contributed, which reflects many of their concerns. *The Germ*, subtitled 'Thoughts towards Nature in Poetry, Literature, and Art', ran for four issues between January and May 1850, and includes poetry, book reviews, short stories, and articles on aesthetics. Among the contributions, F.G. Stephens wrote an essay in *The Germ* distinguishing the characteristics of 'The Purpose and Tendency of Italian Art', which served in some senses as the manifesto for the Pre-Raphaelite movement that they never wrote. Artists should set themselves 'an endeavour to encourage and enforce an entire adherence to the simplicity of nature.' Stephens discusses in particular a Florentine Niello, and works by Ghiberti, Fra Angelico, Masaccio, Fra Bartolommeo, and Ghirlandaio, as well as the artists of the Campo Santo at Pisa, all known from reproductions. He also indicates some of the printed sources through which he, and presumably other members of the Pre-Raphaelite Brotherhood, came to know of these works, by Ottley, Seroux d'Agincourt, Rossini's *Storia della Pittura* and, for Ghiberti, casts from the great bronze doors from the Baptistery in Florence, which were visible in both Somerset House and the Royal Academy. Another contribution, D.G. Rossetti's story 'Hand and Soul', which was included in the first issue, was described by W.M. Rossetti as a 'very serious manifesto of art-dogma', which held that 'the only satisfactory works of art are those which exhibit the very soul of the artist'.[7] The message was elaborated as an extended metaphor, in which an imaginary artist of the Trecento in Florence, Chiaro dell'Erma (based on Fra Angelico), discovers that the only true subject of art is his own soul. The tale was given apparent substance by the inclusion of references to a visit to Florence in the spring of 1847 to study the Trecento, and mention of works in the picture gallery at Dresden, and knowledge of Seroux d'Agincourt. Yet Rossetti never went to Florence, and his knowledge of the other 'sources' was, at best, sketchy.

In fact, had the Pre-Raphaelites been better informed about early Italian art, they would probably never have chosen to label themselves as Pre-Raphaelites, for an interest in the Italian primitives had become almost conventional by 1848. The story of their rediscovery has often been told.[8] The French scholar, Jean-Baptiste Seroux d'Agincourt had led the way, with a pioneering account of the *Histoire de l'art par les monumens depuis sa décadence au IVe siecle jusqu'a son renouvellement au XVIe siecle*, published between 1810 and 1823. Among the artists who worked to provide plates for this publication were the Englishmen John Flaxman and William Young Ottley. The latter, in his *The Italian School of Design* (1818), was dispassionate rather than hostile to the Primitives. It was not, however, until the 1840s that the appreciation of the Italian primitives became widespread. In this context, the influence of A.F. Rio's *De la poésie chrétienne* (1836) cannot be overestimated, and was fundamental for all three of the principal 'rediscoverers', Lord Lindsay, Ruskin, and James Dennistoun, author of the *Memoirs of the Dukes of Urbino* (1851). Rio argued that the only valid means of judging a work of art was not its formal perfection, but the truth of its religious sentiment. In this way, Italian artists of the Trecento and Quattrocento were at once rehabilitated from their role as primitive precursors, to being fully formed and inspired purveyors of religious images in their own right. Although he owed much to contemporary German thought, it was Rio who, for example, established Fra Angelico as the model Christian artist, and resuscitated Carpaccio's reputation.[9] Above all, he believed that every Italian artist, good or bad, was in some sense an expression of a 'national genius'. Rio was lionized in London, where he was instrumental in converting the future prime minister, William Gladstone, to the cause of 'Christian art',[10] and met Ruskin and the popular author, Mrs Anna Jameson, too.

In the very year that the Pre-Raphaelite Brotherhood was formed, a new body was established, the Arundel Society, which had the aim of publishing writings on art and reproductions after paintings, sculpture, and architecture. The most vociferous members of the committee had a particular interest in early Italian painting: Samuel Rogers, Lord Lindsay, and Ruskin, who had recently discovered the Italian primitives on a journey to Italy in 1845. Although these publications were intended for a wide audience, the members for the early years were few, and such publications as the engraving after Giotto's Lamentation in the Arena Chapel (1851-2) can have had limited influence on the general art-viewing public. However, it is recorded that, for example, a slightly later series of 38 watercolours by William Oliver Williams after Giotto's frescoes were enormously enjoyed by D.G. Rossetti when exhibited at the Crystal Palace in 1855-6 – 'A most glorious treat which I had yesterday is the sight of the Giotto tracings made for the Arundel Society, and now in the Crystal Palace. I hope you'll be in time for them. The woodcuts published give no idea.'[11] The woodcuts by the Dalziel brothers were published between 1852 and 1860. They were not a success, and described in *The Art Journal* as 'the one grand mistake of this well purposed Society'. Nor was Ruskin's accompanying text, published as *Giotto and his Works in Padua* (1853–60), and based not on the frescoes themselves, but on the reproductions and the insights in Lord Lindsay's *Early Christian Art*. The Society did not confine itself to Italian primitives, but covered an eclectic mixture of subjects. Moreover, after it had adopted chromolithography for its reproductions in 1856, they became a popular means of decorating middle-class households. The Society became known as 'guardians of the great frescoes of Italy', and the lithographs of Masaccio's work in the Brancacci chapel were held up as examples for 'our artists who belong to the Pre-Raffaellite school'.[12] Although the Society flourished until 1897, its heyday for artists was in the 1850s and 1860s; for the public, it continued into the following decades.

If they had been assiduous in their search for illustrations of 'Pre-Raphaelite' paintings, they would have found them in a number of published works, from Thomas Patch's life of Masaccio (1770) to William Young Ottley's engravings after 'the early Florentine school' (1826) to Lady Callcott's *Description of the Chapel of the Annunziata dell'Arena or Giotto's Chapel in Padua* (1836). There is, however, no evidence that the Pre-Raphaelites knew of or read any of these publications. The opportunities for seeing works by artists of the Quattrocento were limited, but did exist. The pioneering collections of these works, by such figures as the Hon. William Fox-Strangways and William Roscoe of Liverpool, were entirely private, until the former donated part of his collection to Christ Church, Oxford, in 1828 and 1834, where it was hung, rather than displayed, in the library, and was examined by Ruskin in 1842.[13] There is no record of any of the Pre-Raphaelites seeing it there, though Millais, who made frequent visits to Oxford between 1846 and 1852, could well have obtained permission to do so from one of his patrons in the city. It was not until 1850 that Fox-Strangways gave a further portion of his collection to a public gallery. His gift to the University Galleries at Oxford (now the Ashmolean Museum) included a number of important pictures of the Quattrocento, notably Uccello's *Hunt in the Forest*, as well as works by or attributed to Fra Angelico, Barna da Siena, Filippo Lippi, and many others. The one collection where the Italian Primitives were almost wholly neglected was the National Gallery in London, in spite of criticism directly on this point as early as 1836. Indeed, the first significant group of Italian paintings before Raphael, from the School of Botticelli, did not arrive until 1855, together with works by Gozzoli , Mantegna, and others bought by Sir Charles Eastlake.[14] Before his energetic period as Director, the only works of the Quattrocento displayed in Trafalgar Square were Lorenzo Monaco's wings to his *Coronation of the Virgin*, presented by William Coningham in July 1848 with an attribution to Taddeo Gaddi.[15] In the previous month, the authorities of the British Institution had arranged an exhibition of 'a series of pictures from the times of Giotto and Van Eyck'. Although the Flemish pictures were more numerous, and better, than the Italian, there were several works attributed to Fra Angelico and other masters. Once again, there is no evidence that any of the Pre-Raphaelites visited the exhibition.

In spite of these opportunities, mostly apparently missed, the best chance the Pre-Raphaelites had for studying early Italian painting in the original was by travelling on the Continent. In October 1849, a year after the formation of the Brotherhood, Rossetti and Holman Hunt made a tour in France and Belgium. In the Louvre, Rossetti was so struck by Giorgione's *Concert champêtre* that he was inspired him to compose a sonnet for *The Germ*. Holman Hunt remembered that they also admired Fra Angelico's *Coronation of the Virgin* in the Louvre, 'of peerless grace and sweetness in the eyes of both of us', and Rossetti is also recorded as admiring 'some mighty things by that real stunner Leonardo, some ineffably poetical Mantegnas', as well as 'several wonderful early Christians who nobody ever heard of'.[16] In the Low Countries, they admired many early artists, among them Memling at Bruges. This could not be taken as a systematic course of study, however, and when, in later years, Hunt spent some time in Florence and was able to examine a wide range of early masterpieces, he realized that he did not like them at all![17]

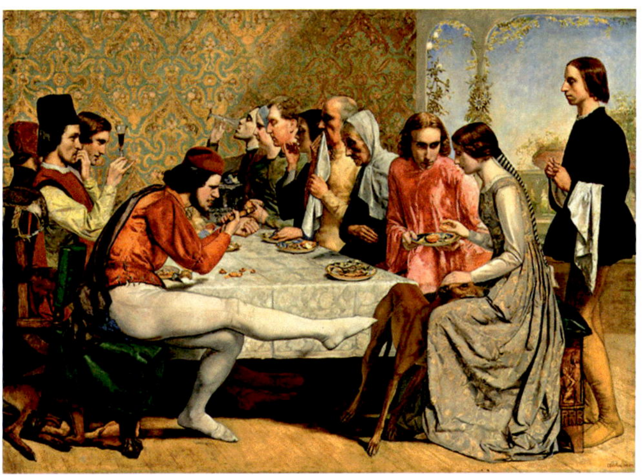

Fig. 5 John Everett Millais (1829–1896), *Isabella*, 1848-9, Oil on canvas, 103 x 142.8 cm, National Museums Liverpool (Walker Art Gallery), WAG1637

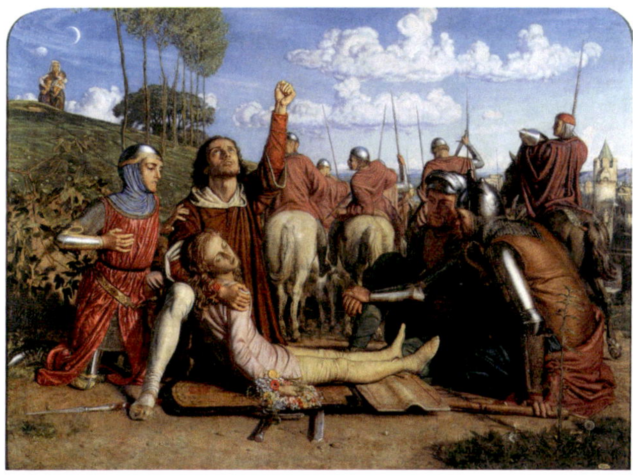

Fig. 6 William Holman Hunt (1827–1910), *Rienzi*, 1848-9, Oil on canvas, 86.4 x 121.9 cm, Private Collection

Among living artists, it was precisely the generation whom the Pre-Raphaelites derided as purveyors of 'slosh' who were instrumental in resuscitating the Primitives, as Francis Haskell has so ably demonstrated. Indeed, he ruefully notes that 'I sometimes feel that before 1848 every painter in England had admired the works of the artists preceding Raphael – except those who were to become the Pre-Raphaelites.'[18] The two painters whose work was decisive in showing the Pre-Raphaelites how they might revitalize English painting were William Dyce and Ford Madox Brown. Dyce had studied in Rome in the 1820s, and he had extensive contact with the Nazarenes, the German 'revivalists' of primitive Italian art. He had developed his own brand of hard-edged and carefully finished 'Raphaelite' painting, and had exhibited a succession of religious pictures which exemplified his High Church leanings. Brown, much younger, indeed nearly a contemporary of the Pre-Raphaelites, had had a sophisticated continental training in Belgium, been strongly influenced by the Nazarenes in Rome, worked on the decoration of the Palace of Westminster, and was immediately sympathetic to the Pre-Raphaelites' aims, although he was never officially a member of the Brotherhood.

In the early years after the formation of the Brotherhood, the Pre-Raphaelites self-consciously chose Italian subjects for their paintings. Yet, apart from Rossetti, their knowledge of Italian literature was largely through the interpretations of English poets, in particular Keats and Browning. So, at the Cyclographic Society, a kind of sketching club in which members were invited to draw from a set subject and criticize each other's efforts, Rossetti proposed eight subjects from Keats's 'Isabella'. So, it was Holman Hunt's painting of *Madeleine and Porphyro*, from Keats's 'The Eve of St Agnes', which led to the close friendship between the two artists. Italian subjects abound in these early years, particularly among the drawings: Millais's *The Death of Romeo and Juliet*, *Isabella*, and so on. But with the best will in the world, none of these drawings can be described as Italianate in style, or even much influenced by Italian art of any period. Their immediate debt is to the stiff outlines of Moritz Retzsch, popular in England as well as on the Continent; and, behind them, the enormously influential outline illustrations of Flaxman.[19] Later, these Italian subjects acquired second-hand, so to speak, reached their apogee in two paintings shown at the Royal Academy in 1849, when the Pre-Raphaelite Brotherhood made their exhibition debut: Millais's *Isabella* (**fig. 5**) and Holman Hunt's *Rienzi* (**fig. 6**). *Isabella* was based on a story from Boccaccio as retold by Keats in his 'Isabella; or, The Pot of Basil'; while the subject of *Rienzi* was taken from Bulwer Lytton's novel *Rienzi, the Last of the Tribunes*. However, Hunt took the precaution of appending in the Royal Academy catalogue an extract from Lytton's novel to explain the subject: 'But for that event, the future liberator of Rome might have been but a dreamer, a scholar, a poet – the peaceful rival of Petrarch – a man of thoughts, not deeds. But from that time, all his faculties, energies, fancies, genius, became concentrated to a single point; and patriotism, before a vision, leaped into the life and

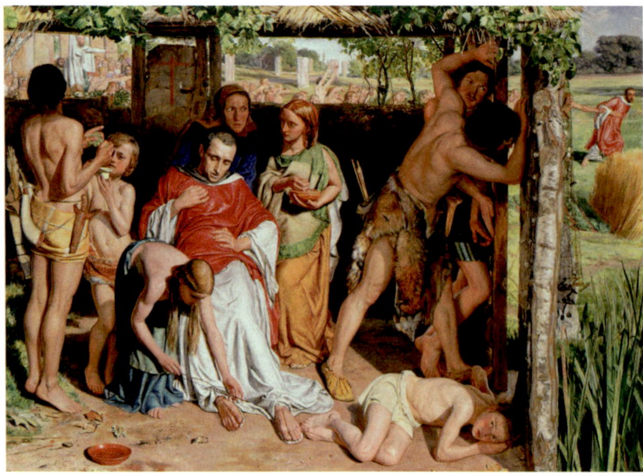

Fig. 7 William Holman Hunt (1827–1910), *A Converted British Family Sheltering a Christian Missionary from the Persecution of the Druids*, Oil on canvas, 111 x 141 cm, Ashmolean Museum, University of Oxford, WA1894.1

vigour of a passion.' The second edition of Lytton's novel was published in 1848, and the revolutions in Italy and elsewhere in that year had brought nationalism to the fore. Hunt's operatic, almost melodramatic, picture was largely painted out of doors, in England, and, although some elements may be said to owe a debt to Italian painting (perhaps to Bernardino da Asola's *Death of St Peter Martyr* of the 1540s, which had been in the National Gallery since 1831), and the composition recalls the lamentation over the dead Christ, no specific borrowings have been adduced,[20] and this hymn to Italian nationalism owes little to Italian art. The same might be said of the group of religious paintings shown at the Royal Academy in the following year: Hunt's *A Converted British Family Sheltering a Christian Missionary from the Persecution of the Druids* (Ashmolean) **(fig. 7)** and Millais's *Christ in the House of his Parents* (Tate). In the same year, Rossetti showed his last truly Pre-Raphaelite painting, *Ecce Ancilla Domini* (Tate). Its unusually tall format is explained by the fact that it was intended to form one wing of a diptych illustrating episodes from the life of the Virgin, of a kind Rossetti would have seen on his recent tour of the Continent. But the style is hardly Italianate. Indeed, it has been suggested that most of these works were far more indebted to Flemish than to Italian painting, and specifically to Van Eyck's Arnolfini Wedding in the National Gallery.[21] In spite of this, contemporary critics described it as 'a work in the manner of Pietro Perugino, and the earlier Italian school', just as they had described the same artist's *Girlhood of the Virgin Mary*, shown in the previous year, as 'Early Christian', 'early religious', 'in the manner of the early school', 'the old missal style', or, in the fanciful nonsense of *The Art Journal*: 'This picture is the most successful as a pure imitation of early Florentine art that we have seen in this country.... With all of the severities of the Giotteschi, we find necessarily the advances made by Pietro della Francesca and Paolo Ucello, without those of Masolino de Panicale.'[22]

So closely had early Italian painting come to be identified with Roman Catholicism, a question of great controversy in England in the 1840s, that defenders of the Pre-Raphaelites attempted to distance their art from the supposed Italian sources, insisting rather on their close study of nature. In a famous letter to *The Times* in 1851, the movement's first champion in print, John Ruskin, recognized that he could not 'compliment them on their choice of *nom de guerre*', for they 'do *not* desire nor pretend in any way to imitate antique painting, as such.' He went on to explain that 'They intend to return to early days in this one point only – that, as far as in them lies, they will draw either what they see, or what they suppose might have been the actual facts of the scene they desire to represent, irrespective of any conventional rules of picture making; and they have chosen their unfortunate though not inaccurate name because all artists did this before Raphael's time, and after Raphael's time did *not* do this, but sought to paint fair pictures rather than represent stern facts, of which the consequence has been that from Raphael's time to this day historical art has been in acknowledged decadence.' In later life, all three of the principal Pre-Raphaelites minimized the influence of early Italian painting, and inevitably emphasized the differences between themselves. Millais, for example, wrote that 'D.G. Rossetti, you must understand, was a queer fellow, and impossible as a boon companion – so dogmatic and so irritable when opposed. His aims and ideals in art were also widely different from ours, and it was not long before he drifted away from us to follow in his own peculiar fancies.... They were highly imaginative and original, and not without elements of beauty, but they were not Nature. At last, when he presented for our admiration the young women which have since become the type of Rossettianism, the public opened their eyes in

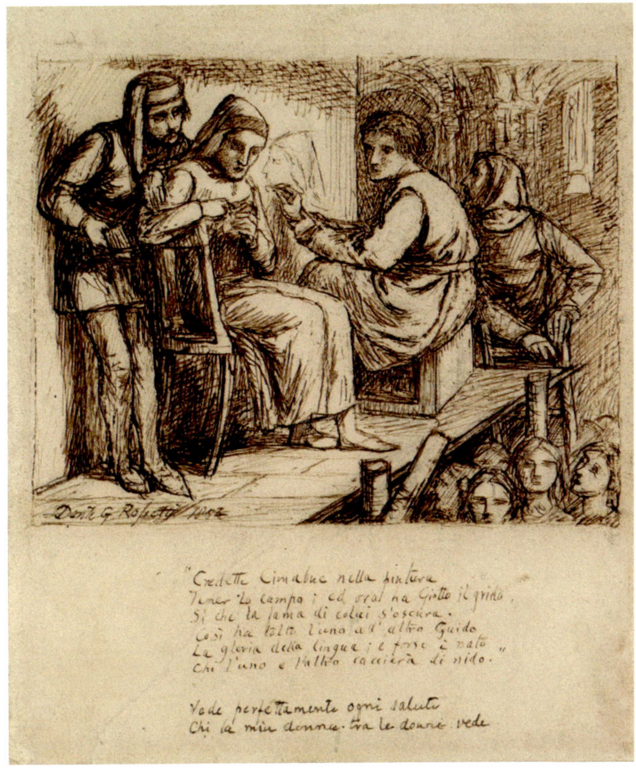

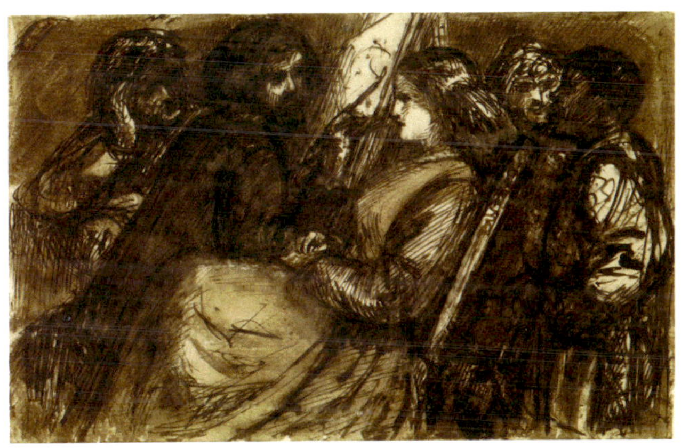

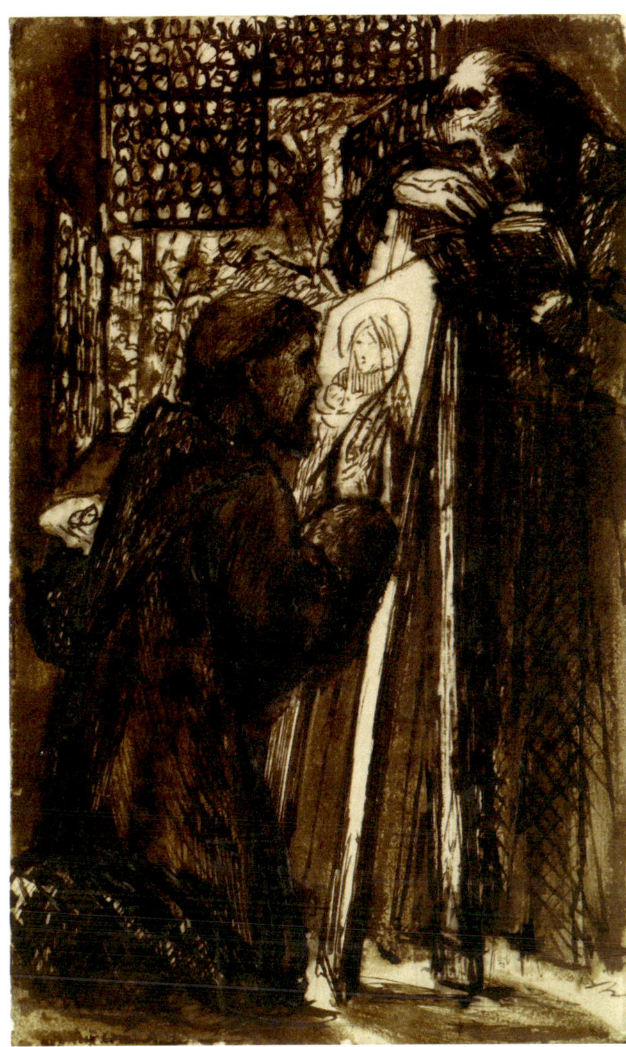

Cat. nos. 5–7 Dante Gabriel Rossetti (1828–1882), (Top left) *Study for 'Giotto painting the Portrait of Dante'* 1852. (Top right) *Fra Angelico painting c.* 1853. (Bottom left) *Giorgione painting c.* 1853. Pen and brown ink and wash on paper, 11.1 x 17.8 cm, Birmingham Museums and Art Gallery. Presented by subscribers, 1903 (1904P450–1)

amazement. "And this," they said, "is Pre-Raphaelitism!" It was nothing of the sort. The Pre-Raphaelites had but one idea – to present on canvas what they saw in Nature.'[23]

Nevertheless, art historians have been not wholly unsuccessful in trying to trace compositional sources for Pre-Raphaelite paintings among works by earlier artists. Among the subjects in Rossetti's early watercolours and drawings, one might naturally expect his depictions of Italian artists to have depended most on Italian models. The drawings and watercolours of Giotto, Fra Angelico, and Giorgione at work (**cats. 5–7**), however, are neither archaeological nor stylistic reconstructions.[24] Only in *Giotto painting the Portrait of Dante* (**cat. 5**) did Rossetti rely on historical fact, and only in the portrait of the sitter: in 1839, Seymour Kirkup discovered Giotto's portrait of Dante in a chapel in the Palazzo del Bargello, and sent a watercolour copy of the head to Rossetti's father, which Dante Gabriel retained all his life.[25] For other works of this period, Rossetti and his friends relied on the plates in Camille Bonnard's *Costumes historiques des* XII, XIV, XV *siècles*, a compilation first published in 1829-30;[26] and Henry Shaw's *Dresses and Decorations of the Middle Ages.*[27] Later in his career, Rossetti came to admire Botticelli, and acquired in 1867 the Florentine master's *Portrait of Smeralda Brandini*

(Victoria & Albert Museum), the composition of which is not dissimilar to Rossetti's own half-length female portraits, although the lush colouring was, as always, more Venetian than Florentine. For the early works of Millais and Holman Hunt, Malcolm Warner has proposed compositional affinities with a variety of works in the National Gallery, not all of them wholly convincing.[28] In *Convent Thoughts* (1850–51; Ashmolean Museum) **(fig. 8)**, by Millais's friend, Charles Alston Collins, there is even an isolated instance of copying from a late mediaeval manuscript: the nun holds a missal based on a leaf from a late fifteenth-century book of hours in Sir John Soane's Museum, another leaf from which had recently been reproduced in a book on *The Art of Illumination*.[29]

It was Burne-Jones who was the only artist who took full advantage of the inspiration of Italian art, in addition to combining the two strains of the original Brotherhood, as exemplified by Ruskin and Rossetti.[30] His formative years were influenced equally by both: he probably read Ruskin at school, certainly read him aloud with William Morris while at Oxford, and was inspired by him to visit the Royal Academy in 1854 and the collection of Thomas Combe in Oxford. It was there that he discovered Rossetti's *Dante Drawing an Angel* **(cat. 8)**, which filled him with the 'greatest wonder and delight' and persuaded him immediately that it was Rossetti, not Millais or Hunt, who was 'the chief figure in the Pre-Raphaelite Brotherhood'. It was Burne-Jones who read Ruskin's *Modern Painters* volume II with its praise of Giotto, and Burne-Jones who was thrilled by Fra Angelico's *Coronation of the Virgin* in the Louvre. The two influences came together in January 1856, when he received his first letter from Ruskin, and had his first meeting with Rossetti. From then on, his art became the battle-ground on which was fought the opposing tenets of Ruskinism and Rossettianism, and it is a measure of his greatness that his own personality gloriously conquered both forces.

In the late 1850s, Burne-Jones shared Rossetti's spirited brand of Mediaevalism, based for subject on old English and French literature, and for style on Dürer's engravings. Ruskin took him in hand, and sent him to Italy in September 1859. With Val Prinsep, he visited Genoa, Pisa, Florence, Siena, Verona, Padua, and Venice. As John Christian notes, he showed independence in looking at Carpaccio and Botticelli years before his mentor discovered them;

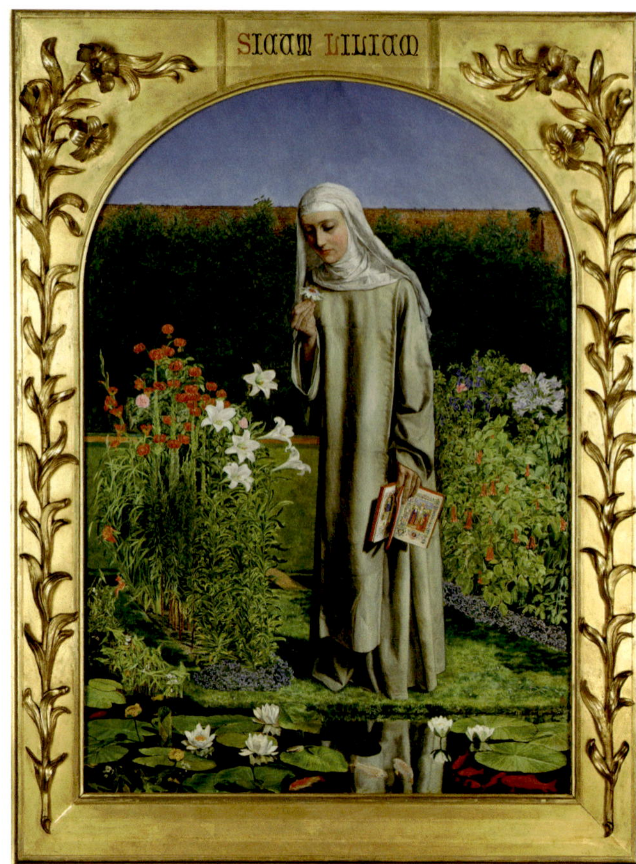

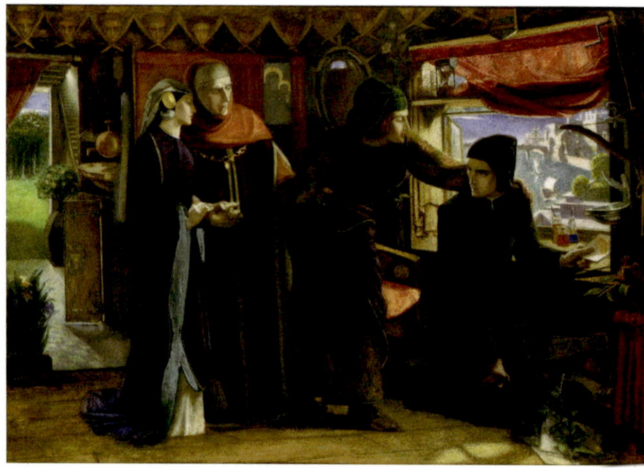

Fig. 8 (Top) Charles Allston Collins (1828–1873), *Convent Thoughts*, 1851, Oil on canvas, 84 x 59 cm, Ashmolean Museum, University of Oxford, WA1894.10

Cat. 8 (Above) Dante Gabriel Rossetti (1828–1882), *Dante Drawing an Angel on the Anniversary of Beatrice's Death* 1853, Watercolour and bodycolour on paper, 42 x 61 cm, Signed in monogram and dated: DGR / 1853, Ashmolean Museum, Oxford, Bequeathed by Mrs Thomas Combe, 1893 (WA1894.16)

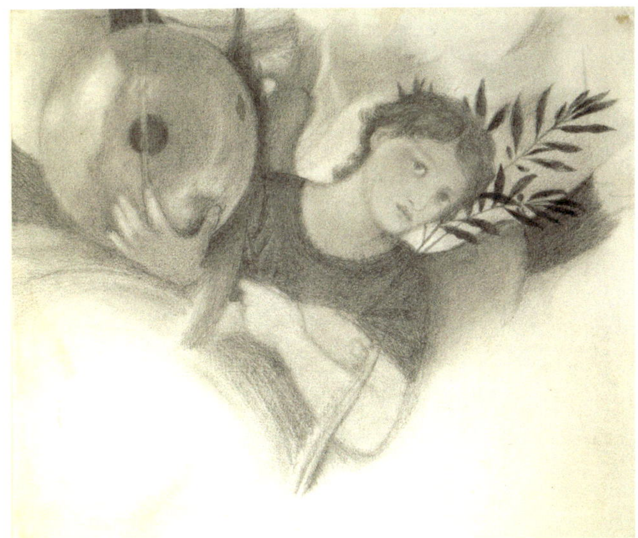

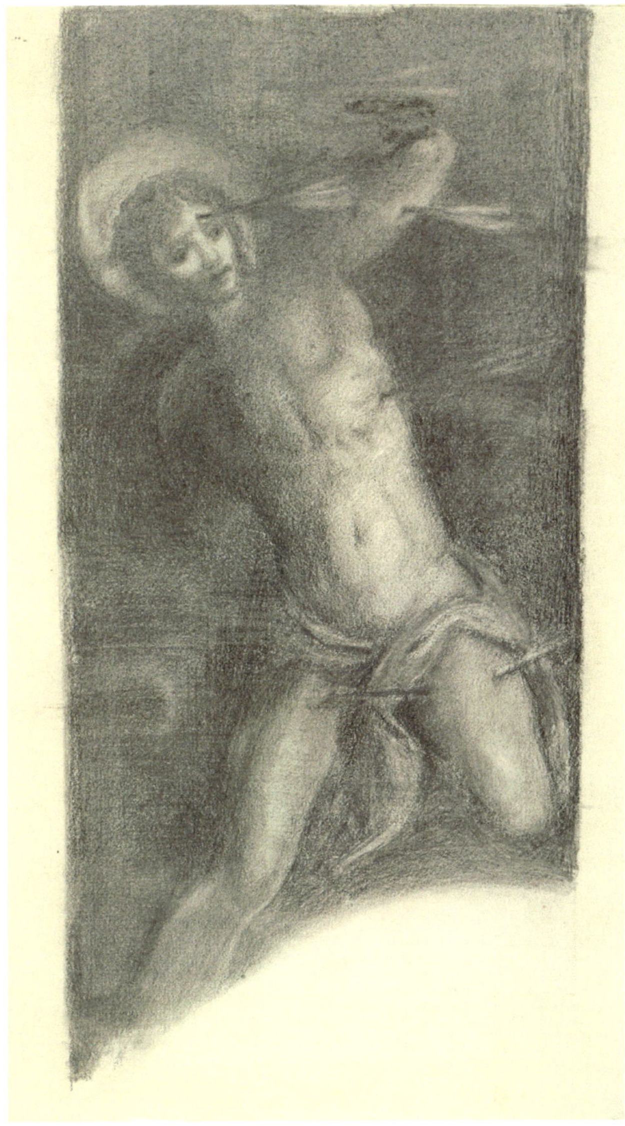

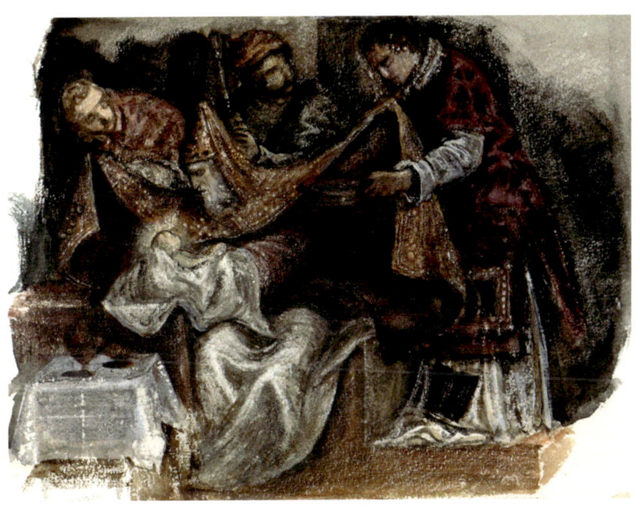

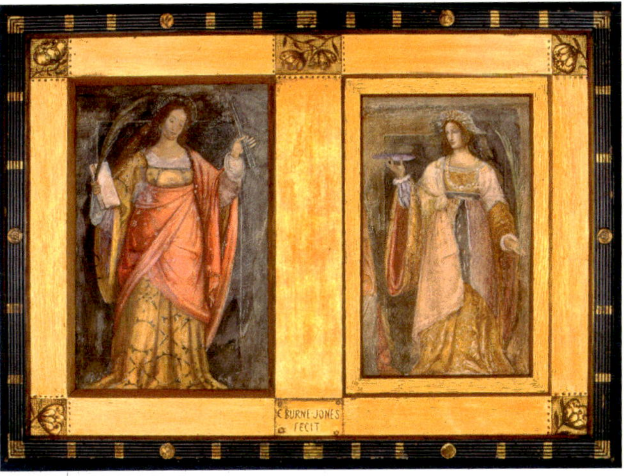

Cat. 49 (Top left) Sir Edward Burne-Jones (1833–1898), *Copy after the 'Allegory of the Battle of Lepanto' by Paolo Veronese* 1862, Pencil and black chalk on paper, 24 x 28.6 cm, Ashmolean Museum, University of Oxford. Ruskin School Collection (Ref. 140)

Cat. 50 (Top right) Sir Edward Burne-Jones, *Study of Tintoretto's 'Saint Sebastian' in the Scuola Grande di San Rocco* probably 1862, Black chalk and pencil on paper, 32.1 x 19.4 cm, Ashmolean Museum, University of Oxford. Ruskin School Collection (Ref. 139)

Cat. 51 (Middle left) Sir Edward Burne-Jones, *Copy after Tintoretto's 'The Circumcision'* probably 1862, Watercolour and bodycolour on paper, 18.1 x 24 cm, Ashmolean Museum, University of Oxford. Ruskin School Collection (Ed. 225)

Cat. 52 (Bottom left) Sir Edward Burne-Jones, *Copies after Bernardino Luini's 'Saint Apollonia' and 'Saint Lucy'* 1862, Watercolour over pencil on paper, 37.5 x 25 cm and 32.5 x 21 cm, inscribed on the original frame: E BURNE-JONES / FECIT. Royal Institution of Cornwall, Royal Museum of Cornwall, Truro.

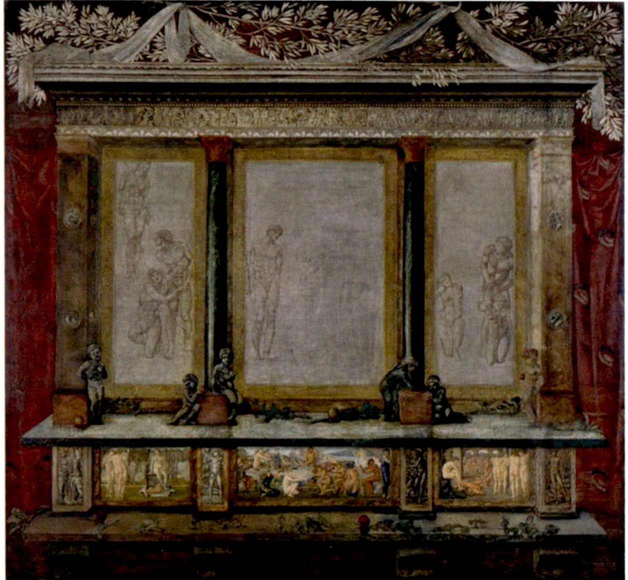

Fig. 9 Edward Burne Jones (1833–1898), *Troy Triptych* (1872–1898), Oil on canvas, 273 x 294.6 cm, Birmingham Museums and Art Gallery, 1922P178

but they generally had 'Ruskin in hand'. The copies Burne-Jones made, mostly of artists Ruskin admired, included Giotto, Masaccio, and Ghirlandaio. It is significant that Burne-Jones was the first to copy from the frescoes in the Campo Santo at Pisa, rather than from reproductions. Once again, Ruskin had led the way, having praised the particular frescoes he copied in his Edinburgh Lecture on Pre-Raphaelitism, and elsewhere. On his second visit to Italy, in 1862, with Ruskin himself, Burne-Jones was enjoined to make copies of Ruskin's new enthusiasms, the Venetians and Luini (**cat. 52**).[31] Most importantly, the pictures he had seen inspired his own compositions of the early 1860s (**cats. 49–52**). During that decade, Burne-Jones's taste in Italian art was moving away from that of his mentor, Ruskin. In particular, he had begun to admire the works of Michelangelo, making copies of the drawings in the University Galleries at Oxford during his vacations there in 1867. Such studies bore fruit in several of Burne-Jones's exhibited works of 1870, which reflect a strong interest in Michelangelo's nudes, notably *Phyllis and Demophoon* and *The Troy Triptych* (**fig. 9**). Indeed, when Ruskin attacked the very Michelangelo drawings that Burne-Jones had copied in one of his Oxford lectures in the summer of 1871, claiming that Michelangelo's treatment of the human figure was 'dishonest, insolent, and artifical',[32] Burne-Jones was mortified, and never quite forgave him.[33] Shortly afterwards, in September 1871, Burne-Jones made his third visit to Italy, in particular to study Michelangelo. His wife, who accompanied him on this trip, recorded that, to study the Sistine Chapel, 'He bought the best opera-glass he could find, folded his railway rug thickly, and, lying down on his back, read the ceiling from beginning to end, peering into every corner and revelling in its execution'.[34] And Burne-Jones's later enthusiasm for Italian art was by no means confined to Michelangelo: the artists he admired most on that trip to Italy included, again according to his wife, Giotto, Orcagna, Uccello, Piero della Francesca, Mantegna, Signorelli, as well as Botticelli, who had suddenly become fashionable after having been completely forgotten until rediscovered by Walter Pater and Ruskin.[35] On his fourth and last journey to Italy, in 1872, Burne-Jones managed to reach Ravenna, before ill health forced him back. On the way, he had visited Florence, Sienna, Volterra, and Bologna, drawing as he went, in particular the works of Botticelli and Mantegna.

Among Rossetti's other followers, Walter Crane made an extended tour of Europe on his honeymoon in 1871-3, carefully studying art of all periods. At Verona, he 'saluted Mr Ruskin's Gothic griffin at the porch of S. Anastasia'; at Venice, the 'glories of the great Venetian painters … and the more primitive but not less beautiful conceptions of Carpaccio, Giov. Bellini, and the early Venetian school'; and at Florence, he was so impressed by Botticelli's paintings in the Uffizi that, some years later, he painted what is virtually a pastiche in his *Renaissance of Venus* (1877; Tate).[36] In 1878, another pupil of Rossetti's, Marie Spartali, settled in Florence with her husband, William Stillman, and continued to send her watercolour illustrations to Dante and Boccaccio to the London exhibitions. More importantly, Charles Fairfax Murray, who had worked in the studios of both Rossetti and Burne-Jones and as a copyist for Ruskin in Italy, took up residence in Florence in 1878, and promoted early Italian art as a dealer, connoisseur, and collector.[37] By the late 1870s, however, both in England and in Italy, the fascination for Italian art was so widespread that it would have seemed perverse for any serious artist to ignore the Primitives any more than the high Renaissance.

Another artist of Burne-Jones's generation, Frederic Leighton, might also be regarded as more truly Pre-Raphaelite than Millais, Rossetti, or Holman Hunt.

As he later remembered, 'for a long time I treated none but subjects from the Italian Middle Ages – going to history, Dante, Boccaccio, and preferring in Shakespeare the Italian plays'.[38] He studied in Frankfurt and Rome, and his first major work, *Cimabue's Celebrated Madonna is Carried in Procession through the Streets of Florence* (**fig. 10**), was greeted with rapture when shown at the Royal Academy in 1855, admired by Ruskin and Rossetti, and bought by Queen Victoria. It was followed by a number of oil paintings and watercolours on early Italian themes, painted in the highly polished style of the Nazarenes, which gave way in the mid-1860s to more classicizing subjects executed in a much softer style. Leighton's eclecticism, and especially his landscape paintings, also illustrate once again the difficulties in seeking a single definition of a Pre-Raphaelite style, for, although he painted assiduously from nature, under the tutelage of Nino Costa and the influence of Corot, he never aimed at the minute descriptions of the Ruskinian landscape painters such as Brett and Inchbold (**fig. 11**).

From the mid-1860s, Costa himself became an essential link between British and Italian artists, largely responsible for promoting the reputations of Pre-Raphaelite artists in Italy, and for introducing progressive Italian painting into the London art world. In the winter of 1865–6, he met George Howard (later 9th Earl of Carlisle) and William Blake Richmond, both of whom became close friends.[39] Howard studied oil painting with Costa, and collected his work assiduously. Richmond, too, acknowledged that 'if what I have painted in landscape has any merit, it is largely due to the early influence of Giovanni Costa'.[40] Both artists were profoundly interested in early Italian art, and they and the other landscape painters who became known as the Etruscans were seen by contemporaries as having adopted a distinctly Italian and Primitive style, and thus, as Giuliana Pieri has argued, as 'quintessentially Pre-Raphaelite'.[41] Their technique was far removed from that of the Ruskinian landscape artists, but no farther than that of, say, Rossetti in 1870 from Rossetti in 1848. Collectors in England were extraordinarily faithful to Costa, to the extent that he showed at the Royal Academy from 1869, and regularly at the Grosvenor Gallery from its establishment in 1877, together with Burne-Jones, Crane, Leighton, and other artists of the Pre-Raphaelite and Aesthetic schools.

Costa was also instrumental in introducing the English Pre-Raphaelites to an Italian audience, for, in spite of the

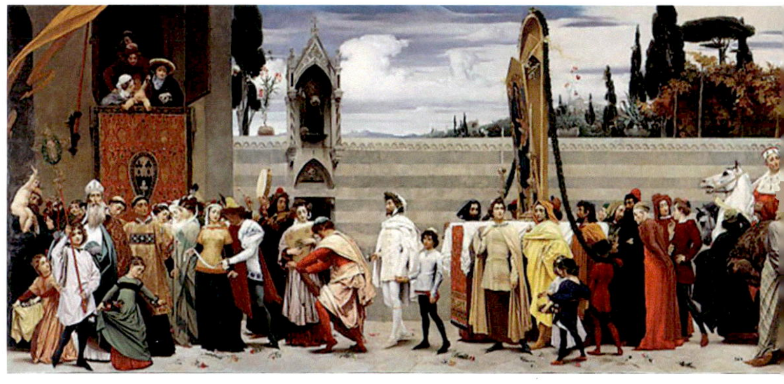

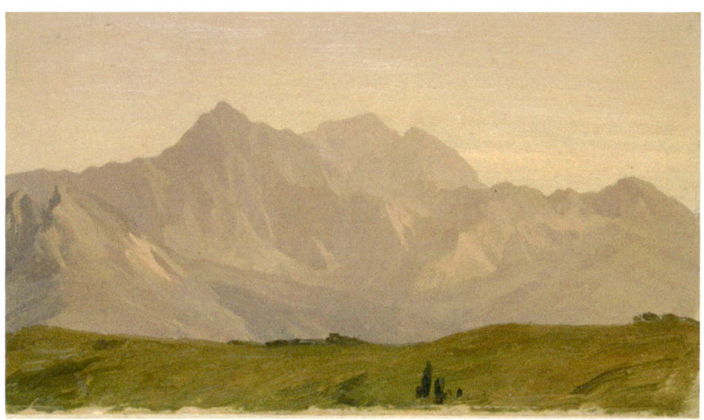

Fig. 10 (Top) Frederic Leighton (1830–1896), *Cimabue's Celebrated Madonna is Carried in Procession through the Streets of Florence* (1853–1855), Oil on canvas, 222 x 521 cm, Royal Collection (on long-term loan to the National Gallery, London)

Fig. 11 (Bottom) Frederic Leighton, *Monte Croce*, Oil on panel, mounted as a drawing, 10 x 17.7 cm, Ashmolean Museum, University of Oxford, WA1950.178.442

presence of the English colony in Florence, there was no opportunity to see their work until 1890, in an exhibition in Rome organised at In Arte Libertas, the society founded by Costa three years earlier.[42] Among the exhibits were several designs by Burne-Jones for his decoration of the American Church in Rome, Rossetti's *Dantis Amor* (**cat. 121**), and other works by the Pre-Raphaelites, which a contemporary critic described as 'a most successful exhibition of the English Pre-Raphaelites, giving a complete survey of the school, from Madox Brown to Burne-Jones, up to the latest followers'.[43] Five years later, the first Venice International Exhibition (Biennale) marked the triumph of Pre-Raphaelitism in Italy, although, since exhibitions held under these auspices were limited to living artists, it gave a very partial view of the movement.[44] Of the members of the original Brotherhood, Rossetti was dead, Millais

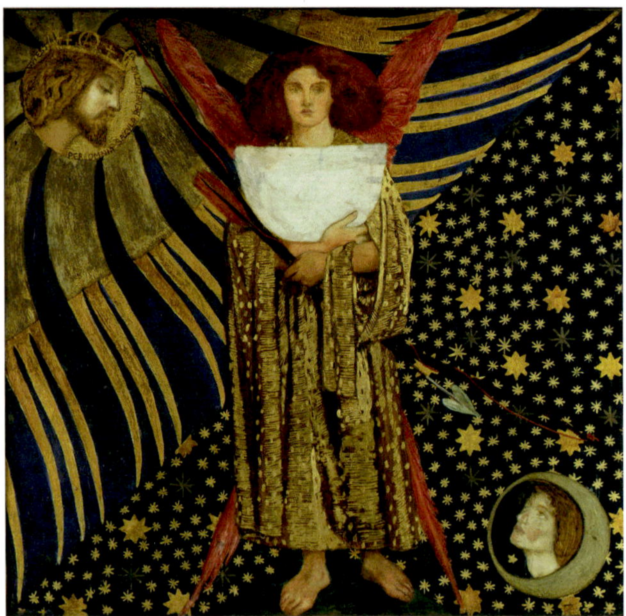

Cat. 121 Dante Gabriel Rossetti (1828–1882), *Dantis Amor* 1860, Inscribed: QUI EST PER OMNIA SAECVLA BENEDICTUS, Oil on mahogany panel, 74.9 x 81.3 cm. Tate. Presented by F. Treharne James, 1920 (N03532)

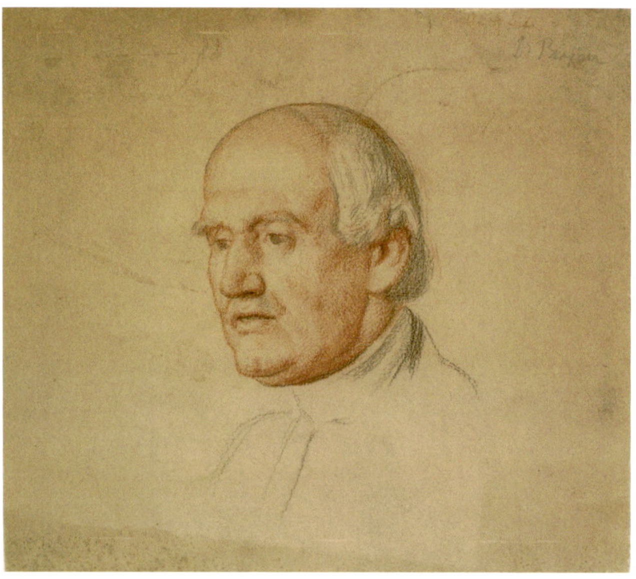

Fig. 12 William Holman Hunt (1827–1910), *Study of the Head of Dr Bloxham for 'May Morning on Magdalen Tower'*, Black and red chalk on brown card, 22.9 x 25.7 cm (irregular), Ashmolean Museum, University of Oxford, WA1970.33

had long since abandoned a Pre-Raphaelite style (as the reviewers were quick to point out), and only Holman Hunt continued in his original, meticulous manner, though his *May Morning on Magdalen Tower* (Lady Lever Art Gallery, Port Sunlight) disappointed the Italian public (**fig. 12**). Only Arthur Hughes and his nephew, Edward Hughes, were felt to live up to the expectations of the Pre-Raphaelite movement. The disappointment arose not only out of the particular pictures shown, but from a more general misapprehension of the development of the Pre-Raphaelitism in England. The artists were much discussed in the Italian press in the late 1870s and 1880s, most notably by Enrico Nencioni, who, in a study of Dante Gabriel Rossetti in 1884, tried to explain the meaning of the term 'Pre-Raphaelite' and how it had frequently been misunderstood – 'Preraffaelismo è parola spesso abusata e sbagliata.'[45]

The great polymath E.H. Gombrich observed in his magisterial survey of *The Preference for the Primitive* that the Pre-Raphaelite style 'is as far removed from the modes of the German Nazarenes as it is from the modes of the Quattrocento, to which it is supposed to pay tribute. Neither in subject-matter, nor in their bright clear colours or narrative manner do these painters display a preference for the primitive, which those words may imply.'[46] As we have seen, the members of the Pre-Raphaelite Brotherhood, which lasted from 1848 to 1852–3, had very limited opportunity to study at first hand paintings made before Raphael. However, even after the Brotherhood had been dissolved, many opportunities occurred, which they mostly failed to exploit. And it was only with what is generally known as the second generation of Pre-Raphaelites, Rossetti's followers such as Burne-Jones, William Morris, Walter Crane, and Marie Spartali, that artists made a conscious effort to see and learn from the art of the Italian Quattrocento. The young men who decided on the label in 1848 can scarcely have imagined how much depended on their choice, or the trouble it would cause, both to their contemporaries, and to later historians. As Rossetti himself remembered, 'the epoch of preraphaelitism was a short one which is quite over yet and will never be renewed.'[47]

1 W. Holman Hunt, *Pre-Raphaelitism and the Pre-Raphaelite Brotherhood*, 2 vols (London, 1905), I, pp. 135–42. It is worth noting that Ruskin later described Lasinio's engravings as 'execrable' – *The Works of John Ruskin*, ed. E.T. Cook and Alexander Wedderburn, 39 vols (London, 1903-12), V, p. 395.

2 quoted by Ruskin himself in his first pamphlet on 'Pre-Raphaelitism', Ruskin 1903–12, XII, p. 339.

3 Hunt 1905, I, pp. 140–1.

4 see, for example, Jason Rosenfeld and Alison Smith, *Millais* (exh. cat., Tate, London, 2007), no. 2.

5 Sir Joshua Reynolds, *Discourses on Art*, ed. Robert R. Wark (New Haven & London, 1975), p. 81.

6 see T.S.R. Boase, 'The Decoration of the New Palace of Westminster, 1841–1863', *Journal of the Warburg and Courtauld Institutes* XVII (1954), pp. 319–58.

7 *The Germ*, ed. W.M. Rossetti (London, 1901), p. 18.

8 Giovanni Previtali, *La fortuna dei primitivi dal Vasari ai neoclassici* (Turin 1956); and Francis Haskell, *Rediscoveries in Art: Some Aspects of Taste, Fashion and Collecting in England and France*, second edn (Oxford, 1980), especially pp. 85–106.

9 R.W. Lightbown, 'The Inspiration of Christian Art', in *Influences in Victorian Art and Architecture*, ed. S. Macready and F.H. Thompson (London, 1985), pp. 3–40.

10 Jonathan Conlin, 'Gladstone and Christian Art, 1832–1854', *The Historical Journal* XLVI (2003), pp. 341–74.

11 *Art and its Images* (exh. cat., Oxford, Bodleian Library, 1975), no. 52.

12 *Art and its Images*, p. 130.

13 Gail S. Weinberg, "First of all First Beginnings": Ruskin's Studies of Early Italian Paintings at Christ Church', *Burlington Magazine* CXXXIV (1992), pp. 111–20.

14 on whom the most recent account is Charles Saumarez-Smith, *The National Gallery: A Short History* (London, 2009), pp. 67–80.

15 Malcolm Warner, 'The Pre-Raphaelites and the National Gallery', *The Pre-Raphaelites in Context* (San Marino, Ca, 1992), pp. 1–11 (p. 3).

16 quoted in Gail S. Weinberg, "Looking backward": Opportunities for the Pre-Raphaelites to see "pre-Raphaelite" art', *Collecting the Pre-Raphaelites: The Anglo-American Enchantment*, ed. Margaretta Frederick Watson (Aldershot, 1997), pp. 52-62 (p. 52)

17 16 Judith Bronkhurst, *William Holman Hunt: A Catalogue Raisonné*, 2 vols (New Haven & London, 2006), I, p. 46

18 Haskell 1980, p. 94

19 see especially Alastair Grieve, 'Style and Content in Pre-Raphaelite Drawings 1848–50', *Pre-Raphaelite Papers*, ed. Leslie Parris (London, 1984), pp. 23–43.

20 Bronkhurst 2006, I, p. 132

21 Warner 1992, pp. 8-9.

22 A useful compilation of contemporary criticism of the Pre-Raphaelites can be found on the website by Thomas J. Tobin, 'The Pre-Raphaelite Critic: Periodical Criticism of the Pre-Raphaelite Movement, 1846–1860' (http://www.engl.duq.edu/servus/PR_Critic/Fulltext.html).

23 J.G. Millais, *The Life and Letters of John Everett Millais, President of the Royal Academy*, 2 vols (London, 1899), I, pp. 52–5.

24 Flavia Dietrich, 'Art History Painted: The Pre-Raphaelite View of Italian Art: Some Works by Rossetti', *The British Art Journal* II (2000), pp. 61–9

25 David Bindman, Stephen Hebron and Michael O'Neill, *Dante Rediscovered, from Blake to Rodin* (exh. cat., Wordsworth Trust, Grasmere, 2007), no. 78.

26 R. Smith, 'Bonnard's *Costume historique* – a Pre-Raphaelite Source Book', *Costume: Journal of the Costume Society* VII (1973), p. 28–37; Gail S. Weinberg, 'Dante Gabriel Rossetti's "Salutation of Beatrice" and Camille Bonnard's "Costumes Historiques", *Burlington Magazine* CXLI (1999), pp. 622–3.

27 Julian Treuherz, 'The Pre-Raphaelites and Mediaeval Illuminated Manuscripts', *Pre-Raphaelite Papers*, ed. Leslie Parris (London, 1984), pp. 153–69 (p. 158).

28 Warner 1992.

29 Treuherz 1984, pp. 151–2.

30 see John Christian, "A Serious Talk": Ruskin's Place in Burne-Jones's Artistic Development', *Pre-Raphaelite Papers*, ed. Leslie Parris (London, 1984), pp. 184–205.

31 John Christian, 'Burne-Jones's Second Italian Journey', *Apollo* (1975), pp. 334-7. See also John Christian, 'Burne-Jones et l'art italien', in *Burne-Jones 1833-1898: Dessins du Fitzwilliam Museum de Cambridge* (exh. cat., Nantes, Charleroi, Nancy, 1992), pp. 33–57; Maria Teresa Benedetti, 'L'arte di Burne-Jones e i suoi viaggi in Italia', in *Burne-Jones: Dal Preraffaellismo al simbolismo* (exh. cat., ed. Maria Teresa Benedetti and Gianna Piantoni; Roma, Galleria nazionale d'arte moderna, 1986), pp. 15–29.

32 Ruskin 1903-12, XXII, p. 98.

33 Lene Ostermark-Johansen, *Sweetness and Strength: The Reception of Michelangelo in Late Victorian England* (Aldershot, 1998), pp. 116–39.

34 Georgiana Burne-Jones, *Memorials of Edward Burne-Jones*, 2 vols (London, 1904), II, p. 26.

35 Michael Levey, 'Botticelli and England', *Journal of the Warburg and Courtauld Institutes*, XXIII (1960), pp. 291–306.

36 Walter Crane, *An Artist's Reminiscences* (London, 1907), p. 121–2, 125.

37 For this whole section, see Sandra Berresford, 'Preraffaellismo ed estetismo a Firenze negli ultimi decenni del XIX secolo', *L'Idea di Firenze: Temi e interpretazioni nell'arte straniera dell'Ottocento*, ed. Maurizio Bossi and Lucia Tonini (Florence, 1989), pp. 191–210. For Murray, see Robert Barrington, 'Copyist, connoisseur, collector: Charles Fairfax Murray (1849–1919)', *Apollo* CCCXCIII (1994), pp. 15–21 .

38 Leonee and Richard Ormond, *Lord Leighton* (New Haven and London, 1975), p. 11.

39 Giuliana Pieri, *The Influence of Pre-Raphaelitism on* Fin de siecle *Italy: Art, Beauty, and Culture* (London, 2007), chapter 4, 'Nino Costa and the Pre-Raphaelite Landscape', pp. 85–110.

40 quoted in Pieri 2007, p. 90.

41 loc.cit.

42 Anna Maria Damigella, *La pittura simbolista in Italia 1885-1900* (Turin, 1981), and Giuliana Pieri, 'The Reception of Pre-Raphaelitism in Italy, 1878–1910', *The Modern Language Review* XCIX (2004).

43 'una mostra molto riuscita di preraffaelliti inglesi, dando un panorama completo di questa scuola, da Madox Brown a Burne Jones, fino agli ultimi seguaci', quoted in Pieri 2007, p. 104.

44 Sandra Berresford, 'The Pre-Raphaelites and their Followers at the International Exhibitions of Art in Venice, 1895–1905', in *Britain at the Venice Biennale 1895-1995*, ed. Sophie Bowness and Clive Philpot (London, 1995), pp. 37-49.

45 Enrico Nencioni, 'Le poesie e le pitture di Dante Gabriele Rossetti', *Fanfulla della domenica*, 17 February 1884, quoted in Peri 2004, pp. 364–81 (p. 369).

46 E.H. Gombrich, *The Preference for the Primitive* (London, 2002) p. 141.

47 quoted in Jan Marsh, *Dante Gabriel Rossetti: Painter and Poet* (London, 1999), p.277.

The Pre-Raphaelites and Italian Literature

Martin McLaughlin

By the time the Pre-Raphaelite movement emerged in 1848, British enthusiasm for Italian culture (and later for Italian independence) was widespread, focusing particularly on Dante and his *Comedy*.[1] Henry Cary's complete translation had been published in 1814 and, thanks to Coleridge's promotion of this version, enthusiasm for Dante's poem extended to the great Romantic poets of the time, so much so that just ten years after the translation appeared, in 1824 Wordsworth could declare 'it has lately become the fashion to extol Dante above measure';[2] by 1850, there were already four complete translations of Dante's *Comedy*; and by 1900, the British reader was able to choose from fifteen different English versions. The poet's centrality in the nineteenth century was encapsulated in Ruskin's famous definition of Dante in *The Stones of Venice* (1851-3) as 'the central man of all the world, as representing in perfect balance the imaginative, moral and intellectual faculties, all at their highest.'[3]

The single most popular episode in Dante's poem was that of Paolo and Francesca (*Inferno*, v) and the ill-starred couple's kiss was represented time and again in romantic art: from William Dyce's painting of 1837 (**cat. 1**), Joseph Noel Paton's Dante Meditating (1850) (**cat. 2**), Alexander Munro's marble statue commissioned by Gladstone (**cat. 3**) and to Rossetti's own paintings of the couple (1855, 1862), down to Charles Edward Hallé's passionate version of 1888. Even outside Pre-Raphaelite circles Francesca was in the minds of artists from Ingres and Blake to Doré and Rodin. For a whole century she was to dominate the British imagination of Italy, from an anthology of Italian verse in translation published in 1798, which opened with the celebrated passage from the *Inferno*,[4] down to the death of Gladstone in 1898: his tomb at Hawarden displayed a relief of the famous lovers.[5]

If the enthusiasm for Dante was widespread outside the Rossetti home, inside the house interest in the Italian poet was intense. Gabriele Rossetti, an Italian exile and Dante scholar, wrote a trilogy of ponderous studies on the poet between 1832 and 1842 which portrayed Dante as a proto-Mason and exile who had used secret codes in his works in order to attack the Papacy (Gabriele had before his exile been a member of the Carbonari, a secret sect bent on political reform in Italy).[6] Young Dante Gabriel would inherit this Dante enthusiasm and this tendency to identify closely with the mediaeval author, but would channel these into more creative outputs. One visual element that played a crucial role in the young artist's interest in the Florentine poet was the fresco of Dante attributed to Giotto, which had been discovered in 1839 on the wall of the Bargello in Florence. Seymour Kirkup sent Rossetti senior a copy in 1840 and his son treasured it throughout his life.[7] The drawing was responsible for changing Dante's iconography from the stern figure of the *Comedy*, epitomized in the Torrigiani and other death-masks, to the youthful poet of the *Vita nuova*. As Rossetti himself put it in *The Early Italian Poets*: 'This is the author of the *Vita nuova*. That other portrait shown us in the posthumous mask – a face dead in exile after the death of hope – should front the first page of the Sacred Poem to which heaven and earth had set their hands.'[8]

Dante Gabriel's earliest drawings are indebted to this iconography of Dante as young poet, but in addition Rossetti in these early works underlines his identification with the mediaeval writer by portraying him not just as a

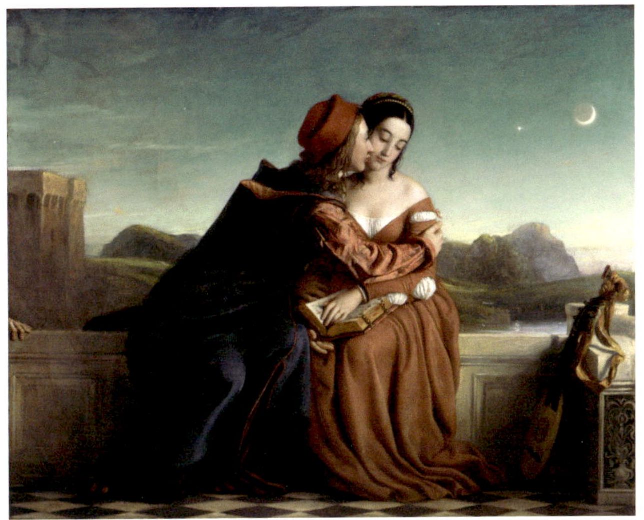

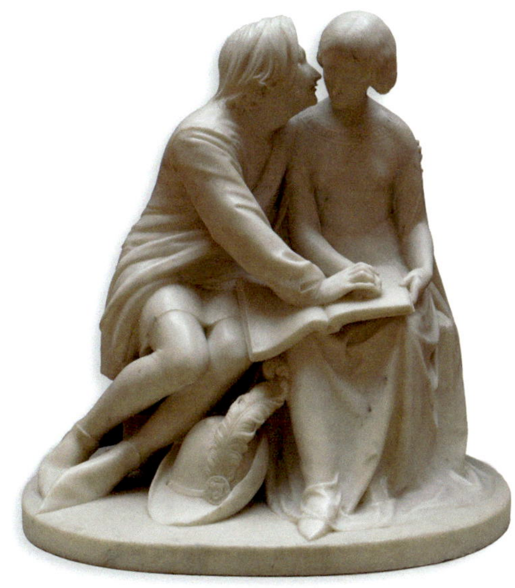

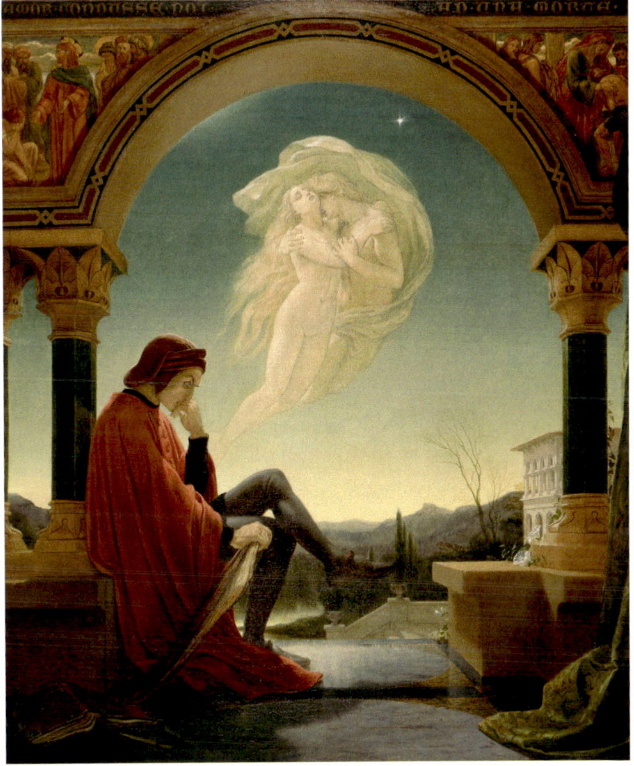

Cat. 1 (Top left) William Dyce (1806–1864), *Francesca da Rimini* 1837, Oil on canvas, 137.6 x 172.7 cm, The National Galleries of Scotland, Edinburgh

Cat. 2 (Bottom left) Sir Joseph Noel Paton (1821–1901), *Dante Meditating the Episode of Francesca da Rimini and Paulo Malatesta* 1852, Oil on canvas, 101 x 89 cm, Inscribed: *Amor. condusse. noi. ad. una. morte.* Bury Art Gallery, Museums and Archives

Cat. 3 (Above) Alexander Munro (1825–1871), *Paolo and Francesca* 1852, Marble, 66 x 67.5 x 53 cm, Signed and dated: Alex. Munro / Sc. 1852, Birmingham Museum and Art Gallery

youthful poet and lover but also as an artist. One of his first works was *Dante Drawing an Angel on the Anniversary of Beatrice's Death,* a drawing of 1849 now in Birmingham, a subject later reprised in the watercolour of 1853 in the Ashmolean. This episode from the *Vita nuova* was the only one which alluded to Dante's artistic qualities. Underneath the drawing Rossetti reproduces the whole passage from the *Vita nuova* (chapter 34), which he had just finished translating. There is an interesting difference in the later watercolour in that amongst Dante's visitors there is now a woman, possibly Gemma Donati, the woman that Dante was to marry.[9] Shortly afterwards another work connected Dante with art even more explicitly: *Giotto Painting the Portrait of Dante*. Here once more Dante's links with painting are stressed in a kind of artistic *mise-en-abîme* in which Dante Gabriel depicts Giotto depicting Dante. The subject reflects the discovery of the Bargello fresco, but Rossetti associates it with a famous passage from *Purgatorio* (Canto XI, 94-99) in which the artistic succession which saw Giotto overtake Cimabue is paralleled by the poetic succession whereby the older poet Guinizelli was superseded by Dante's friend Cavalcanti (who would in turn be outdone by Dante). Rossetti inscribes these six lines beneath the drawing, and their meaning is reflected in the fact that Cimabue is staring at Giotto's brilliant fresco, while Cavalcanti is reading poems by Guinizelli. Yet although the episode is thus linked with the *Comedy*, the fact that this is the youthful Dante being

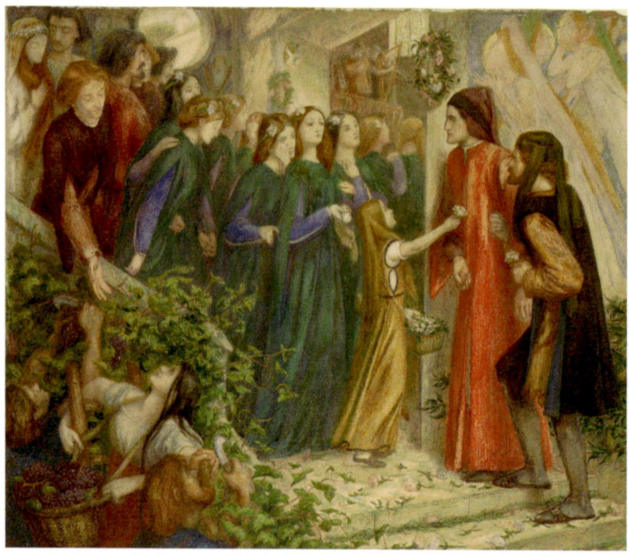

Cat. 13 Dante Gabriel Rossetti (1828–1882), *Beatrice meeting Dante at a Marriage Feast, Denies him her Salutation* 1855, Watercolour and bodycolour over pencil on paper, 34.3 x 41.9 cm, Ashmolean Museum, University of Oxford (WA1942.156)

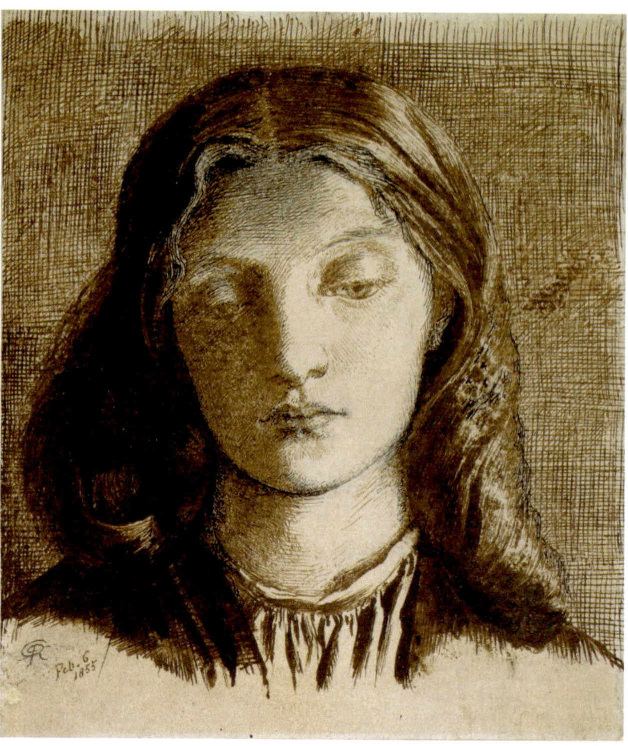

Fig. 13 Dante Gabriel Rossetti, *Elizabeth Siddal*, 1855, Pen and brown and black ink, 13 x 11.2 cm, Ashmolean Museum, University of Oxford, WA1962.17.77

painted, that he is attended by Cavalcanti, and that at the bottom right Beatrice is staring up at Dante as she passes through the chapel, all show that we are in the world of the *Vita nuova*. This is confirmed by the fact that Rossetti also adds the opening two lines from a famous sonnet in the *Vita nuova*: 'Vede perfettamente ogni salute / chi la mia donna tra le donne vede' (*Vita nuova*, 26). Rossetti's comments on the subject are revealing of how the episode embodies several ideals of his: 'I have thus all the influence of Dante's youth – Art, Friendship and Love – with a real incident embodying them'.[10]

Rossetti continued to be inspired by Dante's early work throughout the 1850s: in 1852 he exhibited a watercolour of *Beatrice at a Marriage Feast, Denying her Salutation to Dante*. Ruskin admired the picture and bought a second, almost identical, watercolour of 1855 now in the Ashmolean (**cat. 13**). This depicts the moment when Dante, accompanied by a friend, nearly faints against a painted wall after catching sight of Beatrice in a wedding procession (*Vita nuova*, 14). The detail of the painted wall also accounts for Rossetti's choice of this episode, since once more art, love and friendship are involved. The artist also conflates this episode with an earlier one from the *Vita nuova*, when Beatrice 'denies her salutation' to Dante (*Vita nuova*, 10). In a note to his translation, Rossetti interestingly speculates that the wedding was that of Beatrice herself, hence the poet's swoon.[11] The model for Beatrice here was Rossetti's wife, Lizzie Siddal (**fig. 13**), so in this respect also there is a close intertwining of art and reality. The inspiration he derived from Dante's first work continued throughout the decade. In 1856 he painted his largest ever watercolour, *Dante's Dream on the Day of the Death of Beatrice* (**cat. 14**), once more with Lizzie Siddal as his model. The subject, which he had thought of as far back as 1848, obsessed Rossetti, and in 1871 it would inspire his largest oil painting, though this time the model would be Jane Morris (now in Liverpool; replica of 1879 now in Dundee). On this frame too he would add text: 'Somnium Dantis in extrema Beatricis hora / JUNII DIE. 9 ANNO 1290', and also eight lines from the canzone that mentions this presage of Beatrice's death, 'Donna pietosa', lines 63-70 (*Vita nuova* 23). In both paintings there is also a vision of the city in the background and in the later one a scroll is suspended from the roof with the first verse of Lamentations, 'Quomodo sedet sola civitas', 'How doth the city sit solitary', a phrase used twice by Dante to describe the effect of Beatrice's death on Florence (*Vita nuova*, 28, 30).[12]

In fact, the *Vita nuova* was to be the source of several other major works in Rossetti's mature years. In 1860 he produced *Dantis Amor*, a more symbolic work showing Beatrice and Christ in roundels on either side of Love, but once more Rossetti inserted text which makes clear that this painting too relates to Dante's first work: 'QUI EST PER OMNIA SAECULA BENEDICTUS', the very last words of the *Vita nuova* (42), where Dante hopes to see the sight of his beloved as she enjoys the divine vision. Similarly, *Beata Beatrix* (**cat. 133**), also quotes the opening of *Lamentations*. At the top of the picture the artist once more wrote in Latin the date of Beatrice's death, 'Jun. die 9. 1290', a date which Dante himself makes much play of for he associated Beatrice with the number nine: Beatrice was a miracle, a nine, since three is the root of nine just as the Trinity is the root of a miracle (*Vita nuova*, 29).

Even some of Rossetti's late works go back to his fascination with the *Vita nuova*. The oil painting *La Donna della Finestra / The Lady of Pity* (Fogg Museum, Harvard; see **cat. 125**) was painted in the years 1870-79 with Jane Morris as model, and relates to a key episode in Dante's youthful work, when after the death of Beatrice he is consoled by a woman at a window who shows him much pity and with whom he starts to fall in love (*Vita nuova*, 35-8). Once more, the Dante episode applies to Rossetti's lived experience, since by now he was in love with Jane Morris, the model for this lady of pity. Janey was again the sitter for the drawing *La donna della fiamma* (1870; Manchester City Art Gallery), inspired by four lines from the most important canzone in the *Vita nuova* (ch. 19), 'Donne ch'avete intelletto d'amore' (lines 51-4):

> Whatever her sweet eyes are turned upon,
> Spirits of Love issue thence in Flame,
> Which through their eyes who then may look on them
> Pierce to the Heart's deep chamber every one.[13]

Similarly the watercolour of 1872, *The Salutation of Beatrice* (private collection), shows appended to a tree the most famous sonnet of Dante's first work, 'Tanto gentile'. One final late project Rossetti had in mind was to devise a series of twelve 'autotypes' of Janey, using the new art of photography, to be entitled 'Twelve Coins for One Queen'. In a letter to her of August 1878, Rossetti explains the title he would give to one of them, *Perlascura* (**cat. 128**) by quoting once more from the first major canzone of the

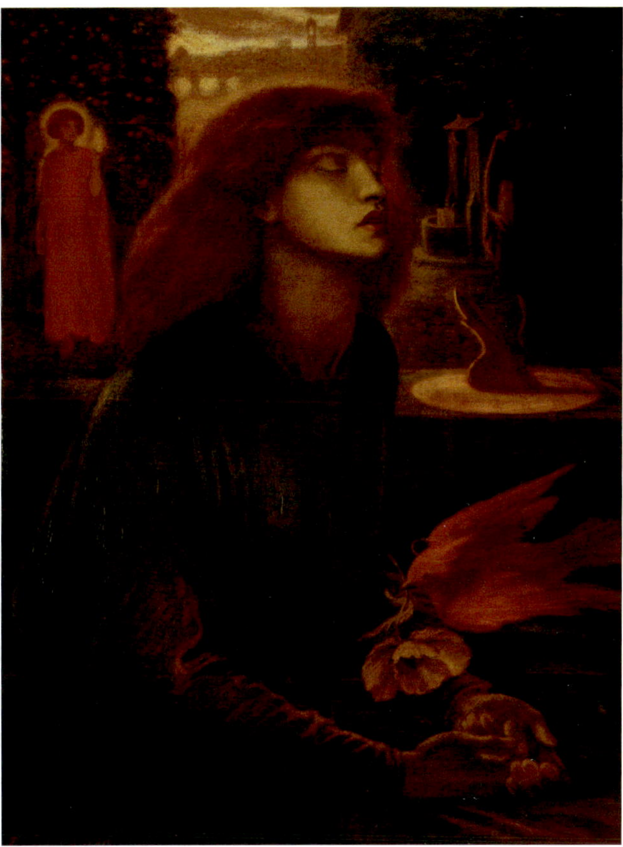

Cat. 133 Dante Gabriel Rossetti, *Beata Beatrix* 1880, Oil on canvas, 86 x 66.7 cm. Signed and dated, DGR 1880. The National Galleries of Scotland, Edinburgh

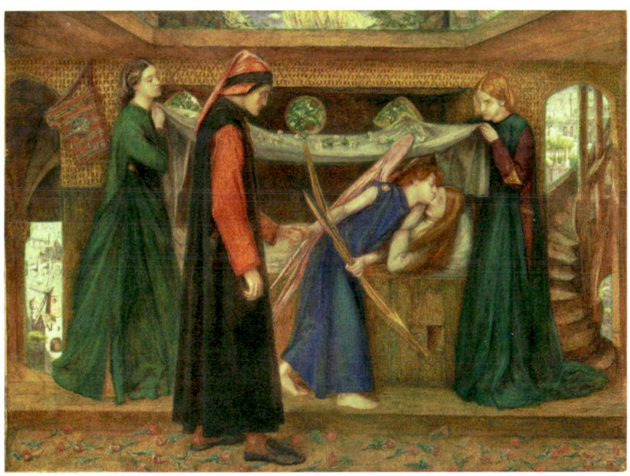

Cat. 14 Dante Gabriel Rossetti, *Dante's Dream at the Time of the Death of Beatrice* 1856, Watercolour and bodycolour on paper, 48.7 x 66.2 cm, Tate. Bequeathed by Beresford Rimington Heaton, 1940 (N05229)

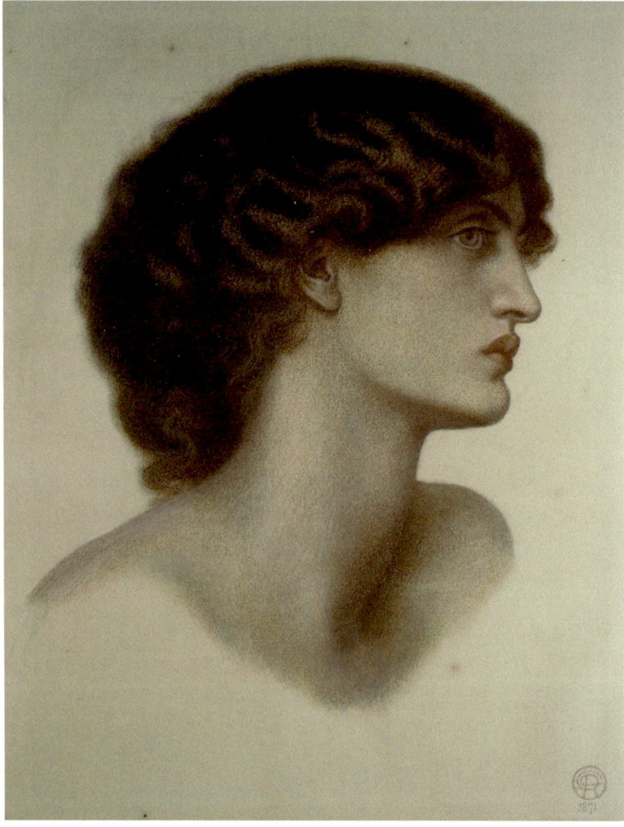

Cat. 128 Dante Gabriel Rossetti, *Perlascura* 1871, Coloured chalk on pale green paper, 55.8 x 43.5 cm, Signed in monogram and dated: *DGR 1871*, Ashmolean Museum, University of Oxford. Bequeathed by Miss May Morris, 1939 (WA1939.4)

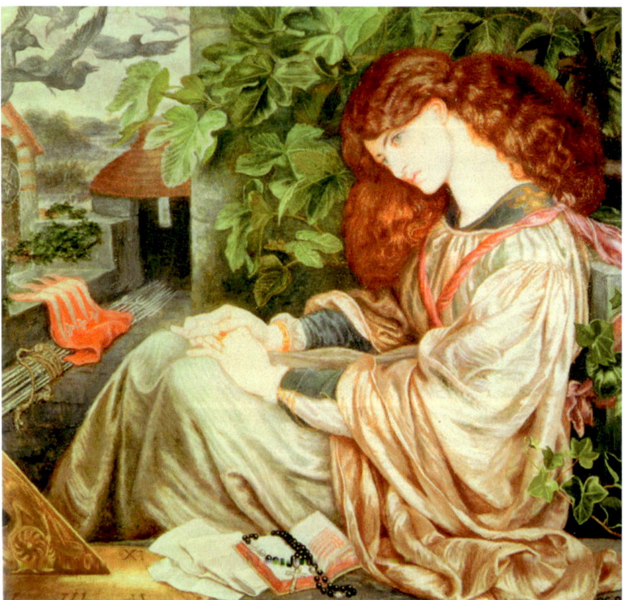

Fig. 14 Dante Gabriel Rossetti, *La Pia de' Tolomei*, 1868-80, Oil on canvas, 105.4 x 120.6 cm, Spencer Museum of Art, University of Kansas

Vita nuova, 'Donne ch'avete intelletto d'amore' (47-50), in fact the four lines preceding those he had used for *La donna della fiamma*:

> She hath that paleness of the pearl that's fit
> In a fair woman, so much and not more;
> She is as high as Nature's skill can soar;
> Beauty is tried by her comparison.[14]

Rossetti was thus haunted by the *Vita nuova* throughout his creative life, from the early *Dante Drawing an Angel* of 1849 to *Perlascura* thirty years later. He was not just a gifted poetic translator of the work, but was also sensitive to the most significant moments in a rather obscure mediaeval text: the turning-point canzone 'Donne ch'avete', the great sonnet 'Tanto gentile', Beatrice's death and anniversary, the 'donna della finestra', and the final prophetic vision all inspired major pictorial works over three decades.[15]

Of course, Rossetti did engage with Dante's major work, the *Comedy*, but he executed far fewer works based on it, compared to the *Vita nuova*, and even then such works tended to come from those sections of the poem that are most redolent of Dante's early poetry: the Paolo and Francesca episode (*Inferno*, v), the Earthly Paradise (*Purgatorio*, xxvii-xxxiii), and in the late 1860s that counterpart of Francesca, Pia de' Tolomei (*Purgatorio*, v) (**fig. 14**). Most of these works belong to the 1850s. The watercolour, *The Salutation of Beatrice in Eden* (Fitzwilliam Museum, Cambridge) was executed between 1850 and 1854, and is based on *Purgatorio*, xxx, 67–74, which describes Beatrice meeting Dante and revealing her face in the Earthly Paradise. Not only is this a moment when Dante's poetry deliberately recalls that of the *Vita nuova*, for he is meeting his beloved for the first time since her death, but in a later diptych of 1859 (National Gallery of Canada, Ottawa), Rossetti paired this moment with the earlier meeting between Dante and Beatrice in Florence narrated in Dante's first work. Shortly afterwards, Rossetti executed another watercolour from the same section of the poem. The meeting with Beatrice is preceded in *Purgatorio*, Canto xxvi by Dante's dream of Leah and Rachel (xxvi, 97–108), the former gathering flowers (the active life), the latter staring at herself in the water (the contemplative life). *Dante's Vision of Rachel and Leah*, of 1855 (**cat. 9**), was one of seven passages proposed by Ruskin as suitable subjects for Rossetti. The vision of Leah and Rachel in

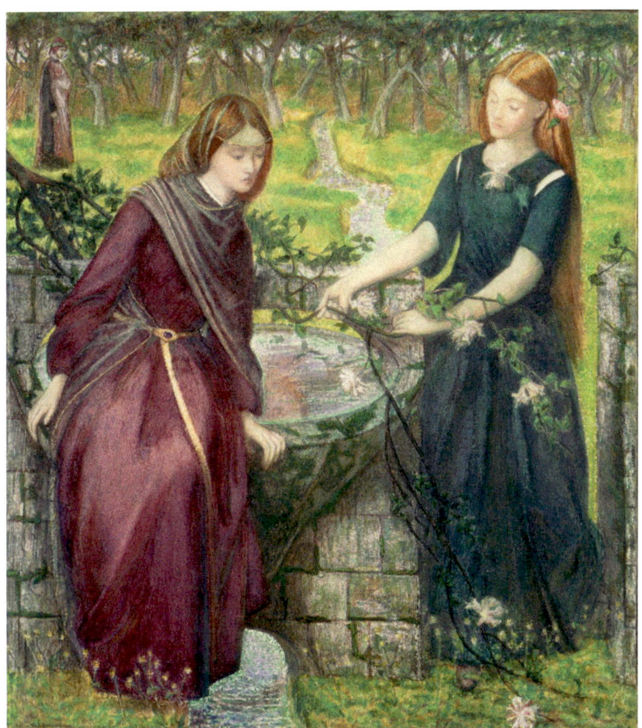

Cat. 9 Dante Gabriel Rossetti (1828–1882), *Dante's Vision of Rachel and Leah* 1855, Watercolour on paper, 35.2 x 31.4 cm, Tate. Bequeathed by Beresford Rimington Heaton, 1940 (N05228)

Dante's poem was the prelude to another female figure, Matilda, the forerunner of Beatrice, and from the same period we have a pen and ink drawing of *Dante's Vision of Matilda Gathering Flowers* (**cat. 12**). However, the most famous sequence of poetry in the *Comedy* recalling Dante's early poetic style is the episode of Paolo and Francesca, where Francesca speaks very much in the language of the author of the *Vita nuova*, so it is not surprising that Rossetti too should have engaged with this episode. The watercolour *Paolo and Francesca* (**cat. 11**), also of 1855, is more complex than other representations, and comprises a trio of panels, in imitation of a mediaeval triptych. Once more the visual is surrounded by the textual: the left panel has Paolo kissing Francesca (no 'mistletoe kiss', according to Ruskin) silhouetted against a window, while the open page of the book they are reading shows Lancelot embracing Guinevere, as in a medieval manuscript, and at the foot of the panel the artist has quoted Dante's lines: 'Quanti dolci pensier, quanto disio' (*Inferno*, v, 113); the central panel depicts Dante and Virgil looking to the right-hand panel, and between them is written Dante's opening phrase to Francesca: 'O lasso!' (v, 112); the right panel shows the two lovers punished in hell by being tossed in a storm reminiscent of their stormy passion, and at the bottom Rossetti completes the rest of the quotation from *Inferno*, v: 'menò costoro al doloroso passo' (v, 114).

Rossetti returned to a subject from the *Comedy* in 1868 when he began painting *Pia de' Tolomei*, an oil which he

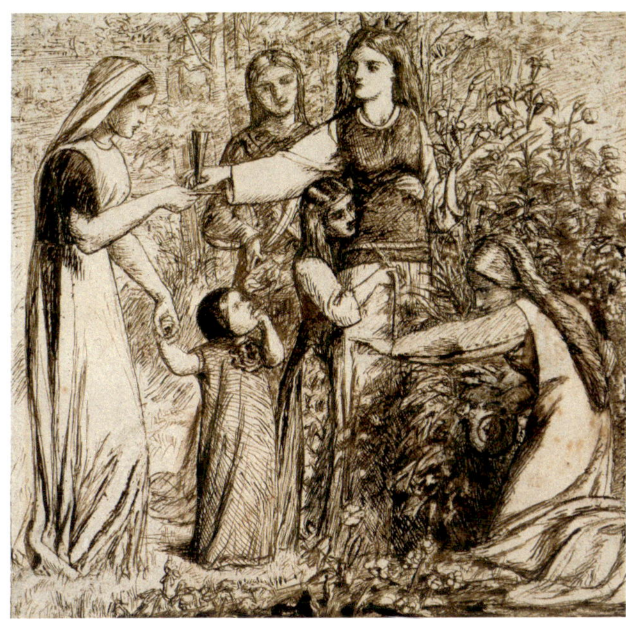

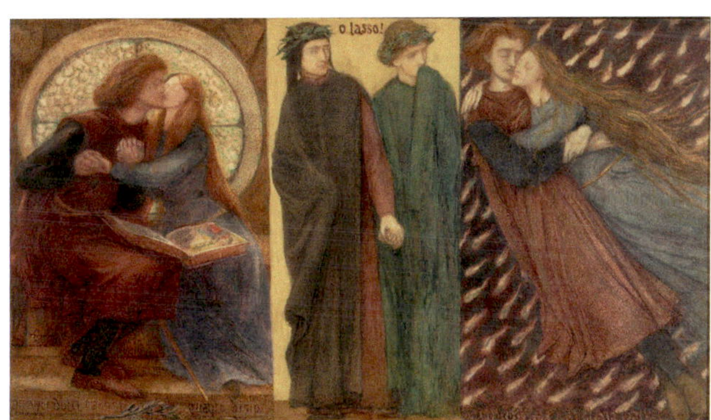

Cat. 12 (Top) Dante Gabriel Rossetti, *Dante's Vision of Matilda gathering Flowers* 1855, Pen and brown ink on paper, 17.8 x 18.5 cm, Ashmolean Museum, University of Oxford (WA1942.157)

Cat. 11 (Bottom) Dante Gabriel Rossetti, *Paolo and Francesca da Rimini* 1855, Watercolour on paper, 25.4 x 44.9 cm, Inscribed at the top: *O lasso!* and along the bottom: *Quanti dolci pensier, quanto disio / Menò costoro al doloroso passo!*, Tate. Purchased with the assistance of Sir Arthur Du Cros, Bart, and Sir Otto Beit, KCMG, through The Art Fund, 1916 (N03056)

completed in 1880, with Jane Morris again as model (now in the Spencer Museum of Art, Kansas University; see **Cat. 124**). In this final work from Dante's masterpiece, Rossetti has once more chosen an elegiac figure, but unlike Francesca who occupies half of Canto V of the *Inferno*, Pia is allotted only six lines in Canto V of the *Purgatorio*. From her few enigmatic lines, we deduce that she died a violent death in the Maremma, probably at her husband's hands, since she mentions the ring with which he had betrothed her. The symbolism of Rossetti's work is evident in that the rosary and prayer-book by her side indicate Pia's piety, while the ravens and marshland outside on the left and the ivy on the right all hint at her impending death. But here too Rossetti's lived existence played a role in the choice of subject: this is a portrait of a woman in an unhappy marriage (just as Janey was) who toys with her wedding ring, surrounded not just by her prayer book but also by old letters.

One other group of works was inspired by Rossetti's profound knowledge of less well known areas of Dante lore. The pen and ink sketch of *Dante at Verona* from 1852 (Birmingham Art Gallery) shows Dante passing a jester on the stairway of Can Grande della Scala's court at Verona. The meeting alludes to a famous episode recounted by Dante's biographers that when in exile in Verona he noticed that Can Grande seemed to enjoy more the company of the jester than that of the poet, and Dante's conclusion is that this is because the ruler has more in common with his buffoon than with a poet. The anecdote is also narrated poetically in Rossetti's long poem 'Dante at Verona', a poem that reverses the praise of Can Grande in *Paradiso*, XVII and turns it into criticism. The oil painting *The Boat of Love*, from 1874-81 (**cat. 127**), derives from perhaps Dante's most famous sonnet outside the *Vita nuova*: in it he imagines that he himself, Cavalcanti and fellow poet Lapo Gianni all go sailing with their three beloveds on a boat steered by Love. Rossetti was connoisseur enough of Dante's minor works to have translated this poem as well as two others dedicated to the hard woman of stone, known to today's Dante scholars as 'La donna della pietra' but whom Rossetti calls Lady Pietra degli Scrovigni, one a sestina and the other a sonnet. The pastel *Lady Pietra degli Scrovigni* (1876; private collection) depicts, unusually for Rossetti, a nude female figure holding a globe which was to reflect the rocky landscape around her, so this clearly referred to Dante's sestina 'Al poco giorno', translated as

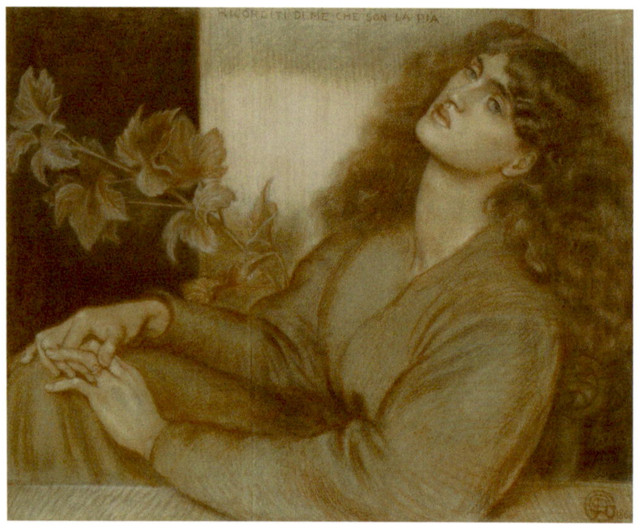

Cat.124 Dante Gabriel Rossetti (1828–1882), *Study for 'La Pia de' Tolomei'* 1868, Coloured chalks on two joined sheets of paper, 65.4 x 82.5 cm, Signed in monogram and dated: *DGR 1868* and inscribed: *Ricorditi di me che son la Pia*, Private collection

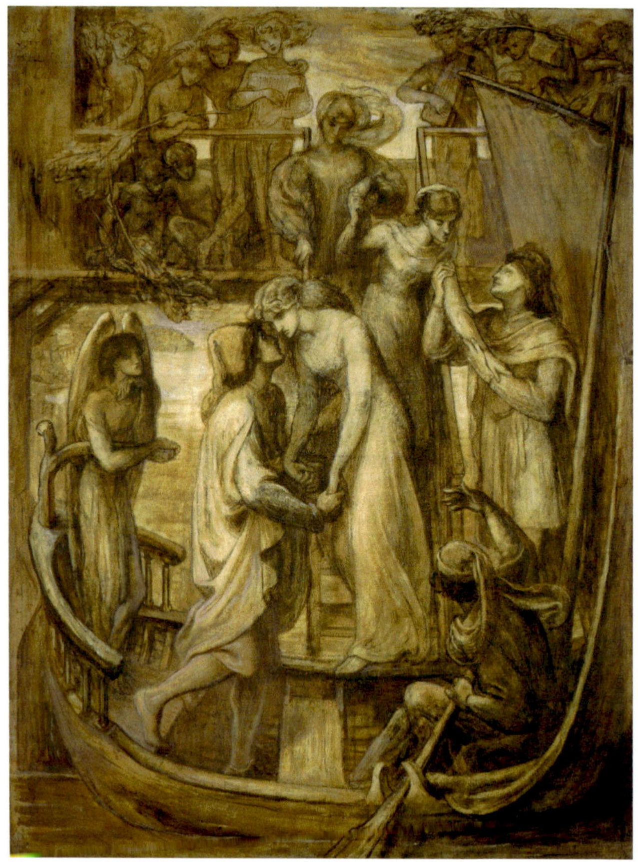

Cat. 127 Dante Gabriel Rossetti, *The Boat of Love* 1874–81, Oil on canvas, 124.5 x 94 cm, Inscribed: *Guido vorrei che tu e Lapo ed io*, Birmingham Museum and Art Gallery (1885P2476)

'To the dim light and the large circle of shade' in *Early Italian Poets* (pp. 267–8). Again the artist is sensitive to the poetry here, since the nudity corresponds precisely to the more explicit sensuality that was typical of the sestina form, and is certainly present in Dante's poem.

One final area of Rossetti's pictorial inspiration from Italian literature regards those subjects that do not derive from Dante. Critics have pointed out that *Bocca Baciata* (Museum of Fine Arts, Boston), *c.*1859–60, marks a turning point in Rossetti's style in a number of ways: it is the first painting to be devoted to a single female subject, the first to portray more carnal tones (the model was Fanny Cornforth (**figs. 15–16**)), and the first to indulge in luxurious clothing in what Rossetti himself called a 'Venetian' style. Famously Swinburne said the work was 'more stunning than can be decently expressed'. But it is also a turning-point in Italian literary terms since this was the first pictorial work by the artist not to be inspired by Dante, but instead by one of the racier stories in Boccaccio's *Decameron* (2.7). The last line of the story tells how the heroine Alatiel 'after sleeping with eight men' and making love 'a thousand times' is finally married to the King of Algarve as though she were still a virgin. At this point the narrator concludes 'bocca baciata non perde ventura, / anzi rinnova come fa la luna ... (a kissed mouth does not lose its freshness, / on the contrary it is renewed just like the moon...)'. Shortly after this, Rossetti extends his 'Renaissance' style with the watercolour of *Lucrezia Borgia* in 1861 (Tate), initiating a move towards Aestheticism. This shows Lucretia in sumptuous garb, washing her hands after poisoning her husband with wine, while in the convex mirror at the back one can see her father Pope Alexander VI helping her doomed husband to walk in order to get the poison fully into his system. The artist's interest in the Borgia family had been aroused earlier since in 1858 he had taken back a watercolour originally entitled *To caper nimbly in a Lady's Chamber / To the lascivious pleasing of a lute* and repainted it in 1863, giving it the new name of *Borgia* (see **cat. 15**). In it we see the Borgia children dancing, Lucrezia slumped on a chair watching them, her father Pope Alexander VI leaning lecherously over her bosom, and her brother Cesare smelling the rose in her hair. Probably the interest in the Borgias stems not from literary texts but from that general interest in Italian Renaissance culture that was typical of mid-nineteenth-century Britain.[16]

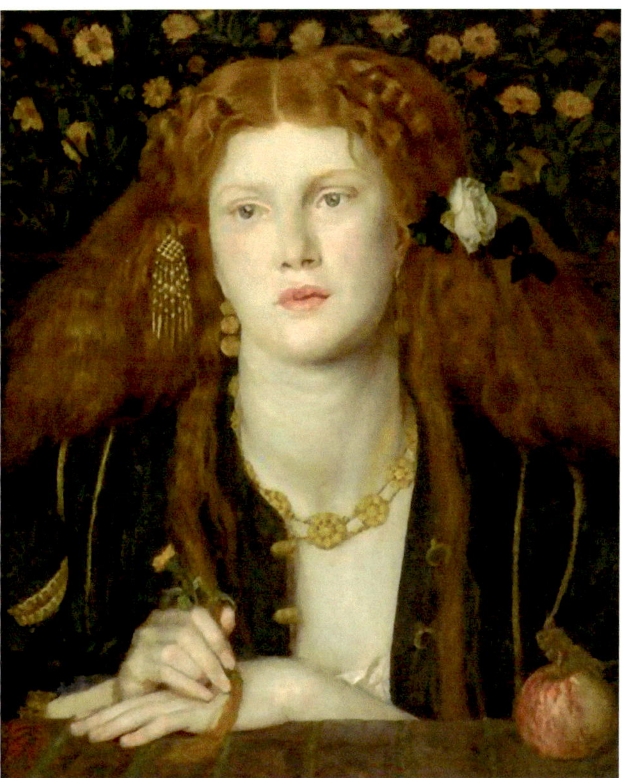

Fig. 15 Dante Gabriel Rossetti, *Bocca Baciata (Lips That Have Been Kissed)*, 1859, Oil on panel, 32.1 x 27 cm, Museum of Fine Arts, Boston, Massachusetts, USA

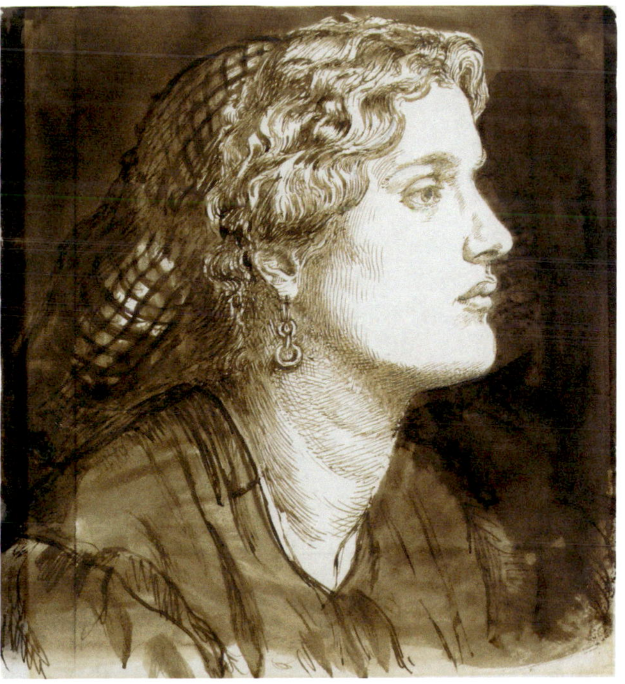

Fig. 16 Dante Gabriel Rossetti, *Portrait of Fanny Cornforth*, c.1860, Pen and brown ink with brown wash on pale blue paper, 22.4 x 21.2 cm, Ashmolean Museum, University of Oxford, WA1977.81

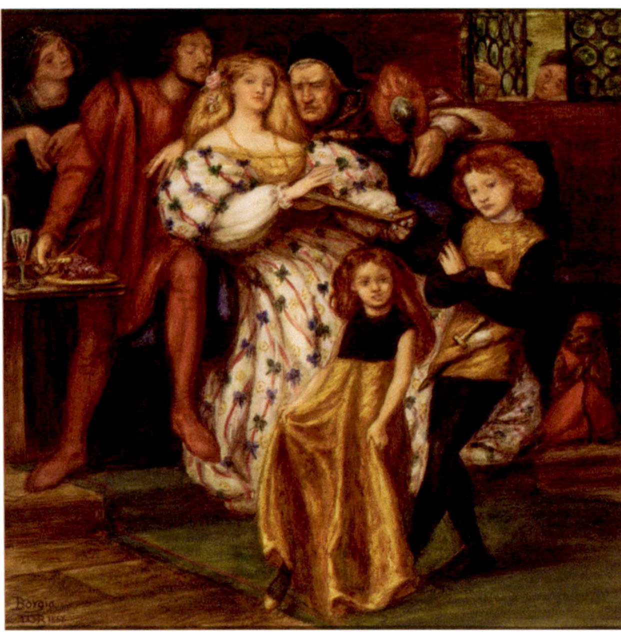

Cat. 15 Dante Gabriel Rossetti, *The Borgia Family* 1863, Watercolour on paper, 36.2 x 37.8 cm, Signed and dated: *D.G.R. 1863*, Victoria and Albert Museum (72–1902)

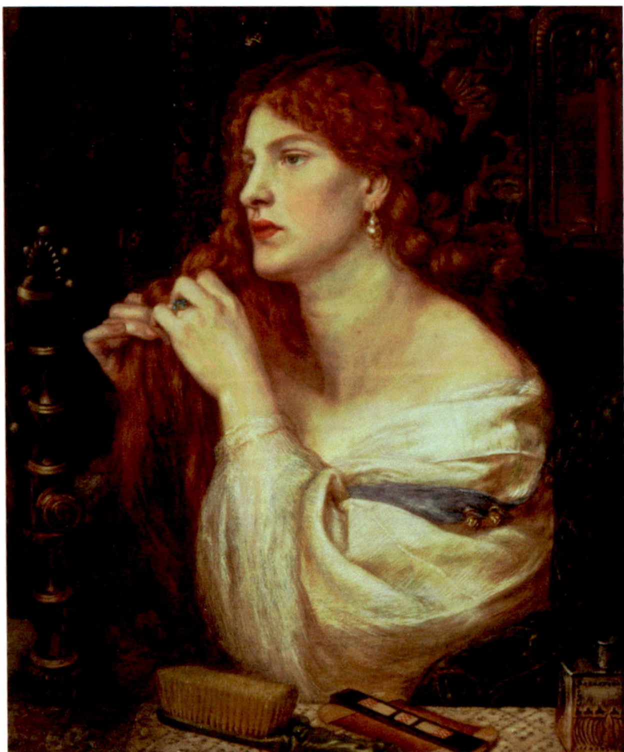

Cat. 122 Dante Gabriel Rossetti, *Fazio's Mistress*, also known as *Aurelia* 1863–73, Oil on mahogany panel, 77.1 x 70.8 cm, Tate. Purchased with assistance from Sir Arthur Du Cros, Bart and Sir Otto Beit, KCMG through The Art Fund, 1916 (N03055)

Fanny Cornforth was also the model for the sumptuous painting *Aurelia (Fazio's Mistress)* (**cat. 122**). Painted in 1863, this appears to have been inspired by the early poet Fazio degli Uberti, whom Rossetti translated in his *Early Italian Poets*. When he repainted it in 1873, he decided to remove the allusion to Fazio, a poet of the age before Dante, since that seemed anachronistic compared to the 'Renaissance' colour of the work. Nevertheless the words of Fazio's canzone 'His Portrait of his Lady, Angiola of Verona', as Rossetti entitles it, clearly allude to the sensual woman that Rossetti represents:

I look at the crisp, golden-threaded hair
Whereof, to thrall my heart, Love twists a net…
I look into her eyes which unaware
Through mine own eyes to my heart penetrate …
I look at the amorous beautiful mouth,
The spacious forehead which her locks enclose, …
I look at her white easy neck, so well
From shoulders and from bosom lifted out…
(*Early Italian Poets*, p. 123).

One final late work, the oil painting *A Vision of Fiammetta* of 1878 (private collection), shows the artist's continued interest in the works of Boccaccio: the painting is inspired by what Rossetti thought was Boccaccio's last sonnet to his lover Fiammetta (now not attributed to Boccaccio), and the artist in his turn wrote an accompanying sonnet for his picture. The flame-coloured dress suggests the name of Boccaccio's beloved and other details reflect the poem that inspired the painting.[17]

Just as influential as his paintings was Rossetti's major non-pictorial work on Italian literature, the largely faithful, often beautiful translations in *The Early Italian Poets*, published in 1861. The first thing that strikes one apart from its poetic qualities is that this is an exhaustive collection, presenting the English reader of the mid-nineteenth century first (in Part I) with an anthology of all the major and minor poets before Dante, and then (in Part II) with the *Vita nuova*, plus the main poems written by Dante and his circle such as Cavalcanti and Cino da Pistoia, even including some texts by two writers who lived until the late fourteenth century, Franco Sacchetti and Boccaccio. Interestingly, despite finding room for these latter poets, the translator accords no space to Petrarch, though he was born before either of them: Pre-Raphaelitism excluded the more rhetorical, almost Renaissance style of Petrarch's poetry.

Rossetti realized that his selection was very broad and at times uneven in quality but he wanted to give a 'full and truthful view of early Italian poetry'.[18] Until that point, English readers could have read Dante's *Comedy* in a number of versions, and in the 1850s the first two complete translations of Petrarch's *Canzoniere* were published, one in 1854, and the other in the popular Bohn's Library series in 1859.[19] In addition, Carlo Arrivabene's anthology of *Poeti italiani* (1855) made available in English translation selections from all the major Italian poets,[20] but Rossetti's anthology was the first to highlight less canonical poets from the early period and offered the first translation of the *Vita nuova* to be published in England. The volume was to have enormous influence on taste in both literature and the visual arts: Rossetti was convinced that Dante's *Comedy* could not be understood without knowledge of the *Vita nuova*. The other criterion which guided the author, apart from that of exhaustiveness, was that of 'beauty', or the aesthetic quality of the poems: time and again he justifies inclusion or exclusion of items on the grounds of their artistic quality, insisting in the Preface that these poems 'possess, in their degree, beauties of a kind which can never again exist in art' (p. xiii). Similarly at the end of the volume he includes three sonnets by Boccaccio 'chosen for their beauty alone' (p. 375), and Rossetti's famous statement on his motives for the translation echoes this criterion: 'The life-blood of rhymed translation is this, – that a good poem shall not be turned into a bad one. The only true motive for putting poetry into a fresh language must be to endow a fresh nation, as far as possible, with one more possession of beauty' (pp. xiii-xiv). So Dante Gabriel was aware of his role in transferring knowledge from one language to another, and his other statement about translation explains his divergence from his father's huge but unread commentaries: 'a translation [...] remains perhaps the most direct form of commentary' (p. xiii). One other element that strikes the reader is the relatively high level of the poet's philology, despite the few flaws pointed out by William Michael Rossetti:[21] although lacking scholarly training, Dante Gabriel carefully lists all his sources, weighs up their reliability (p. xvi), displays a healthy scepticism about dubious attributions, and realizes the importance of the recent discovery in a Florentine library of the manuscript of the medieval poem *L'intelligenza* (p. 168). Allied to this philological sensitivity are his wide ranging cross-references, again remarkable in someone without formal philological grounding: he knows that Dante alludes subtly, we would say intertextually, to Cavalcanti's poems in the *Comedy* (p. 159), he identifies the Latin letter sent by Dante in reply to one of Cino's poems (p. 160), he quotes from *Decameron* 9.4 to shed light on a poem by Cecco Angelieri (p. 164), and so on.

Most interesting of all from our point of view is the fact that almost all of Rossetti's footnotes to the enigmas of the *Vita nuova* are closely linked to his pictorial work. He cites the lines from *Purgatorio*, XI about Cavalcanti succeeding Guinizelli (p. 153), lines which he copies in his drawing of *Giotto Painting the Portrait of Dante*. In his notes on Giotto, he mentions the tradition that Dante had studied drawing with Cimabue (p. 169) and talks of his drawing an angel in the *Vita nuova*. There are also notes on the first meeting of Dante and Beatrice (p. 173), on Dante fainting at seeing Beatrice at a wedding (pp. 195–6), on the symbolism of the date of Beatrice's death (p. 232), and so on, all moments from Dante's early work that would be the subject of a Rossetti drawing or painting. A note that highlights a clash of philology with his criterion of beauty is the one regarding Dante's drawing of an angel. When Dante's visitors arrive, Rossetti's translation states: 'Perceiving whom, I arose for salutation, and said: "Another was with me."' However, his footnote adds: 'Thus according to some texts. The majority, however, add the words, "And therefore was I in thought:" but the shorter speech is perhaps the more forcible and pathetic' (p. 240). For Rossetti, poetry clearly outweighs philology. Another revealing note that is also connected with pictorial works is the one concerning *La Donna della Finestra*. Here Rossetti conjectures, again quite originally, that this woman is none other than Dante's future wife Gemma Donati; if this is so, it confirms what he believes lies at the heart of all true Dante commentary, 'that is, the existence of the actual events even where the allegorical superstructure has been raised by Dante himself' (pp. 246–7). One final note contains links with another portrait: the translator claims he has included the sestina 'Al poco giorno e al gran cerchio d'ombra' because of 'its great and peculiar beauty', though he does acknowledge that it is a 'doubtful conjecture' to associate the poem with the lady Pietra degli Scrovigni (p. 267).

With his paintings and his translations Rossetti initiated a widespread vogue for subjects from the *Vita*

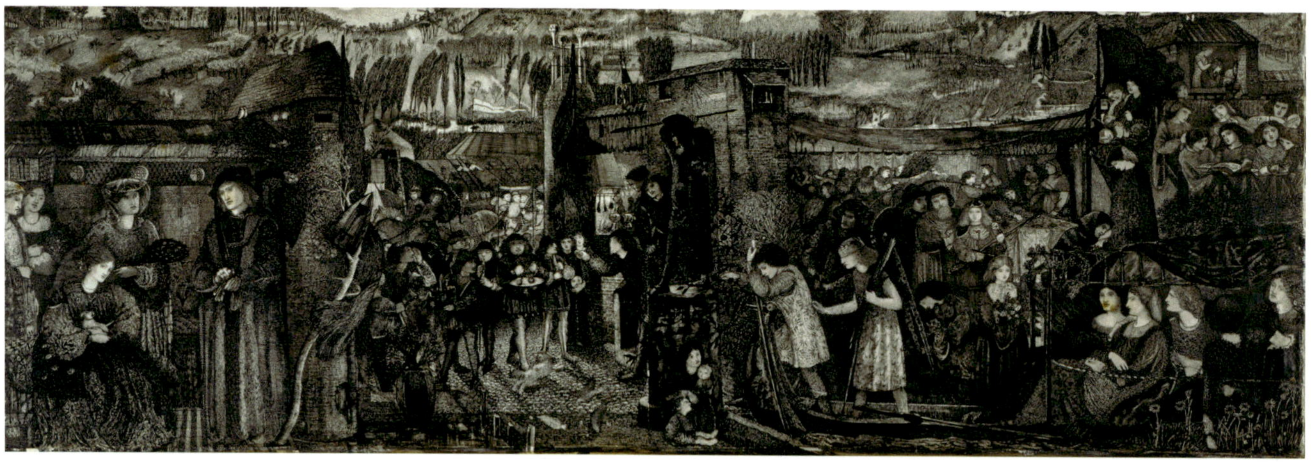

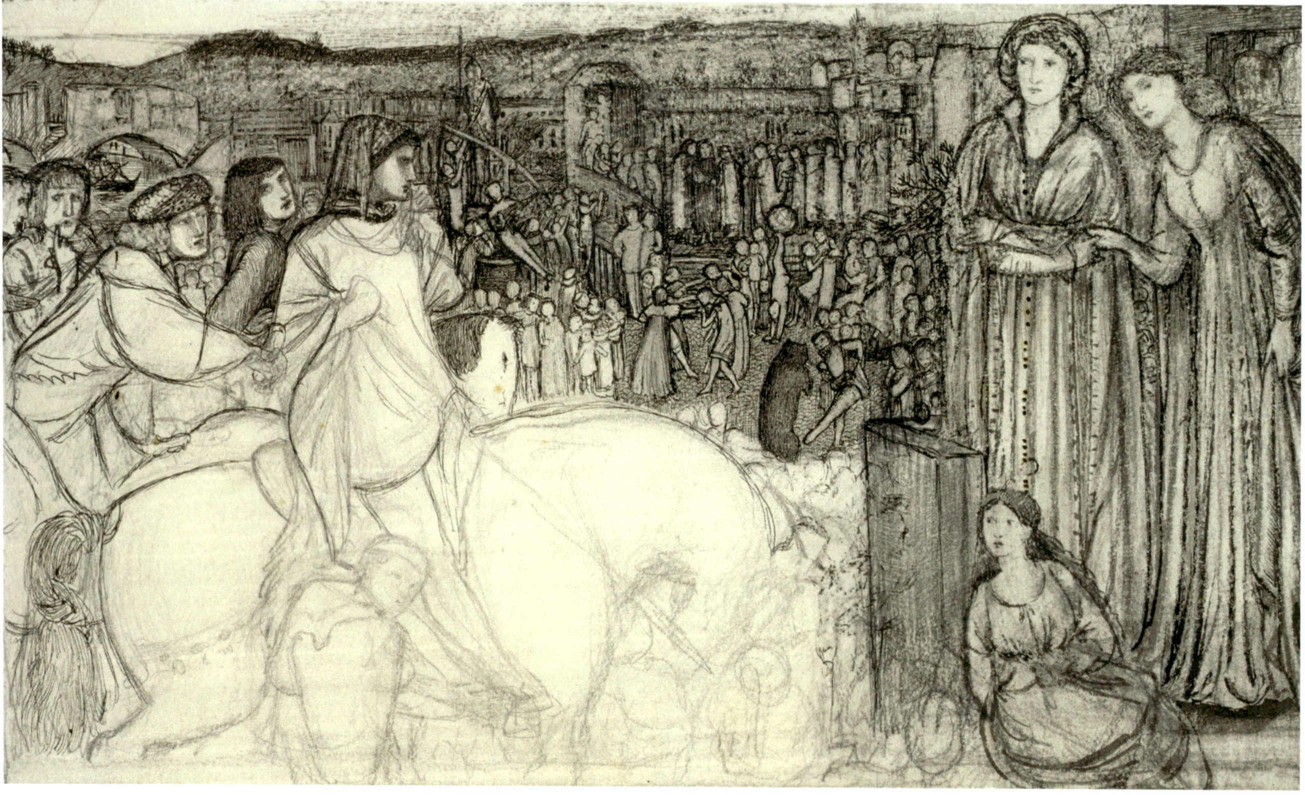

Cat. 17 (Top) Sir Edward Coley Burne-Jones (1833–1898), *Buondelmente's Wedding* 1859, Pen and ink with some grey wash on vellum, 25.5 x 77 cm, Signed: *EBJ*, Lent by the Syndics of the Fitzwilliam Museum, Cambridge

Cat. 18 (bottom) Sir Edward Coley Burne-Jones, *Gualdrada Donati presenting her Daughter to Buondelmonte: The Origin of the Guelph and Ghibelline Quarrel in Florence,* Pen and brush in black ink over pencil on paper, 23.2 x 39.3 cm, Ashmolean Museum, University of Oxford (WA1951.156)

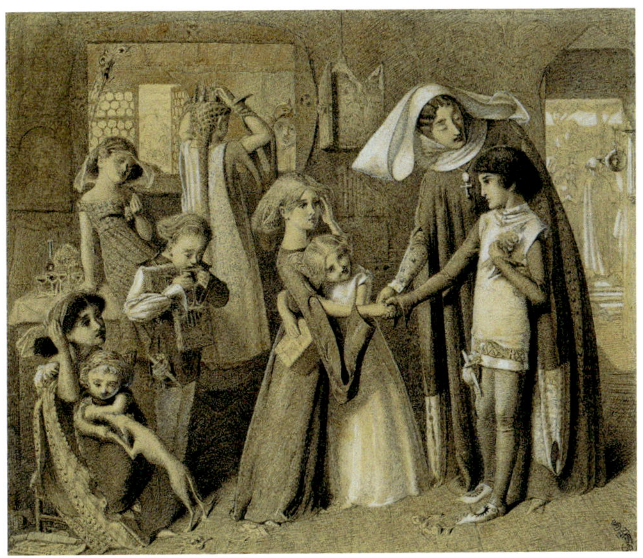

Cat. 16 Simeon Solomon (1840–1905), *Dante's First Meeting with Beatrice* 1859–63, Pen and ink on paper, 19.4 x 22.9 cm, Signed in monogram and dated *12/9/5963*, Tate. Bequeathed by Robert Ross through The Art Fund, 1919 (N03409)

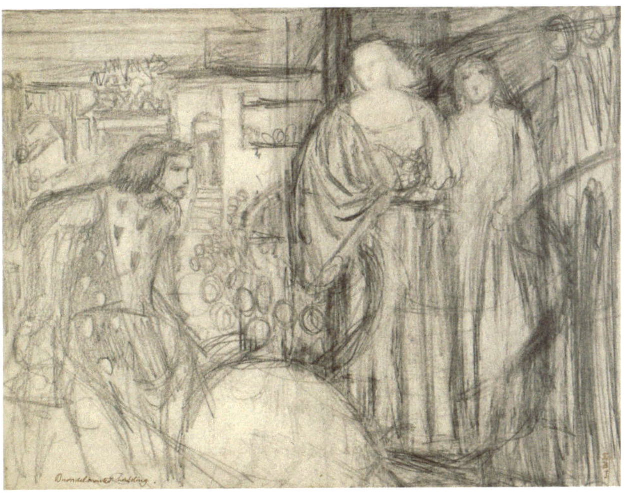

Cat. 20 *Study for 'The Meeting of Buondelmonte and Ciulla, the Origin of the Guelph and Ghibelline Quarrel in Florence'*, Black chalk and pencil on paper, 25.6 x 24.9 cm, Inscribed by Charles Fairfax-Murray, lower left: *Buondelmonte's wedding* and lower right: *E.B.J.*, Whitworth Art Gallery, University of Manchester. Bequeathed by J.R. Holliday, 1927 (D.1927.81)

nuova. Simeon Solomon was inspired to do a striking pen and ink drawing of *Dante's First Meeting with Beatrice*, 1859–63 (**cat. 16**), in order to rival Henry Holiday's version which had been rejected by the Royal Academy in 1860 but exhibited in 1861. Burne-Jones's *Beatrice*, an oil painting from 1870 (private collection), is also like many of Rossetti's paintings in containing an inscription: 'Io vidi donne colla donna mia / non che niuna me sembrasse donna / ma figuravan sol la sua ombra'. Henry Holiday's paintings based on famous moments from Dante's first work were to become immensely popular both at the time and more recently: *Dante Meeting Beatrice as Children* (1860), and *Dante and Beatrice* (1883; Walker Art Gallery, Liverpool). Marie Spartali Stillman, one of Rossetti's models, was also a fine painter in her own right: she executed two versions of *Dante and Beatrice*, one in 1880 where the scene takes place in a church, the other (1881) where Dante is sitting down at a fountain as Beatrice and her friends descend the stairs. She also painted another version where Dante and Beatrice meet as children: *May Feast at the House of Folco Portinari, 1274* (1887). Like Rossetti, she was interested also in subjects from more remote areas of Dante's life and works, such as a watercolour of *Madonna Pietra degli Scrovigni* (1884; Walker Art Gallery, Liverpool), where the woman holds a ball and a winter flowering blackthorn in allusion to Dante's wintry sestina; and a *Dante at Verona*, a gouache and watercolour from 1888 (private collection), which depicts Dante reciting his works to Veronese ladies around a fountain.

Other painters too drew on Italian literary subjects that were not related to Dante, the most popular source being Boccaccio's *Decameron*. However, several of the stories from Boccaccio in these works were mediated through English translations or rewritings. Thus Millais's oil-painting *Cymon and Iphigeneia* (1848; Lady Lever Art Gallery, Port Sunlight) derived from *Decameron* 5.1 but via Dryden's translation of the episode. Similarly the most famous depictions of Isabella and the pot of basil may ultimately come from *Decameron* 2.5, but as the English version of the name indicates – Isabella and not Boccaccio's Lisabetta – the immediate inspiration for Millais's *Isabella* (1849; Walker Art Gallery, Liverpool) and Holman Hunt's *Lorenzo at his Warehouse* (1858–60) and *Isabella and the Pot of Basil* (1866-8; Laing Art Gallery, Newcastle) comes from Keats's famous poem. Burne-Jones' *Buondelmonte's Wedding* (1859; **cats. 17–20**) probably stems from the stories in Boccaccio and in other commentators about the origins of the Guelph-Ghibelline conflict which caused Dante's exile. However, some paintings were definitely and directly inspired by Boccaccio's masterpiece, notably Marie Stillman's *Fiammetta Singing* (1879; Pre-Raphaelite

Inc.) and her extraordinary *The Enchanted Garden of Messer Ansaldo* (1889). The same painter also moved outside the world of Dante and Boccaccio to embrace the third member of the Three Crowns of Florence in her *First Meeting of Petrarch and Laura in the Church of Santa Chiara at Avignon* (1889; private collection). She even drew on Tasso's epic from two centuries after Dante, the *Gerusalemme Liberata*, selecting one of the lyrical highlights of Tasso's epic as her subject for *A Rose from Armida's Garden* (1894; private collection). Marie Stillman is thus perhaps unique amongst Pre-Raphaelite painters in her broad coverage of Italian literature, moving beyond Dante to Petrarch and Boccaccio and down to the distinctly post-Raphaelite poet Tasso (though of course his epic was set in medieval times). The last echo of this interest in Boccaccio is perhaps John Waterhouse's *A Tale from the Decameron*, from 1916 (Lady Lever Art Gallery, Port Sunlight), depicting not a particular tale but Boccaccio's *cornice* where one of Boccaccio's male narrators is seated in a beautiful garden telling his tale to the group of friends.

The Pre-Raphaelites' knowledge of Italian literature was clearly a major source for their art, but as their name suggests, they concentrated on pre-Renaissance texts. Their enthusiasm for such subjects helped shape Romantic sensibility in the course of the nineteenth century as they moved away from the 'Gothic' emphasis on Dante's *Inferno* typical of Flaxman, Fuseli and Blake, to the lyrical moments from the *Comedy* and the *Vita nuova*. Rossetti played a major role in this respect with his pictorial works, his translations and his own poetry. But Dante Gabriel was also knowledgeable about later Italian poetry, including that of his own time: in 1869 he translated Leopardi's poem *Imitazione*, and later published versions of two poems by Niccolò Tommaseo in honour of the writer who died in 1874.[22] But these are isolated cases. When Rossetti and other artists moved beyond Dante, it was primarily towards that other medieval source of narrative moments, Boccaccio's *Decameron*. Some painters such as Marie Stillman might occasionally engage with Tasso, and there may be a hint of Ariosto and the armed Ruggiero's release of the naked Angelica behind Millais's *Errant Knight* of 1870 (Ingres had famously painted the scene in 1819, and Rossetti wrote two fine sonnets to celebrate the painting). However, on the whole the main Italian sources of inspiration for the Pre-Raphaelites were Dante, especially the poet of the *Vita nuova*, and to a lesser extent Boccaccio. This leaves just one puzzle: what is striking is the almost total absence of Petrarch in the work of these artists. Marie Stillman is the exception that proves the rule, and Petrarch may have held an appeal for the female sensibility of the time, since there had been a vogue in the late eighteenth and first half of the nineteenth century for female poets to translate and write about Petrarch.[23] But no other artist drew inspiration from the poems about Laura. One reason for Petrarch's exclusion from the Pre-Raphaelite canon is that his poems are purely lyrical without the strong narrative appeal of the *Vita nuova*, *Comedy,* or the *Decameron*. But there were other factors, as has been suggested: his language was more rhetorical than Dante's and his conceits were less tolerable in English; no great Romantic poets championed him; he did not find a translator as influential as Cary; in addition it was Dante, not Petrarch, who had become the bard of the newly unified Italy in 1861, as shown in the major celebrations of the sixth centenary of the poet's birth in 1865. There was much less fuss about Petrarch's centenary in 1874. Perhaps it was Ruskin who drove the final nail in Petrarch's coffin in England when in his 1871 *Lecture on the Relation between Michelangelo and Tintoret* he aligned the poet with Raphael, saying: 'it is nearly impossible [...] to study Shakespeare or Holbein too much, or Petrarch and Raphael too little'.[24] Even though, in historical terms, Petrarch was two centuries 'pre-Raphael', he was not 'pre-raphaelite'.

1 See amidst the vast bibliography C. P. Brand, *Italy and the English Romantics: The Italianate Fashion in Early Nineteenth-Century England* (Cambridge, 1957); Steve Ellis, *Dante and English Poetry* (Cambridge, 1983); Ralph Pite, *The Circle of our Vision: Dante's Presence in English Romantic Poetry* (Oxford, 1994); *Dante's Modern Afterlife: Reception and Response from Blake to Heaney*, ed. Nick Havely (Basingstoke, 1998); Alison Milbank, *Dante and the Victorians* (Manchester, 1998); Antonella Braida, *Dante and the Romantics* (Basingstoke, 2004); *British Romanticism and Italian Literature*, ed. Laura Bandiera and Diego Saglia (Amsterdam and New York, 2005).

2 Cited in Brand 1957, p. 70.

3 *Comments of John Ruskin on the Divina Commedia*, ed. George P. Huntington, introduction by Charles Eliot Norton (Boston and New York, 1903), p. 3.

4 See William Spaggiari, 'The canon of the classics: Italian writers and Romantic-period anthologies of Italian literature in Britain', in *British Romanticism and Italian Literature* (2004), pp. 27–39 (p. 30).

5 For the figure of Francesca, see Alex MacMillan, 'Dante's nineteenth-century reception: Francesca da Rimini and the idea of Italy', in *Italy's Three Crowns. Reading Dante, Petrarch, and Boccaccio*, ed. Zygmunt G. Baranski and Martin McLaughlin (Oxford, 2007), pp. 73–81. For the relief of Francesca on Gladstone's tomb, see Milbank 1998, p. 152.

6 *Sullo spirito antipapale che produsse la riforma* (*On the Anti-Papal Spirit that Led to the Reformation*; 1832), *Il mistero dell'Amor platonico del medioevo derivato da' misteri antichi* (*The Mystery of Platonic Love in the Middle Ages, Derived from Ancient Mysteries*; 1840), and *La Beatrice di Dante* (*Dante's Beatrice*; 1842): see John Woodhouse, 'Dante and the Rossetti Family', in Baranski and McLaughlin 2007, pp. 82–93.

7 On Kirkup, see John Lindon, 'Dante "intra Tamisi ed Arno" (and Halle-am-Saalle): The letters of Seymour Kirkup to H. C. Barlow', in *Britain and Italy from Romanticism to Modernism. A Festschrift for Peter Brand*, ed. Martin McLaughlin (Oxford, 2000), pp. 121–42.

8 *The Early Italian Poets from Ciullo d'Alcamo to Dante Alighieri 1100-1200-1300, in the Original Metres together with Dante's Vita Nuova*, translated by D. G. Rossetti: Part I: *Poets Chiefly Before Dante*; Part II: *Dante and his Circle* (London: George Routledge & Sons, Limited; New York: E. P. Dutton & Co., 1914), p. 169. Future references will be to this edition.

9 Jon Whiteley, *Oxford and the Pre-Raphaelites* (Oxford, 1989). The idea was expressed by Rossetti himself in a letter of 1854: *Letters of Dante Gabriel Rossetti*, ed. Oswald Doughty and John Robert Wahl, 4 vols (Oxford, 1965-7), I, p. 197.

10 *Letters of Dante Gabriel Rossetti*, I, p. 123.

11 *The Early Italian Poets*, pp. 195-6.

12 For details of the painting in Liverpool, see Mary Bennett, *Artists of the Pre-Raphaelite Circle. The First Generation: Catalogue of Works in the Walker Art Gallery, Lady Lever Gallery, and Sudley Art Gallery* (London, 1988), p. 173.

13 *The Early Italian Poets*, p. 205 (*Vita nuova*, 19).

14 *Dante Gabriel Rossetti and Janey Morris: Their Correspondence*, ed. John Bryson in association with Janet Camp Troxell (Oxford, 1976), p. 75.

15 Of course, paintings such as *Monna Vanna* (cat. 123) allude to another famous episode in the *Vita nuova* 24 where Cavalcanti's beloved Giovanna walks in front of Beatrice and is thus also know as Primavera. But when Rossetti repainted it in 1873, he changed the title to *Belcolore* as being less mediaeval and more befitting the lush, Venetian clothes of the sitter (Alexa Wilding). On *The Daydream* (1880, Ashmolean Museum) being originally called *Monna Primavera*, see John Woodhouse, 'Dante Gabriel Rossetti's translation and illustration of the *Vita nuova*', in McLaughlin 2000, pp. 67-86 (pp. 81-82).

16 Hilary Fraser, *The Victorians and Renaissance Italy* (Oxford, 1992).

17 One other non-Dante literary subject that haunted Rossetti was the anecdote in Condivi's *Life of Michelangelo* about the artist paying his last respects to his Platonic beloved, Vittoria Colonna, and feeling worthy only to kiss her hand. Rossetti intended it to be a counterpart to *Dante's Dream* but no such painting was ever executed. He did, however, write a sonnet on the subject, 'Michelangelo's Kiss' around 1880 (no. 94 in the *House of Life* sonnet sequence). See *Pre-Raphaelite Art in its European Context*, ed. Susan P. Casteras and Alicia Craig Faxon (Madison, NJ and London, 1995), p. 21.

18 *The Early Italian Poets*, p. xiv. Thus he includes the 'scurrilous doggerel' of the exchange between Dante and Forese Donati only for the sake of completeness (p. 370).

19 The first complete translation of Petrarch was by Robert Guthrie Macgregor, *Indian Leisure* (London, 1854); the Bohn Library edition of 1859 contained an anthology of translations by different authors of both the *Canzoniere* and the *Trionfi*: see Peter Hainsworth, 'Translating Petrarch', in *Petrarch in Britain. Interpreters, Imitators and Translators over 700 Years*, ed. Martin McLaughlin and Letizia Panizza (London, 2007), pp. 341–58 (p. 344).

20 Spaggiari 2004, p. 34.

21 *The Works of Dante Gabriel Rossetti*, edited with Prefaces and Notes by William M. Rossetti, Revised and enlarged edition (London: Ellis, 1911), p. 677.

22 *The Works of Dante Gabriel Rossetti*, p. 544 (Leopardi) and pp. 535–36 (Tommaseo).

23 See Silvia Bordoni, "The Sonnet's Claim": Petrarch and the Romantic Sonnet', in Bandiera and Saglia 2005, pp. 81–95, and Luca Manini, 'Charlotte Smith and the voice of Petrarch', ibid., pp. 97–108.

24 See Martin McLaughlin, 'Nineteenth-century British biographies of Petrarch', in McLaughlin and Panizza 2007, pp. 319-40 (pp. 338–40).

Interlocking Patriotisms: Italy and England in the Long Nineteenth Century

Maurizio Isabella

During the nineteenth century, England harboured a profound and passionate love for Italy, which for a long time made the peninsula a favourite of Victorian society. As John Pemble notes, '"Italy" and "culture" were synonymous in popular Victorian conception'.[1] This interest in Italian literature, culture, and history was filtered through Romanticism, and, in consequence, Italy became an imaginary space within which the English were able to give free rein to their emotions and desires. Literary and historical narratives about Italy afforded ample scope for mixing Romantic invention and scholarly rigour. Beyond Romanticism, the cult of the country's artistic and cultural heritage, which had already existed in the preceding century, soon became associated in turn with a whole-hearted identification with the Italian nationalist cause.[2] English travellers who returned to Italy after the collapse of the Napoleonic regime were unanimous in their view that its people, especially in the south, were living in a state of moral and administrative degradation. Conditions in the Papal State and the Kingdom of the Two Sicilies in particular represented the negation of Victorian moral and civic values. Ideas of decadence and the picturesque, aesthetic pleasure and immorality, attractiveness and ethical condemnation, all figured equally in English representations of Italy. According to the scholar Charles MacFarlane, Italy had produced great literature but was also 'the land of brigandism *par excellence*'.[3] British observers gave this sort of condemnation an openly political value, convinced that the main reasons for the decadence were attributable to the Restoration governments, which were prime examples of cruel despotism and administrative incompetence.[4]

It was thanks to this combination of Romantic reappropriation and the projection of England's own values onto Italy, that the Italian Risorgimento became the most widely discussed international political issue in England, and it was celebrated long after its culmination in the fall of Rome in September 1870. In the decades immediately following the collapse of the Napoleonic regime in Italy, it was Italian exiles, together with the literature of the Grand Tour, who determined the way in which the Italian issue was viewed in England. Their moderate political opinions and elevated social status (many were drawn from the nobility) allowed them to enter the country's intellectual and political establishment, and in particular the most exclusive circles of the Whig aristocracy such as Holland House. Writers like Ugo Foscolo, and conspirators like Giuseppe Pecchio and Antonio Panizzi, who had settled in England in the early 1820s after the failure of the political movements at Milan and Parma, used articles in the most important liberal journals to publicise the prejudices and rhetoric which made of the Austrian government in Lombardy and the Veneto the exemplar of absolute barbarism. From the pages of the *Edinburgh Review*, the British public learned that Austria had persecuted moderate liberals like Silvio Pellico and Federico Confalonieri, who were condemned to prison sentences without the right to a fair trial. Italian exiles were also the first to teach the political elite and the liberal public that the Risorgimento was not so much a revolutionary cause as a movement devoted to the introduction of a constitution modelled on that of Great Britain, in the name of civilized principles. The exiles convinced the English, moreover, that the Italian nationalist cause was above all anticlerical, insofar as it singled out the

Papacy as its principal enemy.[5] In this way, the Risorgimento immediately came to be associated with two cornerstones of English patriotism and liberal Whig ideology: on the one hand, with the championing of constitutional liberties and on the other, with the Protestant cause, which viewed the Papacy as the nation's most bitter enemy.[6] Such messages were repeated and amplified in the literary works of Ugo Foscolo and Gabriele Rossetti, in which Dante came to be represented as the founding father of an Italian tradition of exile for the freedom from oppression, or, even, in the case of Rossetti's *Spirito Antipapale* (1832), as a sort of *ante-litteram* Carbonaro committed to the reform of the Papacy.[7]

Compared with the reassuring words of the conspirators of 1820, the revolutions of 1848 presented English public opinion with a more complex, and potentially more disconcerting, reading of the Risorgimento. The democratic and republican principles of Giuseppe Mazzini, who had been resident in England since 1837, did not find universal favour among the ruling classes. In 1848, Palmerston had seen the Piedmontese expansion into Lombardy and the creation of a northern Italian state as an opportunity not only to spread British constitutional freedoms and contain French and Russian influence in Europe, but also to prevent the spread of republicanism on the Continent. Despite the hostility towards the Papacy, and anti-Catholic prejudice, the British governments between 1846 and 1848 had also hoped to reform the Papal State with the consent of Pope Pius IX, who, thanks to his mild reforms, had appeared to both Italian nationalists and the wider European public as being open to change and to liberal principles. In 1849, the British government heard with horror of the news of the birth of the Roman republic under Giuseppe Mazzini.[8]

Nevertheless, during the years around 1848, Mazzini's ideas and the reports of events in Italy had a powerful influence on radical and liberal ideals in Britain. In fact, among Chartists and liberal reformers, a new kind of patriotism took hold that was intrinsically linked to the struggles for emancipation in Italy. English patriotism and internationalism were fused. This was seen in the language of both the radicals and of their liberal counterparts and followers of Mazzini like William Linton, whose 'People's International League' of 1847 had as its express aim to 'rouse the public mind to a recognition of the rights and duties of nations'.[9] Many Chartists saw in Risorgimento republicanism, especially that of Mazzini, an extension of their own patriotism based on the critique of aristocratic corruption and the championing of popular sovereignty, inspired by the memory of the Puritan Commonwealth and the government of Oliver Cromwell. It was not by chance that Mazzini was often associated both with Cromwell and with Milton in the imaginary Pantheon of English radicalism. However, reformers who were in favour of the liberalization of trade and the extension of suffrage, but hostile to the language of socialism and class struggle, saw in Mazzini, and in the Italian revolutions in general, examples of 'moderation' far removed from the extremes of the June revolution in Paris. What attracted liberal reformists like George Dawson were precisely the Mazzinian notions of duty towards one's fellow citizens and co-operation between the classes, as well as the moral and educational aspects of his message. In any case, Mazzini's language, strongly laced with religiosity, made the Risorgimento seem like an act of Protestant reform and a purification of both civil and religious customs. His theology, which denied the divinity of Christ, and his attack on the hierarchy of the Church, were particularly well received amongst dissenters and evangelicals, who like Mazzini found in the Gospel above all a powerful defence of the principles of liberty, democracy, and equality. According to William Adams, Mazzini was 'the greatest teacher since Christ'.[10] The popularity of his religious republicanism explains the existence of a true group of English 'Mazzinists' like James Stanfield, William Lovett, and Emilie Ashurst Venturi, who made the Mazzinian motto 'God and the People' their own.[11]

The end of the wave of revolutions on the Continent and the victory of the reactionaries caused disillusion among radical and liberal forces alike, and confirmed once again the belief that Great Britain remained the only bastion of progress in Europe. In Palmerston's eyes, the social peace maintained during such turbulent times on the Continent only served to prove the enduring qualities of British institutions. The unification of the Italian peninsula that took place between 1859 and 1869 was enormously popular precisely because it confirmed such opinions. Nevertheless, unlike in 1848, the birth of the unified state represented the final victory of English liberty on the Continent over its most bitter rivals: papal despotism, the Austrian and Russian empires, and the authoritarianism of Napoleon III and his ambitions for territorial expansion. The unification of Italy linked the liberal party with 'an international mission on behalf of constitutional, religious and commercial liberty'.[12] Although not a single English politician had predicted the birth of the unified state, its success was seen as resulting from strong ideas and a popular, rather than radical, act of emancipation, which had been achieved without the intervention of foreign powers. For Lord Russell, the events of 1859-69 confirmed the strength of the ideals of England's Glorious Revolution, while for Gladstone, they reinforced the notion of a patriotism founded on England's providential mission to advance humanitarian and constitutional principles throughout the world.[13] In turn, the radicals were able to find in the expedition of Garibaldi and his Mille a popular and democratic contribution to the completion of the Risorgimento.

Garibaldi's international popularity was in fact largely the product of the British press, to the extent that the creation of his myth would have been unthinkable without the mobilization and support that he received from the whole of Victorian society. This support was no doubt increased by the extraordinary development of the media, the public sphere, and British society, unmatched in any other European country. The enthusiasm for Garibaldi's heroic actions, and admiration for the success of his expedition, explain why hundreds of ordinary British men, and many women, felt the need to offer their support and identified with his venture. In the course of the events of 1860 Garibaldi received considerable sums of money from England, collected at a series of public events organised *ad hoc* both by groups of workers and by members of gentlemen's clubs like the Athenaeum. In addition, thousands of volunteers were ready to follow him into battle.[14] Garibaldi's visit to England in 1864 led to the largest public rally of the Victorian era, far exceeding the enthusiasm which greeted the arrival in London of Neapolitan liberals freed from Bourbon prisons in 1859.[15] In London, 500,000 people welcomed and cheered the hero in jubilation, with the result that his carriage took five whole hours to cross the city. His presence inspired a mania for knick-knacks, souvenirs, and topical songs, and stimulated the sale of red shirts. As Lucy Riall has demonstrated, once again the Italian cause, now embodied in the figure of Garibaldi, owed its success to its broad appeal and its capacity to produce extraordinarily diverse, even self-contradictory, reactions and emotions, and to express alternative forms of patriotism. During his stay, Garibaldi was the guest of the Duke of Sutherland, at whose London residence he met Lord Palmerston, Gladstone, Lord Derby, and Lord Russell; but he also paid a visit to Mazzini and participated in events organized both by the Reform Club and at the Crystal Palace, where an audience was specially organized for the working classes. According to *The Times*, Garibaldi's visit had become a demonstration of national unity, in which people of every social class had rushed to honour him.[16] But without doubt the popular enthusiasm for the hero, and the presence of trade-union representatives at the public rallies, were due to a reappropriation of his cause which did not necessarily sit harmoniously with the more reassuring, liberal-moderate interpretation of the Risorgimento. Garibaldi's sudden decision not to visit Manchester, Newcastle, or Glasgow was immediately attributed to the wish of the government not to excite radical and anti-institutional feeling, and Queen Victoria and the conservatives were greatly relieved when he left after twelve days.[17]

The same interweaving of England's celebration of its own identity with a sincere commitment to Italian nationalism, and the same plurality of political interpretations, can be found in the vast artistic, historical, and literary production dedicated to Italy in the Victorian period. British historiography devoted to the Italian Middle Ages and Renaissance was extensive and highly influential in this period. Victorian men of culture were divided on the merits and demerits of the two ages, each interpreted as a supreme moment of economic, artistic, and literary civilization and civil harmony. As is well known, John Ruskin viewed the Middle Ages as the high point in the development of freedom and cultural expression, and the Renaissance as a period of despotism and decadence, whilst writers such as John Addington Symonds, author of the popular *Renaissance in Italy* (1875-86), regarded the Renaissance – a period in which despots had become the expression of democratic regimes – as representing the true zenith of Italian history, and of Italian culture in general.[18] In both cases, the more or less explicit message that Italian history communicated to Victorian readers was that England now represented what Italy had been for the world during the Middle Ages or the Renaissance. The study of Italy provided reflections on the causes of such splendour (which could give rise to a certain complacency on the part of the public regarding the superiority of its homeland), but also on the more or less imminent possibilities and reasons that could have caused a decline. On the other hand, the idea that the Victorian era represented a new Renaissance was reinforced by the spread of public and private architecture in London and Manchester that imitated the Florentine *palazzo*. At the same time, British histories of the Middle Ages and Renaissance and of art, including that of the Pre-Raphaelites, reinterpreted those centuries in a proto-national light, projecting the patriotism of nineteenth-century Italy backwards in time. Thus the Italian Risorgimento also represented a second Renaissance, a revival of Italian civilization after centuries of decadence. As Symonds wrote in the conclusion to the final volume of his work on the Renaissance, which concentrated on the decadence of Italian culture in the Counter-Reformation, 'Thanks be to God, that I who pen these pages, and that you who read them, have before us in this year of Grace the spectacle of a resuscitated Italy!'[19]

However, although in the eyes of the general public and those of the political elite the new state reflected the values of liberalism and English patriotism, its social and civil conditions remained similar to those described by travellers on the Grand Tour at the beginning of the century. As British observers soon discovered, the overwhelming majority of Italians were still a long way from overcoming the vices produced by centuries of political despotism and religious fanaticism. We should thus interpret the efforts of the *British and Foreign Bible Society* to convert Italians to Protestantism through preaching and the diffusion of the Bible in the years following unification as being in line with its belief that the principles of liberalism, and the defeat of Papal despotism, could only successfully take hold through the spiritual regeneration of the people.[20]

Moreover, Italy was still regarded as a new power and as a second-class nation, born at the centre of an area – the Mediterranean – in which British naval dominance was almost undisputed. The gulf between the two countries, in economic terms, was massive. As Eugenio Biagini has noted, the standard of living in the peninsula made Italy comparable to a developing country today, and in 1860 Italy had far more in common with the countries of the Mediterranean basin than it did with England.[21] Two episodes in particular clearly illustrate the attitude of the British government towards Italy, and show the arrogance and superiority complex of the imperial power towards the fragile and fledgling unified state they also reflect the preoccupation and disappointment with the moral, social, and civil conditions of the peninsula. In 1863, the British Minister for Trade tried to incorporate into a trade agreement between the two countries, designed to liberalize the exchange of goods, a clause to protect religious freedom. Such a treaty, born in a climate of optimistic faith in the advantages of free trade which was shared by the liberal elites of both countries, demonstrates how in commercial politics too, the British government continued to maintain hostility towards Catholicism and wanted to protect Protestant minorities and encourage the spread of the Reformation. By itself, this kind of clause was not rare, indicating how the liberal creed was combined with a desire to export its own cultural and religious values as well. However, it was still generally applied only to countries outside Europe (the only exception in the past being Portugal), and in particular countries in Africa and South America. The Italian government, in the person of the Minister for Foreign Affairs, Visconti Venosta, naturally greatly resented this request, which put Italy on a par with semi-civilized countries and demanded the protection of a liberty already guaranteed by the constitution. The clause was consequently deleted from the treaty before it was ratified in 1863.[22]

On other occasions, England treated Italy like an imperial annex when it felt its own interests to be directly under threat. In 1870 the Royal Navy did not hesitate to send warships to the coast of Sardinia to defend one of its vice-consuls from repeated death threats. Martino Zamponi, a Sardinian citizen and the British vice-consul in the ports of Olbia and Terranova, found himself embroiled in a feud with rival families which cost the life of his son. Having been unable to obtain reassurances from the Italian government, the consul, Walker, did not hesitate to ask the British Navy to send a warship to Cagliari and Terranova. This resulted in the immediate end to the threats and feud against vice-consul Zamponi, but also angered the Italian government, which found itself humiliated by a gesture that put Italy on a par with countries on Africa's Mediterranean coast.[23]

The difficult struggle against banditry, the vendettas against a vice-consul, and the violence against Protestants – sixteen protestants were massacred at Barletta in March 1866, following a fiery sermon during Sunday mass – confirmed to the English that the new state was incapable of guaranteeing respect for the law, the control of its territory, or the security of its citizens, and that England was therefore justified in treating Italy as a country of limited sovereignty. After unification, the British press continued to report news stories that called into doubt the complete regeneration of Italy, and outlined a long journey towards civilization. The efforts to evangelize Italy also turned out to be in vain. The organizers of the *Italian Bible Society*, founded in 1872, had to face the fact that Italy remained a Catholic country even after the breakthrough at Porta Pia: their meetings for the most part attracted only foreigners resident in Rome.[24] And yet the end of the Risorgimento did not signal the decline of British enthusiasm for Italy, nor the end of the identification of British and Italian patriotism. Both its love affair with Italy – a country of innumerable and immeasurable beauties in landscape and art – and the cult of the Risorgimento persisted well beyond the twilight of the Victorian era, despite disillusionment with the real conditions of the country. In particular, it was George Macaulay Trevelyan's literary-historical work that passed onto the next century an interpretation of the Risorgimento which embraced all the values and expectations that the Victorian era had projected onto these events, more enthralling than any novel. Trevelyan's link with the 'Victorian' Risorgimento was in one sense direct: his father George's house had been the meeting place of Italophiles like John Ruskin and the Pre-Raphaelites, and his father had himself gone to Italy in 1867 in the hope of joining Garibaldi. In Trevelyan's Garibaldian trilogy, published between 1907 and 1911, we find in fact much of the cultural tradition that had made Italy so attractive during the preceding century: the tradition of the Grand Tour; the typical sentimentalism of English expressions of solidarity for the struggle for Italian independence, described as a fight between good and evil and as the unstoppable affirmation of progress, according to the Whig view of history; and finally, an echo of Mazzinian values cleansed of any trace of republicanism.[25] With an optimism that reflected the electoral victories and reforms introduced by the liberal party at the beginning of the twentieth century, Trevelyan concluded his trilogy with these words: 'To us Englishmen, Garibaldi will live as the incarnate symbol of two passions not likely soon to die out of the world, the love of country and the love of freedom'.[26]

1 John Pemble, *The Mediterranean Passion: Victorians and Edwardians in the South* (Oxford, 1987), p. 60.

2 Maura O'Connor, *The Romance of Italy and the English Political Imagination* (Basingstoke, 1998).

3 Charles MacFarlane, *The Lives and Exploits of Banditti and Robbers in all Parts of the World*, 2 vols (London, 1822), I, p. 5.

4 Nelson Moe, *The View from Vesuvius: Italian Culture and the Southern Question* (Berkeley & London, 2002).

5 See, for example, Giuseppe Pecchio, 'Political condition of the Italian States', *Edinburgh Review*, 55 (1832), pp. 362–97.

6 Maurizio Isabella, *Risorgimento in Exile: Italian Émigrés and the Liberal International in the Post-Napoleonic Era* (Oxford, 2009), pp. 202–8.

7 *Sullo spirito antipapale dei classici antichi d'Italia. Disquisizione di Gabriele Rossetti, professore di lingua e letteratura italiana nel Collegio del Re in Londra* (London, 1832).

8 Saho Matsumoto-Best, *Britain and the Papacy in the Age of Revolution 1846–1851* (Rochester, 2003).

9 Maurizio Isabella, 'Italian exiles and British politics before and after 1848', in *Exiles from European Revolutions: Refugees in Mid-Victorian England*, ed. S. Freitag (Oxford 2003), pp. 59–87; Margot C. Finn, *After Chartism: Class and Nation in English Radical Politics, 1848–1874* (Cambridge, 1993), pp. 70–77; O'Connor 1998, pp. 72–9.

10 W.E. Adams, *Memoirs of a Social Atom*, 2 vols (London, 1903), I, p. 263.

11 Eugenio Biagini, 'Mazzini and Anticlericalism: The English Exile', in *Giuseppe Mazzini and the Globalisation of Democratic Nationalism 1830–1920*, ed. Christopher Bayly and Eugenio Biagini (Oxford, 2008), pp. 145–66.

12 Jonathan Parry, *The Politics of Patriotism: English Liberalism, National Identity and Europe, 1830–1886* (Cambridge, 2006), pp. 221–257 (p. 221).

13 Parry 2006, pp. 230; 255–6.

14 Lucy Riall, *Garibaldi: Invention of a Hero* (New Haven & London, 2007), pp. 294–6.

15 On the arrival of the Neapolitan exiles, see Isabella 2003, p. 78.

16 Riall 2007, pp. 330–44.

17 ibid., pp. 338–9.

18 Hilary Fraser, *The Victorians and Renaissance Italy* (Oxford, 1992).

19 J.A. Symonds, *Renaissance in Italy: The Catholic Reaction*, 2 vols (London, 1886), II, p. 435.

20 Danilo Raponi, 'Religious Reformation and National Unity: British Protestants and Italy', in *New Perspectives in British Cultural History*, ed. by Rosalind Crone, David Gange, and Katy Jones (Cambridge, 2007), pp. 78–89.

21 Derek Beales and Eugenio Biagini, *The Risorgimento and the Unification of Italy* (London, 2002), p. 177.

22 Danilo Raponi, 'An "anti-Catholicism of free trade"? Religion and the Anglo-Italian negotiations of 1863', *European History Quarterly*, 39 (2009), pp. 633–52.

23 O.J. Wright, 'Sea and Sardinia: Pax Britannica versus Vendetta in the new Italy (1870)', *European History Quarterly*, 37 (2007), pp. 398–416.

24 Raponi 2007, pp. 82–3.

25 George Macaulay Trevelyan, *Garibaldi's Defence of the Roman Republic* (London, 1907); *Garibaldi and the Thousand* (London, 1909); *Garibaldi and the Making of Italy* (London, 1911). Lucy Turner Voakes, 'The Liberal Heroism of Trevelyan's Garibaldi: the Risorgimento and English Literary History, *c.* 1867–1911', forthcoming, in *Modern Italy*, and also Lucy Riall, 'Rappresentazioni del Quarantotto italiano nella storiografia inglese', in R. Camurri, *Memoria, rappresentazioni e protagonisti del 1848 italiano* (Verona, 2006), pp. 21–37.

26 Trevelyan 1911, p. 297.

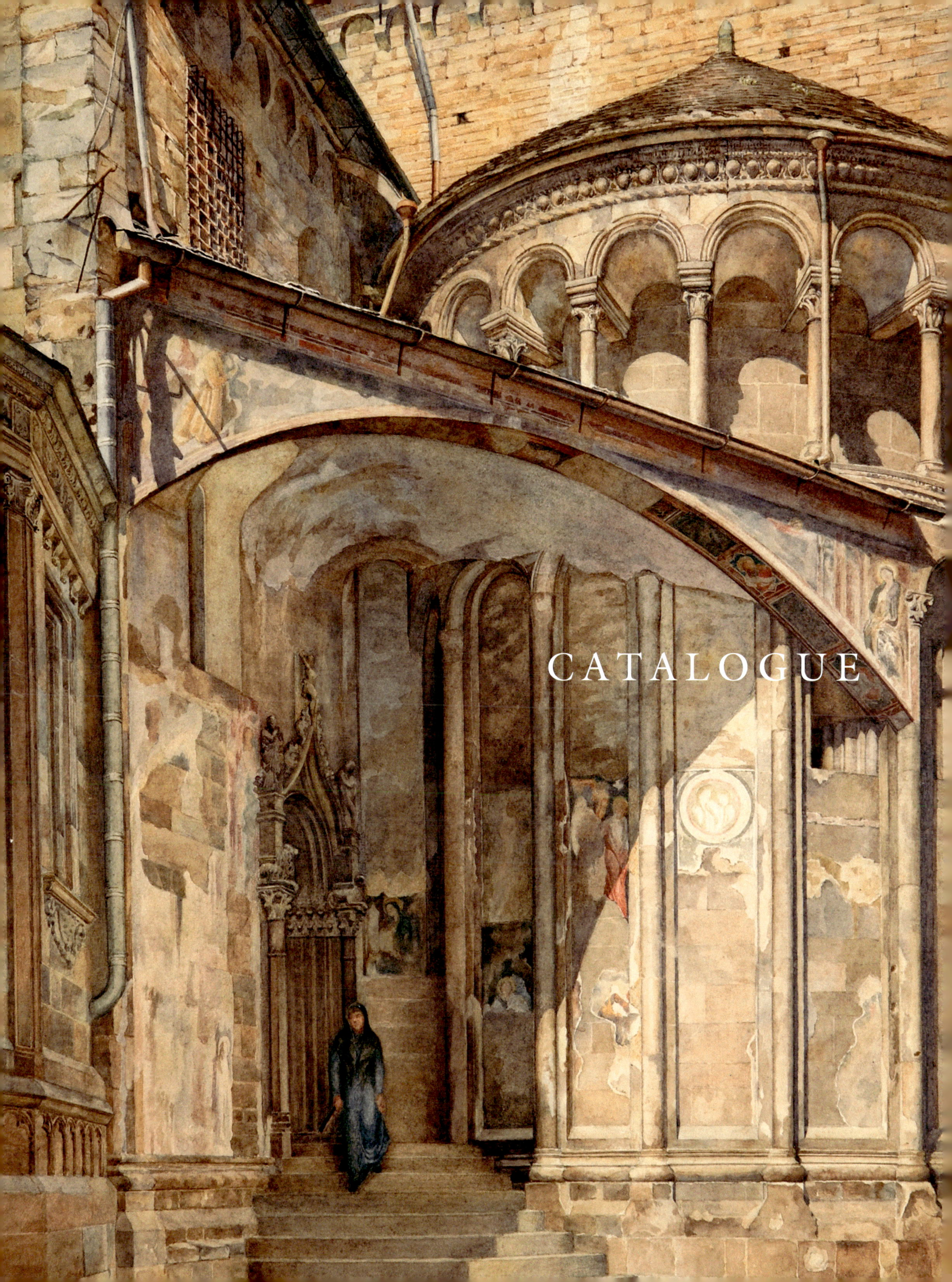

CATALOGUE

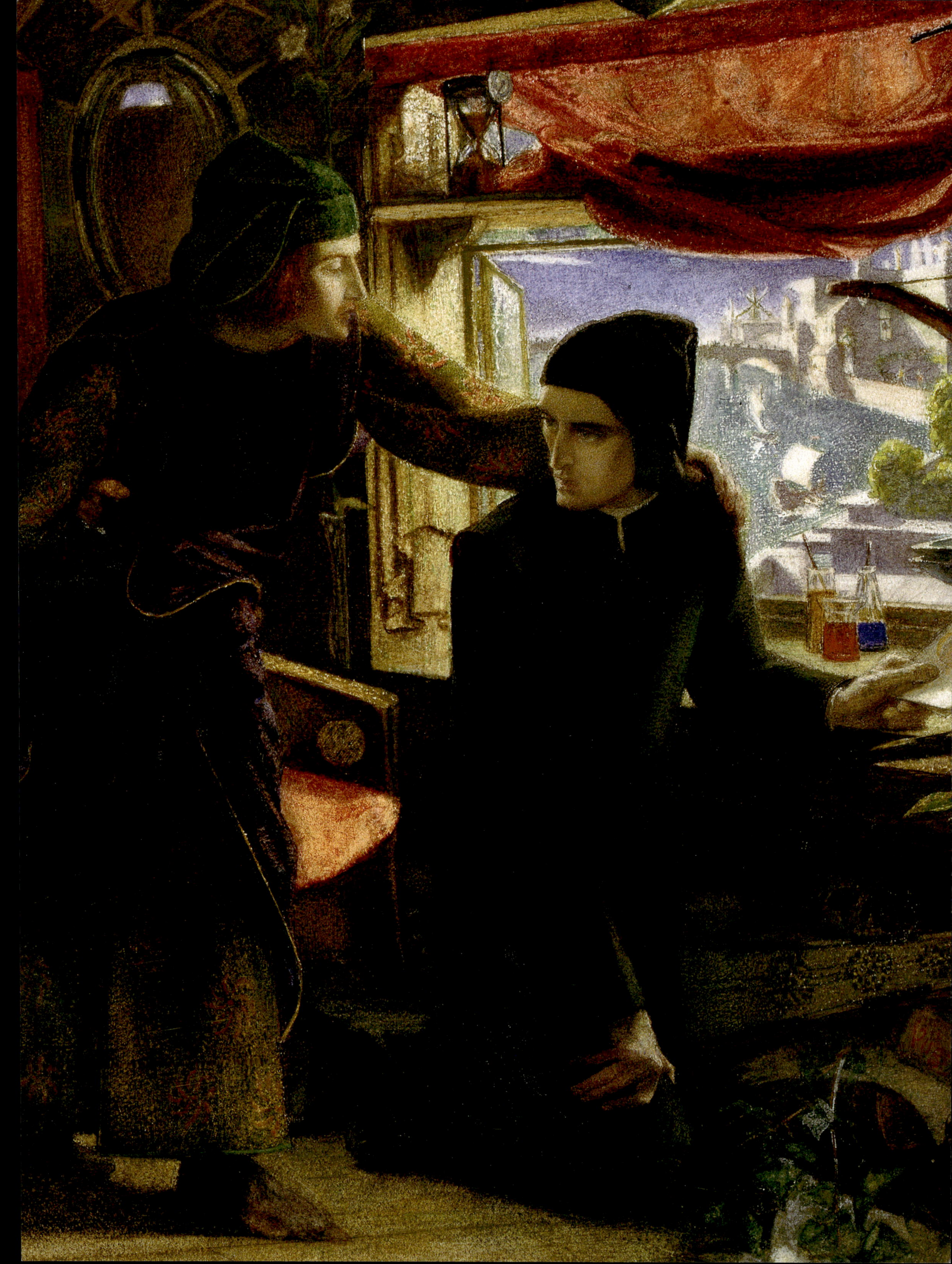

I

THEMES FROM ITALIAN HISTORY AND LITERATURE

The members of the Pre-Raphaelite Brotherhood probably had as little first-hand experience of Italian literature in the original as they did of Italian art before Raphael. Only the Rossettis spoke and read Italian fluently. The first paintings exhibited by the Pre-Raphaelites were based on Italian subjects as interpreted by English authors, notably the poets Robert and Elizabeth Browning, John Keats, and the plays of Shakespeare set in Italy. Two paintings shown in the first Royal Academy exhibition after the formation of the Brotherhood, in 1849, had Italian subjects: Holman Hunt's *Rienzi* (private collection), which was based not on any historical account of the life of Cola di Rienzi, but on Bulwer Lytton's novel *Rienzi, the Last of the Tribunes*; and Millais's *Isabella* (Walker Art Gallery, Liverpool), from Keats's poem, 'Isabella, or the Pot of Basil', itself derived from Boccaccio. Dante Gabriel Rossetti also used episodes from Shakespeare, Tibullus, and other authors, as well as illustrations from Italian history, such as the depictions of Italian artists at work, or the imaginary monk, *Fra Pace* (1856; private collection), the single drawing which persuaded Burne-Jones to become an artist. However, he identified most closely with the poet Dante, in both personal and artistic terms, and many of his greatest works of the 1850s are illustrations of passages from the *Divine Comedy* and the *Vita Nuova*. Among them was the episode of Paolo and Francesca, which he suggested to the sculptor Alexander Munro, and which had by this time been treated by many artists, both in England and on the Continent, notably by the associate of the Nazarenes in Rome, William Dyce. Joseph Noel Paton's paintings of Italian Renaissance subjects were probably indebted to his association with the young Pre-Raphaelites, although he greatly admired Dyce as well. His preoccupation with Dante endured from 1851, when he showed a *Death of Paolo and* Francesca at the Royal Scottish Academy, until 1878, when he was preparing a painting of *Paolo and Francesca – Inferno*. In the 1840s and 1850s, Rossetti was also working on his translations of Italian poetry and of Dante's *Vita Nuova*, published in 1861 as *Early Italian Poets*, to some acclaim. Among Rossetti's disciples, Simeon Solomon reinterpreted one of his subjects with his own eccentric draughtsmanship; while Burne-Jones was apparently instructed by Ruskin to illustrate an episode from Italian history never treated by Rossetti, as well as less recondite subjects such as Lucrezia Borgia.

1
William Dyce (1806–1864)
Francesca da Rimini 1837
Oil on canvas, 137.6 x 172.7 cm
The National Galleries of Scotland, Edinburgh
Ref: Babington 2006, no. 16

When this picture was shown at the Royal Scottish Academy in 1837, the title in the catalogue was supplemented by a long extract from Boccaccio which explained that Guido da Polenta had arranged for his daughter Francesca to marry Gianciotto, the eldest son of his enemy, the master of Rimini. Because Gianciotto was hideously deformed, he decided to marry her by proxy, and sent his handsome younger brother Paolo. On seeing Paolo, Francesca believed that he was her future husband, and fell in love. Unlike Dante, therefore, who treated the episode in the *Divine Comedy*, Boccaccio maintained that the lovers were wholly innocent.

In its original form the composition was much more readily identifiable with earlier treatments of the subject by Ingres, who delighted in showing the evil and ugly elder brother discovering the two lovers together behind an arras, stealing a kiss. However, after Dyce's death, the canvas was acquired by the Royal Scottish Academy as 'the principal work he had executed before he left Scotland', and, in 1881, the figure of Gianciotto was removed on the instructions of Sir Noel Paton; only his hand remains on the parapet. Even in its present state, it reveals Dyce's inexorable leaning towards Raphael, and the influence of the Nazarenes he had met in Rome in the 1820s.

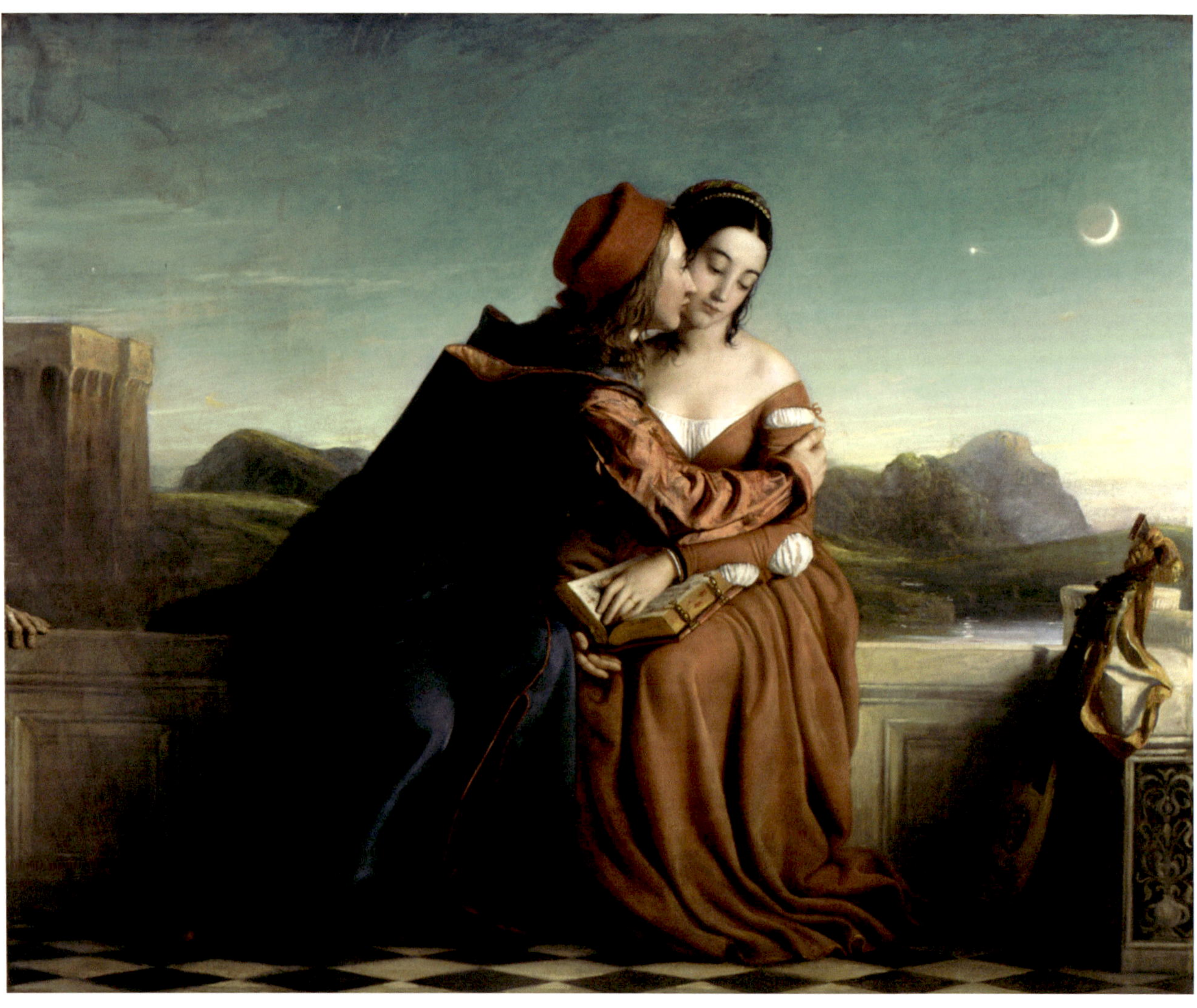

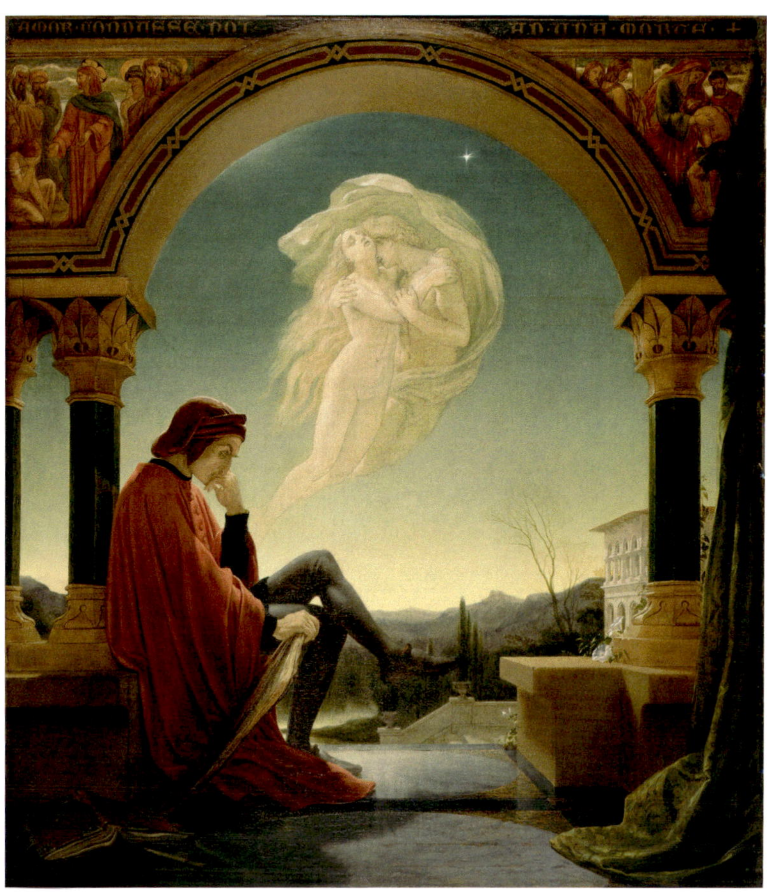

2
Sir Joseph Noel Paton (1821–1901)
Dante Meditating the Episode of Francesca da Rimini and Paulo Malatesta 1852
Oil on canvas, 101 x 89 cm
Inscribed: *Amor. condusse. noi. ad. una. morte.*
Bury Art Gallery, Museums and Archives

Paton enjoyed considerable success in his native Scotland: he was elected a full member of the Royal Scottish Academy at the early age of 29, and appointed Queen's Limner in Scotland in 1866. During his studies at the Royal Academy in London in 1843–4, he met Millais, who became a lifelong friend. Although he was an ardent nationalist and illustrated many themes from Scottish history, it is for his literary subjects that Paton is best remembered, notably his two illustrations from Shakespeare's *Midsummer Night's Dream, The Reconciliation of Oberon and Titania*, and *The Quarrel of Oberon and Titania* (National Gallery of Scotland), which were exhibited to great acclaim in 1847 and 1849 respectively. Following the example of both Dyce and D.G. Rossetti, Paton exhibited a series of works depicting the story of Paolo and Francesca during the early 1850s, probably inspired by Keats as much as Dante. They included *The Death of Paolo and Francesca* (exhibited in 1851), and *Dante Meditating the Episode of Francesca da Rimini and Paulo Malatesta*, which was shown at the Royal Scottish Academy in 1852. The architectural composition, with subsidiary scenes in spandrels, serves as a reminder that Paton had been one of the artists commissioned to decorate the new Palace of Westminster in the 1840s. The scenes in the spandrels show the Christ and the Woman taken in Adultery (above Francesca) and the Return of the Prodigal Son (above Paolo). Both parables illustrate the virtue of mercy and forgiveness. The inscription, from Canto v of the *Divine Comedy*, reads 'Love leads us to a single death'. When the picture was exhibited, the critics were generally favourable. *The Scotsman* fully understood the significance of the subject, describing it as 'one of those still, but momentous hours, in which immortal thoughts are inspired into great minds, and given as a heritage to mankind for ever. … The picture, on the whole, is the grandest thing Mr Paton has yet given us; more simple, impressive and sublime. The details, where the severity of the treatment allows of any, are, as usual, exquisitely painted, the pale white convolvulus that climbs up the marble colonnade is lovely, and the architecture is very gracefully put in'. He did, however, complain of a certain coldness in Dante's expression.[1] Two years later, Paton showed a painting entitled *The Dead Lady*, of the subject that Rossetti had considered the pendant to *Dante's Dream*, Michelangelo kneeling at the bedside of Vittoria Colonna (untraced).

1 *The Scotsman*, 6 March 1852

3

Alexander Munro (1825–1871)
Paolo and Francesca 1852
Marble, 66 x 67.5 x 53 cm
Signed and dated: *Alex. Munro / Sc. 1852*
Birmingham Museum and Art Gallery
Ref: Pointon 1975, pp. 90–92; Parris 1984, no. 44; Read and Barnes 1991 no. 21; Wildman 1995 no. 19

W.M. Rossetti remembered that his brother 'never had a more admiring or attached friend than Munro', and several of Munro's early works are indebted to D.G. Rossetti's example. The most notable is this group of *Paolo and Francesca*, which is based on one of a series of compositional drawings made by Rossetti in 1849. Both sculpture and drawing may ultimately be derived from Flaxman's engraving of 'The Lovers Surprised', first published in 1793. They illustrate the passage from the *Divine Comedy* when the young pair spent hours reading of Lancelot and Guinevere, and fell in love. In Cary's translation, which was probably that used by Munro, the passage reads:

> One day
> For our delight, we read of Lancelot,
> How him love thrilled. Alone we were, and no
> Suspicion near us. Oft-times by that reading
> Our eyes were drawn together, and the love
> Fled from our alter'd cheek. But at one point
> Alone we fell. When of that smile we read,
> The wishes smile, so rapturously kiss'd
> By one so deep in love, then he, who ne'er
> From me shall separate, at once my lips
> All trembling kiss'd. The book and writer both
> Were love's purveyors. In its leaves that day
> We read no more.

Munro completed the plaster version of his group in time to show it at the Great Exhibition at the Crystal Palace in 1851, where it was seen by W.E. Gladstone, M.P. for the University of Oxford. He commissioned the marble version, having been assured by Munro that 'the freshness of the idea which is very well expressed in the clay can be reproduced without loss in the marble.' The marble was exhibited at the Royal Academy in 1852, when the *Morning Chronicle* observed that Munro had rejected 'Academic idealism' for 'Gothic naturalism'.[1]

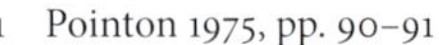

1 Pointon 1975, pp. 90–91

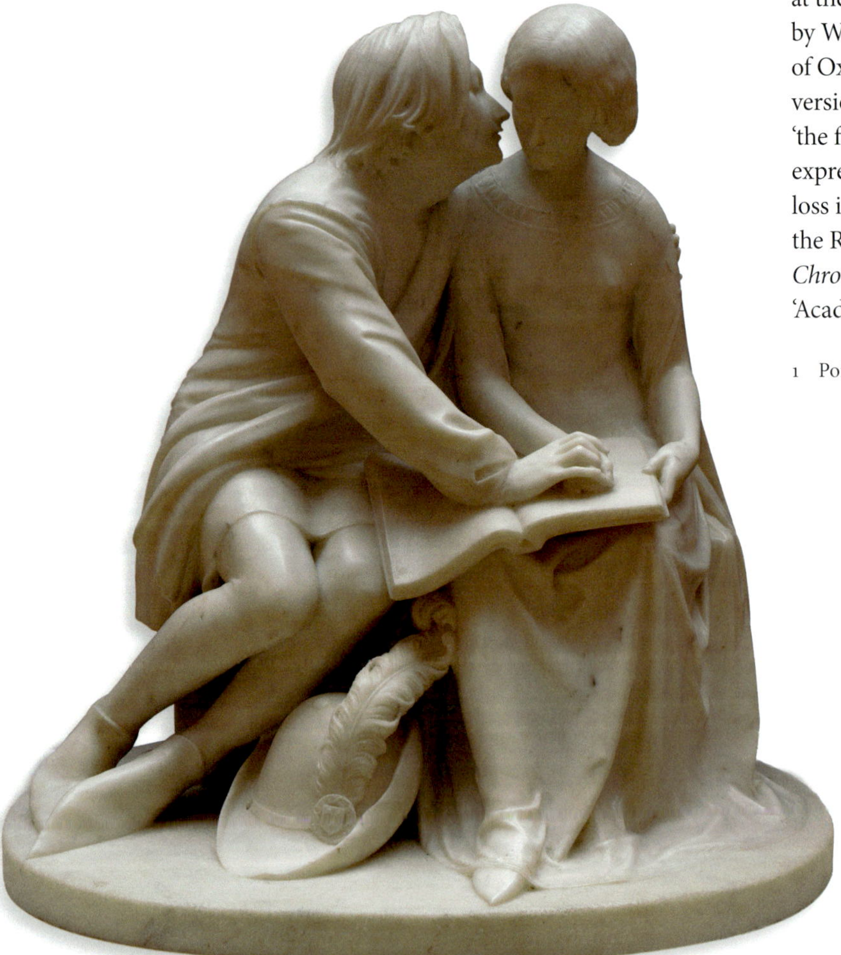

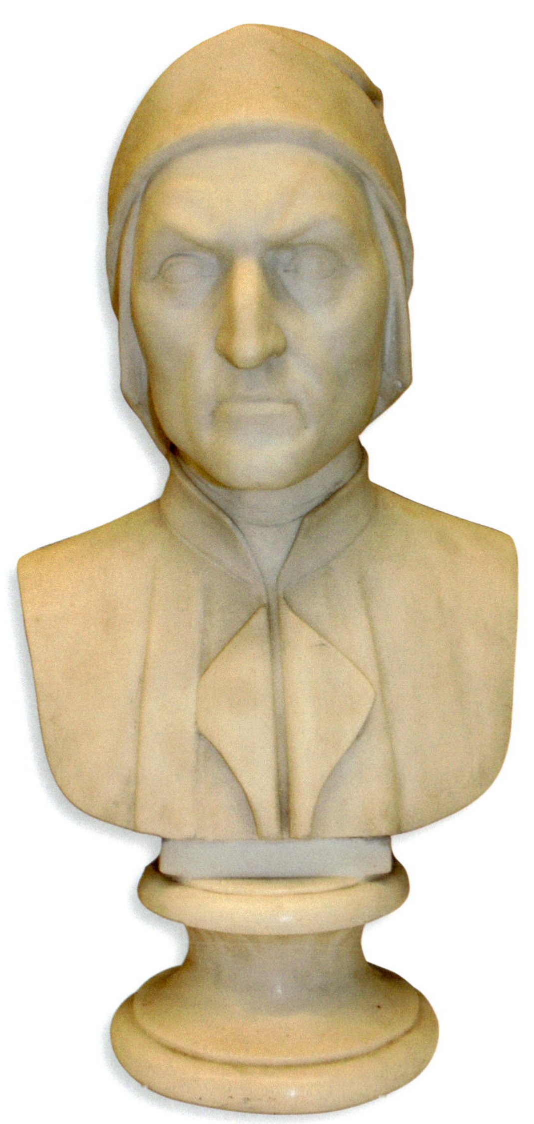

4
attributed to Alexander Munro (1825–1871)
Dante ?1856
Marble, 59.5 x 31 x 25 cm
The Mistress and Fellows of Girton College, Cambridge
Ref: Read and Barnes 1991 p. 48

Although Dante's reputation in England had risen considerably since the publication of Cary's translation of the *Divine Comedy* in 1814, his bust was still one of the rarest of writers to decorate libraries in Great Britain.[1] Indeed, only a single bust before 1850 is recorded, that exhibited at the Royal Scottish Academy in 1849 by William Brodie, based on a mask owned by the Lord Advocate of Scotland, Andrew Rutherford (untraced). It was perhaps natural that, after the success of his group of *Paolo and Francesca*, Munro should have gone on to sculpt a bust of Dante, which he exhibited it at the Royal Academy in 1856. Although it has not been conclusively identified, it is probably that photographed by Lewis Carroll in 1859, which is of a similar format to Munro's bust of Giuseppe Mazzini, made on a visit to London in 1857, and is signed.[2] The present bust has traditionally been attributed to Munro, although it is quite different from the signed bust, more conventional, but impressively modelled.

1 see, for example, Baker 1991
2 see Taylor and Wakeling 2002, pp. 159–60

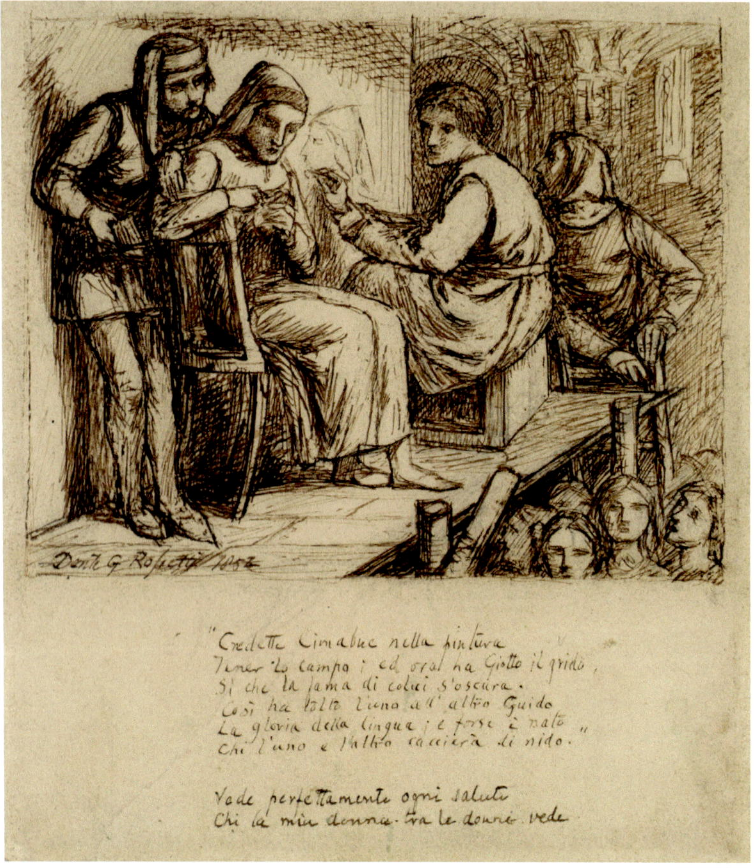

5

Dante Gabriel Rossetti (1828–1882)
Study for 'Giotto painting the Portrait of Dante'
1852
Pen and brown ink on paper, 19 x 16.8 cm
Signed and dated: *Dante G. Rossetti 1852* and
Inscribed:
"Credete Cimabue nella pintura
Tener lo camp; ed ora ha Giotto il grido,
Sic he la fama di colui s'oscura.
Cosi ha tolto l'uno all'altro Guido
La Gloria della lingua; e forse e nato
Chi l'uno e l'altro cacciera di nido."
Vede perfettamente ogni salute
Chi la mia donna -tra le donne - vede.
Tate. Bequeathed by J.R. Holliday, 1927. (N04283)
Ref: Surtees 1971, no. 54A

The inscription explains the subject, from Canto XI of the *Purgatorio*, which appears in Cary's translation as:

> Cimabue thought
> To lord it over painting's field; and now
> The cry is Giotto's, and his name eclips'd.
> Thus hath one Guido from the other snatch'd
> The letter'd prize: and he perhaps is born,
> Who shall drive either from their nest

followed by two lines from the *Vita nuova*, translated by Rossetti as:

> For certain he hath seen all perfectness
> Who among other ladies hath seen mine:

Cimabue peers over Giotto's shoulder as he paints a portrait of Dante on the walls of the Bargello Chapel, while Guido Cavalcanti holds a book by Guido Guinicelli, whose fame he has eclipsed. The conflation of the texts enables Rossetti to show Beatrice passing below the platform in a wedding procession. The main subject was recorded by Vasari and apparently confirmed by the discovery of the portrait of Dante in the Bargello in 1840. This drawing served as the study for a magnificent watercolour dated September 1852,[1] which Rossetti described in a letter to his friend, Thomas Woolner, as combining 'all the influence of Dante's youth – Art, Friendship, and Love – with a real incident embodying them.'

1 private collection of Lord Lloyd-Webber; Surtees 1971, no. 54

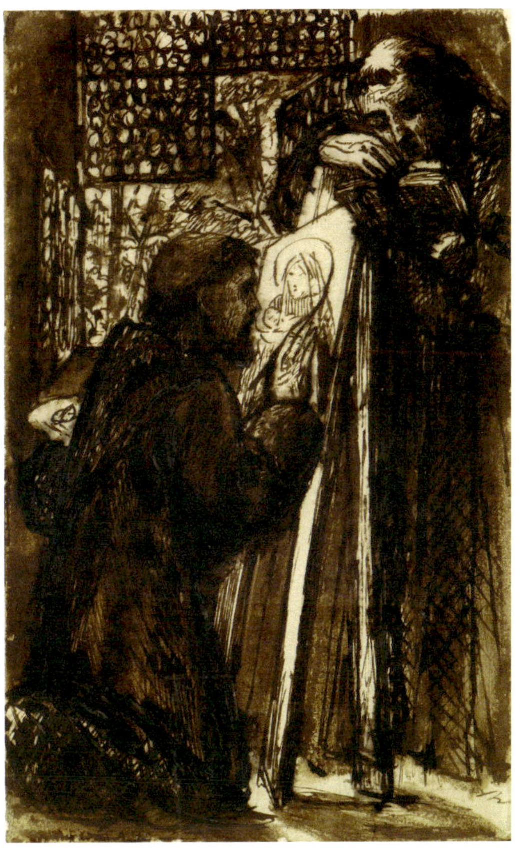

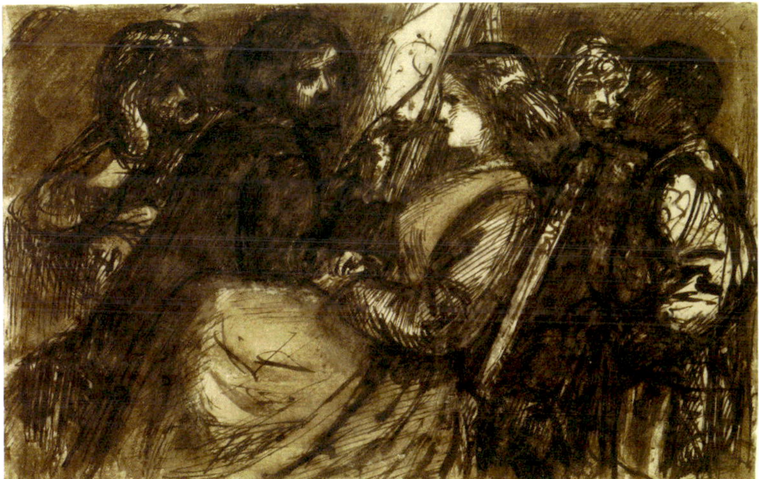

6
Dante Gabriel Rossetti
Fra Angelico painting c. 1853
Pen and brown ink and wash on paper, 17.8 x 11.2 cm

7
Giorgione painting c. 1853
Pen and brown ink and wash on paper, 11.1 x 17.8 cm
Birmingham Museums and Art Gallery. Presented by subscribers, 1903 (1904P450–1)
Ref: Surtees 1971, no. 694–5

Both Fra Angelico and 'Giorgioni' (*sic*) appear in the list of Immortals compiled by Rossetti and Holman Hunt on behalf of the Pre-Raphaelite Brotherhood in August 1848. When the pair visited Paris in the following year, they particularly admired Fra Angelico's altarpiece of *The Coronation of the Virgin*. Also, Rossetti was inspired to write a sonnet on Giorgione's *Concert champêtre*, published in *The Germ*. These two drawings reflect therefore the artist's own personal predilections. Although the drawings are of different formats, they are on sheets of similar sizes and form a pair. For the Victorians, Fra Angelico was the epitome of the spiritual painter in the service of God and art, and Rossetti's story 'Hand and Soul', published in *The Germ*, owes much to his perception of Fra Angelico. In the drawing, Fra Angelico is seen painting whilst one of the other brothers reads to him from the scriptures or some other holy book. By contrast, Giorgione came to be regarded as the epitome of the sensual painter, the originator of the warm colouring and soft modelling of the Venetian school. Both scenes are entirely imaginary.

8

Dante Gabriel Rossetti (1828–1882)
Dante Drawing an Angel on the Anniversary of Beatrice's Death 1853
Watercolour and bodycolour on paper, 42 x 61 cm
Signed in monogram and dated: *DGR / 1853*
Ashmolean Museum, University of Oxford.
Bequeathed by Mrs Thomas Combe, 1893 (WA1894.16)
Ref: Surtees 1971, no. 58; Treuherz 2003, no. 42

Rossetti's first drawing of this subject, made in 1849, was also his first illustration from Dante's *Vita nuova*, and his first work to be signed with the initials 'P.R.B.' (Birmingham Museum and Art Gallery). It shows Dante sitting alone on the first anniversary of the death of his beloved Beatrice, drawing an angel. Chancing to turn his head, he noticed other people standing watching, and excused himself by saying, 'Another was with me'. This watercolour, Rossetti's largest so far, was completed in 1853, and is one of the most complex and richly coloured of his early works. It brought the artist to the attention of John Ruskin, who wrote to him for the first time on 10 April 1854 to tell him that he thought this watercolour 'a thoroughly glorious work – the most perfect piece of Italy, in the accessory parts, I have ever seen in my life – not of Italy only – but of marvellous landscape painting.'[1]

1 Fredeman 2002–10, I, p.335

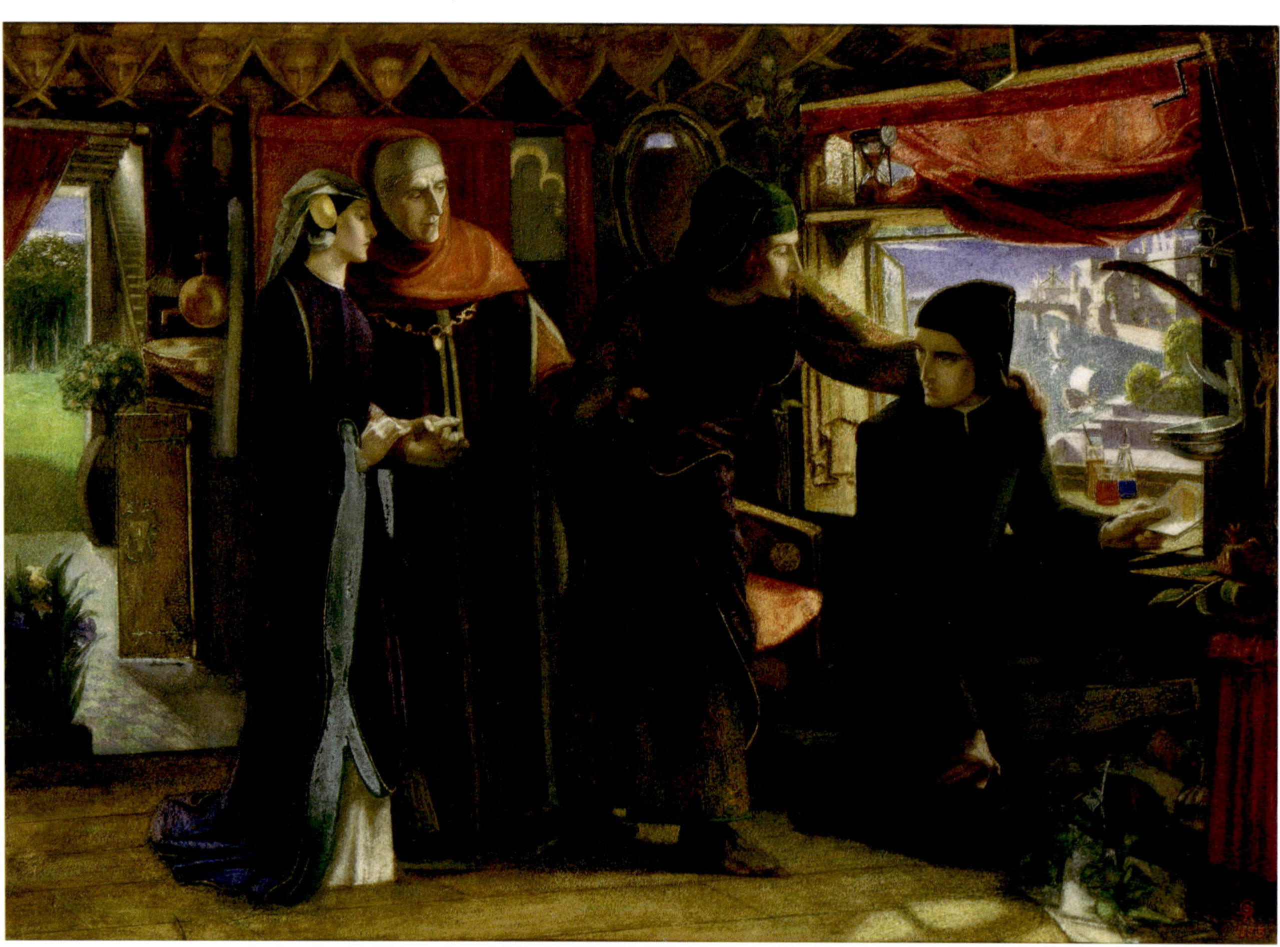

9
Dante Gabriel Rossetti
Dante's Vision of Rachel and Leah 1855
Watercolour on paper, 35.2 x 31.4 cm
Tate. Bequeathed by Beresford Rimington Heaton, 1940 (N05228)
Ref: Surtees 1971, no. 74; Hewison 2000, no. 118; Treuherz 2003, no. 45

In 1855, in the hope of encouraging Rossetti to paint subjects more intellectual than romantic, Ruskin commissioned two watercolours illustrating the *Purgatorio*: *Dante's Vision of Matilda gathering Flowers* (untraced; see cat. 12), and *Dante's Vision of Rachel and Leah*. At the end of the year, he had ceded the latter to Ellen Heaton, noting that 'it is only imperfect because Rachel does not sit easily – but stiffly, in a Pre-Raphaelite way – at the fountain's edge – and because her reflection is wrongly put in the water – but it is very lovely – and I think you might like to have it for some time at any rate.' He also admitted that Rossetti was very fond of this drawing himself. The watercolour shows Rachel admiring her own reflection in the water, while Leah gathers flowers to adorn herself. The figures are generally taken as allegories of the active and the contemplative life.

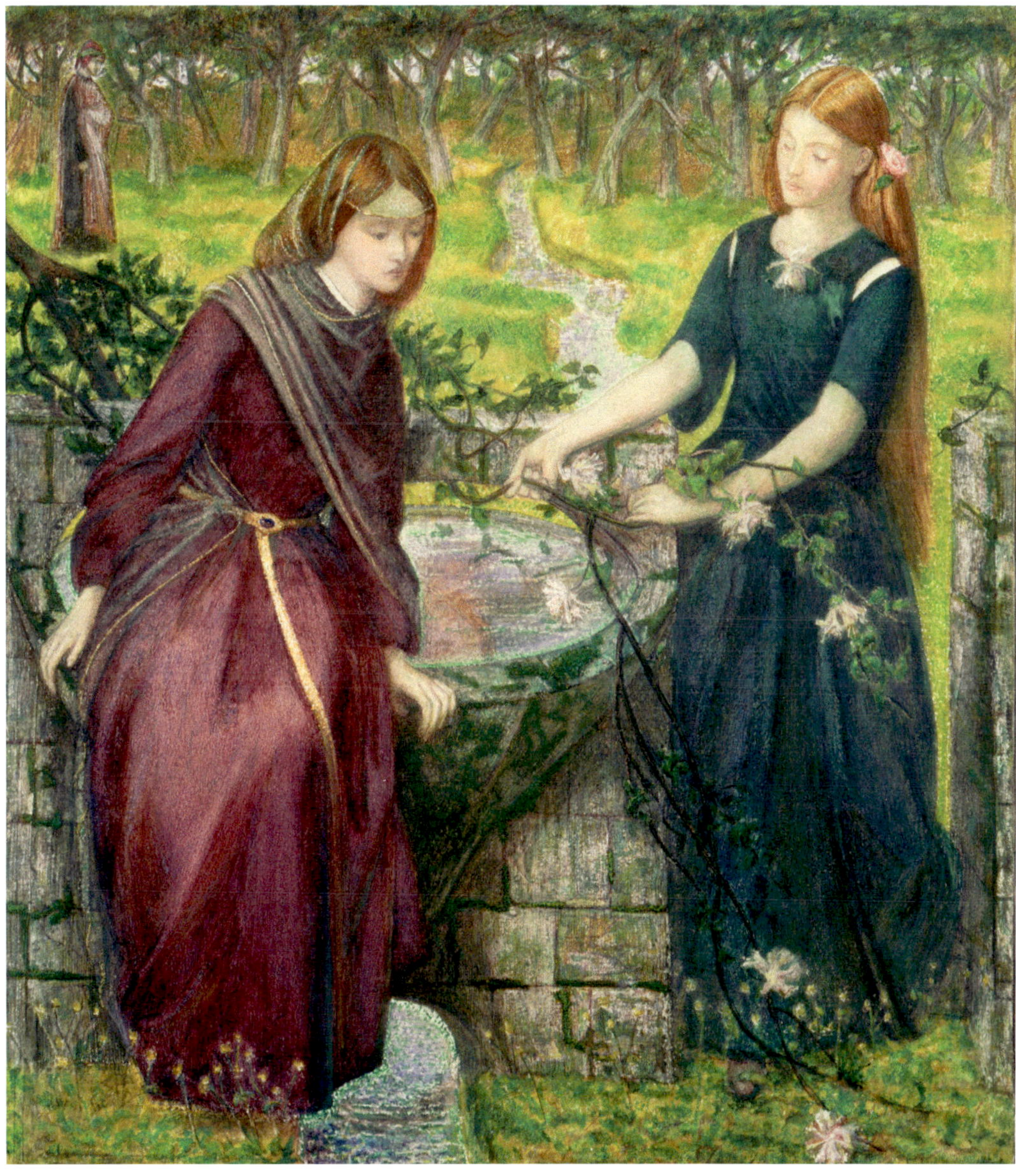

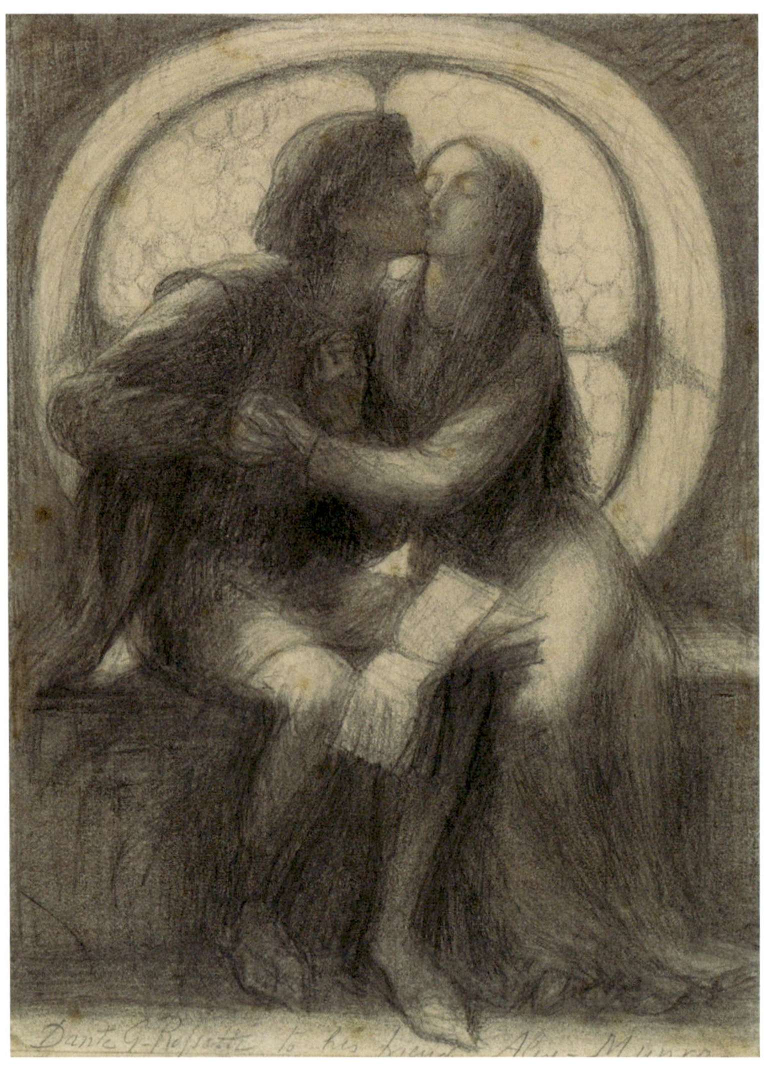

10
Dante Gabriel Rossetti
Study for 'Paolo and Francesca da Rimini' 1855
Pencil on paper, 22.6 x 16.7 cm
Signed and dedicated along lower edge:
Dante G. Rossetti to his friend Alex. Munro
The British Museum (1981–11–07–17)
Ref: Surtees 1971, no. 75A

This drawing corresponds fairly closely to the left-hand panel of the watercolour (**cat. 11**), save that, to heighten the passion of the moment, the book is shown about to fall to the ground. It is dedicated to Alexander Munro, who paid Rossetti the compliment of translating his early ideas for the group of lovers into marble (**cat. 3**). Although it is generally described as a study for the watercolour, and may have originally been so, its high degree of finish might suggest that Rossetti subsequently worked it up before giving it to Munro.

11

Dante Gabriel Rossetti
Paolo and Francesca da Rimini 1855
Watercolour on paper, 25.4 x 44.9 cm
Inscribed at the top: *O lasso!* and along the bottom: *Quanti dolci pensier, quanto disio / Menò costoro al doloroso passo!*
Tate. Purchased with the assistance of Sir Arthur Du Cros, Bart, and Sir Otto Beit, KCMG, through The Art Fund, 1916 (N03056)
Ref: Surtees 1971, no. 75; Hewison 2000, no. 117

Rossetti's most elaborate treatment of the Paolo and Francesca story, this was painted in 1855 as one of a series of watercolours commissioned by Ruskin. On the left, the two lovers have left off reading from the story of Lancelot, and embrace passionately; in the centre, Dante and Virgil contemplate the ill-fated pair; while, on the right, Paolo and Francesca whirl through the second circle of Hell, reserved for the lustful. Inscribed on each panel is an appropriate quotation from Dante's *Inferno*, V: 'Alas, by what sweet thoughts, what fond desire, Must they at length to that ill pass have reach'd!' Rossetti had been contemplating a tripartite composition since 1849, when his brother recorded in the *Pre-Raphaelite Journal*' that 'Gabriel... intends that the picture shall be in three compartments. In the middle, Paolo and Francesca kissing, on the left Dante and Virgil in the second circle; on the right the spirits blowing to and fro' (19 November 1849).[1] Such a scheme was no doubt inspired by triptychs Rossetti had seen on his recent tour of France and the Low Countries. The watercolour was painted in a week in October or November 1855, in order to raise money to relieve Elizabeth Siddal, who was reported destitute in Paris. Ruskin paid for it, and recommended it to Mrs Heaton as 'a most gloomy drawing – very grand – but dreadful ... Prudish people might perhaps think it not quite a young lady's drawing. I don't know.' However, he also offered her the companion drawing of *Dante's Vision of Rachel and Leah* (**cat. 9**), which she naturally preferred.

1 Fredeman 1975, p.27

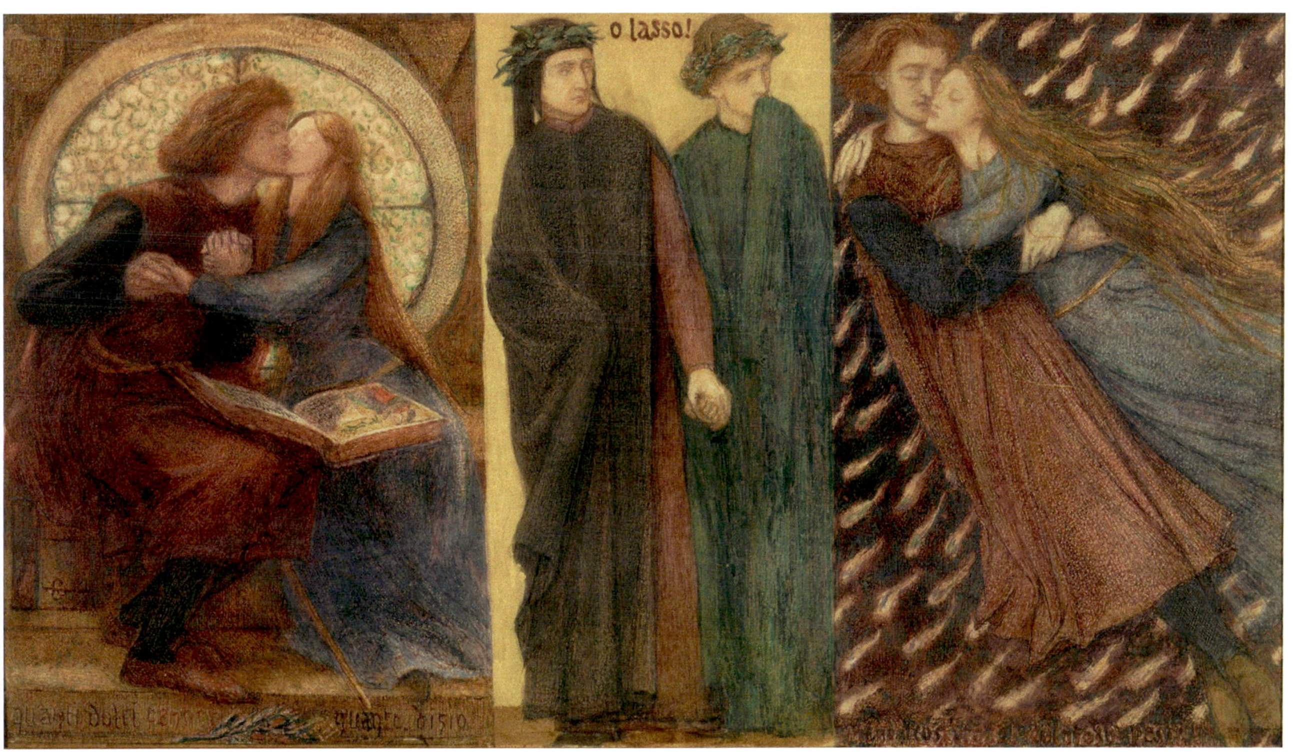

12
Dante Gabriel Rossetti
Dante's Vision of Matilda Gathering Flowers 1855
Pen and brown ink on paper, 17.8 x 18.5 cm
Ashmolean Museum, University of Oxford (WA1942.157)
Ref: Surtees 1971, no. 72A

This is the only surviving preparatory study for the watercolour of the same title commissioned by Ruskin in 1855 (now untraced). The subject is taken from Dante's *Purgatorio*, canto XXVIII: Dante sees Matilda gathering flowers in an ancient wood, singing as she goes. Rossetti does not follow the text closely, but ignores the river symbolically separating Dante from Matilda, and, rather than show her alone, adds a number of attendants. She is seen cutting a lily while receiving a tall glass from a servant. On her head, she wears a crown, while a girl attaches a girdle round her hips, and two women and a child look on.

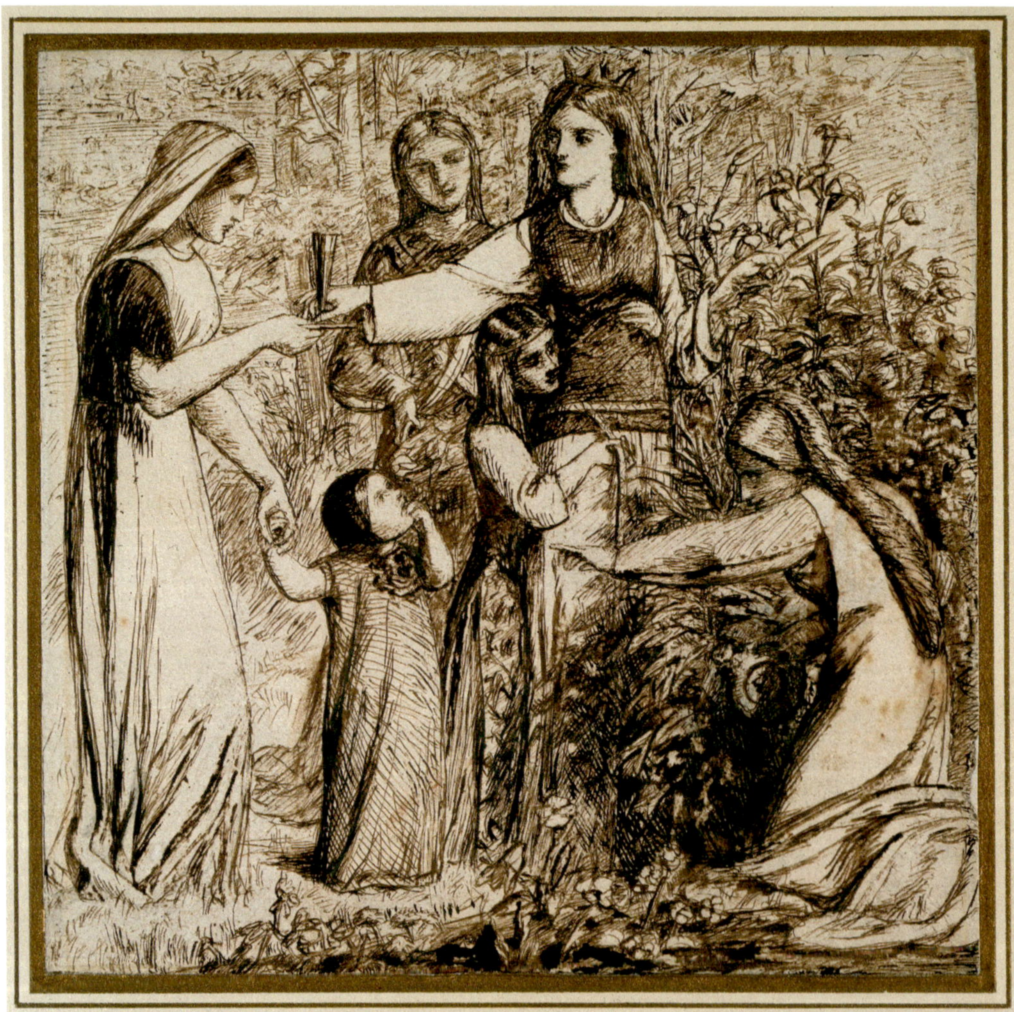

13

Dante Gabriel Rossetti
Beatrice Meeting Dante at a Marriage Feast, Denies him her Salutation 1855
Watercolour and bodycolour over pencil on paper, 34.3 x 41.9 cm
Ashmolean Museum, University of Oxford (WA1942.156)
Ref: Surtees 1971, no. 50 R1; Treuherz 2003, no. 39

The subject was one of the 'opportunities for pictorial illustration' that Rossetti found in Dante's *Vita Nuova* in 1848: Beatrice, walking in a procession of young bridesmaids for a wedding feast, sees Dante but, believing that Dante has paid undue attention to another woman, ignores him, and he staggers back against the frescoed wall. In 1851, Rossetti made a watercolour of the subject,[1] which Ruskin described in a letter to Holman Hunt as 'a most glorious piece of colour. The breadth of blue-green and fragmentary gold is a perfect feast.' This was sold to Henry Tamworth Wells, but Rossetti borrowed it back in 1855 to make this replica, which he sold to Ruskin for £40. The composition is one of Rossetti's most crowded, with the married couple relegated to upper right corner, in order to accommodate the wedding procession, the incident on the staircase at lower left, the frescoes behind Dante, and a glimpse of the wedding interior. The figure of Beatrice was modelled on Elizabeth Siddal.

1 Surtees 1971, no. 50

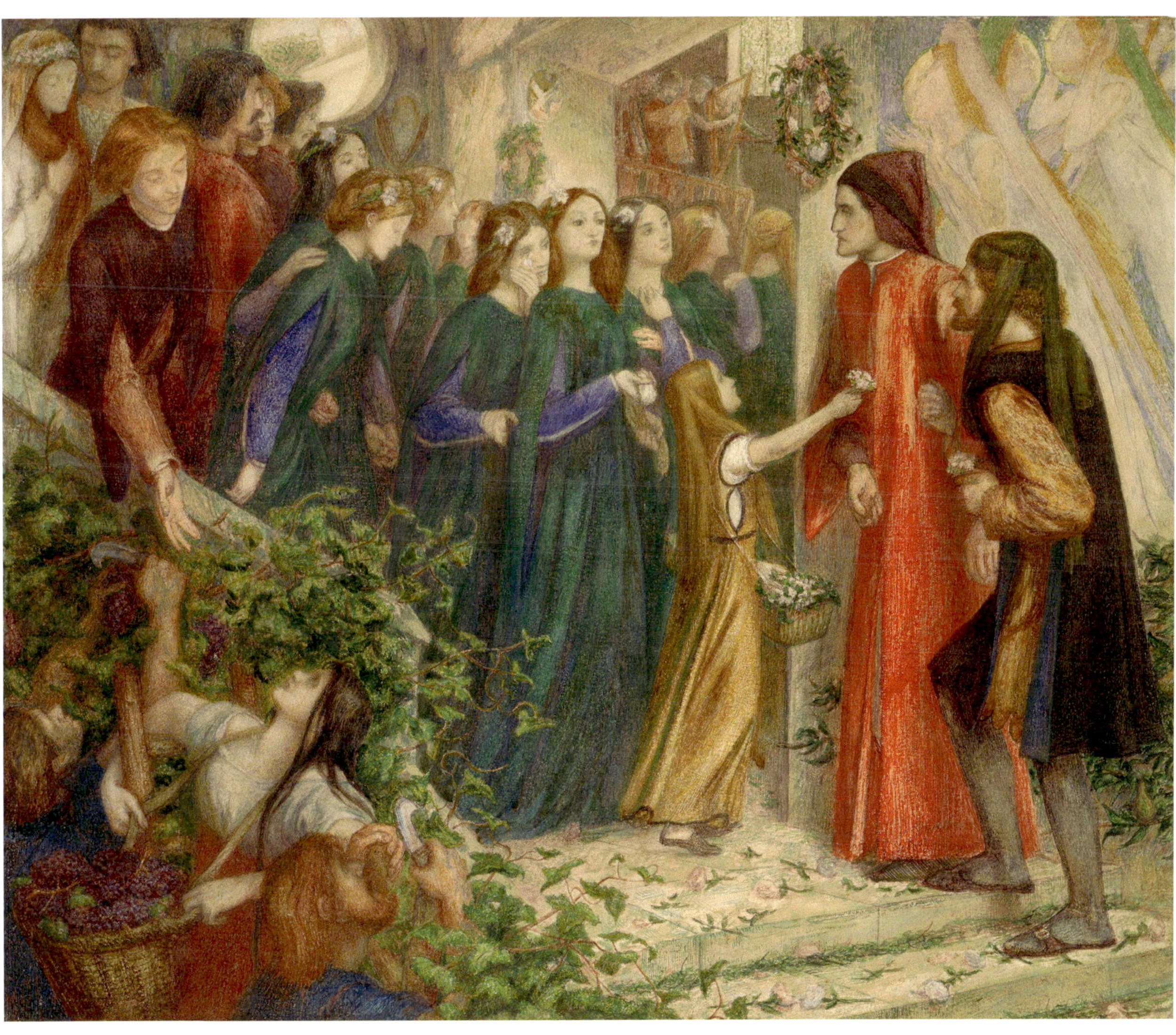

14

Dante Gabriel Rossetti

Dante's Dream at the Time of the Death of Beatrice 1856

Watercolour and bodycolour on paper, 48.7 x 66.2 cm
Tate. Bequeathed by Beresford Rimington Heaton, 1940 (N05229)
Ref: Surtees 1971, no. 81; Parris 1984, no. 218

Rossetti first considered this subject from the *Vita nuova* in 1848, and it remained a favourite throughout his life, as an illustration of love broken by death. This watercolour, the largest Rossetti ever painted, was begun in 1855, and completed in the following year for Ellen Heaton. The subject is a dream that Dante had while ill, and, conscious of his own mortality as a consequence, imagined a series of scenes, culminating in the death of his beloved Beatrice. Rossetti described the scene in a letter to Mrs Heaton: 'The lines illustrated are: These idle fantasies / Then carried me to see my lady dead; / And when I entered, / With a white veil her friends were covering her; / And in her mild look was a quietness / Which seemes as if it said, I have found peace…. The figures (all foreground ones) are, Dante, the dead Beatrice, two other ladies & an angelic figure representing Love, who is introduced as a person throughout the Vita Nuova; & there is a good deal of accessory matter, the drawing being, unless I am much mistaken, considerably more than double the size of the Rachel & Leah, and it is in every respect a much better drawing than that one, which I undertook not at my own suggestion, and the subject of which never interested me'. Dante walks on the ground, while the principal group is raised above him on a dais. At his feet are red poppies, symbolizing dreams, and he is brought into his dream by the hand of Cupid, who kisses Beatrice on her deathbed. The theme of love conquered by death was a favourite of Rossetti's, and he later treated this particular subject in his largest oil painting (**see cat. 126**).

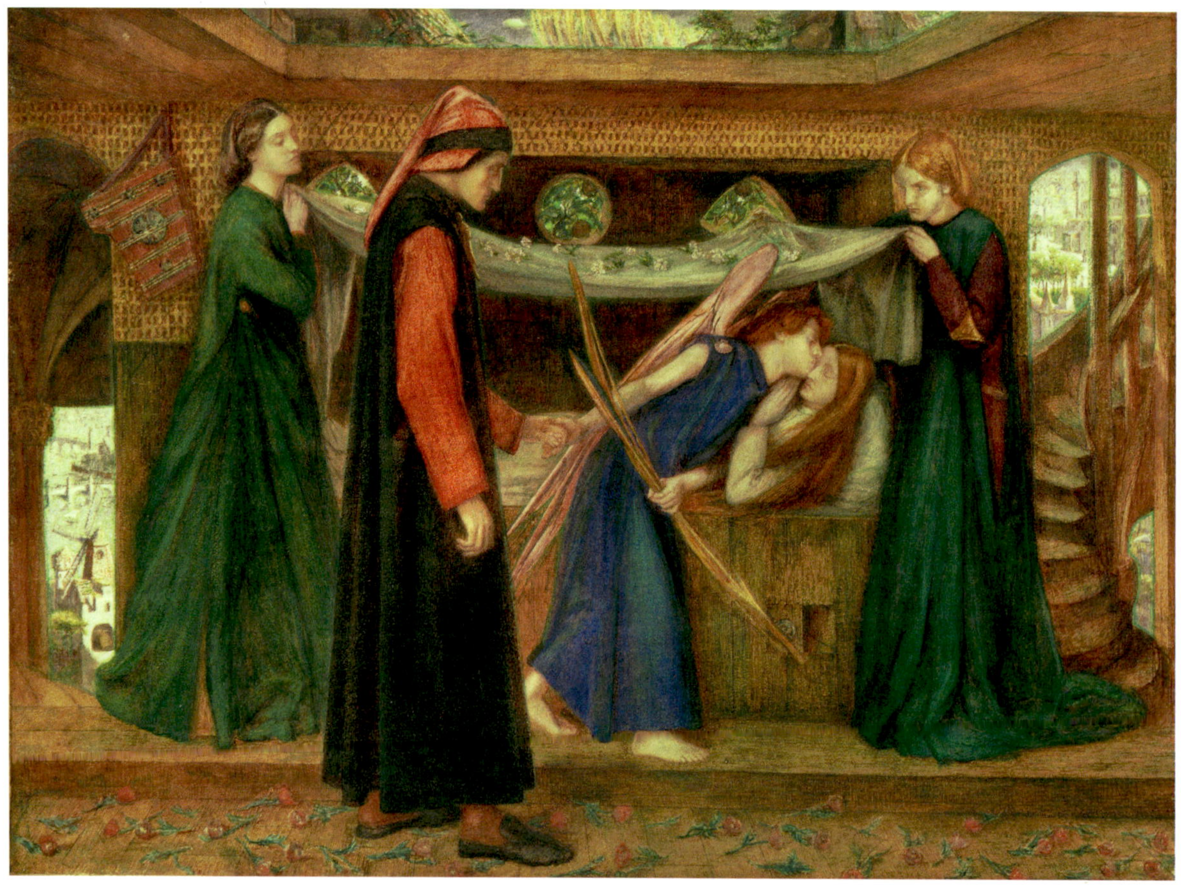

15
Dante Gabriel Rossetti
The Borgia Family 1863
Watercolour on paper, 36.2 x 37.8 cm
Signed and dated: *D.G.R. 1863*
Victoria and Albert Museum (72–1902)
Ref: Surtees 1971, no. 48

By the time he came to paint this watercolour, Rossetti had adopted the practice of adding titles to finished works, rather than creating pictures to illustrate specific titles. However, the origins of this subject go back as far as 1850. In that year, Rossetti completed a drawing of a similar composition inscribed with lines from Shakespeare's *Richard III*, Act I scene 1: 'To caper nimbly in a lady's chamber / To the lascivious pleasing of a lute'.[1] The first watercolour of the subject was begun in 1851, and acquired by George Price Boyce, who allowed Rossetti to work on it intermittently until it was eventually completed in 1859.[2] From a rather demure scene of music-making, the composition had become a celebration of the erotic power of music. The female playing the lute is Lucrezia Borgia, notorious for her seductive and wicked ways; behind her is her brother Cesare, while behind them is the figure of Pope Alexander VI. In contrast to the earlier treatment, the costume is now luxurious and colourful. This slightly larger version, less linear and more painterly, was executed between October 1862 and July 1863.

1 Birmingham Museum and Art Gallery; Surtees 1971, no. 47
2 Tullie House Museum and Art Gallery, Carlisle; Surtees 1971, no. 48

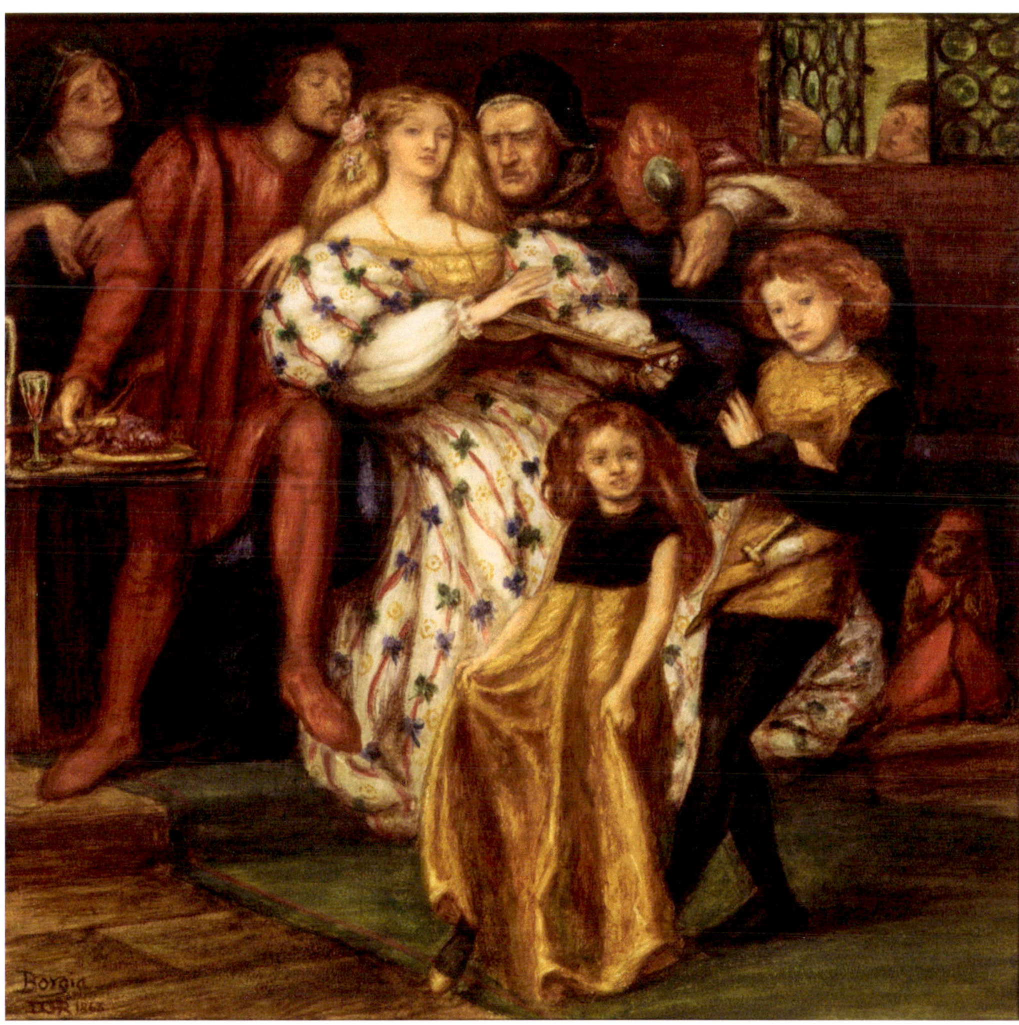

16
Simeon Solomon (1840–1905)
Dante's First Meeting with Beatrice 1859–63
Pen and ink on paper, 19.4 x 22.9 cm
Signed in monogram and dated *12/9/5963*
Tate. Bequeathed by Robert Ross through The Art Fund, 1919 (N03409)
Ref: Parris 1984, no. 228; Cruise 2005, no. 16

The curious date indicates that the drawing was begun in 1859 and completed in 1863. It was thus one of the first secular, rather than biblical, subjects attempted by Solomon, and strongly influenced by his friendship with Rossetti. It shows an episode recorded in the *Vita Nuova* of Dante meeting Beatrice for the first time, when she was in her ninth year, which was supposed to have taken place on 1 May 1275. When the drawing was first exhibited, in 1859, the critic in *The Times* wrote it as 'an illustration … of the extreme length to which quaint ugliness can be carried', and its artist as 'a very young pre-Raffaelite – nay almost pre-historical artist'. The crowded composition, with its abundance of subsidiary figures and almost pedantic depiction of details, is certainly wilfully naïve. In addition to its obvious debt to Rossetti, the figures of Dante and Beatrice surely owe their stilted poses and short necks to Millais's *The Woodman's Daughter*, exhibited in 1852 (now in the Guildhall Art Gallery).

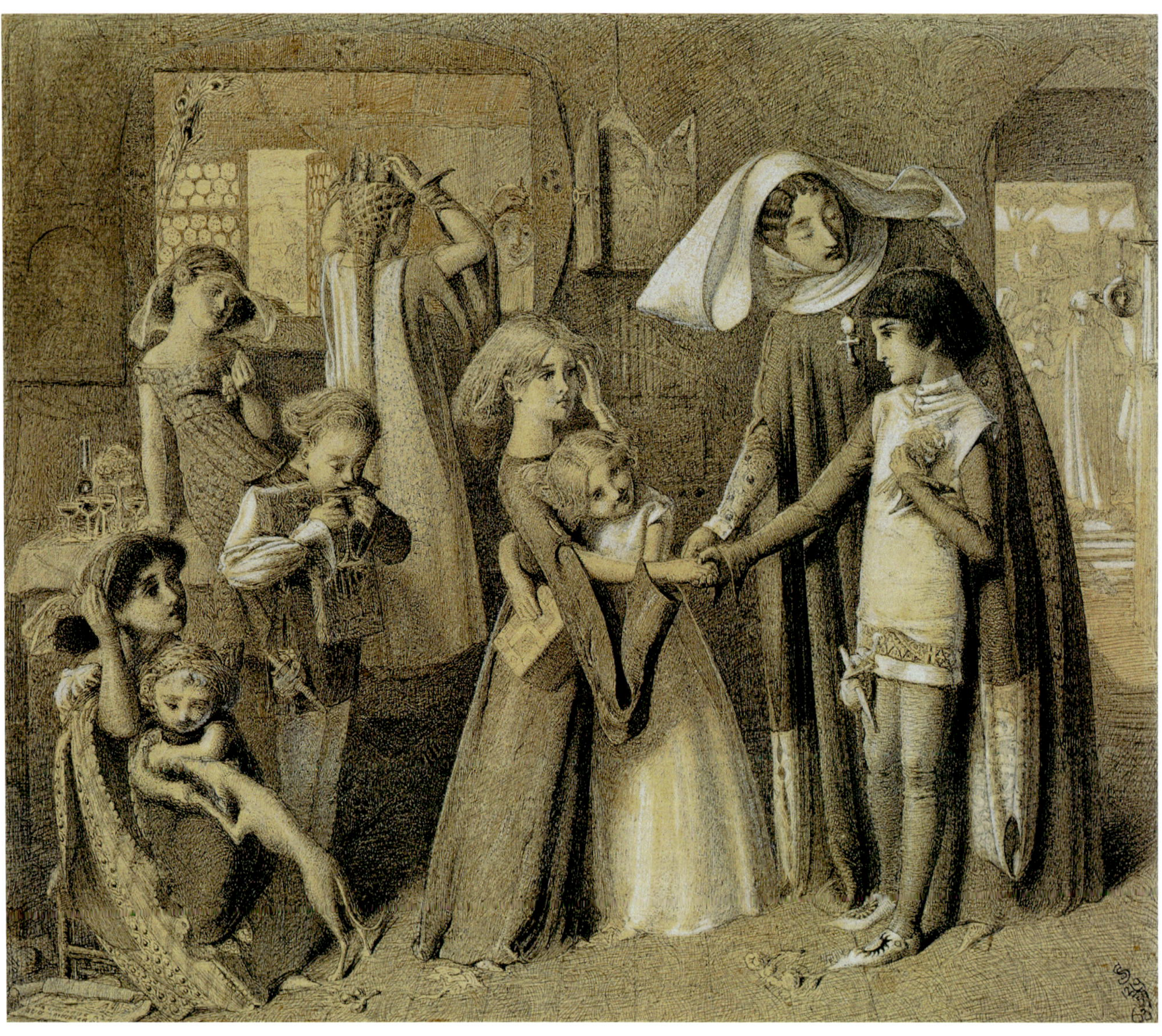

17–20

Sir Edward Coley Burne-Jones (1833–1898)
Buondelmonte's Wedding 1859
Pen and ink with some grey wash on vellum, 25.5 x 77 cm
Signed: *EBJ*
Lent by the Syndics of the Fitzwilliam Museum, Cambridge.
Ref: Wildman and Christian 1996, no. 7

Gualdrada Donati presenting her Daughter to Buondelmente: The Origin of the Guelph and Ghibelline Quarrel in Florence
Pen and brush in black ink over Pencil on paper, 23.2 x 39.3 cm
The Ashmolean Museum, University of Oxford (WA1951.156)

Two Studies for 'Buondelmonte's Wedding'
Black chalk and Pencil on paper, 23.5 x 31.1 cm, 23.5 x 27 cm
Tate. Bequeathed by J.R. Holliday, 1927 (A01161–2)

Study for 'The Meeting of Buondelmonte and Ciulla, the Origin of the Guelph and Ghibelline Quarrel in Florence'
Black chalk and pencil on paper, 25.6 x 24.9 cm
Inscribed by Charles Fairfax-Murray, lower left: *Buondelmonte's wedding* and lower right: *E.B.J.*
Whitworth Art Gallery, University of Manchester.
Bequeathed by J.R. Holliday, 1927 (D.1927.81)
Ref: Christian 1973

One of Burne-Jones's earliest projects was for a 'large oil picture of the Wedding of Buondelmonte'. The painting was never completed, but the artist made a number of preparatory drawings exploring the composition, and a highly finished design in pen and ink on vellum. The subject shows Buondelmonte de' Buondelmonti, a Florentine nobleman, who was betrothed to a girl of the Amidei family. However, when riding through the city, he was accosted by the widow, Gualdrada Donati, who persuaded him that the Amidei girl was not good enough for him, and that he should marry her own beautiful daughter. When he did so, the Amidei took offence. On Easter Day 1215, when Buondelmonte was riding over the bridge, he was brutally murdered at the foot of the pillar with the statue of Mars. The Donati were of the Guelph faction, and the Amidei of the Ghibelline, and the murder was the catalyst to the bloody war between the two parties which ended with the victory of the Ghibellines in 1289. The incident is referred to by Dante in both the *Inferno* and the *Paradiso* and recounted by Machiavelli and Sismondi. It had also been treated by several artists in the 1840s and early 1850s, most notably G.F. Watts, whose painting of *The Origin of the Guelph and Ghibelline Quarrel in Florence* (Watts Gallery, Compton) Burne-Jones would have known. The preparatory studies for this composition concentrate on the meeting of Buondelmonte, on horseback, with Ciulla, the daughter of Gualdrada Donati. The Ashmolean drawing is the most resolved, and was presumably the last in the sequence. The finished drawing on vellum shows the widow Donati presenting her daughter to Buondelmonte on the left; while on the right, Buondelmonte's bride, of the Amidei family, arrives by barge, guided by the blind-folded figure of Cupid. The bridge over the Arno and the pillar with the statue of Mars, the scene of Buondelmonte's murder, are clearly visible. The drawing was apparently begun in January 1859, when George Price Boyce noted in his diary for 17 January that 'Jones showed me the commencement of a pen and ink drawing for Ruskin – subject from Florentine history'.[1] It was not completed until December 1859, after Burne-Jones had returned from his first journey to Italy. John Christian suggests that both subject and style were indebted to Ruskin, who was keen to wean his protégé away from the influence of Rossetti, and who would have urged him to look at early Italian art before he went abroad. Ruskin also owned a copy of Sismondi, which he could have lent Burne-Jones. Christian further notes that both the preliminary drawings and the finished composition are indebted to the frescoes in the Campo Santo at Pisa, especially Orcagna's *Triumph of Death*, which Burne-Jones had recently studied. The extraordinarily crowded composition, each element drawn in obsessive detail, is the most extreme example of Burne-Jones's self-consciously archaic style, and may not have been intended altogether seriously.

1 Boyce 1980, p.

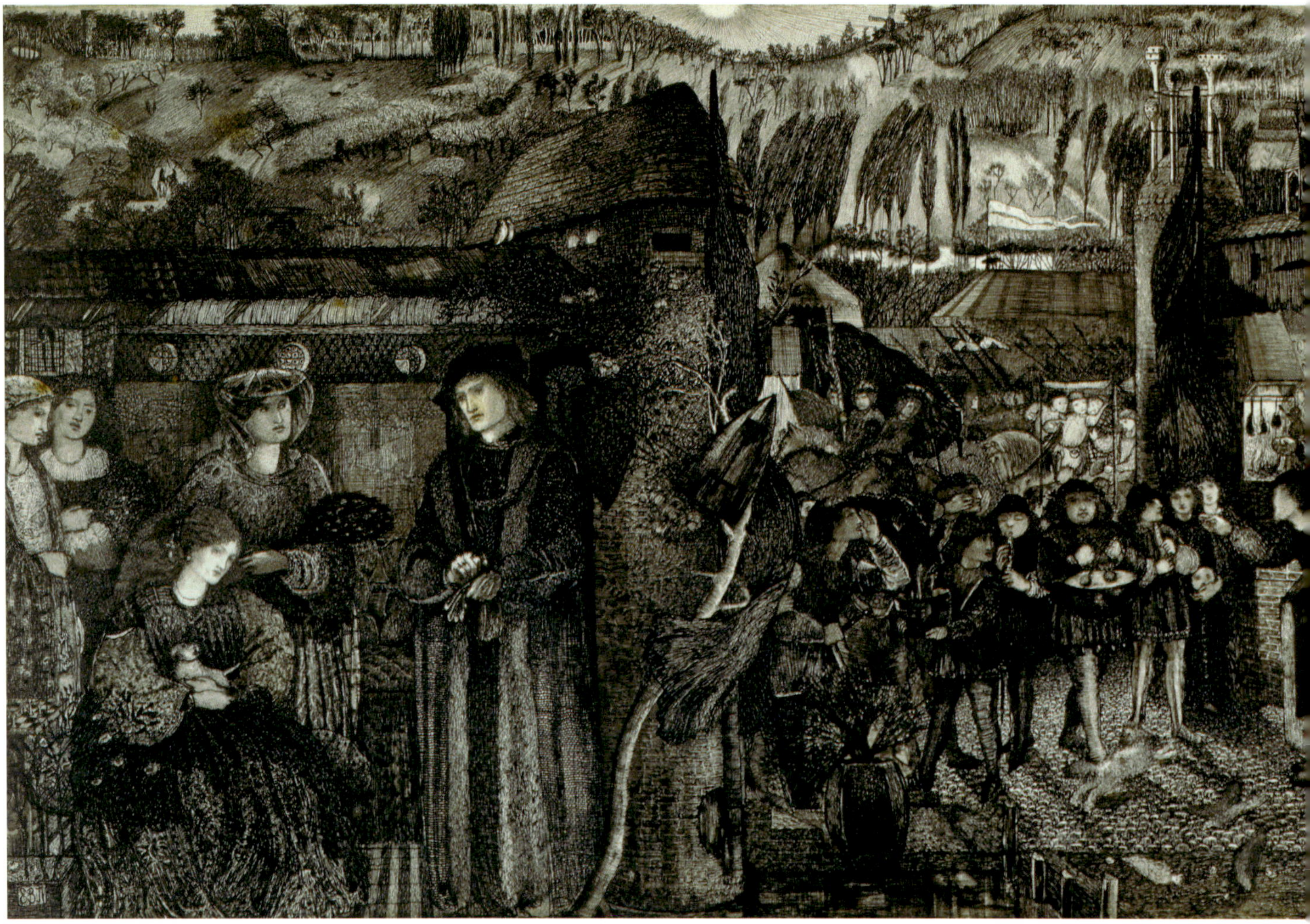

17

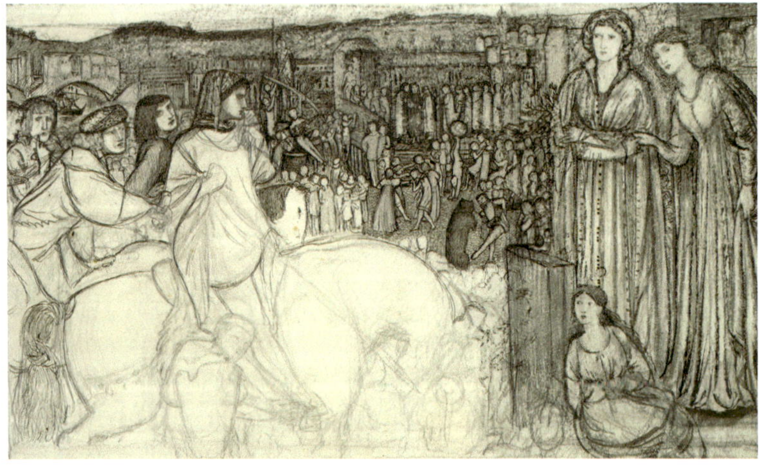

18

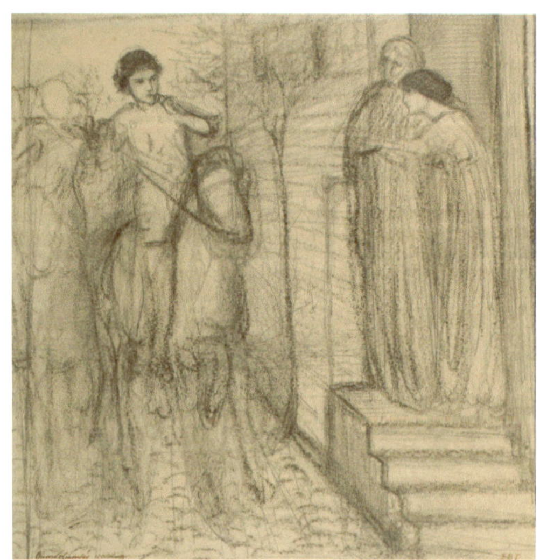

19a

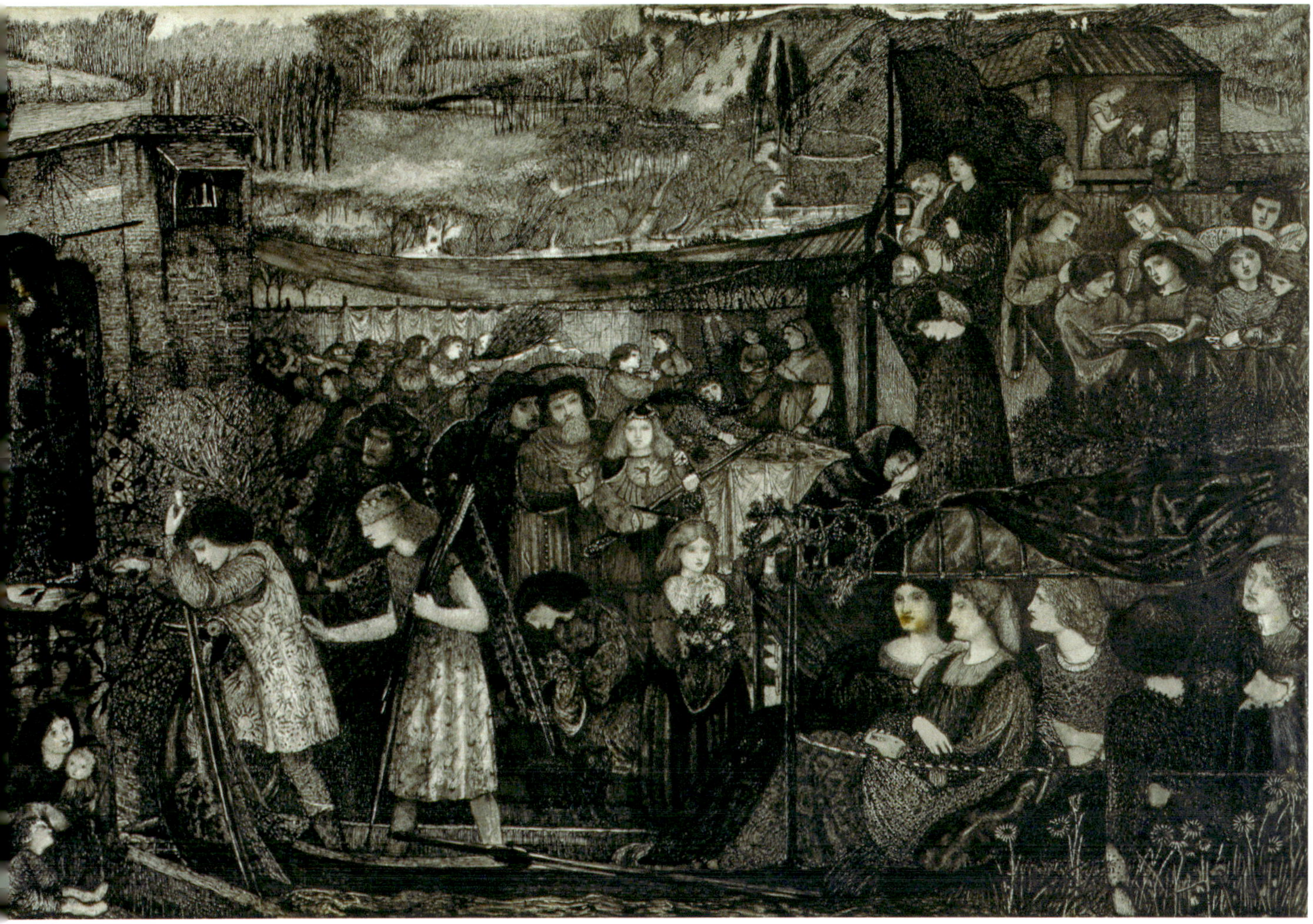

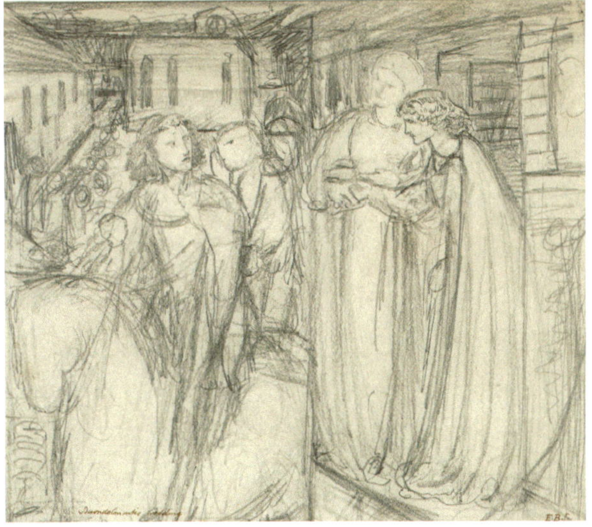

19b

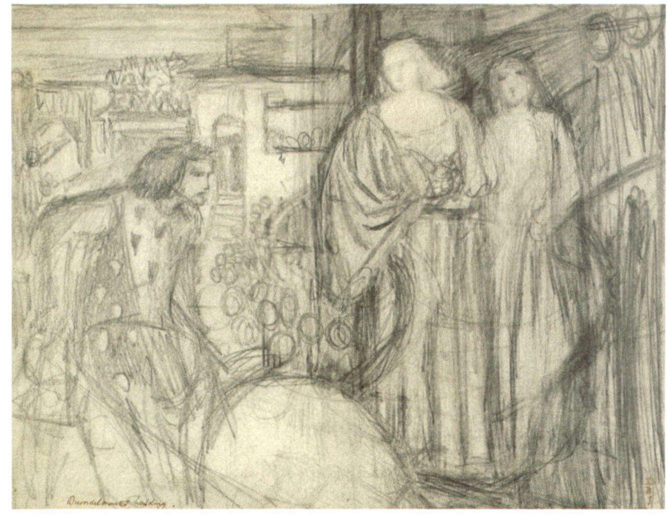

20

21
William Dyce (1806–1864)
The Meeting of Jacob and Rachel 1857
Oil on canvas, 48.4 x 66 cm
Signed in monogram and dated: *WD 1857*
Private collection
Ref: Pointon 1979, p. 196

Jacob and Rachel was Dyce's most successful composition, and he produced four slightly different versions. The first, exhibited at the Royal Academy in 1850, was so popular that Dyce commissioned a copy of it from the young Holman Hunt. The second version (Leicester City Art Gallery) follows the first, whilst the third was admired by Gladstone and Prince Albert when it was shown at the Royal Academy in 1853 (now in the Hamburg Kunsthalle). The last was perhaps undertaken as a private commission, and is a reduced version of the Leicester picture. Although the figure of Rachel is, typically for Dyce, almost a pastiche of Raphael, that of Jacob is indebted in its strong anatomical profile to the Bolognese School, in particular to Guercino. Various commentators have noted that the composition may be related to works by Nazarene artists Dyce had met in Rome, in particular to Schnorr von Carolsfeld's *Bilderbibel.* The subject itself, taken from Genesis 29.11, had a strong personal relevance to Dyce, since it referred to the story of Jacob, who was kept waiting fourteen years before being allowed to marry his first love, Rachel; Dyce, aged 46, had married Jane Brand, aged only nineteen, in 1850.

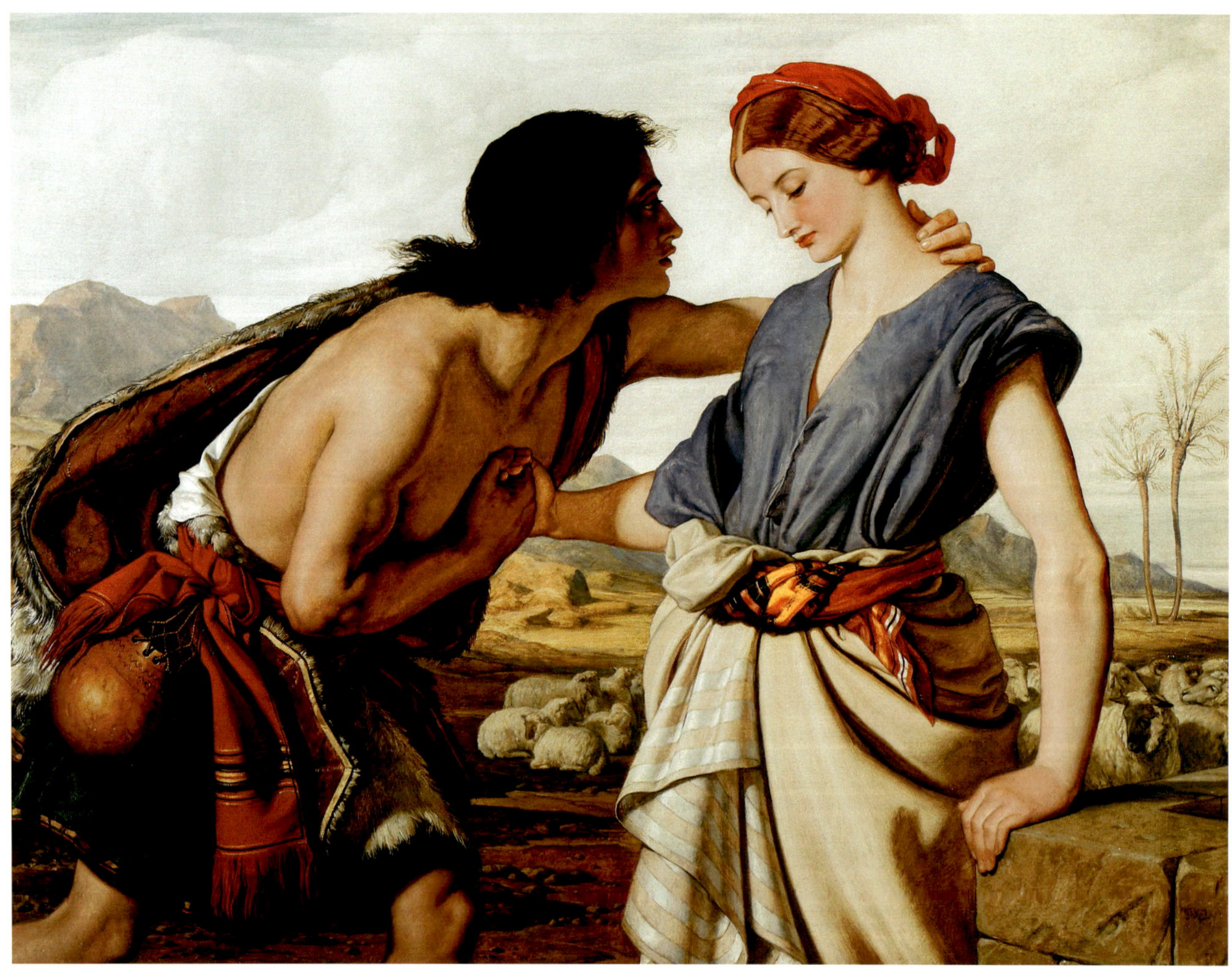

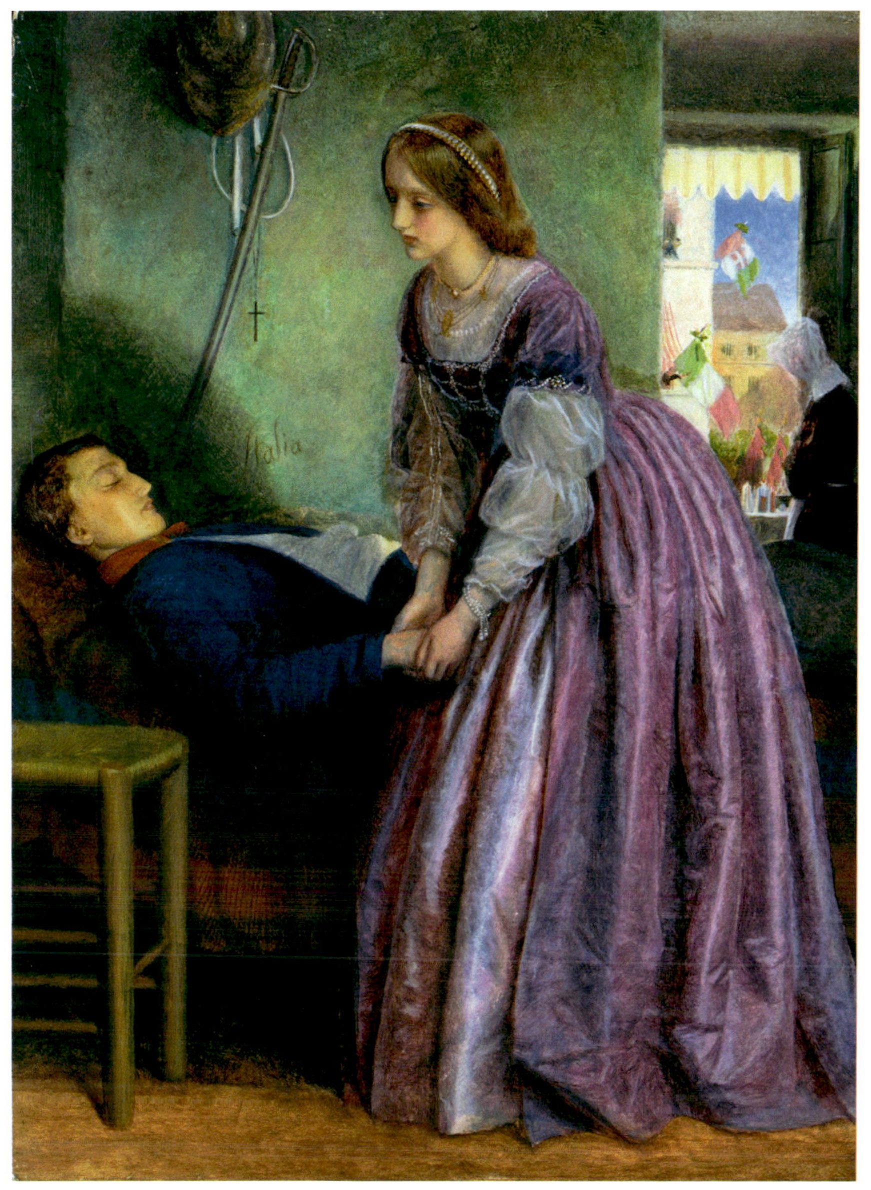

22

Arthur Hughes (1832–1915)
That was a Piedmontese 1860
Oil on panel, 40.5 x 30 cm
Inscribed on the wall, *Italia*
Tate. Bequeathed by Beresford Rimington Heaton, 1940 (N05244)
Ref: Roberts and Wildman 1997, no. 51

Elizabeth Barrett Browning (1806–1861) lived mostly in Florence from 1846 until her death, and was a passionate advocate of Italian nationalism. Indeed, a tablet on the Brownings' house, Casa Guidi, in Florence, describes her as 'fece del suo verso aureo anello tra Italia e Inghilterra'. Although her poetry was illustrated by several of the Pre-Raphaelites, only Hughes's painting shows an Italian subject. It was Ruskin who suggested the subject to Mrs Heaton, who commissioned the painting in 1860: 'If Hughes felt at ALL up to doing "That was a Piedmontese; and this is the Court of the King", it would give a permanent and public value to the picture well worth the extra effort'. The lines are from Mrs Browning's ode to Italian unity, 'A Court Lady'. While he was painting the picture, Hughes confessed that 'I don't like "fervid, impassioned exclamation" and have an especial horror of all such in pictures. I prefer the quieter moment that must have followed it and which I feel I can be more successful in'. Privately, Ruskin thought the painting exquisitely painted, 'a little treasure', but quite wrong as an illustration to Mrs Browning's poem, for 'the whole *gist* of the poem is that the woman puts on her richest *Court* dress … Hughes has not in the least felt or understood this'.

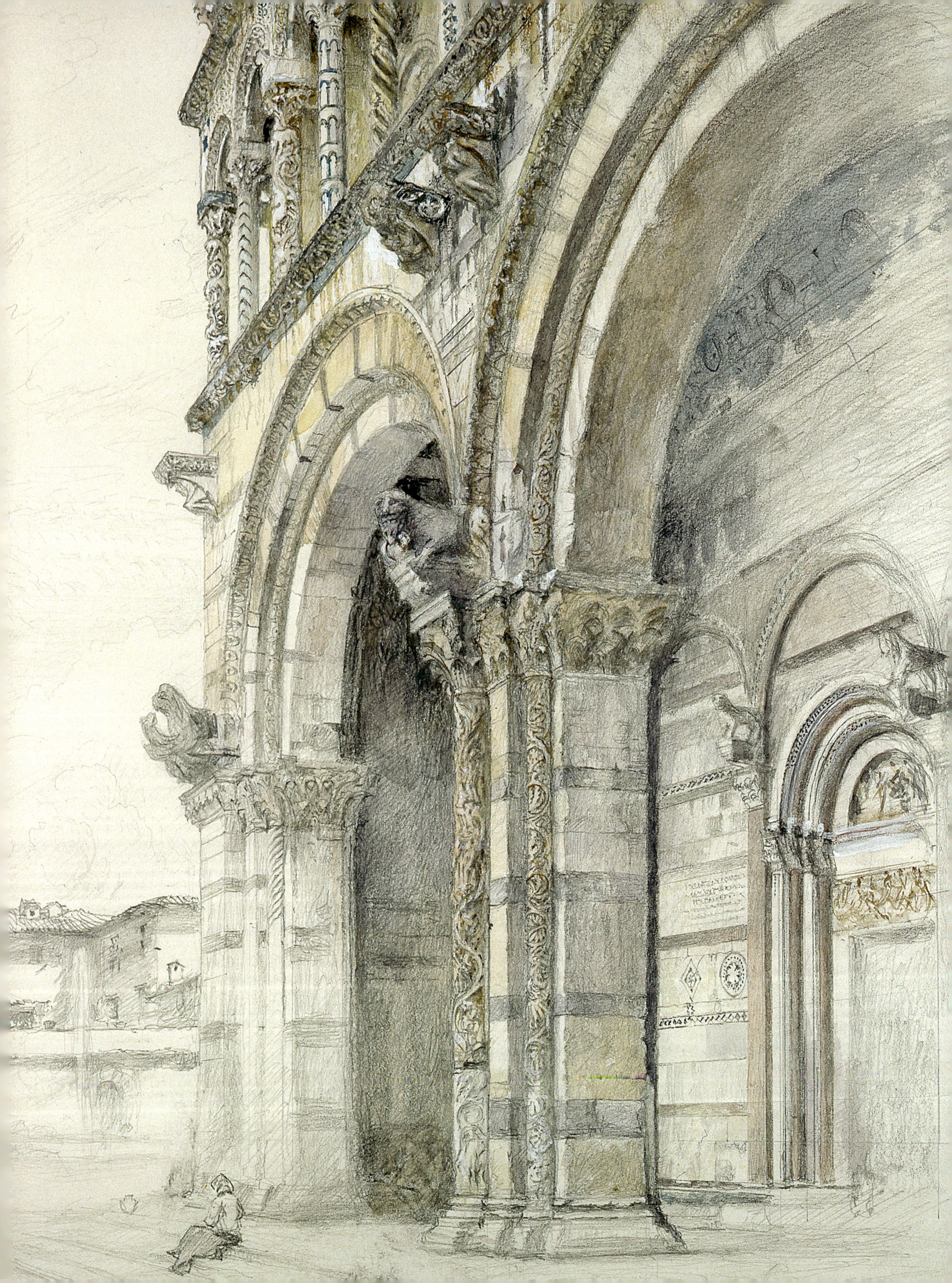

II

RUSKIN AND ITALY

Ruskin loved Italy – her people, her landscape, her history, and her buildings. He was an habitual traveller in all parts of Europe as well as within the British Isles, but it was Italy that gave him the greatest delight and feeling of expectation. It was also the country which gave rise to the most intense anxiety, verging on despair, as he witnessed the desecration of a unique architectural and artistic heritage.

His awareness of Italy was both imaginative and visceral, coloured by works of art which evoked the country but also with a close familiarity with her towns and countryside. In 1832, as a thirteenth-birthday present, he received Samuel Rogers's collection of poems *Italy*, illustrated with vignette engravings by J.M.W. Turner. The following year he stepped on Italian soil for the first time, while in 1835 he made the first of many visits to Venice. In 1845 he was permitted to travel to Italy without his mother and father, undertaking a long and exhaustive tour of Tuscany and then moving on to Venice in preparation for the second volume of *Modern Painters*. In 1849-50, and again in 1851-2, he was in Venice making historical research and studying buildings in preparation for the three volumes of *Stones of Venice*. In the 1850s and 1860s he made occasional visits to Italy; in 1862 with Burne-Jones, and in 1869, he coincided with Holman Hunt in Venice. In his later years he made long stays in Venice and returned to Rome and Tuscany, his last Italian travels being in 1888.

Many of the main themes of Ruskin's written work were first explored in the course of visits to Italy. Whether travelling with others or during his increasingly frequent solitary sojourns, he was stimulated by the places he visited, by the works of art and buildings that he studied, and by what he learned about the country's history and patterns of social life, towards a new comprehension of the interconnections between faith, economics, and art, and the fulfilment that men and women find in their daily lives. Thus, the study of the history of Venice that led to *Stones of Venice* was also the inspiration of a vision of how society might operate more harmoniously (expressed in 1860 in *Unto this Last*). For Ruskin, it was the baleful influence of the Renaissance (in his mind, a phenomenon comparable in its impact to the British Industrial Revolution), that eliminated and made impossible the personal, the idiosyncratic, and the sincerely faithful.

The Pre-Raphaelites were versed in Ruskin's early writings, notably the first and second volumes of *Modern Painters*. In the 1850s, Ruskin became the advocate and defender of the Pre-Raphaelite movement, believing it to be a fitting school of art for a Protestant nation, and one that expressed essential virtues. He believed passionately in the power of great art to reform and to inspire, and that people of all kinds should be able to learn from the first-hand experience of works of art. He celebrated works of art that were intensely felt and meaningful in the human predicaments they described, and which avoided all theatricality, conceit, and academic convention. His own drawings – and Ruskin drew instinctively and compulsively, believing that drawing was a spur to more intensive looking and therefore to a heightened understanding of what lay before one – are the most personal record of his engagement with the places he visited.

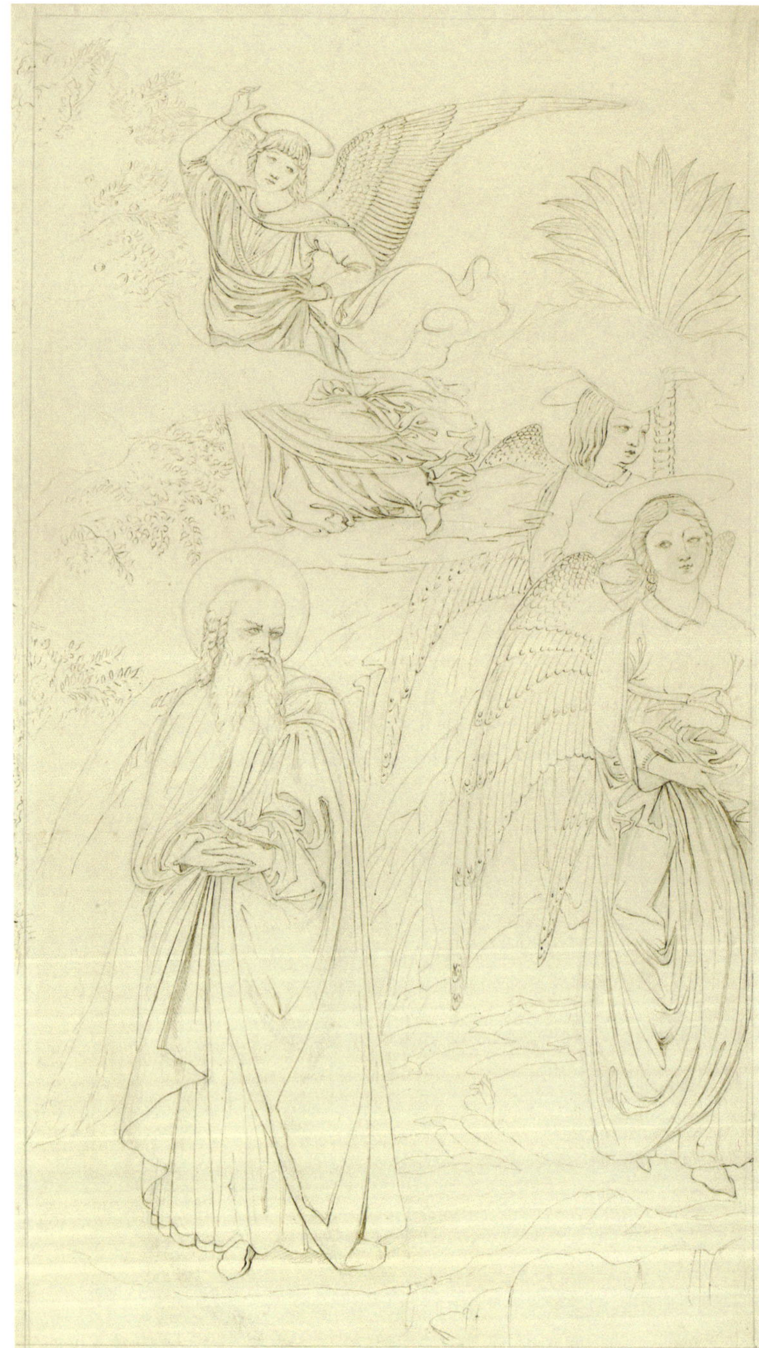

23
John Ruskin (1819–1900)
Drawing of Abraham Parting from the Angels from Benozzo Gozzoli's 'Story of Abraham and Hagar' in the Camposanto, Pisa 1845
Pen and ink over pencil on paper, 47.6 x 31.6 cm
Ashmolean Museum, University of Oxford.
Ruskin School Collection (Std 25)
Ref: Clegg and Tucker 1993, no. 32

Ruskin spent the summer of 1845 in Tuscany, looking at works of art of all kinds in preparation for the second volume of *Modern Painters*, which he intended as an account of historic schools of painting. In Pisa he studied the frescoes of the Campo Santo, already famous throughout Europe from the engraved plates of Carlo Lasinio. Ruskin was appalled by the state of neglect he found, describing the frescoes as 'much injured even *since* I was here [...] while for want of glass, and a good roof, these wonderful monuments are rotting every day'.[1]

The drawings he made in the Campo Santo are starkly linear, with careful attention paid to the drapery folds and distribution of the figures. In Gozzoli's fresco, as elsewhere in the Campo Santo, Ruskin was struck by the accuracy with which the Old Testament stories were told: 'I never believed the patriarchal history before, but I do now, for I have seen it. You cannot conceive the vividness & fullness of conception of these great old men'.[2] He was delighted by the way Abraham is seen to take leave of the angels who had come to inform him of the destruction of Sodom and Gomorrah, noticing that one angel remained behind, as described in Genesis, a point of detail he regarded as a 'simple, hard reading real Bible truth', which allowed Gozzoli's painting to be regarded as suitably 'protestantized'[3] and therefore a fitting exemplar to British artists and students. Both Lasinio's engravings and Ruskin's descriptions of the Campo Santo frescoes in *Modern Painters* volume II were vital formative influences upon the Pre-Raphaelites.

1 Shapiro 1972, p. 61
2 Shapiro 1972, p. 67
3 quoted in Clegg & Turner 1993, p. 38

24

John Ruskin

Pencil Outline of a Part of the Fresco of 'The Friends of Job' in the Camposanto, Pisa, Attributed to Taddeo Gaddi 1845
Pencil on paper, 34.8 x 45.3 cm
Ashmolean Museum, University of Oxford. Ruskin School Collection (Std 24)
Ref: Clegg and Tucker 1993, no. 33

Having completed his study of Gozzoli's work in the Campo Santo (**cat. 23**), Ruskin moved on to the fresco showing *Stories of Job*, then believed to be the work of Giotto and now tentatively ascribed to Taddeo Gaddi or to a follower. His aim was to look closely at each of the Pisa frescoes in order to be able to distinguish and characterise the different types of painting seen there, and to be able to construct a theoretical development of style.

This particular fresco had suffered grievously from damp penetration over centuries. By Ruskin's account, 'Giotto's Job is all gone – two of his Friends' faces and some servants are all that can be made out'.[1] In addition, parts of the composition were blocked from view by tombs, including some of quite recent construction. All this heightened the sense of urgency with which he approached the task of drawing the remains of the fresco, and his whole-hearted commitment, both mental and technical. For four days he drew in pencil, searching for accuracy and expression. His treatment of the hands posed particular difficulties: 'They are as badly drawn as they can be, but there they are all full of life and feeling, running out at the very finger ends'. And yet, the drawing when finished was 'as Giottesque as can be', more useful Ruskin believed as a record than any of the engraved copies of the frescoes that had been produced, and from which he had 'learned a vast deal in doing it'.[2]

The Campo Santo frescoes were largely destroyed in 1944.

1 Shapiro 1972, p. 62
2 Shapiro 1972, pp. 70–1

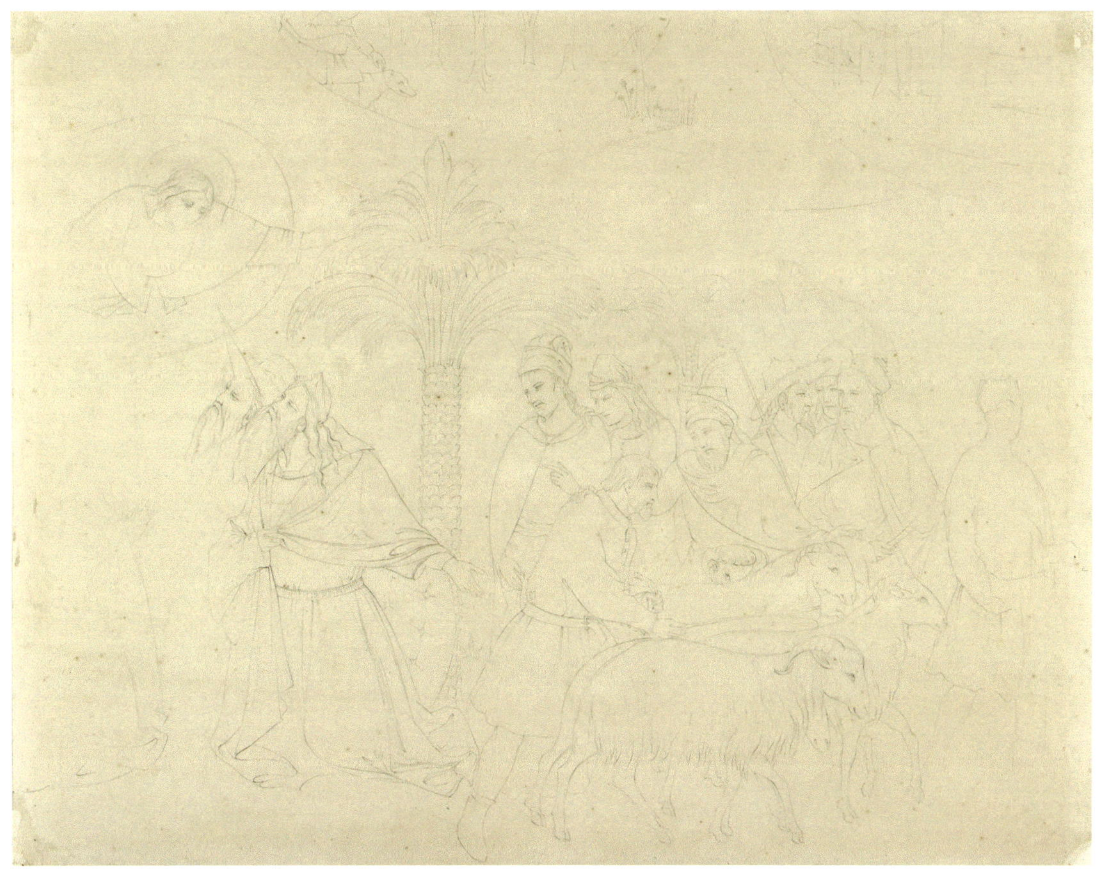

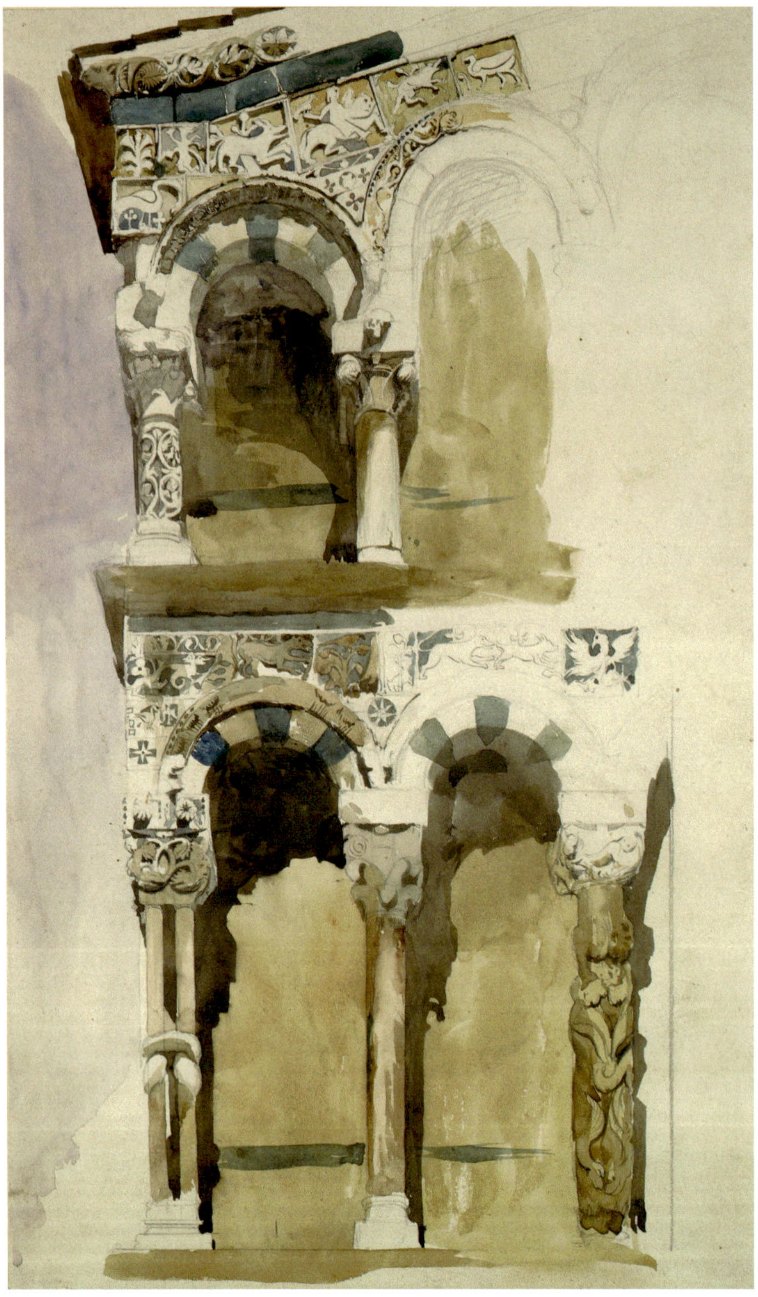

25
John Ruskin
Part of the Façade of the Destroyed Church of San Michele in Foro, Lucca 1845
Pencil and watercolour on paper, 40.7 x 24.6 cm
Ashmolean Museum, University of Oxford. Ruskin School Collection (Ed. 84)
Ref: Clegg and Tucker 1993, no. 72; Hewison 2000, no. 69

In a letter to his father of 6 May 1845, Ruskin described the routine of his days in Lucca. Among the places that it was his habit to visit and study each morning – 'writing as I go, all I can learn about the history of the churches, and all my picture criticism'– were S. Frediano, S. Romano, and the Duomo. After lunch, he was 'ready to set to work, [sitting] in the open warm afternoon air, drawing the rich ornaments on the façade of St Michele'. He went on to describe the subject of cat. 25: 'It is white marble, *inlaid* with figures cut an inch deep in green porphyry, and framed with carved, rich, hollow marble tracery'.[1]

There are three principal frontal drawings of the façade of S. Michele in the Ashmolean. One is dated 1845,[2] and it may be assumed that all were made that summer, although Ruskin returned to Lucca with his parents in the following year. In addition, Ruskin commissioned a daguerreotype of the exterior of the church, and himself made a soft-ground etching of the left-hand arch, perhaps after another photograph, which was reproduced in *The Seven Lamps of Architecture*.

The construction of S. Michele began in 1143, as is indicated by the date carved on a column of the central archway, while the façade was completed early in the thirteenth century. It is of the Romanesque Pisan-Lucchese type, with tiers of columned arcades running across the width of the façade, gradually decreasing in height in the third register to accommodate the slanting roof line of the aisles.

1 Shapiro 1972, p. 54
2 Ashmolean Museum, University of Oxford. Ruskin School Collection (Ed. 83)

26

John Ruskin

Copy after the Central Portion of Tintoretto's 'The Crucifixion' in the Scuola Grande di San Rocco, Venice 1845

Pencil, chalk, ink and watercolour on paper, 27 x 53.5 cm

Ruskin Foundation (Ruskin Library, University of Lancaster)

Ref: Hewison 2000 no. 135

The experience of Tintoretto's paintings changed Ruskin's life: in them, he discovered an art of exhilaration and emotion. As he recalled in *Præterita*: 'But for that porter's opening [the door of the Scuola], I should [...] have written The Stones of Chamouni, instead of The Stones of Venice [...] but Tintoret swept me away into the "mare maggiore" of the schools of painting which crowned the power and perished in the fall of Venice; so forcing me into the study of Venice herself; and through that into what else I have traced or told of the laws of national strength and virtue.'[1]

Ruskin's copy of the *Crucifixion* captures the dynamic frenzy and compositional complexity of the original, with loosely blocked figures, shadowed peripheries, and a centrifugal subjection of all parts of the scheme to the crucified figure of Christ. Always beguiled by touching incidental detail – Ruskin described to his father the motif of a donkey feeding on the remaining strewn palm leaves from Christ's entry into Jerusalem – he also understood Tintoretto's genius in drawing his composition together, by having filled it 'with such various and impetuous exertion, that the body of the Crucified is, by comparison, in perfect repose.'[2]

Tintoretto's work in the Scuola began in the Albergo in 1564 with his commission-winning *St Roch in Glory*. The *Crucifixion*, which is displayed on the end wall of the same room, was begun in the following year. By the middle of the nineteenth century, these paintings were in perilous condition, dirty and discoloured, and affected by damp. By drawing them, Ruskin trained himself to trace their main lines and to search for obscure pictorial detail. The studies are therefore an exercise in intensive looking, as well as serving as an aid to memory.

1 Ruskin 1903–12, XXXV, p. 372w

2 Ruskin 1903–12, IV, pp. 270–1

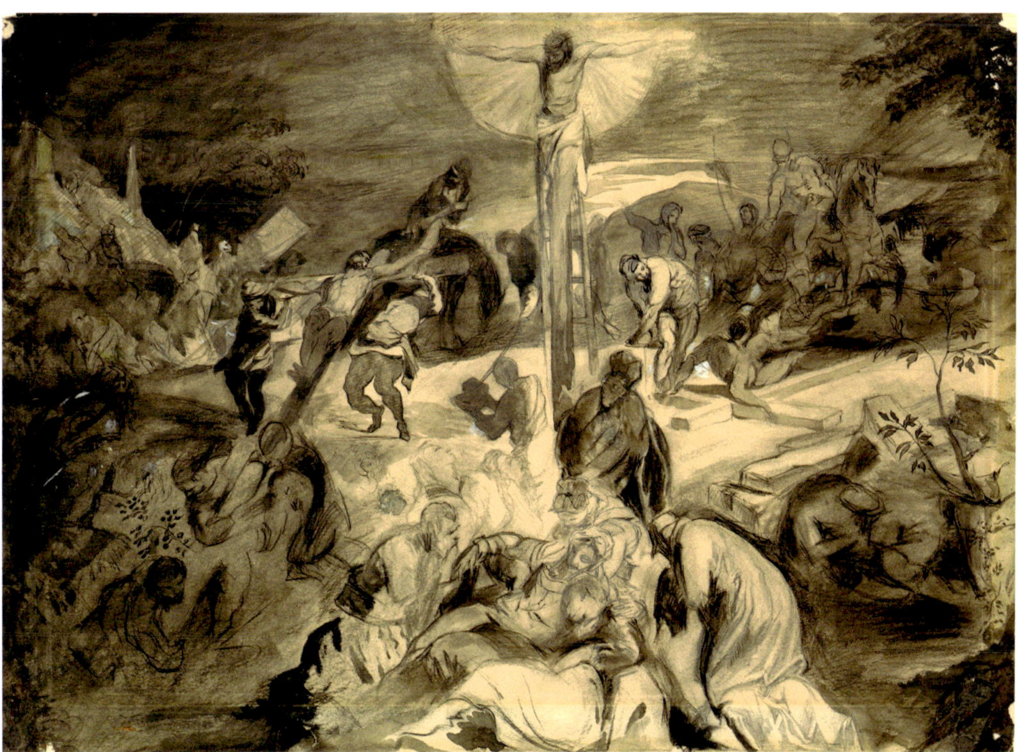

27 (a–f)

Six daguerreotypes of architectural subjects
Verona: Duomo. North Griffin (reversed)
Verona: St Anastasia Gate Gate Tomb (reversed)
Verona: Signorio Tomb from North East Verona: Tomb of Can Mastino II from behind figure (reversed)
Verona: Signorio Tomb from the South East (reversed)
Detail of the Façade of S. Michele, Lucca
Ruskin Foundation (Ruskin Library, University of Lancaster) Ref: Costantini and Zannier 1986, figs. 43, 39, 35, 33, 36, 71
RF Dag. 30, 35, 41, 43, 44, 69

Five of these daguerreotypes of architectural subjects were presumably acquired by Ruskin during one of the visits that he made to Verona from Venice in either 1849–50 or 1851–2. He had bought commercially made photographs of this type since 1840, finding such images useful as *aide-mémoires* to be consulted in conjunction with his own drawings when writing about buildings. In 1849, Ruskin took with him to Venice photographic equipment which he and his servant John Hobbs had learnt to use. When compared with those made by professional photographers, Ruskin's own daguerreotypes may be recognised by their distinctive and sometimes idiosyncratic compositions. Ruskin and Hobbs showed a delightful indifference to the tidy framing of subjects, cropping out parts that a commercial photograph would have included, and ignoring the perspectival convergence which the professional photographer would have corrected. Some were mechanically reversed so that the subject was seen the right way round; others were left in mirror image. As with Ruskin's drawings, these photographs were made to provide information about specific architectural features, and were not regarded as works of art in their own right.

Ruskin knew how useful photography was, but came to believe that a drawn image could convey more information about a building, not only because the draughtsman had colour at his disposal, but because the line and texture of a drawing allowed expression that the mechanical process of photography seemed not to permit. On occasions, as for example in his drawing of *The South Side of the Basilica of St Mark's* **(cat. 28)**, he copied a photograph to produce a living record of the building. There will have been a similar visual interchange between these photographs of Gothic tombs, arches, and details of church buildings in Verona, and his drawings of the same motifs.

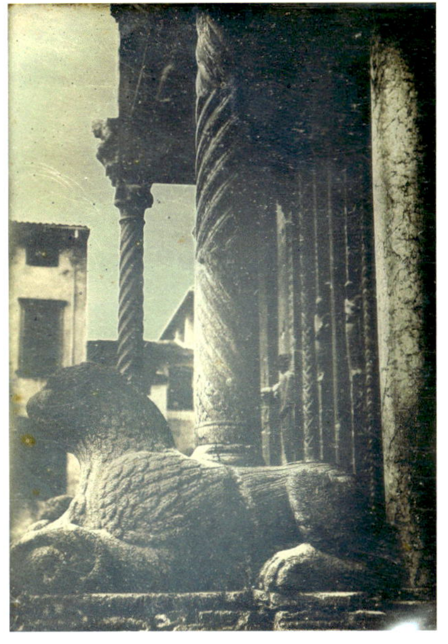
a

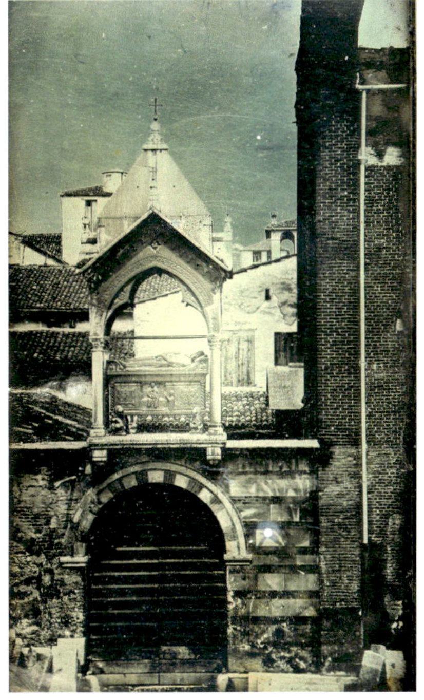
b

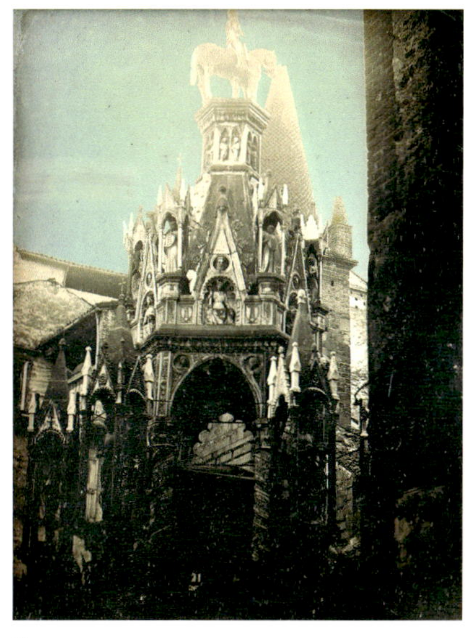
c

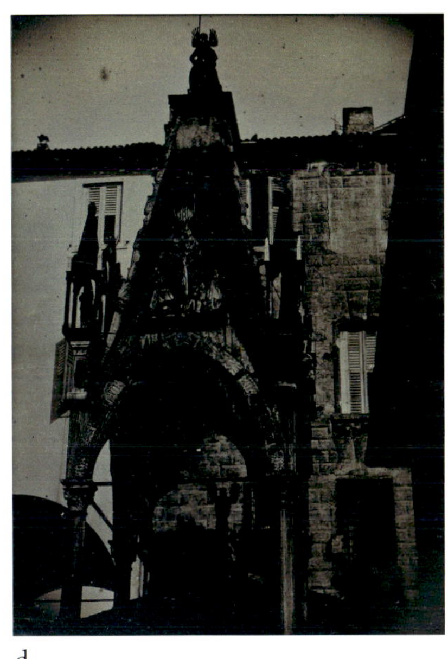
d

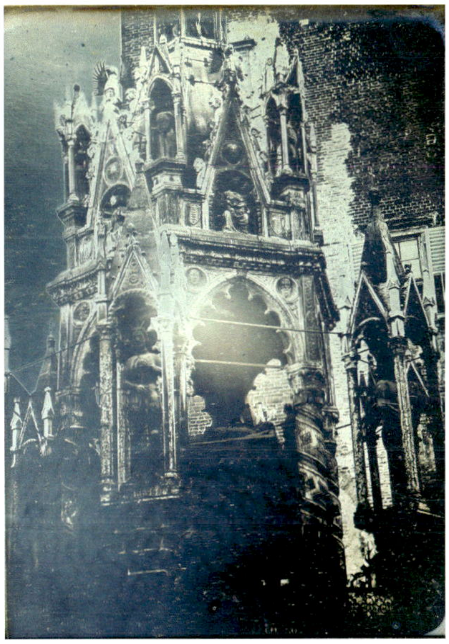

e

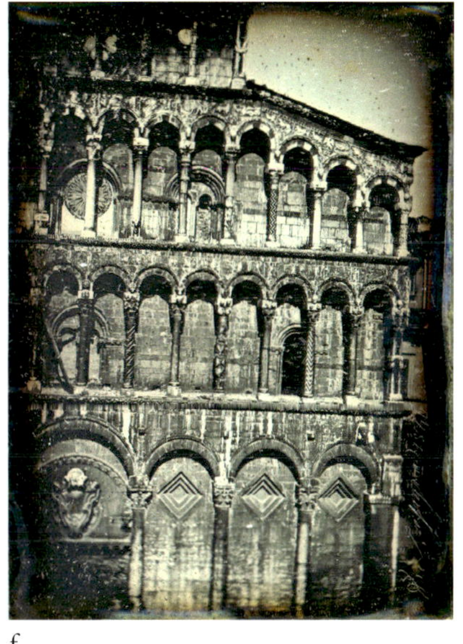
f

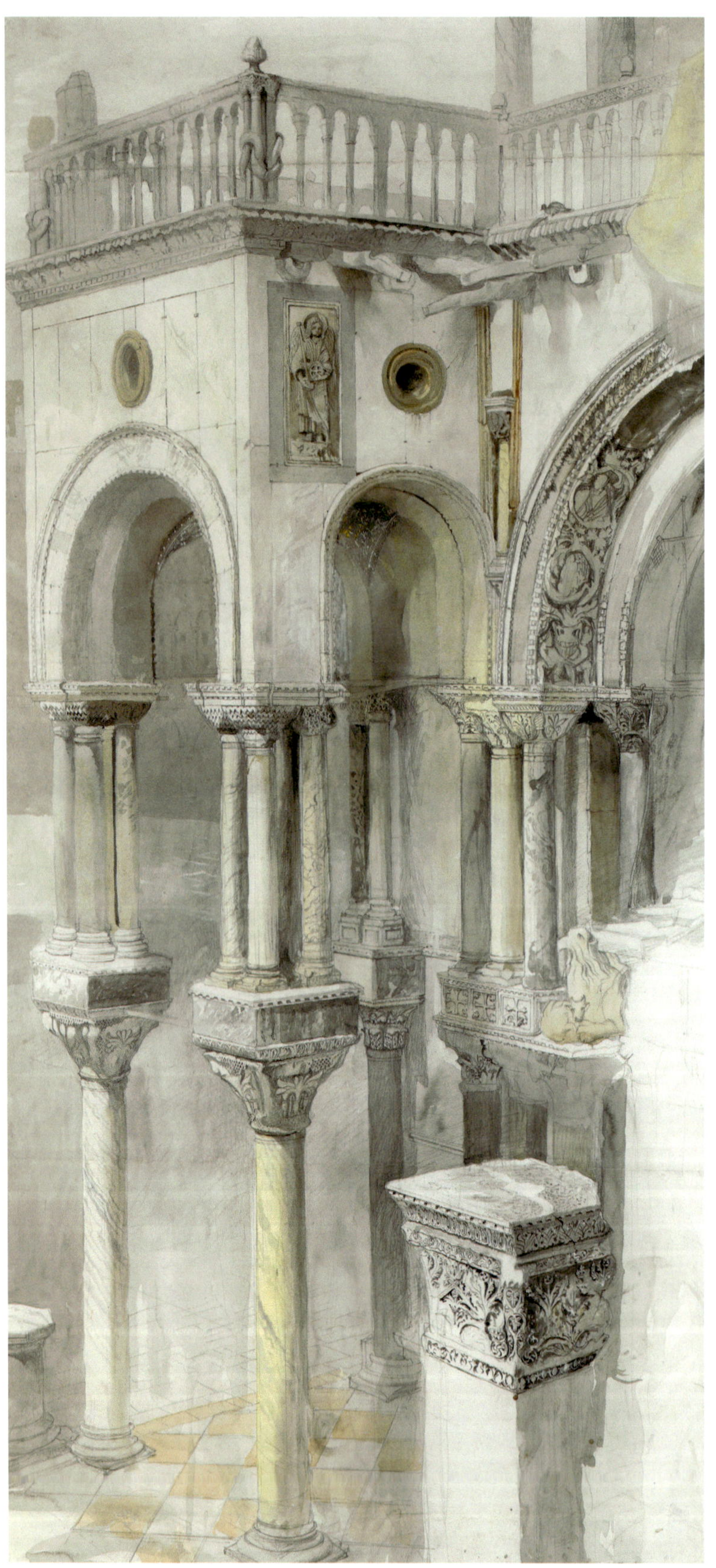

28
John Ruskin
The South Side of the Basilica of St Mark's, Venice, from the Loggia of the Doge's Palace
c. 1851
Pencil and watercolour, heightened with white, on three joined pieces of paper, 95.9 x 45.4 cm
Private collection, courtesy of Andrew Wyld
Ref: Hewison 2000, no. 80

This large and impressive drawing was scaled up from a daguerreotype made under Ruskin's direction by his servant John Hobbs during the first of the two research tours for *The Stones of Venice*, in 1849–50. The photograph was taken from the loggia of the Doge's Palace and also shows the walled-up Porta da Mar, together with one of the St Jean d'Acre columns. The plate was corrected so that the image appeared the right way round, allowing Ruskin in turn to show the forms of architecture clearly and with emphasis on elements such as the 'Lily Capitals' surmounting the columns at the lower left, although without adjustment for perspective. The drawing was apparently intended to serve as the basis for a lithographic plate for the volume *Examples of the Architecture of Venice*, published in three parts in 1851, but was never finished.

Ruskin regarded the loggia of the Doge's Palace as a particularly good vantage point from which to examine the south side of the basilica. In 1854 he recommended G.P. Boyce to draw from 'one point, as far as I know, never done' (a statement which demonstrates that Ruskin's own drawing really was copied from the photograph rather than done *in situ*). Boyce was 'to make friends with the old porter of the Ducal Palace – and get into the upper loggia at the corner. [From there] St Marks portico comes in somehow so [Ruskin gives a sketch] – with the top of the broken square capital of the St Jean d'Acre pillar underneath – and St Marks place behind most beautifully'.[1] Boyce's own watercolour of St Mark's, in fact taken from pavement level, is cat. 45.

1 Boyce 1980, p. 120

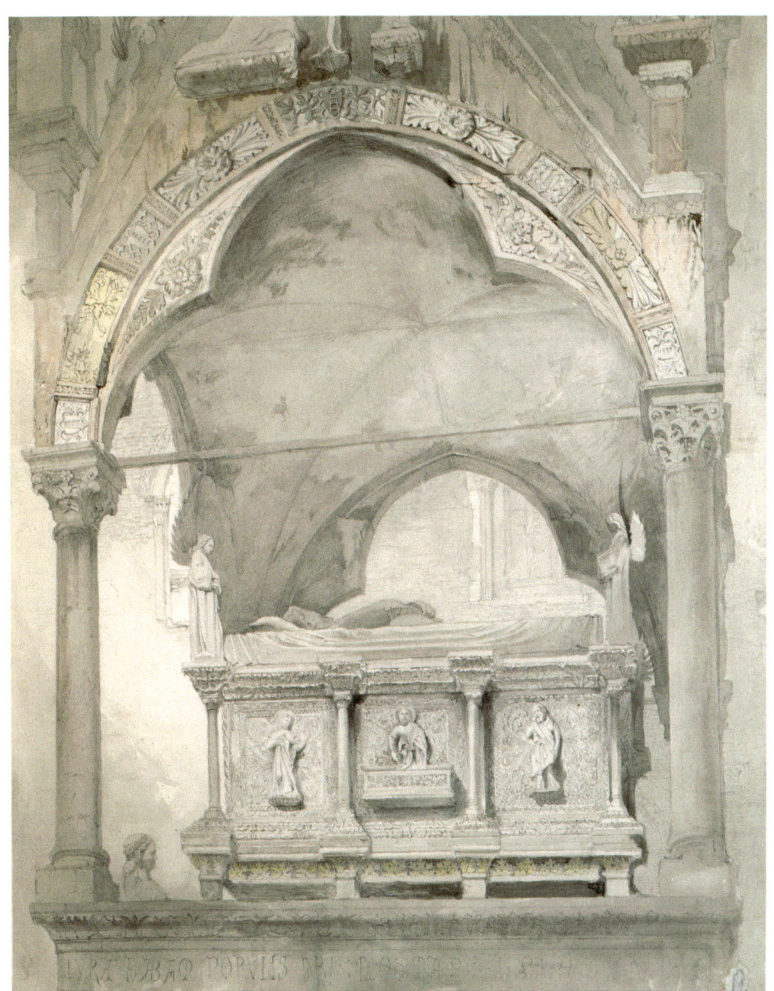

29
John Ruskin
Study for Detail of the Sarcophagus and Canopy of the Tomb of Mastino II della Scala at Verona
1852
Pencil and watercolour on paper, 45.9 x 36 cm
Ashmolean Museum, University of Oxford.
Ruskin School Collection (Ref. 59)
Ref: Hewison 2000, no. 87

Ruskin frequently visited Verona in his early years, usually when *en route* for Venice. In 1851–2, when he was working on the second and third volumes of *Stones of Venice*, he travelled to Verona several times, and took the opportunity of making a series of drawings of the open-air tombs of the fourteenth century in the city. As he wrote to his father on 6 June 1852: 'I think the Gothic of Verona more and more superb every time I examine it'.[1] Ruskin was fascinated by the various Scaliger tombs, analysing them as he had the ducal tombs in Venice in terms of a mounting hubris, which was reflected in their increasing degree of ornamentation. He frequently recommended them to other artists: the entire structure of the tomb of Mastino II della Scala, seen from a different angle, is seen in Boyce's watercolour of 1854 (**cat. 48**).

Ruskin's drawing shows the side view of the tomb of Mastino II della Scala, the construction of which began in 1345. An effigy of the ruler of Verona, who died in 1351, lies on his sarcophagus, with an angel at each corner and with the figure of Christ rising from the tomb between those of the Baptist and the Virgin on its side. Above is seen the soaring trefoil arch of the Gothic canopy. In this drawing, Ruskin fulfils one of the essential principles of his own architectural draughtsmanship, and one that he frequently advised others to follow, which was to approach closely to the subject and to allow the forms of the building represented to fill the sheet, while at the same time avoiding all peripheral or incidental detail. In this way, drawings were intended to serve a primarily documentary purpose, and to be informative for those who might never visit the places themselves.

1 Bradley 1955, p. 297

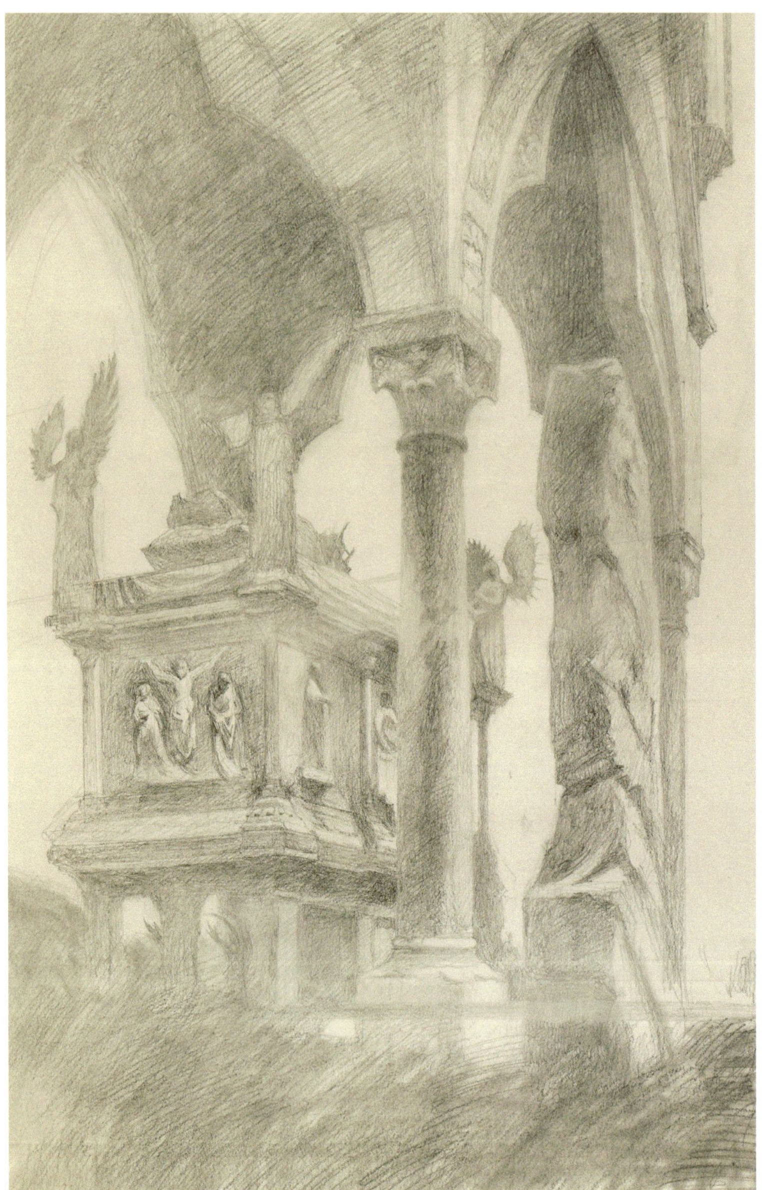

30
John Ruskin
Study for the General Chiaroscuro of the Sarcophagus and Canopy of the Tomb of Mastino II della Scala at Verona 1852
Pencil on paper, 50.7 x 33.3 cm
Ashmolean Museum, University of Oxford. Ruskin School Collection (Ref. 58)

This drawing of the tomb of Mastino II emphasises the contrast of tone between the lit parts and the shadowed underside of the Gothic canopy. Ruskin was particularly interested in the way buildings were lit and the dramatic effects of irradiating light on a structure. In the case of the Scaliger tombs, he noticed that they were often seen in shadow because the direct light of the sun was blocked. To his perception, this was a determining element in the aesthetic impact of the complex, and one that he feared might be disrupted by the reconstruction of the surrounding buildings.

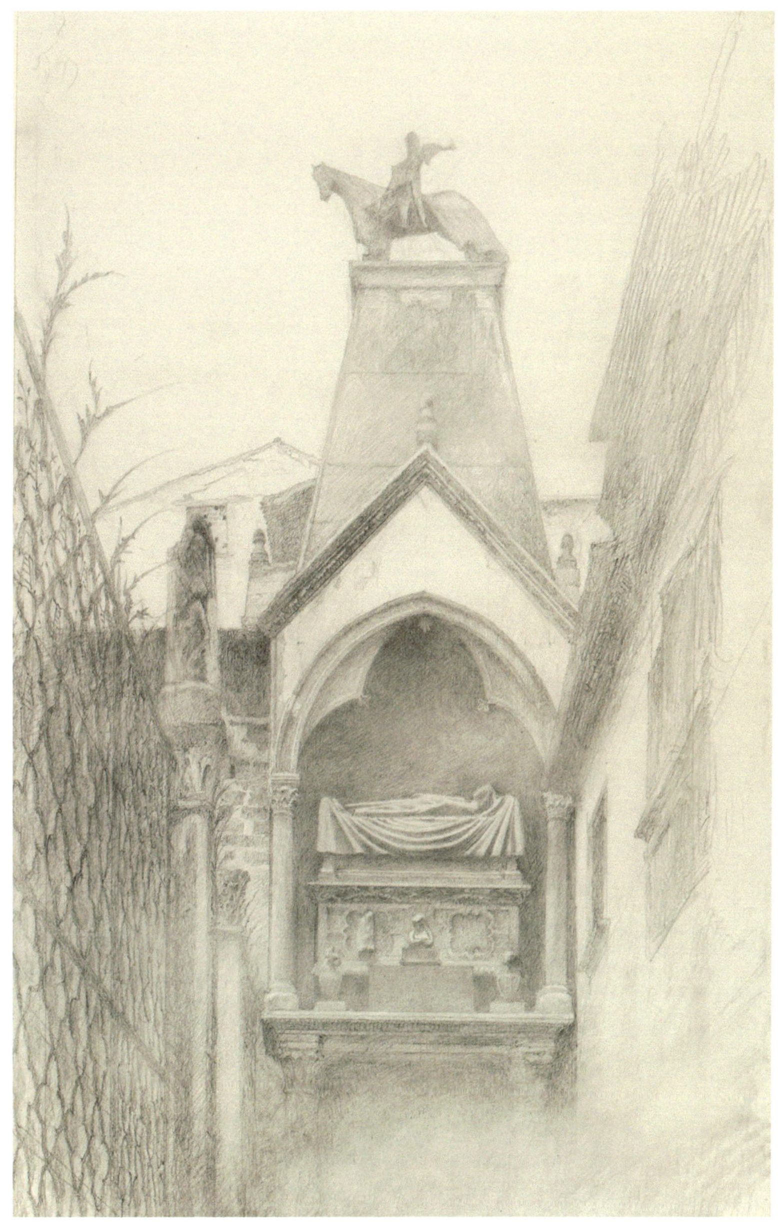

31
John Ruskin
Study of Tomb of Can Grande della Scala at Verona 1869
Pencil on paper, 50.7 x 32.3 cm
Ashmolean Museum, University of Oxford.
Ruskin School Collection (Ref. 57)

On 10 June 1869 Ruskin described to his mother the trouble that he had with this drawing of the Can Grande tomb, and compared his own work with that of J.W. Bunney: 'He is doing most lovely work for me – coloured drawings of the buildings, large – while I myself draw the detail'. Of his own draughtsmanship, he reported candidly: 'Alas! the judgment is still far before the manual power. I was quarter of an hour yesterday vainly trying to draw a fold of Can Grande's mantle. But I do better than anyone else would. For no one else would even try'.[1]

Can Grande I died in 1329. His monument, made by the Master of S. Anastasia and the first in the sequence of Scaliger tombs, consists of a sarcophagus supported by two hounds, with the effigy resting on top. Above the canopy stands a tall plinth with Can Grande mounted on horseback at the top. Ruskin here shows the ironwork enclosing the cemetery, which incorporates emblematic ladders, the crest of the della Scala family; above, jagged stems of leaves made of wrought-iron flare upwards like flames.

Although Ruskin contemplated a full volume, or perhaps even a series of volumes, devoted to the Romanesque and Gothic architecture of Verona, the principal outcome of his study there was his lecture 'Verona, and its Rivers', given at the British Institution on 4 February 1870.

1 Ruskin 1903–12, XIX, p. li

32
John Ruskin
The Gryphon bearing the North Shaft of the West Entrance of the Duomo, Verona
1869
Watercolour and bodycolour over pencil on paper, 22 x 35.7 cm
Ashmolean Museum, University of Oxford. Ruskin School Collection (Ed. 82)

In *Modern Painters* volume III, published in 1856, Ruskin explained how the principle of 'truth to nature' might even be applied to the representation of a mythic beast, comparing the Verona gryphon with a 'false grotesque from classical architecture',[1] and supporting his argument with an etching after his own drawing of the head of the gryphon. On 22 June 1869 he wrote to his mother from Verona to tell her how he was getting '"quite round" my favourite Griffin': 'I am painting him on the other side from that I engraved in *Modern Painters*, and the marble of him comes all into beautiful orange and grey, and I'm continually finding out new feathers and sinews in him that I did not know of'.[2] In the lectures he gave on sculpture in 1870, *Aratra Pentelici*, he explained that the 'Griffin representing Christian life is restraining the dragon in its claws'.[3]

Although Ruskin displayed this drawing with the illustrations of Italian Gothic art in the Oxford Drawing School, the cathedral of Verona, dedicated to S. Maria Matricolare, was begun after the earthquake of 1117, and its façade and spiral-decorated marble columns date from the Romanesque period.

1 Ruskin 1903–12, V, p. 140
2 Ruskin 1903–12, XIX, p. li
3 Ruskin 1903–12, XX, p. 362

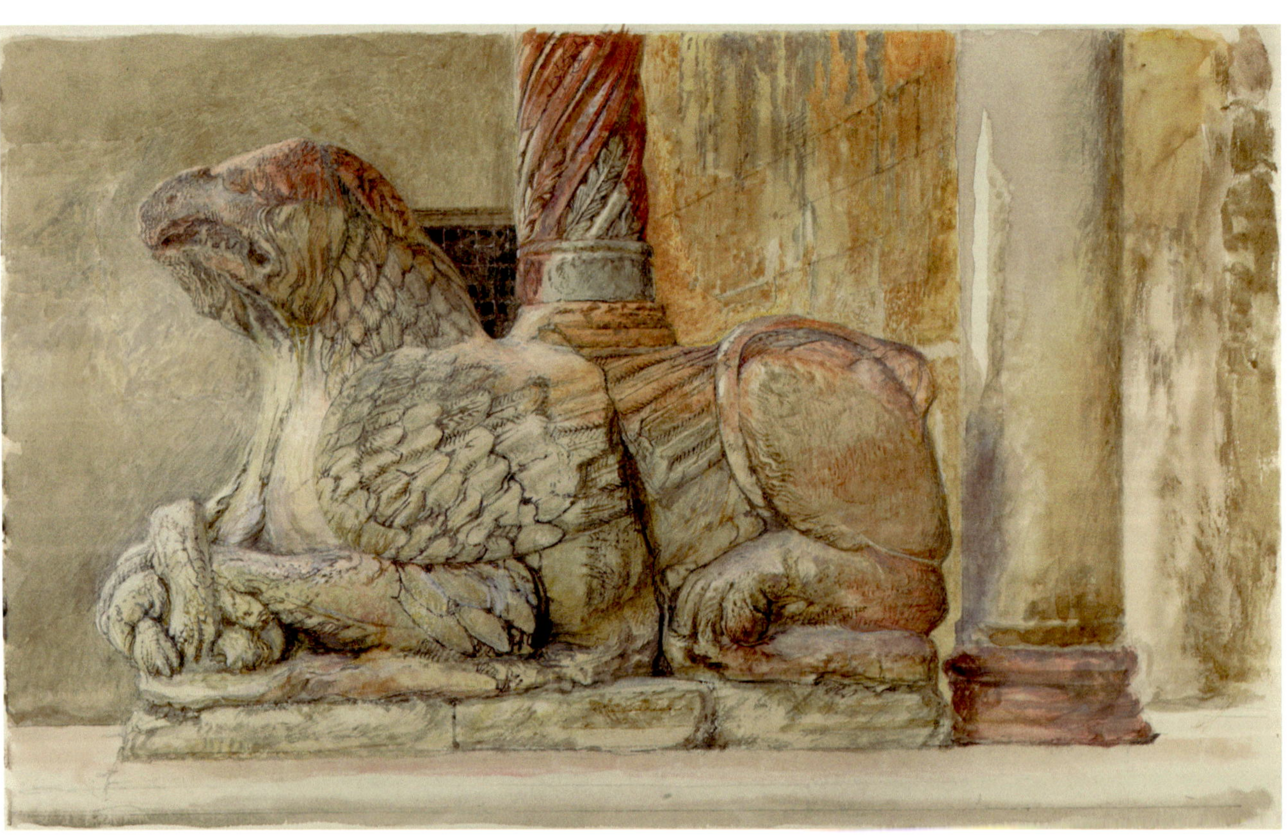

33
John Ruskin
View from the Palazzo Bembo to the Palazzo Grimani, Venice 1870
Pencil and watercolour on paper, 35.3 x 50.8 cm
Ashmolean Museum, University of Oxford.
Ruskin School Collection (Ref. 66)

In the course of his later visits to Venice, Ruskin made a series of careful pencil views of the buildings of the Grand Canal, employing a diminishing perspective across the width of the sheet. Although this type of drawing may be seen to have originated in the Venice palace views that he had made in 1841 in imitation of the work of Samuel Prout, by the 1870s Ruskin was prepared to evoke the architectural forms in calligraphic short-hand rather than seeking to describe each element. In this move towards generalisation, at least in the more distant parts of the composition, he conformed to a broader evolution of taste, and may have been aware, for example, of the astonishingly abstract views of Venice by Inchbold **(see cat. 87)**.

Ruskin made a short stay in Venice in May and June 1870, travelling with his cousin Joan Severn and others. Cat. 33 was drawn from a moored gondola close to what is now the Rialto vaporetto stop, with the bridge itself immediately behind. On the left is the Palazzo Bembo, a late Gothic reconstruction of a Byzantine structure, with barges moored on the Riva del Carbon; farther down, at centre right and facing directly onto the canal, is the imposing Palazzo Grimani, built to the design of Sanmicheli; and beyond is the Byzantine Ca' Farsetti.

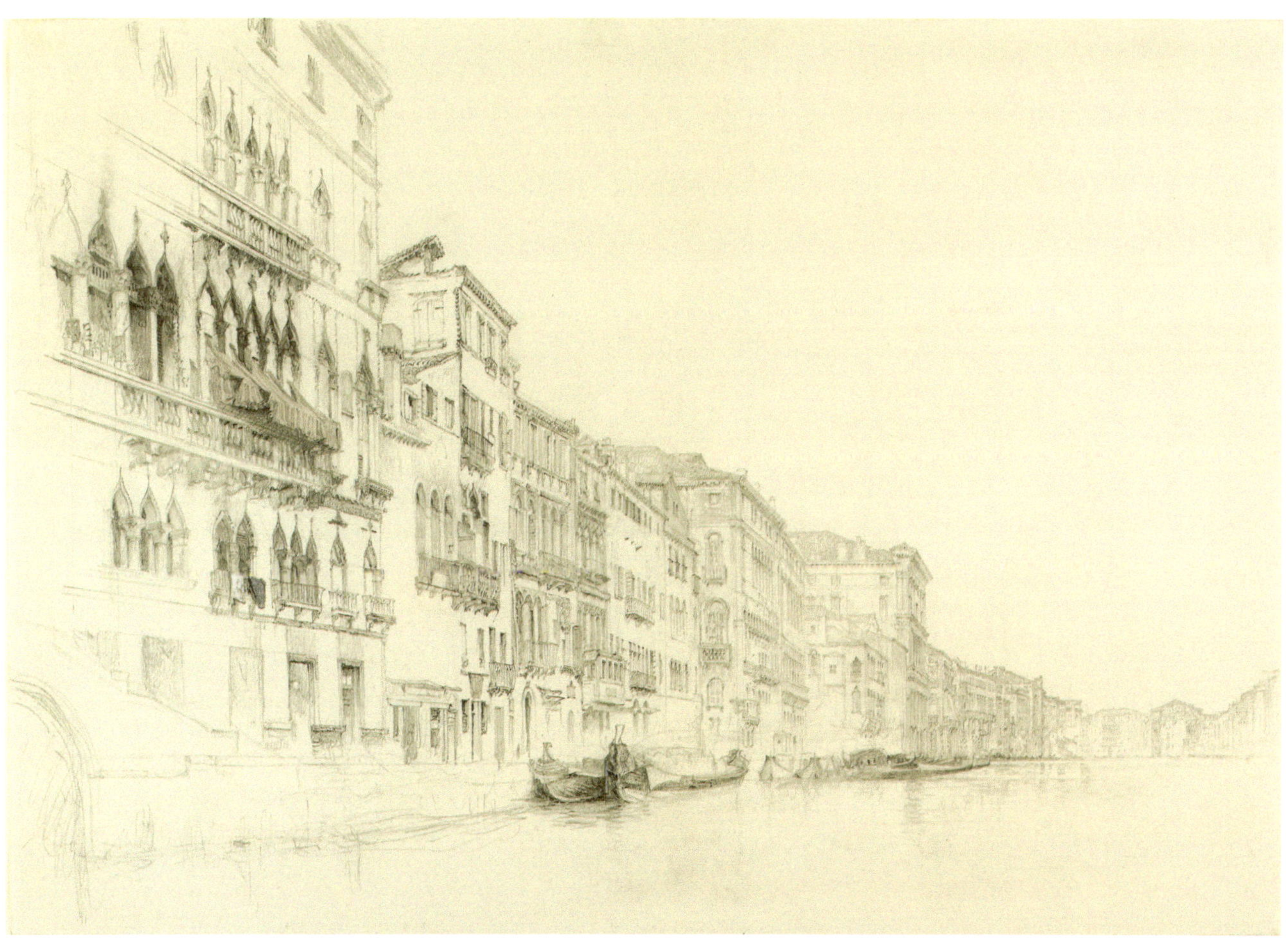

34
John Ruskin
Study of a Panel of the Font, Baptistery, Pisa
1872
Watercolour and bodycolour over pencil, 51.2 x 36 cm
Ashmolean Museum, University of Oxford.
Ruskin School Collection (Ref. 100)
Ref: Clegg and Tucker 1993, no. 273

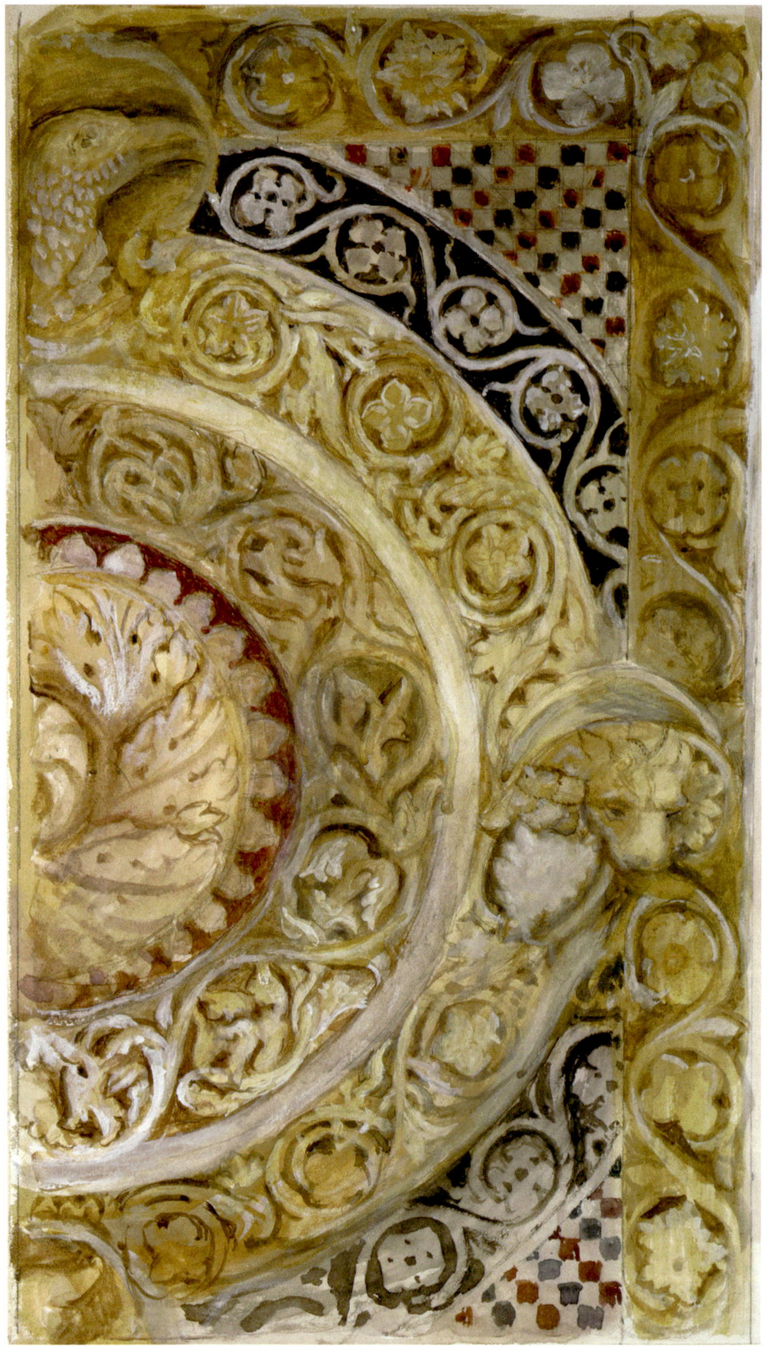

All his life, Ruskin was attracted by abstract pattern and the ornamentation of surfaces. He loved inlaid masonry and mosaic decoration, and as early as 1849, in *The Seven Lamps of Architecture*, had contrasted the flat decorated planes of southern architecture, exemplified by buildings in Lucca, Venice, and Pisa, with the three-dimensional and dynamically curvilinear Gothic of the north. His pleasure in the complexity of pattern and colour, without needing to consider a structural context or to be especially concerned with how the decoration served or obscured the stability of the building, was a defining characteristic of his approach to architecture.

From this may be extrapolated larger principles of looking and observation: Ruskin drew what lay before him that he might appreciate forms more clearly; on the other hand, there was also a purely sensuous aspect to his inspection of materials, relishing what he saw without necessarily caring what it was. The drawing of the Pisa font panel may be thus considered as an exercise in delight, to gratify what Ruskin occasionally referred to as the 'innocence of the eye'.

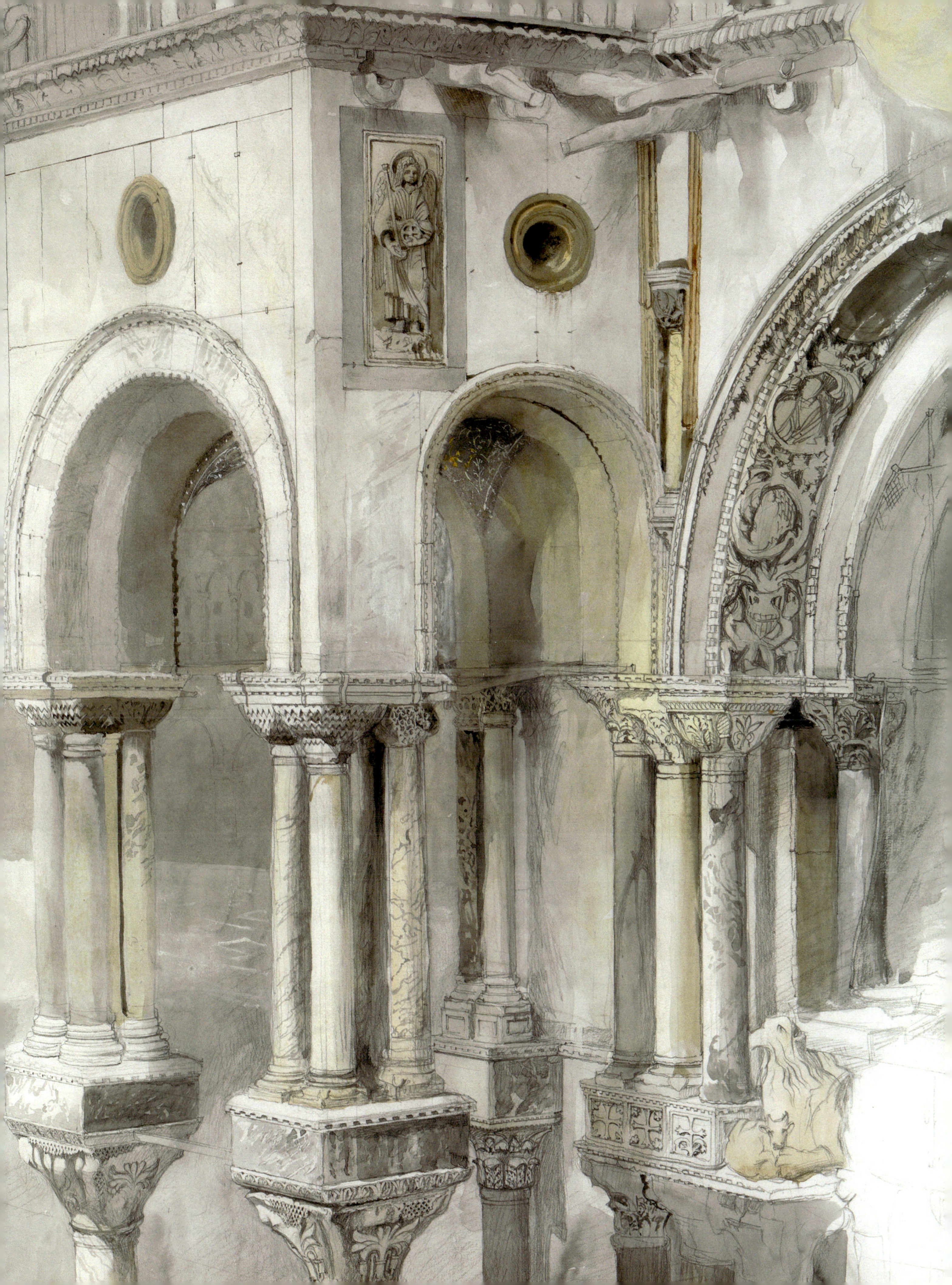

35

John Ruskin

The Baptistery, Florence: Study of the Upper Part of the Right-hand Compartment on the South-west Façade 1872

Watercolour and bodycolour over pencil on paper, 52 x 34.6 cm

Ashmolean Museum, University of Oxford. Ruskin School Collection (Ref. 120)

Ref: Clegg and Tucker 1993, no. 123; Staley and Newall 2004, no. 76

In March 1872, in his newsletter ostensibly addressed to the 'working men of England', *Fors Clavigera*, Ruskin announced his purpose of going to Florence to draw the baptistery in connection with the lectures on architecture that he was preparing to give at Oxford, where he had been Slade Professor since 1869. Although the lectures, which were published as *Ariadne Florentina*, eventually focused on the art of engraving, nonetheless he found the opportunity to say that the 'whole history of *Christian* architecture and painting begins' in this building, and that it might be regarded as the consummation of an ancient Greek tradition of architecture, (as 'the last building raised on the earth by the descendants of the workmen taught by Dædalus').[1] He was fascinated by the way in which a structure whose origins were thought to be late Roman was decorated in a style which made it quintessentially Tuscan. He allowed himself to consider the marble facings in isolation as 'white substance, cut into, and filled with black and dark green'.[2] Ruskin was instinctively drawn to flat surface and pattern rather than space and structure, and celebrated the baptistery as something 'on the surface of which the eye and intellect are to be interested by the relations of dimension and curve between pieces of encrusting marble of different colours, which have no more to do with the real make of the building than the diaper of a Harlequin's jacket has to do with his bones'.[3]

Although each of the six flanks of the baptistery are apparently similar, with a blind arcade of white and green marble (from the quarries of Luni and Prato respectively) forming the central register, Ruskin had noticed that in fact 'there wasn't a single space in all the octagon and all the panelling that matched another'. In this drawing, Ruskin paid close attention to the exact pattern and distribution of the architectural elements: 'I painted [...] one compartment of it with the best care I could – [and] never took more pains with a drawing'.[4] It shows the upper part of the right-hand compartment that faces towards the south-west on to the Piazza S. Giovanni. Only those on the south-west and north-west flanks have such narrow window spaces, and only that facing the south-west has square patterns in the upper part that meet but do not overlap with the semicircular band running round the inside of the blind arch. Looking even more closely, it may be observed that the cracks and joint marks in the marble facings shown in the drawing remain visible in the building today, even including the small square repair marks in the white panel on the right of the window. However, two of the three rectangular sheets with half disk tops in the lower part (those on each side, but not that in the centre), as well as parts of the green marble, including the pediment of the window, have been repaired or replaced since the time of Ruskin's drawing.

Ruskin constantly encouraged artists to draw buildings which might be threatened with destructive restoration, and his own drawings were often intended to fulfil this purpose, although they were seldom as meticulous as this example. It was exactly Ruskin's intention that this particular piece of scrupulous observation allows the viewer to detect which parts of the fabric are restorations and what is original.

1 Ruskin 1903–12, XXIII, p. 413

2 Ruskin 1903–12, XXII, pp. 343–4

3 Ruskin 1903–12, XX, p. 217

4 Ruskin 1903–12, XXIII, p. 241

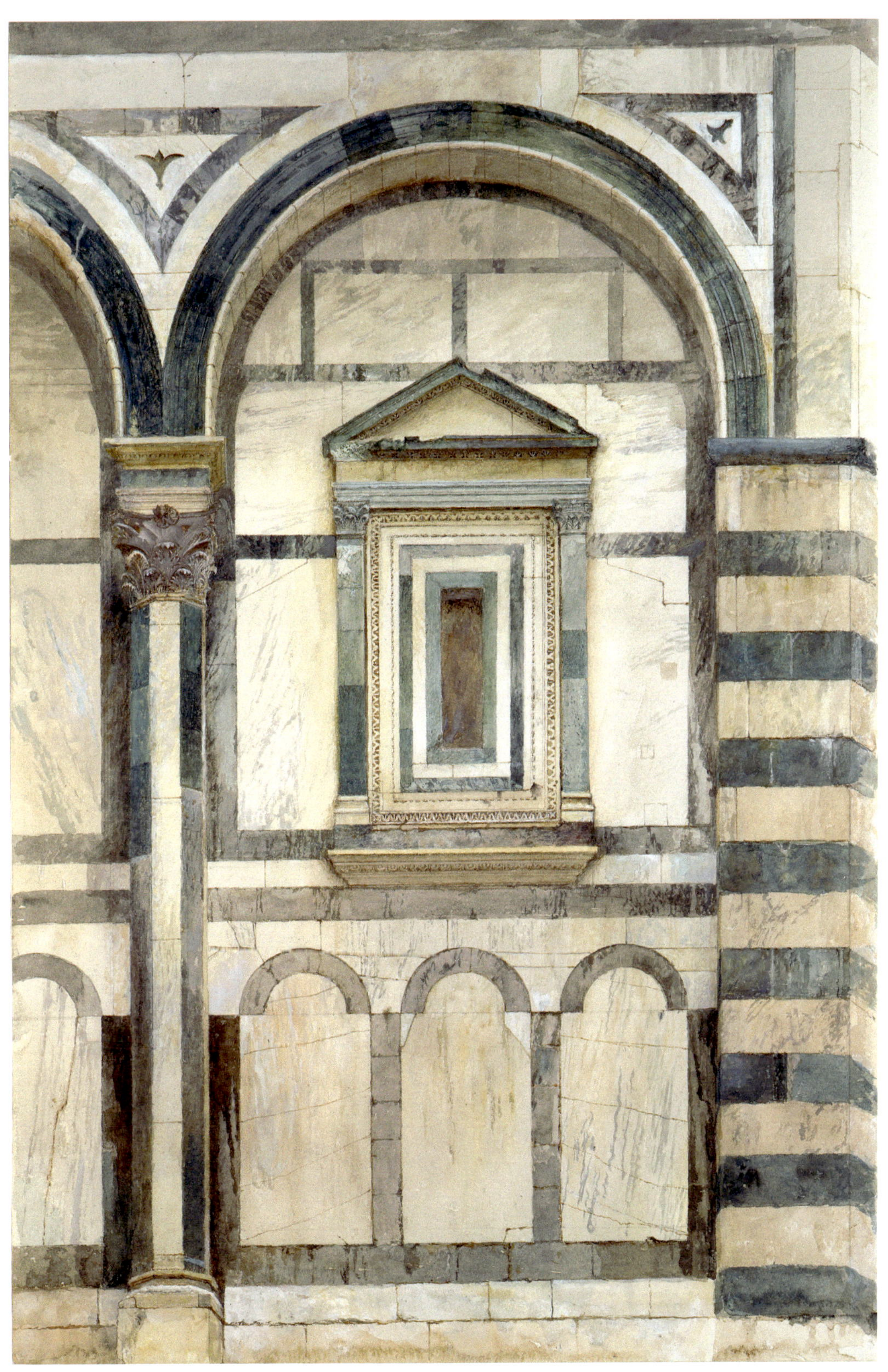

36
John Ruskin
The Tomb of Frederick II in the Cathedral of Palermo 1874
Watercolour and bodycolour over pencil on paper, 49.5 x 32.9 cm
Ashmolean Museum, University of Oxford. Ruskin School Collection (Ref. 84)

English friends living in Sicily invited Ruskin to Palermo in the spring of 1874. His first impression was discouraging; he found 'a town built of large stones the colour of mud, with an iron *curled* balcony to every window and everybody's shirts, chemises, petticoats,

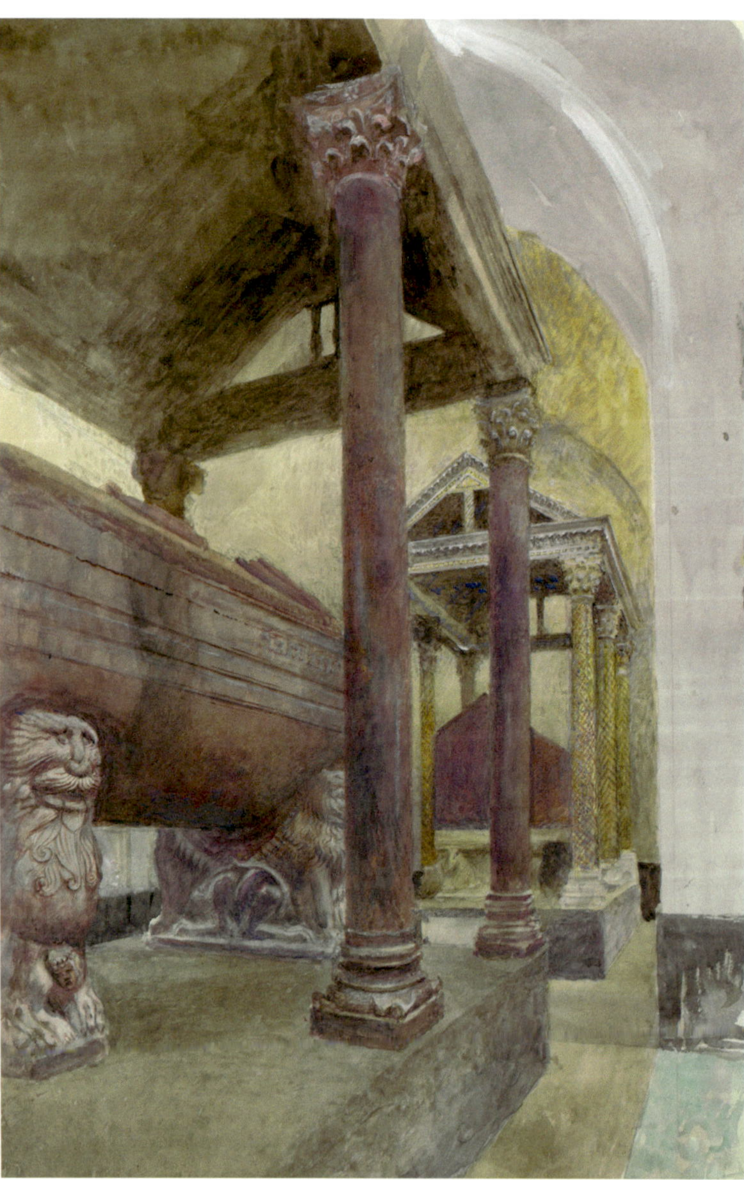

and bedclothes hung out over them to dry'. However, on 22 April he recorded the things that had made a positive impression upon him in the city, writing: 'Fifthly, I've seen the tomb of Frederick II, and knelt at it! and am going to draw it to-morrow – God willing'.[1] The tomb, of 'Corinthian porphyry and gold',[2] was for Ruskin the 'perfect type of Greek-Christian form [...] temple over sarcophagus'.[3] Ruskin had thought of writing a biography of Frederick and in his lecture *Val d'Arno* in the previous year discussed his periodic clashes with the papacy.

The tombs of the Norman kings of Sicily were originally placed in the choir of the cathedral, but in 1781, in the course of Ferdinando Fuga's reconstruction of the church, were moved into two communicating chapels off the south aisle. On the left is the tomb of Frederick II, almost certainly that which King Roger II had commissioned for himself but which Frederick stole from the cathedral in Cefalù in 1213 (leading to his excommunication). Roger rests in the one behind, also made of porphyry over a carved marble base and with a marble baldachino.

The chilly neo-classical interior of Palermo cathedral in its late eighteenth-century form was exactly what Ruskin most disliked. Curiously, he appears not to have commented on the tragic loss of what must have been the most astonishing church in Palermo, Archbishop Walter Offamilio's defensive citadel in the heart of the city, built in the 1180s in competition with William II's Benedictine foundation, Monreale.

1 Ruskin 1903–12, XXIII, pp. xxxii–xxxiii
2 Ruskin 1903–12, XXXI, p. 26
3 Ruskin 1903–12, XXXIII p. 477

37
John Ruskin
Tomb of Ilaria del Carretto in the Duomo of San Martino, Lucca 1874
Watercolour and bodycolour on pencil on paper, 20.3 x 30.5 cm
Ashmolean Museum, University of Oxford. Ruskin School Collection (Ref. 79)
Ref: Clegg and Tucker 1993, no. 237; Hewison 2000, no. 237

Ruskin's first account of the tomb of Ilaria del Carretto was in a letter to his father of 6 May 1845. Having described its different parts, he concludes: 'It is impossible to tell you the perfect sweetness of the lips and closed eyes, nor the solemnity of the seal of death which is set upon the whole figure. The sculpture – as art – is in every way perfect: truth itself, but truth selected with inconceivable refinement of feeling'.[1] In the Epilogue to *Modern Painters* volume II of 1883, he stated categorically that Jacopo della Quercia's statue of Ilaria was his 'ideal of Christian sculpture'.[2]

This drawing is one of three of the tomb made by Ruskin in the summer of 1874. Ruskin's meditation upon the death of a beautiful young woman brought a cruel sense of his own loneliness and of personal failure. As he explained in *Fors Clavigera*, studying it had once turned him 'from the study of landscape to that of life'.[3] In 1874, however, he informed his readers: 'I feel the separation between me and the people round me, so bitterly, in the world of my own which they cannot enter; and I see their entrance to it now barred so absolutely by their own resolves'.[4] Still later, in 1878 – and with thoughts of the loss of Rose La Touche racking his consciousness – he meditated on the transition between life and death: 'And through and in the marble we may see that the damsel is not dead, but sleepeth: yet as visibly a sleep that shall know no ending until the last day break, and the last shadow flee away; until then, she "shall not return"'.[5]

1 Ruskin 1903–12, IV, p. 122 n. 1
2 Ruskin 1903–12, IV, p. 347
3 Ruskin 1903–12, XXVIII, p.146
4 Ruskin 1903–12, XXVIII, p. 146
5 Ruskin 1903–12, XXXIV, p. 171

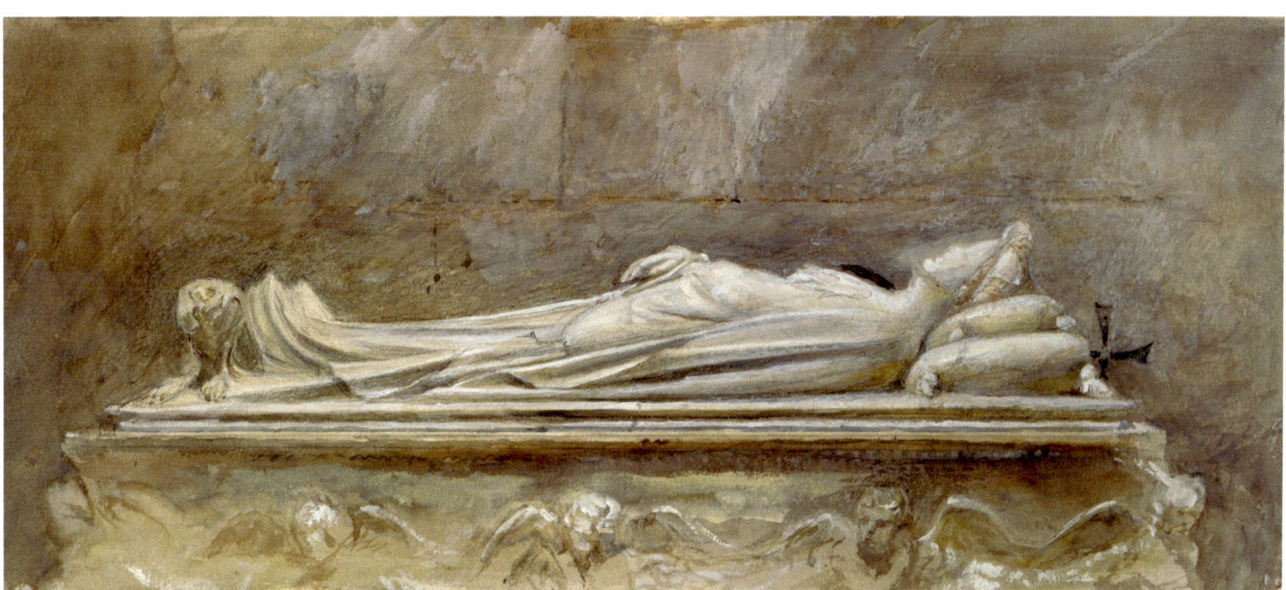

38
John Ruskin
Drawing of Tintoretto's 'Circumcision' in the Scuola Grande di San Rocco, Venice 1869
Pencil, watercolour, and bodycolour on paper, 34.8 x 39.2 cm
Ashmolean Museum, University of Oxford. Ruskin School Collection (Ref. 97)

Ruskin 'discovered' Tintoretto in 1845, describing his first visit to the Scuola Grande di San Rocco to his father: 'I never was so utterly crushed to the earth before any human intellect as I was to-day – before Tintoret. Just be so good as to take my list of painters and put him in the school of Art at the top – top – top of everything, with a big black line underneath'.[1] There are frequent references to Tintoretto in *Modern Painters* volume II, written in 1846, and detailed analysis of the symbolical or allegorical meaning of specific works. For Ruskin, Tintoretto became the essential Venetian artist, representing the virility of expression that he associated with the city.

From the time of his completion of his researches for *Stones of Venice*, in June 1852, until 1869, Ruskin avoided Venice, perhaps because he felt that his work there was complete, but also because of the sad associations after the humiliating failure of his marriage. When he finally returned in 1869, he visited the Scuola with Holman Hunt, and made the present study.

The Circumcision was the last canvas to be installed, in about 1587, as part of the cycle of New Testament subjects that decorate the Ground Floor of the Scuola. Ruskin gave an ecstatic account of it in his *Venetian Index*[2] (although subsequent authors have recognised it to be largely the work of Tintoretto's studio).

1 Ruskin 1903–12, IV, p. xxxviii
2 Ruskin 1903–12, XI, pp. 409–10

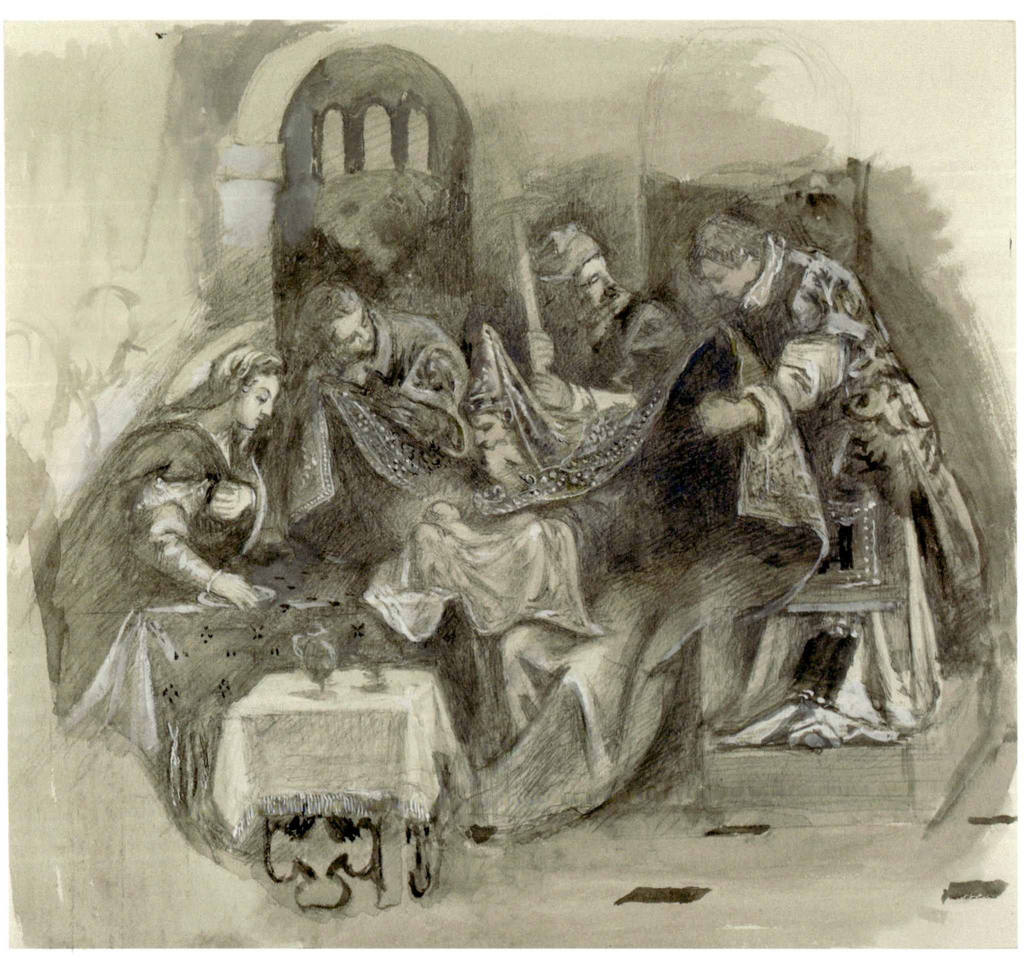

39
John Ruskin
Study of the Child in Tintoretto's 'The Circumcision' in the Scuola Grande di San Rocco, Venice 1869
Watercolour and bodycolour over pencil on paper, 34.1 x 50.6 cm
Ashmolean Museum, University of Oxford. Ruskin School Collection (Ref. 96)

Much of Ruskin's analysis of specific works in the various cycles of paintings by Tintoretto at the Scuola Grande di San Rocco was dependent on his observation of individual details within the compositions. These in turn he interpreted as symbols – often finding typological connections between the Old and New Testaments – as well as taking delight in the artist's inventiveness and the treatment of incidental details. His reading of the S. Rocco paintings – which, as products of the Counter-Reformation, might in the first place have seemed so alien to his spiritual inclination – led him to a new appreciation of how the iconography of a work might instruct a spectator, both literally and subliminally. Holman Hunt remembered telling J.E. Millais how Ruskin 'describes pictures of the Venetian School in such a manner that you see them with your inner sight, and you feel that the men who did them had been appointed by God, like old prophets, to bear a sacred message'.[1] To a large extent, therefore, the spiritual intensity of the first phase of Pre-Raphaelitism, and especially the works of Hunt, was dependent on Ruskin's study of Italian painting of the sixteenth century.

When Ruskin and Hunt visited S. Rocco together in 1869, they read the account Ruskin had given of Tintoretto's works. Ruskin, who by then no longer believed in God, explained to the profoundly faithful Hunt: 'I am led to regard the whole story of divine revelation as a mere wilderness of poetic dreaming [...] there is no Eternal Father to whom we can look up, that man has no helper but himself', and concluding that 'Tintoretto did not believe any more than I do the fables he was treating'.[2]

1 Hunt 1905, I, p. 90
2 Hunt 1905, II, pp. 265–7

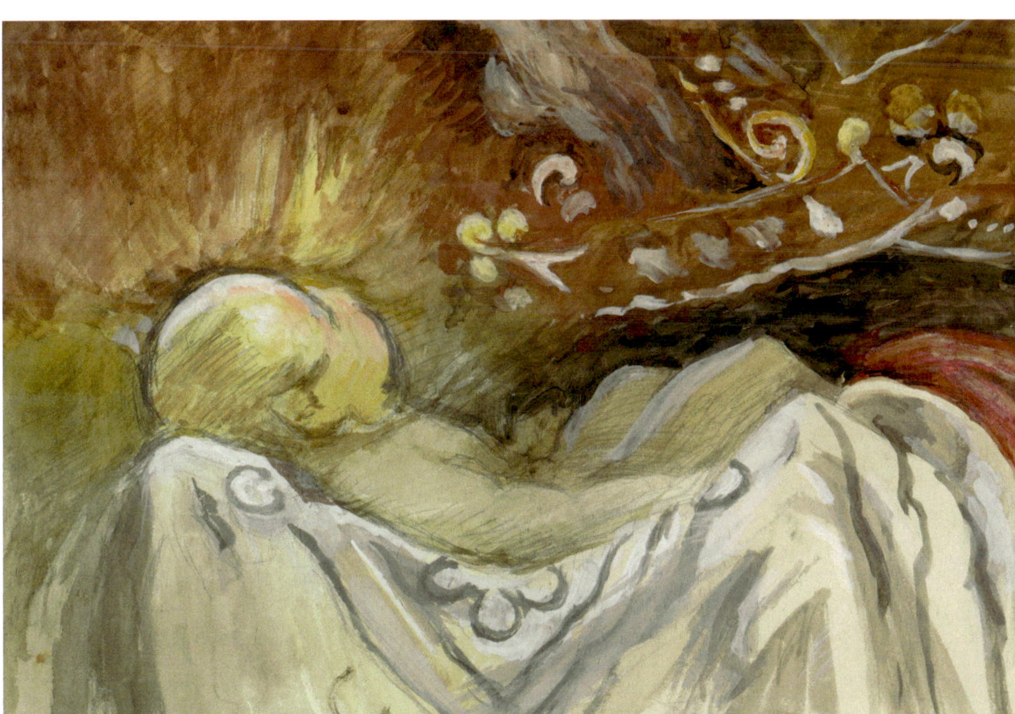

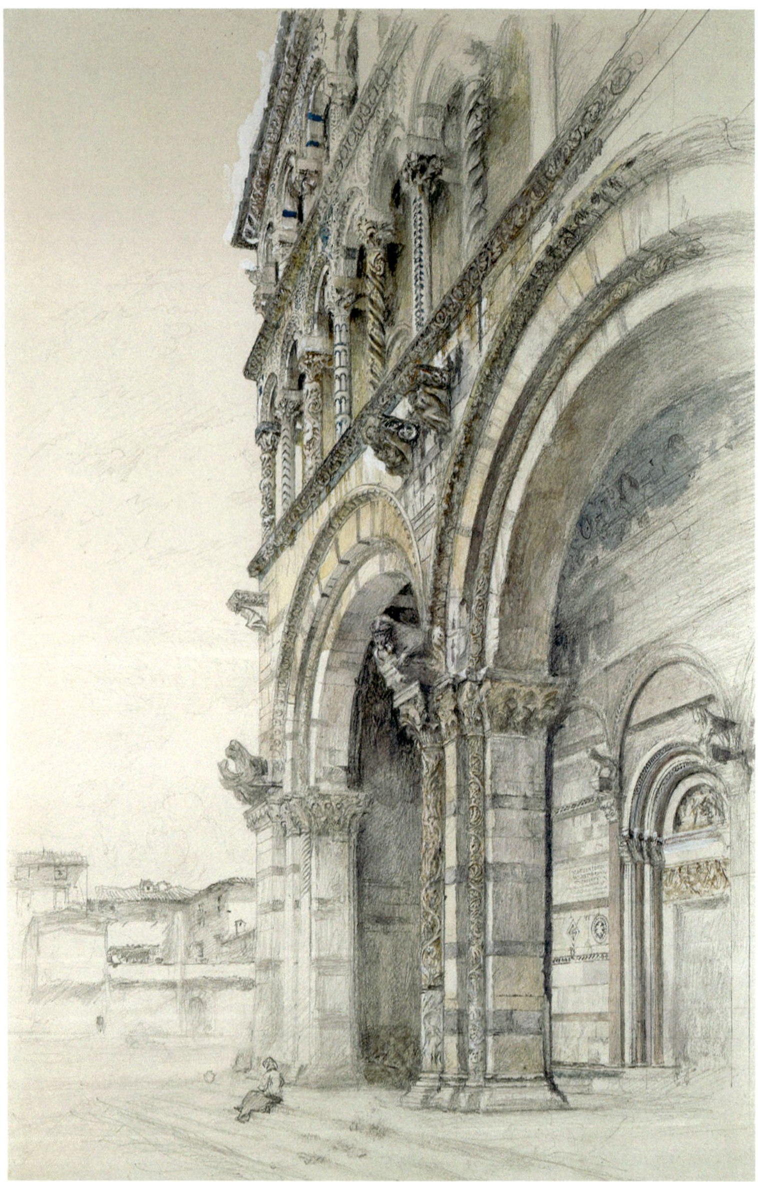

40
John Ruskin
The Duomo of San Martino, Lucca 1874
Pencil, watercolour and bodycolour on paper, 50.2 x 33.5 cm
Ashmolean Museum, University of Oxford. Ruskin School Collection (Ref. 85)

This view of the façade of S. Martino shows two of the three deep arches that form the west front of the cathedral at ground level, and the loggias and arcades of Romanesque columns above, seen at an oblique angle which gives a dynamic quality to the composition. The drawing derived from the same visit to Lucca in July and August 1874 during which he devoted so much effort and emotional energy to his studies of the tomb of Ilaria del Carretto (**see cat. 37**). Much of what he saw during this tour of Tuscany caused him distress, as many buildings appeared to have been damaged by restoration. Lucca, however, unlike Pisa and Florence, appeared relatively unscathed, although he was horrified by the damage that had been inflicted on the church of S. Romano.

41
John Ruskin
Drawing of Carpaccio's 'Dream of St Ursula' from 'The Legend of St Ursula' 1876
Watercolour and bodycolour over Pencil on paper, 29.4 x 27.6 cm
Ashmolean Museum, University of Oxford. Ruskin School Collection (WAL. 9)

Ruskin was captivated by the work of Vittore Carpaccio (*c.* 1460–1526) from the time that it was first recommended to him by Burne-Jones in 1869. In 1870 he described Carpaccio's work as 'faultless' in execution,[1] saying elsewhere that he was 'the greatest master of gradation'.[2] In September 1876 Ruskin persuaded the authorities in the Accademia in Venice to place Carpaccio's *Dream of St Ursula* in a private room where he might study it closely and meditate upon it. This meticulous copy of the whole composition was made for the Drawing School in Oxford, and therefore had an

1 Ruskin 1903–12, XIX, p. 443
2 Ruskin 1903–12, XV, pp. 497–8

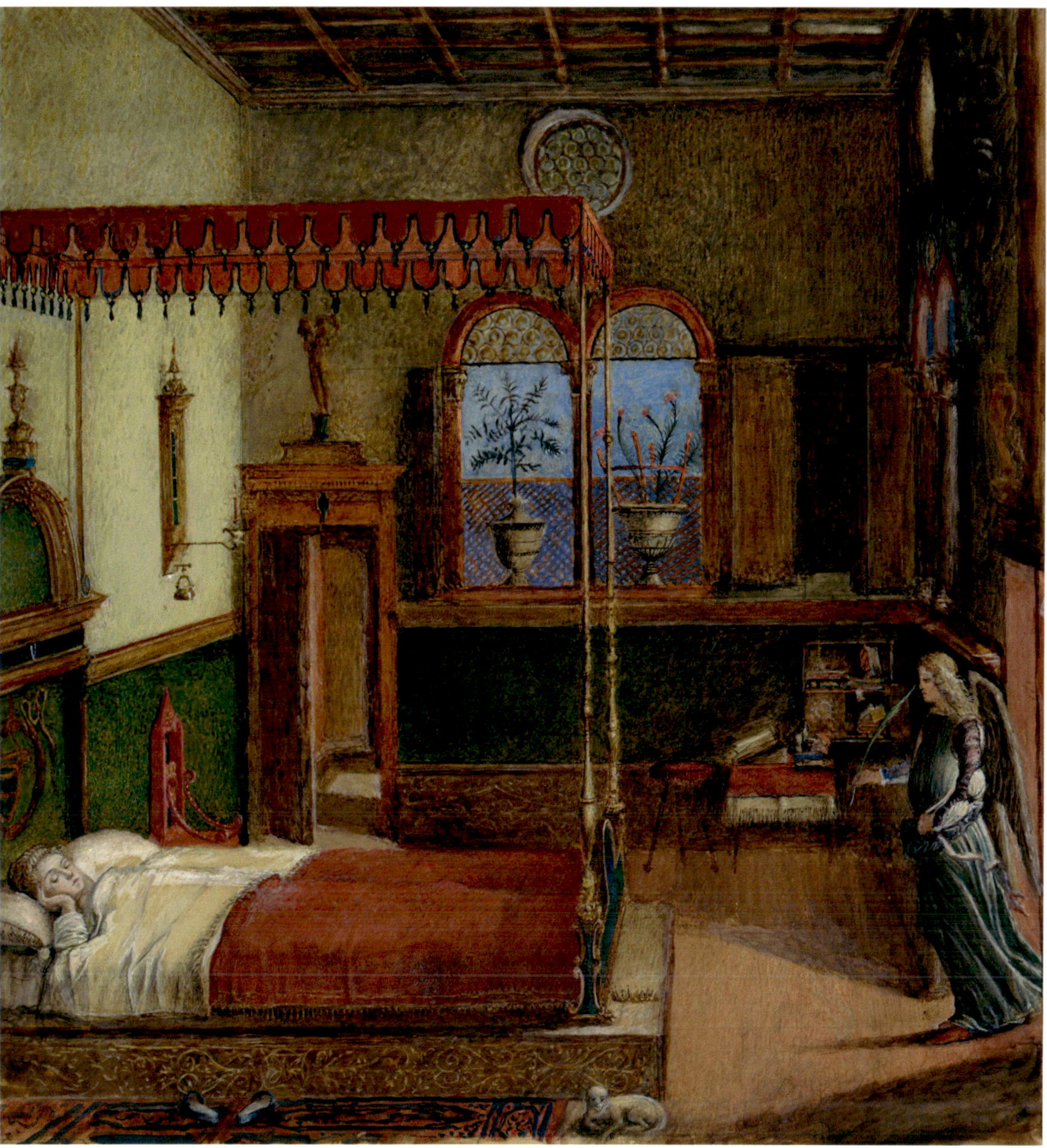

ostensibly didactic purpose. The subject shows an angel appearing to the saint in a dream to tell her of her martyrdom, but also to reassure her that she should accept death because she will be welcomed into Heaven. Ruskin has carefully noted the various symbolical motifs: the flood of light from heaven as the door is opened; the pots of carnations and verbena on the window ledge, representing earthly and heavenly love; and the holy image lit by a smoking candle on the left wall.

For Ruskin, the composition represented 'No dream, but a vision'. Its apparent reality was in fact a strange hallucination on his part, as he identified the saint with a young Irish girl named Rose La Touche with whom he had been obsessively in love but who had died in 1875. As his febrile imagination was driven to incipient mania by a sense of loss and longing, he constructed a bizarre system of coded messages – which he believed to have been directed to him from Rose – from the emblems shown in the painting, and which was corroborated by chance encounters and incidental events that he experienced that winter in Venice.

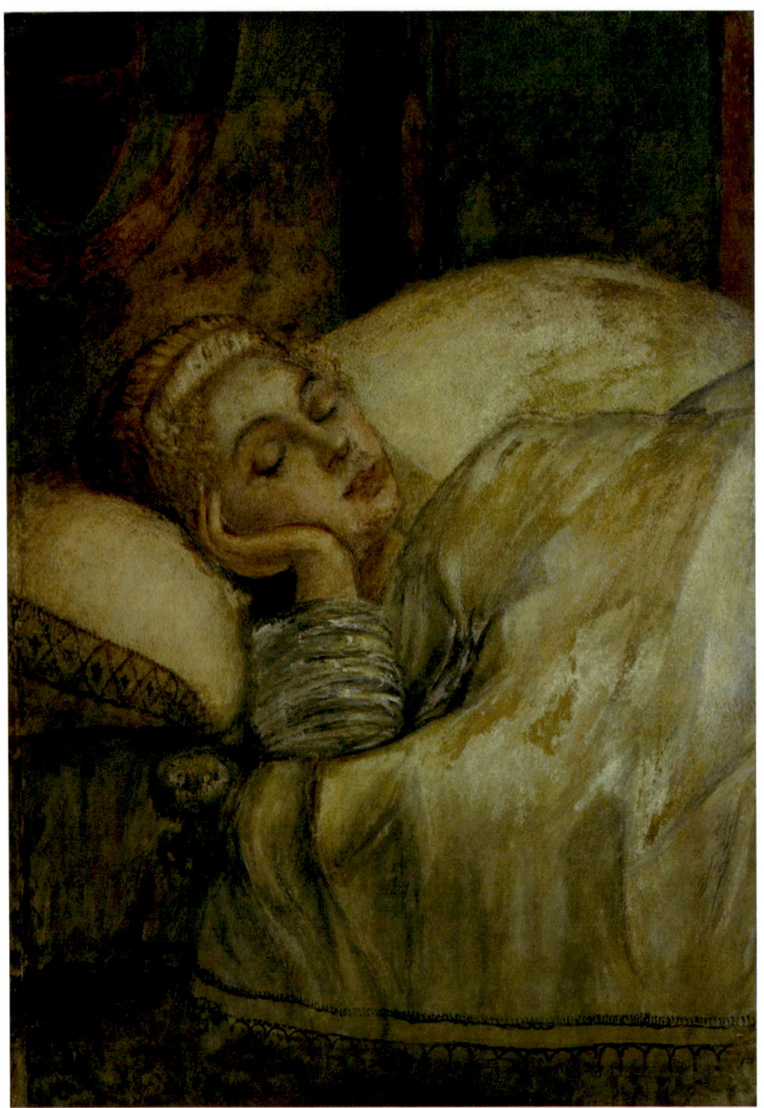

42
John Ruskin
Head of St Ursula, from Carpaccio's 'Dream of St Ursula' 1877
Watercolour on paper, 57 x 40 cm
Somerville College, Oxford
Ref: Hewison 2000, no. 244

In addition to the scale drawing of the entire composition (**cat. 41**), Ruskin made three copies of separate details in *The Dream of St Ursula*. Here the sleeping saint is shown with her head resting on the pillow and supported on her hand. Her yellow hair and pale complexion may have reminded Ruskin of Rose La Touche, who was herself blonde and blue-eyed. However, the connection between the saint and the Irish girl had reached such a point of confusion that he could no longer clearly distinguish between the two. Ruskin's mental equanimity was breaking down, his plight exacerbated by the bleakness of Venice in winter and by his sense of his own isolation. In 1878 he suffered a complete mental breakdown, the first of a series of bouts of insanity that dogged him for the remaining years of his life.

43
John Ruskin (1819–1900)
Study of Verbena in Carpaccio's 'Dream of St Ursula' 1876–7
Watercolour on paper, 37 x 31 cm
Sir Stephen Oliver

The second of the studies of details in *The Dream of St Ursula* was inspired by the vase of greenery resting on the windowsill on the far wall of Ursula's chamber.

On Christmas Eve, 1876, after a session copying the Carpaccio in which he had found himself in 'a dream of very right and high spirit, about St Ursula and Rosie',[1] Ruskin returned to the Calcina Hotel on the Zattere to find a pot of dianthus left as a Christmas present by his Irish friend, Lady Castletown. On Christmas morning he dwelt upon the apparent significance of the gift in *Fors Clavigera*: 'Last night, St Ursula sent me her dianthus "out of her bedroom window, with her love"'.[2] He continued: 'She sent me the living dianthus [...] but she had sent me also, in the morning, from England, a dried sprig of the other flower in her window, the sacred vervain'. Ruskin's interest in the symbolism attached to different flowers, which in this case supported Rose's supposed message of comfort to him, was assisted by the botanist and keeper of the herbarium at Kew, Professor Daniel Oliver, to whom the present drawing was given, and was further explored by Ruskin in his book *Proserpina*.

1 Ruskin 1956, III, p. 922
2 Ruskin 1903–12, XXIX, p. 30

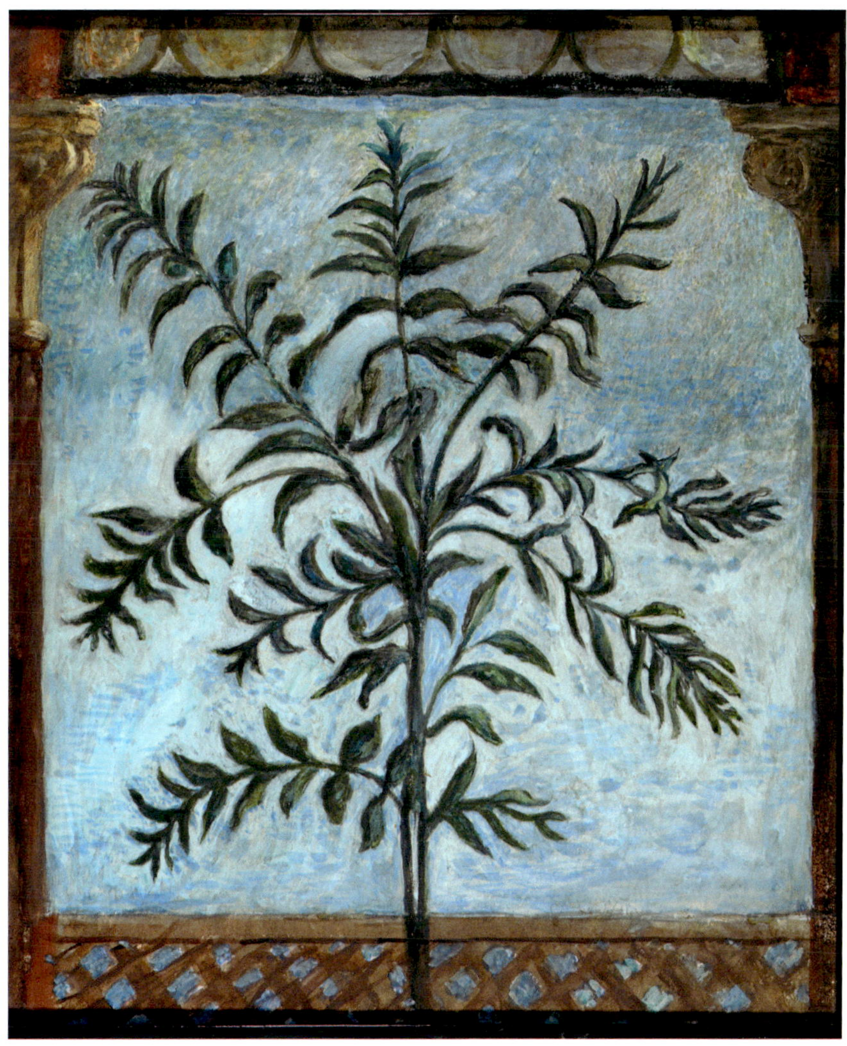

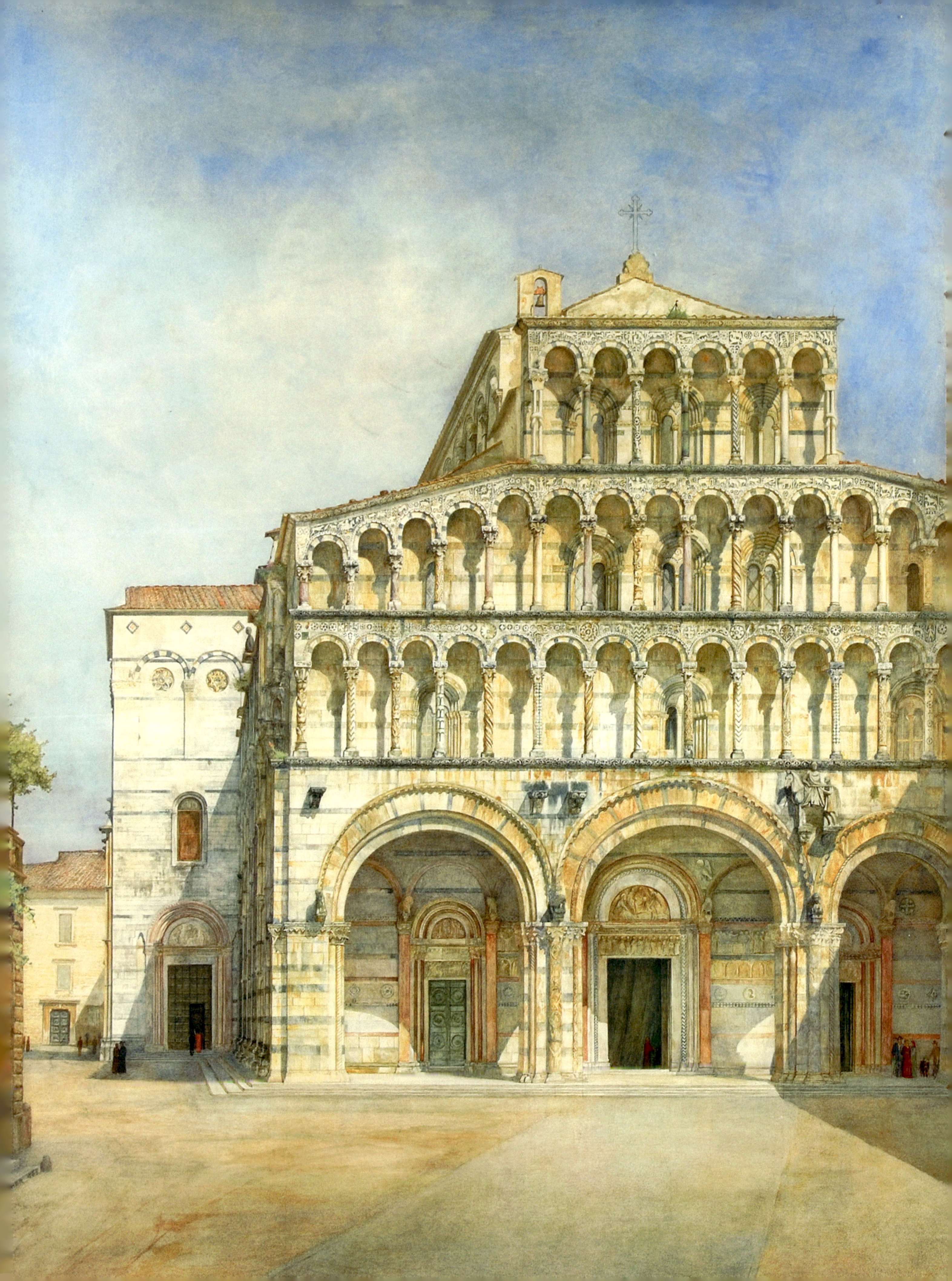

III

RUSKIN'S DISCIPLES IN ITALY

John Ruskin did not regard himself as a professional artist, but instead used draughtsmanship as a most personal means of recording places and things that were important to him. His large collection of daguerreotypes likewise served as a reference library of images with which to support his memory, but on the whole he found drawings – his own and those by other artists – richer and more expressive than photographs.

From the mid-1840s Ruskin was obsessively concerned with the damage that was being done to Italy's architectural heritage, either by outright demolition, or through the destruction brought on by warfare and insurrection (in 1849 his express purpose in going to Venice was to see what injury to the fabric of the city had occurred during the Manin revolt against the Austrians), or – most insidious of all – as a consequence of injudicious restoration. His lifelong project to draw the buildings that he believed were at risk, and to persuade others to do likewise, began as informal recommendations to friends, as for example when he advised G.P. Boyce to see the Scaliger Tombs in Verona in 1854. Later, however, Ruskin's approach became more systematic, and he employed a succession of artists to make drawings of specific buildings and copies of paintings. Much of this material was specifically intended for the two educational institutions he founded: the Drawing School at Oxford (1871) and the Guild of St George at Sheffield (1878).

Ruskin was a hard taskmaster who had very specific ideas about how buildings should be drawn. Artists were expected to concentrate on architecture and decoration, and to avoid incidental detail or peripheral distractions. Furthermore, he required his copyists to approach as closely as they could to the building in view and if possible to treat it square-on, in order to make architectural forms and decoration visible in detail. However, he did not allow his artists to sink into a purely mechanical method of drawing; works were to be lively and vivid, and to convey the artist's emotional response to what was seen. These twin expectations were difficult to reconcile, and, in addition, Ruskin's reactions to the work made on his behalf were coloured by his own fluctuating emotional and mental state.

The principles that governed the Pre-Raphaelite representation of buildings and works of art were in a sense analogous to those which made Pre-Raphaelite figure paintings so distinctive: textures and colours were to be meticulously replicated and facial expressions and gestures were to be explicit and unambiguous.

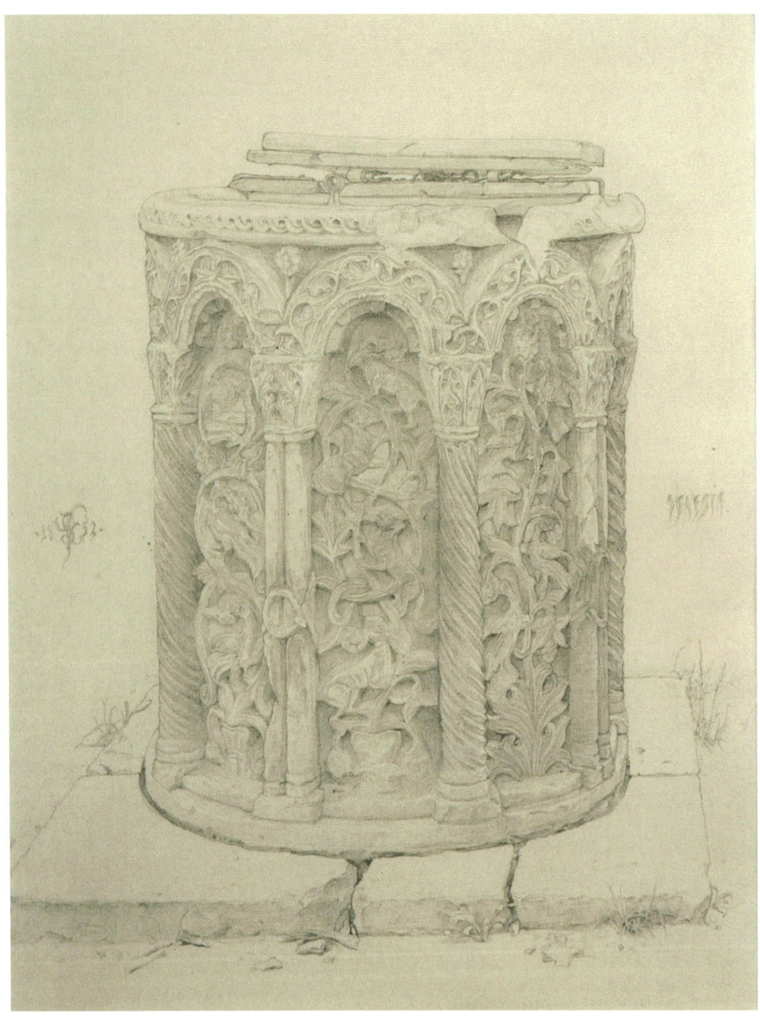

44
Frederic Leighton (1830–1896)
A Byzantine Well-head 1852
Pencil on white paper, 25.4 x 19.3 cm
Signed and dated: *18FL52* and Inscribed: *VENEZIA*
Private collection
Ref: Jones 1996, no. 2

Leighton had a very cosmopolitan artistic education, studying in Paris, Florence, London, and Berlin, but his early drawing style was indebted to his years at the Städelsches Kunstinstitut in Frankfurt, directed by the Nazarene painter, Philip Veit. In August 1852, Leighton left Frankfurt to establish himself in Rome, where he would settle into a studio in the via della Purificazione in November. On the way, he stopped at Venice for several weeks. In a note home to his family in England, he described how 'You are sitting, early in the morning, in a spacious and picturesque court; you have got your sketch-book, and you are busily poring over a drawing of a beautiful old Saracenic well; you are intent on doing it well.' The well was in the courtyard of Palazzo Olivetti, off the Salizzada San Samuel, and Leighton's drawing is one of his earliest set pieces, a tour de force of virtuoso draughtsmanship, dependent not so much on his German training as on his reading of Ruskin. As he wrote about this time, 'I long to find myself again face to face with Nature, to follow it, to watch it, and to copy it, closely, faithfully, ingenuously – as Ruskin suggests, "choosing nothing and rejecting nothing".' Stephen Jones describes the drawing as 'a deliberate exercise in Ruskinian exactitude.'[1] It is not surprising that Ruskin admired the drawing enormously, describing it as 'perfect' and borrowing it as an illustration for his Slade lectures at Oxford in 1883, together with Leighton's most celebrated drawing, the similarly Ruskinian *Study of a Lemon Tree* made at Capri in 1859 (private collection).

1 in Jones 1996, *loc.cit.*

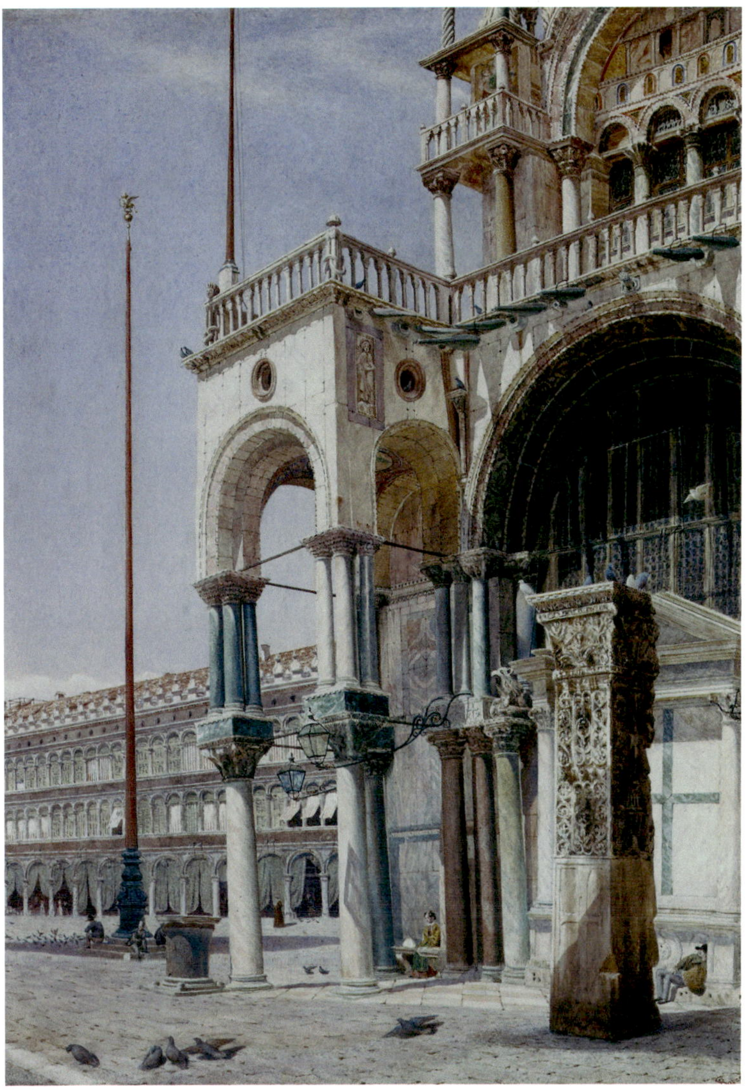

45
George Price Boyce (1826–1897)
St Mark's, Venice: South-west Angle 1854
Watercolour on paper, 54.6 x 38.2 cm
Private collection
Ref: Egerton and Newall 1987, no. 13

During the early 1850s, Boyce met several of the main exponents of the Pre-Raphaelite style: Rossetti and Ford Madox Brown in *c.* 1851, Millais in 1852, and Ruskin in 1854. When Ruskin and his father visited Boyce to examine his collection of watercolours by Rossetti, Ruskin also expressed admiration for Boyce's own landscapes and architectural subjects and, hearing about his projected European tour, volunteered advice on where he should go and what he should paint. In particular, he suggested that, when Boyce was in Venice, he should make careful studies of the exterior of St Mark's in clear daylight and at close range. As he wrote on 14 June 1854: 'I congratulate myself, in the hope of at last seeing a piece of St Mark's done as it ought to be done: [...] it answers precisely to your wishes, as expressed in your note, "*near* subject – good architecture – colour & light & shade".'[1] A fortnight later he recommended that Boyce should apply for permission to ascend to the loggia of the Doge's Palace in order to look down on the south flank of the basilica, a view that he was to treat in a drawing of his own a few years later (**see cat. 28**).

The south-west portico of St Mark's, along with its counterpart at the north end of the façade, had been constructed in the thirteenth century, incorporating materials brought to Venice after the sack of Constantinople during the Fourth Crusade in 1204. Obscured by the St Jean d'Acre column – another piece of war booty – is the Porta da Mar, the former entrance to the basilica from the sea, which was walled up in 1501 to create the Zen Chapel. Ruskin felt passionately about St Mark's, reflecting on the spirituality and creative invention that was more evident in 'a single angle of that church than would serve to build a modern cathedral'.[2] He was also desperately anxious about the destructive restoration and by the threat of wholesale reconstruction. In 1845 he wrote to his father: 'I am barely in time to see the last of dear old St Mark's. They have ordered him to be "pulito" [...] off go all the glorious old weather stains, the rich hues of the marbles which nature, mighty as she is, has taken two centuries to bestow, and already the noble corner farthest from the sea – that on which the sixth part of the age of the generations of man was dyed in gold – is reduced to the colour of magnesia – the old marbles displaced and torn down'. His own drawings of St Mark's and those that he encouraged others to make were intended both as a record of the building and as a means of allowing the beauty of its historical fabric to be better and more widely known.

1 Boyce 1980, p. 119
2 Ruskin 1903–12, IV, p. 307

46

George Price Boyce

San Giorgio Maggiore from the Piazzetta, Venice – Moonlight 1854

Watercolour on paper, 18.7 x 28 cm

Signed in monogram and dated 54; Signed in monogram and dated on *verso*, *Venice – Aug. 54 – GPB;* Inscribed on the mount, *San Giorgio Maggiore from the Piazzetta, Venice. Aug. 1854* and on the *verso* of the mount, *Moonlight sketch of San Giorgio Maggiore from the Piazzetta – Venice GPBoyce Aug 1854 sketched by lantern light*

The Trustees of the British Museum

Ref: Egerton and Newall 1987, no. 17; Staley and Newall 2004, no. 127

While Boyce was staying in Venice in the summer and early autumn of 1854, he made a number of small, informal studies of unexpected views. Earlier in the year, on 21 April 1854, when he met Ruskin, he recorded in his diary: 'He was very and pleasant and encouraging in manner' but, 'on my expressing my liking for after sunset and twilight effects, he said I must not be led away by them, as, on account of the little light requisite for them, they were easier of realization than sunlight effects.'[1] In a spirit of independence, perhaps of defiance, Boyce painted several exquisite nocturnal effects. **cat. 46** was taken from the bench that surrounds Sansovino's Loggetta and shows the south-west corner of the Ducal Palace as well as the columns of St Mark and St Theodore and the distant San Giorgio. The real subject of the drawing, however, is the moonlight effect.

After the so-called Manin revolution in 1848 and its suppression by Austrian troops in the following year, Venice returned to a state of subjugation. Social conditions were bad and few tourists visited the city. Boyce's watercolour shows the railings installed by the Austrians to close the arcade of the Doge's Palace to provide a sentry position. It also shows the cannon placed at the south-west corner of the building, which represented both a symbol and the reality of the foreign occupation, and which was commented upon with smouldering resentment by residents and visitors alike. More positively, the Austrian authorities had made attempts before and after the revolution to improve the infrastructure of the city, by constructing a causeway and improving street lighting. Boyce, characteristically observant, carefully included the gas lamps in the Piazzetta which had been denounced by Ruskin as 'grand new iron posts of the last Birmingham fashion'.[2]

1 Boyce 1980, p.
2 Shapiro 1972, pp. 198–9

47

George Price Boyce

Near the Public Gardens, Venice 1854

Watercolour on paper, 19 x 27.3 cm

Signed and dated, *GPB 54*; Inscribed on *verso*, *Near the public gardens, Venice GP Boyce Sept 1854*

Private collection

Ref: Egerton and Newall 1987, no. 16

This is one of the most beautiful of Boyce's informal studies of Venice made in 1854. The restrained palette and fluent technique seem to some scholars to anticipate Whistler. The view, with buildings seen 'end on', and sailing ship moored in the lagoon, is wholly original, although the shimmering effects in the sky and water perhaps owe something to a slightly older generation of watercolour artists such as John Linnell or Samuel Palmer. It probably shows the angle of the Riva dei sette martiri and the widest street in Venice, now called Via Giuseppe Garibaldi.

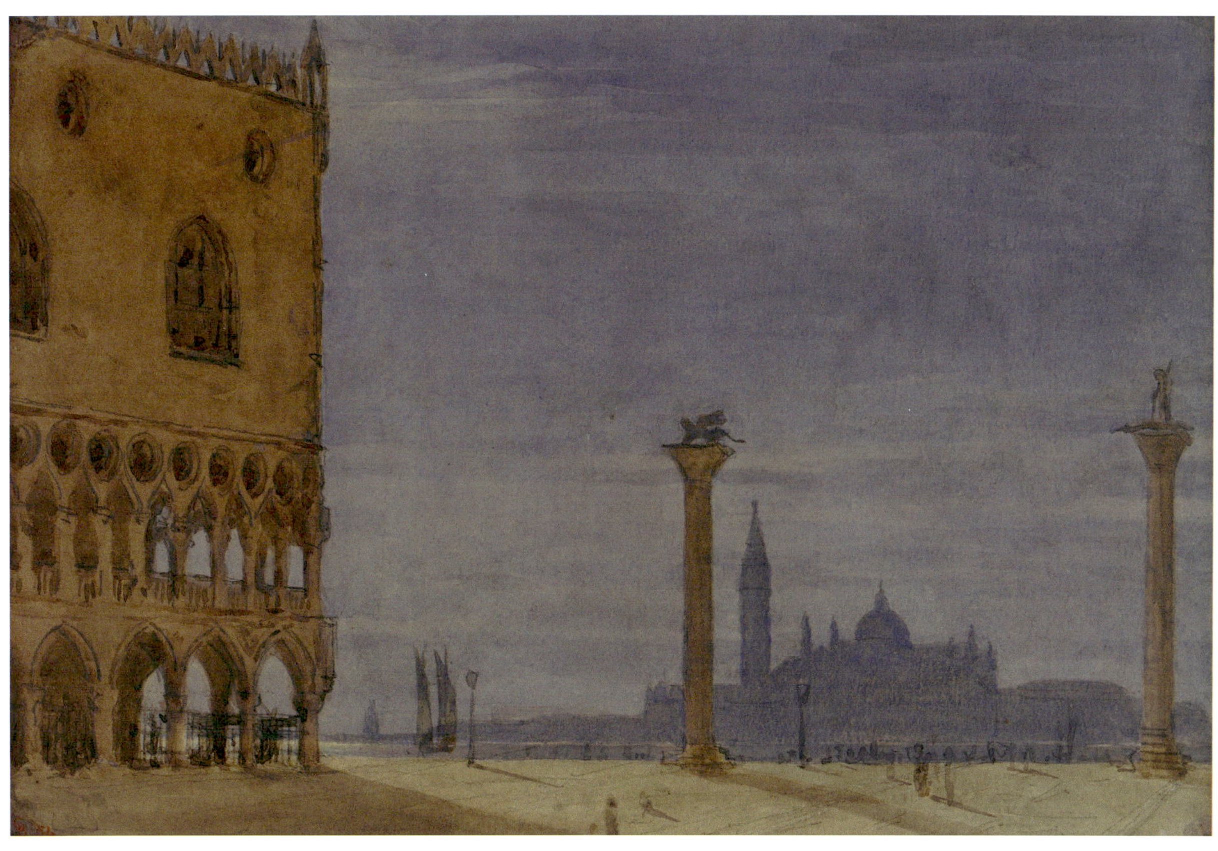

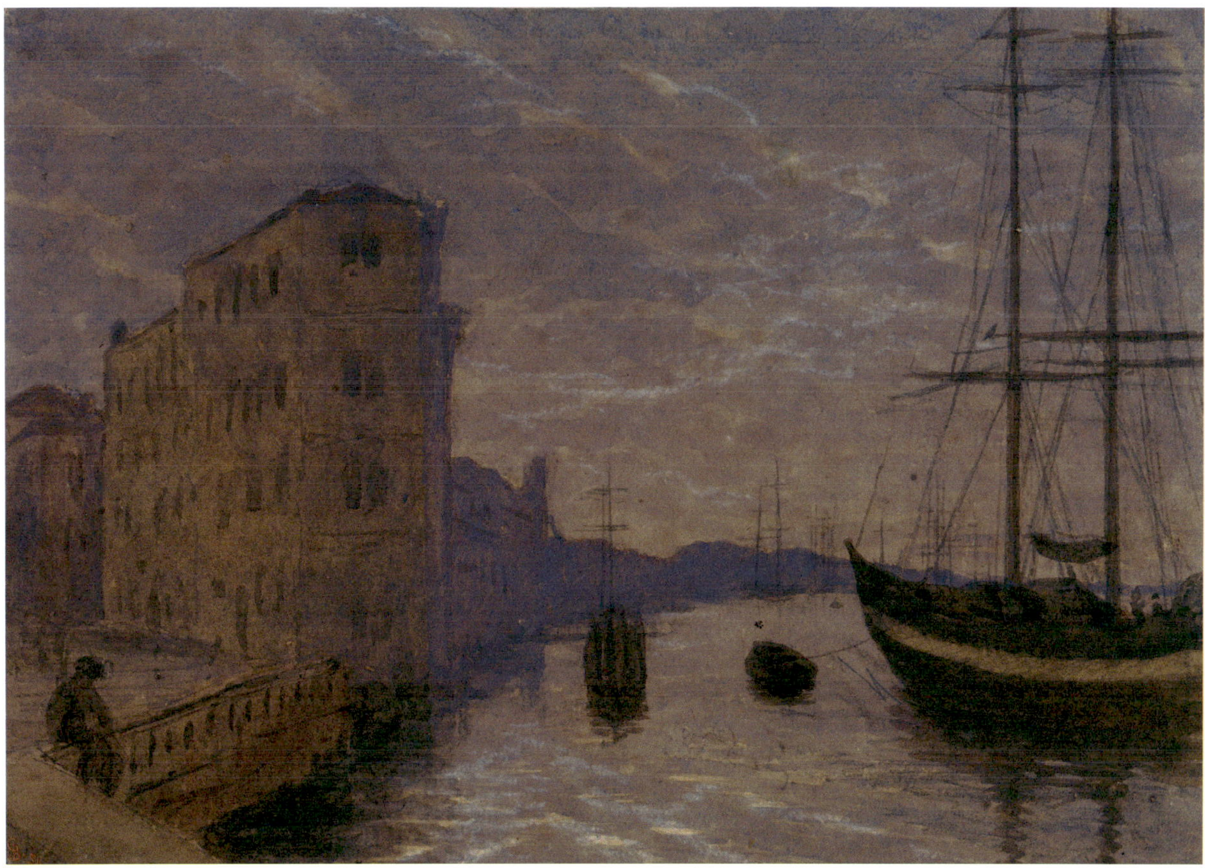

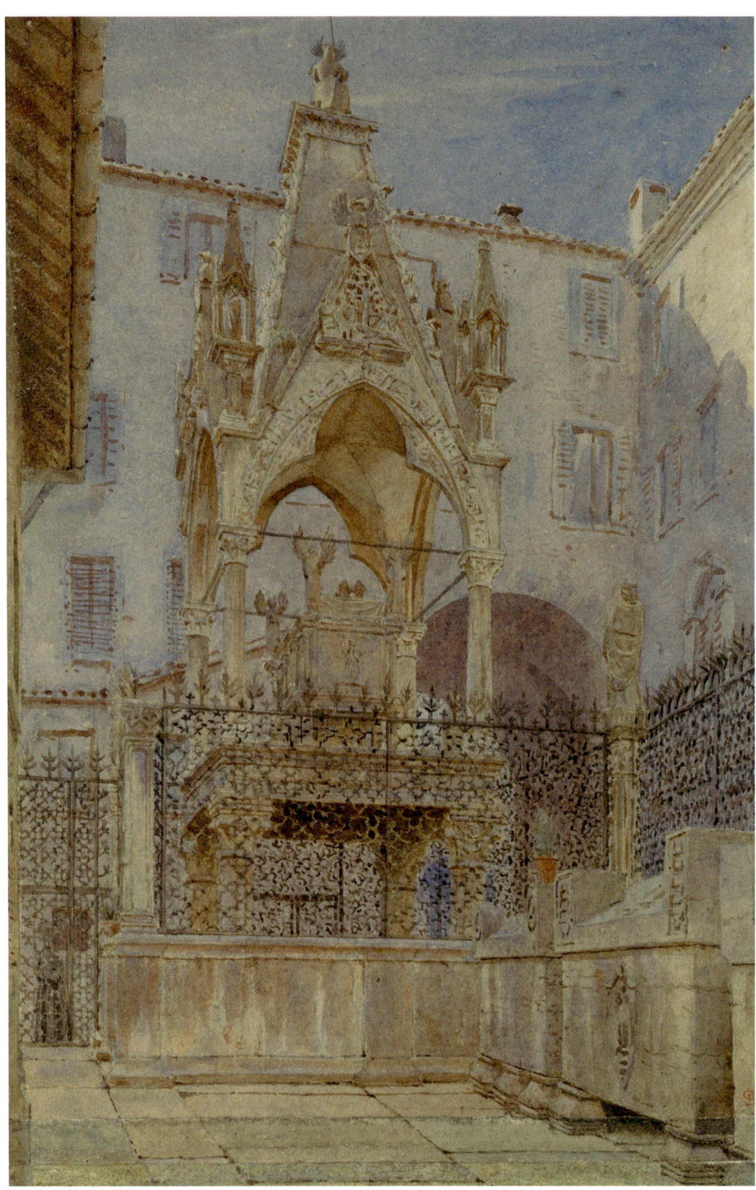

48
George Price Boyce
Tomb of Mastino II della Scala 1854
Watercolour on paper, 39.4 x 27 cm
Private collection
Ref: Egerton and Newall 1987, no. 19; Staley and Newall 2004, no. 57

Boyce went on from Venice to Verona at the end of 1854, following Ruskin's recommendation that 'after you have done with St Marks [you should] quit the Venetian canals, and to make a most careful study of the Porch of the *Duomo* of Verona, which in its Gryphon sculpture, is the finest thing I know in North Italy – while, of course – the little group of the Scala Monuments is altogether unrivalled *in the world* for sweet colour & light and shade; and in these times, there is no knowing how long it may stand'.[1] The present drawing, taken from a vantage point within the enclosure of iron railings that forms the small cemetery, shows the monument to Mastino II della Scala, who died in 1351. The autumnal sun lights up the tops of the surrounding buildings.

1 quoted in Boyce 1980, p.119

49
Sir Edward Burne-Jones (1833–1898)
Copy after the 'Allegory of the Battle of Lepanto' by Paolo Veronese 1862
Pencil and black chalk on paper, 24 x 28.6 cm
Ashmolean Museum, University of Oxford.
Ruskin School Collection (Ref. 140)
Ref: Christian 1975, p. 335

Ruskin sponsored Burne-Jones's two early visits to Italy, in the autumn of 1859 and the spring of 1862. In return for Ruskin's generosity, Burne-Jones had undertaken to make copies of paintings and frescoes under his direction. Whereas the drawings from the first trip are generally brief notations made for Burne-Jones's own benefit, those deriving from the second are generally larger and more formal, and were deliberately done to fulfil Ruskin's need for documentary accounts of works of art that he feared might be deteriorating or otherwise at risk.

Ruskin accompanied Burne-Jones and his wife Georgiana part of the way on the second trip. They went out through Paris and Switzerland, and arrived at Milan on 31 May. Burne-Jones and his wife then went on to Venice for several weeks, where Ruskin joined them in mid-July. Burne-Jones made a number of copies for Ruskin, of which this drawing, which he described as 'a little head of Paolo in the Ducal Palace', was the first. It shows the angel holding the olive branches together with Christ's left hand, in Veronese's *Allegory of the Battle of Lepanto* in the Sala del Collegio of the Palazzo Ducale, which Ruskin later called 'an unrivalled Paul Veronese'. Burne-Jones described his drawing to Ruskin as one of 'four rotten little sketches', but confessed that he was pleased with the result, 'so much more faithful than those I did under your eye'. In fact, Burne-Jones's drawing bore so strongly the artist's own mannerisms, that Ruskin mistakenly described it not as a copy after Veronese, but as an original study for *The Days of Creation*, one of a series of compositions of the 1870s also used as designs for stained glass.

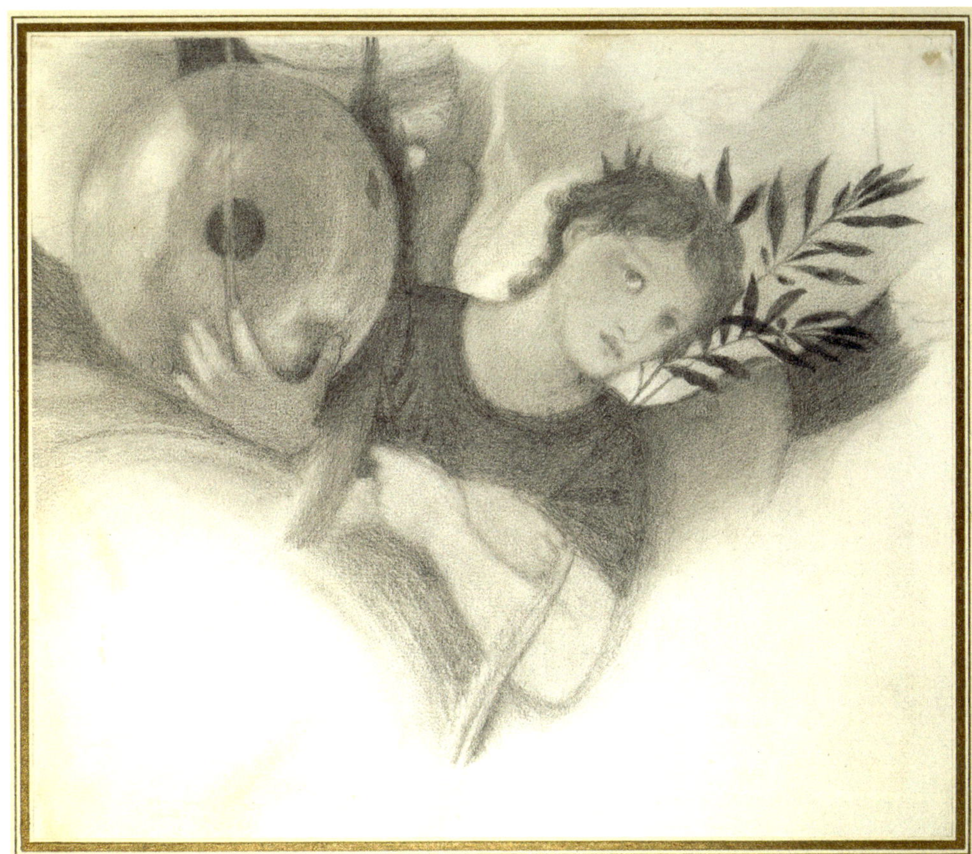

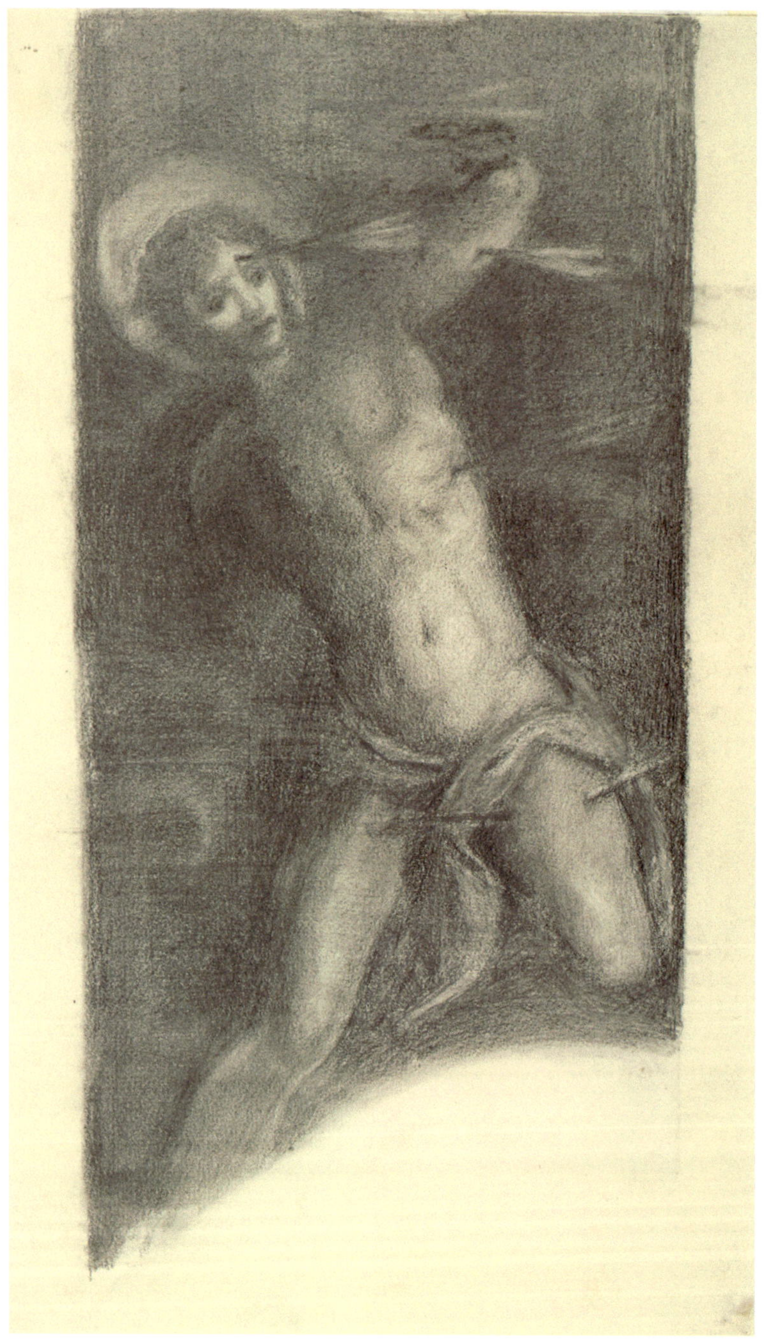

50
Sir Edward Burne-Jones (1833–1898)
Study of Tintoretto's 'Saint Sebastian' in the Scuola Grande di San Rocco probably 1862
Black chalk and Pencil on paper, 32.1 x 19.4 cm
Ashmolean Museum, University of Oxford.
Ruskin School Collection (Ref. 139)
Ref: Christian 1975, p. 335

It is usually assumed that the series of drawings and watercolours Burne-Jones made of details from paintings by Tintoretto in the Scuola Grande di San Rocco in Venice date from his second journey to Italy, in 1862.

Tintoretto's *St Sebastian* occupies the right-hand compartment of the back wall of the Upper Hall of the Scuola di San Rocco, and was, like the pendant figure of St Roch, painted in *c.* 1578–81. The saint is seen naked apart from a loin-cloth; his powerful body is twisted and seems to sway as arrows rain down upon him and pierce his flesh. Burne-Jones was increasingly interested in the representation of the musculature of male bodies in the 1860s, drawing from antique sculpture as well as from paintings, and paying particular attention to the art of Michelangelo. Ruskin became increasingly disapproving of the direction his erstwhile disciple was taking, which would lead in due course to works such as *The Wine of Circe* (private collection) and *Phyllis and Demophoön* (Birmingham Museums and Art Gallery).

51
Sir Edward Burne-Jones
Copy after Tintoretto's 'The Circumcision'
probably 1862
Watercolour and bodycolour on paper, 18.1 x 24 cm
Ashmolean Museum, University of Oxford.
Ruskin School Collection (Ed. 225)
Ref: Christian 1975, p. 335

Like the copy of Saint Sebastian (**cat. 50**), this watercolour was probably made during Burne-Jones's stay in Venice in 1862. Ruskin gave it to his Drawing School in Oxford, and praised it for showing 'the value of subdued tints in pale colour', as well as giving an 'idea of the subdued tones of dark colour employed in the higher schools of the Venetians after their complete acceptance of chiaroscuro as a collateral power'.[1]

1 Ruskin 1903–12. XXI, p. 140

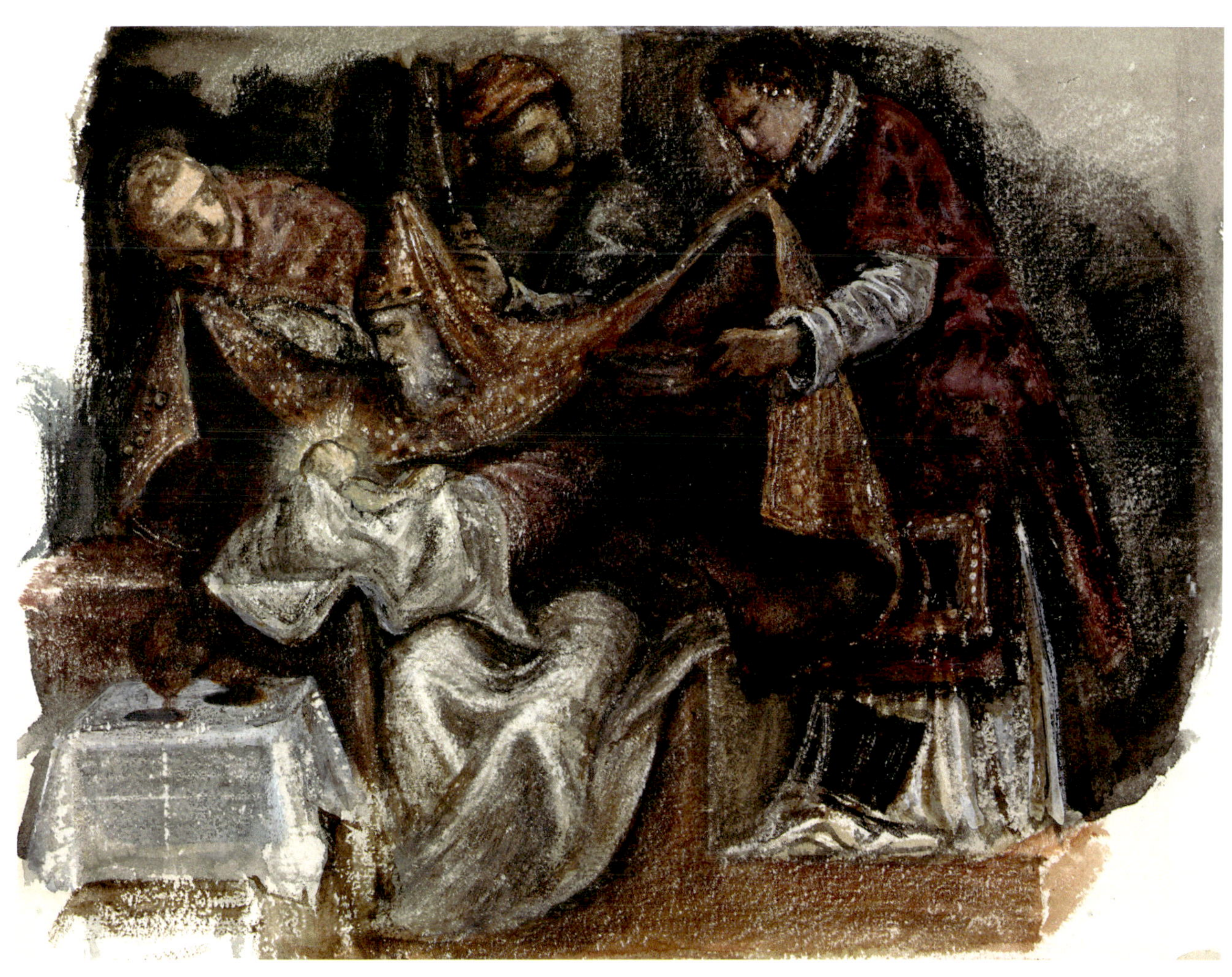

52

Sir Edward Burne-Jones

Copies after Bernardino Luini's 'Saint Apollonia' and 'Saint Agatha' 1862

Watercolour over Pencil on paper, 37.5 x 25 cm and 32.5 x 21 cm

Inscribed on the original frame: *E BURNE-JONES / FECIT*

Royal Institution of Cornwall, Royal Museum of Cornwall, Truro

Ref: Wildman and Christian 1998–9, no. 20

While still in Venice, Burne-Jones received a letter from Ruskin announcing that he was making an actual size copy of Bernardino Luini's *St Catherine* in the church of San Maurizio,[1] and reminding him that he had also agreed to make copies there. In her reminiscences, Georgiana Burne-Jones recalled 'the "Monasterio" to which we went in Milan, with Mr Ruskin, to see Luini's pictures … was a large church that had been used as a military hospital during the Franco-Sardinian War with Austria, and still bore marks of rough usage'. She then quoted from a letter in which her husband described the difficulties he faced: 'I am drawing from a fresco that has never been seen since the day it was painted, in jet darkness, in a chapel where candlesticks, paper flowers and wooden dolls abound freely. Ruskin, by treacherous smiles and winning courtesies and delicate tips, has wheedled the very candlesticks off the altar for my use […] and I draw every day now by the light of eight altar candles; also a fat man stands at the door and says the church is shut if anybody comes'.[2] Luini's frescoes in the convent hall were painted in 1522–4 for Alessandro Bentivoglio. Saints Apollonia and Lucy appear on the left wall, and Saints Catherine and Agatha on the right. Burne-Jones's copy therefore shows one from each of Luini's pairs of saints. Luini's figures are identified by their attributes: Apollonia, deaconess of Alexandria, with the pincers used to wrench out her teeth, and Agatha holding a shallow dish containing her breasts. Oddly, Burne-Jones carefully omits Agatha's attribute, so that the dish she is holding appears to be empty.

The Milanese artist Bernardino Luini (fl. 1512–died 1532) was known in Britain in the period from his *Christ among the Doctors*, which was part of the bequest of the Revd Holwell Carr to the National Gallery in 1831. Later, in *Modern Painters* volume II, published in 1845, Ruskin included him in a list of five artists 'despised until I spoke of them, – Turner, Tintoret, Luini, Botticelli, and Carpaccio'.[3] In the early 1860s the Arundel Society was considering the feasibility of issuing an edition of chromolithographs of Luini's frescoes, which probably accounted for Ruskin's particular interest in the artist in 1862. A few years later, Ruskin praised Luini's work in *The Cestus of Aglaia* (published as nine papers of the Laws of Art in 1865 and 1866): 'He is the only man who entirely united the religious temper which was the spirit-life of art, with the physical power which was its bodily life […] ten times greater than Leonardo; – a mighty colourist, […] Luini has left nothing behind him that is not lovely'.[4]

1 now in the Ashmolean Museum, Ruskin School Collection; see Hewison 1996, no. 19

2 Burne-Jones 1904, I, p. 248

3 Ruskin 1903–12, IV, p. 355

4 Ruskin 1903–12, XIX, p. 130

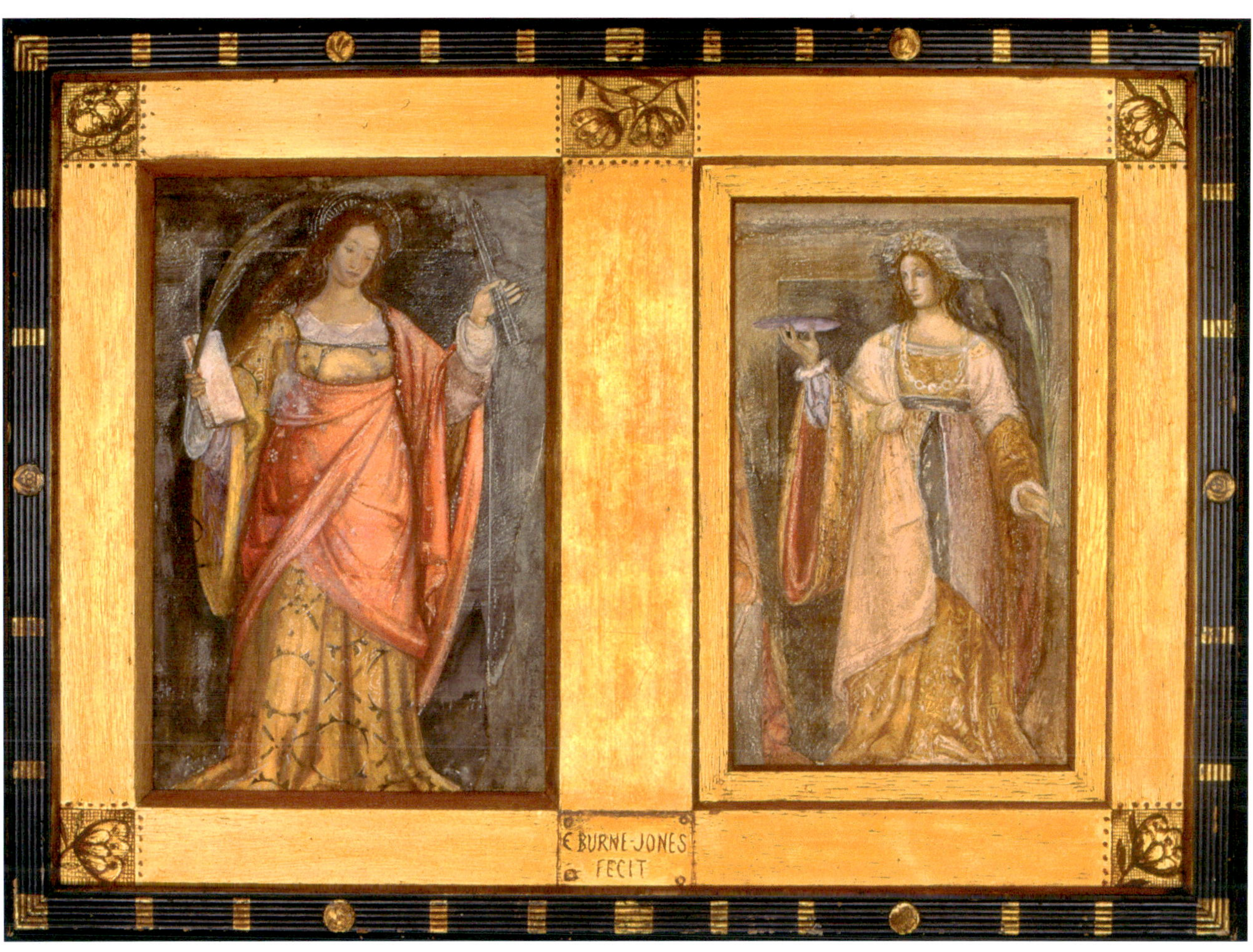
E BURNE-JONES
FECIT

53
Sir Edward Burne-Jones
A Dream of the Nine Muses 1871
Bodycolour on canvas, varnished, 27 x 35.5 cm
Lent by the Syndics of the Fitzwilliam Museum, Cambridge. Bequeathed by Sir Sidney Colvin through the National Art Collections Fund, 1927

Burne-Jones's third visit to Italy took place in September 1871, shortly after he had taken personally Ruskin's damning criticism of Michelangelo's work as 'an attempt to execute something beyond his power, coupled with a fevered desire that his power may be acknowledged.'[1] Lady Burne-Jones described the trip as 'a real homecoming after his nine years of absence.' He visited Rome for the first time, and was disappointed, but 'the landscape of Italy was his lasting delight, especially in the volcanic regions where hills rose suddenly from the plain and cities grew out of the hills.' She records the circumstances surrounding the creation of *A Dream of the Nine Muses*: 'On his way to Rome, between Monte Fiascone and Viterbo, Edward fell asleep and had a dream of the nine Muses on Mount Helicon, so distinct that he drew it on awaking.'[2] The subject is unusual in the nineteenth century, and Burne-Jones's evocation of the austere landscape of Boeotia very different from earlier depictions of the lush green hills animated with classical temples. Here, in a rather stylised landscape surely inspired by the Sienese masters of the Quattrocento, notably Giovanni di Paolo, the muses are not individually identified, but are distributed to decorative effect around the well-spring.

1 Ruskin 1903–12, XXII, p. 87
2 Burne-Jones 1904, II, pp. 24–5

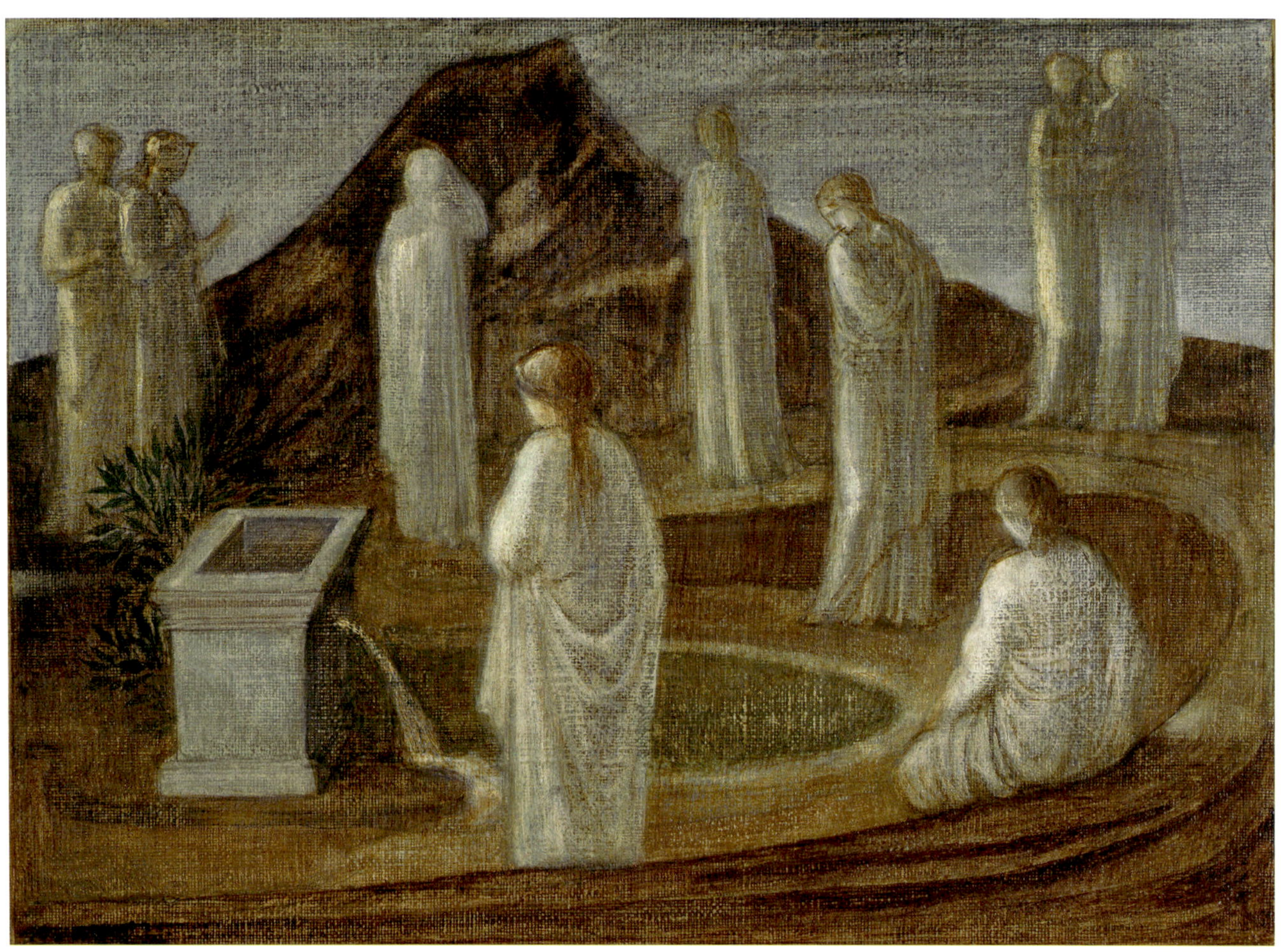

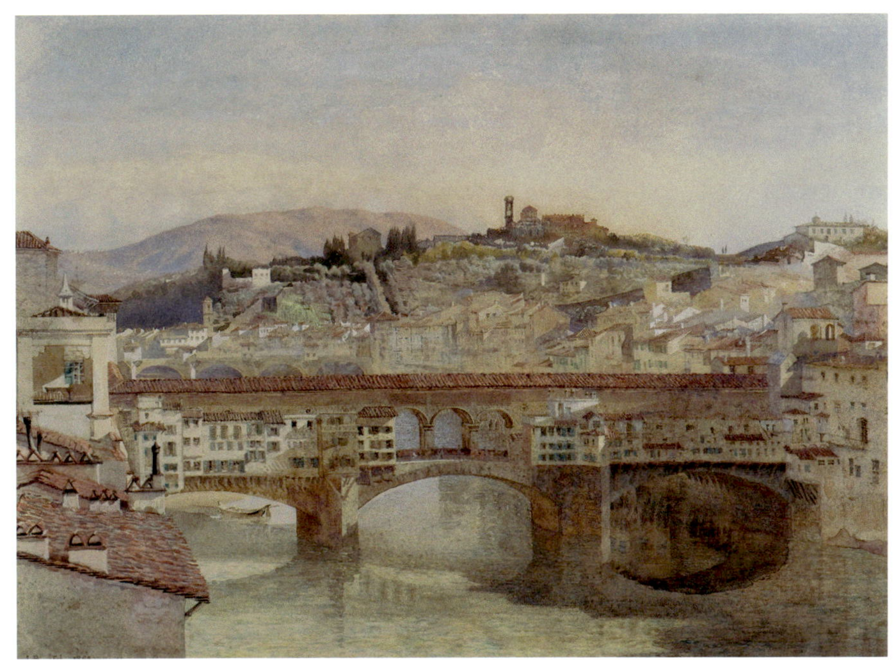

54
John Brett (1831–1902)
The Ponte Vecchio, Florence 1862
Watercolour on paper, 21.6 x 29.2 cm
Signed and dated: *J.B. Feb. 1862*
Private collection
Ref: Payne 2010, pp. 70–72 and cat. no. 407

Brett shared many of Ruskin's interests, including geology and the physical sciences, and in 1860 Ruskin described him as 'one of my keenest-minded friends'.[1] Later, their relationship broke down: as Ruskin wrote in 1865, 'I will associate with no man who does not more or less accept my own estimate of myself. For instance, Brett told me, a year ago, that a statement of mine respecting a scientific matter (which I knew à fond before he was born) was "bosh". I told him in return he was a fool; he left the house, and I will not see him again "until he is wiser"'.[2]

Following an Alpine tour in the summer and autumn of 1861, Brett travelled to Florence, where he spent the winter. This watercolour was drawn from the rooftop of his lodgings on the Lungarno close to the Ponte Sta Trìnita in February 1862. The view is towards the east, with the Ponte Vecchio as the focus of the drawing, with the Ponte alle Grazie beyond, and the gabled façade and campanile of S. Miniato breaking the horizon at the centre right.

Brett returned to London in March 1862. Shortly afterwards, he attended a breakfast party with a friend, Arthur Munby, who recorded Brett's view that 'the old nobility and even the professional classes are awed and crushed by mob rule; that the lawlessness is as great as ever, and the unity no nearer'. However, Brett praised 'the Pope's government and holds Louis Napoleon to be an unselfish hero'. These were most unusual attitudes for an Englishman; most regarded the papacy as an obstruction to the cause of Italian unification, while Emperor Napoleon III's imperial ambitions within Europe were the object of widespread resentment and even alarm. Brett was probably being deliberately perverse, as Munby concluded for, despite being 'able and intelligent [...] his love of paradox and his chivalrous proud devotion – self-opinionated too – to unpopular causes [are] very pleasantly provoking'.[3]

A year later, in February 1863, *The Ponte Vecchio, Florence* was purchased by Ruskin's father, John James Ruskin, for 30 guineas. Ruskin senior later remained on good terms with Brett, offering professional support even when Brett saw little or nothing of John Ruskin himself.

1 Ruskin 1903–12, VII, p. 360
2 Ruskin 1903–12, XXXVI, pp. 493–4
3 quoted in Payne 2010, p. 72

55 (a and b)
John Brett
Two Studies for 'Val d'Aosta'
Watercolour over pencil, heightened with white and with gum arabic on paper, 24.5 x 19.5 cm
Watercolour and bodycolour on paper, 16.5 x 25.4 cm
Private collection of Lord Lloyd-Webber
Lit: London 2003, no. 105–7; Newall 2007; Payne 2010, pp. 45–8, and cat. nos. 274–5, 287

In his Academy Notes for 1858, Ruskin wrote of Brett's *The Stonebreaker*: 'If he can paint so lovely a distance from the Surrey downs and railway traversed vales, what would he not make of the chestnut groves of the Val d'Aosta!' Brett took up the suggestion, and spent nearly five months painting in and near the Val d'Aosta between June and November 1858, working on the *Val d'Aosta* he intended to present at the Royal Academy in the following year. During that time, he took the opportunity of visiting Ruskin at Turin, but there seems little truth in the traditional assumption that Ruskin effectively collaborated in the conception and execution of Brett's painting. Indeed, certain parts are decidedly unpalatable to Ruskin, as he later acknowledged. Brett took considerable pains to choose his vantage point, which, as Newall has established, was from the Mont Torretta, looking down over the castle and village of Saint Pierre towards the Testa del Rutor and Monte Paramont, with the Rutor glacier at the far left on the horizon. The preparatory sketches and watercolours show that he considered a view from lower down the Mont Torretta, which included the prominent landmarks of the castle of Saint Pierre (where Brett was lodging) and the Castel d'Argent, visible in Cat. 54. Both were carefully omitted from the finished painting, for Brett was less interested in the historical associations of the site, than in its geological structure. He was still deeply religious, and Payne has argued that the sleeping girl prominent in the foreground should be interpreted as a symbol of fallen humanity in a beautiful landscape. Newall, however, has associated the painting with a passage in Ruskin's *Modern Painters* volume IV, in which he describes 'The Mountain Gloom', an apparently idyllic landscape populated by peasants downtrodden by the Roman Catholic church. Ruskin chose to ignore any symbolic meaning, and, when the picture was exhibited at the Royal Academy in 1859, instead praised the depiction of 'what a Piedmontese valley is like in July', but criticised it as 'Mirror's work, not Man's'. *Val d'Aosta* failed to sell, and, perhaps out of guilt, Ruskin himself bought it.

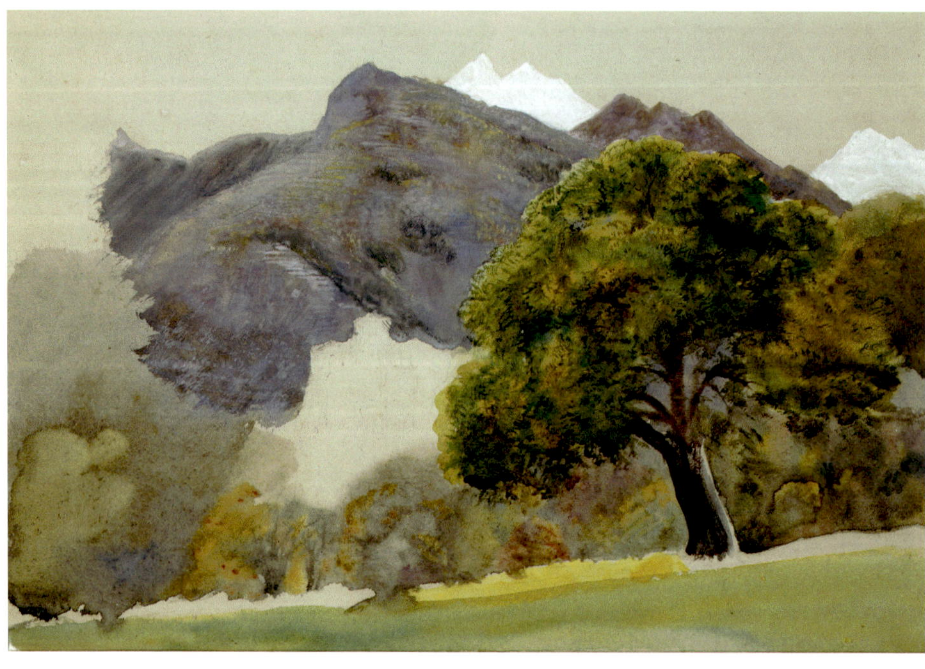

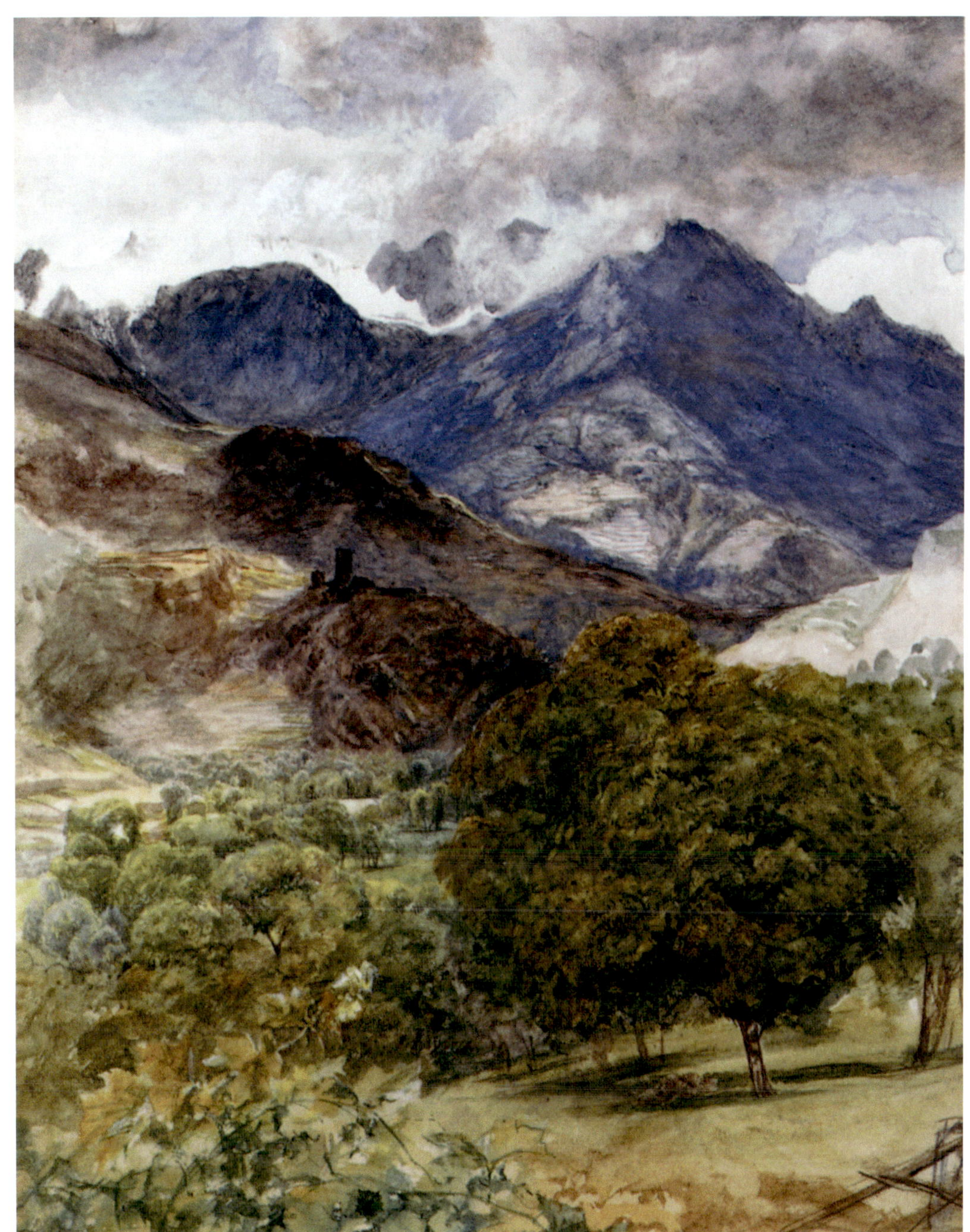

56
John Brett
Florence from Bellosguardo 1863
Oil on canvas, 60 x 101.3 cm
Tate. Presented by Thomas Stainton in memory of Charles and Livinia Handley-Read, 1972
Ref: Staley and Newall 2004 no. 71; Payne 2010, pp. 74–7 and cat. no. 421

John Brett spent the winters of 1861–2 and 1862–3 in Florence. His extraordinary panoramic view of *Florence from Bellosguardo* was painted during the second of these sojourns. In Florence he was welcomed into the literary circle of Isabella Blagden, who had been a friend of Robert Browning when he was living in Florence, and at whose house, the Villa Brichieri at Bellosguardo, Brett may have stayed.

Brett admired and was inspired by the poetry of Robert and Elizabeth Browning, who had lived in Florence since 1845, and where she died in 1861. In a letter of 1863 Brett told Robert Browning that his poem 'Old Pictures in Florence' had 'always floated uppermost in my memory while I was painting the picture and directly determined its character'. Furthermore, he asked whether the following lines from the first and second verses might be appended to the entry in the catalogue of the forthcoming Royal Academy exhibition:

And washed by the morning water-gold,
Florence lay out on the mountain-side.
River and bridge and street and square
Lay mine, as much at my beck and call,
Through the live translucent bath of air,
As the sights in a magic crystal ball.

Browning was happy to give his permission, even allowing Brett to change 'morning' to 'evening' to make the lines compatible with his picture. He went on to recommend his wife's 'Aurora Leigh' (1856) as offering an even more evocative description of the city.

If the inspiration of the painting was in part literary, it remains an astonishing *tour de*

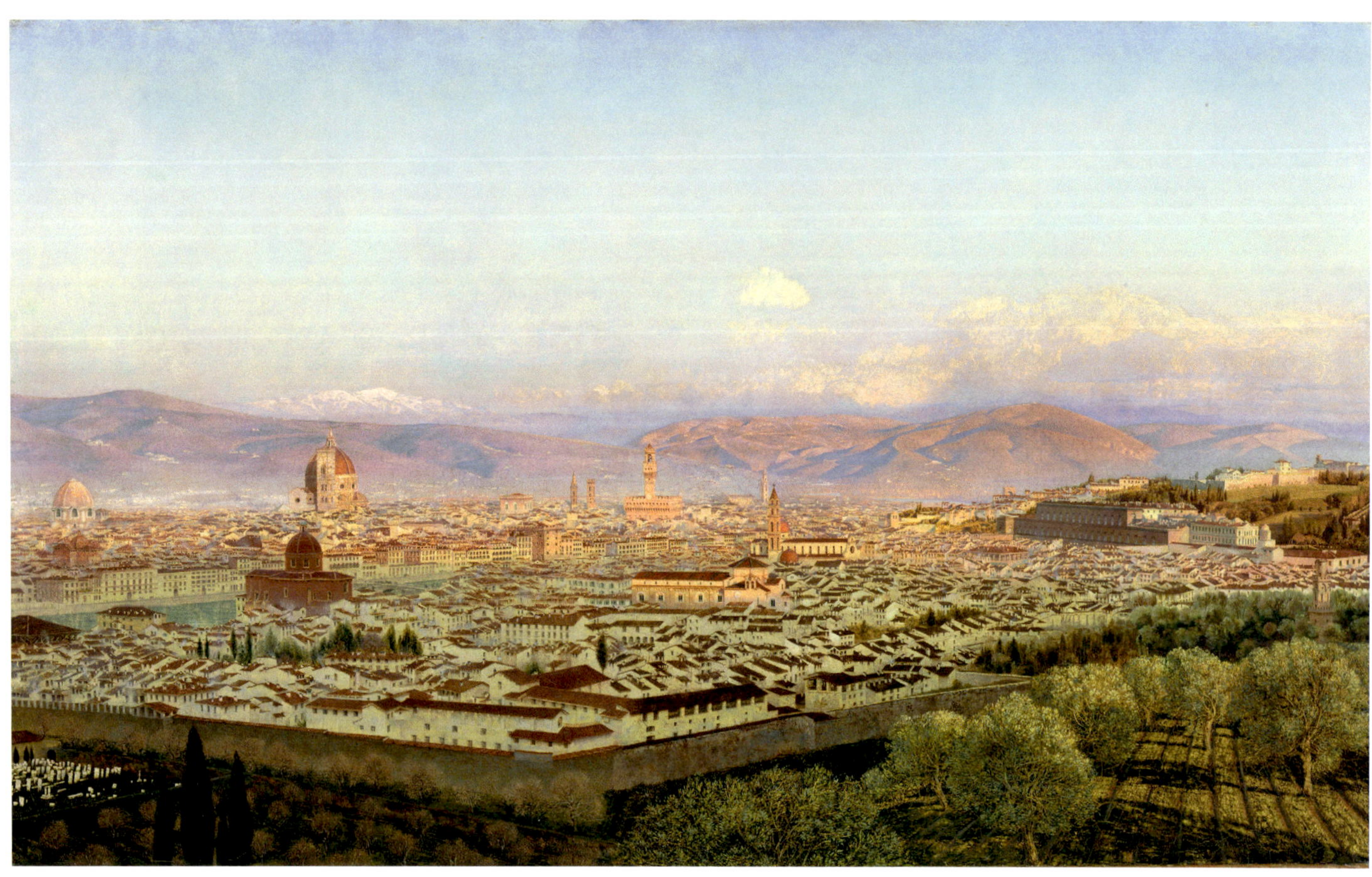

force of topographical observation. The view is taken from the hillside to the north-west of Bellosguardo itself, looking from the Villa Fioravanti (not from the Villa Brichieri, as has previously been suggested).[1] Only from this point are the distant landmarks of the city clearly visible and seen in correct orientation to one another; from left to right, they are the Sagrestia Nuova, the Duomo (its façade not yet ornamented with coloured marbles), the Palazzo Vecchio, Santa Maria del Carmine, Santo Spirito, and the Pitti Palace. Fiesole is visible on the hillside to the north, while the distant Apennines are capped with snow. The multitude of motifs – roofs, walls, and windows spread across the central part of the composition – are drawn together and made visually tantalising by the vibrant texture of repeated pattern and by the rich and glowing atmospheric effect as the winter sun irradiates the scene from low in the sky behind the artist's right shoulder. Brett had a particular propensity for landscape vistas in which the immediate foreground remains suspended, leaving the middle and distant elements to seem unconnected with the vantage point. He enjoyed extraordinarily long sight and seems deliberately to have looked for subjects that lent themselves to being seen at long range. In his view of Florence, as in many of his other works of the 1860s, the viewer experiences a feeling of vertiginous detachment as he inspects a landscape about which so much apparent information is given, but to which there seems to be no opportunity for physical access.

One topographical oddity, indicative of some vague symbolical association in Brett's mind, is the placing of the Jewish cemetery in the left foreground outside the city walls. This seems to have been a deliberate manipulation because the Jewish cemetery in Florence – still operating in the 1860s and then about a century old – was, in fact, within the city boundaries, in the Viale Ludovico Ariosto and close to the Porta San Frediano. In purely visual terms, this departure from strict topographical accuracy works well, with the white gravestones showing brightly out of the shadowed lee of the mediaeval wall and serving as a repoussoir matched by olive groves on the right.

Florence from Bellosguardo and another painting by Brett, *Norbury on the Mole* (Lord Lloyd-Webber), were rejected by the Royal Academy selection committee in 1863. This was seen as a deliberate rebuffal by the artistic establishment of the emergent progressive landscape school, of which Brett was the acknowledged head, and caused much comment both in artistic circles and in the press. Brett was then invited by Holman Hunt to participate in a private exhibition of works rejected by the Academy, to be held at the Cosmopolitan Club in Charles Street in the summer of 1863.[2] However, he preferred to show the two rejected paintings in his own studio in Pump Court in the Temple, causing much resentment within the Pre-Raphaelite circle. *Florence from Bellosguardo* was much admired at Pump Court and promptly sold to the financier and trustee of the National Gallery, Lord Overstone, whose collection included masterpieces by both old and modern masters, among them Claude's *Enchanted Castle* (National Gallery, London).

1 see Staley & Newall 2004, p. 123
2 see McEvansoneya 1996

57
John Brett
Capri in the Evening 1863
Oil on canvas, 55.9 x 139.7 cm
Private collection
Ref: Payne 2010, pp. 86–7 and cat. no. 473

After the considerable scandal surrounding his two submissions to the Royal Academy in 1863, Brett returned to Italy. He travelled by sea from Gravesend, and had arrived at Naples by 9 September 1863. During the winter, he completed two oils which were shown at the Royal Academy in 1864: *Massa, Bay of Naples* (Indianapolis Museum of Art) and *A North-west Squall in the Mediterranean* (untraced), as well as a number of watercolours, notably *Near Sorrento* (Birmingham Museum & Art Gallery). From December 1864, Brett was on Capri, where he was joined by a number of friends. Among them was Georgina Weldon, who recorded in her diary that Brett painted his view of *Capri in the Evening* in the true Pre-Raphaelite method, outdoors. Mrs Weldon, wearing her 'Capri dress', was presumably the model for the figure sitting on the wall in the foreground. The picture was Brett's main submission to the Royal Academy in 1865, where it was rejected. After the success of the previous year, this further rejection is surprising: Payne has suggested that the format of the painting – it is nearly three times as wide as it is high – may have been too unconventional. However, the picture sold easily to Alfred Morrison, who had already bought *Massa, Bay of Naples*, and whose influence possibly persuaded the Royal Academy to accept the view of Capri for the summer exhibition in 1866.

Capri in the Evening shows the setting sun lighting up the Monte Tiberio on the right, and the Punta Campanella on the left, from a spot slightly to the west of the present-day Marina Grande. It was the third in the sequence of pictures painted according to the principles Brett had developed on board ship when he first landed in the Bay of Naples in the previous year, notably in the use of blue turning to green or grey in the shadows. The elongated format contributes greatly to the atmosphere of timeless calm that Brett wished to convey, as do the decorative orange and lemon trees carefully placed in a field of newly sown grain in the foreground.

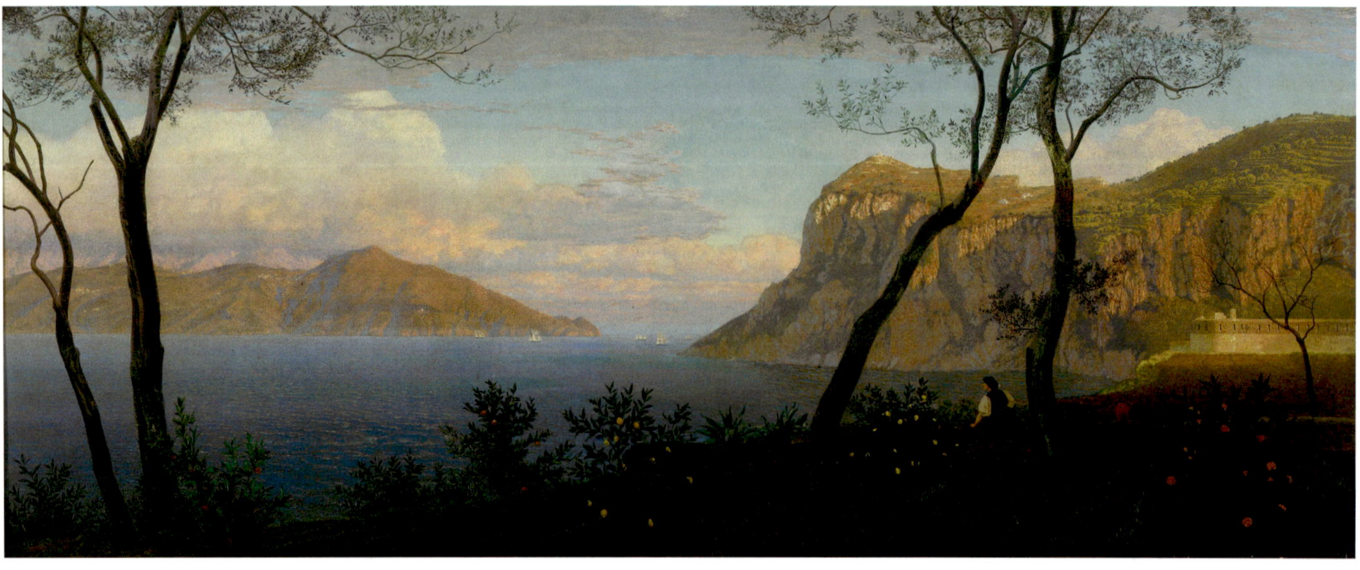

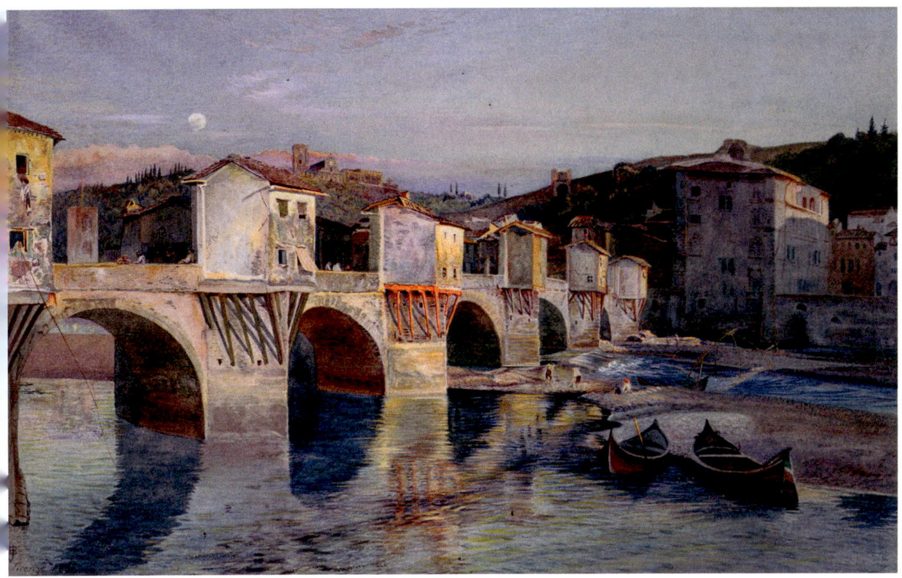

58
John Wharlton Bunney (1828–1882)
Ponte alle Grazie, Florence 1866
Watercolour on paper, 32.3 x 49.5 cm
Signed and dated: *JB 66*
Museums Sheffield
Ref: Staley and Newall 2004, no. 73

Bunney was working as a clerk in the offices of the publisher Smith, Elder & Co when he attended the Working Men's College in London in the period 1855–61. He showed precocious skill as a draughtsman and exhibited a nature study entitled *By the Wayside* at the Royal Academy in 1856. The following year, when participating in the touring exhibition of Pre-Raphaelite art in the United States, he was described in the catalogue as a pupil of both Ruskin and Rossetti. In 1859, Ruskin sponsored Bunney to travel to the Alps to paint and draw Alpine scenery, and in the following year, he employed him for the first time to make copies of works of art in Venice, claiming that it is 'nobler work to preserve other people's great things, than do little things of one's own'.[1] In about 1863, Bunney decided to live permanently in Italy, settling first in Florence, and moving to Venice in 1870. He depended for his precarious livelihood on the sale of landscape and topographical subjects in the London exhibitions, as well as on his work as a copyist. In the late 1870s, he was much involved in the campaign to protect St Mark's from 'restoration', and from 1877 until 1881 he worked on his great oil of the west front of St Mark's, which by his own estimate took him 600 days (although a recent commentator has suggested that this figure should not be taken literally).[2]

Bunney's watercolour of the mediaeval Ponte alle Grazie in Florence shows the bridge from the north bank of the Arno, with the church of S. Miniato on the distant hillside to the south-east. The bridge was constructed on nine arches in 1345 and buildings used as chapels and oratories were gradually added on the piers, overhanging the river and supported by wooden struts, as seen in the drawing. These were demolished in 1876 to allow the bridge to carry a railway line, and the whole structure was destroyed by the retreating German army in August 1944. Although Bunney is thought of principally as a meticulous topographical draughtsman, this work, which was intended for the Royal Academy in 1870 (although apparently not shown), is especially atmospheric, with the warm light of evening reflected in the surface of the river, and the moon rising on the distant horizon. Ruskin ostensibly mistrusted such transient 'effects', but, some years later, he wrote that Bunney's 'pretty drawings of sunsets making me cry with envy'.[3]

1 quoted in Morley 1984, II, p. 33
2 see Bunney 2007
3 quoted in Morley 1984, II, , p. 35

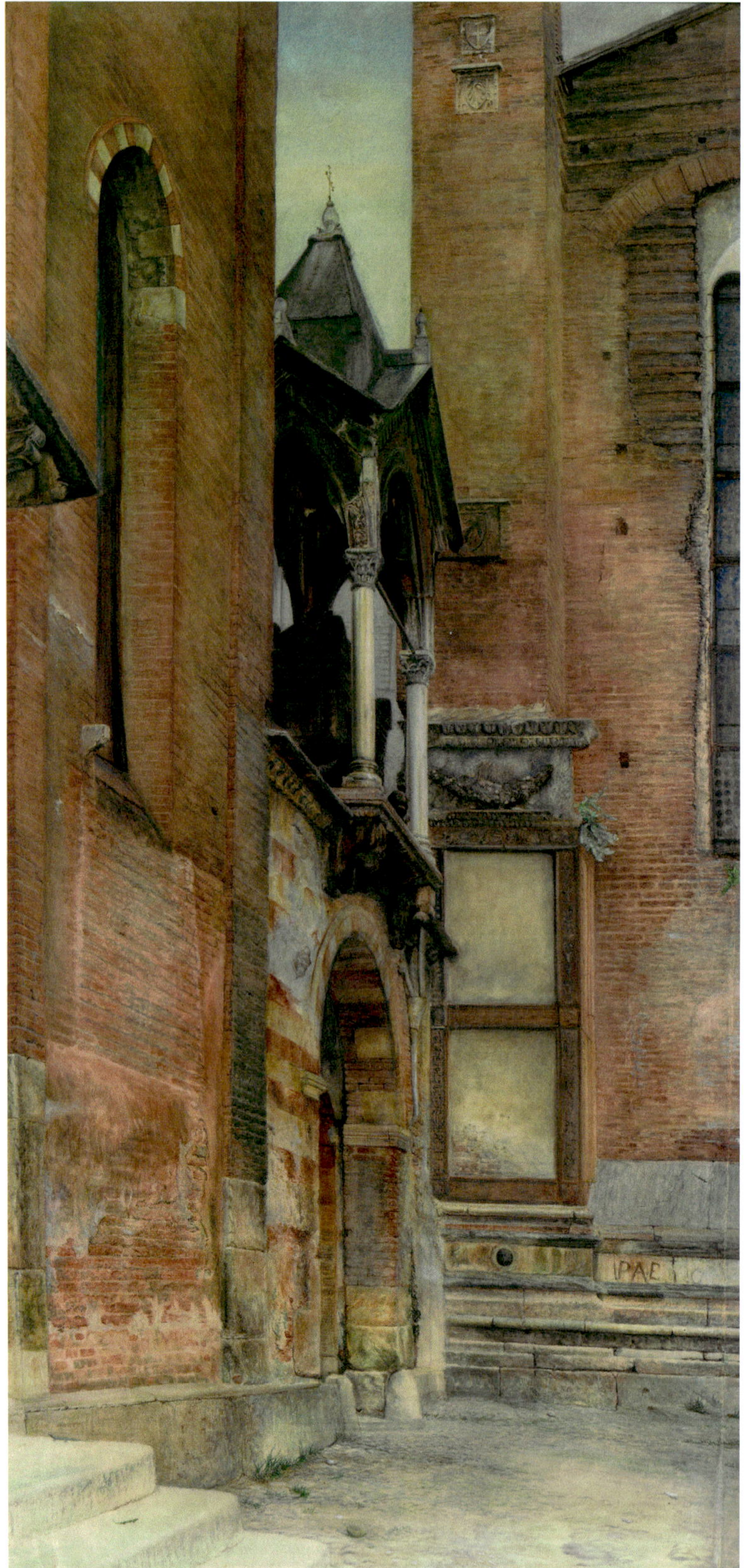

59
John Wharlton Bunney (1828–1882)
Castelbarco Tomb, Verona 1869
Watercolour and bodycolour over Pencil on paper, 98 x 48 cm
Signed and dated: *Verona 1869 John Bunney*
Ashmolean Museum, University of Oxford.
Ruskin School Collection (WAL 6)

Ruskin frequently recommended Verona to friends and artists, and in 1857, he declared that the city 'contains [...] perfect examples of the great twelfth-century Lombardic architecture, which was the root of all the mediæval art of Italy, without which no Giottos, no Angelicos, no Raphaels would have been possible: it contains that architecture, not in rude forms, but in the most perfect and loveliest types it ever attained – contains those, not in ruins, nor in altered and hardly decipherable fragments, but in churches perfect from porch to apse, with all their carving fresh, their pillars firm, their joints unloosened. Besides these, it includes examples of the great thirteenth and fourteenth century Gothic of Italy, not merely perfect, but elsewhere unrivalled.'[1]

Bunney went to Verona to make architectural drawings for Ruskin in September 1868, and remained there until 6 October 1869. When Ruskin joined him in May 1869, they noticed that scaffolding poles had been erected round the Castelbarco tomb and restoration work was about to begin. Ruskin persuaded the authorities to remove the poles so that he and Bunney might record the tomb in its unrestored state. Bunney began this drawing of the tomb on 26 May and had completed it by 15 June. It gives an oblique view of the Gothic canopy of the tomb of Guglielmo di Castelbarco (d. 1320), which stands above the doorway of a suppressed convent at the side of the church of S. Anastasia. Ruskin later incorporated it in his Drawing School at Oxford, describing it as 'a most careful drawing, leaving little to be desired in realization of the subject. It is taken so near the tomb as to make the perspective awkward, but I like this quaint view better than more distant ones.'[2]

1 Ruskin 1903–12, XVI, p. 66
2 Ruskin 1903–12, XIX, p. 453

60

Arthur Burgess (1843–1886)
Sculpted Moulding on Tomb of Mastino II della Scala 1869
Charcoal heightened with white bodycolour on paper, 25.4 x 188 cm
Collection of the Guild of St George, Museums Sheffield (R 140)
Ref: Morley 1984, II, pp. 47–8

Burgess was introduced to Ruskin in 1860, apparently by Octavia Hill, and entrusted with the task of making illustrations both from botanical text books and from specimens to be used in Ruskin's *Proserpina* and other books. Burgess's plates are extraordinarily delicate, and an invaluable complement to Ruskin's texts. In the summer of 1869, Burgess accompanied Ruskin to Verona to make drawings of the Scaliger tombs. As Ruskin remembered in 1887, 'Arthur did everything I wanted of him at Verona in perfectness. He drew the mouldings of the Scala Tombs as never architecture had been drawn before; he collated and corrected my measurements; he climbed where I could not; and at last made a model in clay of every separate stone in the Castelbarco Tomb, showing that without any cement the whole fabric stood on its four pillars with entire security'.[1]

Cat. 60 is one of Burgess's meticulously scaled charcoal studies of details of the Scaliger tombs. Some of them were used to illustrate Ruskin's lecture on 'Verona and its Rivers', given in February 1870. The usefulness of these large drawings in the lecture hall was what presumably encouraged Ruskin to arrange for Burgess to be permanently employed at Oxford to make diagrams and display boards in connection with his Slade lectures.

1 Ruskin 1903–12, XIV, p. 351

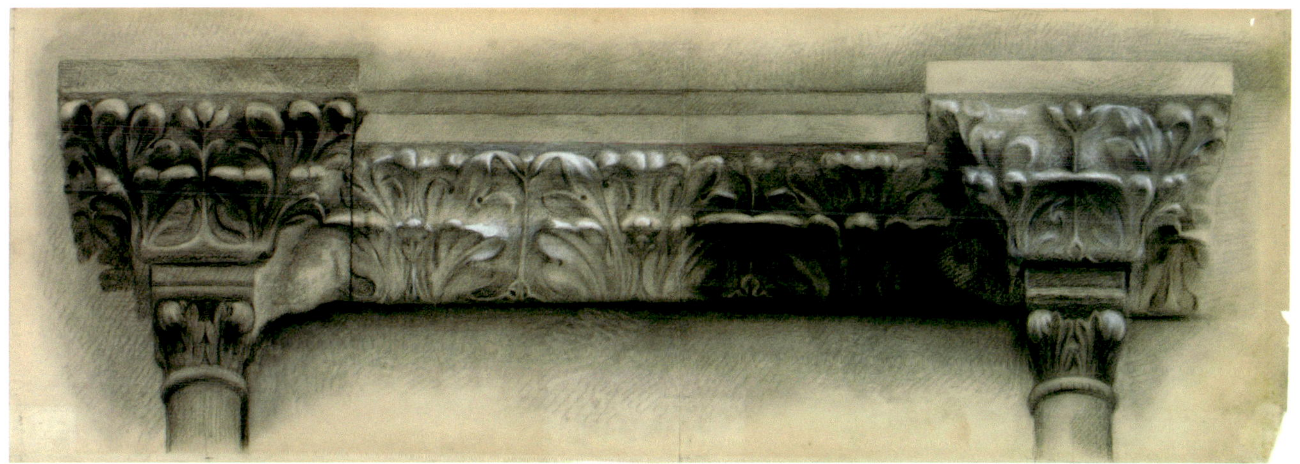

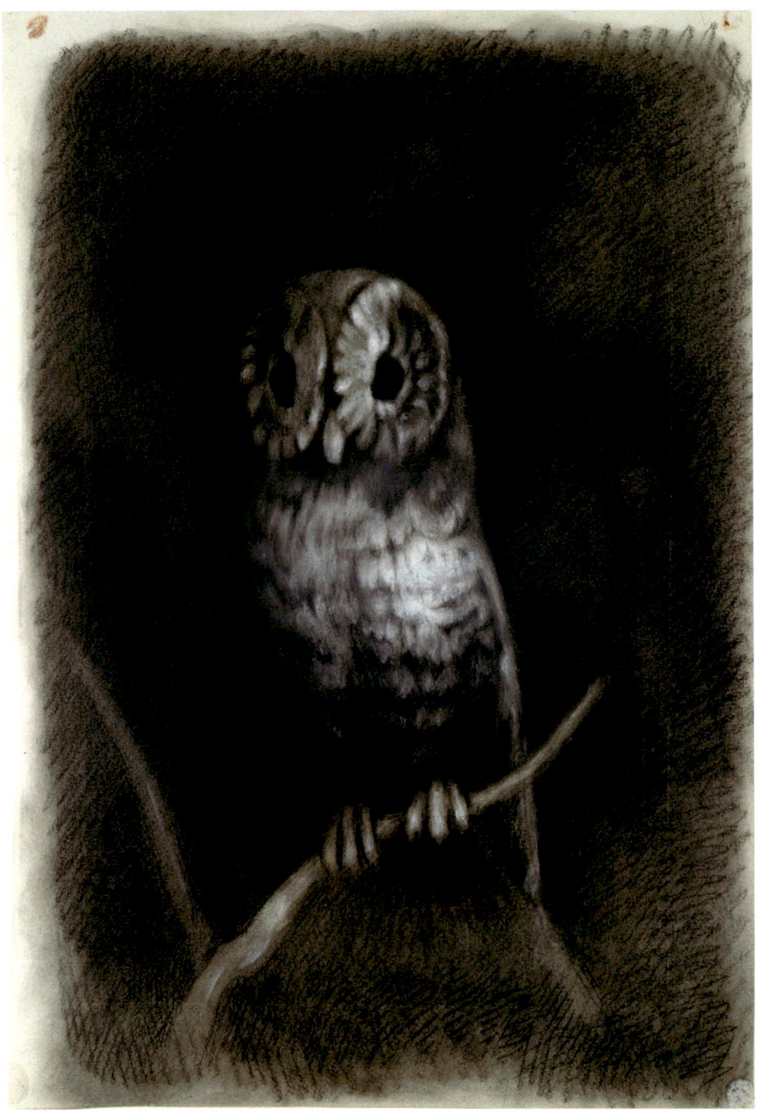

61

Arthur Burgess

Owl, Copied from a Photograph of Mantegna's Fresco of 'The Martyrdom of Saint James' in the Church of Eremitani, Padua 1872

Charcoal, black and white chalks on paper, 49.8 x 34.6 cm

Ashmolean Museum, University of Oxford. Ruskin School Collection (Rud. 46)

Ref: Hewison 1996, no. 31

Burgess's drawing shows a detail from Mantegna's fresco in the Cappella Ovetari, in the church of the Eremitani in Padua (which now exists only in a fragmentary state following the devastation of the church in 1944).

The drawing was made from a photograph, and in a chalk technique that seems almost to simulate the surface quality of mezzotint (Burgess had worked as an engraver before being employed to make drawn copies). Ruskin gave it to the Oxford Drawing School and praised it unreservedly in his published catalogue: 'This wonderful study of Mr Burgess is to show a great draughtsman's manner of using the brush. Seen at a proper distance it represents Mantegna's fresco work in a quite marvellous manner. For advanced students it is also an admirable exercise in chalk-drawing.'[1] After Burgess's early death, Ruskin wrote of him as 'such a draughtsman in black and white as I never knew the match of, with gifts of mechanical ingenuity and mathematical intelligence in the highest degree precious to me.'[2]

Ruskin studied Mantegna's fresco in Padua in the summer of 1870. He discussed Mantegna's work in his lecture *The Eagle's Nest* in 1872, where he coupled him with Dürer as an artist 'polluted and paralyzed by the study of anatomy'.[3] He also used the lecture to launch a broad attack on scientific materialism and the teaching of science at Oxford. It is likely that Burgess's drawing was intended as an illustration to this lecture.

1 Ruskin 1903–12, XXI, p. 179
2 Ruskin 1903–12, XIV, p. 351
3 Ruskin 1903–12, XXII, p. 122

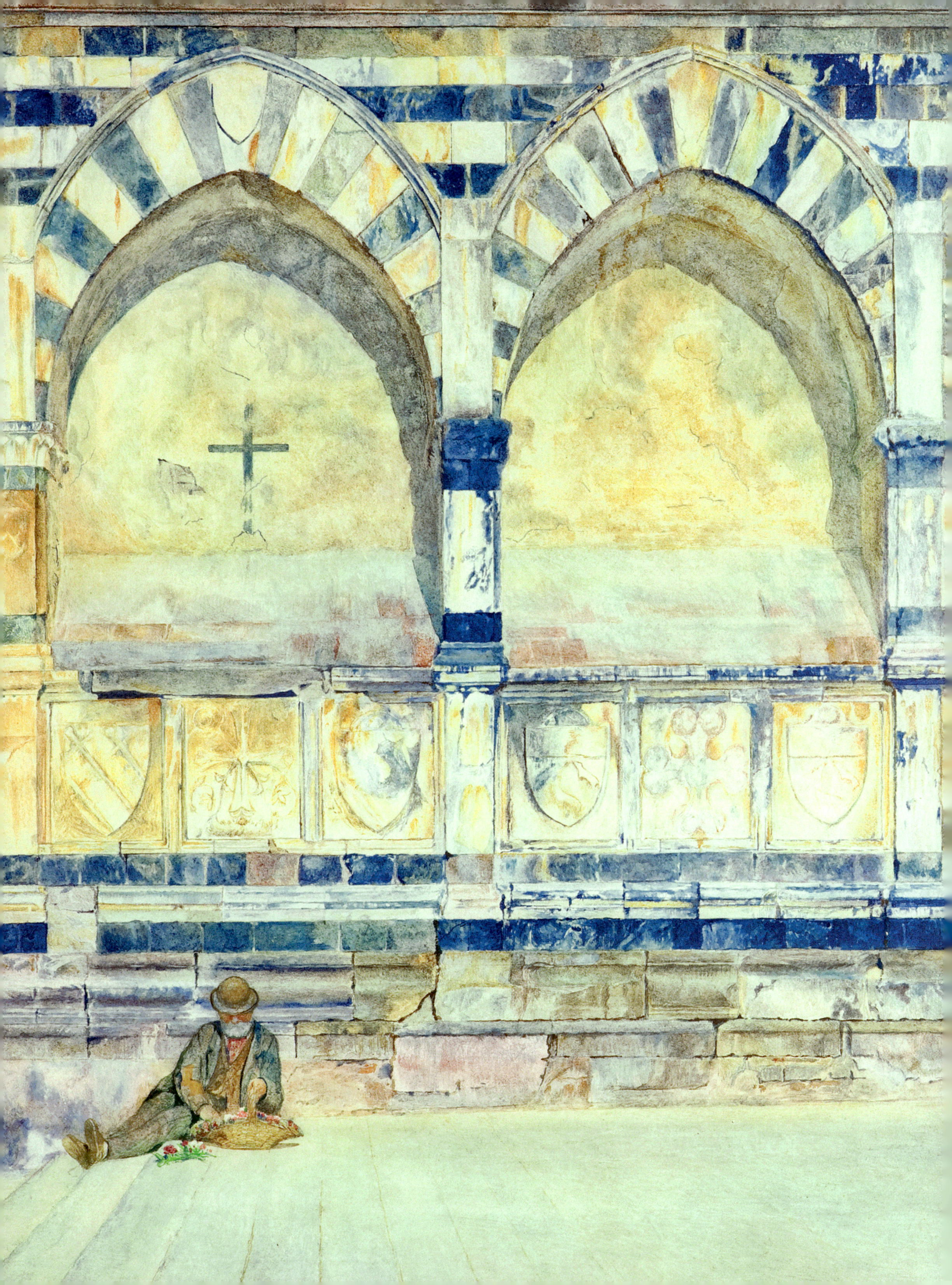

62

Henry Roderick Newman (1843–1917)
The Three Arches of Santa Maria Novella, Florence 1877
Watercolour and Pencil on paper, 42.5 x 52 cm
Signed and dated: *H.R. Newman / 1877*
Ruskin Foundation (Ruskin Library, University of Lancaster)
Ref: Staley and Newall 2004, no. 77

In *Mornings in Florence*, published in 1876, Ruskin exhorted the reader to pause for a moment outside the church of Santa Maria Novella to look at 'the small detached line of tombs on the left, untouched in its sweet colour and living weed ornament'. This he would 'fain have painted, stone by stone'.[1] In due course Ruskin owned two watercolour views of the arcade, by H.R. Newman and by T. M. Rooke (**cats. 62 and 74**).

In 1877, when Ruskin was shown a view by Newman of the piazza and façade of Santa Maria Novella, he wrote directly to the American artist to express his delight in it, going on to say, 'I have not for many and many a day seen the sense of tenderness and depth of colour so united – still less so much fidelity and affection joined with a power of design which seems to me, though latent, very great'. He continued with a wry observation on Newman's having made 'a poetical harmony of colour out of an omnibus stand', and the further suggestion that he might go on to draw 'those three old arches, seen right in front on the left of the steps going up to Sta Maria Novella. If they are still uninjured and wear their weeds, there's nothing lovelier in Florence'.[2]

The three arches form an extension of the embrasures, known as the *avelli*, which run across the lower register of the façade of the Dominican church, and which are continued in a long arcade which encloses the graveyard. Each opening is enclosed by a Gothic canopy decorated with white and grey-blue marble, done in the decorative style that originated in the marble facing of the Baptistery and which became a distinctive feature of the Tuscan Romanesque, and contains the tombs and family vaults of noble Florentine families. A year before Newman drew the arches on the left Ruskin had himself attempted the subject but had been driven off by the nuisance of stone-throwing urchins. The present drawing, 'carried out', as Ruskin said in 1882, 'with more patience than I possessed', seems to have been bought by Ruskin for the Guild of St George collection but subsequently mislaid or given away.

Newman began training as a doctor before he enrolled at the National Academy of Design in New York. In 1870 he travelled to Europe, staying briefly in Paris before settling in Florence, where he lived for the rest of his life. Even before he left the United States, his landscape watercolours fulfilled Ruskinian principles of truthful observation. However, he was never dependent on Ruskin's employment, but always able to find a market for his landscape and architectural subjects among visitors to Italy and also in London exhibitions. In addition to his scrupulous architectural subjects, he made landscape compositions of a wider perspective and more atmospheric type, and on a massively expanded scale, such as his *Lagoon at Venice* (which was more than two metres wide). Newman also made flower drawings, making a speciality of anemones; these were also much admired, and coveted, by Ruskin.

1 Ruskin 1903–12, XXIII, pp. 382–3
2 Ruskin 1903–12, XXX, p. lxxiii

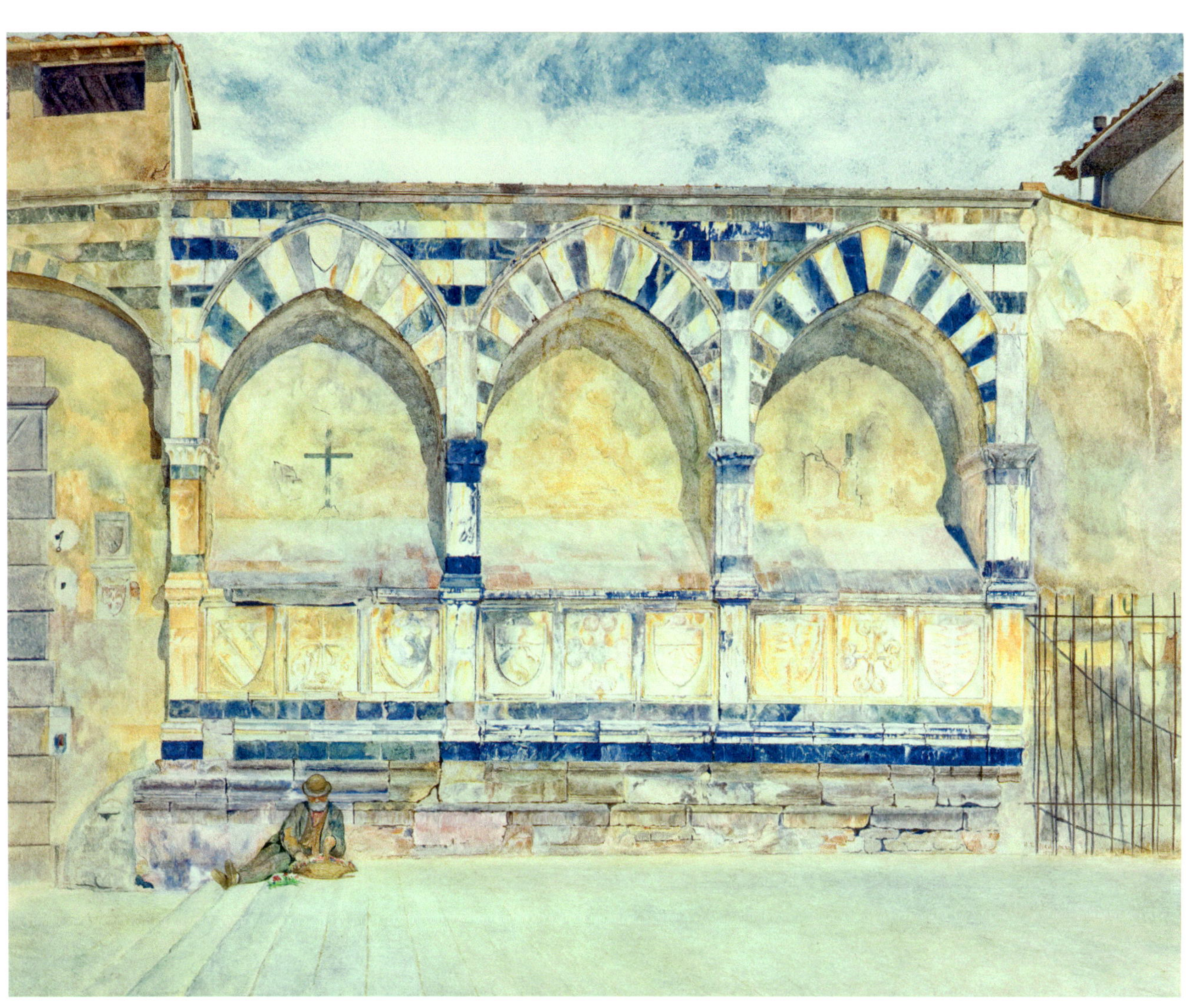

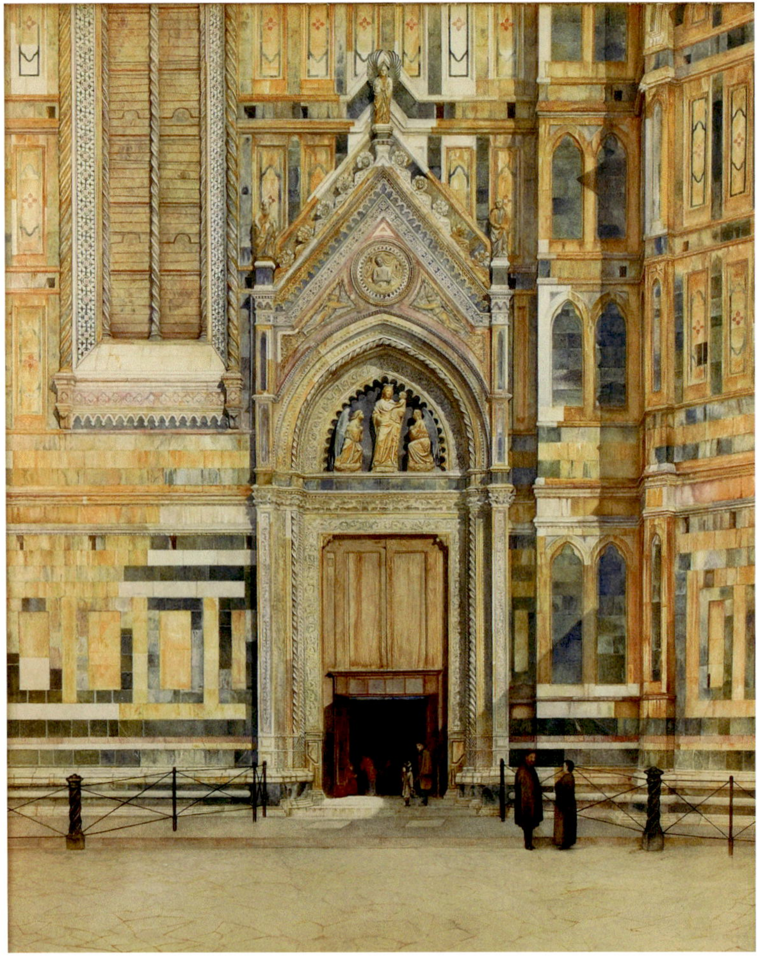

63
Henry Roderick Newman (1843–1917)
South Door of the Duomo, Florence 1881
Watercolour and bodycolour on paper, 79.3 x 65 cm
Signed and dated: *Henry Roderick Newman 1881*
Collection of the Guild of St George,
Museums Sheffield (R21)
Ref: Morley 1984, II, p. 123

Ruskin bought this drawing and another showing the Duomo and east face of the Baptistery in Florence in 1881, intending them for display in the museum of the Guild of St George. In his account of the collection he described the view of the south door of the Duomo as 'exquisitely rendered in the colour of the marble, remaining still uninjured by restoration, except in the clearly visible white patches of fresh stone and the upper crockets of the gable'. The sculpted decoration of the Gothic Porta dei Canonici was carved by Lorenzo d'Ambrogio and Piero di Giovanni Tedesco, Jacopo di Piero Guidi, and Nicolo Lamberti in the 1390s. A campaign of restoration of this part of the cathedral had to be temporarily suspended so that Newman could make his drawing.

Ruskin placed the two Florence drawings beside Verocchio's *Madonna and Child* in the Guild of St George Museum, 'to show how, for 500 years, Italy remained steadfast to what may be, in all its branches, called "art of precision", doing everything as accurately, finely, and thoroughly as possible'.[1]

1 Ruskin 1903–12, XXX, p. 208

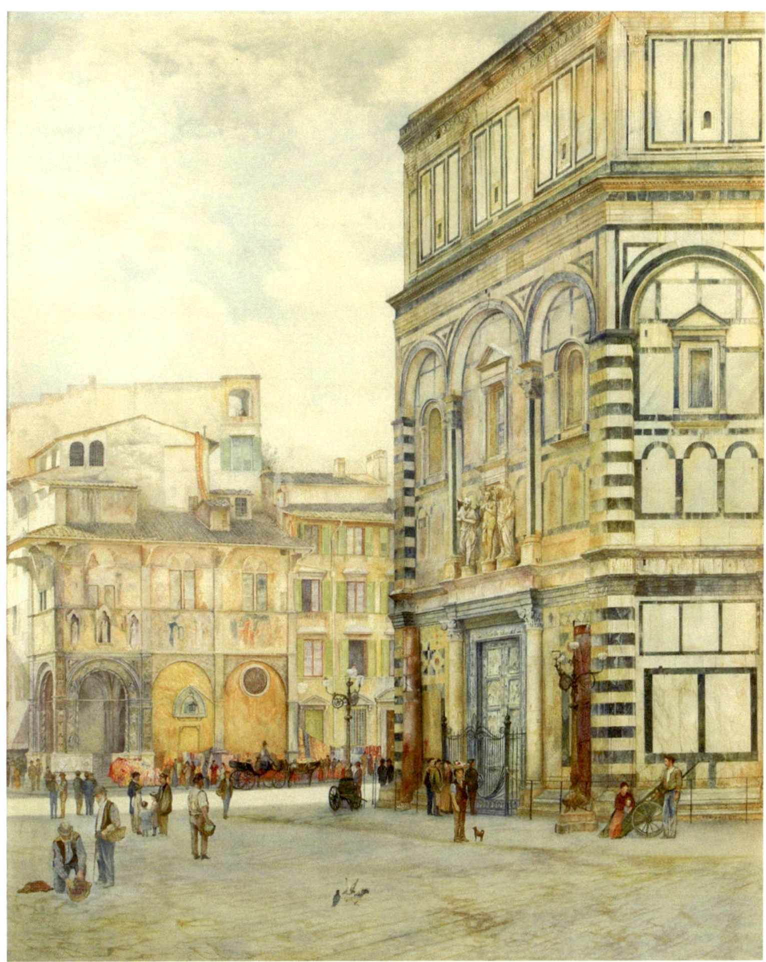

64
Henry Roderick Newman
The Baptistery of San Giovanni, Florence 1881
Watercolour and bodycolour on paper, 78.1 x 63.8 cm
Collection of the Guild of St George,
Museums Sheffield (R19)
Ref: Morley 1984, II, pp. 122–3

Newman's drawing shows the east side and main entrance of the Florence Baptistery, seen across the Piazza San Giovanni. The sculptural decoration of the building, notably Lorenzo Ghiberti's 'Gate of Paradise' bronze door, made in 1425–52, and the *Baptism* attributed to Sansovino above, are clearly visible though they are not drawn with the same meticulous detail that Ruskin himself had employed in his drawing *A Compartment of the Baptistery, Florence* (**cat. 35**). Out of view, on the left side, stand the cathedral and campanile.

The Baptistery assumed enormous significance in Ruskin's theoretical perception of the development of architectural forms in the 1870s. As he explained in a lecture at Oxford on Ghiberti in November 1874, 'all that is needful for you to learn essentially of the history of Italian architecture may be learned on the little area, scarcely larger than a peasant winnows his corn upon, of smooth pavement between the Baptistery of Florence and Giotto's Tower'.[1] It may be assumed that Newman had read Ruskin's Oxford lecture and included the many figures in his composition in response to Ruskin's colourful account of the inconvenience of 'omnibus traffic' and 'hawkers of small-ware'.

Ruskin bought the watercolour shortly after it was made for a hundred guineas, and placed it in the Museum of the Guild of St George. In his projected catalogue of the collection, he described it as 'an exquisitely careful rendering of the effect of the marble walls of this building, seen in half light, reflected from the façade of the Duomo'. In addition he referred to 'the gate [as] the one of which the valves were executed by Ghiberti with a skill which has ever since been the admiration of Europe'.[2]

1 Ruskin 1903–12, XXIII, p. 239
2 Ruskin 1903–12, XXX, p. 208

65

William Gershom Collingwood (1854–1932)
The Head of Ilaria del Carretto, from the Tomb Sculpture by Jacopo della Quercia 1882
Watercolour and bodycolour on paper, 17 x 25 cm
Signed and dated and Inscribed, *ILARIA DI CARETTO / G. Collingwood. Lucca 1882*
Collection of the Guild of St George, Museums Sheffield (R498)
Ref: Morley 1984, II, p. 60; Clegg and Tucker 1993 no. 262

Ruskin had made drawings in S. Martino at Lucca in 1872 and 1874, and had described the sculptural decoration of the church in *Fors Clavigera*. His series of drawings of the tomb of Ilaria del Carretto **(cat. 37)** were made in a concerted campaign of several weeks in 1874. He made a further attempt to convey the tender beauty of the statue when he returned to Lucca in 1882, confiding despairingly to his travelling companion, W.G. Collingwood, 'I was thinking last night that the drawing which I am now trying to make of Ilaria in the weakness and despair of declining age, might possibly be the last I should make before quitting the study of Italian and even all other, art, for ever'.[1] Collingwood's drawing of the head of Ilaria del Carretto was perhaps made to console Ruskin when his own drawing proved a disappointment.

1 quoted in Morley 1984, II, p. 60

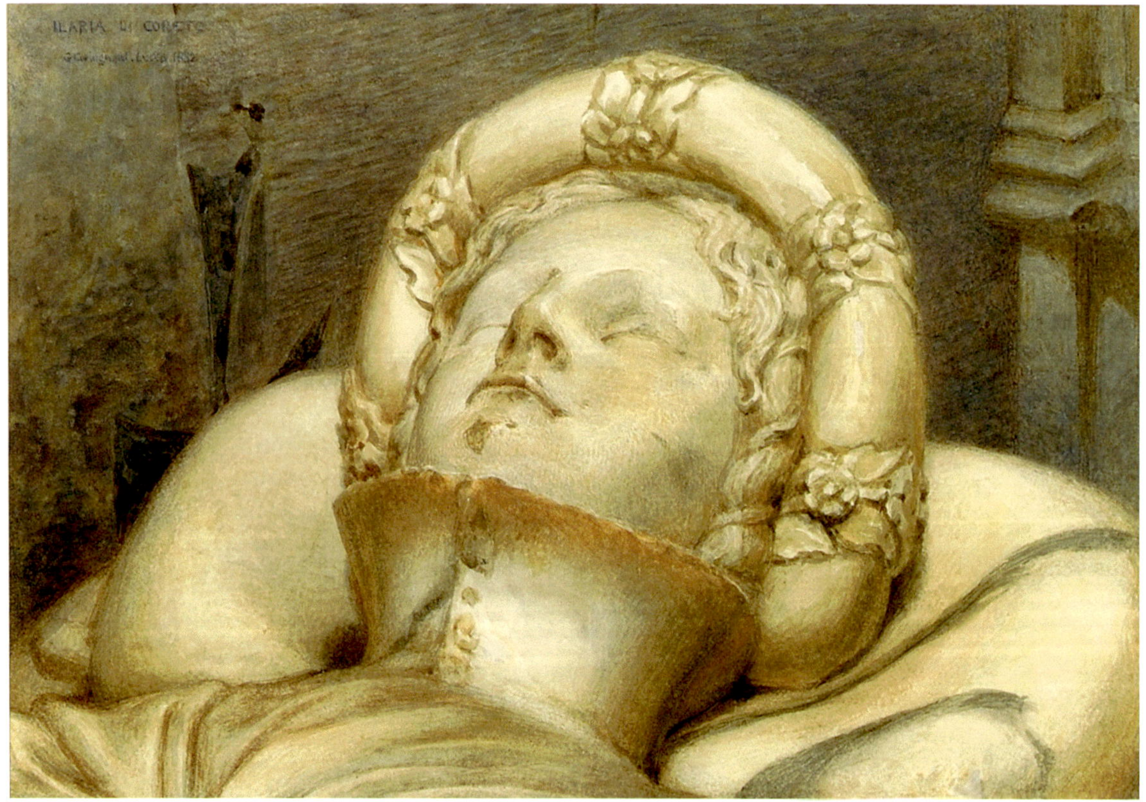

66

Thomas Matthews Rooke (1842–1942)
Drawing of Mosaics in the Vault of the Chancel of San Vitale, Ravenna 1884
Watercolour, bodycolour and gold paint over pencil on wove paper, 40.8 x 52.1 cm
Ashmolean Museum, University of Oxford.
Ruskin School Collection (Ref. 166)

Rooke worked as a designer for William Morris before becoming a studio assistant to Burne-Jones. In 1878, Burne-Jones recommended him to Ruskin, saying that 'There is a very high place in Heaven waiting for him, and HE DOESN'T KNOW IT'.[1] Ruskin first employed Rooke to make drawings of the mosaics in St Mark's in Venice, which he feared were to be irreparably damaged, like the floor: as he wrote to Burne-Jones, 'Mr Rooke must begin at once, on bright days with the single figures on the walls of the aisles'.[2] Later that same season, Ruskin, who still considered Rooke as being on probation, directed him to copy the mosaic which he called the 'Clergy, People and Doge', warning, 'Then I shall see clearly how we respectively feel'. In April and May 1884, Rooke and Frank Randal worked together at Ravenna, again copying mosaics, which, although today among the most celebrated in Italy, were, according to Ruskin, 'not really known at all'. At the time, Ruskin was planning to discuss the mosaics in the second chapter, 'Ponte della Pietra', of his projected history of Christendom, *Our Fathers have told us*, which, however, he never completed. Rooke made at least two studies of the mosaics in Ravenna: this general view of the vault of the chancel in San Vitale, and a study of three female saints in San Apollinare Nuovo.[3]

1 quoted in Morley 1984, II, p. 175
2 ibid.
3 now in Sheffield; Morley 1984, II, pp. 190–91

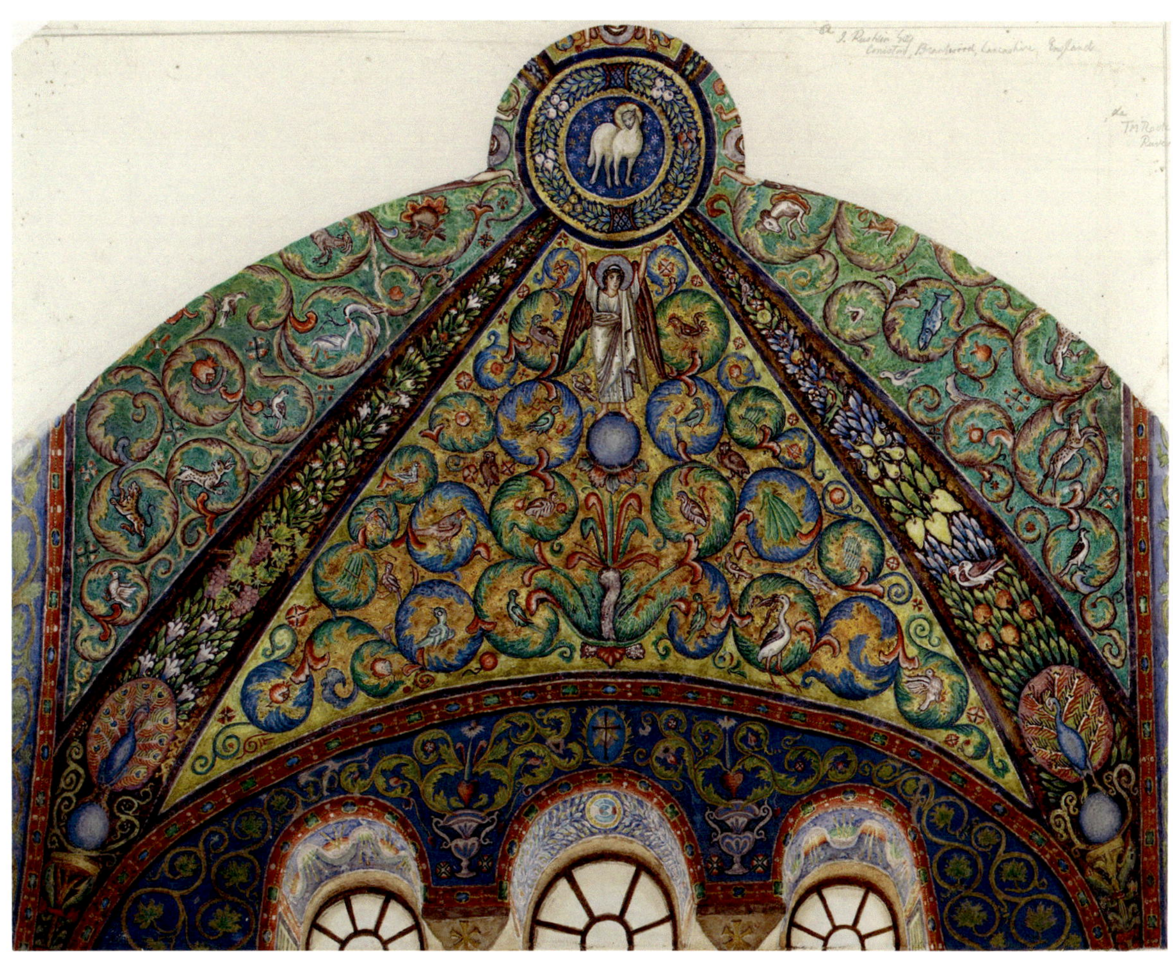

67–68
Frank Randal (c. 1858–1910)
Mosaic Roundels of Sts Bartholomew and Matthew at San Vitale, Ravenna 1884
Watercolour on paper, 31.5 x 20 cm
Inscribed: *Apostle Medallions. Choir Arch. S. Vitale Ravenna / April & May 1884*

Mosaic of St Luke at San Vitale, Ravenna 1884
Watercolour on paper, 39 x 17 cm
Inscribed: *St. Luke / N. Side of Choir, S. Vitale Ravenna / May 1884*

Collection of the Guild of St George, Museums Sheffield (R33, R20)
Ref: Morley 1984, II, p. 161

The details of Randal's early life are sketchy, but he first worked for Ruskin in the summer of 1881, and seems to have been financially dependent upon commissions for the Guild of St George in the period 1881–6. He had extraordinary skill as a draughtsman: in 1883, Ruskin wrote to him enthusiastically about a series of ornithological drawings – 'The zoo birds are treasures' – but encouraged him to 'try to get a similar power in landscape outlines'.[1]

Ruskin sent Randal to Ravenna with T.M. Rooke in the early summer of 1884 to record the Byzantine mosaics. He also hoped that Randal would learn a meticulous technique from the ever-reliable Rooke. In the event, when Ruskin received Randal's drawings in August, he was so impressed by their quality that he mistook them for the work of Rooke. Ruskin's only complaint was in connection with a study of a capital and iron work in the church of S. Vitale (now in the collection of the Guild of St George), of which he said: 'Please another time don't give a week's work to draw an iron grating that hides a capital'.[2]

1 Morley 1984, II, p. 127
2 quoted in Morley 1984, II, p. 160

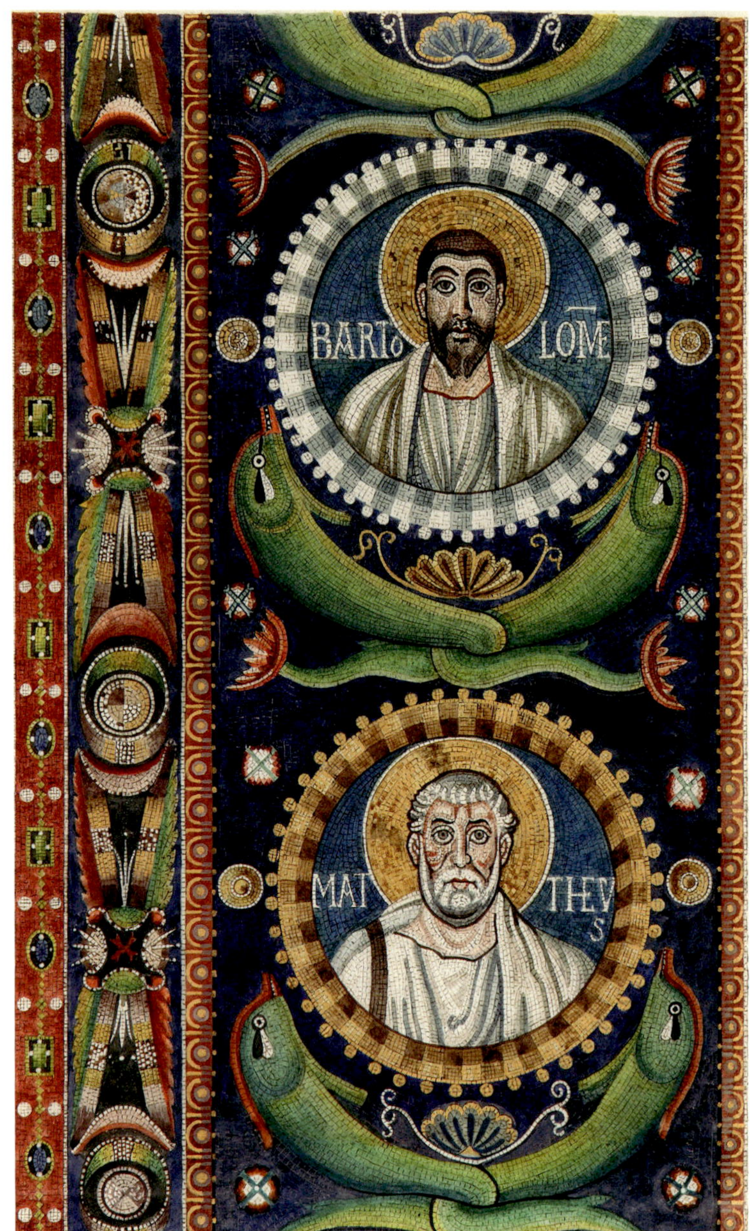

067

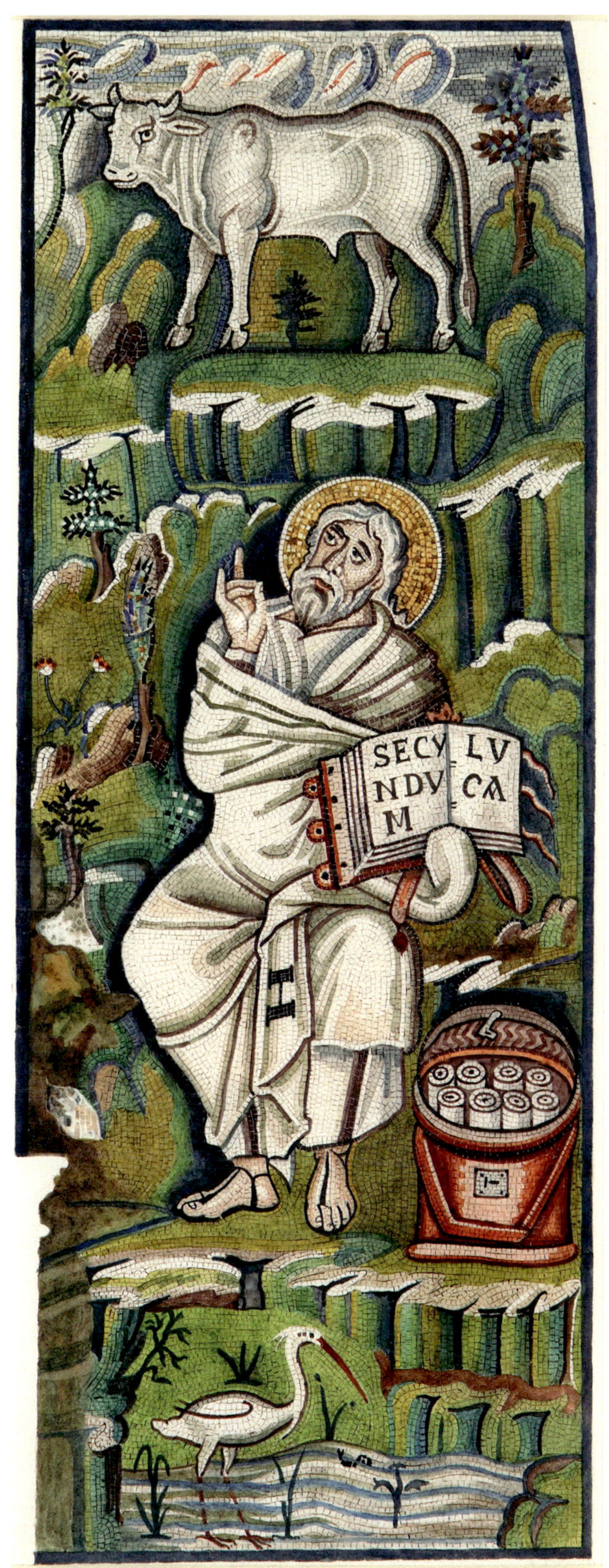

068

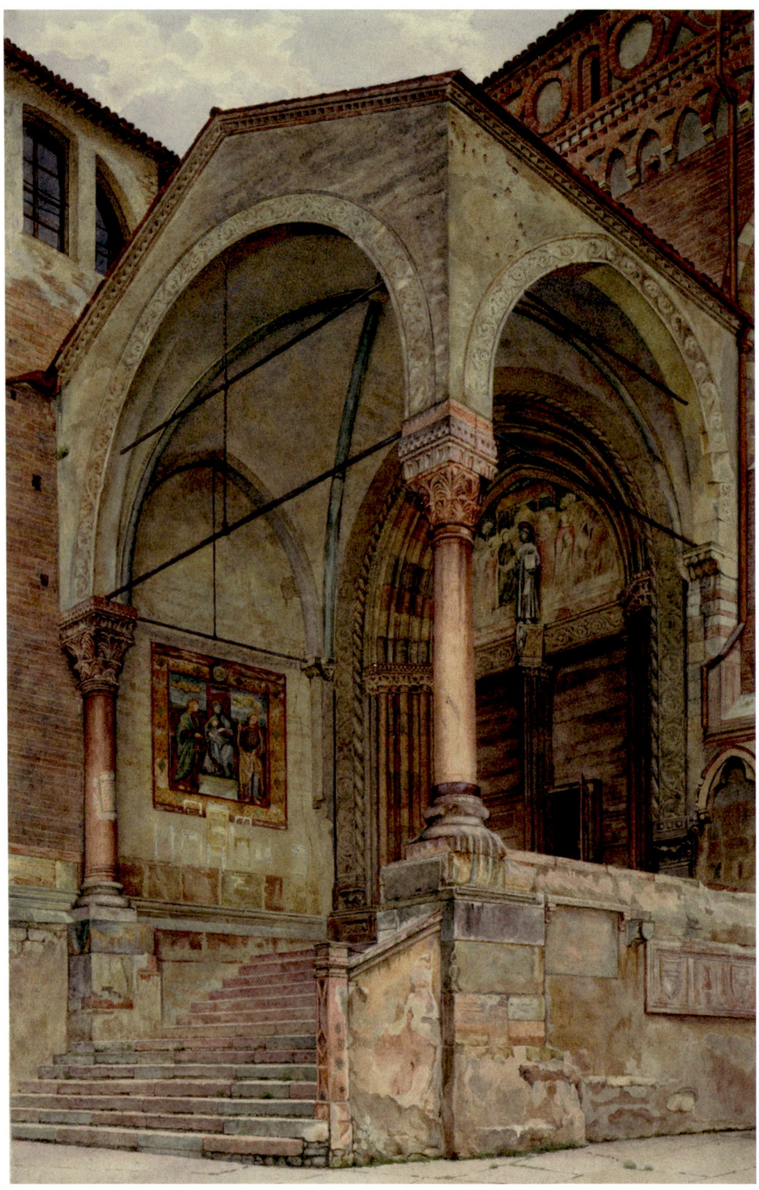

69
Frank Randal (*c.* 1858–1910)
The North Porch of San Fermo Maggiore, Verona 1884
Watercolour on paper, 37.9 x 25.4 cm
Ashmolean Museum, University of Oxford. Ruskin School Collection (Rud. 23bis)

In the late summer and autumn of 1884, Randal worked in Verona with the Italian copyist Alessandro Alessandri, of whom Ruskin said: '[He] speaks English and you will learn much from his exquisite stone colouring'.[1] Randal made a series of drawings of different parts of the lower and upper churches of San Fermo, begun in 1065. This drawing shows one of the entrances to the upper church, which was rebuilt in the Gothic style in the early fourteenth century.

Ruskin strongly criticised the later drawings Randal sent back from Italy, but, in a sad postscript to one of Ruskin's letters, his servant Baxter noted that, 'I think it right to tell you that the poor master is not at all himself at present – therefore anything he says strongly is no evidence of what he really thinks'.[2]

1 Morley 1984, II, p. 128
2 Morley 1984, II, p. 129

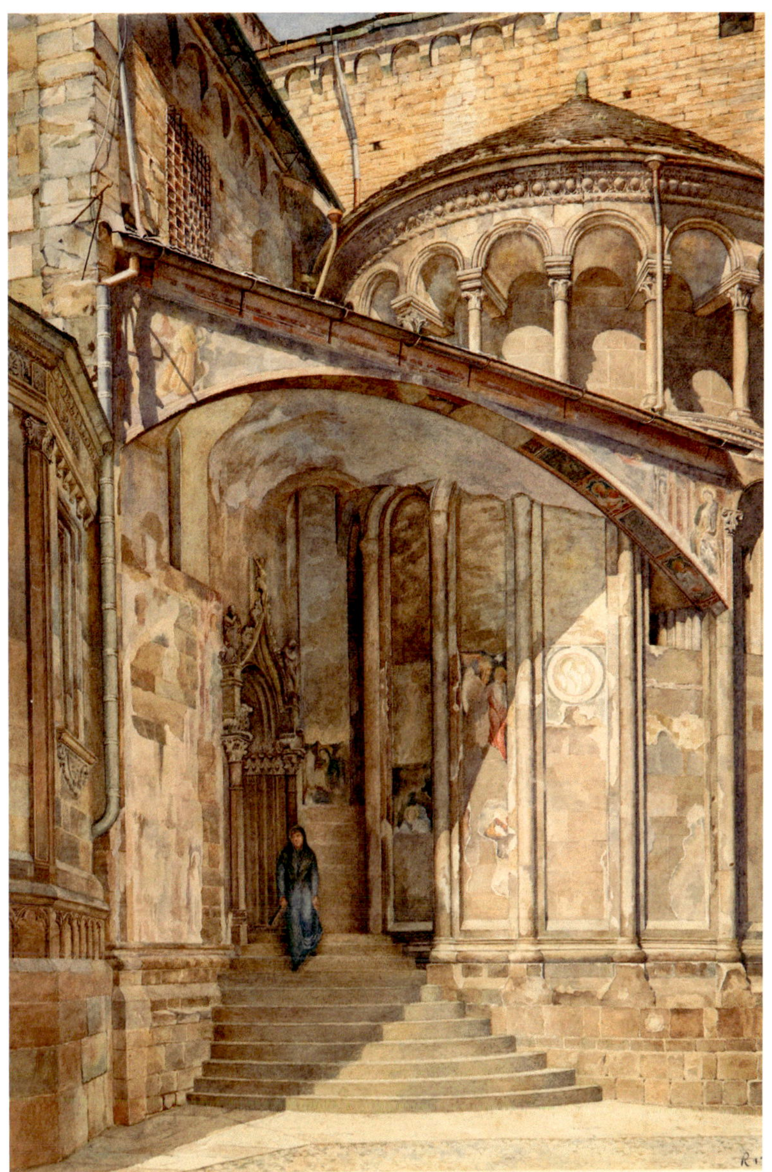

70

Frank Randal

Angle of the Choir and Transept, Santa Maria Maggiore, Bergamo 1885

Watercolour and bodycolour on paper, 27 x 25 cm

Inscribed on *verso*: *Angle of the Choir and Transept (with absidal chapel) Santa Maria Maggiore Bergamo / Aug. & Sept. 1885 / (date over doorway 1357)*

Collection of the Guild of St George, Museums Sheffield (R1741)

Ref: Morley 1984, II, p. 168

Randal moved on from Lecco to Bergamo in July 1885, with the purpose of making a series of studies of the town's principal church, Sta Maria Maggiore. In due course he sent eight drawings to the museum of the Guild of St George, of which six survive.

In September 1885 Randal was told that his employment by the Guild was to be ended, as Ruskin himself was to cease commissioning copies and architectural studies on account of his own deteriorating health. This was despite Ruskin's previous reassurance that, 'whatever happens to me, I trust the members of the Guild [...] will not allow your conscientious and admirable work to be broken off'.[1] In fact, Ruskin was well enough by the end of the year to invite Randal to his house at Brantwood so that they could paint and draw together.

1 quoted in Morley 1984, II, , p. 168

71

Frank Randal (c. 1858–1910)
The Resegone of Lecco 6.30 p.m. 1885
Watercolour and bodycolour on paper, 22.2 x 33.3 cm
Inscribed: *The Resegone of Lecco Como / June & July 1885. 6.30 pm.*
Collection of the Guild of St George, Museums Sheffield (R16)
Ref: Morley 1984, II, p. 166

The inscription on this drawing has never been correctly read, and consequently its significance has not been understood. The subject of the drawing is Monte Resegone in the Italian Alps, on the border between the provinces of Bergamo and Lecco. It derives its name from the word for a saw in the local Lombard dialect, *resega*, and is also known as the Monte Serrada; both refer to the distinctive serrated crest of the mountain. As Randal would have been aware, Monte Resegone is described several times in the most celebrated Italian novel of the nineteenth century, Manzoni's *I promessi sposi* (1828), written in praise of Italian nationalism and strongly critical of the Austrian rule of Lombardy.

Randal has paid close attention to the limestone strata seen as broad ridges and grassy platforms which link together the pyramidal blocks, and to the nine peaks forming the serrated crest. The strong shadows of the early evening show the mountain forms in three-dimensional clarity.

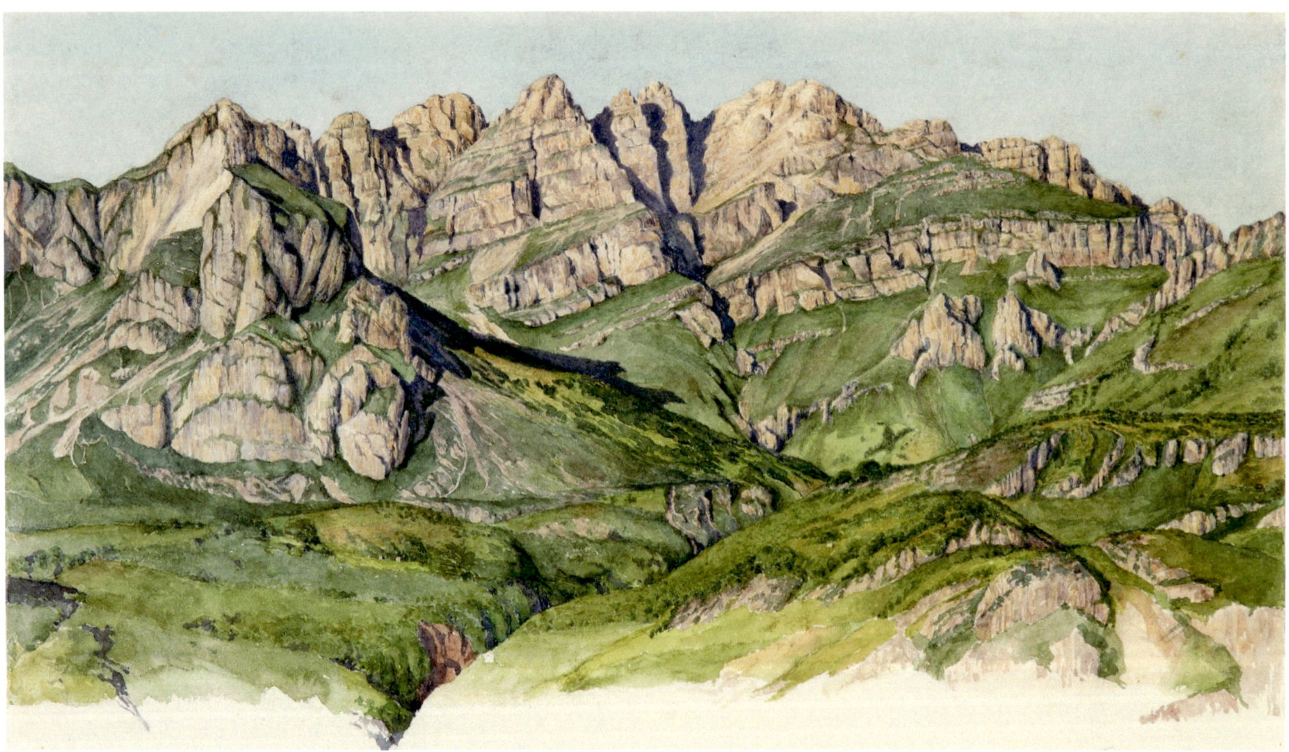

72
Frank Randal (c. 1858–1910)
The Passo del Fo, Lecco 1885
Watercolour and bodycolour on paper, 17.2 x 24.8 cm
Inscribed: *Lecco 1885. 8 am.*
Collection of the Guild of St George,
Museums Sheffield (R2140B)
Ref: Morley 1984, II, p. 166

By December 1884, Ruskin felt that Randal and his painting companion, Angelo Alessandri, had worked so hard in Verona that they deserved a holiday. He therefore instructed them to travel to Lecco, at the southern tip of the eastern reach of Lake Como, where they were to 'get a warm cell of lodging, under the rocks, with windows to the lake, and study skies and distant mountains, till further orders; and row and fish, if the days are fine, but don't work more than five minutes of sketch in pencil out of doors'. Ruskin was still trying to persuade the artists he employed of the virtue of brevity and impression, so concluded: 'I find many of my drawings at home over five minutes of pencil most valuable, and you both want that sort of practice'.[1]

Randal is recorded as having made a large number of landscape drawings in northern Italy that winter and spring, but only the present pair seem to have survived. Of a drawing of Monte Grigna (untraced), Ruskin wrote with admiration in February 1885: 'Had you stayed all winter at Lecco only to do this sketch, I should have considered the time well spent. It is entirely right and beautiful, and it happens just now that I am more interested in mountains than anything, and in clouds next [...]'.[2] He also sent him off-prints of additions he had recently made to *Modern Painters* IV, which bore the sub-title 'Of Mountain Beauty'.

1 Ruskin 1903–12, XXX, p. lxxii
2 ibid.

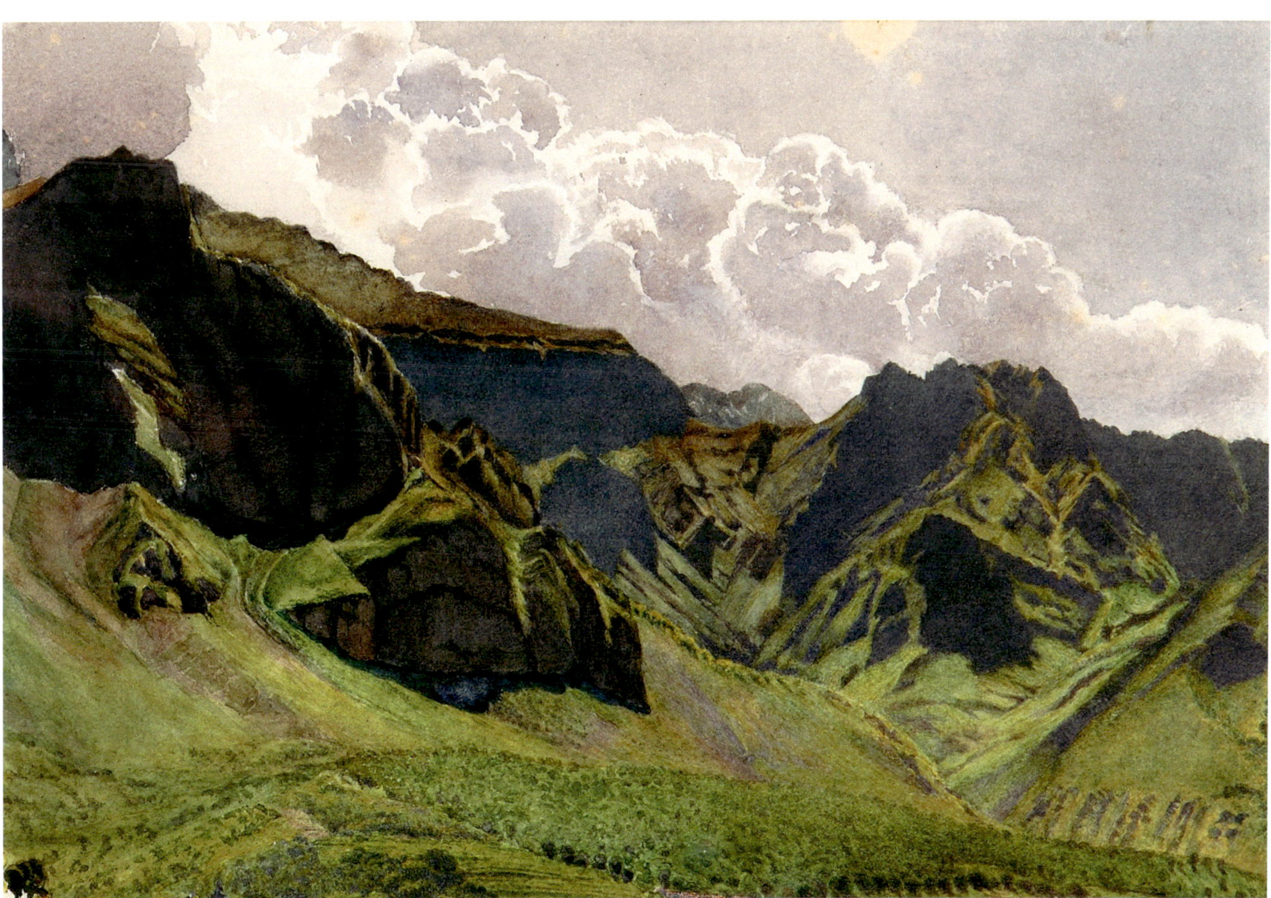

73

Henry Roderick Newman (1843–1917)
The Façade of the Duomo, Lucca 1885
Watercolour and bodycolour on paper, 77.5 x 63.5 cm
Signed and dated: *H.R. Newman 1885*
Collection of the Guild of St George,
Museums Sheffield (R23)
Ref: Morley 1984, II, p. 126; Clegg and Tucker 1993, no. 261

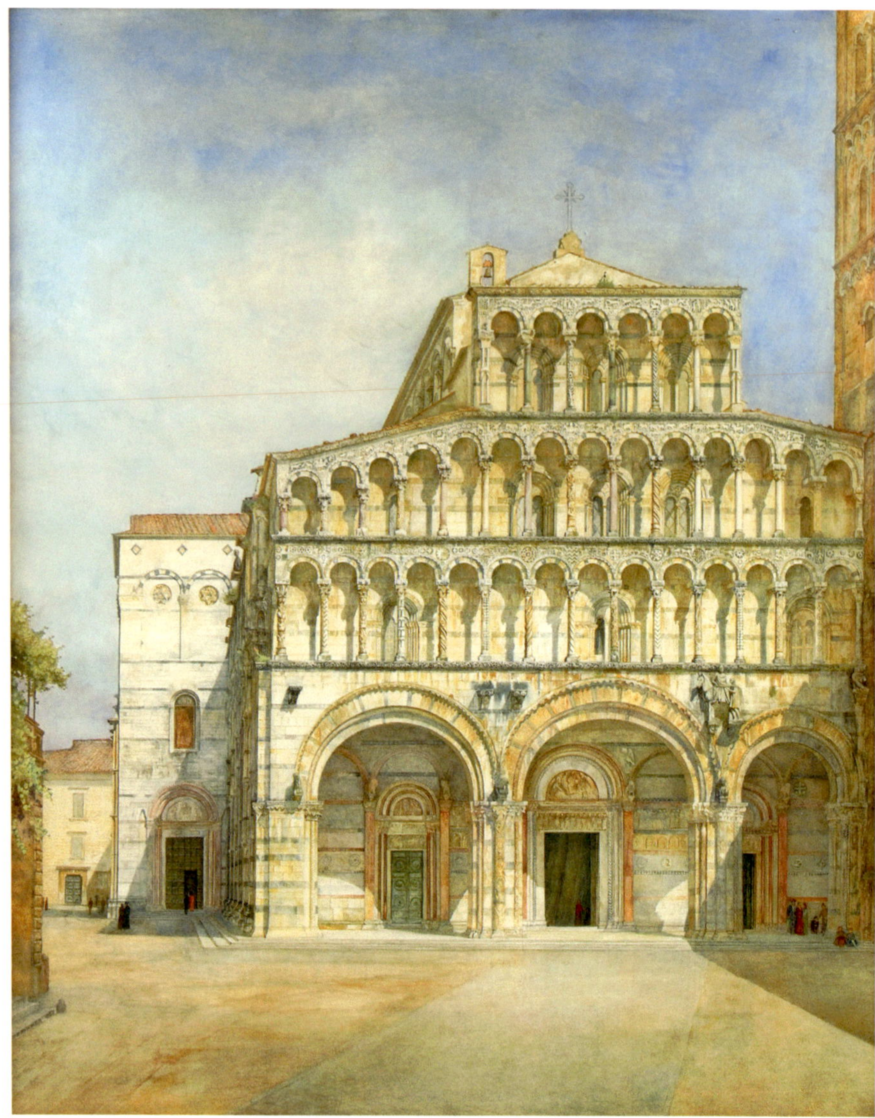

When Newman joined Ruskin and W.G. Collingwood in Lucca in the autumn of 1882, he began a series of drawings of the façades and architectural detail of Romanesque churches in the city. Ruskin bought several of the drawings Newman made while they were together, including a detail of a column from the cathedral,[1] which he deposited in his Drawing School at Oxford, where it joined a drawing by Ruskin himself of the façade of San Martino from an oblique angle in 1874.

Ruskin commissioned Newman's drawing of the façade of the Duomo in 1885, providing him with a pencil and bodycolour sketch to indicate the required perspective and format (now in the Ruskin Library, Lancaster University). To some degree Ruskin seems to have been losing faith in Newman, finding his characteristic use of a reduced range of pale browns, yellows, and pinks in the architecture, and striking blues for the sky, inadequate for the purpose of providing information about buildings. He angrily inscribed his own drawing: 'Drawn for the plan of composition of picture to be done by Henry Newman, who lost himself and me, alike, in his unhappy egotism of ultramarine – Rose Madder & yellow ochre!'[2] In 1887 Ruskin resorted to an invidious comparison of Newman's work with that of his other principal acolyte: 'All that Rooke does is entirely delightful to me [while by contrast] Newman is too laborious, just now. He has martyred himself to lemon yellow and Ultramarine'.[3]

The church of San Martino – the bishopric of Lucca since the eighth century – was reconstructed in 1060 under the orders of Anselmo da Baggio, later Pope Alexander II. The asymmetrical façade, which abuts the campanile, consists of three registers of carved colonnettes, capitals and round arches supporting an architrave of inlaid stone. Newman's watercolour is so carefully drawn that the sculpted decoration of the columns, including that showing Nicola Pisano's *Adoration of the Magi* and another decorated with a Tree of Life, can be read as if one were standing on the spot.

1 *Study of a Column from the Central Colonnade on the West Front of the Duomo di San Martino, Lucca* (WA. RS.LC.46)
2 quoted in Clegg & Tucker 1993, p. 132
3 quoted in Leith 1996, p. 34

74
Thomas Matthews Rooke (1842–1942)
Three Tombs beside Santa Maria Novella, Florence 1887
Watercolour on paper, 27.8 x 30.4 cm
Inscribed: *In Piazza / Santa Maria Novella / 1887*
Collection of the Guild of St George, Museums Sheffield (R34x)
Ref: Morley 1984, II, pp. 206–7; Clegg and Tucker 1993 no. 268

Rooke made the last of his copies for Ruskin during a stay in the winter of 1886–7, where he was 'to work chiefly on things perishing'. His first task was to draw the Badia Fiesolana, but 'on days when you don't care to go as far as Fiesole',[1] Ruskin suggested that he should work at Santa Maria Novella, where he made this drawing of the tombs that Newman had drawn much less meticulously ten years earlier (**cat. 62**).

1 quoted in Clegg & Tucker 1993, p. 136

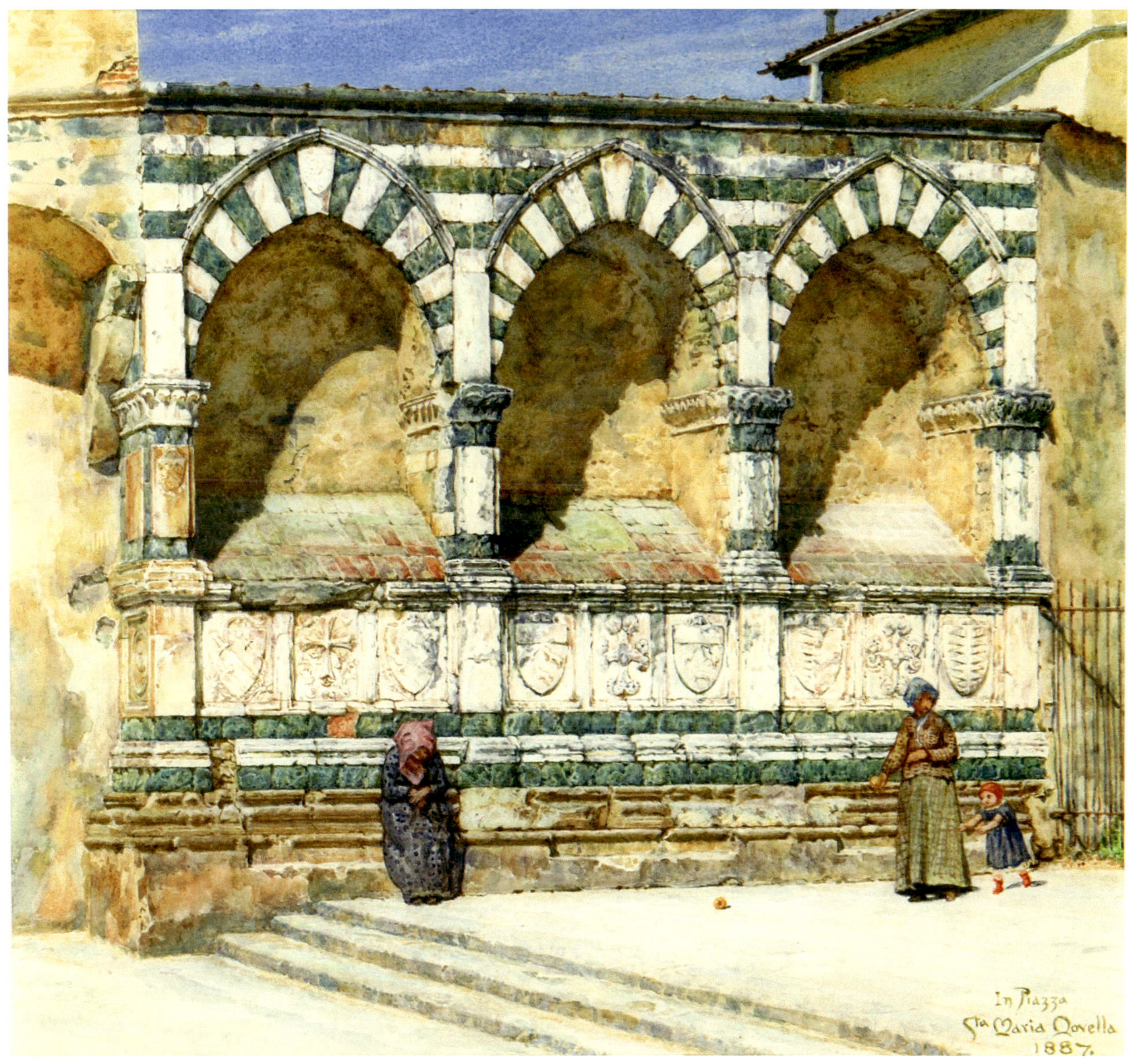

75

Henry Roderick Newman (1843–1917)
San Martino, Lucca 1887
Watercolour with touches of white bodycolour over Pencil on paper, 63.1 x 43.3 cm
Birmingham Museum & Art Gallery

In contrast with his earlier view of San Martino **(cat. 73)**, this later example corresponds almost exactly in its dramatically oblique perspective of the central and left-hand openings of the main arcade to Ruskin's own drawing of 1874 **(cat. 40)**, and was perhaps made in deliberate emulation of that study. However, there is no indication that it was made in the hope that Ruskin might acquire it – by this time, Newman was finding a wider clientele for his drawings.

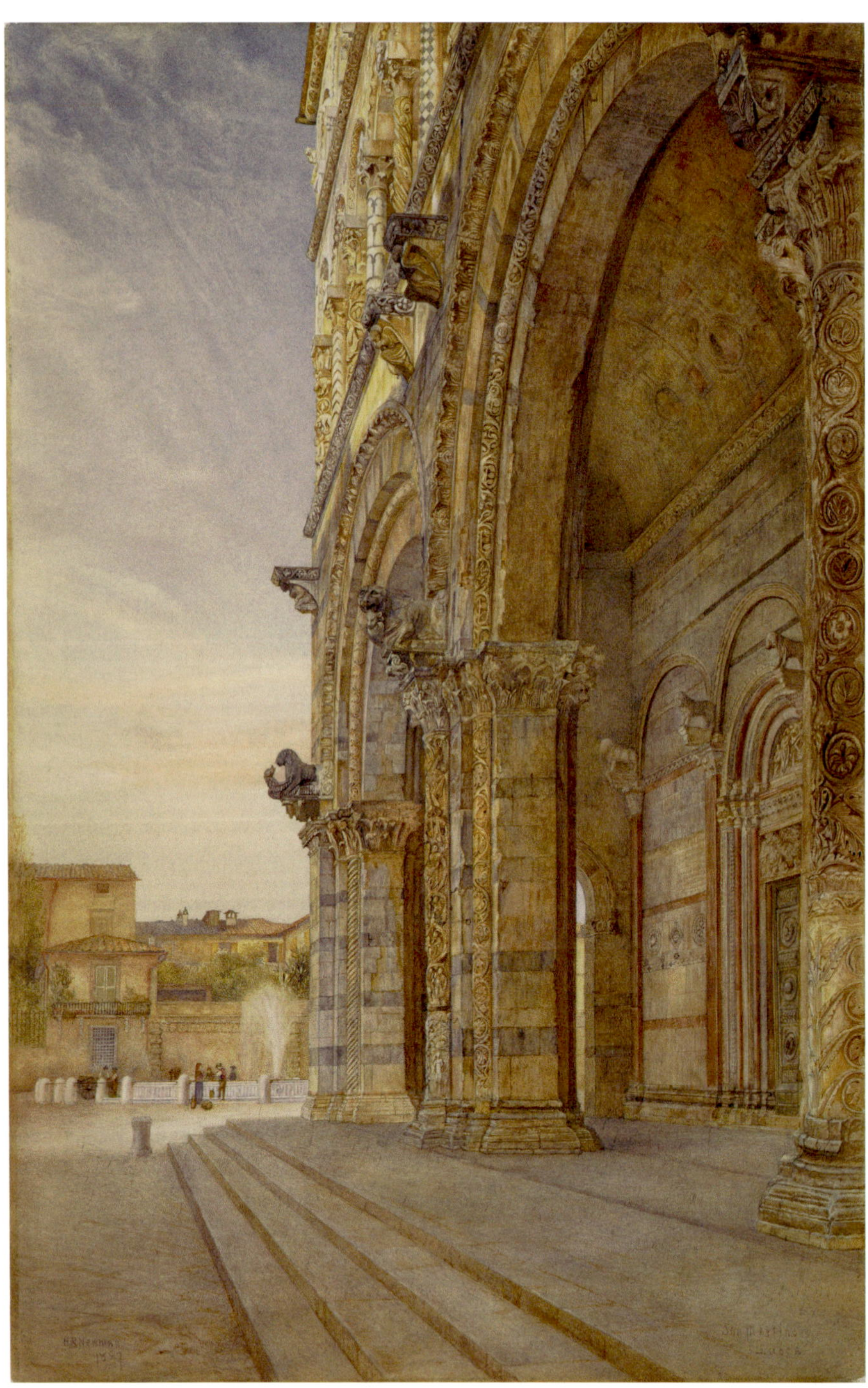

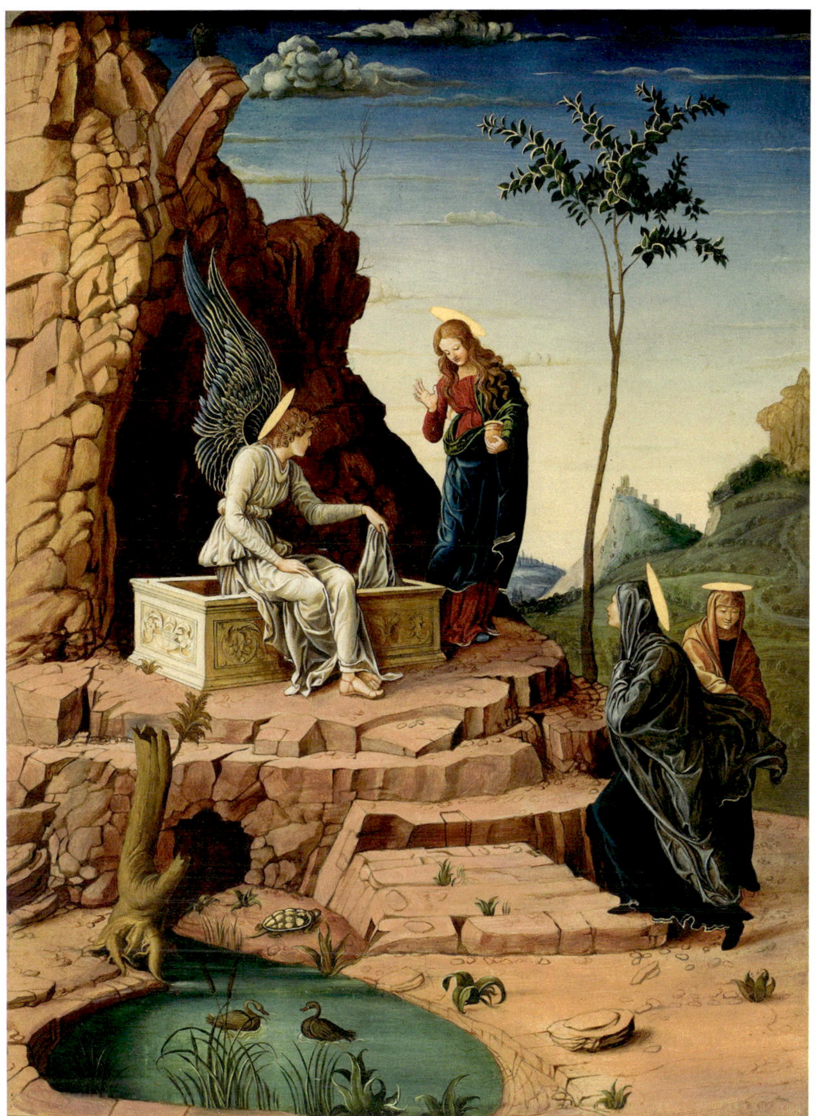

76
George Howard, 9th Earl of Carlisle (1843–1911)
after Andrea Mantegna (c. 1430/1–1506)
The Maries at the Sepulchre
Oil on panel, 42 x 31 cm
Inscribed on *verso*: *A Legros / de la part de son élève / G. Howard 1er mars 1869 / copie d'Andrea Mantegna / appartenant à Lord Taunton*
Private collection

After taking his degree at Cambridge, George Howard became the first pupil of the French artist, Alphonse Legros (1837–1911), in November 1865. The two remained firm friends, and it was on the strength of commissions for copies from Howard that Legros made his own trip to Italy in 1872, where he was especially impressed by the work of Masaccio. It was no doubt through Legros's influence that Howard made this copy after a painting attributed to Mantegna: since his early years, Legros had had a taste for the 'Primitives', and transmitted his enthusiasm to his pupils, being largely responsible for the revival of interest in metalpoint drawings. The original painting is one of a series of three scenes of the passion of Christ by a follower of Mantegna, and was bequeathed to the National Gallery by George Howard's aunt, Lady Taunton, in 1892. The copy is the same size as the original, and meticulously exact, demonstrating Howard's real feeling for early Italian painting as well as his considerable technical prowess.

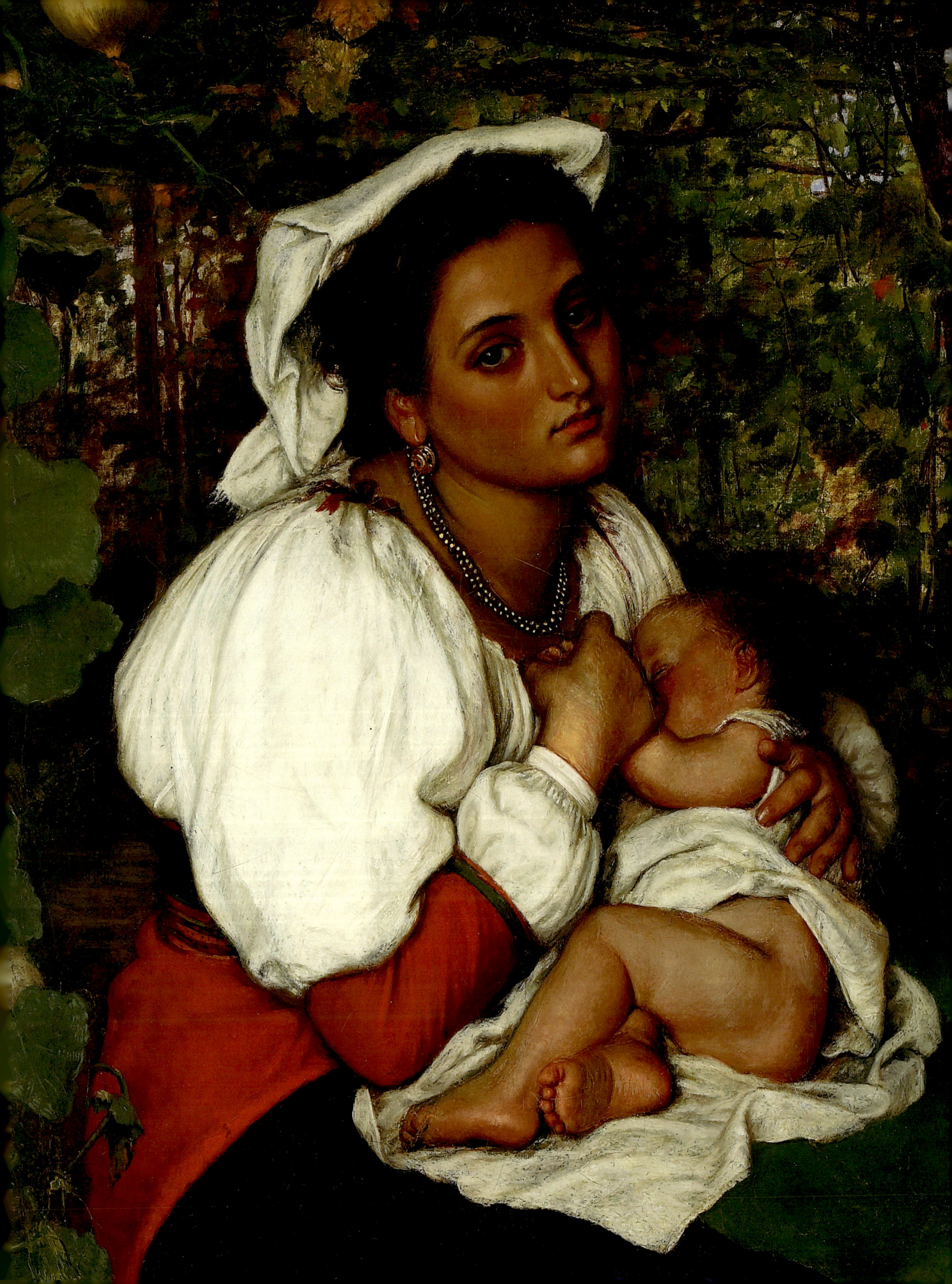

IV

OTHER PRE-RAPHAELITE TRAVELLERS IN ITALY

Of the original members of the Pre-Raphaelite Brotherhood, only two, W.M. Rossetti and Holman Hunt, spent extended periods in Italy. Millais included the peninsula on his tour of Europe in 1865, but his visit had no lasting effect on his art; and D.G. Rossetti never succeeded in reaching his father's homeland, in spite of his fluency in the language and abiding interest in the history and literature of the country. Even Holman Hunt, whose glorification of Italian nationalism, *Rienzi*, was one of the first Pre-Raphaelite paintings to be exhibited, was much more interested in finding suitably authentic backgrounds to his biblical and religious paintings in the Holy Land and the Near East. Indeed, his first visit to Italy, in the winter of 1866–7, came about only because he was unable to reach the Holy Land owing to an outbreak of cholera. This stay was beset by tragedy, as his new wife, Fanny Waugh, died of miliary fever less than two months after the birth of their son. He returned to Italy in 1868, travelling as far south as Naples, and made a number of watercolours and oil paintings. W.M. Rossetti felt that Italy was 'my native country almost in equal degree with England', and travelled there often. He worked with his brother on his translations of Dante, and published separate studies of his work. In later life, he became influential in promoting Italian literature, especially in Oxford, where he was a lecturer and examiner. He also served on the jury of the first Venice Biennale in 1895. W.M. Rossetti's most important visit to Italy took place in 1873, when he took part in the expedition organised by William Bell Scott. Lucy Madox Brown, whom he married in the following year, was one of the party; D.G. Rossetti pulled out at the last minute.

Among the immediate associates of the Brotherhood, Burne-Jones was the most assiduous traveller. His first visit to Italy in 1859 was made at the behest and expense of Ruskin, but he later came to view Italy as his artistic and spiritual home. Holman Hunt's pupil, Edward Lear, had lived in Rome between 1837 and 1848, and later travelled extensively before settling at San Remo in 1871. J.W. Inchbold had studied and painted with Ruskin in Switzerland, but, by the time of his visit to Venice in 1862–4, he had largely abandoned Ruskin's precepts in both oils and watercolours. Walter Crane chose Rome and Naples for his extended honeymoon in 1871–3, a period which had a decisive effect on his art.

77
William Holman Hunt (1827–1910)
Il Ponte Vecchio, Florence
Watercolour on paper laid down on panel, 25.4 x 54.6 cm
Victoria and Albert Museum, London (196–1894)
Ref: Staley and Newall 2004, no. 142; Bronkhurst 2006, no. D251

Hunt married Fanny Waugh in December 1865, but she died a year later while the couple were making an extended stay in Florence. Although Hunt's main preoccupation during this period was his painting illustrating Keats's *Isabella and the Pot of Basil* (Laing Art Gallery, Newcastle), he found time, both as a relaxation from the emotional turmoil of the painting, and as a technical exercise, to execute this watercolour. Hunt was living at 14 Lung'Arno Acciajoli, and, every day, he walked to his studio at 16 via delle belle donne, where he worked from 8.30 a.m. until dusk. From his lodgings, he had this view of the west side of the Ponte Vecchio, which spans the Arno at its narrowest point, and is one of the few mediaeval bridges surviving to be still crowned with its full complement of shops, overhanging the structure of the bridge itself. As he had already done in *London Bridge on the Occasion of the Marriage of the Prince and Princess of Wales* (1863; Ashmolean), Hunt explores in his view of the Ponte Vecchio the combination of moonlight and artificial light to illuminate the scene.

The watercolour was greatly admired when it was exhibited at the Dudley Gallery in London in 1872. Later, artists such as Leighton, Burne-Jones, T.M. Rooke, and Hunt's friend Charles Crowley are all recorded as being enthusiastic. The first owner was John Graham, the brother of William Graham, the great patron of Burne-Jones (**cats. 126-7, 132**).

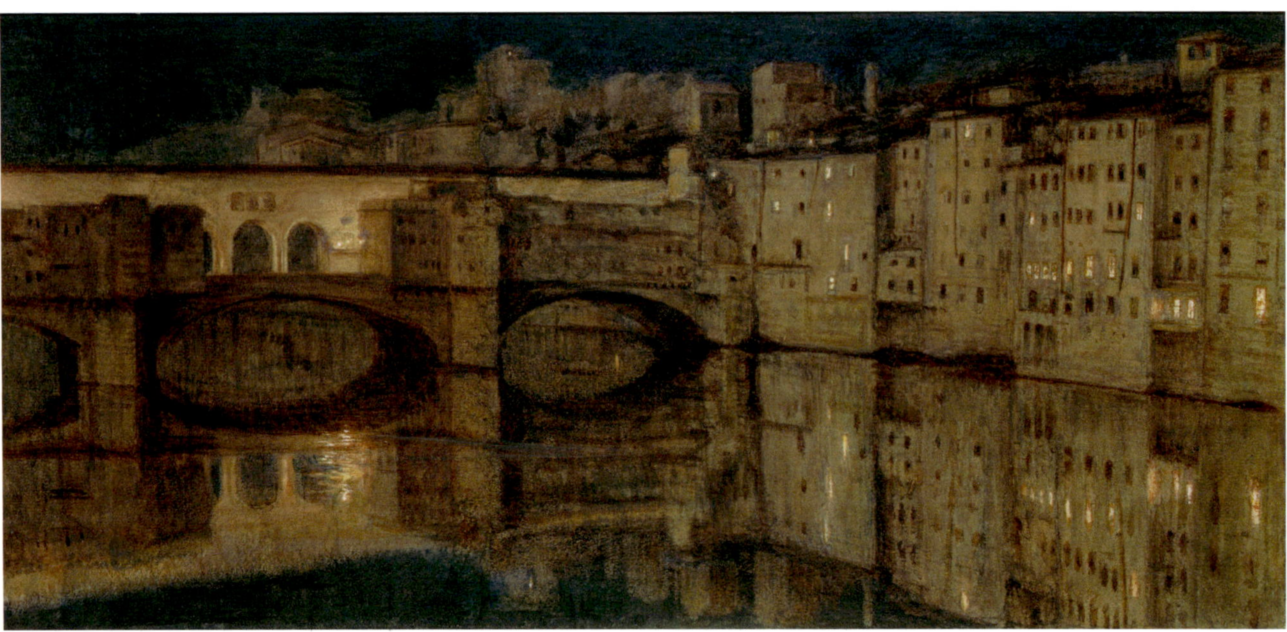

78

William Holman Hunt

A Festa at Fiesole

Watercolour with scratching out and pencil, 34.9 x 50.5 cm

Signed in monogram and inscribed lower left: *Whh 68 / FIESOLE*

Private collection

Ref: Staley and Newall 2004, no. 75; Bronkhurst 2006, no. D255

During his second stay in Florence, in June 1868, Hunt went up to Fiesole to escape the summer heat, and reported that he was 'for the sake of the open air working at water colour landscapes'. The second of these watercolours, *A Festa at Fiesole*, eventually formed part of a series of four Italian landscapes exploring the effects of the brilliant summer sunshine on the countryside, which the artist later considered 'far the best drawings I have ever done.' It was begun on 6 July 1868, when Hunt visited Fiesole with J.W. Bunney and they discovered that it was the feast of St Romolo, one of the patron saints of the town. The view was taken from the garden walls of the Villa Medici on the old road to Florence, looking over the valley of the Arno. The inclusion of a young boy looking wistfully at the group of retreating soldiers adds anecdotal interest not included in the other watercolours in the series.

When this work was exhibited at the Old Watercolour Society in 1870, the reviewers complained of the awkward composition, and, especially, the effect of the sun shining through the trees. F.G. Stephens had already warned Hunt that 'the meteorological effects …will be, I fancy, *caviare* to the million'. Hunt explained that 'the green halo round the sun in the cypress grove at Fiesole … is rather an optical than a meteorological effect.'

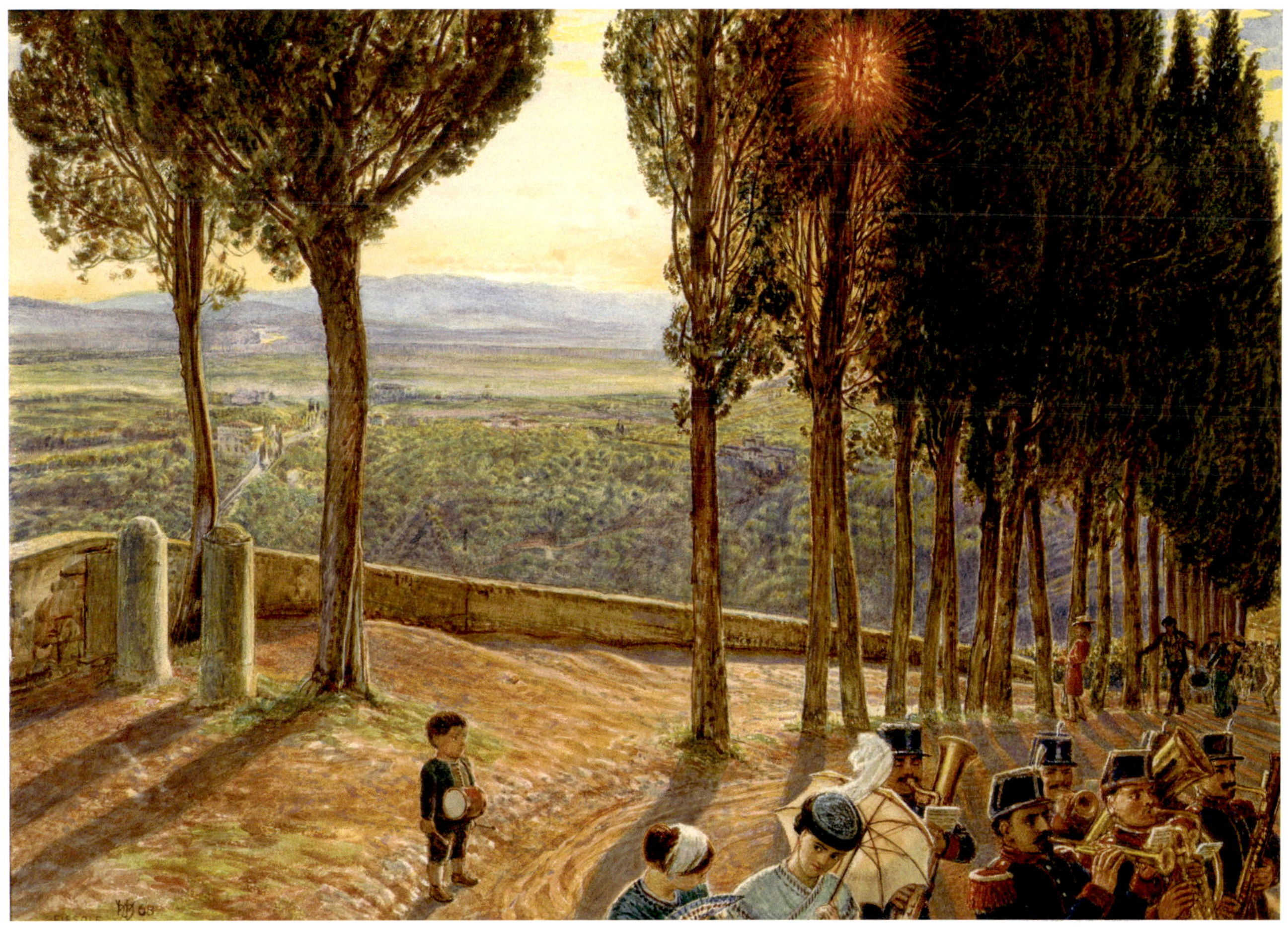

79

William Holman Hunt

Interior of the Cathedral at Salerno 1868
Watercolour with traces of white bodycolour, scratching out, and pencil, 25.3 x 35.5 cm
Signed in monogram and inscribed: *Whh 1868 / SALERNO*
Private collection
Ref: Bronkhurst 2006, no. D257

From his stay at Fiesole in the summer of 1868, Hunt moved on to Naples on 14 July. He remained until September, also visiting Salerno and Ravello, before returning to Florence in December. While at Salerno, he naturally visited the cathedral, celebrated above all as the burial place of the Evangelist, St Matthew. Although it was consecrated by Gregory VI in 1084, the present structure is largely a Baroque reconstruction after an earthquake in 1688.

Hunt began this watercolour while waiting for the key to the crypt. It shows the view towards the west door from the altar, with the choir in the middle distance, and the twelfth-century mosaics in the foreground. Bronkhurst notes that the treatment of the foreground is 'consciously experimental, the light dissolving rather than intensifying form'. She also observes that, because architectural detail was not Hunt's aim, the two Cosmati pulpits, among the glories of the interior, are almost hidden, while the less interesting pulpit in the choir is carefully depicted. The enormous scale of the interior is indicated by the candelabrum on the left, which stands over 17 feet (5 metres) high, dwarfing the choristers.

The watercolour is significant as the first work Hunt exhibited after his election as an Associate of the Old Watercolour Society in February 1869. It was shown with a moonlight scene, *Moonlight at Salerno*,[1] as a contrasting pair of architectural interior and landscape, day and night, brilliant sunshine and moonlight. As he told Stephens, 'I did them for the sake of the effect and sentiment of the light'. Stephens wrote that they 'combine the splendour of enamel with the solidity, finish, and wealthy colouring of oil.' He went on to describe the interior as 'an effect of brilliant daylight on the gorgeously decorated church... we are looking from the place of the high altar over the many-hued pavement of *opus Alexandrinum*, past slabs of precious marbles, rosy and red, to the vista of the arcaded nave. The whole is suffused with light at its fullest power without glare, and, superb as the multifarious details are, aerial perspective is perfectly preserved in the greatest variety of tints and wealth of tones.'

1 untraced; Bronkhurst 2006, no. D258

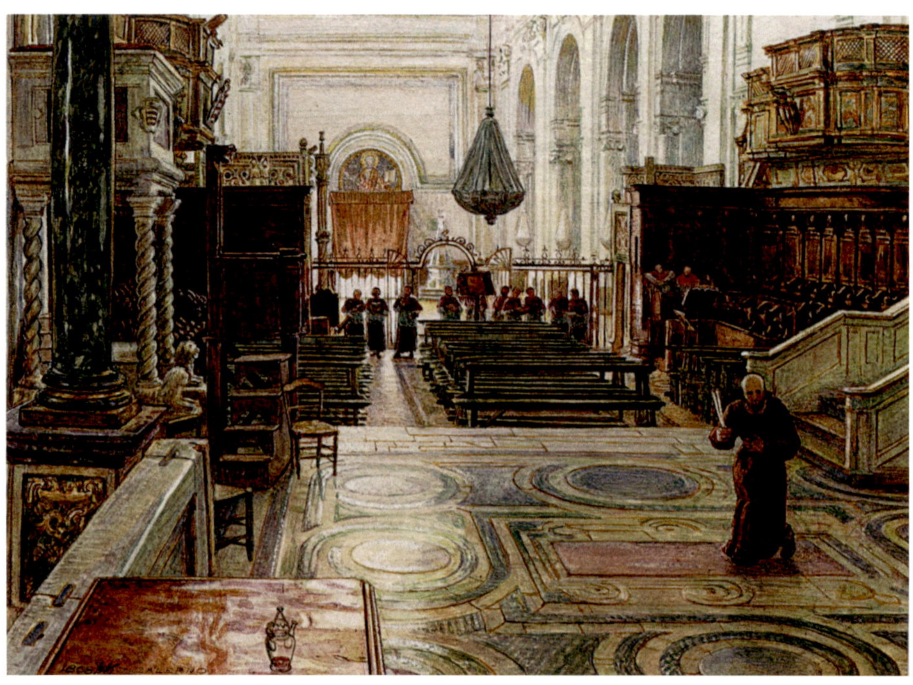

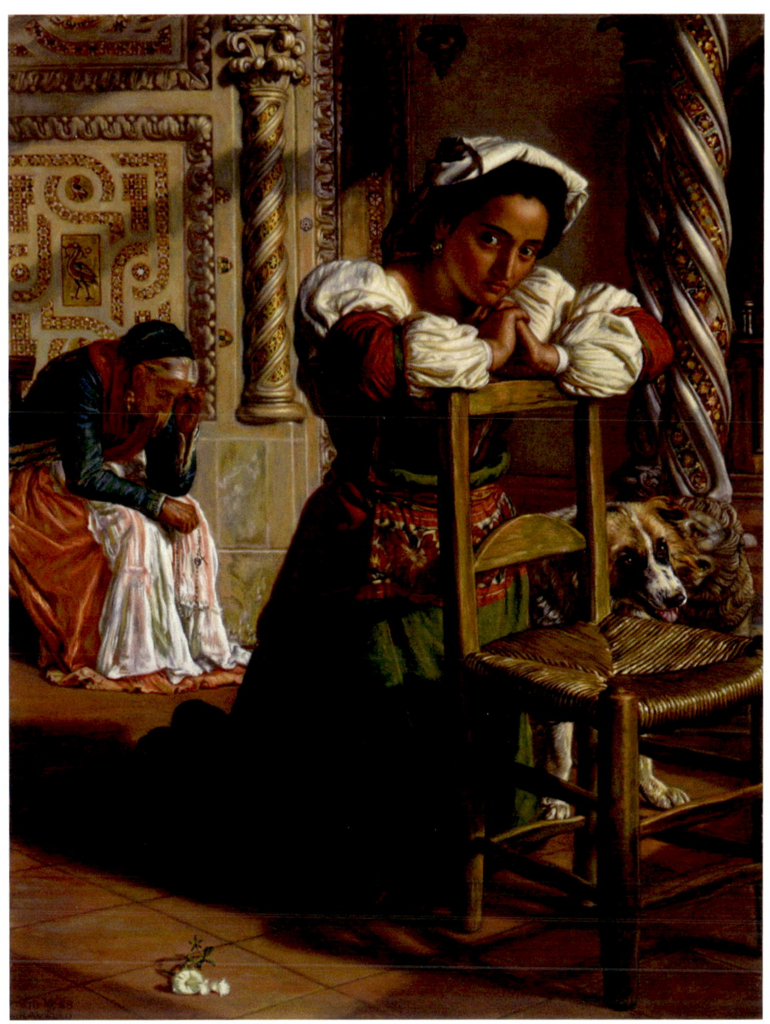

80
William Holman Hunt
Past and Present 1863–8
Oil on canvas, 61.2 x 47 cm
Signed in monogram and dated and inscribed: *Whh 1868 / Ravello*
Aberdeen Art Gallery and Museums Collections
Ref: Bronkhurst 2006, no. 100

On 25 August 1863, Hunt wrote to F.G. Stephens that, 'My plans are now to finish all my work and then to take a pot-boiler of an Italian girl with me to Naples to paint a background.' He had begun the painting earlier in the summer, evidently intending it to be another of his single figure compositions made principally for money. The chair, of a common type of rush-bottom, and two sets of beads were apparently borrowed by Hunt, through the intermediary of his Catholic friend, J.H. Pollen, from the church where he worshipped. The model for the figure presumably wears her own costume, and was one of the Italian colony in London; she also sat to Hunt's friend and pupil, Martineau, for his *Woman of San Germano* (**cat. 85**). Having presumably completed the figure in 1863, Hunt made no progress with the picture until his second trip to Italy in 1868. Eventually, he spent some weeks during August and September 1868 at Ravello, staying with a friend. Fortunately, he noted, 'The locality is right enough for the costume, for the people of the neighbourhood wear it'. The background was painted in the Cathedral of San Pantaleone. Hunt's view shows two of the six spiral columns resting on the backs of lions which support the pulpit designed by Nicola di Bartolomeo da Foggia in 1272, together with the Cosmati mosaics on the wall, to which Hunt has added a column to balance those of the pulpit. He worked with characteristic slowness on the painting, and only completed it after his return to Florence in the autumn. The title, which is not Hunt's own, refers to the contrast between the piety of the old woman in the background and the distracted, even coquettish, glance of the main figure, who takes her dog to church and has dropped a posy of flowers on the floor.

81
William Holman Hunt
An Italian Child
Oil on canvas, 52.1 x 49.1 cm
Signed in monogram and dated: *Whh 69*
Private collection, on long loan to the National Museum Liverpool (Lady Lever Art Gallery)
Ref: Bronkhurst 2006 no. 112

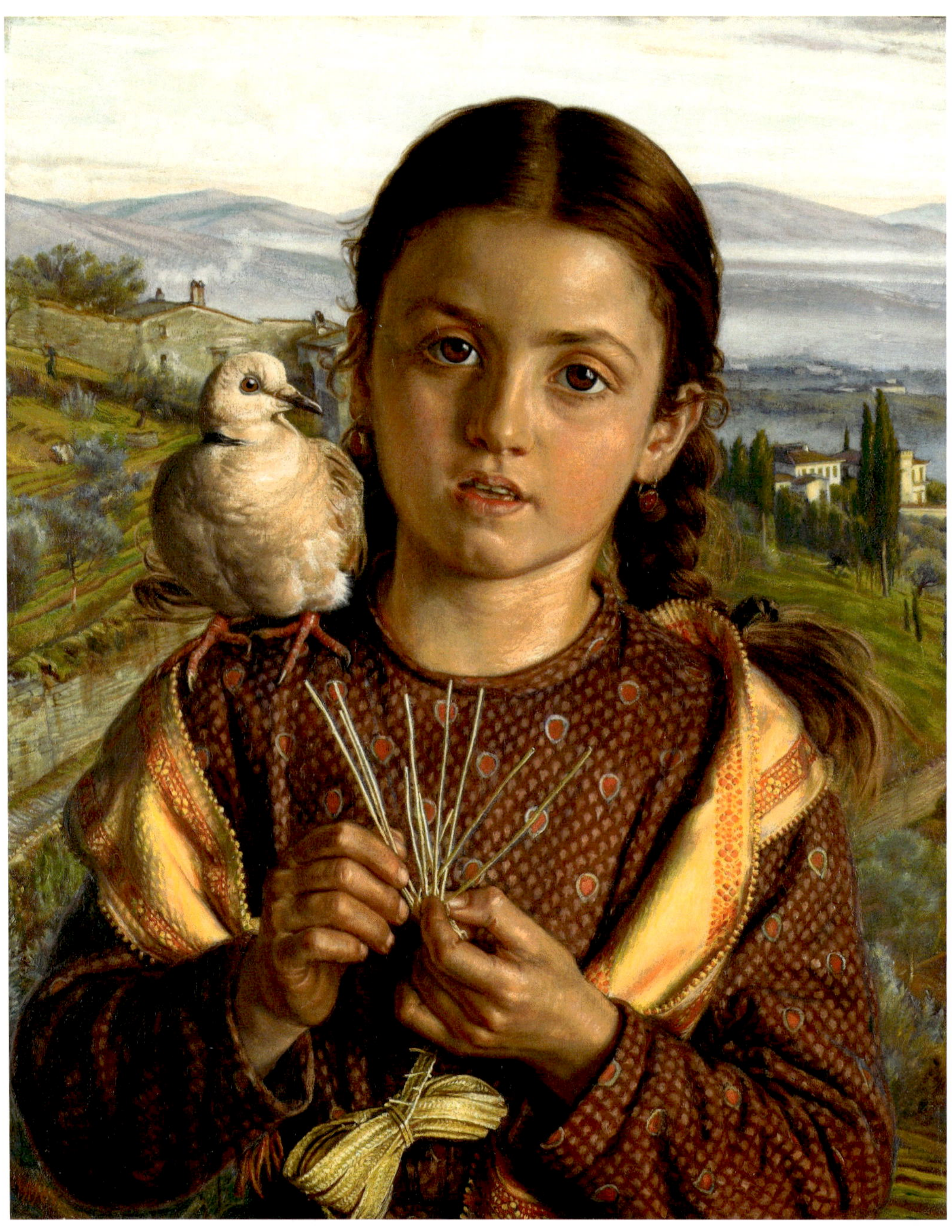

82
William Holman Hunt (not exhibited)
Caught!
Oil on canvas, 34.9 x 31.1 cm
Signed in monogram and dated: *Whh 69*
Private collection
Ref: Bronkhurst 2006 no. 113

Having left his own baby son with relatives in England, Hunt was naturally enchanted by the two children of the gardener at the Villa Medici in Fiesole, where he was the guest of William Blundell Spence, picture dealer, archaeologist, and author of *The Lions of Florence* and other works. He made a number of studies of the girls, all apparently with a view to painting a picture. By 3 February 1869, he could write from Florence to F.G.Stephens that he had nearly completed the 'two heads of children which I began up at Fiesole two or thee months since.' *An Italian Child* and its pendant, *Caught!*, were among the portraits of children that Hunt described as 'potboilers', and he was relieved when he had 'done with the long weary task of keeping the little unruly savages moderately attentive to their work.' The two pictures were completed by mid-March 1869. In his memoirs, Hunt described the larger picture as 'a damsel as a Tuscan straw-plaiter of the type of gentle features peculiar to the cities of the Apennines, such as Perugino loved to paint.' Bronkhurst notes that the composition may have been influenced by works by the Renaissance Old Masters, among them Raphael and Perugino. *Caught!* shows the younger daughter surprised in some unspecified misdemeanour. She is unlikely to have created the long curling apple peel on the window sill, which may be intended as a symbol of lost innocence. Although the two pictures are of different sizes, they form a contrasting pair, the elder girl in an expansive landscape setting in the valley of the Arno, the younger indoors, constricted by a wall and a chair.

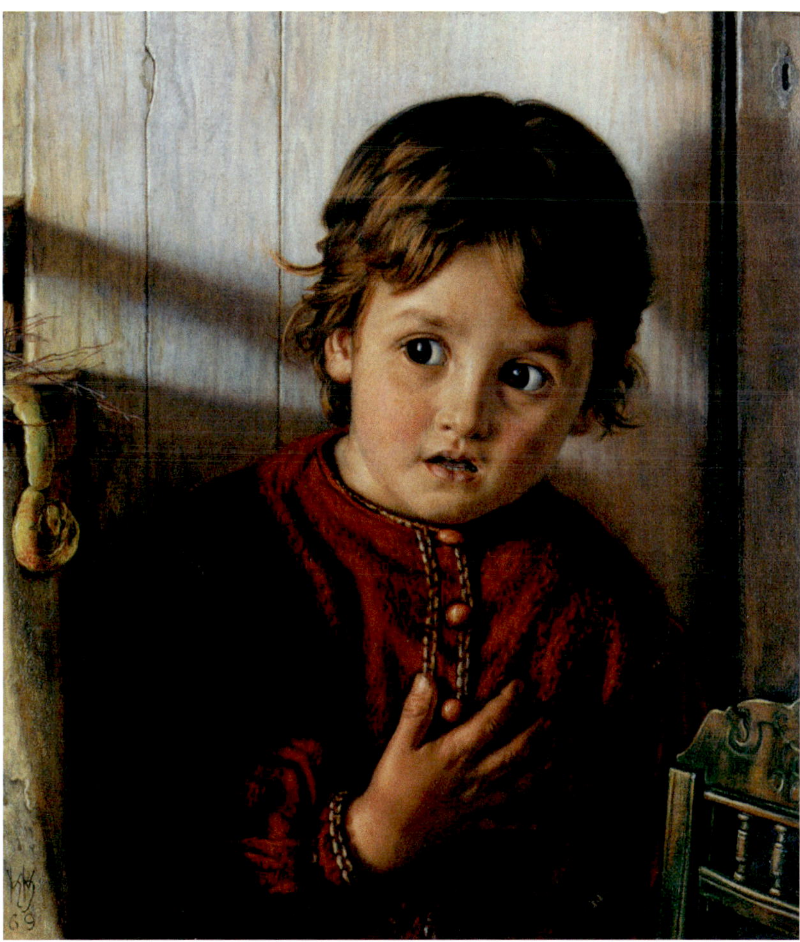

83

Edward Lear (1812–1888)
Florence from the Villa San Firenze
Oil on canvas, 64.8 x 128.2 cm
Signed in monogram and dated: *EL 1862*
Inscribed verso: *View of Florence, taken from Villa San Firenze near San Miniato, painted for Thomas Fairbairn, Esq., from drawings I made on the spot in 1861.* [signed] *Edward Lear*
U.K. Government Art Collection (GAC 6950)
Ref: Bronkhurst 1983, p. 592

Edward Lear was probably the greatest traveller of all artists in the nineteenth century. He passed through Florence on his first visit to Italy in November 1838, where he found a 'hurly-burly of beauty and wonder'; nevertheless, 'the whole place is like an English watering-place'.[1] Although he made oil sketches on this first trip to Italy, it was not until he had met Holman Hunt in 1852 that he was able to satisfy his ambition to become a serious painter in oils. It has been argued that Lear painted only one picture according to true Pre-Raphaelite principles, outdoors,[2] but he remained close to Hunt and had great influence on several Pre-Raphaelites travelling in the Near East.

Lear spent most of June 1861 at Florence, with a commission from his old patroness, Lady Waldegrave, for a view of the city from the Villa Petraia. His initial impression was enchantment: 'Florence, with all the begemmed & villa sparkling hills, more exquisite than one could fancy.' Unfortunately, enchantment soon turned to disappointment, and he found the view from the Villa Petraia 'a little disappointing, the foliage being meagre, & little at command. Yet it MUST be done.' An alternative view, from the Villa Albrizzi, associated by Lear with Galileo, was 'grand but wanting the River'. It was not until 12 June, the day he witnessed Cavour's funeral, that he went up to San Miniato, to the south-east of the city, and 'found I could get into the Villa S. Firenze, the REAL view of Turner. It is very glorious, and I shall set to work at it thoroughly!'[3] And thoroughly he worked, drawing solidly from 2.30 until 7 p.m between 14 and 22 June, every day except the 20th, when his servant and companion George arrived. His technique was unusual: he divided the view into four sections, and drew and then inked in each one separately. The first included the stand of cypress trees on the left; the second showed the

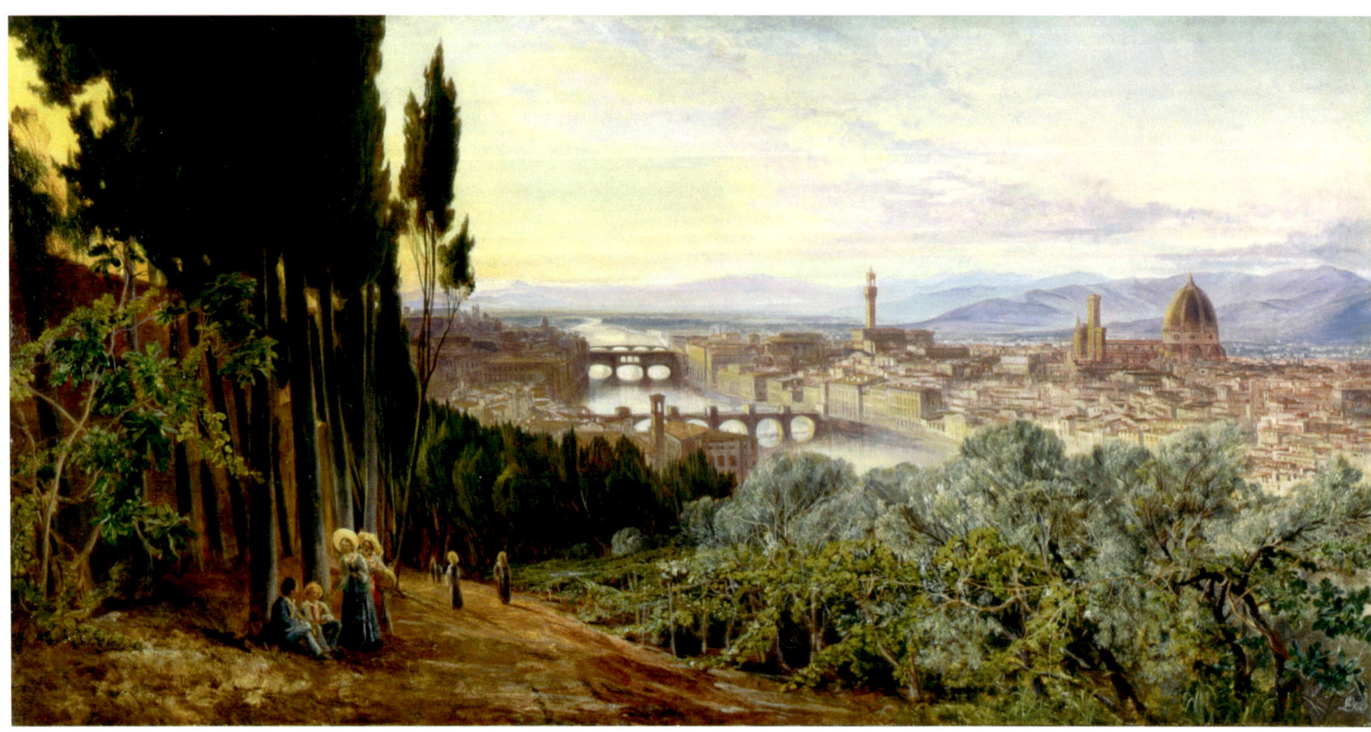

south bank of the river and the two bridges – the Ponte alle Grazie and the Ponte Vecchio; the third included the north bank of the river and the Palazzo Vecchio; while the fourth concentrated on the cathedral.[4] After he had finished these four large detail drawings on 21 June, he reluctantly took up the view commissioned by Lady Waldegrave, from the Villa Petraia; as he recorded on 22 June, 'next comes the Villa Petraija in earnest'. In spite of this resolve, he made a last visit to the Villa San Firenze on 28 June and 'drew cypresses between showers of rain.'[5] Two days later, he left the city.

On the basis of his drawings made in Florence, Lear began the oil paintings in his studio in Corfu. The first was for Lady Waldegrave, on which he was working 'ferociously' in August 1861, but he found the task of painting the detailed townscape far from congenial: 'Today I [must] fidget over all the houses all the hours. No life is more SHOCKING to me than the sitting motionless like a petrified gorilla as to my body & limbs hour after hour – my hand meanwhile, peck, peck pecking at billions of little dots & lines, while my mind is fretting & fuming through every moment of the weary days work.'[6] However, he had completed the picture by 12 October 1861, and in February 1862, was at work on the view of *Florence from the Villa San Firenze*, which had been commissioned by Sir Thomas Fairbairn, a prominent industrialist and an important patron of the Pre-Raphaelites. Desperately short of money, Lear completed Fairbairn's painting in late April or early May 1862.[7] Unlike Brett, whose almost contemporary view of Florence deliberately ignores pictorial convention **(cat. 56)**, Lear has chosen a picturesque view in which the details, as carefully placed as Brett's, are subordinate to the general effect of the city and its setting. It is indeed almost the same view that Turner had shown in several watercolours, one presumably intended for Charles Heath's *Picturesque Views in Italy*, which was never published, and another engraved for *The Keepsake* in 1828.[8] Characteristically, however, Turner broke up the composition by placing prominent trees in the centre, dividing the city in two; Lear takes no such bold step, but leaves his cypresses conventionally where they grew.

1 quoted in Levi 1995, p. 73
2 Treuherz 2002
3 Lear Diaries, 6, 7, 8, and 12 June 1861. Lear's first drawing, a rapid general view dated 12 June, was sold at Sotheby's 10 March 1988, lot 146
4 The drawings respectively with Agnew's, 1965; Sotheby's 7 July 1965, lot 58; with Agnew's, 1960; and with Agnew's, 1961. Photographs are in the Witt Library
5 presumably the rain-spattered drawing in the Tate (N02799)
6 Strachey 1907, p. 189
7 Strachey 1907, p. 229
8 Wilton 1979, nos 726–9

84

Edward Lear (1812–1888)
The Plains of Lombardy from Monte Generoso
Oil on canvas, 24 x 47 cm
Signed in monogram, *EL*
Ashmolean Museum, University of Oxford.
Bequeathed by the Revd Henry Fanshawe Tozer, 1916
WA 1916.39

Lear moved into the Villa Emily, San Remo, in 1871, and spent the summers from 1878 to 1883 at Monte Generoso, to the west of Como on the Italian-Swiss border. He found the area very beneficial to his health and that of his servant, George, and enjoyed the company of a large number of friends and acquaintances among the other guests: 'I constantly expect to see the Sultan, Mrs Gladstone, Sir Joshua Reynolds and the twelve Apostles walk into the Hotel.'[1] Indeed, almost the only disadvantage was the noise of children – 'the row of forty little ill-conducted beasts' at meals was 'simply frightful'.[2] Although ostensibly on holiday, Lear made many drawings of the view from the summit, and even considered using it in his projected series of 'paintings-sympathizations' evoking the poems of Tennyson, as one of the possibilities appropriate to the lines 'On some vast plain before a setting sun', from 'Guinevere'; the others were views in the Himalayas, Egypt, and Syria.[3] This oil painting was one of nine of various subjects begun on 2 February 1880, all based on sketches from Lear's portfolio, and ranging from Ravenna to Gwalior and Malabar, from his Indian journey in 1873–4; Lear never adhered strictly to the Pre-Raphaelite principle of painting from nature, though he retained the brilliant white ground and luminosity he had learnt from Holman Hunt all his life. *Monte Generoso* was sold to Henry Tozer, an Oxford classicist and geographer and the author of a commentary on Dante, who also made an important collection of Lear's watercolours. It is among Lear's most intense late works, the composition and colouring both simplified and sophisticated.

1 Strachey 1911, p. 267
2 Strachey 1911, p. 246
3 Pitman 1988, pp. 189–92

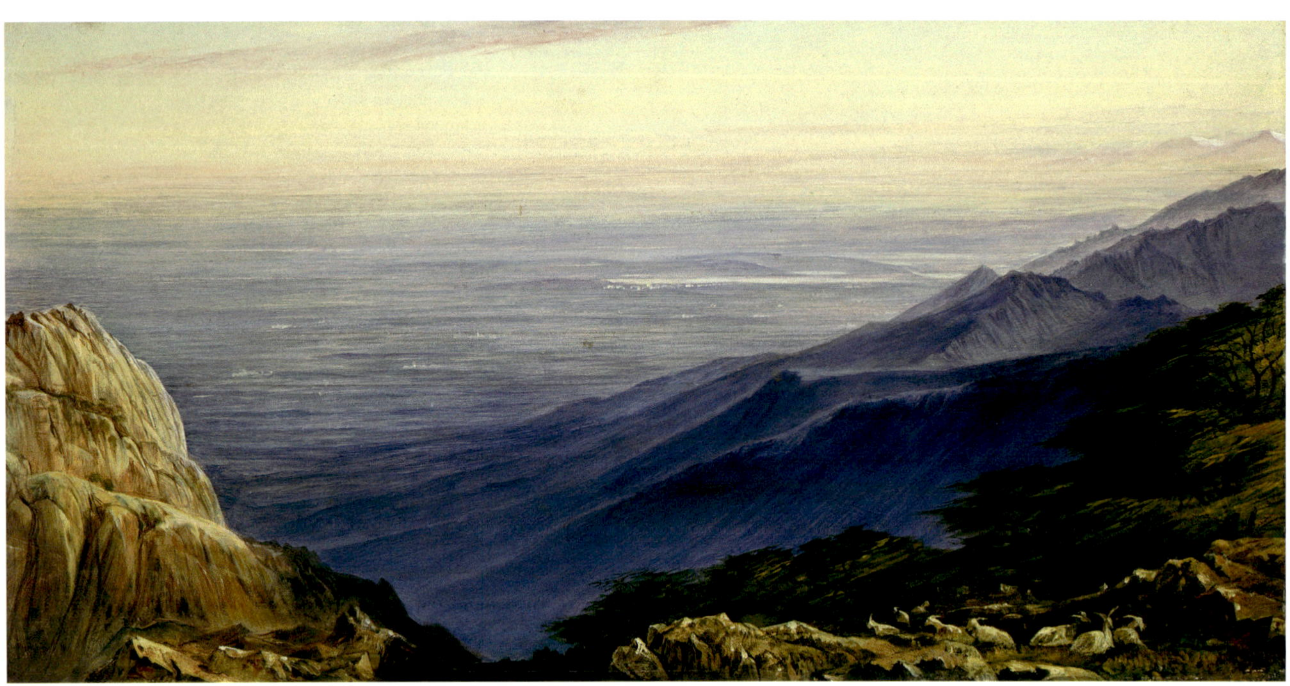

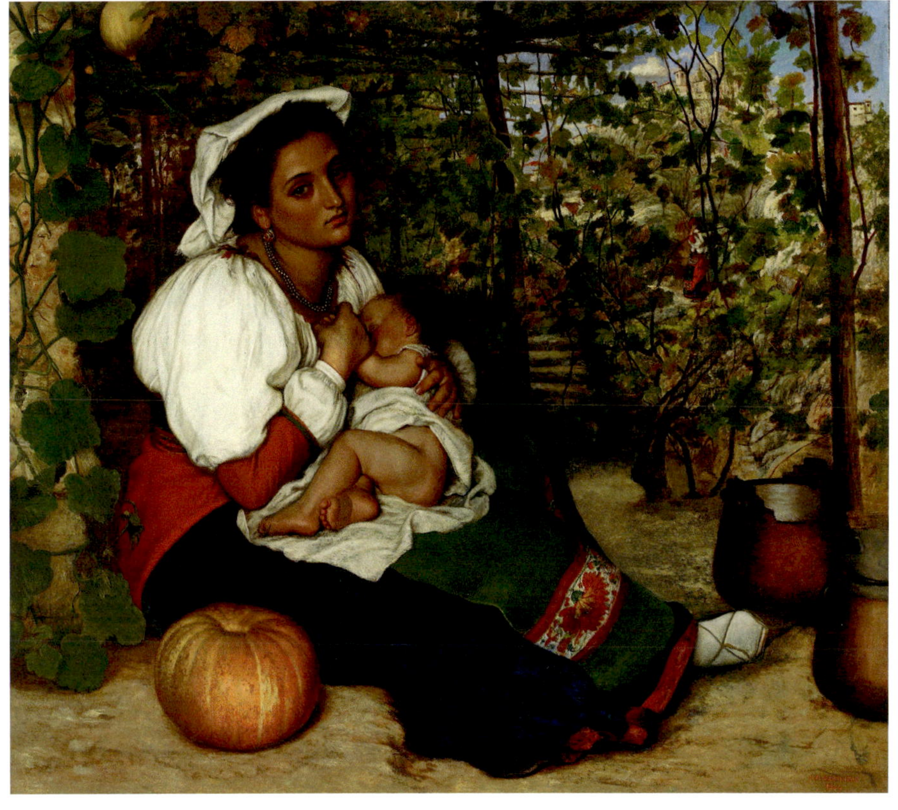

85
Robert Braithwaite Martineau (1826–1869)
A Woman of San Germano
Oil on canvas, 57.5 x 65.2 cm
Signed and dated: R.B. MARTINEAU 1864
Accepted by H.M. Government in lieu of inheritance tax and temporarily allocated to the Ashmolean Museum, 2009
Ref: Martineau 1924, pp. 207–8; Martineau 1942, p. 100

Martineau studied painting with Holman Hunt from 1851, shared his studio until 1857, and remained close to his master all his life; they held a joint private exhibition in 1864. He was an important member of the Pre-Raphaelite circle, exhibiting with them in Russell Place in 1857, and serving as treasurer of the Hogarth Club. He was the model for one of the figure's in Ford Madox Brown's *Work* (1856–63; Manchester City Art Gallery), and the subject of one of Hunt's most impressive portraits in chalk.[1] He worked very slowly, in a true Pre-Raphaelite technique, and Hunt deplored his habit of 'painting over and over again his yesterday's work while still wet.' His output was thus very small – he completed fewer than twenty paintings before his premature death at the age of 43.

A Woman of San Germano was exhibited at the Royal Academy in 1864. It seems to show the same model as that in Hunt's *Past and Present* (**cat. 80**), in the same dress, and would therefore have been substantially painted in London. Moreover, there is no record that Martineau ever travelled to Italy, so he may have based the background on prints or it may even be imaginary. The type of peasant woman (*contadina*) and her picturesque costume was one that many European artists had painted, especially during the 1820s and 1830s, but is otherwise almost unknown among the Pre-Raphaelites.[2] The model may have been one of the large Italian colony in the area around Holborn in London in the 1860s, which included a significant element from the Liri valley, which included San Germano (now Monte Cassino), and which was part of the Neapolitan region of Campania. The women wore Neapolitan costume, and covered their heads with handkerchiefs, as is seen in the paintings by Martineau and Hunt.[3] The meticulous detail of the woman's costume and the tenderness of her pose as she holds her sleeping child are matched by the care with which the elements of still life – cooking pots and pumpkin – and the pergola of vines are painted. Martineau also no doubt intended the viewer to understand references to compositions of the Virgin and Child by the Italian Old Masters.

When he exhibited this picture at the Royal Academy in 1864, together with *The Knight's Guerdon* (Ashmolean), the critic in *The Times* complained that he expected more important works from this artist, but acknowledged that both paintings 'have his distinctive quality of rich and subtly modulated colour' (11 May 1864).

1 Walker Art Gallery, Liverpool; Bronkhurst 2006, no. D196

2 a young girl wearing a similar costume appears in a photograph by Julia Margaret Cameron of 1869; see Cox and Ford 2003, pl. 914

3 see Sponza 1988, pp. 13, 19, 248

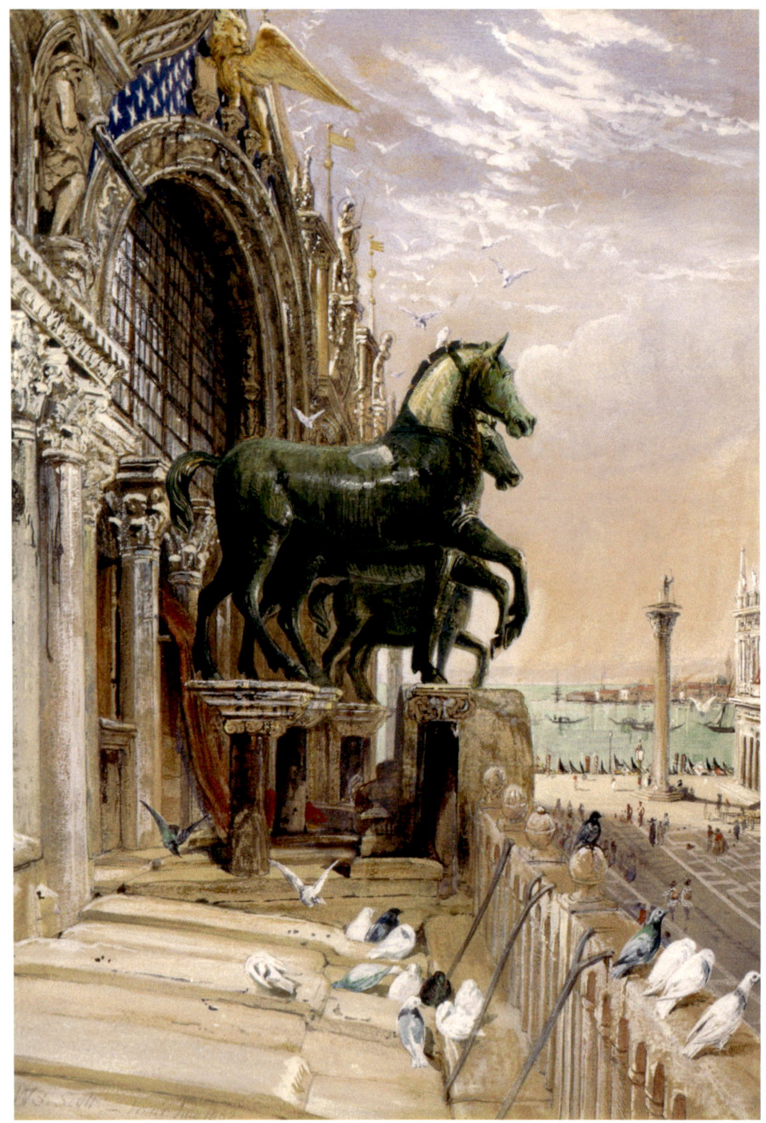

86
William Bell Scott (1811–1890)
Upper Portion of the Façade of St Mark's, Venice
Watercolour on paper, 35.6 x 25.3 cm
Signed and dated: *W.B. Scott Venice July 1862*
Victoria & Albert Museum (A.L. 4358)

In *The Stones of Venice*, Ruskin described the upper part of the façade of St Mark's as 'a confusion of delight, amidst which the breasts of the Greek horses are seen blazing in their breadth of golden strength'.[1] They had been sent from the Hippodrome at Constantinople in 1204, and were frequently supposed in the nineteenth century to have been cast in the workshop of Lysippus. Although they might have seemed an obvious choice of subject for artists, there are surprisingly few depictions of them in detail, in spite of their easy accessibility.

Scott had planned a journey to Italy with W.M. Rossetti and D.G. Rossetti in 1862. However, following the suicide of his wife, Elizabeth Siddal, in February, D.G. Rossetti withdrew, and W.M. Rossetti and Scott travelled alone. Scott had already begun his watercolour of the bronze horses of St Mark's when J.W. Inchbold met him in July 1862, and was apparently mortified to hear that Inchbold proposed to attempt a similar view.[2] Inchbold nevertheless proceeded to paint *The Green Horses of St Mark's*, exhibited at the Royal Academy in 1873 and now untraced. Scott's watercolour is carefully worked up and signed for sale.

1 Ruskin 1903–12, X, p. 83
2 Newall 1993, p.

87

John William Inchbold (1830–1888)
On the Lagoon, Venice
Oil on canvas, 40.6 x 72.5 cm
Inscribed: *The Certosa Venise / from Giardino Publico* and signed in monogram
Leeds Museums and Galleries (City Art Gallery)
Ref: Newall 1993, no. 15

During his early years, Inchbold was the great pioneer of the Pre-Raphaelite landscape painted according to the principles laid down by Ruskin. At the Royal Academy in 1855, Ruskin called Inchbold's *The Moorland: Tennyson* 'the only thoroughly good landscape in the rooms of the Academy … the appreciation of truth in it is so intense, that a single inch of it is well worth all the rest of the landscapes in the room.'[1] However, by 1857, Ruskin felt that Inchbold 'had entirely gone off the rails',[2] and they gradually drifted apart.

Inchbold spent the years 1862–4 in Venice, perhaps for the sake of his health. Among the works painted during this period are a number of remarkable landscapes in oil. Unlike his paintings of the previous decade, which tend to be obsessively detailed and take almost literally Ruskin's order to 'reject nothing' from nature, the Venetian views are much more spacious and less claustrophobic in feeling. He seems to have been instinctively drawn to the less populated parts of the city, such as the islands of San Pietro di Castello and Sant'Elena, and his views are generally taken looking away from the tourist attractions, out over the lagoon, with the city reduced to a narrow band of buildings on the horizon, between the expanses of water and sky. Even the painting entitled *The Redentore, Venice*, shows Palladio's church almost subsumed by the vegetation in the gardens in the foreground.[3] *On the Lagoon, Venice* is the most extreme of these views, and shows no significant landmarks at all. The artist's inscription is confusing: although it indicates that he painted the view looking out from the Public Gardens towards the island of La Certosa, in fact, it must have been painted from the north or east side of Castello or Sant'Elena. It was perhaps because of their unconventional subject-matter that Inchbold's views of Venice seem not to have found a ready market when he returned to England in 1864.

1 quoted in Newall 1993, p. 12
2 quoted in Newall 1993, p. 14
3 Newall 1993, no. 17

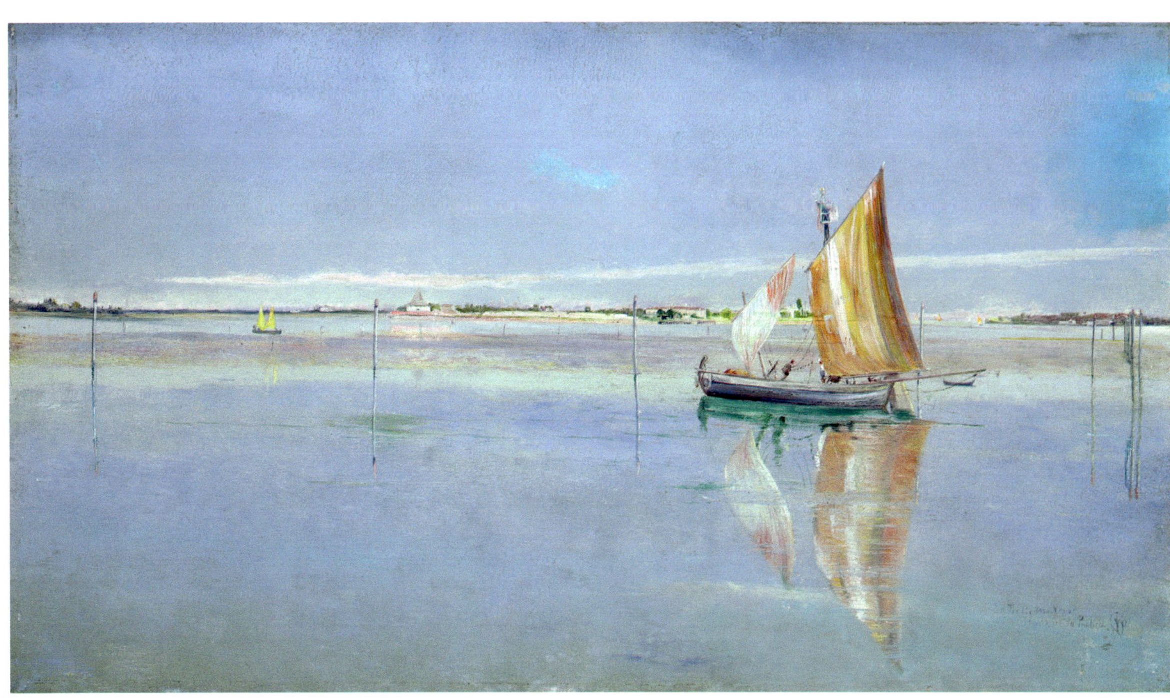

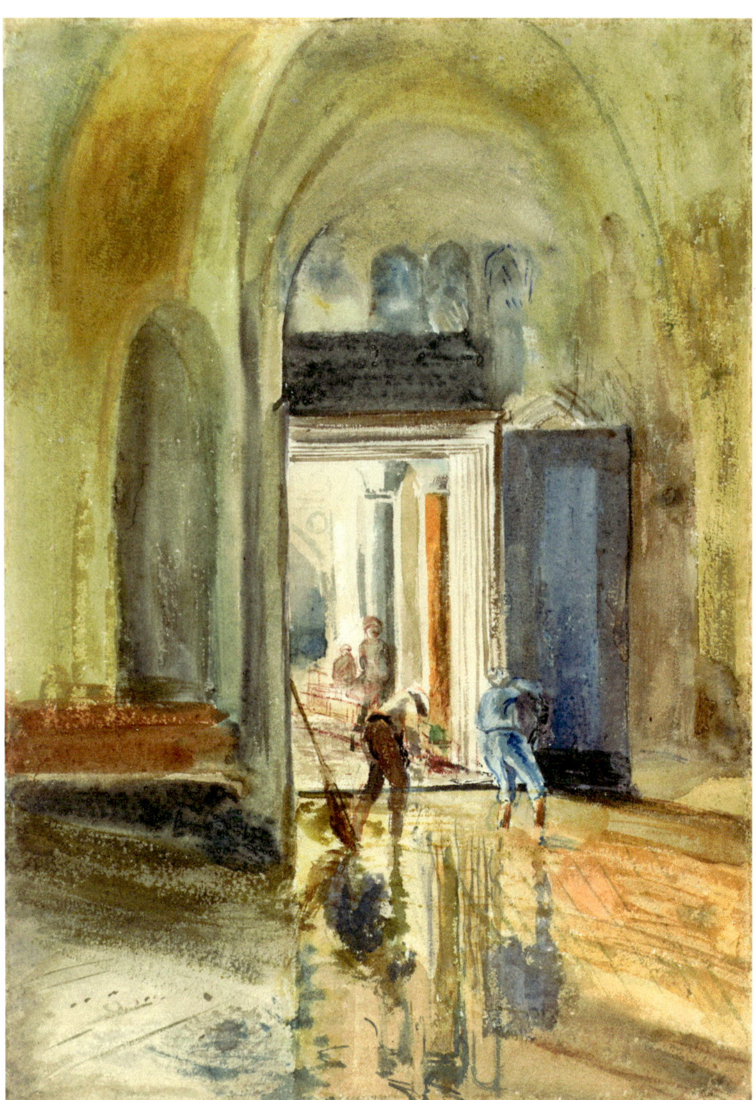

88
John William Inchbold (1830–1888)
Inundation at St Mark's
Watercolour and pencil on paper, 36.1 x 25.8 cm
Inscribed: *Inundation at St Marcs / 1863–4*
Tate. Purchased as part of the Oppé Collection with assistance from the National Lottery through the Heritage Lottery Fund, 1996 (T09026)
Ref: Newall 1993, no. 16

In addition to his oil paintings, Inchbold also made numerous watercolours during his extended stay in Venice. They are much freer in technique, and generally made as studies rather than finished works for sale. Apart from *Venice, Nocturne: San Giorgio Maggiore* (Tate), which shares the wide expanse of lagoon and sky with many of the contemporary oil paintings, the subjects of the watercolours are generally more informal. This is one of the most topical, describing the scene during the winter of 1863–4 when the basilica of St Mark's was flooded. The vigorous movement seen in the men sweeping out the water is unusual in Inchbold's work.

89
John William Inchbold
Vesuvius and the Bay of Naples from Posilippo
Watercolour on paper, 25.3 x 35.4 cm
Signed and dated: *J W Inchbold 1887*
Victoria & Albert Museum (261–1898)
Ref: Newall 1993, no. 56

Although the date has traditionally been read as '1857', Newall has convincingly associated this watercolour with the year '1887', both from documentary sources and on stylistic grounds. Inchbold spent the winter of 1886–7 travelling on the French Riviera and in Italy: in December 1886, he was in Rome, and intending to visit Naples early in the new year.

Inchbold's is the classic view looking east from Posilippo, across the Bay of Mergellina and the Castel del'Ovo towards the volcanic peaks of Somma and Vesuvius. It is probably identical to the watercolour, otherwise untraced, of *Vesuvius from Virgil's Tomb* sold in the artist's studio sale. As with his views of Venice, Inchbold has again taken a view looking out onto a panoramic landscape, rather than inwards towards a notable tourist attraction, in this case the tomb of Virgil, which had been a place of pilgrimage since the Renaissance.

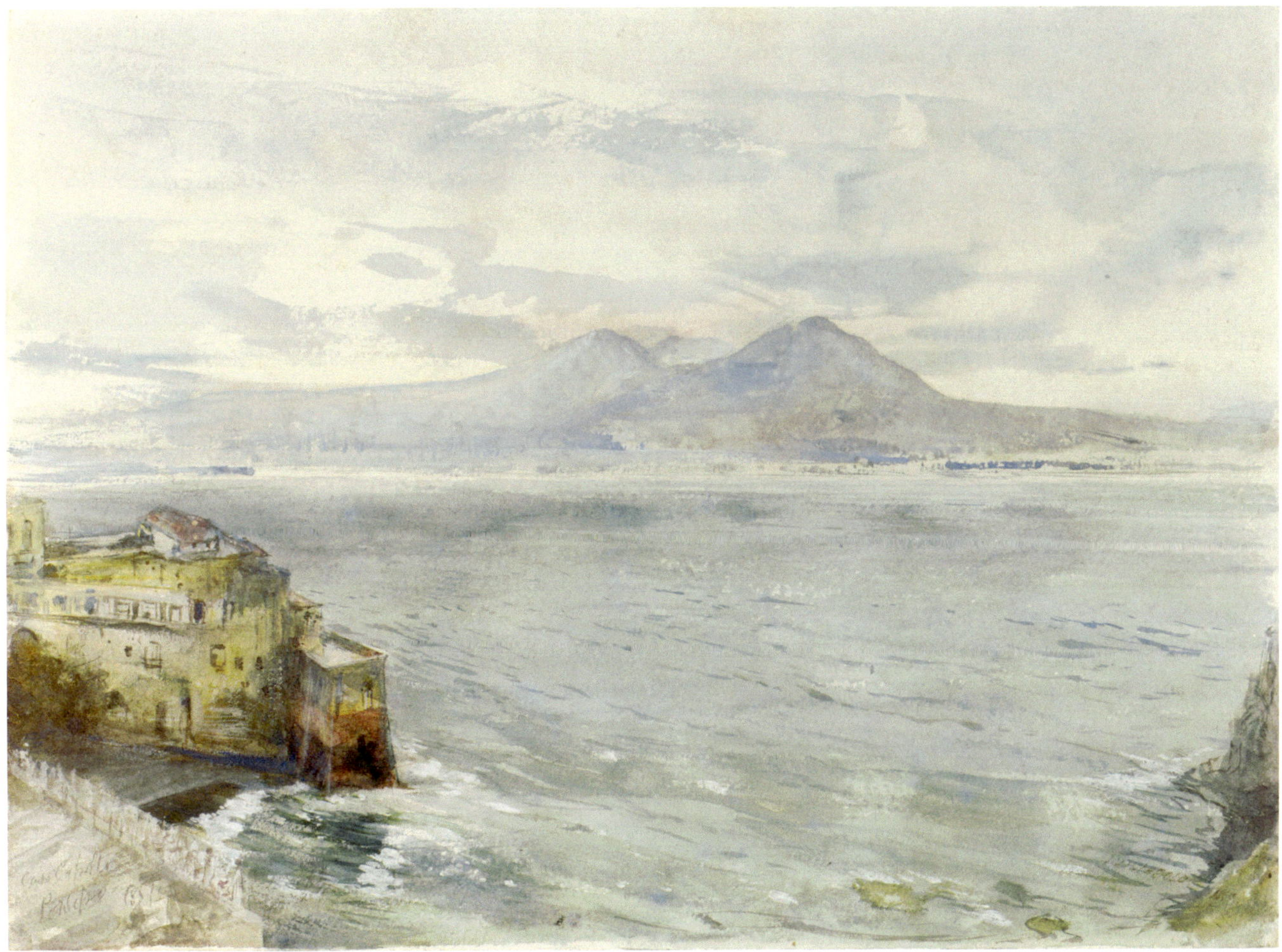

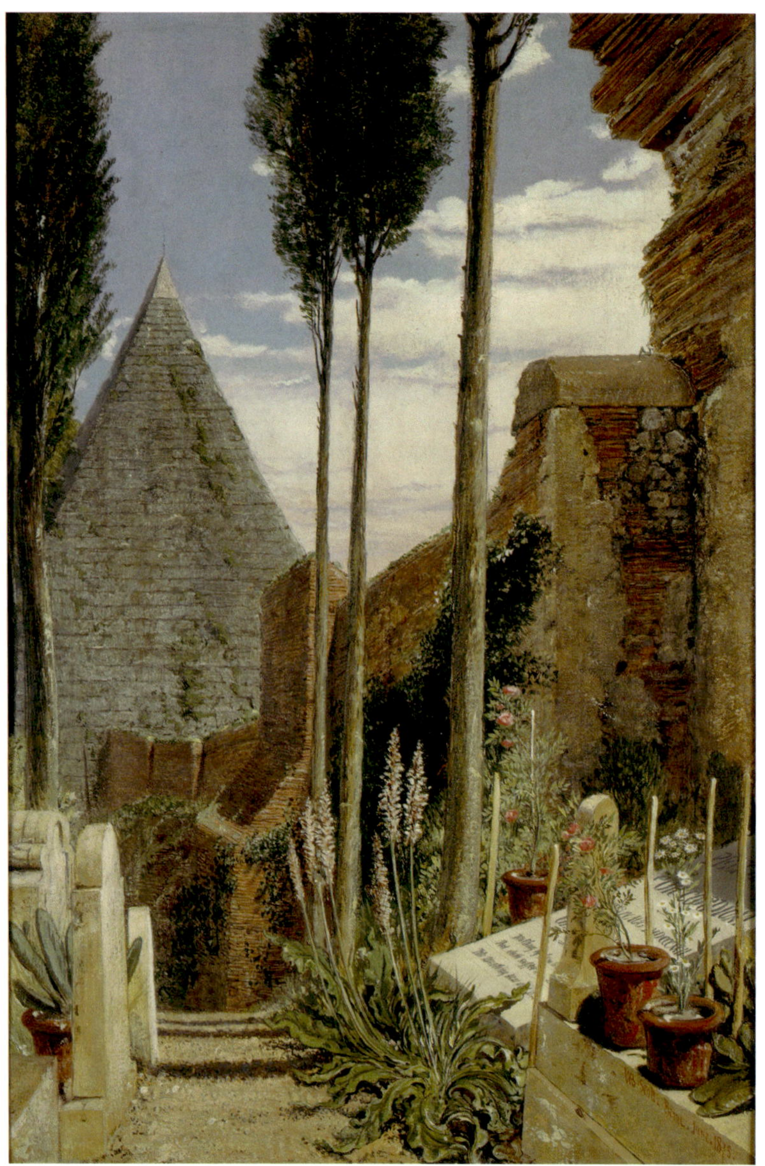

90
William Bell Scott
Shelley's Grave in the New Protestant Cemetery at Rome
Oil on canvas, 48 x 33 cm
Signed and dated: *W.B. Scott Rome. June 1873.*
Ashmolean Museum, University of Oxford.
Presented by Miss Alice Boyd, 1893 (WA1893.2)
Ref: Liversidge & Edwards 1996 no. 39

Scott made his last visit to Italy in the company of his wife, his patroness Alice Boyd, his friend W.M. Rossetti, and Ford Madox Brown's daughter, Lucy. They travelled via Genoa and Pisa to Rome, and stopped at Venice on the return journey. As a friend and admirer of D.G. Rossetti, Scott also had pretensions as a painter-poet, and published editions of the poems of Shelley and Keats in 1873. It was natural that he should paint the tombs of Shelley and Keats while in Rome, both out of personal interest, and because they had become places of pilgrimage for all English visitors, for whom the parallel fates of the young poets romantically buried in a foreign country were irresistible.

Shelley was drowned off the coast of Lerici, and his body washed ashore near Viareggio on 18 June 1822. It was cremated on the beach, and the ashes buried in the Protestant Cemetery in Rome in the following year. As in his view of Keat's grave, Scott shows the grave stone with the inscription carefully legible: *PERCY BYSSHE SHELLEY / COR CORDIUM / NATUS IV AUG. MDCCXCII / OBIIT VIII JUL. MDCCCXXII / Nothing of him that doth fade / But doth suffer a sea-change / Into something rich and strange.*

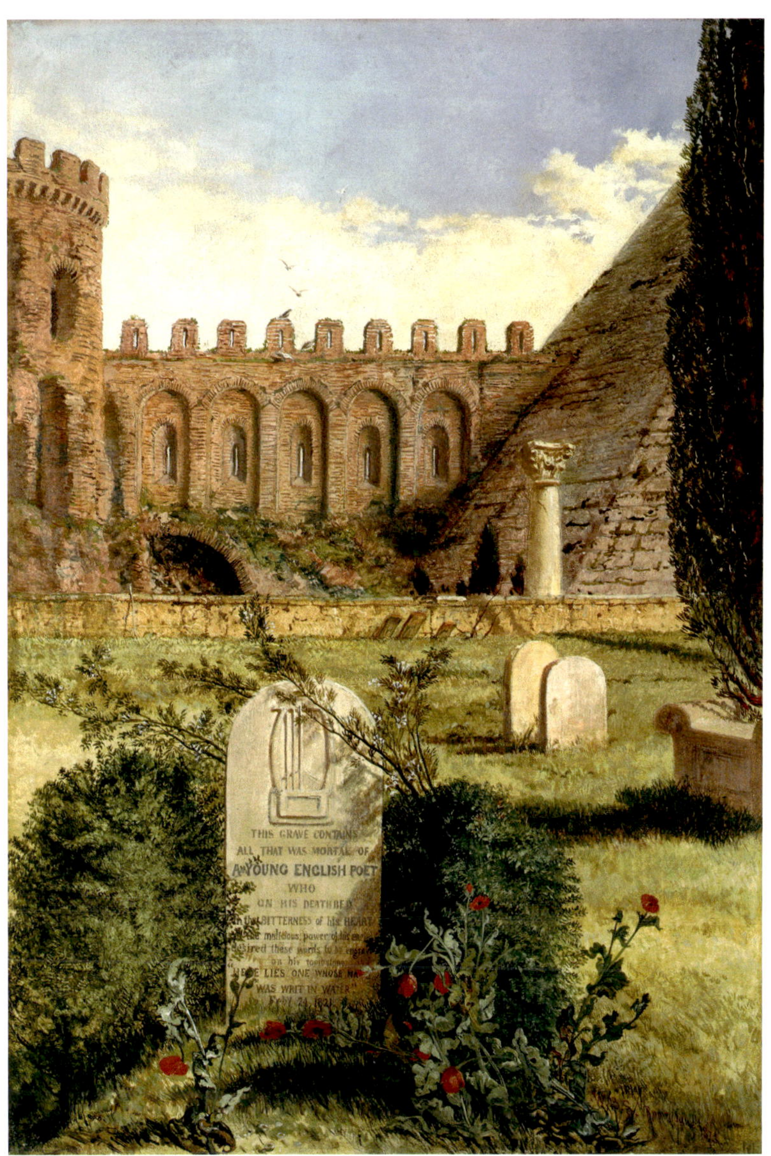

91
William Bell Scott
Keats's Grave in the Old Protestant Cemetery at Rome
Oil on canvas, 48 x 33 cm
Signed and dated: *W.B.S. Rome June 1873*
Ashmolean Museum, University of Oxford.
Presented by Miss Alice Boyd, 1893 (WA1893.3)
Ref: Liversidge & Edwards 1996 no. 38

In his preface to *Adonais*, Shelly described this scene: 'John Keats was buried in the romantic and lonely cemetery of the protestants in that city, under the pyramid which is the tomb of Cestius, and the massy walls and towers, now mouldering and desolate, which formed the circuit of ancient Rome. The cemetery is an open space among the ruins covered in winter with violets and daisies. It might make one in love with death, to think that one should be buried in so sweet a place.' Keats died in his lodgings in the Piazza di Spagna in Rome on 23 Februrary 1821, and was buried in the Protestant Cemetery. His friend Joseph Severn arranged the tombstone, whose inscription is carefully transcribed by Scott: *THIS GRAVE CONTAINS ALL THAT WAS MORTAL OF A YOUNG ENGLISH POET WHO ON HIS DEATH-BED In the BITTERNESS of his HEART* [at] *the malicious power of his* [enemies] *desired these words to be engrav*[ed] *on his tombstone 'HERE LIES ONE WHOSE NAME WAS WRIT IN WATER' Feby 24 1821.* A few years later, in 1877, the young Oscar Wilde described the site of Keats's tomb as 'the holiest place in Rome'.

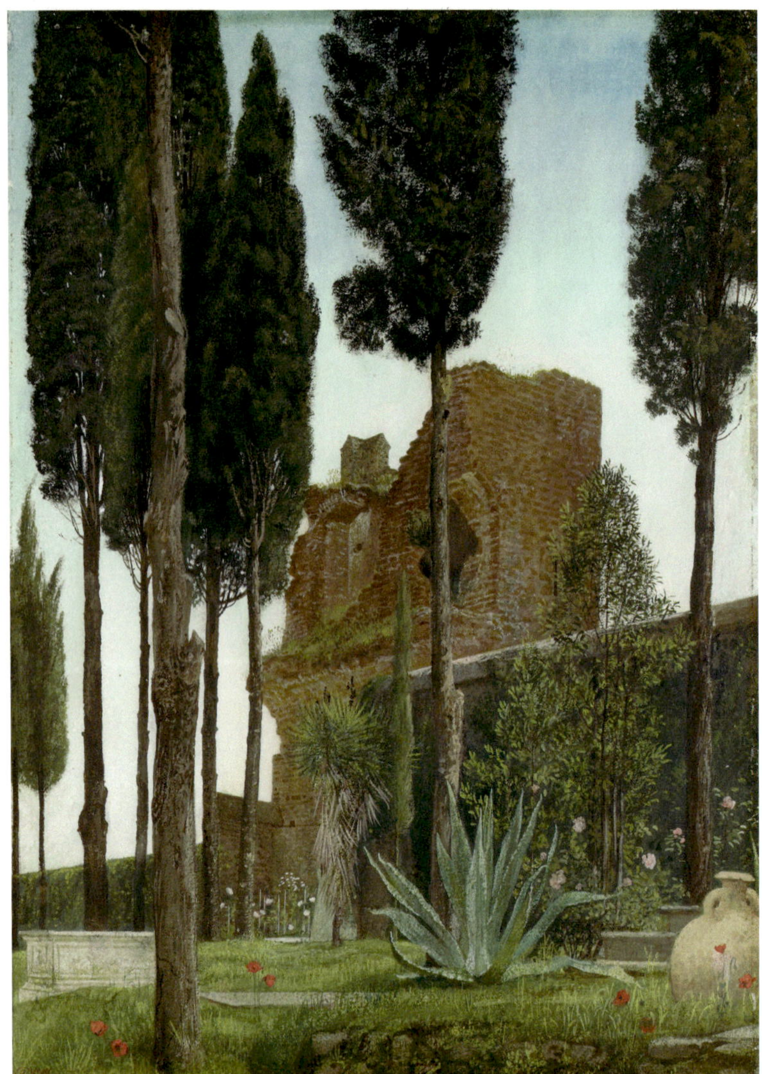

92
Walter Crane (1845–1915)
The Grave of Shelley
Watercolour and bodycolour on paper, 34.5 x 27.7 cm
Signed in monogram and dated: *MAY / 1872*
Ashmolean Museum, University of Oxford.
Presented by Lady Mary Murray, 1942. (WA1942.77)

Walter Crane was already an experienced artist when he saw the work of Burne-Jones for the first time at the Old Watercolour Society's exhibition in 1865; he particularly admired the 'magic world of romance and pictured poetry' in Burne-Jones's work. His landscape painting, however, owes more to the example of Burne-Jones's friend and patron, George Howard, both in the use of bodycolour, and the expansive compositions.

Crane married Mary Andrews on 6 September 1871 and the couple spent eighteen months on their extended honeymoon in Italy. In the spring of 1872, Crane received a commission from George Howard to make a drawing of Shelley's tomb in the Protestant cemetery. He expressed himself 'really delighted', as he was such an admirer of the poet that he was 'glad to pay my little tribute to him… even if the place where he is buried were less beautiful than it is.'[1] Crane had completed the drawing by the time he left Rome on 18 May 1872 , and sent it to Howard, together with a sonnet he had written in the cemetery, later published in his *Reminiscences*.[2] Unlike Scott (**cat. 90**), Crane takes a distant view of Shelley's tomb, nestling at the foot of one of the most substantial surviving portions of the Aurelian Wall, and surrounded by flowers. Indeed, the drawing is a more general evocation of the magical mood of the cemetery, commented on by so many visitors, than an elegy to Shelley himself.

1 letter from Crane to Howard, 11 April 1872 (Castle Howard MSS)

2 letter from Crane to Howard, 31 May 1872 (Castle Howard MSS); Crane 1907, p. 152

93

Walter Crane

The Grave of Keats

Watercolour and bodycolour on paper,
24.3 x 34.1 cm
Signed in monogram and dated: *ROMA / 1873*
Ashmolean Museum, University of Oxford.
Presented by Lady Mary Murray, 1942 (WA1942.78)

Following their return from the summer in Naples, the Cranes spent the winter of 1872–3 in Rome. Walter spent much of his time sketching outdoors, and his wife recorded in her diary that he worked on this drawing of Keats' grave in the Protestant Cemetery on 11–12 May 1873.[1] Although both drawings of the tombs were commissioned by George Howard, they do not form a pair. It is tempting to wonder whether the careful, almost punctilious, depiction of Keats's grave, with its inscription almost entirely legible, was an answer to criticism from Howard that the view of Shelley's grave was too generalized. The site of Keats's grave, in the older part of the cemetery, certainly called for a more conventional composition, although, in taking his view slightly from the side, Crane has been able to include more of the pyramid of Caius Cestius than would have been possible in a straightforward frontal view.

Both drawings were given by Howard to his eldest daughter, Lady Mary, who, as a child, accompanied him on his visits to Crane's studio in Rome in the winter of 1871–2, on their way to and from a holiday in Naples.

1 Crane, Journal

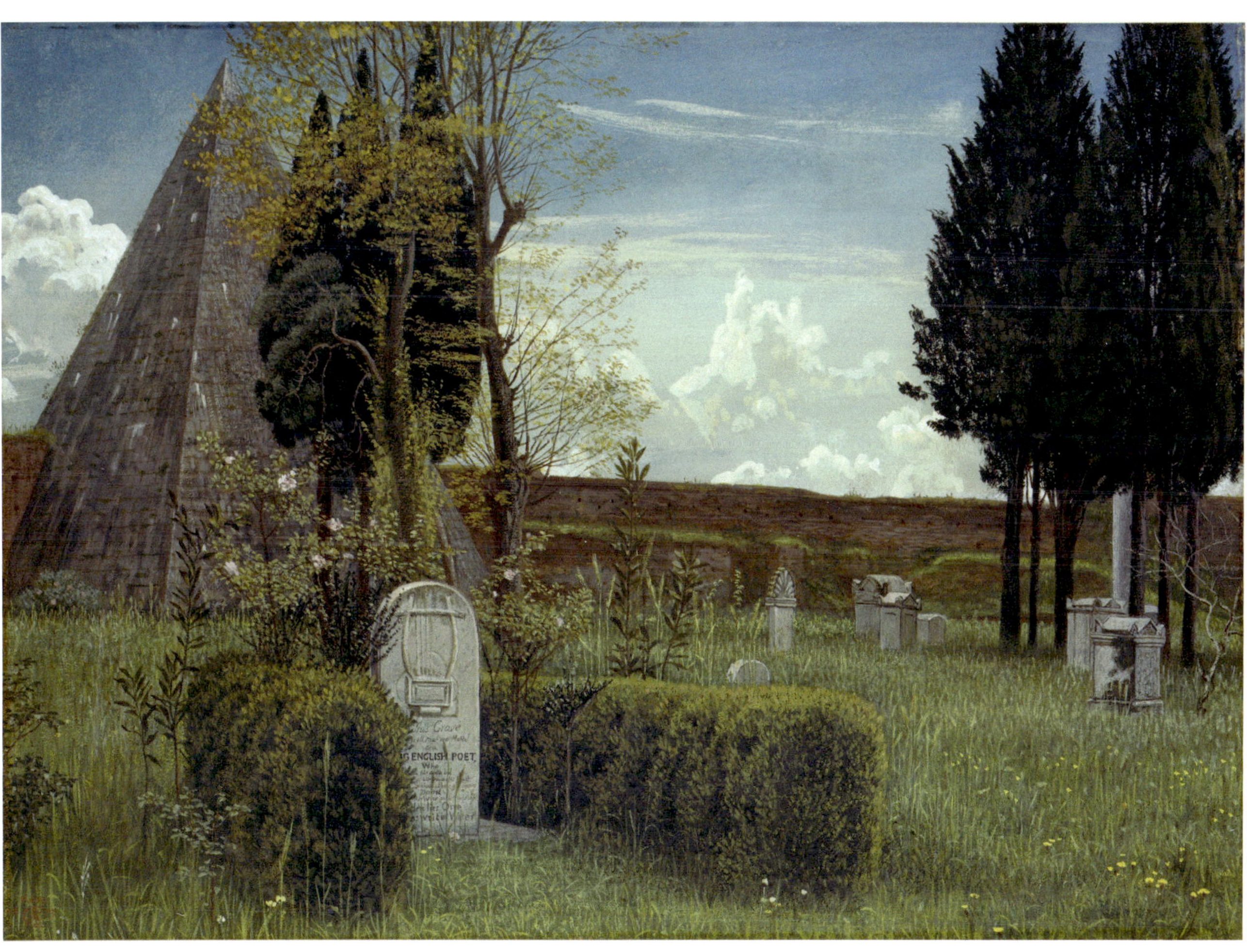

94
Walter Crane
Vietri on the Gulf of Salerno, from Cava dei Terreni
Watercolour and body colour on paper, 20.1 x 30.1 cm
Whitworth Art Gallery, University of Manchester (D.1954.5)
Ref: Smith and Hyde 1989, no. C17

During their long, hot summer in Naples and the surrounding area in 1872, the Cranes spent a fortnight at Cava dei Terreni, which they found 'delightfully quiet after noisy Amalfi'.[1] In his *Reminiscences*, Crane described the village as 'a delightful spot among hills and chestnut woods, a little inland from the sea, commanding a view of the Gulf of Salerno and the town of Salerno.'[2] They lodged in an old house, and went on many walks in the surrounding countryside. Among the watercolours he made in this period was this view looking south-east towards Vietri. It was probably taken from the terrace of his lodgings, where he noted that there was a vineyard 'where, as one walked, the pendent bunches "into our hands themselves would reach"'.[3]

1 Crane, Journal, 25 September 1872
2 Crane 1907, p. 146
3 ibid

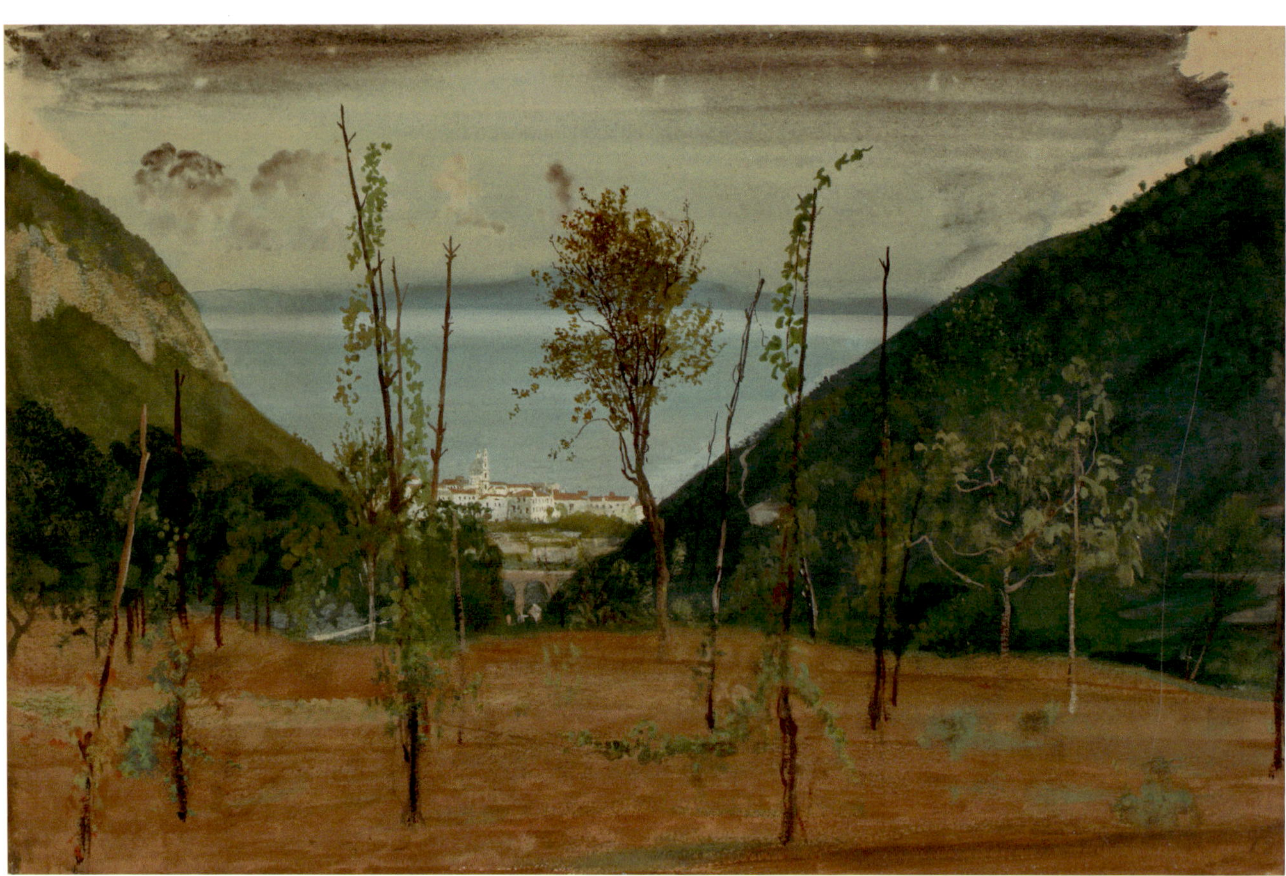

95
Walter Crane
Cava dei Terreni 1872
Watercolour and body colour on paper, 34 x 25 cm
Signed in monogram and dated: *WC 1872 /CAVA DEI / TERRENI*
Private collection
Ref: Smith and Hyde 1989 no. C18

Another of the drawings made during Crane's stay at Cava dei Terreni, between 25 September and 9 October 1872, this may show the 'charming old formal garden behind [his lodgings] with box hedges and pomegranate trees and hydrangeas'.[1] However, it has also been suggested that it may depict the more informal garden of the monastery of SS Trinita di Cava, near Corpo di Cava, which Crane is known to have visited on 1 October 1872. The unruly profusion of vegetation is unusual in Crane's works of this period, which generally emphasise an orderly and decorative composition.

1 Crane 1907, p.146

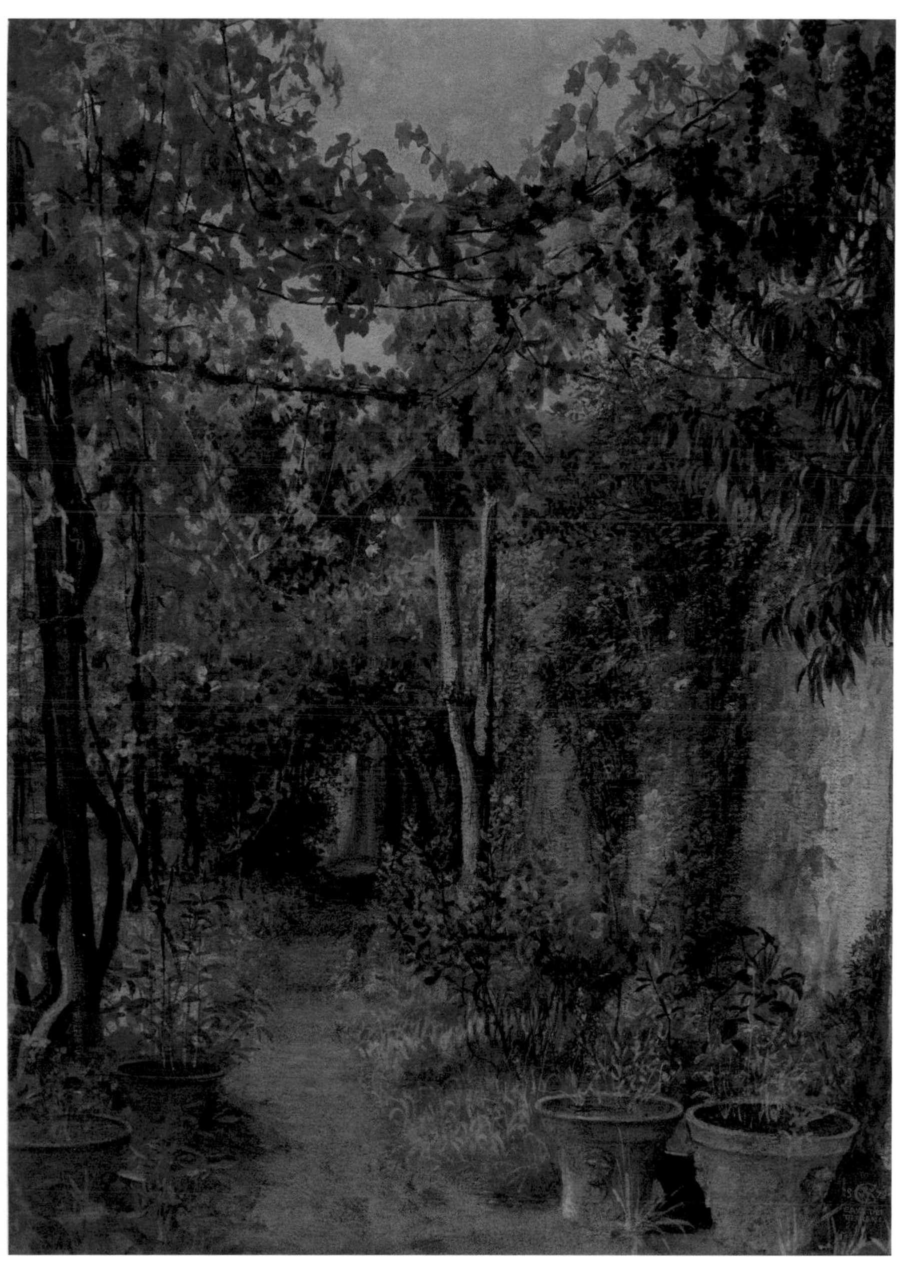

96
Walter Crane
An Italian Villa
Watercolour on paper, 18.9 x 35.2 cm
Signed in monogram and dated: *WC 1872*
Whitworth Art Gallery, University of Manchester. Presented by the Friends of the Whitworth, 1973 (D.1973.11)

The splendid neo-classical villa set in a large park planted with pine and cypress trees has unfortunately not been identified. The site of the villa is probably either in Rome or Naples or their surrounding countryside. From Crane's published *Reminiscences* and his unpublished diaries, we know that he made studies at the Villa Volkonsky and the Villa Haig in Rome, and it is possible that the latter is the subject of this watercolour. Crane visited the Villa Haig on several occasions in March 1872, describing it as 'a charming house, surrounded with a terraced garden and vineyards, and commanding lovely views of Rome'.[1] It was situated on the Monti Parioli, and occupied by the two elderly sisters, the last of their line of Haig of Bemersyde. After the death of the second in 1878, the villa presumably changed hands and was renamed, but its current name, or whether it even survives, is not known.

1 Crane 1907, pp.134-5

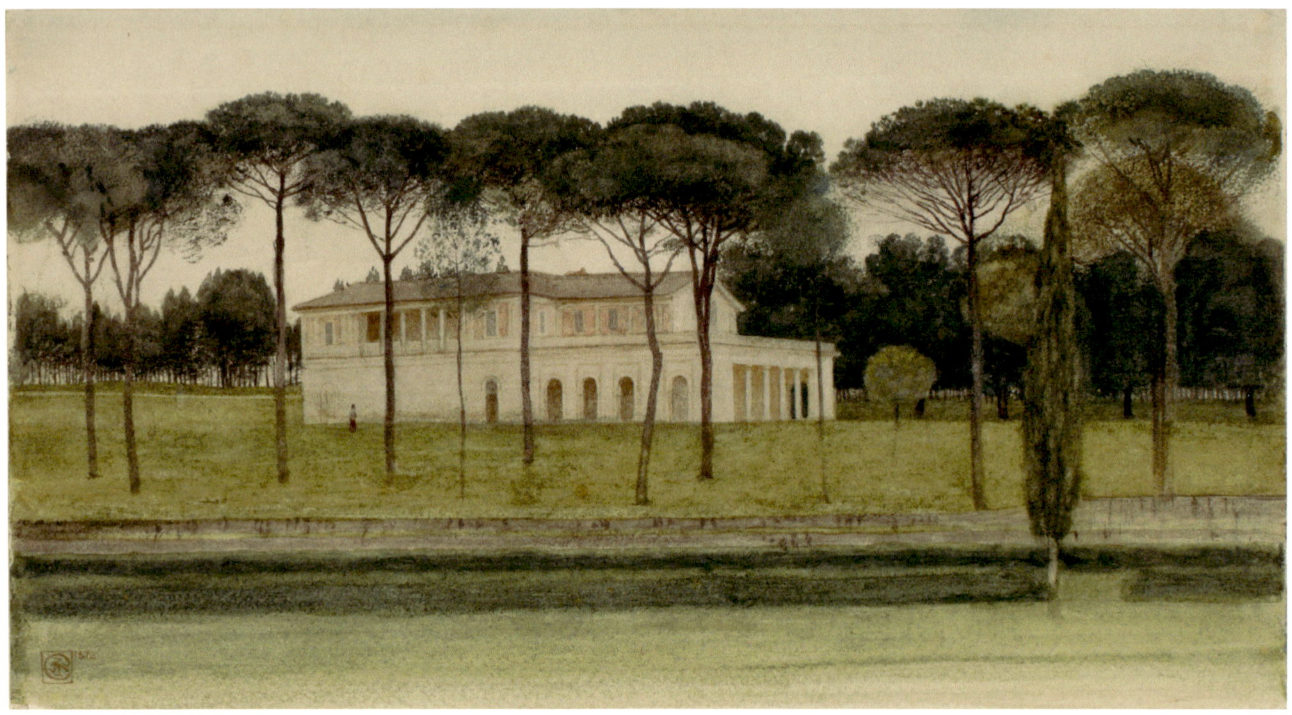

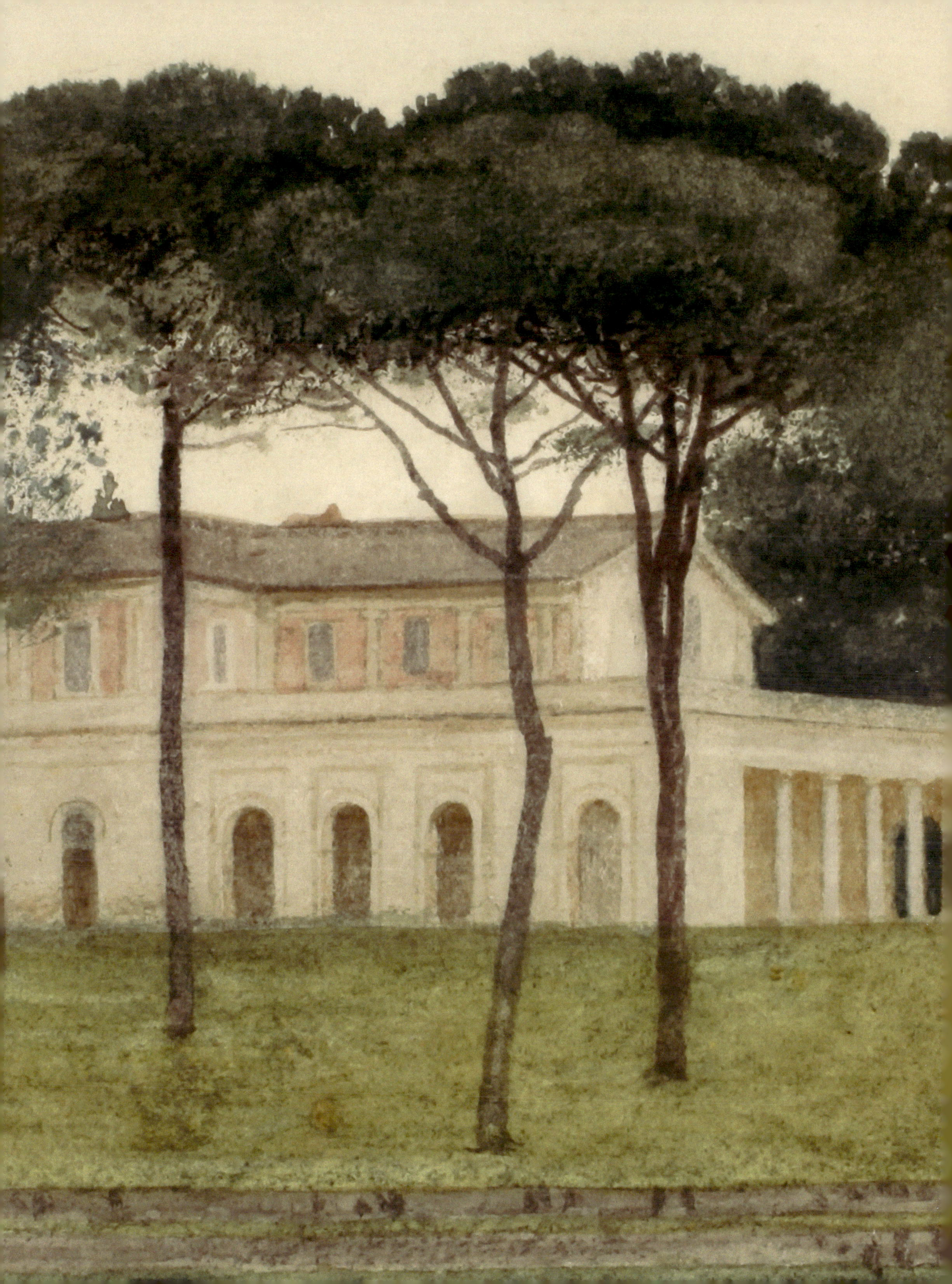

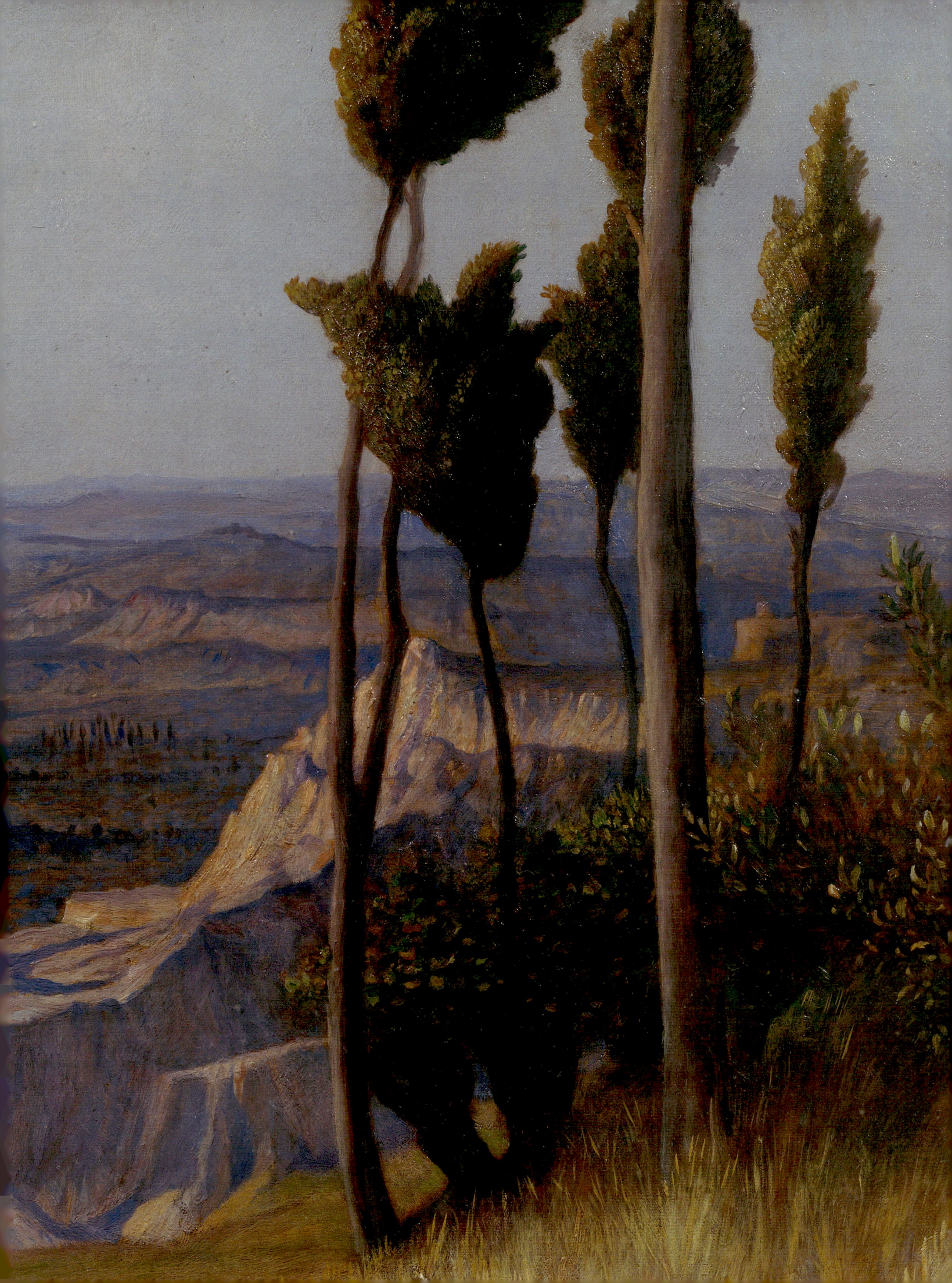

V

GIOVANNI COSTA AND THE ETRUSCANS – PAINTERS OF THE ITALIAN LANDSCAPE

The Etruscans were a group of English painters who loved Italy and made frequent painting expeditions there, and who were personal friends and artistic acolytes of the Italian painter Giovanni Costa. This informal association was formed in Rome in the winter of 1883–4. Among the members were Matthew Ridley Corbett, George Howard, and William Blake Richmond. They adopted their name essentially as a tribute to Costa himself, who seems to have had the nickname 'the Etruscan'. However, it was seldom applied in the press when the artists exhibited in London, either at the Grosvenor Gallery, where they frequently showed from its inception in 1877, or at the New Gallery, which took over the Grosvenor's role for progressive artists, and where the Etruscans tended to migrate in the later 1880s.

The distinctive landscape type favoured by the Etruscans was of a pronounced horizontal format, often with the outlines of distant mountain ranges placed across the width of the composition, or with river bank or coastal plain. It had its origin in the artistic principles devised by Costa in the course of expeditions into the Roman Campagna, often in company with the English painters George Heming Mason and Frederic Leighton, in the early 1850s. Together, they developed a technique of sketching in *plein air*, often on panels or on paper or card, in which they sought to convey the structure and atmospheric effect of the landscape in as direct and painterly a way as possible. These essentially private exercises served as a means of visual training, and were quite distinct from the large-scale figurative works which were painted in the studio, and which, especially in the case of Costa, could occupy them for many years at a time.

From the late 1850s onwards a wider circle of English artists gravitated towards Costa. Leighton, who, after long years of apprenticeship in Germany, France and Italy, settled in London in 1859, frequently recommended friends to him in the course of their travels in Rome or Florence. In the later years of Costa's life, a younger generation of English landscape painters gathered around him at his home at Marina di Pisa, where he moved in 1885. Leighton formed a collection of works by Costa, and in turn encouraged him to exhibit in London. Costa gradually came to depend on a circle of British patrons, of whom the most prominent were the Revd Stopford Brooke and George Howard. Owning works by Costa seems to have become a self-conscious expression of sympathy for the cause of Italian liberation, and, after the Risorgimento, a means of identifying oneself as an italophile.

Although the paintings of Costa and the Etruscans are not conventionally regarded as being Pre-Raphaelite, the links between these artists and the Pre-Raphaelites in the broader sense are close. In London, Costa met and exhibited with several of the painters of the second generation of the Pre-Raphaelites, notably Burne-Jones. Moreover, Costa's art was to some degree moulded by his contact with British art and patronage, while at the same time he was a vital formative influence upon the work of a rising generation of English artists.

97
Giovanni Costa (1826–1903)
They Sleep by Day to Fish by Night 1853–6
Oil on panel, 12 x 47.6 cm
Private collection
Ref: Newall 1989, no. 1

In 1853 Costa and George Mason went on a painting expedition to the Lazio coast south of Rome. They spent several weeks at Ardea, where they made sketches from nature and prepared motifs for large-scale paintings – Costa was working at the time on his *Women Stealing Wood on the Shore near Ardea on an Evening when the Libeccio blows* (Castle Howard Collection). Olivia Rossetti Agresti described how the two men 'spent their whole time out of doors, painting as long as daylight lasted, and passing the nights *à la belle etoile*'.[1] One night, they were woken by the cries of fishermen struggling to land their boat in rough weather; they assisted by hauling on a rope that was thrown to them on the beach. The following day, when the fishermen were resting before setting out again, Costa made a drawing of the figures[2] and possibly an initial oil sketch for this painting. It shows the morning after the storm, when conditions had settled, with the golden light of the sun casting long shadows over the landscape, and the crests of the waves showing brightly against the otherwise shadowy surface of the sea.

This small painting was bought by Leighton in 1856 or 1857, and was the first work by Costa that he acquired. Its crisp handling and strong feeling for the quality of light, as well as its wide format and the careful division of the composition into zones determined by sky, horizon, sea, and foreground, are qualities that may be associated with the Macchiaioli painters, whom Costa met at the Caffè Michelangiolo after he settled in Florence in 1859. They may also be regarded as a first demonstration of the principles that were to be carried forward by Costa's English followers. At some stage Costa made an expanded version of the composition, which he showed at the New Gallery in 1890.[3]

1 Agresti, 1904, p. 68
2 reproduced in Nicholls 1982, fig. vi
3 a detail of which is reproduced in ibid, fig. vii

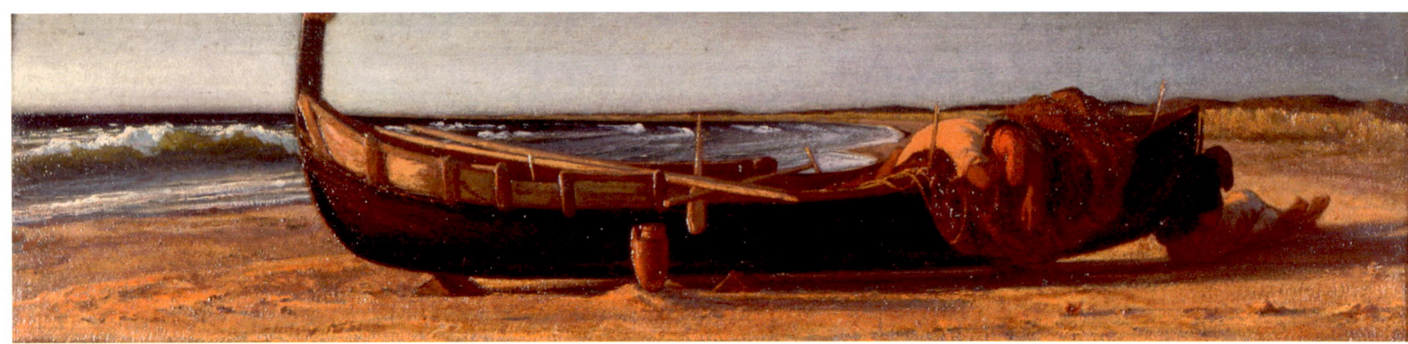

98
Giovanni Costa
Porto d'Anzio 1853
Oil on panel, 12.5 x 37.1 cm
The Gere Collection
Ref: Riopelle 1999, no. 19

This oil sketch of Porto d'Anzio has the appearance of having been made directly from the motif and in the open air, and was presumably painted on the expedition made by Costa and Mason in 1853. The horizontal format serves to emphasise the scale of the wide, flat coastal landscape; more than half of the composition is devoted to the sky, with beautiful observation of cloud formations. The horizon is delicately interrupted by the tips of trees rising from the dense forest which forms the foreground. Costa reveals himself as an instinctive colourist, who captures the freshness of the landscape by his choice of subtle greens, pinks, blues and greys, which are at the same time entirely naturalistic but also tellingly luminous. The whole composition is unified by the texture of the oak panel showing through the paint layer.

It was to a large extent under Costa's influence that both George Heming Mason and Frederic Leighton began to make oil sketches of a similar type.

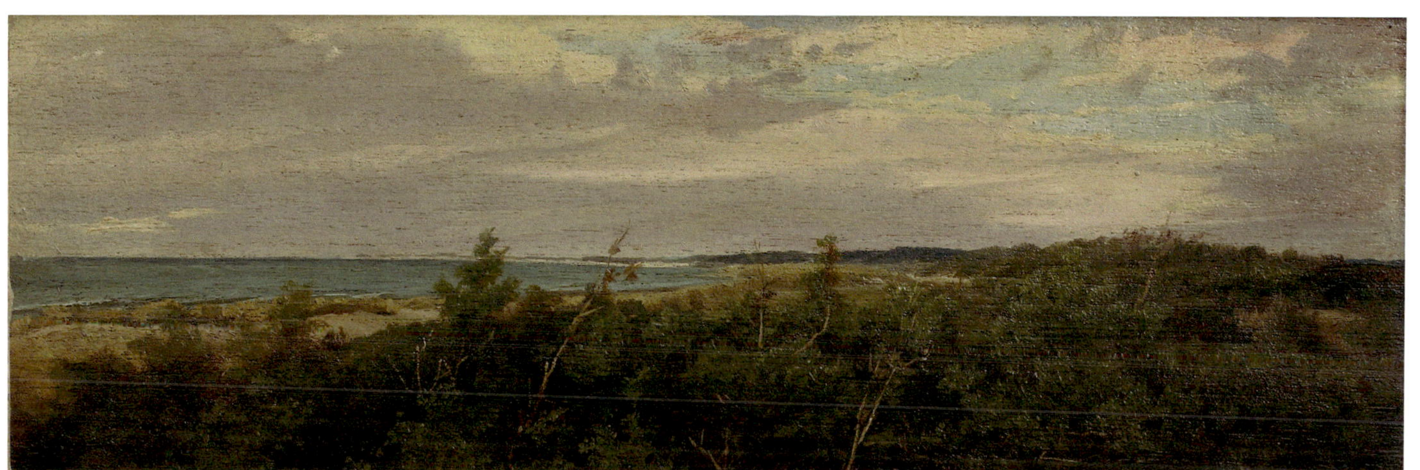

99
Giovanni Costa (1826–1903)
Ruins in the Alban Hills c. 1855
Oil on paper, laid down on to canvas, 28.5 x 43.5 cm
Ashmolean Museum, University of Oxford. Purchased with the assistance of The Art Fund, the Friends of the Ashmolean, and Mme Alice Goldet, 2003 (WA2003.139)

This recently discovered work probably dates from early in Costa's career, during the period he was living principally at the Pensione Martorelli at Ariccia as a fugitive from Rome after the failed uprising against the foreign occupation of Italy in 1848, and following the re-establishment of Papal authority in 1850. In the course of the decade he made frequent painting expeditions into the remote countryside of the Campagna, exploring both the Lazio coastline between Ostia and Anzio, and the hills and volcanic lakes close to Albano.

The painting is treated with a freedom and freshness which makes it immediately recognisable as an oil sketch painted in the open air. Moreover, it was done on paper rather than panel or prepared canvas, a method favoured by French *plein-air* oil sketchers and which tends to indicate a spontaneous adoption of a subject, without particular forethought or deliberation. It shows the ruins of a Roman building against a backdrop of precipitous mountains and rocky outcrops. Although the precise site in the Alban Hills has not been identified, Dario Durbè has recently suggested that the view shows the remains of the Roman Bath complex of Cellomaio, the fabric of which survives as part of the medieval town of Albano Laziale. These had been built by the Emperor Caracalla to reward the legionaries who had assisted him in the murder of his brother, Geta.

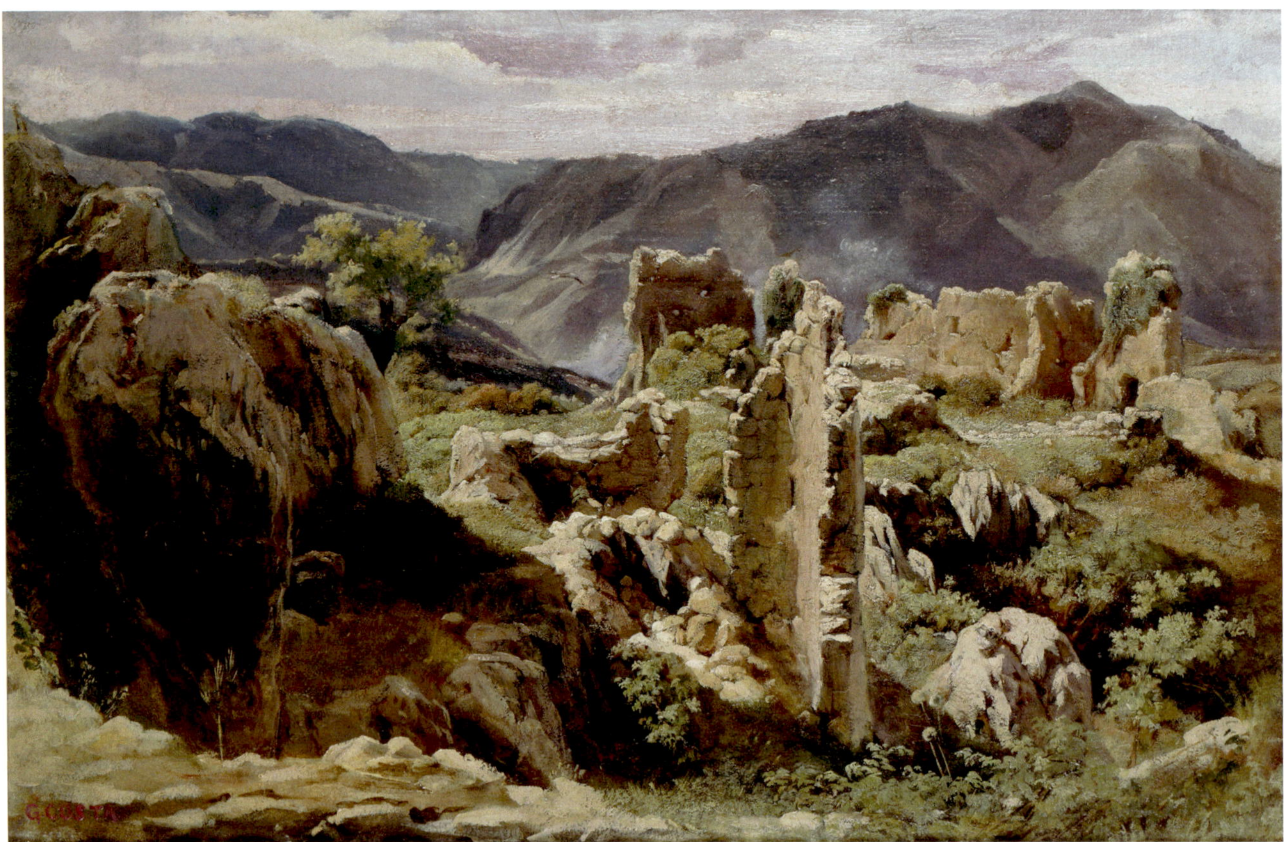

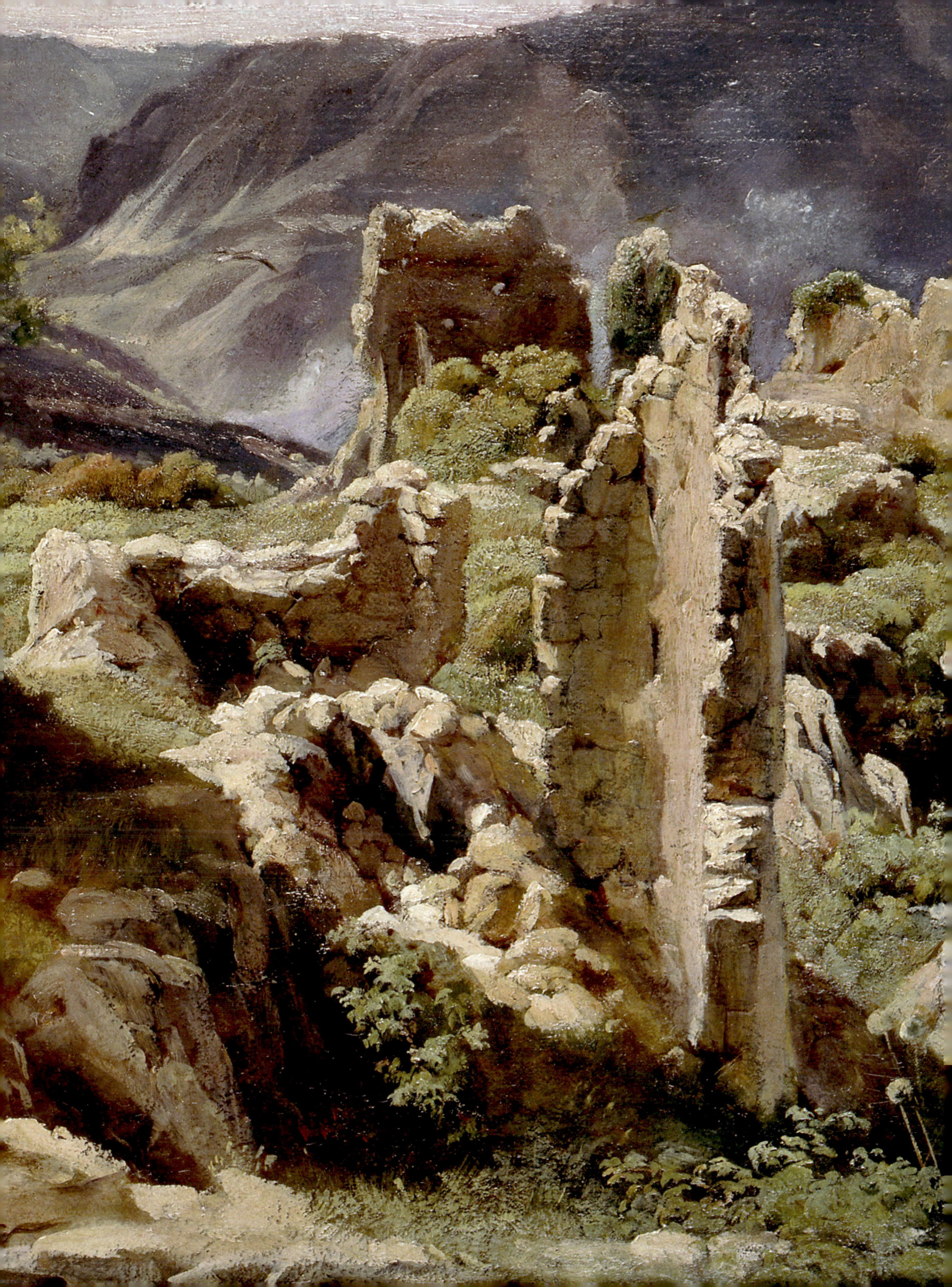

100
George Heming Mason (1818–1872)
Villa Borghese c. 1852–3
Oil on paper mounted on board, 13.5 x 36.1 cm
The Gere Collection
Ref: Riopelle 1999, no. 56

Mason arrived in Italy with his brother in 1843, but it was not until the early 1850s that he began to paint in earnest. His meeting with Giovanni Costa at Ariccia in 1852 was decisive for his technique and his choice of subject matter. An early inscription indicates that Mason's view was made in the grounds of the Villa Borghese in Rome, whose gardens had been painted by generations of landscape artists. The sketch shows scenery which is densely wooded in the middle ground and with a complex outline of different varieties of tree growing in the park, all seen against a distant outline of snow-crested mountains, the whole treated with rich and painterly strokes of colour. Contrasting with the sombre greens and near blacks of the centre, in the foreground a patch of ochre appears to denote a wall or building.

These were the essential traits that became characteristic of the Etruscans in the 1880s. Mason, however, was by then long dead, having returned to Staffordshire to marry and pursue his career as a painter of idyllic subjects which are English in their setting but Theocritan in their mood, and for which he gained enormous esteem but almost no commercial success.

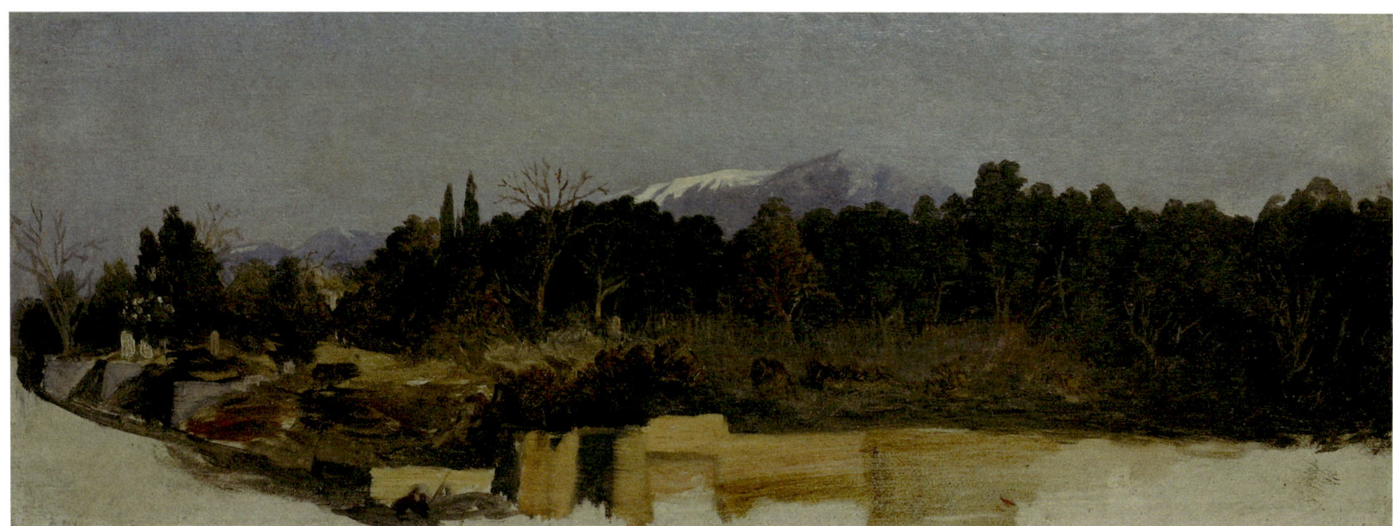

101
George Heming Mason
Italian Peasant Women in the Campagna Driving an Ox c. 1855?
Oil on canvas, 23 x 41.5 cm
Private Collection

Mason developed steadily as an artist, and his first exhibit at the Royal Academy, *Ploughing in the Campagna* in 1857,[1] was on an ambitious scale. It was also probably intended to rival similar subjects by the hugely successful Rosa Bonheur, in capturing the particular character of an agricultural landscape. *Italian Peasant Women* is closely related to another work of this title signed and dated 1855 (private collection), which, however, shows the three women in an open landscape, whereas the exhibited version includes a clump of trees on the right and gateposts on the left. Whether either picture was painted in the open air, as Costa's example would have demanded, cannot be ascertained. After his return to England in 1858, Mason continued to paint such subjects: *Wind on the Wold* (Tate), painted in 1863, shows another peasant girl driving a pair of cows through a more animated English landscape.

1 Walker Art Gallery, Liverpool

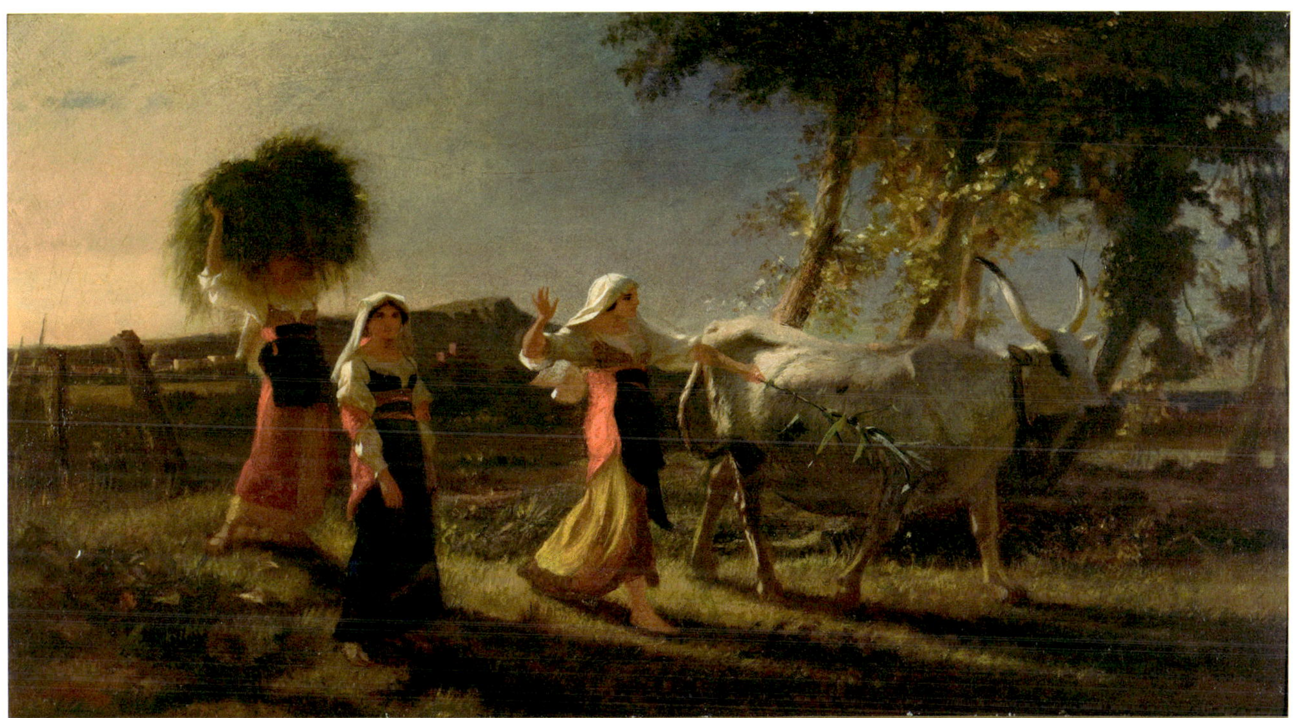

102
Frederic Leighton (1830–1896)
Staircase of a House at Capri 1859
Oil on canvas, 27.6 x 29.8 cm
Private collection
Ref: Jones 1996, no. 17

Leighton had long wanted to visit Capri, having expressed the wish to make 'a trip to Naples, Capri, Ischia, Amalfi, and all the spots about which artists rave'.[1] Capri had attracted English travellers in the eighteenth and early nineteenth centuries; British troops were garrisoned on the island during the Napoleonic wars, while in later years Henry Wreford, special correspondent for *The Times* in Rome and Naples and an untiring supporter of the cause of Italian liberty and unity, settled there. Leighton's enthusiasm for Capri probably owed more to his contact with European writers and artists than with English-speaking painters: from the 1820s onwards, the island was much visited by travelling Germans, including the neo-classical poets Stolberg, Stegmann, Rückert, and Platin, and the painter Karl Blechen, the illustrator Joseph von Führich, and a group of painters who named themselves 'Die Odyseer' to mark their admiration for Homeric legend. The French painter J.J. Henner, winner of the *Prix de Rome* in 1858, visited the island in the course of his Italian sojourn.

Leighton was twenty-eight when he visited Capri in the early summer of 1859. He remained for five weeks, staying at a locanda run by Michele Pagano, one of the few hotels on the island, although it was 'of modest pretensions, [it was] especially recommended to gentlemen alone [and was] a favourite resort of artists who occasionally spend several months in the island'.[2] He seems to have intended the stay as a deliberate withdrawal from the hectic life that he had previously led in the art worlds of Rome and Paris

In addition to the series of small but delicious oil sketches (**see cats. 103, 105**), he painted various panoramic views of the island and made a large number of immaculate drawings of buildings and vegetation, of which the most celebrated is the *Study of a Lemon Tree* (private collection).

Leighton's landscape painting owes much to a European tradition of extempore oil sketching aimed to capture the momentary effects of light and atmosphere that enliven the scene. Although his earliest recorded landscapes date from 1859, they are strongly dependent on the example of his close friend, Giovanni Costa, with whom he went on painting expeditions in the Roman Campagna from 1859 onwards. He seems also to have taken close account of works by French landscape artists working in Italy, notably Corot, whose work of the 1820s he would surely have studied while he was living in Paris between 1855 and 1859. Leighton was fascinated by the way in which Corot used oil colour to evoke the luminescence of the landscape, and his particular affection for the twilight effects of dawn and dusk. The present subject shows a house at Capri, with a beam of sunlight penetrating the soft shadow of the upper story and shining brightly on the base of a column cut from the distinctive white limestone quarried on the island. As Leighton's biographer recalled: 'No one, I believe, has ever painted the luminous quality of white, as it is seen under heated sunlight in the South, with the same charm as Leighton. The sketches he made of buildings at Capri are quite marvellously true in their rendering of such effects'.[3]

Leighton painted landscape for his own delight and as a means of training his eye to harmonious patterns and conjunctions of colour and texture, not for the purpose of building up a repertoire of pre-formed natural details which might then be slotted into his large-scale figurative compositions.

1 Barrington 1906, I, p. 172
2 Baedeker's guide to *Southern Italy* (1867)
3 Barrington 1906, II, p. 18

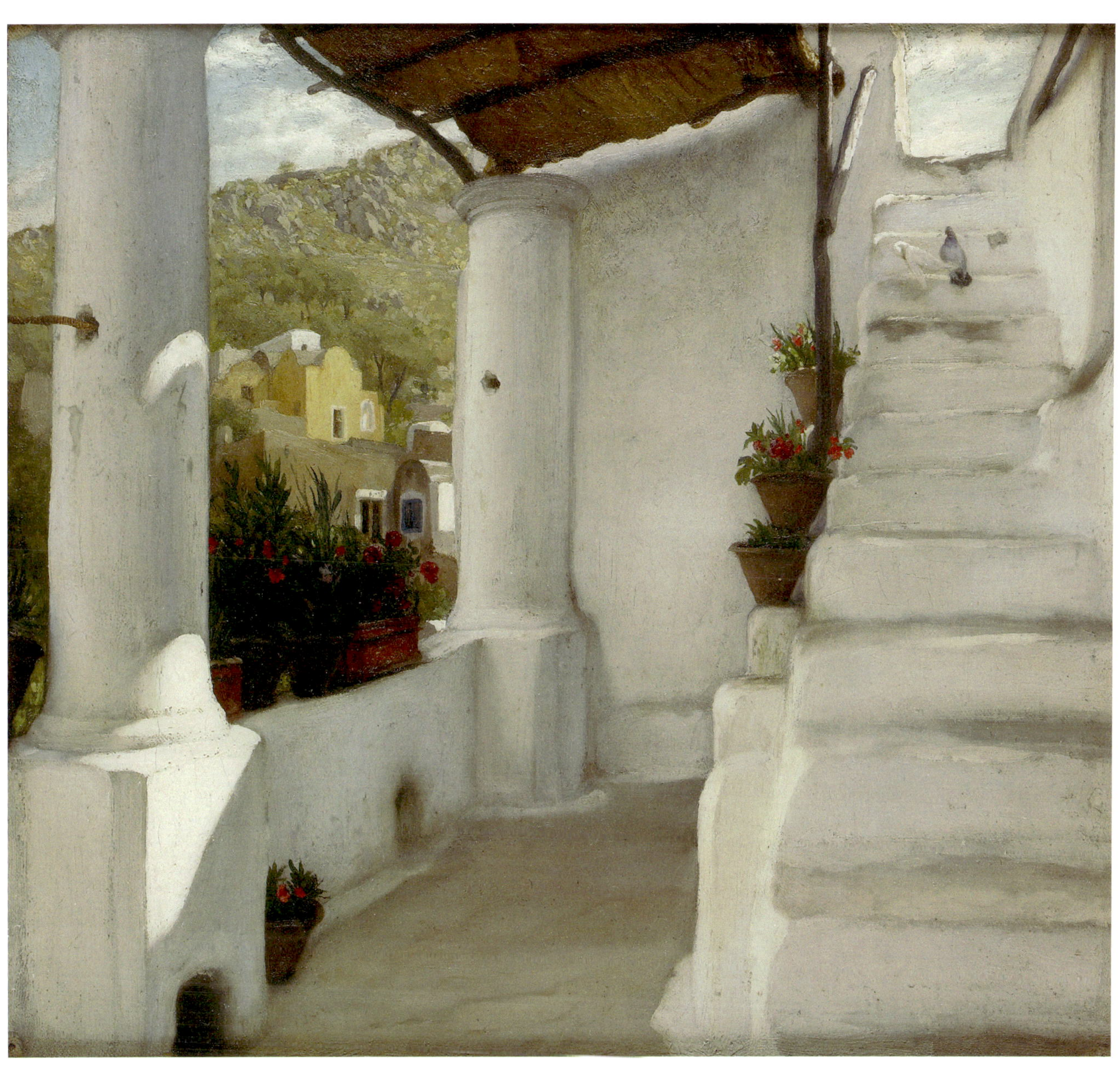

103
Frederic Leighton (1830–1896)
A Street Scene at Capri 1859
Oil on canvas, 32 x 24.5 cm
Private collection
Ref: Jones 1996, no. 16

Leighton seems to have intended his Capri oil sketches of 1859 as a series, with buildings and gardens shown at different times of day and glimpses of the labyrinthine alleyways and terraces combining to give a cumulative impression. This was an exercise that he was to repeat in the course of subsequent travels abroad: in 1867, he made a succession of studies of the sea and islands of the Aegean, and in the following year he painted some thirty oil studies in Egypt, working at different times of day and with different effects and directions of light on the river banks observed from a Nile steamer. In his diary, he described the Egyptian project as 'a sort of discipline'.[1]

1 Barrington 1906, II, p. 158

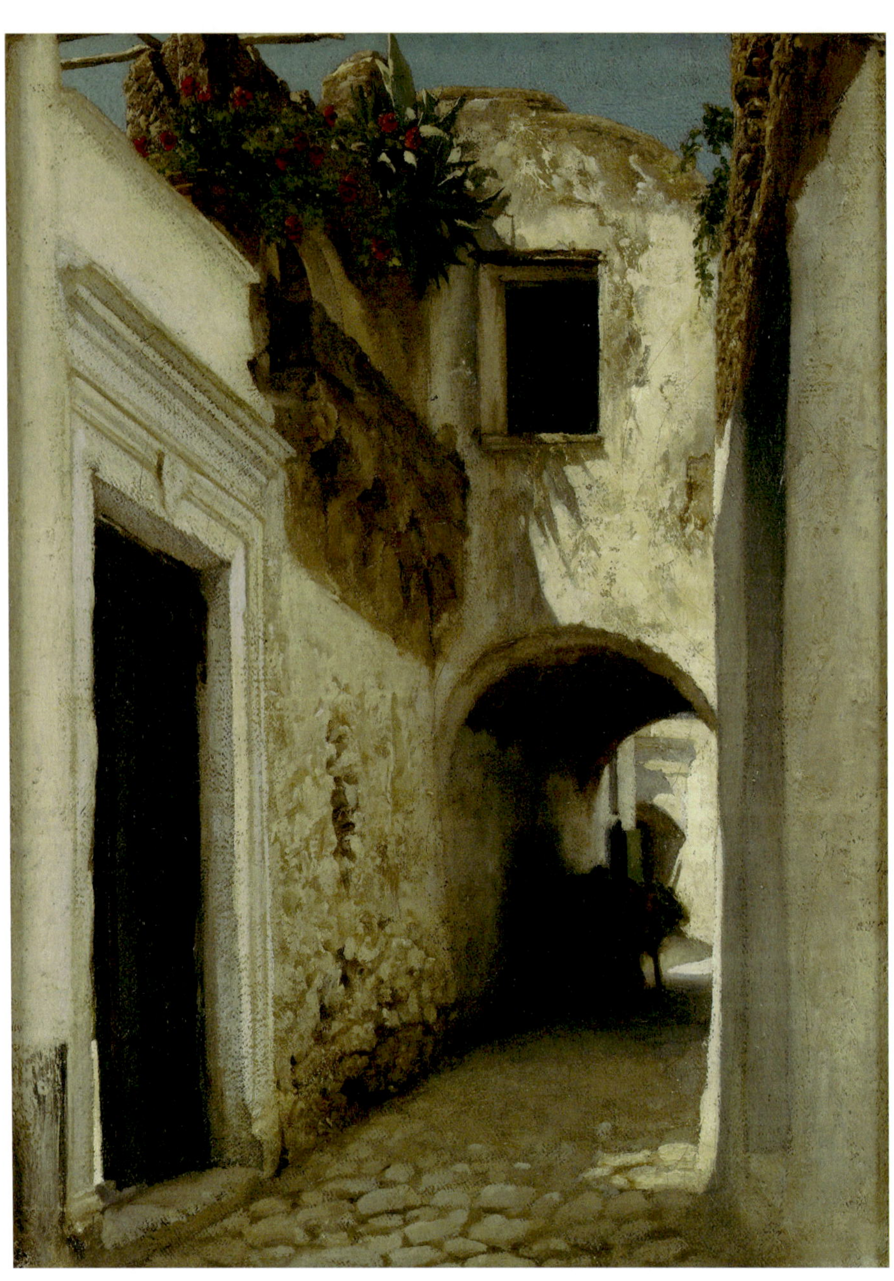

104
Frederic Leighton
The Villa Malta 1860s (?)
Oil on canvas, 27.2 x 41.5 cm
The Gere Collection
Ref: Jones 1996, no. 51; Riopelle 1999 no. 51

The Villa Malta in Rome stands on an area of land that forms a southerly extension to the grounds of the Villa Medici, close to the top of the Spanish Steps and the church of Sta Trintà dei Monti. It was thus near Leighton's studio in the Via della Purificazione, which he occupied from 1852 to 1855, and near that of his close associate, Giovanni Costa, in the Via Margutta. The villa had previously belonged to the Prince von Bülow, and had served as a gathering place for a distinguished circle of German writers and artists. Leighton may have been particularly interested in it because of his own strong connections with German intellectual life.

The boldness and freedom of the sketch, and the confidence with which the artist has allowed rich broad brushstrokes to remain visible in some areas, while in others leaving the grain of the canvas to show through more thinly applied veils of pigment, is characteristic of Leighton's mature landscape style, and demonstrates his complete assimilation of both French and Italian *plein-air* sketching traditions. It was long attributed to Corot, whose sketches made in Italy in the 1820s Leighton intensely admired when he was living in Paris in the 1850s. Leighton certainly met Corot in Paris, either in the late 1850s or early 1860s, and may have been introduced to him by Costa in 1862 or 1863. In 1865 Leighton bought Corot's cycle of the four times of day from the Decamps sale in Paris (now in the Loyd Collection, on long-term loan to the National Gallery), and in later years he recalled Corot's advice on the particular colours suitable for landscape painting.

Leighton did not exhibit his landscape sketches at the Royal Academy, even after he was elected president in 1878. However, he occasionally lent them to alternative exhibition venues such as the Society of British Artists and the Grosvenor Gallery, where they were displayed with works by Costa in 1879. However, they were never for sale, but were instead displayed on the walls of his studio in Holland Park Road, shown in plain gold frames and hung one above another from dado to frieze. The view of the Villa Malta can be seen in a photograph of the studio taken at the time of the artist's death.

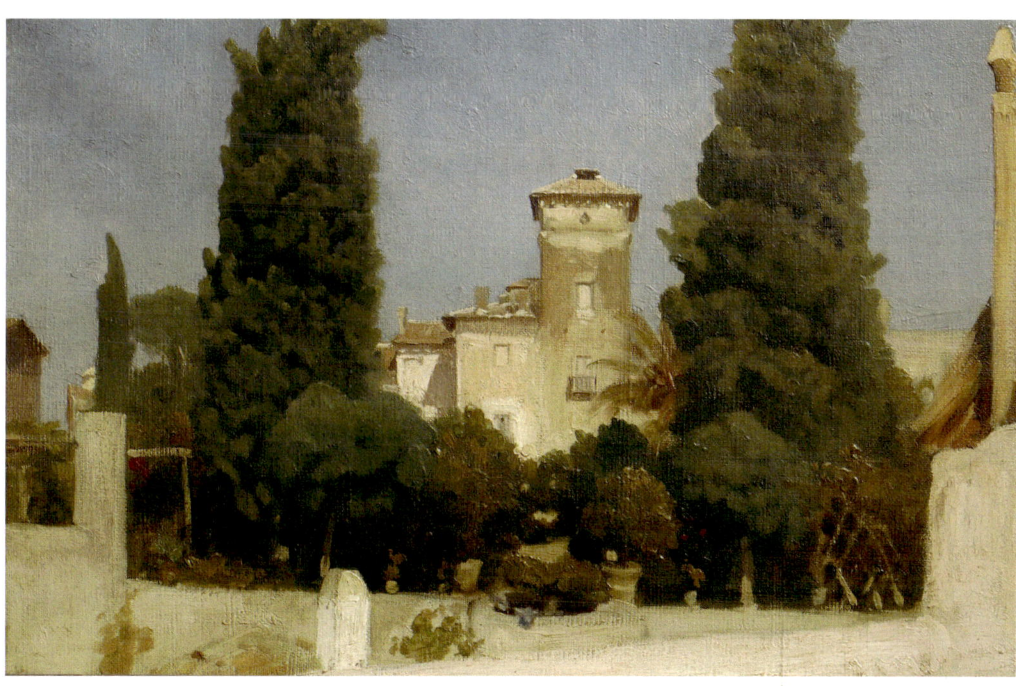

105
Frederic Leighton (1830–1896)
View in Capri 1860s (?)
Oil on canvas, 21.2 x 29.3 cm
The Gere Collection
Ref: Riopelle 1999, no. 49

More than a dozen Capri views by Leighton were included in his posthumous studio sale, and a number remain unidentified. Cat. 105 is likely to have been one of these, and is certainly visible in photographs of his studio taken after his death.

Although Leighton's stay in Capri in 1859 is well documented, it is clear that he returned to the island on subsequent occasions, and some of his works must date from these later visits. The present view is likely to have been made in the 1860s when he was most strongly influenced by the French tradition of *plein-air* sketching. It shows the distinctive white box-shaped houses with their low saucer-domed roofs, with the light flaring on the expanse of sea on the left in an effect of *contre-jour*.

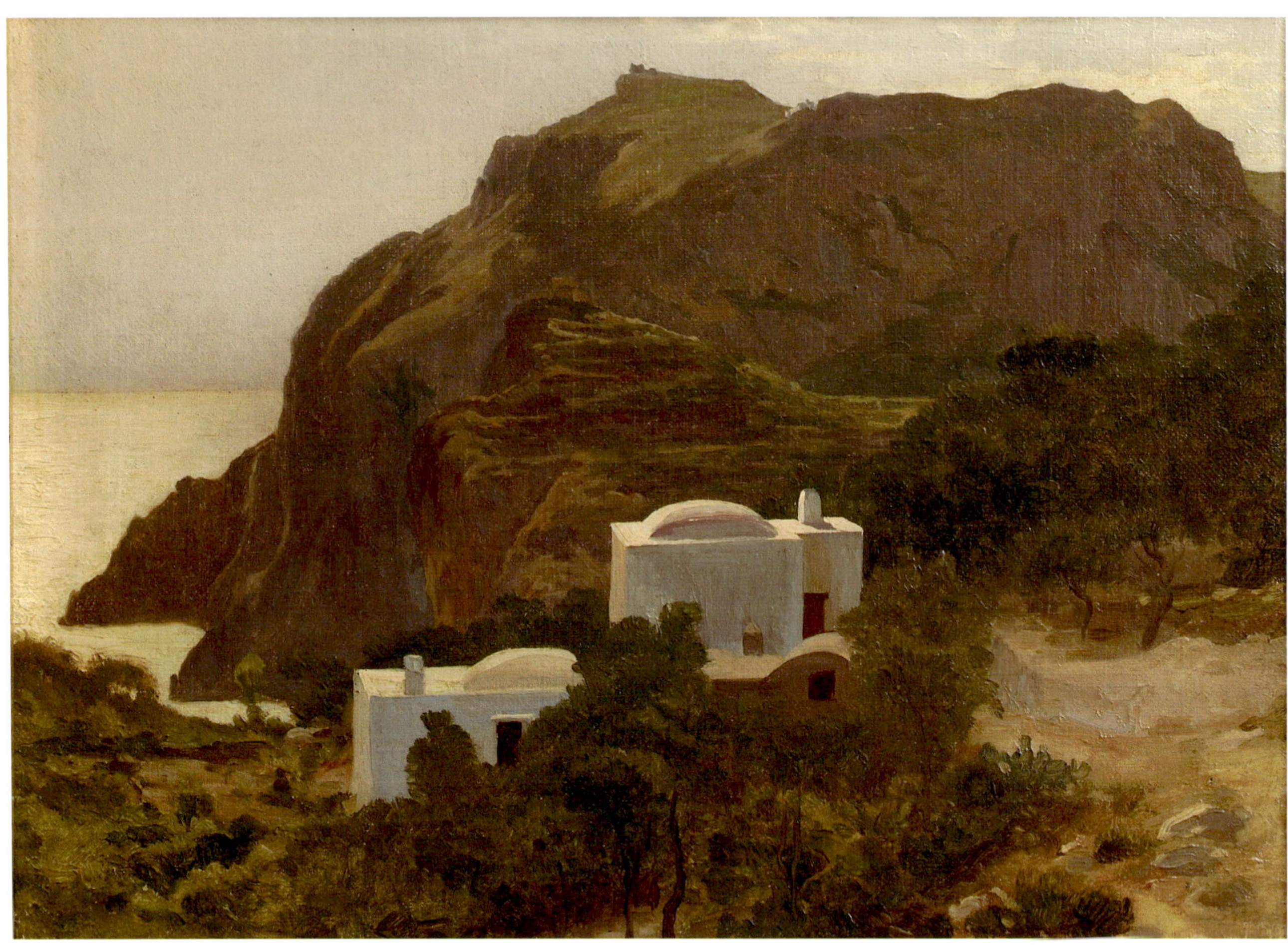

106
Giovanni Costa (1826–1903)
The Faraglioni Rocks, Capri – An October Morning 1875–7
Oil on canvas, 29.5 x 45.5 cm
From the Castle Howard Collection
Ref: Newall 1989, no. 25

Costa and his wife and daughter spent several months on Capri in the autumn of 1875. Their stay coincided with the English artists Walter Maclaren and Edgar Barclay. Among the works Costa had in hand was a figure subject entitled *The Salt-stealer*, which was intended as a political protest against the high rates of taxation on the sale of salt and the concomitant offence of gathering salt where it had dried on the sea-shore. This view shows the distinctive limestone blocks in the sea off the south-eastern tip of Capri, seen from high on the south coast above the Marina Piccola, with morning sunlight blazing on the sea. In the foreground, a white-skirted woman lies on the ground eating grapes from a vine.

Referring to the picture in a letter to George Howard when it was shown in an exhibition of his works at the Fine Art Society in 1882, Costa noted that he worked on it over a period of two years.[1] It was one of a large number of works acquired by George Howard and displayed at his Yorkshire seat, Castle Howard.

1 Dini and Frezzotti 2009, p. 218

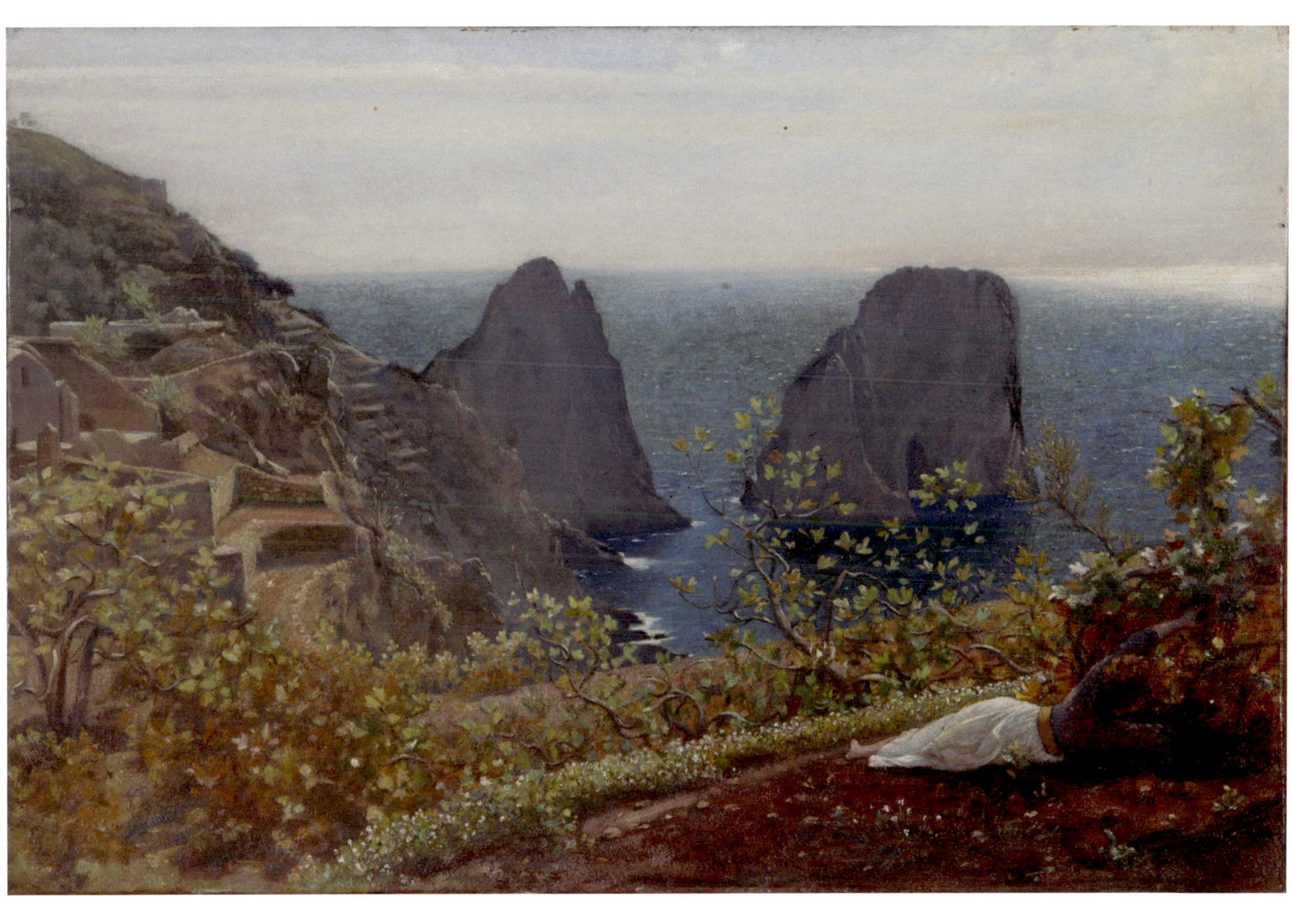

107

George Howard, 9th Earl of Carlisle
(1843–1911)
Keats's Grave in the Protestant Cemetery, Rome mid-1870s
Watercolour and bodycolour on paper, 27.8 x 38.1 cm
Private collection

Having commissioned the two watercolours of the tombs of Keats and Shelley from Walter Crane in 1872–3 (**cats. 92 and 93**), George Howard later made his own view of Keats's grave. Whereas Crane showed the tomb frontally, with much of the inscription visible, Howard's watercolour more tactfully shows the stone obliquely, so that the sculpted relief of the lyre is hard to see, and as part of a composition in which the cypresses and pines in the cemetery make a dense and complex background. Comparison with Crane's drawing shows that the laurels on either side of the grave are more fully grown in Howard's, suggesting that it was made a year or two later.

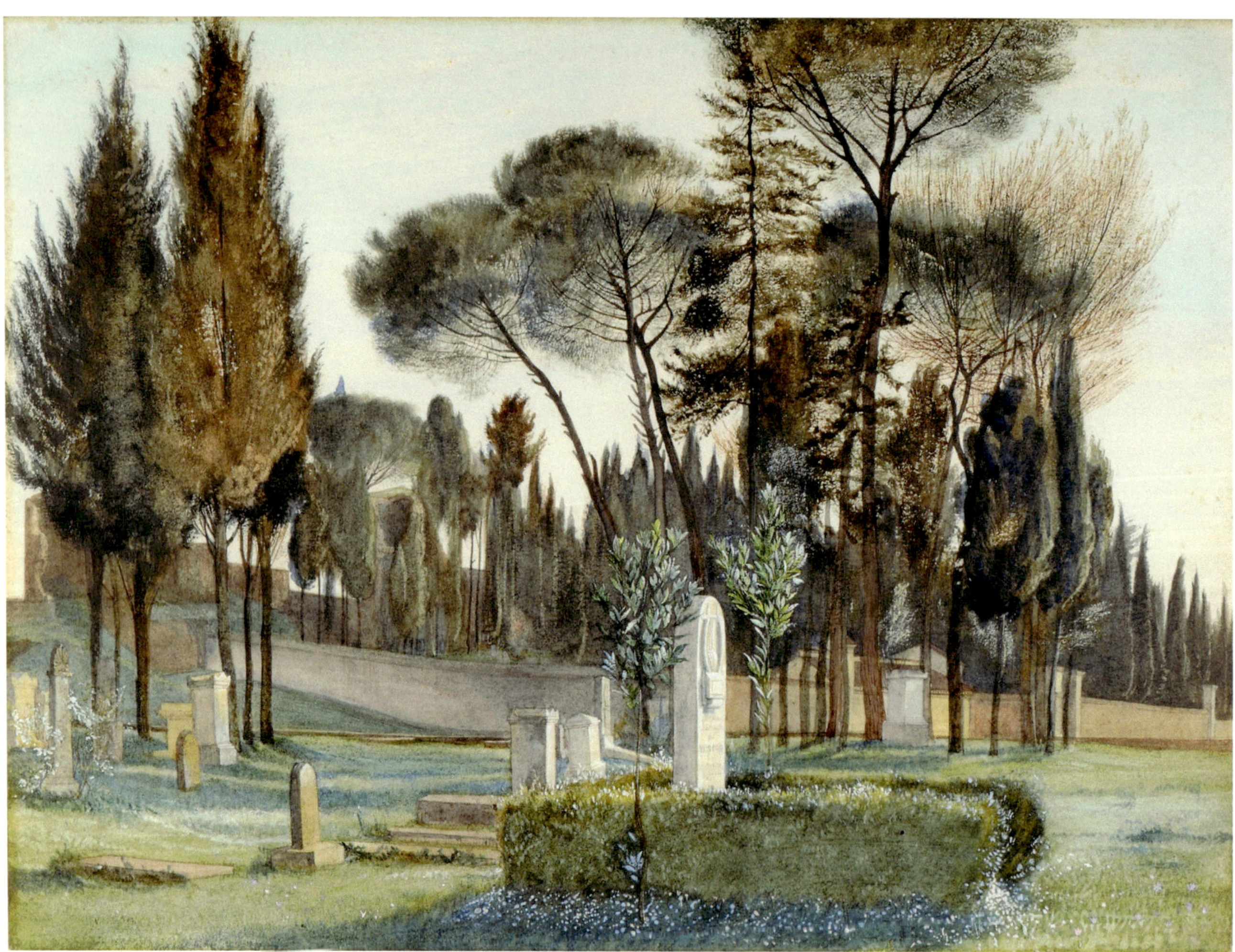

108

William Blake Richmond (1842–1921)

Near Viareggio, where Shelley's Body was Found

1875

Oil on canvas, 91.5 x 228.5 cm

Manchester City Art Galleries

Ref: Newall 1989 no. 23; Reynolds 1995, pp. 112–3

This epic vision of a landscape in the process of being subsumed by darkness shows the Tuscan coastline with the Carrara Mountains on the horizon. It was intended as a memorial to the English poet Percy Bysshe Shelley, who had drowned off the Tuscan coast in 1822 and whose body had been burned on a funeral pyre on the shore at Viareggio.

Shelley's tragic death and the supernatural associations of this particular coastline haunted the minds of English visitors. The Revd Stopford Brooke, who had written about the Romantic poets and who knew several of the Etruscans, described a visit to Viareggio and the weird event that he witnessed:

> I went to Viareggio, to see the place where Shelley's body was burned. That too was romantic enough to satisfy me […] One little cottage was near, and the woman came out and brought me with the most delightful and interested talk to the very spot where the Inglese, as they called Shelley, was burned […] The mountains, which press down too close and too high to the shore, were fortunately half concealed by huge storm-clouds pressing up against their flanks and breaking into white vapour above their peaks. I saw the ghost of Shelley flitting by in a drift of mist, and his eyes were soft and burning. 'I am now,' he cried, 'a creature of the earth and water, and the nursling of the sky.' 'Alas,' I said, 'why? But perhaps that is best.' 'Yes, that is best,' he said, and the thin fleece in which he was melted in the sun.[1]

William Blake Richmond had painted in the Roman Campagna with Costa in the late 1860s, and, under his influence, developed a style which depicted landscape in simplified, even abstract, forms which emphasised both volume and structure. Costa completed his *Scirocco Day* (private collection) at about the time Richmond conceived *Near Viareggio*, and the two works may be to some extent complementary – each includes the motif of a male figure stripped to the waist and carrying a load upon his shoulders.

When the painting was shown at the Royal Academy in 1875, William Michael Rossetti recognised the 'half-naked man bronzed almost to blackness […] advancing upward from the sea-beach, carrying a burden of faggots; intended probably to lead the mind on to the idea of Shelley's funeral-pyre, without, however, strictly representing anything belonging to those events which invest the coast of Via Reggio with so tragic and so sublime an interest'.[2]

1 Jacks 1917, II, pp. 521–2

2 Rossetti 1876, p. 519

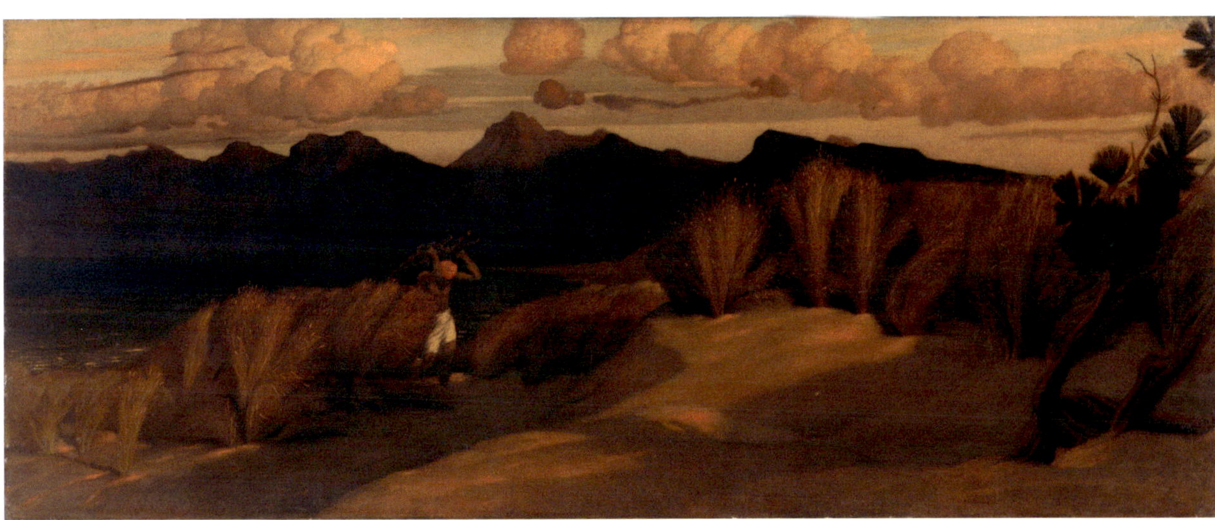

109
Giovanni Costa (1826–1903)
A View of Monte Amiata, Tuscany 1880s (?)
Oil on panel, 21 x 39 cm
Ashmolean Museum, University of Oxford.
Bequeathed by John Roscoe, 1931 (WA1931.57)
Ref: Newall 1989, no. 37

Costa's view shows the distinctive volcanic profile of Monte Amiata on the distant horizon, against the western sky at evening. The mountain stands between the villages of Castel del Piano and Abbadia S. Salvatore in southern Tuscany, and rises to an altitude of 1738 metres. Its flanks and the surrounding countryside are given over to the cultivation of sweet chestnuts, cereals, grapes, and olives. Since the Etruscan period cinnabar (red mercuric sulphide) has been extracted from mines on the slopes of Monte Amiata. Its man-made equivalent, vermillion, has been used by artists and decorators since ancient times, as Costa was presumably aware.

Costa's visit to Monte Amiata is not recorded by his biographer or referred to in his own memoirs. Even in the last years of his life, he continued to roam the Italian countryside in summer and autumn, showing a particular preference for places of long historical or mythical association. In 1881–2 he painted a view of Monte Catria, a limestone massif near Gubbio in Umbria, which may be compared with the view of Amiata: in both pictures, the mountain ridge is seen from the far distance at dusk or early morning, so that the landscape foreground is suffused by long shadows marked by diagonals which lead the eye into the distance.

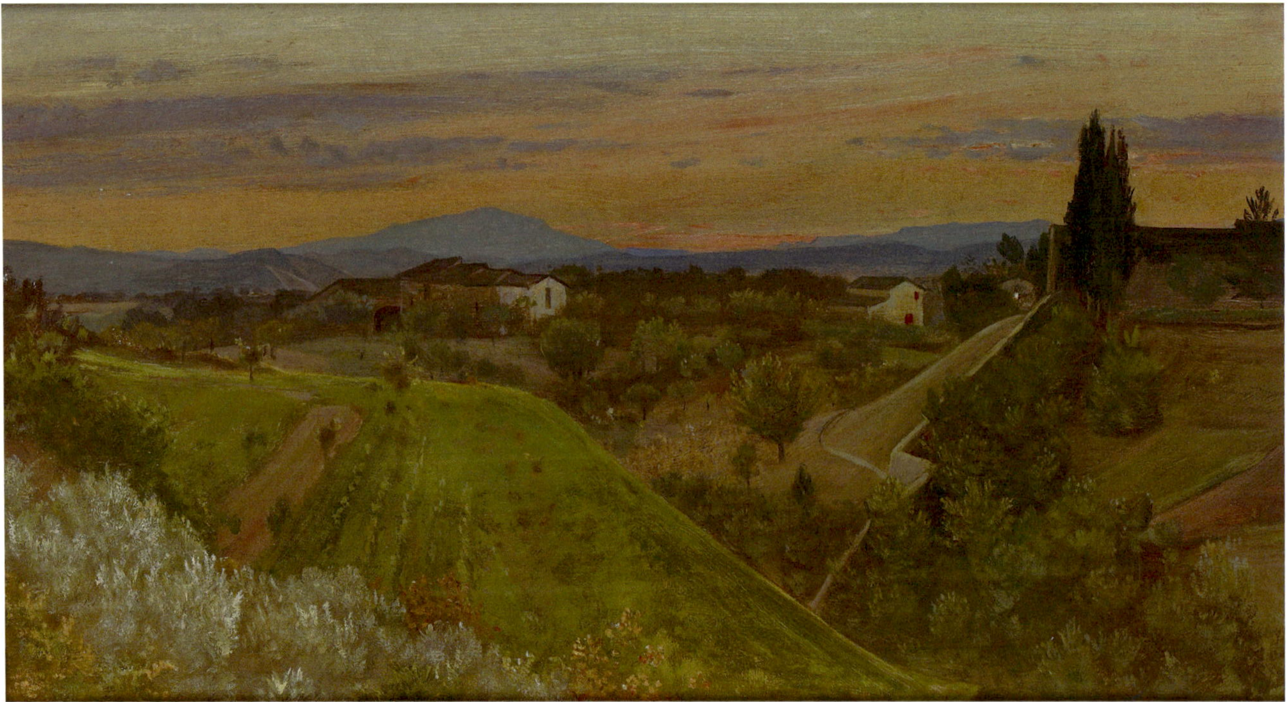

110
Matthew Ridley Corbet (1850–1902)
Montecelio, from the Villa d'Este, Tivoli 1883–4
Oil on canvas, 19.7 x 33 cm
Private collection

Corbet settled in Rome in the winter of 1880–81, living at 20 Via di San Basilio and joining a group of young artists in the city, which included the sculptor Alfred Gilbert and the American painter Elihu Vedder. He soon made the acquaintance of Giovanni Costa, from whom he learned how to refine his landscape compositions by the use of subdued and harmonious colour. In the winter of 1883–4, Corbet was a founder member of the Etruscan school, and he later showed with Costa in the exhibition 'In Arte Libertas'. This painting, which exemplifies the crispness and clarity of Corbet's early style, has recently been identified as a view of Montecelio, a village to the north-west of Tivoli among the Cornicolani Hills which stands on the site of the Roman Corniculum.

Although the city of Rome and the surrounding Campagna were Corbet's favourite painting grounds in the first half of the 1880s, he also made expeditions to the south, joining the community of artists that formed around Charles Caryl Coleman at Capri in about 1882, and to the countryside near Perugia, where he shared a rented farm house with Gilbert and his family.

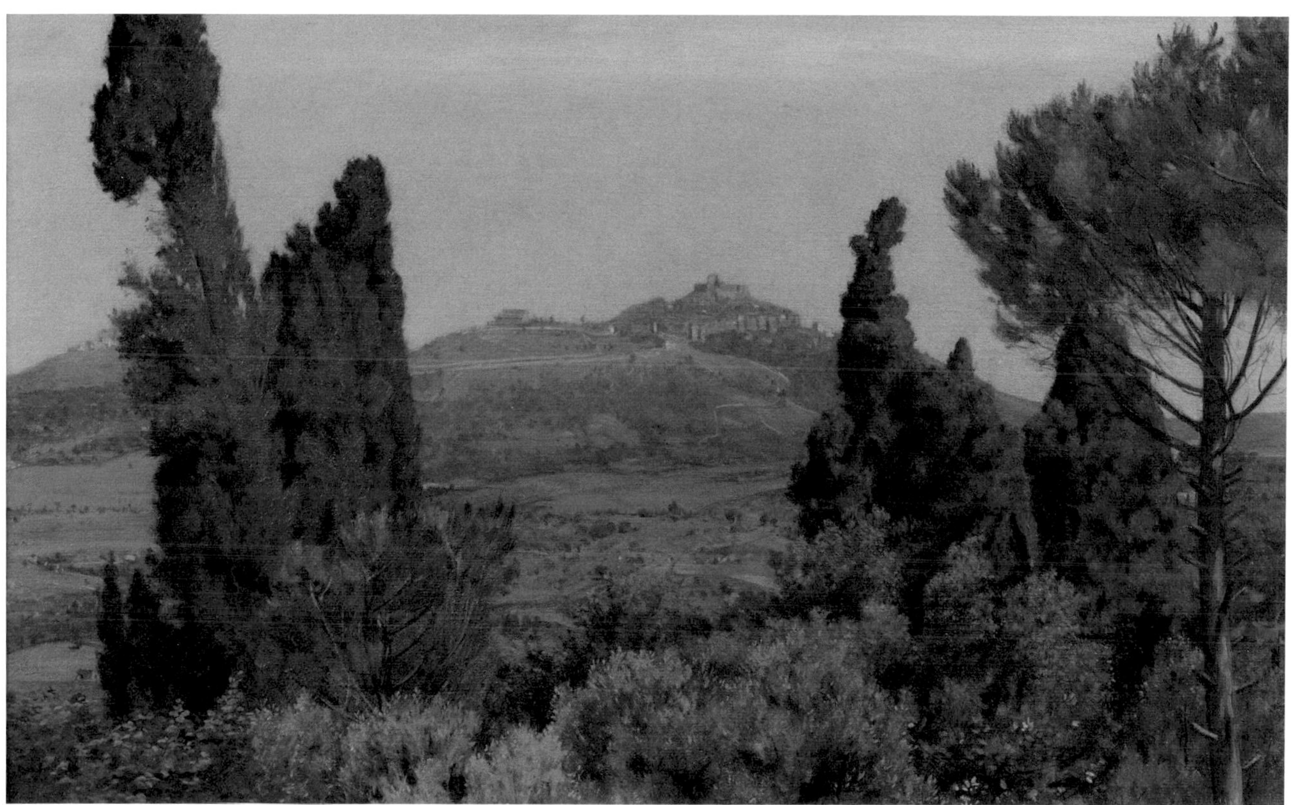

111

George Howard, 9th Earl of Carlisle (1843–1911)
The Baths of Caracalla, Rome ?1886
Oil on canvas 76 x 165 cm
U.K. Government Art Collection

112

George Howard, 9th Earl of Carlisle
The Baths of Caracalla, Rome 1886
Watercolour and bodycolour on paper, 24 x 54 cm
From the Castle Howard Collection
Ref: Newall 1989, no. 46

Howard's view taken from inside the ruins of the Baths of Caracalla in Rome was presumably made in the summer of 1886, when he spent three months in the city and is known to have painted with Costa on the Palatine. The brick and concrete construction was made during the reign of the emperor Caracalla between AD 211 and 216. The baths are estimated to have been capable of accommodating up to 10,000 people, putting them on a scale to compare with the Baths of Trajan. Furthermore, despite the quarrying of building materials in the Middle Ages, and further spectacular depredations under Pope Paul III, who removed all the remaining marble and granite columns and gigantic statuary for display in the Palazzo Farnese, the building is sufficiently well preserved to give a powerful sense both of the scale and organisation of an imperial bath complex.

Howard's view is towards the south-east, with the ancient city walls close to the Porta S. Sebastiano and the Porta Latina beyond what was then the open countryside and hills on either side of the Appian Way shown in the distance. On the left side of the composition are seen what appear to be the late sixteenth-century church of S. Ceraseo de' Appia and the Renaissance Casa del Cardinale Bessarione. The structure of the Baths themselves is shown divided by the central axis which formed an atrium off which the swimming pool (*natatio*), the cold hall (*frigidarium*), and the hot room (*caldarium*) were placed.

In choosing this subject, Howard has relished the shapes and textures of the sun-baked ruins – which are treated in a pallid and unified range of pinks, greys and browns, and which blend harmoniously with the wider landscape – while at the same time he succeeds in giving an impressive sense of the vast volume of the ancient fabric. A note of 'dolce far niente' is introduced by the presence of two young women wearing clothes that protect them from the sun. A green lizard – one of the artist's favourite motifs, introduced to denote the southern landscape – appears in the centre close to the lower edge.

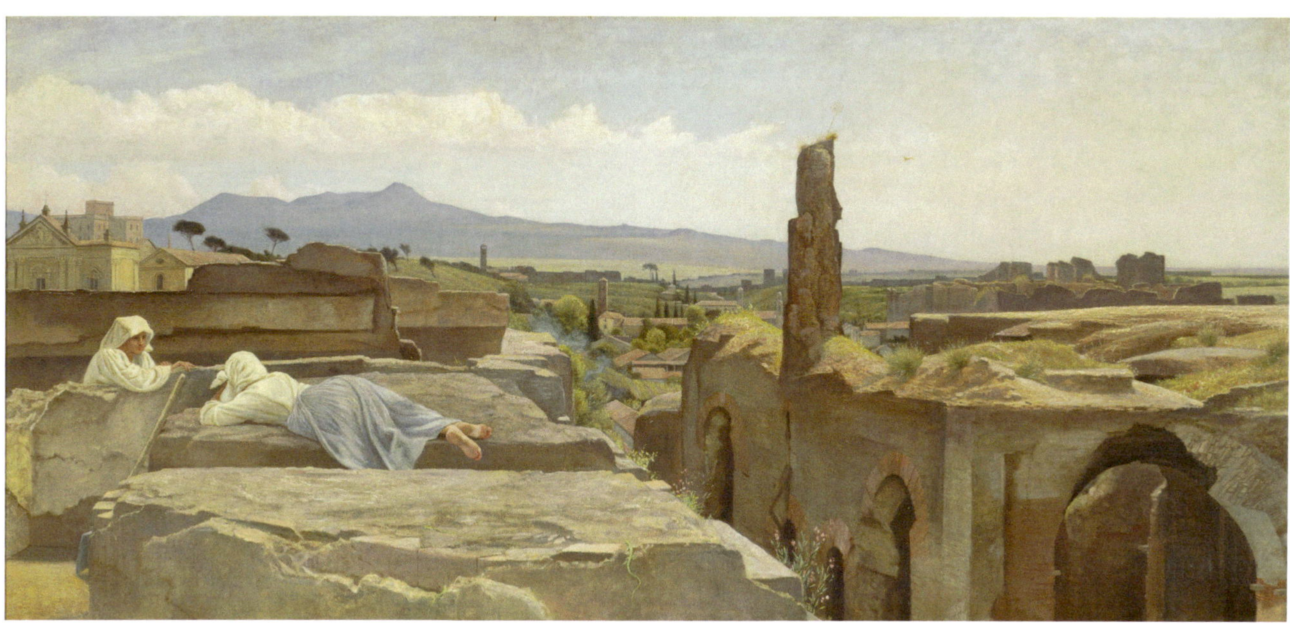

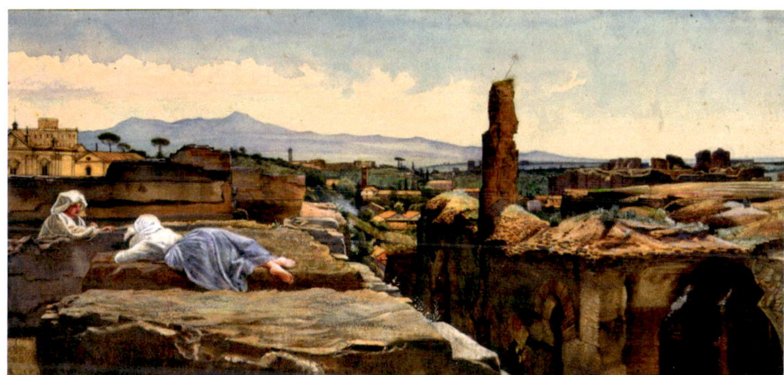

113
George Howard, 9th Earl of Carlisle
(1843–1911)
A View within the Baths of Caracalla, Rome
1886 (?)
Watercolour on paper, 35.6 x 26 cm
From the Castle Howard Collection

This drawing was presumably done in the course of the same visit to Rome as the large oil subject (**cat. 111**), but from a lower vantage point in order to show the great piers of concrete faced with brick as well as intact parts of the arched roof of the central atrium.

Costa disapproved of the medium of watercolour, finding it flimsy, insubstantial, and inexpressive. Howard, despite his reliance on the Italian painter and implicit faith in his advice on artistic matters, nonetheless had a strong predilection for watercolour. This was in a sense a family tradition, as his mother Mary Parke had been a talented amateur artist and a pupil of Peter De Wint.

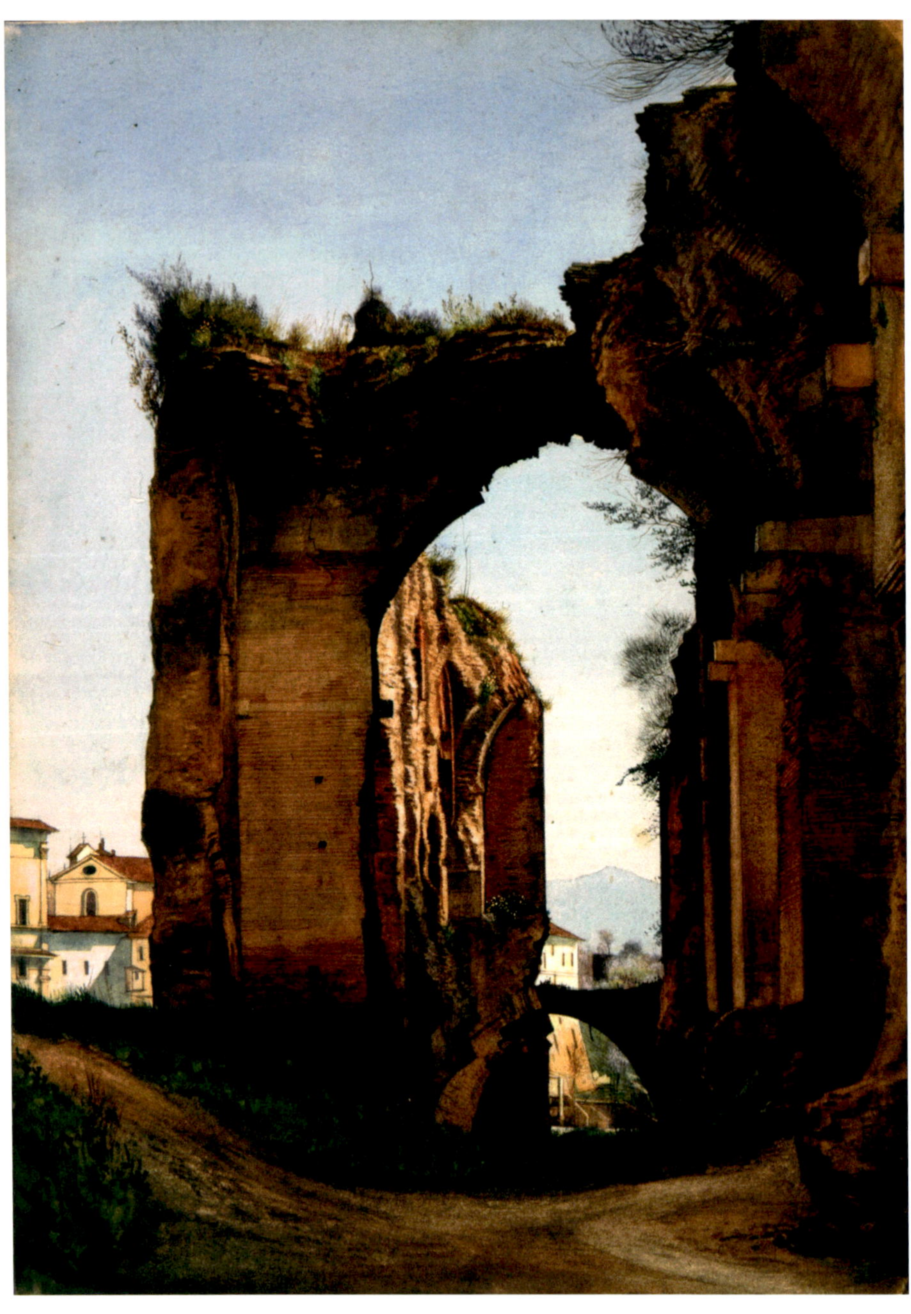

114
William Blake Richmond (1842–1921)
The Sea, Bocca d'Arno 1889 (?)
Oil on panel, 25 x 62 cm
Ashmolean Museum, University of Oxford. Bequeathed by Mrs H.F. Medlicott, 1950 (WA1950.47)
Ref: Reynolds 1995, pp. 68–9

Richmond had known Costa since about 1866, and was perhaps introduced to him by Frederic Leighton. As he recalled: 'Costa's work was a revelation to me, it made me see nature in a new light, it inspired me with desire. I saw in it absolute sincerity, a feeling for form which was Greek, for colour refined and strong, if reticent, and always harmonious [...] It was never "pretty", always beautiful, sometimes austere. I can compare it with no one else's'.[1]

In 1868 Richmond rented a house for his family close to the mouth of the River Arno. On other occasions, when travelling alone, he lodged at a pensione at Gombo. He returned to the Tuscan coast in the summer of 1889, staying at the house that Costa had bought at Marina di Pisa four years previously. It seems likely that the present view at Bocca d'Arno was painted on this last occasion.

1 Stirling 1926, pp. 206–7

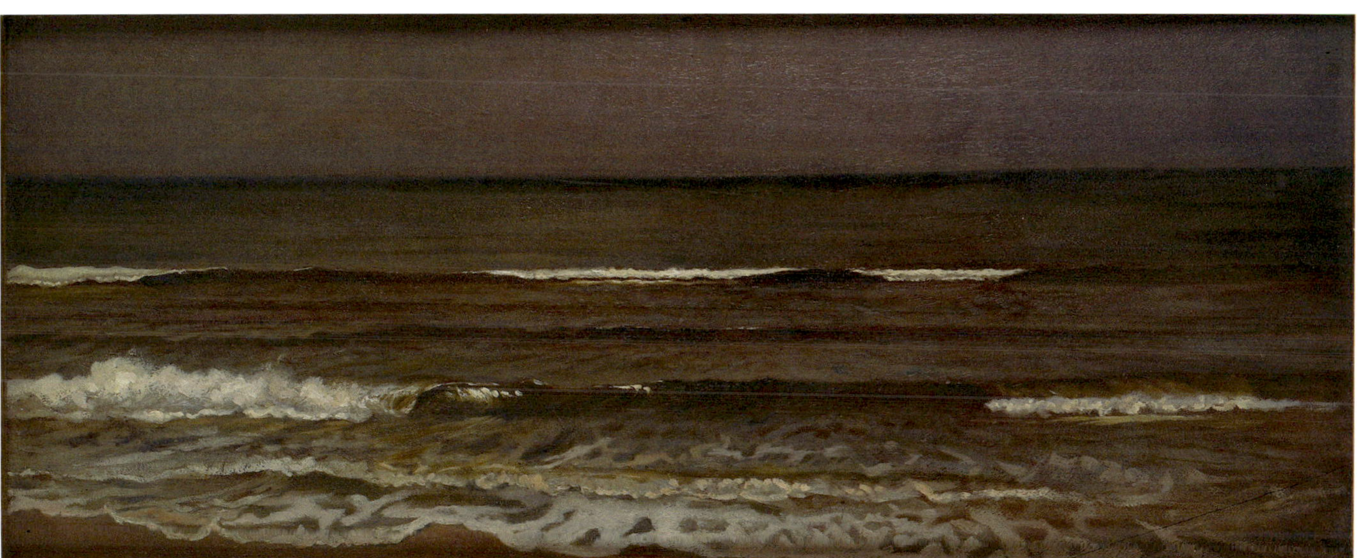

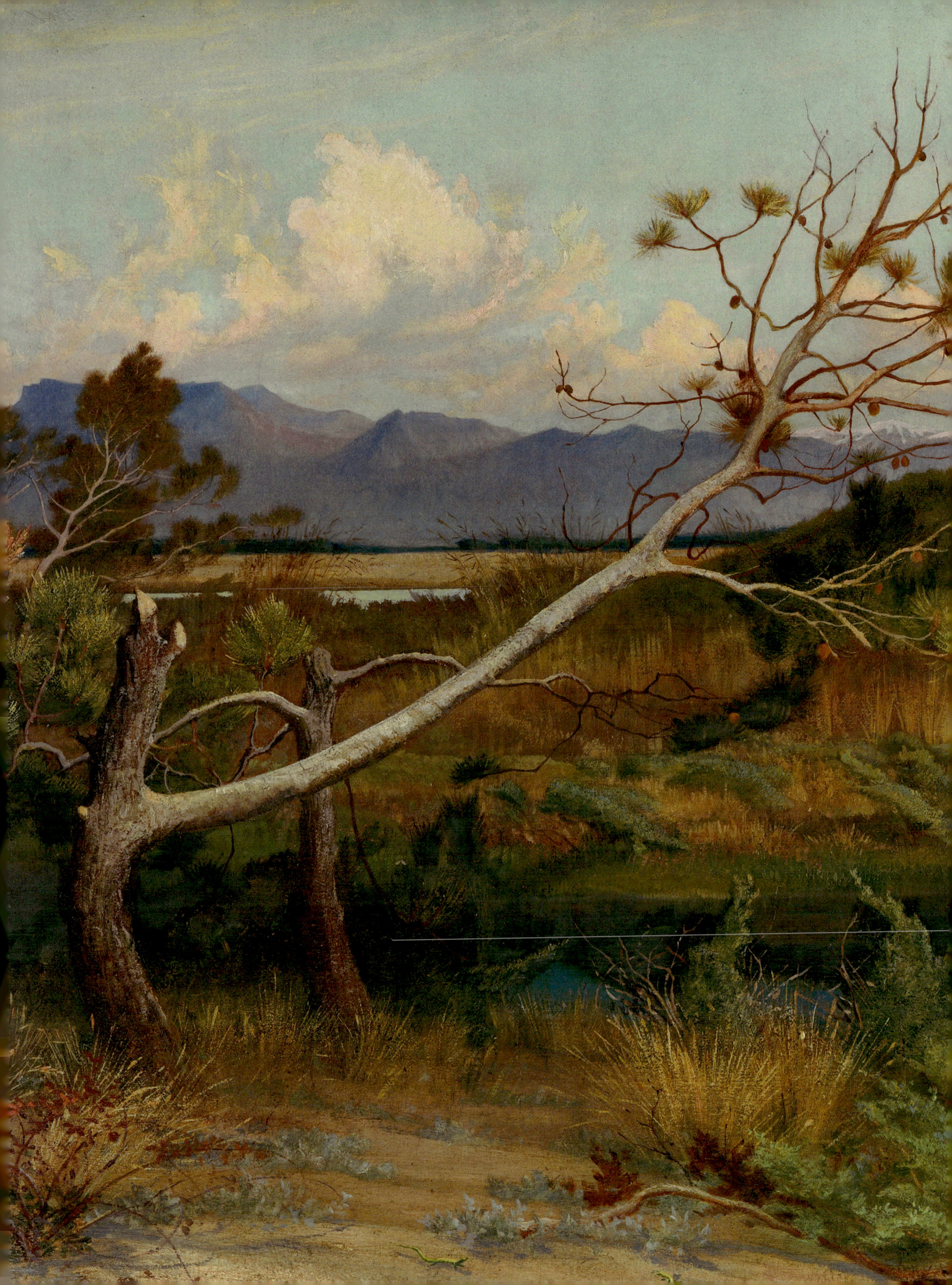

115
George Howard, 9th Earl of Carlisle
(1843–1911)
The Fort at Bocca d'Arno 1889–91
Oil on canvas, 48.2 x 108 cm
Private collection
Ref: Newall 1989, no. 70

Costa bought a house at Marina di Pisa in September 1885, and he spent most summers and autumns there for the rest of his life. Stopford Brooke described this Tuscan setting on a visit in 1895:

> I drove to the Bocca d'Arno, and spent an afternoon on the seashore and by the river at its opening into the sea. That *is* a place for artists. The sea, the river, the dark forest-line, the distant mountains, the long, low shore, are all in their right place, at their right distance, and in their due proportions; and it is drenched in sentiment, not human, but of Nature's very self. Then I went to drive in the pine forest, and to wander through it by the Fiume Morto to the sea; and I walked a long time through those wild solitary woods, where the nightingales were singing in a madness of joy. I had last been there in '75, twenty years ago, and the place was full of associations to me. I knew it well. [1]

Howard's view is towards the north, with the familiar outline of the Carrara Mountains forming the horizon. The surface of the river, flowing to the sea which is out of view on the left side, is glimpsed as a silver fillet at the centre of the composition; in the foreground is a sinister pool of still, dark water. Dominating the centre is a maritime pine tree, broken and contorted by the prevailing winds from the sea. The building on the headland on the right was a notable landmark known as the 'fortino'. Nearby was Costa's own house, described by his biographer as a 'charming villa on the sea front, with the pine woods coming right down to the garden wall'.[2]

George Howard and his daughter Cecilia had visited Costa in November 1889, when he may have begun the present view. A photograph of the broken pine tree and the expanse of still water stretching across the middle ground (possibly in fact a view of the Fiume Morto, as described by Brooke), exists in an album compiled by the artist (now in a private collection), indicating that the painting was in part worked on in the artist's studio in England, before being exhibited at the New Gallery in 1891. While staying with Costa in 1889, Howard bought back one of his own works entitled *Bocca d'Arno* (Castle Howard Collection), which shows the shoreline with a woman gazing out to sea, and a distant outline of the Carrara Mountains; he showed it at the New Gallery in the following year.

1 Jacks 1917, II, p. 521
2 Agresti, 1904, p. 251

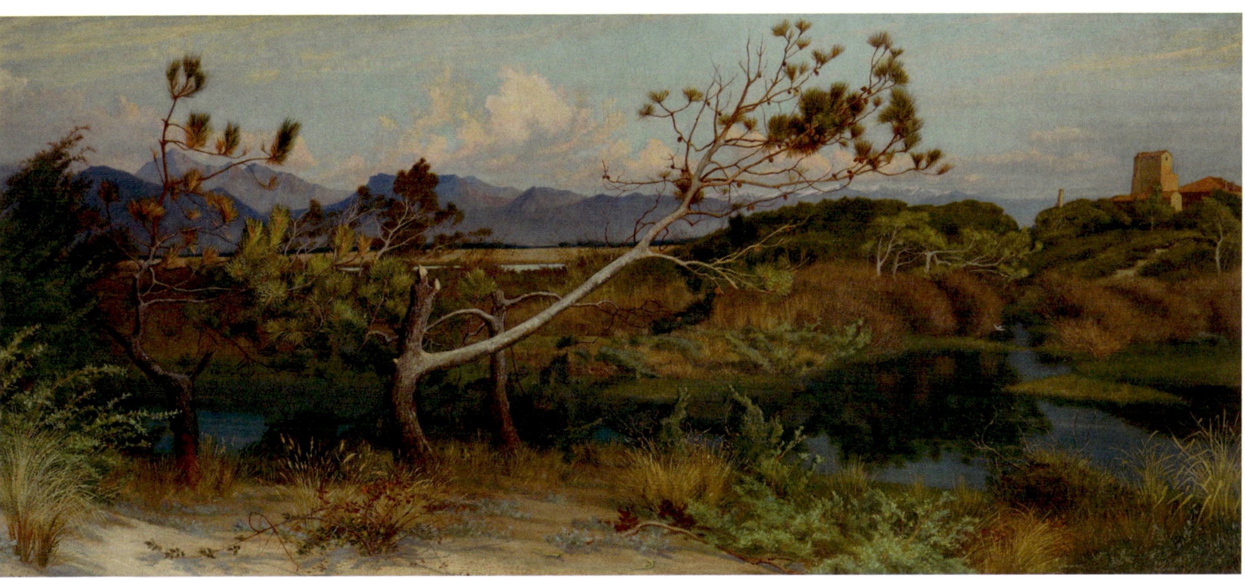

116
William Blake Richmond (1842–1921)
The Plains of Tuscany from Volterra 1892
Oil on canvas, 39.4 x 59.7 cm
Signed and dated: *W.B.R. 1892*
Private collection
Ref: Newall 1989 no. 75; Reynolds 1995, pp. 242, 298

Richmond told Costa's biographer, Olivia Rossetti Agresti, that 'if what [he] had painted in landscape has any merit, it is largely due to the early influence of Giovanni Costa',[1] who advised him to 'cut from it small detail.[2].

Richmond's landscape painting ranged in scale from the awe-inspiring *Near Viareggio* **(cat. 108)** to small oil sketches on wooden panels. Some may be regarded as complete works of art, while others were aids to memory or intended as preparatory studies for details in figure compositions. Cat. 116 was shown at the New Gallery summer exhibition of 1895. It shows the sandstone banks known as the Balze, which form the perimeter of the city of Volterra and which drop steeply to the lower level of the wide Pisan Plain towards the north and west. The effect is one of late-afternoon light, so that the ravines that have been cut in the soft Pliocene rock formations – which is eroding so quickly as to have swallowed up a succession of buildings and cemeteries which once stood on open ground outside the town – are seen in stark definition. A group of cypresses occupy the foreground, their strange, attenuated trunks defining the interstices of the composition.

1 Agresti 1904, p. 132
2 quoted in Newall 1989, p. 20

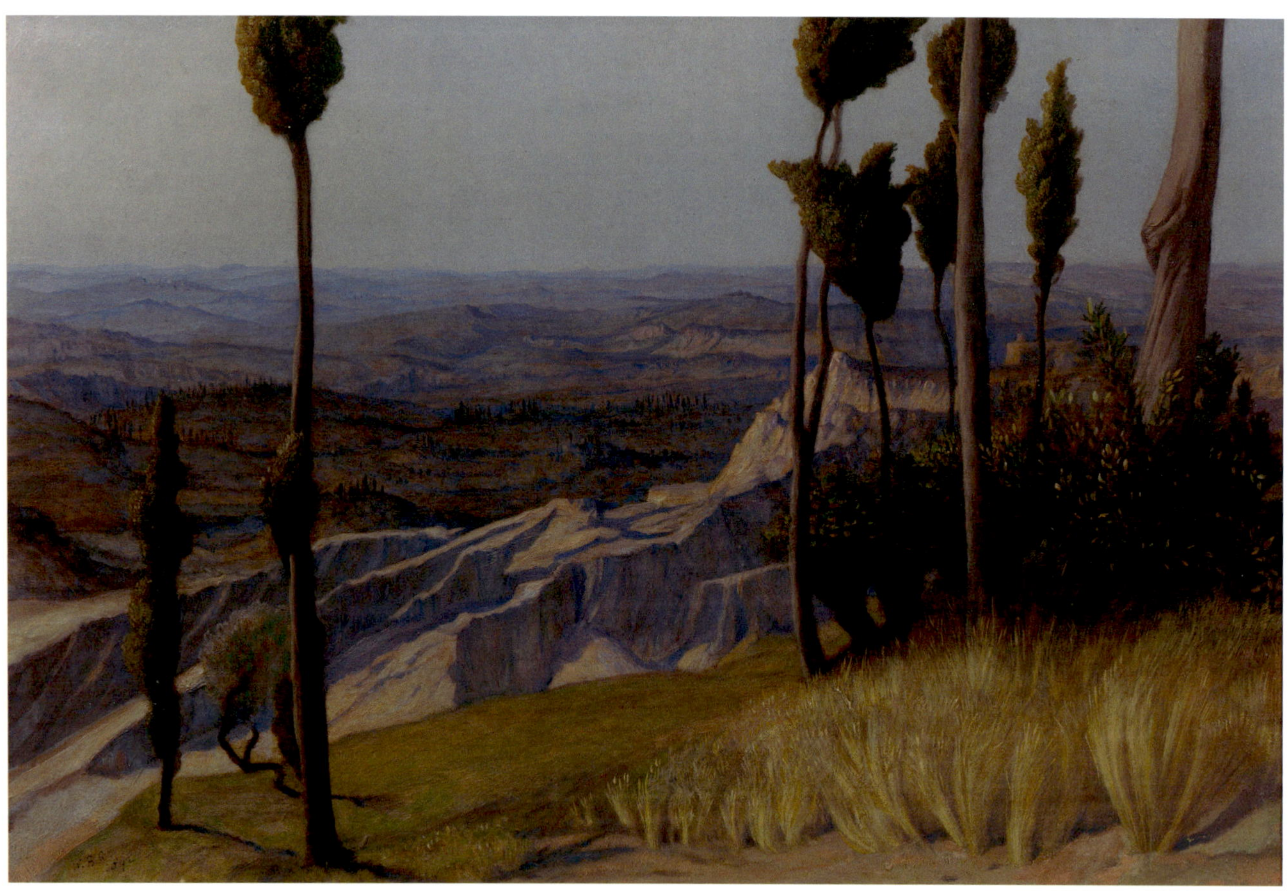

117
Matthew Ridley Corbet (1850–1902)
From Volterra, Looking towards the Pisan Hills
1898–9
Watercolour on paper, 50.2 x 69.2 cm
Signed and dated: *M.R. Corbet 1898–9*
Private collection
Ref: Newall 1989 no. 78

From 1885, Corbet made frequent visits to Bocca d'Arno, staying with Costa or lodging at the Albergo Ascani at Marina di Pisa. In the following years, he made a thorough exploration of the coastal plain between Livorno and Viareggio, as well as of the hills inland around Volterra and to the north of Lucca. His success in capturing the characteristic effects of the Italian countryside was noted by an obituarist: 'His knowledge of Italy is not that of a tourist; it is that of a poet-painter, whose imagination is stirred by the cadence of the hills, the magic of dark cypresses silhouetted against the evening sky, the elusive beauty of olive-clad slopes, the "temper" of that country whose every valley, as mists steal silently across, is charged with memories'.[1] Cat. 117 is towards the north-west, with the Pisan Hills between Lucca and Pisa forming the distant horizon and valley of the Arno providing the vaporous middle ground.

Corbet treated the Tuscan landscape with careful observation of the topography and a use of colours that subtly convey the effects of autumn as well as the quality of light at the end of the day. This is the kind of evocation of the Italian landscape that delighted London audiences in the 1880s and 1890s. Corbet exhibited at the Grosvenor and New Galleries, as well as at the Royal Academy, where this view from Volterra was shown in 1899.

1 *Art Journal*, 1902, p. 93

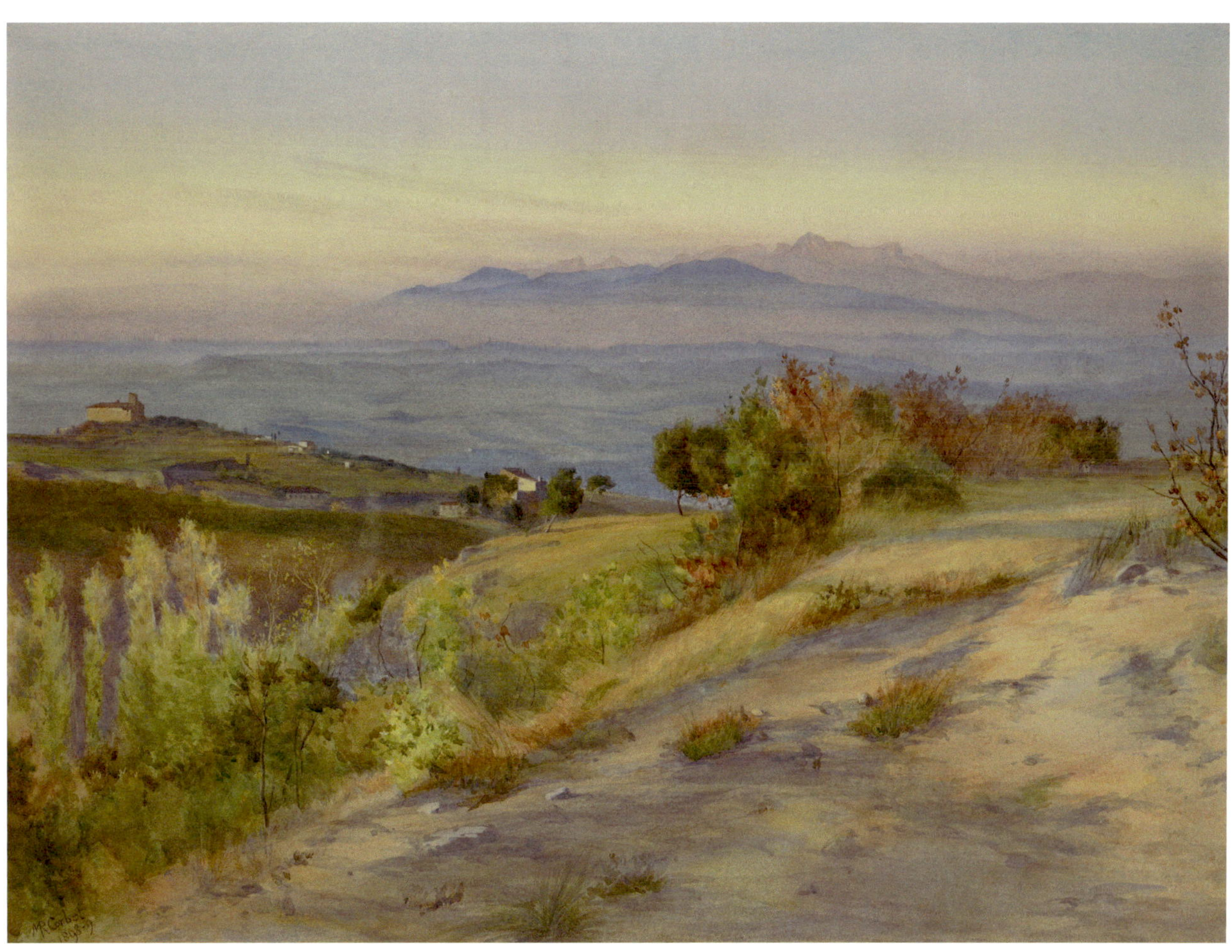

118
Giovanni Costa (1826–1903)
After a Shower near Pisa
Oil on panel, 13.3 x 29.2 cm
The Gere Collection
Ref: Riopelle 1999, no. 20

This undated panel shows the countryside between the River Arno and the pine forests to the north of S. Rossore, and was probably painted in the late 1880s or early 1890s.

Costa's late style was marked by brighter colours and the elimination of black in the shadows, a development that may have been influenced by contemporary Post-Impressionism. Likewise, his distinctive style of dabbing colour onto the canvas or panel to create a sparkling and vibrant texture suggests analogies with the technique of the French Pointillists, as Riopelle has noted.[1] Costa remained entirely cosmopolitan in his old age, and certainly had opportunities to study French painting in exhibitions in Paris and elsewhere. On the other hand, the collectors of his works remained almost exclusively English – the present painting belonged to the print publisher and dealer, Robert Dunthorne – and there was a parallel development towards a painterly texture and greater brightness of colouring in English landscape painting in the last years of the nineteenth century.

1 Riopelle 1999, p. 68

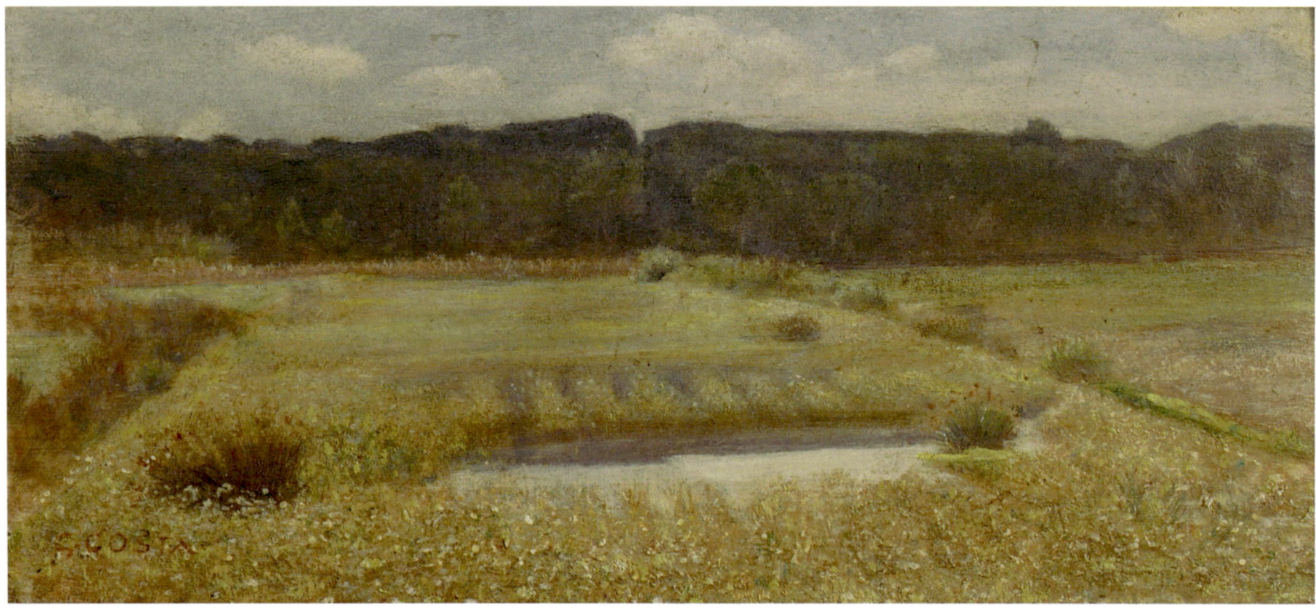

119

George Howard, 9th Earl of Carlisle (1843–1911)
Terraces near Amalfi with Rustics working in the Foreground 1910
Watercolour and bodycolour on paper, 36.5 x 53.5 cm
From the Castle Howard Collection

George Howard and his wife, Rosalind Stanley, were both interested in Italian politics and were in touch with several leaders of the campaign for Italian unification. Among them was Giuseppe Mazzini, who visited the Howards at their London home in December 1871, after his release from prison following the final capture of Rome and consequent amnesty for political prisoners.

The Howards made their first visit to Italy in December 1865, and made frequent tours in different parts of the country until the 1880s. On occasions they invited friends to travel with them – for example Jane Morris and her children, who stayed with them at Bordighera in 1881 – and on other occasions they coincided by arrangement or chance with artist friends in Italy. In later years George and Rosalind tended to drift apart, and after he succeeded as 9th Earl of Carlisle in 1889, she devoted much of her time to the management of the Yorkshire and Cumberland estates, while he continued to draw and paint, and accepted public responsibilities such as serving as a trustee of the National Gallery. The couple had stayed on the Amalfi peninsula early in 1872, but the present drawing was in fact made at Sorrento in March 1910, shortly before the artist's death.

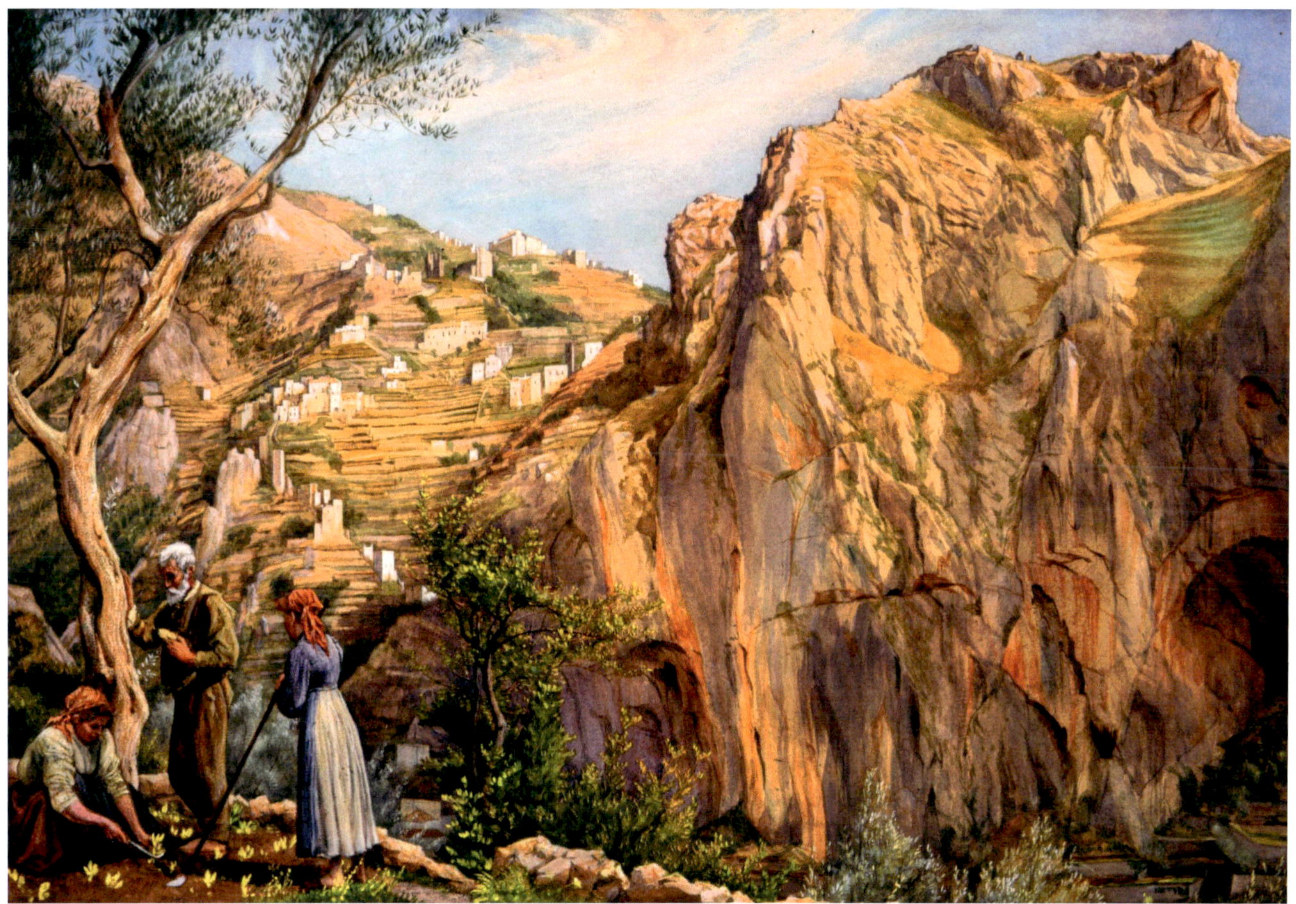

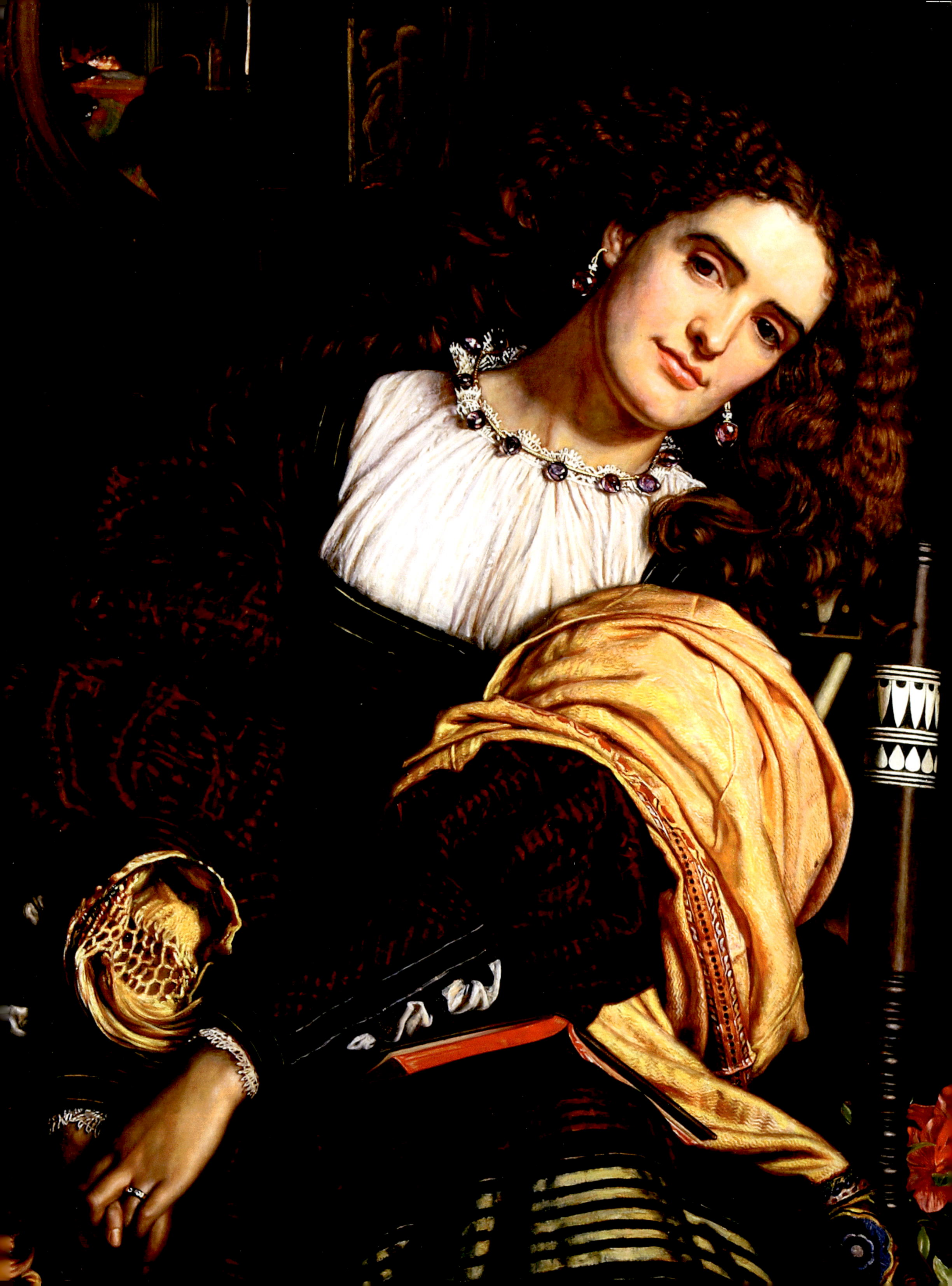

VI

AESTHETICISM – THE INSPIRATION OF THE RENAISSANCE

From the middle of the nineteenth century, a growing aesthetic sophistication, stimulated by an increasing exposure to ideas from continental Europe, meant that progressive English painting shed its traditional documentary and story-telling functions. The prompting of dreams and fantastic imaginings, and of veiled meaning and resonant imaginative association, became the goal of advanced painters, and is the defining trait of the new school of artists that arose in the wake of Pre-Raphaelitism.

D.G. Rossetti was the member of the Pre-Raphaelite Brotherhood who had the most sophisticated understanding of how a work of art might operate on the imagination, and it is significant that he was a poet as well as a painter. Although he had previously struggled to master the techniques of oil and watercolour, he emerged in the late 1850s as the most influential of all the Pre-Raphaelites, and became the leader of a group of younger artists, including Burne-Jones and Arthur Hughes, which transformed Pre-Raphaelitism into a school concerned with subliminal and other-worldly subjects. Rossetti's painting *Bocca Baciata* of 1859 (now in the Museum of Fine Arts, Boston), which took its inspiration from a line in Boccacio – 'the mouth that has been kissed loses not its freshness' – marks the arrival in English art of a distinctive languorous and voluptuous quality, in place of the earnestness and ingenuousness that had characterised the art of the Pre-Raphaelite Brotherhood.

Rossetti was intimately familiar with Italian poetry and literature. Burne-Jones, his disciple in the late 1850s, made four visits to Italy, each of which had a profound effect on his art. In 1859 he travelled to Venice on Ruskin's recommendation to look at works that Ruskin had described. In 1862 he returned expressly to copy from Tintoretto. The impact of sixteenth-century Venetian painting was overwhelming, and it was he rather than Ruskin himself who 'discovered' and led the cult for Carpaccio. In 1871, in the course of a visit to Rome, Burne-Jones revelled in the genius of Michelangelo, who by that time had become the inspiration of his figurative classicism. This enthusiasm for Michelangelo was profoundly disturbing to Ruskin, who openly denigrated the master in his lecture at Oxford in 1871, *The Relation between Michael Angelo and Tintoret.* Burne-Jones took the attack personally, and it led to a rift between the two men.

In the same period, Algernon Charles Swinburne and Walter Pater wrote about Italian sixteenth-century art in way that inspired a generation and led British culture to find weird and alarming beauties and strange associations in the art of Titian, Leonardo, and Michelangelo. Swinburne's advocacy of the sixteenth century was a spur to painters such as Burne-Jones and Simeon Solomon, while Walter Pater's prose, notably his description of the *Mona Lisa* in *The Renaissance* (1873), served as a plea that individuals should respond intensely to beauty, and that works of art should only be judged for their aesthetic merit and without consideration of their supposed moral character. Thus the study of Italian post-Renaissance art became a principal inspiration of the movement known as 'art for art's sake', and in due course led to the decadence.

120
Simeon Solomon (1840–1905)
The Painter's Pleasaunce 1861
Watercolour and bodycolour with scratching out and varnish on paper, 25.6 x 33.1 cm
Signed and dated: *SS. / 2/12/61*
Whitworth Art Gallery, University of Manchester (D.1911.4)
Ref: Parris 1984, no. 233; Cruise 2005, no. 49

By the time Solomon came to paint this watercolour, depictions of episodes from the lives of historic artists had become almost commonplace, both in England and in France. Among them, Solomon would surely have seen both Leighton's *Cimabue's Madonna* (1855) and Dyce's *Titian's First Essay in Colour* (1857) when he was a student. In the more immediate Pre-Raphaelite circle, Rossetti had made a number of drawings of such subjects in the early 1850s **(see cats. 5–7)**, which Solomon would have known of, even if he had not seen them. *The Painter's Pleasaunce* was not intended to evoke a specific artist – the archaic spelling and even the use of the word 'pleasaunce' indicating a period long ago but timeless – although the rich colouring have led some commentators to suggest that the subject may be Giorgione. Certainly, many of the details suggest that the interior is Italianate, but it would be wrong to go any further, as it is also entirely fanciful. The artist is absorbed in his work, while his model is amused by a kitten and her faithful hound keeps watch. A serving girl stands ready behind the artist to offer her wine and cakes, and stares coyly out at the viewer.

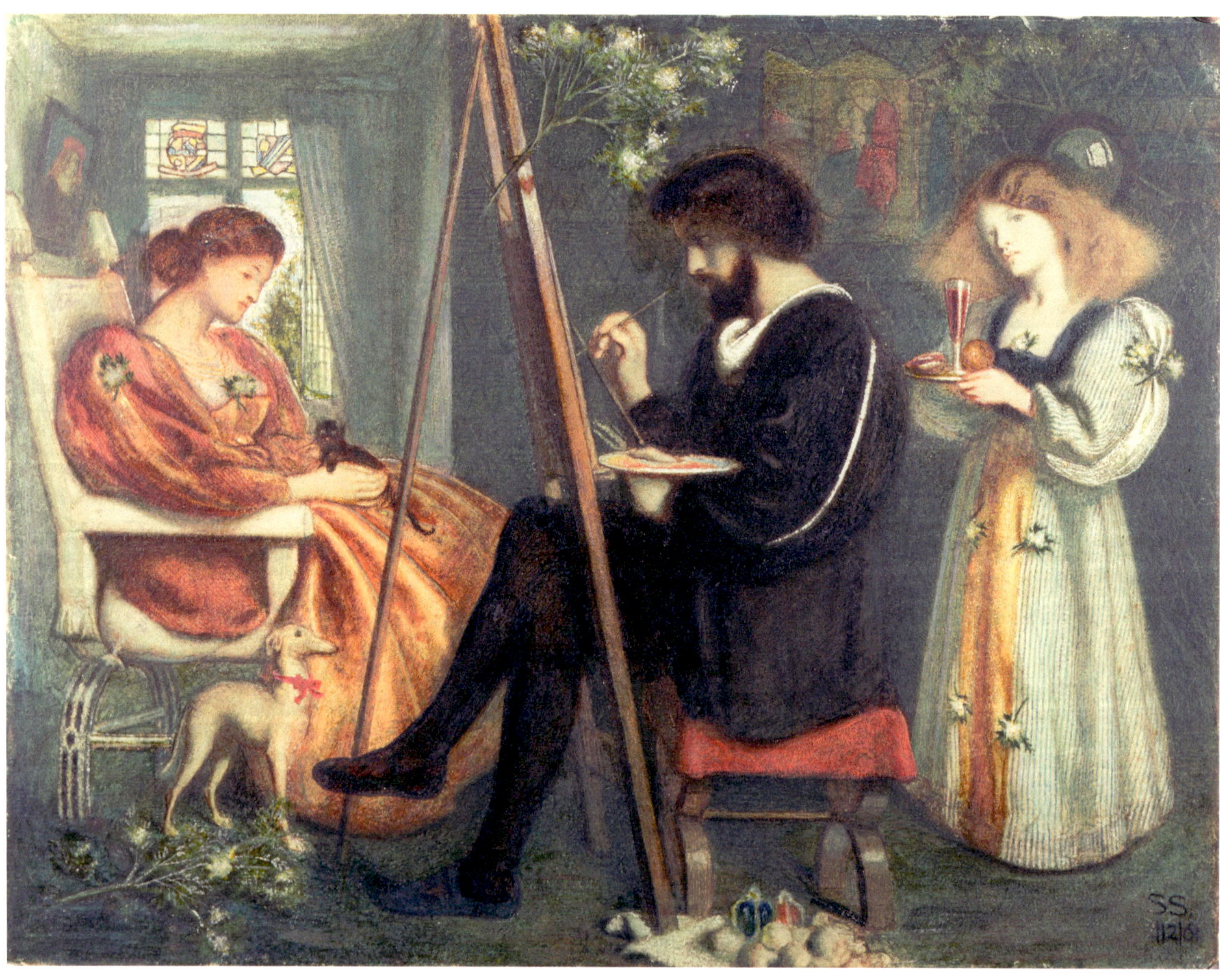

121
Dante Gabriel Rossetti (1828–1882)
Dantis Amor 1860
Inscribed: *QUI EST PER OMNIA SAECVLA BENEDICTUS*
Oil on mahogany panel, 74.9 x 81.3 cm
Tate. Presented by F. Treharne James, 1920 (N03532)
Ref: Surtees 1971, no. 117; Parris 1984, no. 104

This painting originated as one of three panels of a cupboard door which formed the upright back of a large settle, designed by Rossetti and made by Henry Price, a carpenter employed by William Morris, for use in the rooms that Morris and Burne-Jones occupied in Red Lion Square. When Morris married Jane Burden in April 1859, Rossetti painted the two side panels, *The Salutation of Beatrice on Earth* and *The Salutation of Beatrice in Heaven* (National Gallery of Canada, Ottawa) as a wedding present to the couple. In 1860 the settle, with the side panels incorporated, was reassembled at the Red House at Bexley Heath, which had been built for the Morrises by Philip Webb. The present panel was made to go at the centre, with the patterning of its background and diagonal division into fields decorated with emblematic swirling flames and stars, and with a head of Christ in the upper and left-hand part representing the sun, and one of Beatrice (for which Lizzie Siddal was the model) in the lower and right-hand part, the moon, symbolical of day and night. At the centre stands the red-winged figure of Love, modelled on Jane Morris herself – with flowing auburn hair and wearing a gold and brown robe and holding in his arms a sundial which, had the painting been completed, would have indicated the time of Beatrice's death on 12 June 1290, at the ninth hour of the day (as seen in the preparatory drawing for the composition), along with a bow and arrow. Also on the preparatory drawing are various further quotations from Dante's *Divine Comedy*, making clear the significance of the subject. This was a scheme that Rossetti had contemplated since the late 1840s (the earliest design for the multiple-composition, dated 1849, is in the Fogg Art Museum, Harvard University).

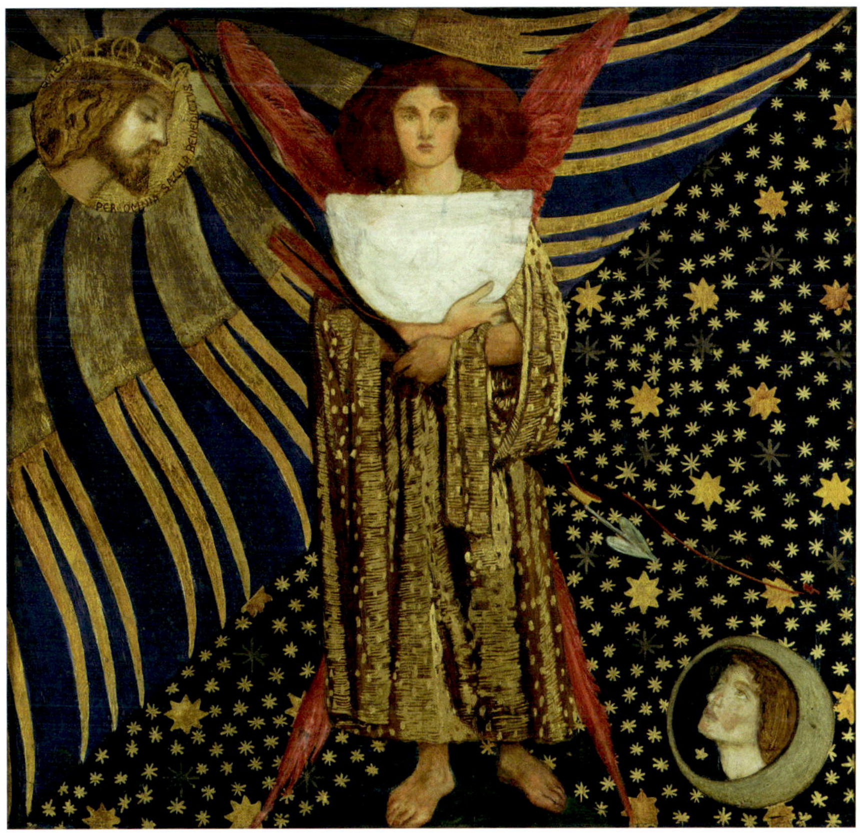

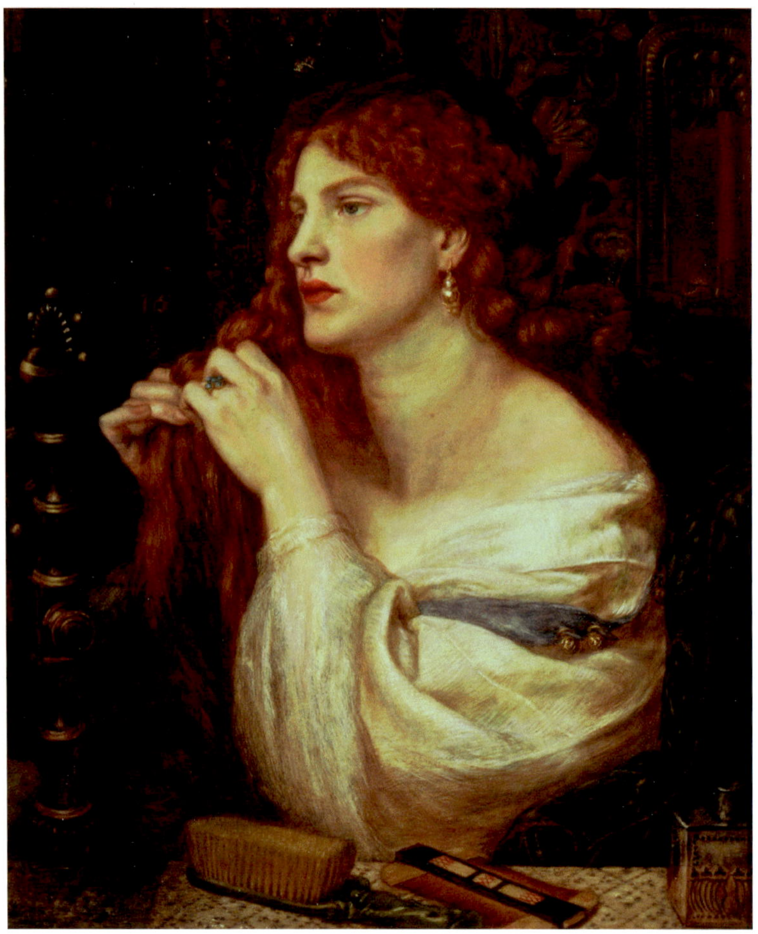

122
Dante Gabriel Rossetti (1828–1882)
Fazio's Mistress, also known as *Aurelia* 1863–73
Oil on mahogany panel, 77.1 x 70.8 cm
Tate. Purchased with assistance from Sir Arthur Du Cros, Bart and Sir Otto Beit, KCMG through The Art Fund, 1916 (N03055)
Ref: Surtees 1971, no. 164; Treuherz 2003, no. 100

Rossetti's painting was inspired by a poem by the fourteenth-century Italian Fazio degli Uberti, which he translated as 'His Portrait of his Lady, Angiola of Verona' and published in *Early Italian Poets* (1861). In it, the poet listed the particular beauties of his paramour: 'crisp, golden-threaded hair', 'amorous beautiful mouth', 'lips, red as an open rose', 'white easy neck', and 'large arms, so lithe and round'. This hymn of physical admiration and desire concludes with a note of uncertainty:

Song, thou canst surely say, without pretence,
That since the first fair woman ever made,
Not one can have display'd
More power upon all hearts than this one doth;
Because in her are both
Loveliness and the soul's true excellence: –
And yet (woe's me!) is pity absent thence?

The figure of Angiola is seen at a dressing-table laid with a brush, comb and scent bottle, and a looking-glass to the left, holding the tresses of her hair as she gazes in unseeing reverie. The room is claustrophobically furnished with tapestry, a sconce, and a shadowed open space with heavy furniture and metalwork. Although the pretext for the painting was literary, Rossetti never intended it as a straightforward illustration of the verse. As he wrote to Ellen Heaton when he began the picture, 'I am now painting a lady plaiting her golden hair. This is an oil and chiefly a piece of colour',[1] to be judged for its decorative quality and erotic allure.

The painting depicts a room in Tudor House, the seventeenth-century mansion in Chelsea which Rossetti occupied after the death of Elizabeth Siddal. The figure is the artist's mistress Fanny Cornforth, blonde-haired and voluptuous, whose sensuous presence was the inspiration for the type of half-length figures of beautiful young women, who allow themselves to be the object of admiration but refuse to engage directly with their male admirers. In this sense, *Fazio's Mistress* is a successor to *Bocca Bacciata* (Museum of Fine Arts, Boston), which was also a portrait of Fanny. That it was a good likeness is testified by Rossetti himself, who received the painting back for retouching in 1873 and who wrote to her: 'I have got an old picture of you here which I painted many years ago. It is the one where you are seated doing your hair before a glass. Rae, to whom it belongs, has sent it to me as it wants some glazing, but *I am not working at all on the head*, which is exactly like the funny old elephant [Rossetti's love-name for Fanny], as like it as I ever did'.[2]

1 quoted in Surtees 1971, p. 92
2 quoted in Surtees 1971, p. 93

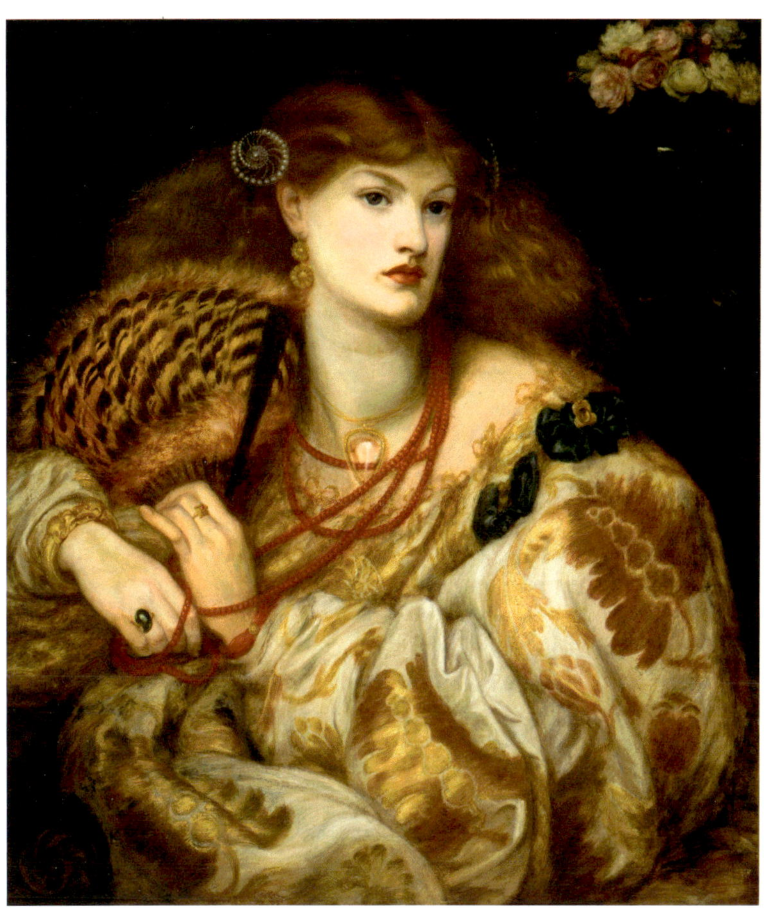

123
Dante Gabriel Rossetti
Monna Vanna, also known as *Belcolore* 1866
Signed with monogram: *DGR*
Oil on canvas, 88.9 x 86.4 cm
Tate. Purchased with assistance from Sir Arthur Du Cros, Bart and Sir Otto Beit, KCMG through The Art Fund, 1916 (N03054)
Ref: Surtees 1971, no. 191

Monna Vanna exemplifies the type of non-narrative representation of female beauty, painted in what Rossetti regarded as the Venetian style, and is effectively a portrait of the professional model, Alexa Wilding. The title was taken from the *Vita Nuova*, XXIV, in which Dante sees two ladies, Vanna and Bici, translated by Rossetti as Joan and Beatrice: 'The first is christen'd Spring; The second Love'. However, it has no particular significance other than to emphasise the Italianate character of the subject. The original title was given in a letter from Rossetti to the collector John Mitchell in September 1866: 'I have a picture close on completion – one of my best I believe, and probably the most effective as a room decoration which I have ever painted. It is called *Venus Veneta*, and represents a Venetian lady in a rich dress of white and gold – in short the Venetian ideal of female beauty'.[1] In 1873, when he retouched both this picture and *Fazio's Mistress* (**cat. 122**), Rossetti devised new titles for both: *Belcolore* for the present work, and *Aurelia* for *Fazio's Mistress*. As he explained to George Rae, both the old 'names [were] derived from 13th century sources & quite out of place with such modern looking pictures'.[2] Thus in the early 1870s, Rossetti was moving further towards an abstract exploration of the female persona.

The clasp worn in the model's hair, consisting of a spiral of pearls, and the multi-stranded necklace of red coral, are among Rossetti's favourite properties in the period, seen in a number of his works.

1 Fredeman 2002–10, III, p. 472
2 Fredeman 2002–10, VI, p. 339

124

Dante Gabriel Rossetti (1828–1882)
Study for 'La Pia de' Tolomei' 1868
Coloured chalks on two joined sheets of paper, 65.4 x 82.5 cm
Signed in monogram and dated: *DGR 1868* and inscribed: *Ricorditi di me che son la Pia*
Private collection
Ref: Surtees 1971, no. 207B

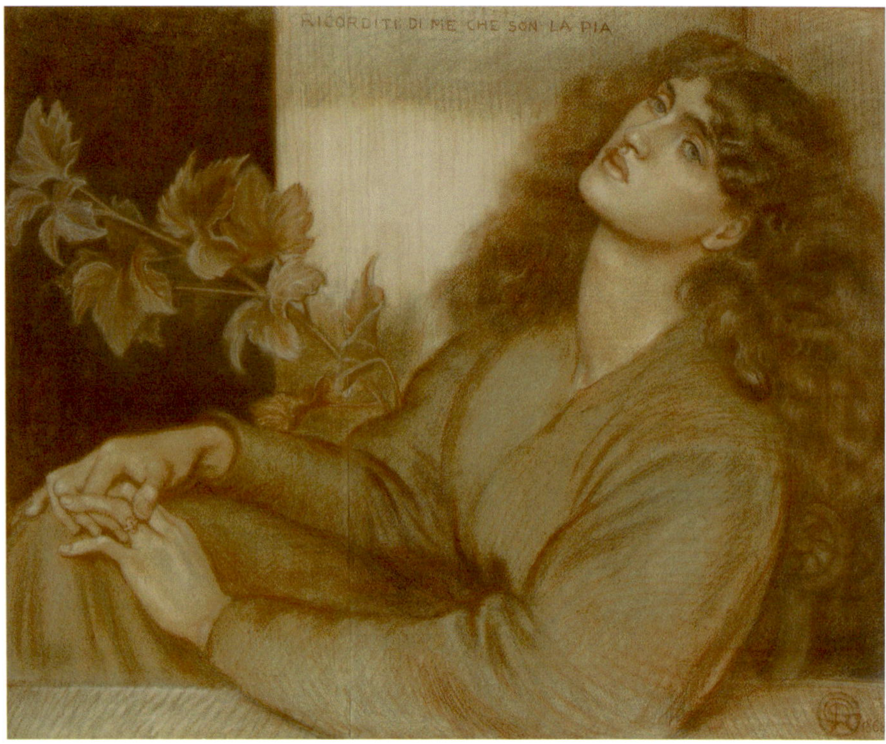

This is an early study for the figure in Rossetti's painting *La Pia de' Tolomei*, begun in 1868 but not completed until 1881.[1] The subject illustrates a passage in Dante's *Purgatory*, Canto V, which tells how a beautiful young woman named Pia de' Tolomei was imprisoned by her husband, Nello della Pietra, in a remote castle in the Maremma; in the sadness of her isolation she pined away and died. Rossetti made two large compositional studies for the painting: this one shows the figure with her head thrown back, and is inscribed with the line from Dante, 'Remember me, who am La Pia'. The second drawing is much closer to the finished oil painting, with the head of the figure leaning forward, and the inscription of the following line from Dante, *Siena mi fè, Disfecimi Maremma* ('Siena made me, Maremma unmade me').[2] In both compositions, Pia holds the wedding ring that binds her to her cruel husband.

Jane Morris was the model for both the compositional studies and the finished painting. They were made at a time when Rossetti's feelings for her were becoming more intense, and she had become the inspiration for much of his poetry and his pictures. They had first met in 1857, when he was working in the debating chamber of the Oxford Union. She was the daughter of an ostler, without formal education, but already a forceful personality, and extremely beautiful. She married William Morris in 1859. Rossetti may always have been attracted to her, but in the early years of her married life their relationship remained within the bounds of propriety. However, in the second half of the 1860s, it became a love affair, and relations between Jane and William Morris lapsed into cold formality.

The remorse that Rossetti must have felt as he found himself in love with the wife of one of his oldest friends, combined with the complications and deceptions necessitated by the affair, preyed on the painter's already febrile state of mind. Several times in his later career he chose subjects which made tacit comment on Jane's situation in a loveless marriage. Proserpine, for example, was obliged to live in the Underworld as the wife of Pluto and only permitted to return occasionally to the land of the living. The present subject from Dante implies a similar commentary on Jane's predicament, as it illustrates an unloving husband who compels his wife to forgo all pleasures and contact with the world and thus denies her the will to live.

1 Spencer Museum of Art, University of Kansas, Lawrence; Surtees 1971, no. 207

2 Surtees 1971, no. 207A; Treuherz 2003, no. 140

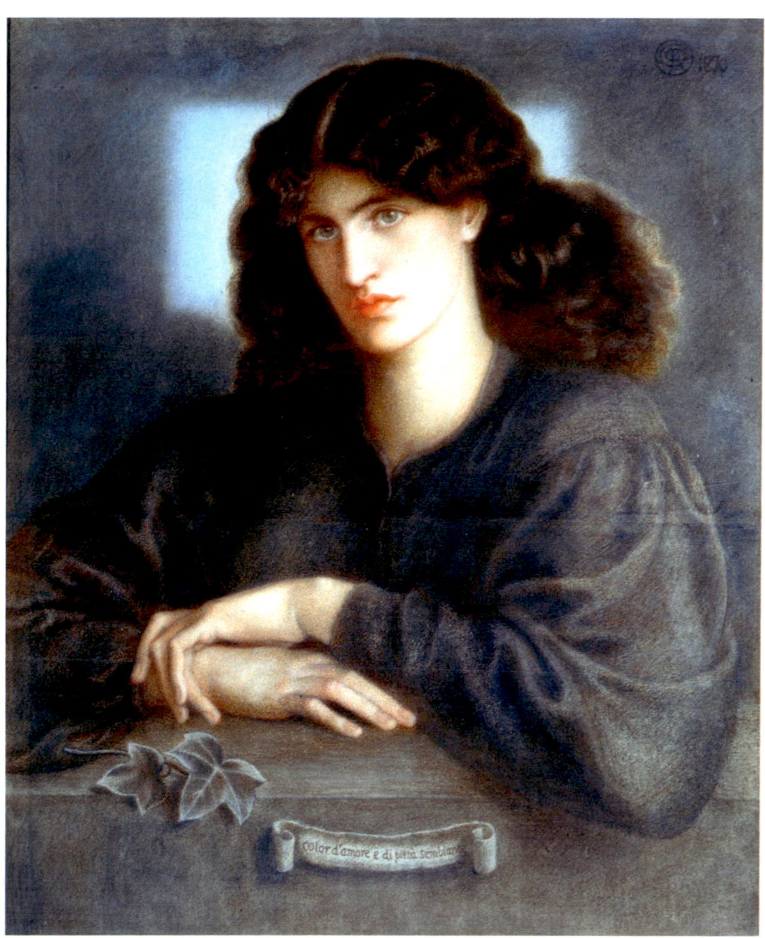

125
Dante Gabriel Rossetti
La Donna della Finestra 1870
Coloured chalk on paper, 85 x 72 cm
Signed in monogram and dated: *DGR / 1870* and inscribed on a scroll: *Color d'amore e di pietà sembiante*
Bradford Art Galleries and Museums
Ref: Surtees 1971, no. 255A; Treuherz 2003, no. 143

The subject, from the *Vita Nuova*, was yet another that Rossetti had planned to paint as early as 1848. It described how a lady looked down from a window and saw Dante weeping in the street after the death of Beatrice. The model for the drawing was Jane Morris, recognisable by her lustrous and flowing hair. The line of poetry on the scroll is from the section of the *Vita Nuova* describing the compassionate lady; in Rossetti's own translation, it reads, 'Love's pallor and the semblance of deep ruth / Were never yet shown forth so perfectly / In any lady's face, chancing to see / Grief's miserable countenance uncouth...'. The composition thus evokes Rossetti's feelings for Jane Morris, who would have consoled him after the death of his wife, Elizabeth Siddal; and a more general expression of compassion or pity.

The device of placing a panel of light against the back wall of the space which the figure is supposed to occupy was one which Rossetti frequently utilised in his later career, as a means of giving depth to the composition. An oil version of the subject, painted in 1879 (Fogg Art Museum, Harvard University), shows the figure seated behind a parapet and with a glimpse through the open windows of a terrace.

126
Dante Gabriel Rossetti
Study of Dante for 'Dante's Dream' 1871
Black chalk on two pieces of paper, 77.5 x 33 cm
Private collection

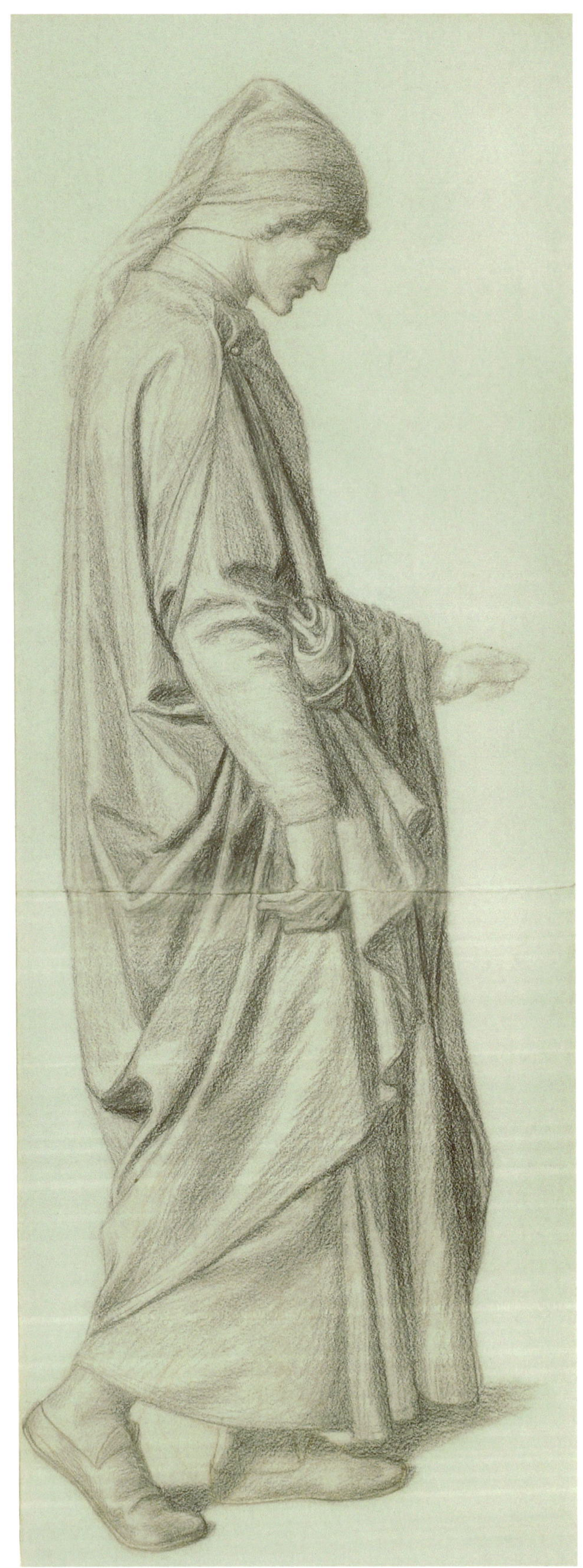

In addition to the single figures of the late 1860s and 1870s, Rossetti was considering a number of large Dante subjects for his patrons, F.R. Leyland and William Graham. The largest, *Dante's Dream*, was completed in 1871 and offered to Graham, who declined to buy it because of its size (Walker Art Gallery, Liverpool). Numerous studies of individual figures survive for the second version of *Dante's Dream*. Most were based on Rossetti's friends: Jane Morris sat for Beatrice, and Alexa Wilding and Marie Spartali Stillman for the female attendants. The model for Dante himself was Marie Spartali's husband, William James Stillman (1828–1901), an American artist closely associated with both Rossetti and Ruskin. Dante's pose in the huge oil is more fluid than it had been in the watercolour of 1856, with the position of his feet and the folds of his drapery much more animated. Although the oil follows this preparatory drawing closely, Rossetti revised the position of Dante's right hand in the finished composition, so that it is languidly rather than firmly held by the figure of Love.

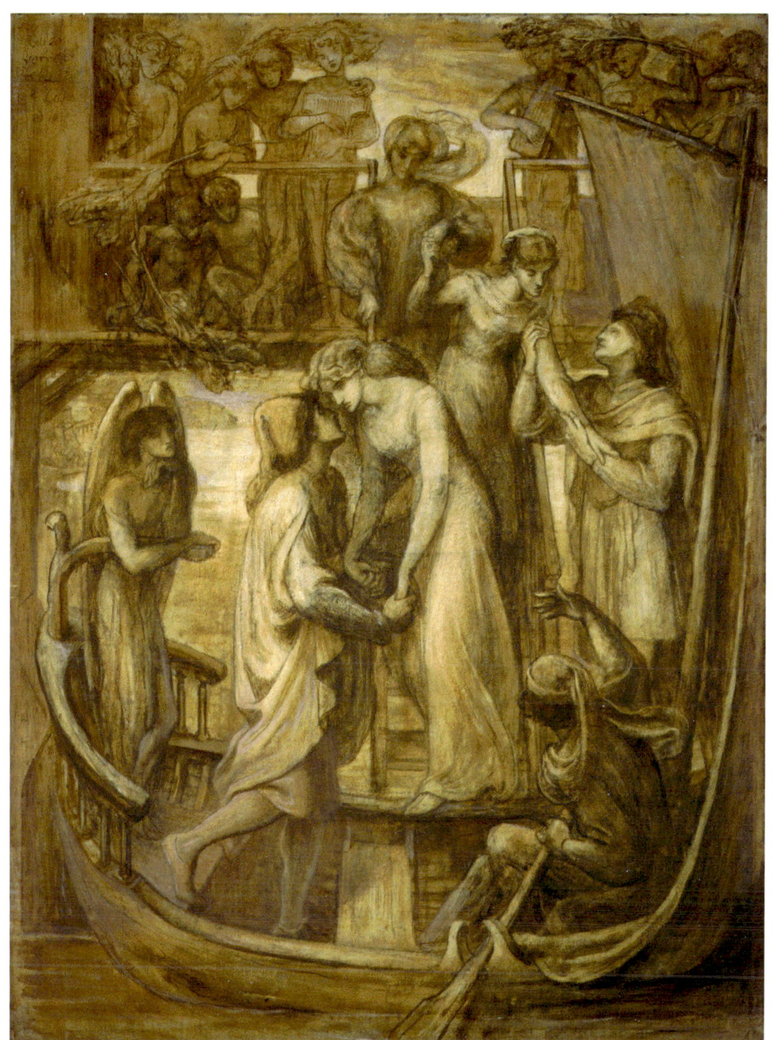

127
Dante Gabriel Rossetti
The Boat of Love 1874–81
Oil on canvas, 124.5 x 94 cm
Inscribed: *Guido vorrei che tu e Lapo ed io*
Birmingham Museum and Art Gallery (1885P2476)
Ref: Surtees 1971, no. 239; Parris 1984, no. 141

The subject of *The Boat of Love* was taken from a sonnet addressed by Dante to Guido Cavalcanti, which Rossetti had included in his *Early Italian Poets*: 'Guido, I wish that Lapo, thou, and I, / Could be by spells conveyed, as it were now, / Upon a barque, with all the winds that blow / Across all seas at our good will to hie.' The figures in Rossetti's painting are therefore Dante handing Beatrice into the boat, and Cavalcanti supporting Giovanna behind; Lapo sits in the boat. In December 1871, Rossetti wrote to Leyland describing the composition: 'In it, Dante and his two friends are in the enchanted ship, while Love brings Beatrice and two other ladies down the steps of a pier to join them for their love-voyage.... The pier, river, and city beyond, with the ship in the foreground, and a row of children along the pier at the top of the picture, bearing branches for a love-pageant, make a delicious ensemble, and will, I know, bring out what I have in me.... So strong is the subject in my mind that I have set about getting a model of the ship made to paint from, having my authority from a beautiful one in a composition by Benozzo Gozzoli, in the Campo Santo of Pisa.' The boat was constructed by Rossetti's studio assistant, Henry Treffrey Dunn, in the basement of Rossetti's house. It was built 'on a very roomy scale but he had so many figures in his design comprising the boating party, that it would have been impossible to have crammed them all in with ease and comfort to themselves'. This monochrome oil sketch was begun in 1874 for William Graham but abandoned unfinished when patron and artist could not agree terms.

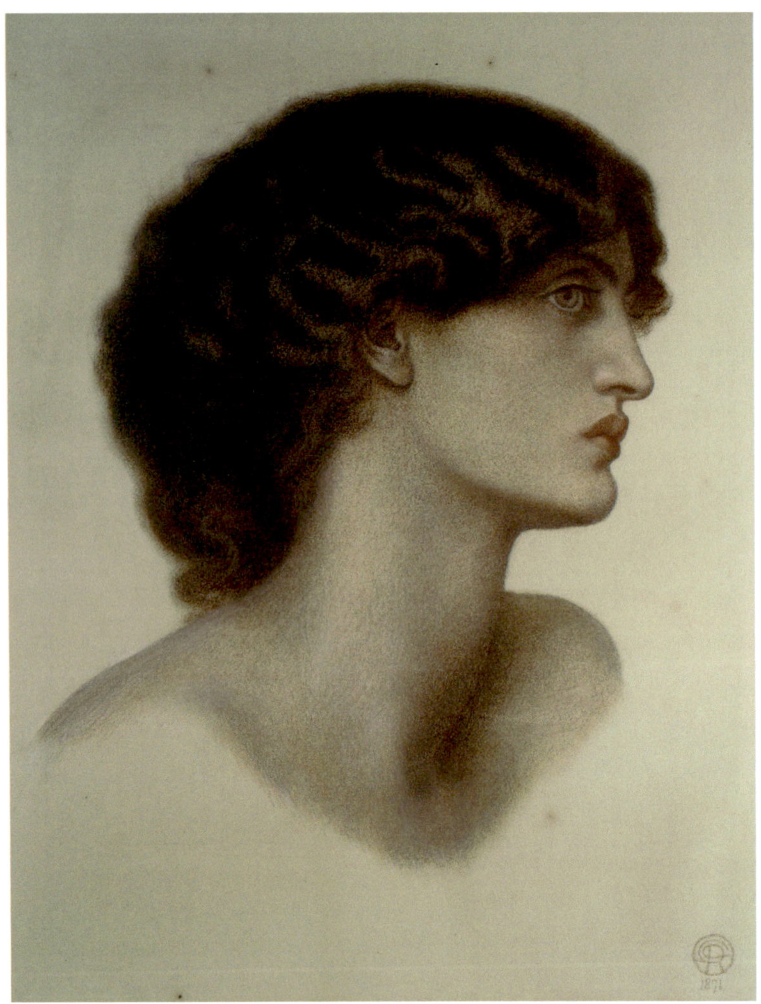

128
Dante Gabriel Rossetti
Perlascura 1871
Coloured chalk on pale green paper, 55.8 x 43.5 cm
Signed in monogram and dated: *DGR 1871*
Ashmolean Museum, University of Oxford.
Bequeathed by Miss May Morris, 1939 (WA1939.4)
Ref: Surtees 1971, no. 225

This is one of four drawings of Jane Morris by Rossetti bequeathed to the Ashmolean by her daughter, in accordance with her wishes. It was made in 1871, and in composition is the least elaborate of the four. In 1877, the drawing was reproduced in autotype, and in February 1878, Rossetti decided to call it '*Twilight* which title seems to be received as very appropriate to the shadowed eyes and penetrating sweetness of the expression.' A few days later, he had 'thought of another name for that profile head, *Perlascura* (i.e. dark pearl, as an Italian female name….The name is exact for complexion).' He then decided to include the drawing in a much larger project: as he wrote to Mrs Morris in August 1878, he 'thought of bringing out some dozen autotypes of you in a book – done on a moderate scale so as to make a large folio shape. I might call them "Perlascura: Twelve Coins of One Queen".' He went on to explain that the title was suggested by lines from the *Vita nuova*: 'She hath that paleness of the pearl that's fit / In a fair woman, so much and not more; / She is as high as Nature's skill can soar; / Beauty is tried by her comparison.'[1] Each drawing was to be accompanied by a sonnet by Rossetti himself, but the project was never completed. Although there is no definitive list of the drawings of Mrs Morris that Rossetti intended to include, only the profile portrait, *Perlascura* itself, would have been appropriately described as a coin.

1 Bryson and Troxell 1976, p. 75

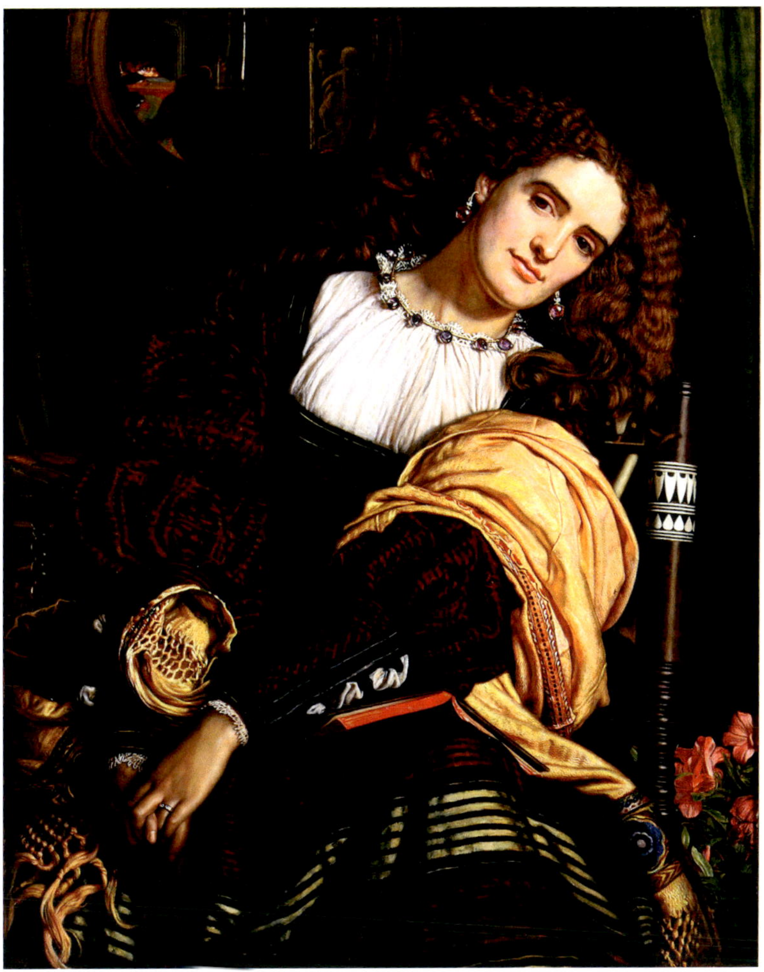

129
William Holman Hunt (1827–1910)
Il Dolce far Niente 1859–66
Oil on canvas, 99 x 82.5 cm
Signed in monogram and dated: *WHH 1866*
The Schaeffer Collection, courtesy of Nevill Keating Pictures
Ref: Bronkhurst 2006, no. 93

In his autobiography, Hunt described how he began work on *Il Dolce Far Niente*: 'Having long been engaged on works of scale below life-size, it seemed wise now to take up the painting of figures of full proportions. Through the kindness of friends a young lady sat to me, and I commenced a picture which I called "Il Dolce Far Niente". I made use of the Egyptian chairs, which, having been borrowed and painted by other artists, were no longer attractive to me for Oriental subjects. I was glad of the opportunity of exercising myself in work which had not any didactic purpose. The picture, however, had to be laid by for the time, and finished at a later period from another model'.

Hunt seems originally to have based the painting on the figure of Annie Miller, a professional model for whom he had conceived a hopeless infatuation. However, relations between the two broke down late in 1859, partly because she wished to work for other artists, and Hunt put aside the painting. He returned to it in 1865, using the features of Fanny Waugh, whom he married on 28 December 1865.

In describing the picture as one 'which had not any didactic purpose', Hunt was distinguishing it from the great majority of his works. Generally he sought to uplift or edify his audiences by treating themes from the scriptures or by inventing morally or spiritually improving themes. Here, however, he evoked a mood of languor, into which the spectator is invited to join by the figure's gaze. In this sense, it corresponds to paintings of a similar erotic mood by artists such as Rossetti, whose *Bocca Baciata* Hunt had seen, and left bewildered – 'Rossetti is advocating as a principle mere gratification of the eye ... I disavow any sympathy with such [a] notion'. Frederic Leighton, likewise, was at this time painting his series of portraits of the Italian model 'La Nanna', which made a great impact at the Royal Academy in 1859. However, Bronkhurst has convincingly suggested that the prominent engagement ring and the cosy domestic fireside scene visible in the mirror may refer to the model's impending marriage, and the painting thus have more autobiographical content than is usually acknowledged.

130 (Top)
Sir Edward Burne-Jones (1833–1898)
Venus Concordia 1871
Pencil on paper, 30.3 x 48.4 cm
Whitworth Art Gallery, University of Manchester (D.1921.34)

131 (Bottom)
Sir Edward Burne-Jones (1833–1898)
Venus Discordia 1871
Pencil on paper, 29.8 x 48.1 cm
Whitworth Art Gallery, University of Manchester (D.1921.34)

In the late 1860s, Burne-Jones's love of Michelangelo's nudes became evident in a number of his own compositions. The most notorious was the watercolour *Phyllis and Demophoon* (Birmingham Museum and Art Gallery), which attracted great controversy when exhibited at the Old Watercolour Society in 1870. In the following year, Burne-Jones began work on one of his most complex oil paintings, a polyptych in the Italian taste illustrating episodes from the *Siege of Troy.* This comprised three main panels showing the Judgement of Paris, Helen carried off to Troy, and Helen watching Troy burn; together with a predella containing the Feast of Peleus and complementary subjects of Venus Concordia and Venus Discordia, divided and flanked by four small upright panels illustrating the theme of Amor vincit omnia. Burne-Jones never completed the polyptych (now in Birmingham Art Gallery), but developed each of the elements into larger works. The two drawings of *Venus Concordia* and *Venus Discordia* are highly finished, and were used by T.M. Rooke as the basis for the large canvases he blocked out for his master in 1872–3. They remained unfinished and appeared in Burne-Jones's studio sale in 1898 (now in Plymouth and Cardiff respectively). The first shows Venus seated on her throne, holding the apple she has won, with Cupid resting at her feet and the Graces to her right. The companion drawing represents the triumph of the baser human passions, with Venus huddled uncomfortably on a dark throne, watching the shivering forms of the four Vices, Anger, Envy, Suspicion, and Strife. The fighting figures in the background are reminiscent of Pollaiuolo's famous engraving of the *Battle of the Nude Men*, while the heavy forms of the nudes are indebted to Burne-Jones's study of Michelangelo.

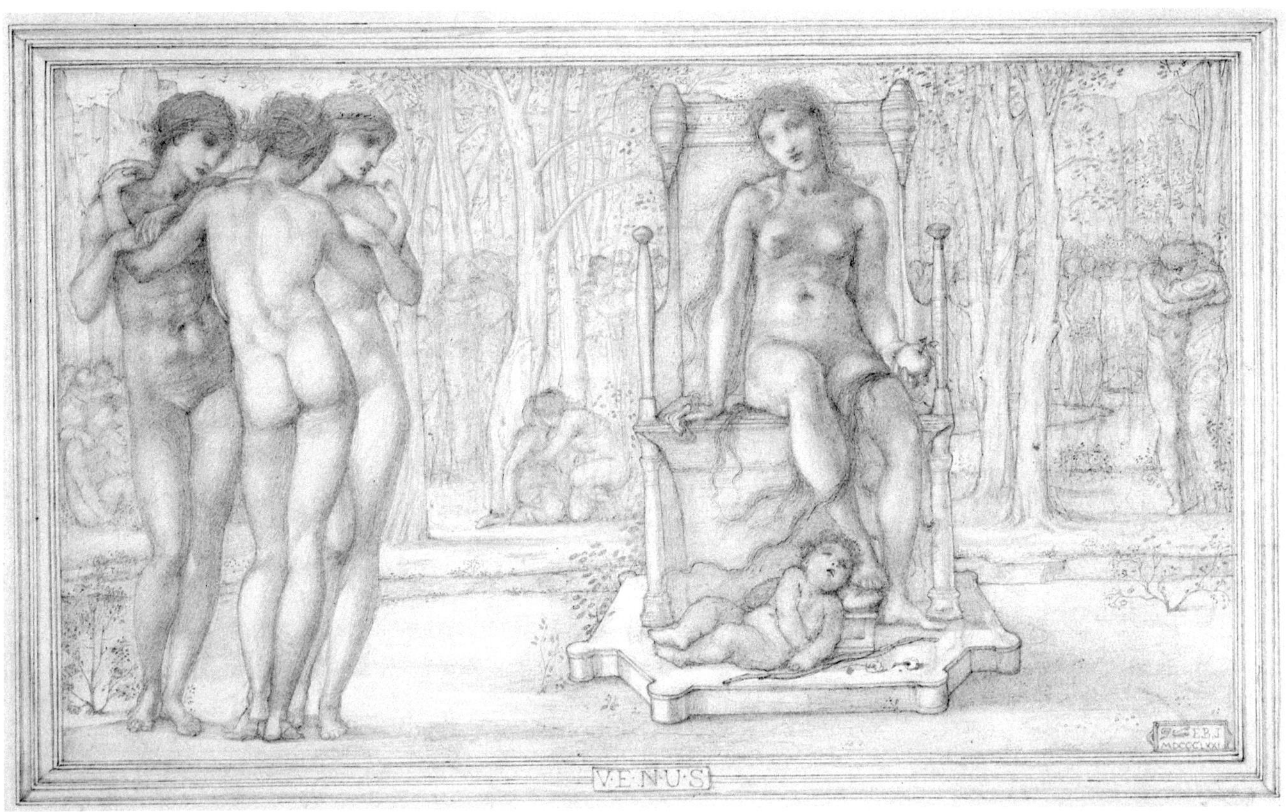
V·E·N·U·S
E.B.J.

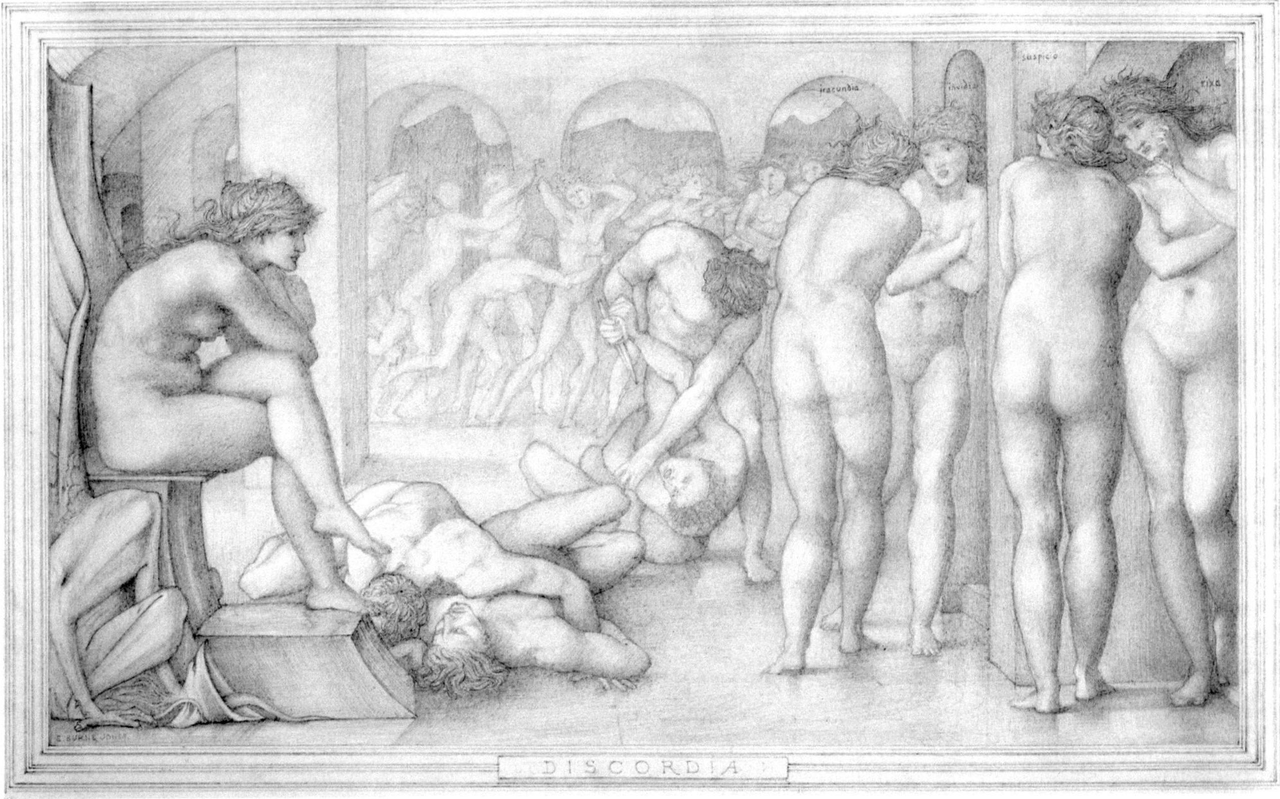
DISCORDIA

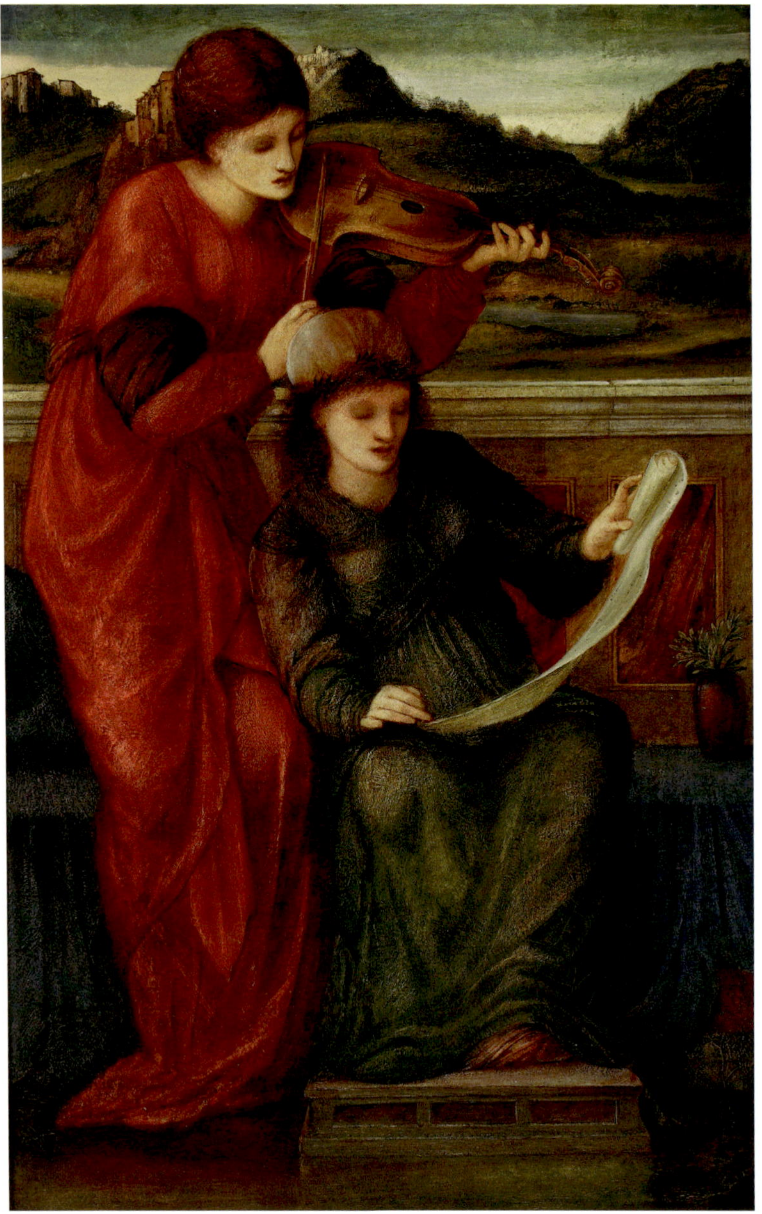

132
Edward Burne-Jones (1833–1898)
Music 1877
Oil on canvas, 67.7 x 43.5 cm
Ashmolean Museum, University of Oxford. Accepted by H.M. Government in lieu of inheritance tax on the estate of Miss Jean Preston and allocated to the Ashmolean Museum, 2008 (WA2008.15)

Burne-Jones began work on the first version of *Music* in 1875, describing it in his record of work as 'a small picture of two girls with a viol and a scroll of music'. The picture was completed in the following year, as 'two girls with viol and scroll, in red and green dresses'.[1] In 1877, Burne-Jones painted a second version of *Music*, which he noted as 'finished replica of two girls with viol and scroll. Graham'. The name 'Graham' is generally assumed to refer to the artist's great patron, William Graham, who served as M.P. for Glasgow between 1865 and 1874, and who was one of the few collectors who bought major works by both the Pre-Raphaelites and the Old Masters, including Italian pictures painted before Raphael. In fact, although it was William Graham who commissioned *Music* from Burne-Jones, he did so on behalf of his brother, John, in whose posthumous sale the picture appeared in 1894.[2]

Music is one of the most Italianate of all Burne-Jones's compositions, painted when his obsession with Italian art was at its height. It shows two female figures, one playing a viola da braccio, the other holding a scroll of music and singing. The placing of the figures on a balcony in front of an expansive landscape is reminiscent of the paintings of the Virgin and Child by Bellini, while the landscape itself suggests the hill towns of northern Italy. The theme of music-making, treated repeatedly by Burne-Jones and other English artists associated with the Aesthetic Movement such as Rossetti, Leighton, and Albert Moore, was seen to originate in the *concert champêtre* of Giorgione, of which Swinburne had written ecstatic praise. Music was perceived as an art form that depended entirely on the sensuous response of the listener and which required no interpretation for its appreciation, hence Walter Pater's edict that painters should raise their work to 'the condition of music' so that the medium might be freed from a prosaic documentary or narrative purpose.

1 For the earlier version, see the catalogue entry by John Christian for Christie's sale of 14 March 1997, lot 56; see also London 2003, no. 42

2 Christie's, 5 May 1894, lot 48. See the letter from William Graham to Burne-Jones, 22 April 1876: 'the little picture of 2 girls with music instruments that are to be for my brother', in Garnett 2000, p. 258

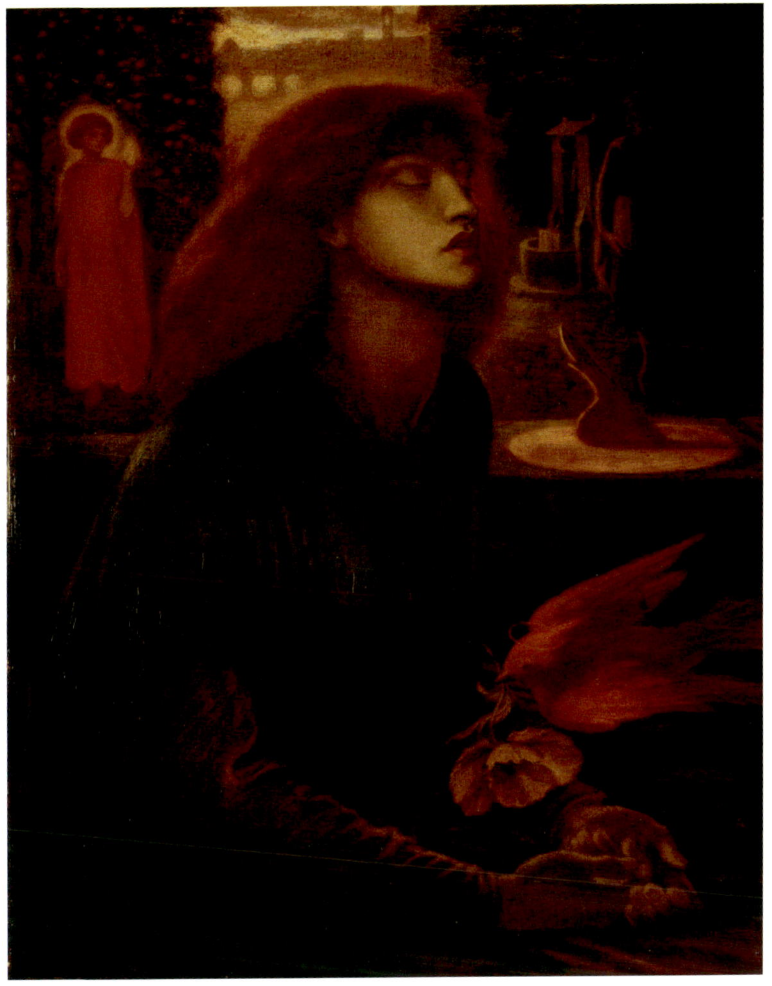

133
Dante Gabriel Rossetti (1828–1882)
Beata Beatrix
Oil on canvas, 86 x 66.7 cm
signed and dated, *DGR 1880*
The National Galleries of Scotland, Edinburgh
Ref: Surtees 1971, no. 168 R.6

Although *Bocca baciata* of 1859 is generally regarded as the first of Rossetti's single half-length figures, the first version of *Beata Beatrix* was apparently 'begun many years' before 1863, when the artist wrote to Mrs Heaton that he might take it up again and complete it. It was the most personal of all Rossetti's subjects from the *Vita nuova*, and also became, though it may not have been conceived as, an evocation of the death of his wife, Elizabeth Siddal, who died in 1862. In a letter to Lady Mount Temple, whose husband bought the first version of the composition, Rossetti explained that it 'is not at all intended to represent Death ... but to render it under the resemblance of a trance, in which Beatrice seated at the balcony over-looking the City is suddenly rapt from Earth to Heaven'. In his explanation of the version of the composition painted for William Graham in 1872, Rossetti emphasised that it was not intended a literal representation of the death of Beatrice, but 'as an ideal of the subject, symbolized by a trance or sudden spiritual transfiguration'. Beatrice sits with her hands open to receive the poppy of death, carried by a white dove. She sees a vision of Heaven through closed eyelids. Behind her is a sundial, the shadow falling on the hour of nine. As Rossetti noted, Dante insisted on the number nine in connexion with Beatrice – he met her at the age of nine, she died at nine o'clock on 9 June 1290, and was herself '"a nine", that the the perfect number, or symbol of perfection'. In the background are the figures of Dante standing beside a well, and Love holding a burning heart. Between them is a view of the Ponte Vecchio in Florence. The symbolism of the composition is extensive, and made more complicated by the conflation of Beatrice with Siddal.

The subject continued to haunt Rossetti, who completed a replica in chalks in 1869 (Fogg Art Museum, Harvard University), another in oils in 1872 for William Graham 'for lucre' (Art Institute of Chicago), another in chalks in the same year for the collector Leonard Rowe Valpy, yet another, left unfinished at Rossetti's death, completed by Ford Madox Brown (Birmingham Art Gallery), and this final version of 1880. It, too, was painted for Valpy, but never delivered. By this late date, the figure of Beatrice is no longer based on that of Elizabeth Siddal, but a more idealised female form, the colouring is warmer and less realistic, and the mood even more elegiac than in the earlier oils.

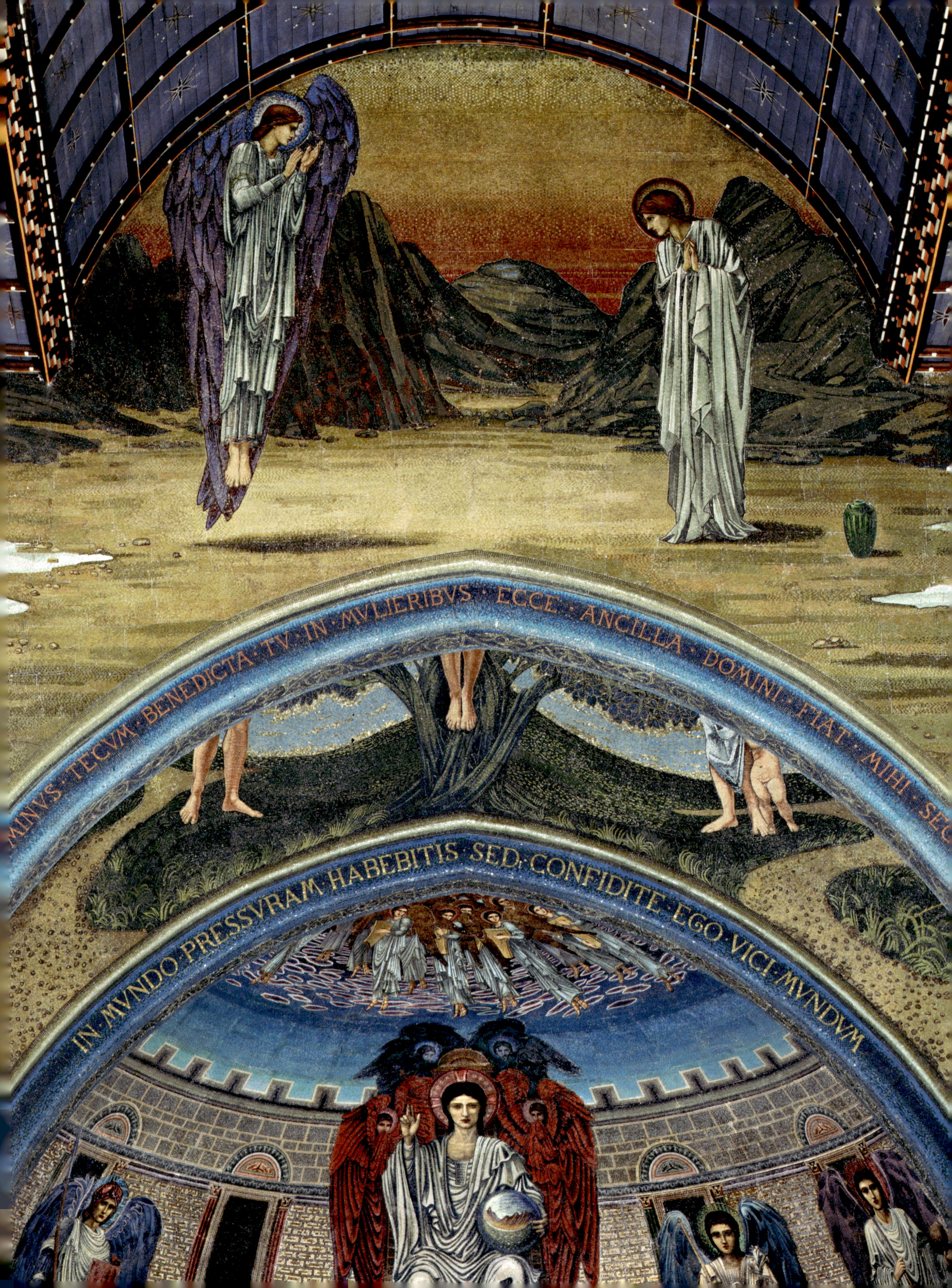
MINVS · TECVM · BENEDICTA · TV · IN · MVLIERIBVS · ECCE · ANCILLA · DOMINI · FIAT · MIHI · SEC
IN MVNDO PRESSVRAM HABEBITIS SED CONFIDITE EGO VICI MVNDVM

VII
BURNE-JONES'S DESIGNS FOR THE AMERICAN CHURCH IN ROME

Following the establishment of the Italian republic in 1870, the new liberal government allowed protestant churches to be built within the walls of Rome. In 1871, the rector of the American Episcopalian congregation, Robert Nevin, began to raise money for a new church on the via Nazionale. The architect was G.E. Street, who made something of a speciality of designing Anglican churches abroad – in Geneva, Paris, and Constantinople –and who, by coincidence, was commissioned to design two churches in Rome at almost the same time; the other was for the English congregation in the via del Babuino. The American church was constructed between 1872 and 1876, but the architect's ambitious plans to decorate the apse with mosaics, announced in 1875, only came to fruition in 1881, when Junius Morgan provided funds for the mosaics in the semi-dome. Street turned to his old friend Burne Jones to provide the designs.

For Burne-Jones, the invitation fulfilled a dream he had had for much of his life. Twenty years earlier, after visiting Torcello and Venice on his second journey to Italy in 1862, he had discussed with Ruskin the possibility of creating and decorating a chapel 'with hierarchies and symbols and gods',[1] but the plans came to nothing. On his third visit to Italy, in 1873, he had visited Ravenna and, in spite of illness, been greatly impressed with the celebrated mosaics there. In spite of the revival in the use of mosaics in public buildings in England, Burne-Jones and Morris did not include them in their work at Morris and Company, so the American commission was Burne-Jones's only opportunity to do 'big things … and vast spaces and for common people to see them and say Oh! – only Oh!'[2]

Street formally commissioned Burne-Jones in July 1881 to design a mosaic for the apse – it is likely that he had envisaged only this one mosaic, and the arches were to be left striped, like the rest of the nave. However, after Street's death in December 1881, Burne-Jones had second thoughts, as he wrote to George Howard in February 1882:

> the Roman Church I shall give up – Street is dead who could have stood between me + the cloth + could have helped me also with the workmen – but I cannot + will not be hurried about work - + I shall write this week + thrown up the affair – having already wasted many a precious hour upon it – but I see it would be a life of torment + I am not fit for it.[3]

It was apparently at this stage that Dr Nevin intervened personally, not only to confirm the existing commission, but to entice Burne-Jones with further work, the decoration of the two arches in the apse, which Street had left as striped brickwork like the remainder of the church. Burne-Jones worked slowly and reluctantly, and described the project as 'an unthankful task that no one will ever care for, but for the sake of many ancient loves I am doing it; for love of Venice and Ravenna and the seven impenetrable centuries between them, and for love of many old studies and odds and ends of things I like.'[4] He eventually completed the design for the Heavenly Jerusalem in 1884. It incorporated the figure of Christ enthroned flanked by the Archangels with their attributes, and a blank arch for Lucifer, in a very personal interpretation of the Byzantine style suitable for such an interior. The preparatory work involved both a compositional study, six highly finished studies of the individual figures, and a lath and plaster model of the semi-dome roughly painted by Burne-Jones. The six

134

Sir Edward Burne-Jones (1833–1898)

Study for 'The Annunciation'

Watercolour and body colour on brown paper,

52.1 x 74.9 cm

Extensively inscribed

St Paul's within the Walls, Rome

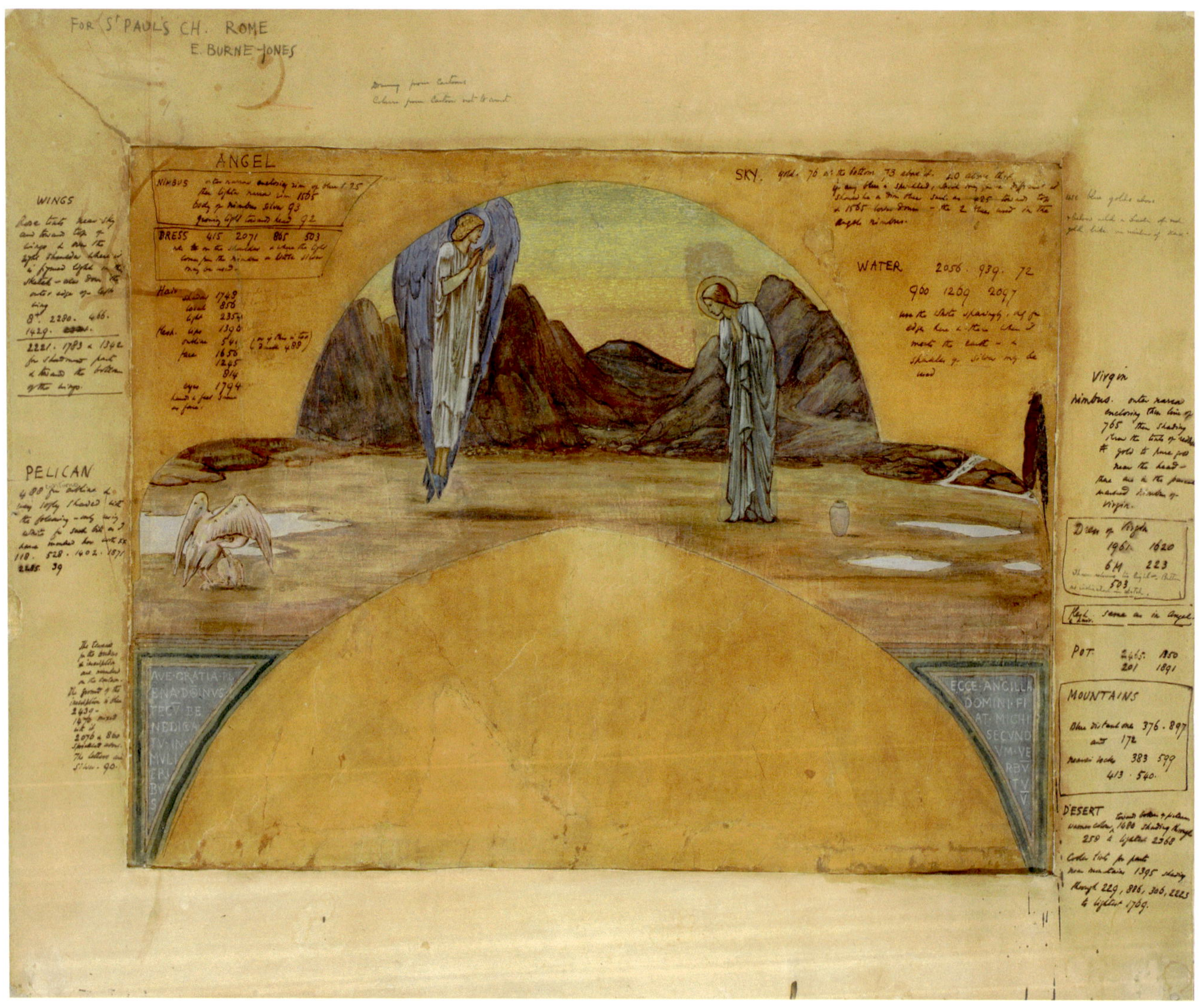

studies were retained by Burne-Jones, and hung in his summer house at Rottingdean. The most time-consuming task was the precise translation of Burne-Jones's designs into mosaic. The Venezia-Murano Company, directed by Giovanni Castellani, undertook the laborious task. Burne-Jones and William Morris 'used to give part of their Sunday morning time to sorting out colours used by the Venezia-Murano Company from a cabinet of tesserae which had been brought to the garden studio, and they made duplicate lists of the numbers on the tesserae which, when the work began to be executed, formed a means of communication with the workmen.'[5] Burne-Jones sent out to Murano full-scale cartoons and long lists of numbers corresponding to individual shades for the tesserae. The cartoons were divided into sections, and each one covered with tesserae by the workmen. The sections were then joined together to judge the whole effect, and then divided again to be installed separately in the apse. The first sample was disastrous, but, fortunately, Rooke happened to be in Venice, and he, Castellani, and Nevin succeeded in producing a second sample which Burne-Jones noted was 'as good as ever I hoped for'.[6] The Heavenly Jerusalem was unveiled on Christmas Day 1885.

For Burne-Jones, this was only the beginning of the project, for he envisaged covering the whole of the church in mosaic. One possibility excited him greatly: 'On one wall, there is a space of forty feet sheer down, where I mean to shoot Lucifer and his knights out of a glittering heaven'.[7] He worked on this design throughout 1887 and 1888, but it was never executed as a mosaic **(see cat. 143)**. However, the death of one of the parishioners in Rome, Hickson Field, on 18 April 1888, enabled Nevin to continue the scheme in the apse, when he persuaded Field's widow to provide funds in memory of her husband. Burne-Jones apparently sent finished drawings of subjects to Rome for the approval of Mrs Field, and Dorment suggests that these may be the works visible in a photograph of Burne-Jones's house taken c. 1890 – the *Nativity*, *Annunciation*, and *Tree of Life*, as well as the glory of angels above Christ's head. Mrs Field selected the *Annunciation* **(cat. 137)**. This takes place not in the conventional interior, with Mary interrupted in her reading by the archangel Gabriel, but in the desert, where, according to the apocryphal Book of James (11.1) and other sources, Mary had taken a pitcher to fill it with water. On the left is a pelican, a symbol of Christ's sacrifice, which causes its breast to bleed to feed

135
Sir Edward Burne-Jones
Study for 'The Heavenly Jerusalem'
Watercolour and body colour on five pieces of brown paper, 52 x 137.2 cm
St Paul's within the Walls, Rome

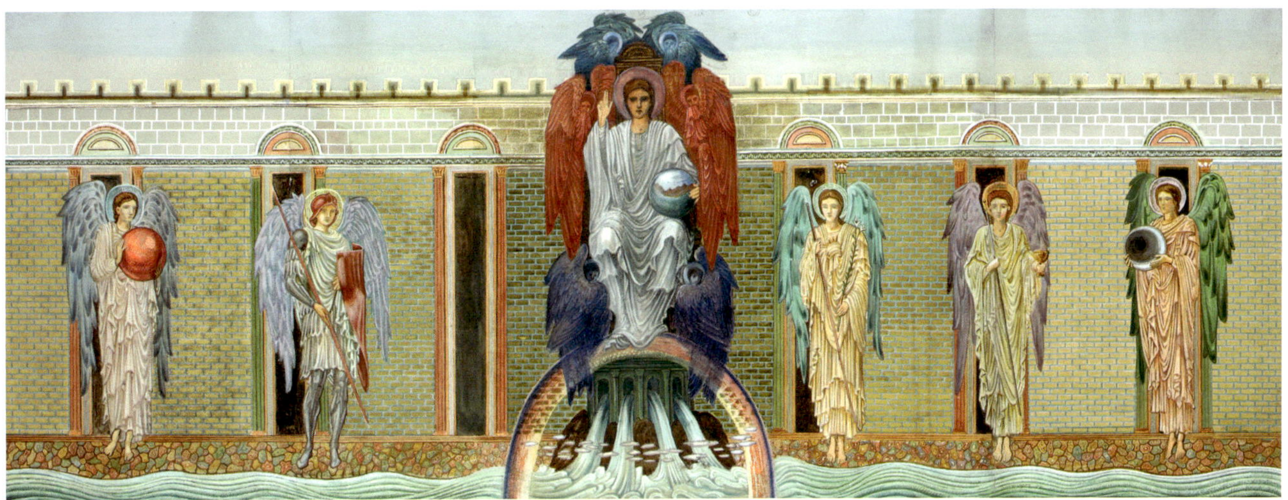

its young. For the translation into mosaic, Burne-Jones adopted a more efficient method of sending packets of the tesserae themselves with the cartoon, each labelled 'mountains', 'deserts', and so on. He took the precaution, however, of making a new compositional sketch with careful instructions to the mosaicists (**cat. 134**).

The design for the final mosaic, the *Tree of Life*, was begun as early as the winter of 1885–6, but it was not until the summer of 1891 that it was mentioned again – 'now someone has offered to pay for another arch to be covered, and there I shall make the design I had set my heart on – of a great flowering tree.'[8] He described this composition as 'a mystical thing – Christ hanging with outspread arms but not crucified: the cross is turned into a big tree all over leaves, and the stems of the tree are gold...a great flowering tree growing all over the space, myriads of leaves to it – every leaf as big as a man's hand – and in the tree a very pale Christ. On one side of it is Adam and on the other Eve, and two toddlers, and these shall stand for mankind.' The figures are flanked by sheaves of wheat and lilies, symbolic of many passages in the Bible. Burne-Jones was especially pleased with the design, believing that 'it said as much as anything I have *ever* done';[9] but acknowledged, even emphasized, that 'everything is done to make it not a picture ... and few will understand it.'[10] Indeed, when the large bodycolour version (**cat. 142**) was shown at the New Gallery in 1888, 'no one even looked at it.'[11] The mosaics of both the *Annunciation* and the *Tree of Life* were unveiled on 18 November 1894.

The final element of the scheme, in the choir, was *The Earthly Paradise*, which was executed in mosaic long after Burne-Jones's death, under the supervision of his pupil, Rooke. It shows five disparate groups of figures ranged in front of a Byzantine church reminiscent of St Mark's, Venice, in the background. On the far left are the ascetics, with St Francis among them; then the matron saints, including Mary Magdalen and Martha. In the centre are five Fathers of the Greek church and four of the Latin church, with St Paul in the centre. To the right is a procession of female martyrs, each identified by her attribute: St Catherine with the wheel, St Barbara with a tower, St Cecilia with an organ, St Dorothea with roses, and St Agnes with the lamb. On the far right is a group of saints in armour and on horseback, patrons of European nations: George of England, James of Spain, Patrick of Ireland, Andrew of Scotland, and Denis of France. Within this group is also the single figure on foot of Longinus, the Roman soldier whose lance pierced the side of Christ. At the wish of Nevin, and rather incongruously, Rooke gave many of these figures the faces of important members of the Anglican communion, American and Italian heroes, including Garibaldi, and benefactors to the American church. Among them are Nevin himself (who had died in Mexico in 1906), Burne-Jones in the figure of St John Chrysostom, and Lady Burne-Jones as St Barbara. The final mosaic was unveiled on 1 December 1907.

Burne-Jones never saw his mosaics in Rome, although he was sent photographs of them. They had preoccupied him for the last eighteen years of his life. However, he found the difficulties in ensuring their execution wearing: when he was approached to make mosaics in the dome of St Paul's Cathedral in London, he is recorded as saying that 'I love mosaics better than anything else in the world' but 'I couldn't face it'.[12]

Ref: Burne-Jones 1904, II, pp. 114–15, 134–5, 141–4, 159–60, Dorment 1978; Benedetti 1978; Benedetti and Piantoni 1986, nos. 109–112; Millon 2001; London 2003, nos. 58–9, 62

1 quoted in Dorment 1978, p. 73
2 Burne-Jones 1904, II, p. 13
3 quoted in Dorment 1978, p. 74
4 Burne-Jones 1904, I, p. 134
5 Burne-Jones 1904, II, pp. 141–2
6 Burne-Jones 1904, II, p. 144
7 Burne-Jones 1904, II, p. 159
8 quoted in Dorment 1978, p. 81
9 Rooke 1981, p. 34
10 Burne-Jones 1904, II, pp. 159–60
11 Rooke 1981, loc. cit.
12 Burne-Jones 1904, II, p. 219

136
Sir Edward Burne-Jones
Study for 'The Earthly Paradise'
Body colour and chalk on brown paper, 54 x 139.8 cm
St Paul's within the Walls, Rome

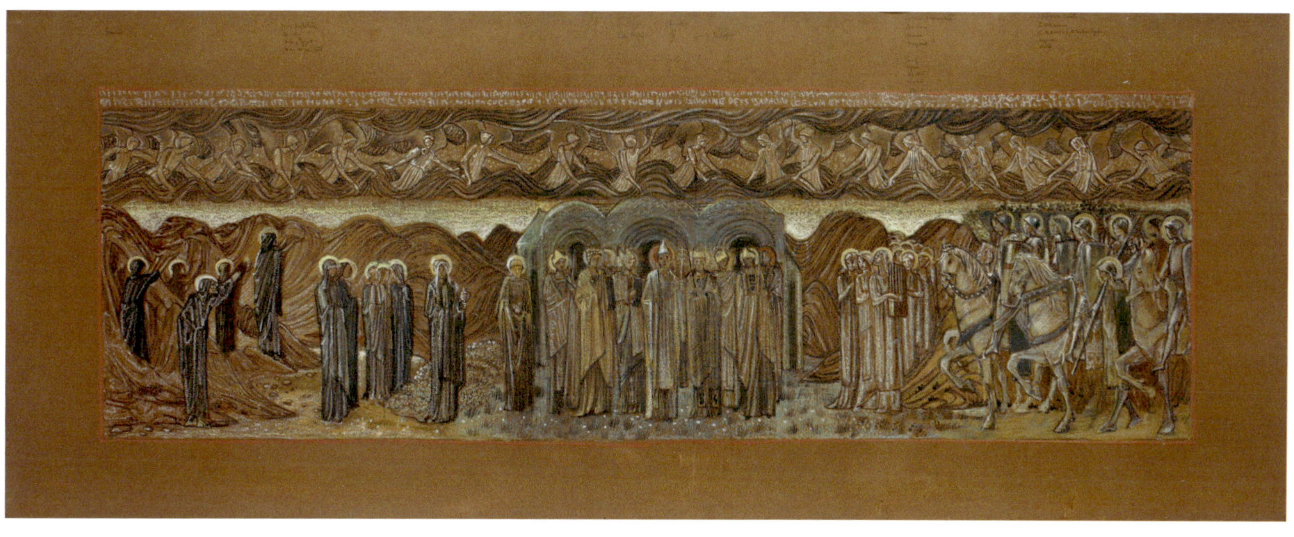

137
Sir Edward Burne-Jones
The Annunciation
Body colour over pen and brown ink, with silver and gold paint, 51.5 x 71.3 cm
Richard Dorment

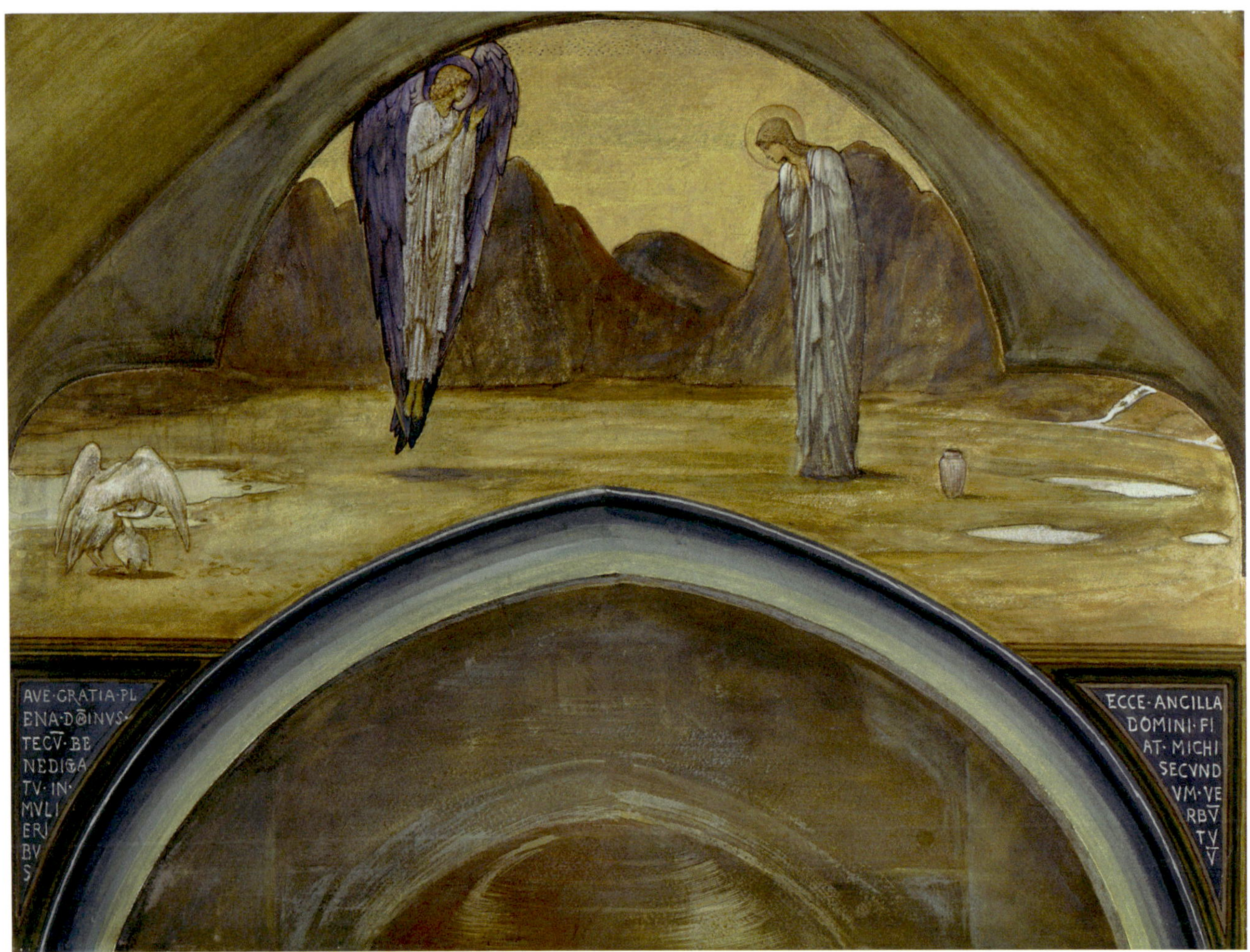

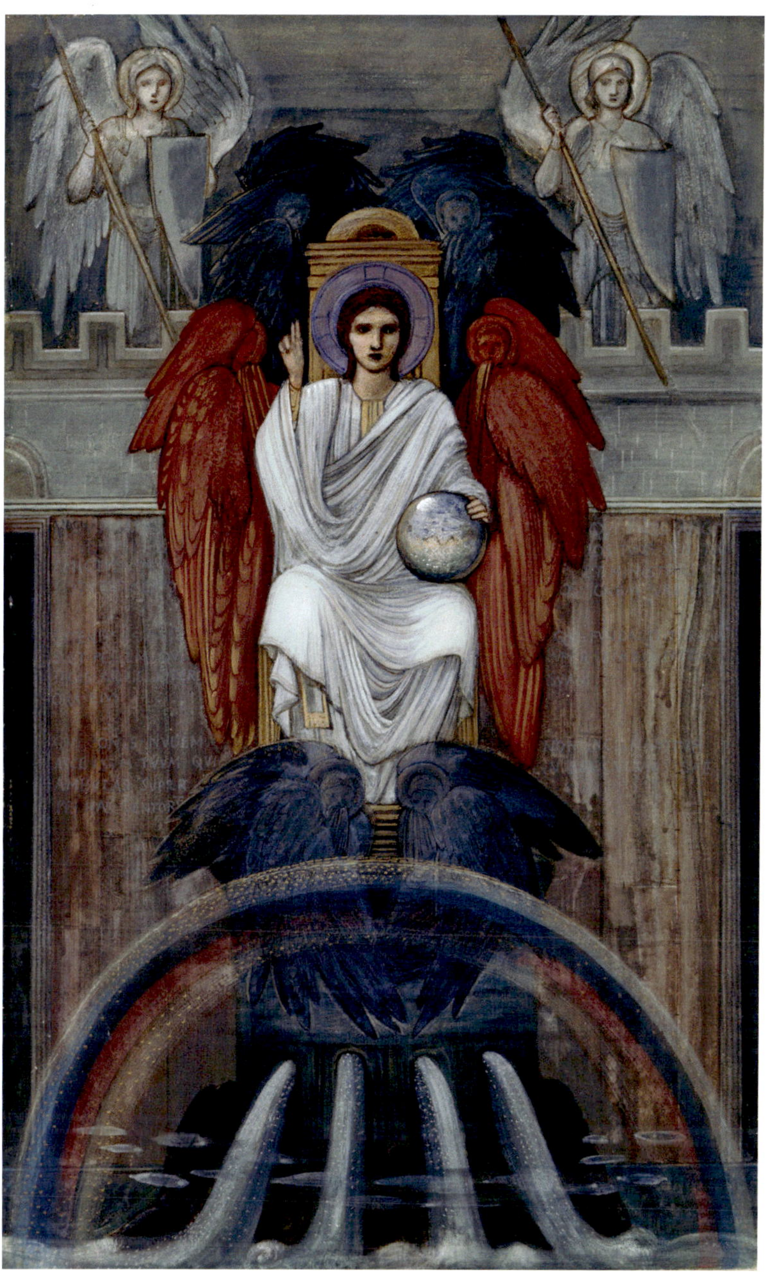

138
Sir Edward Burne-Jones
Christ enthroned
Pastel, body colour, and gold paint on board, 68.6 x 42.5 cm
Private collection of Lord Lloyd-Webber

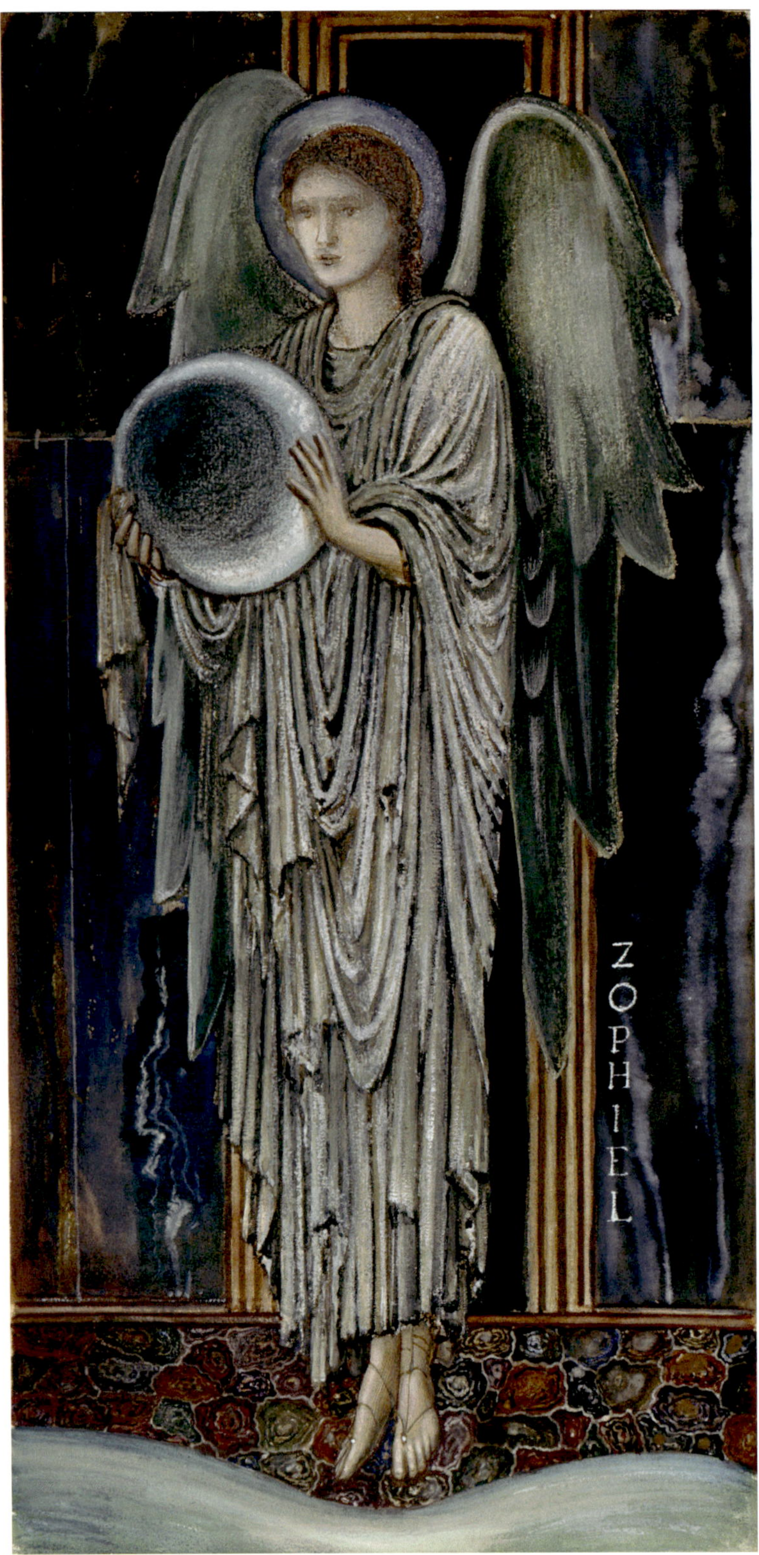

139
Sir Edward Burne-Jones
The Archangel Zophiel
Body colour on board, 51.5 x 26.5 cm
Inscribed, lower right, *ZOPHIEL*
Private collection of Lord Lloyd-Webber

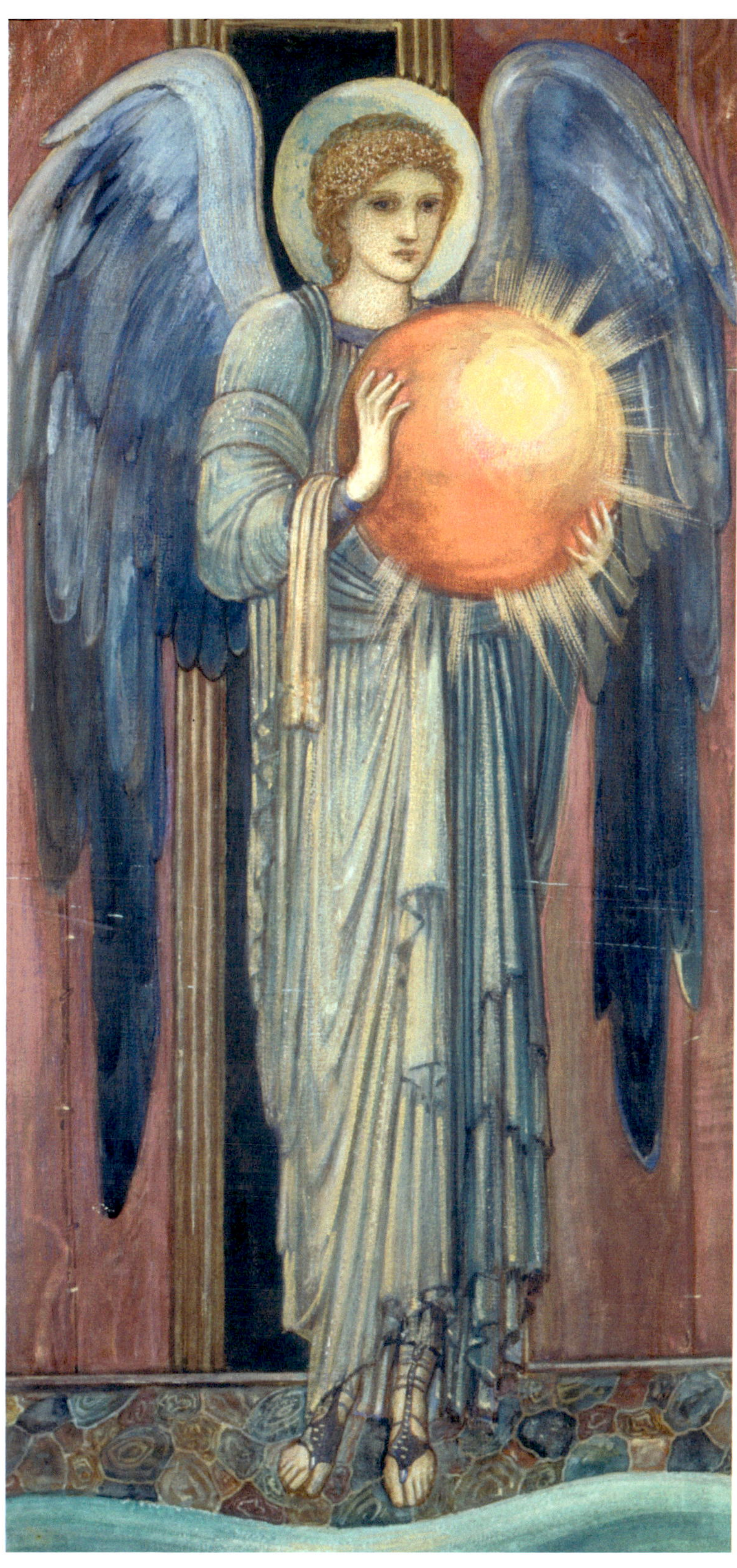

140
Sir Edward Burne-Jones
Uriel, Archangel of the Sun
Body colour on board, 68.6 x 42.6 cm
Board of Trustees of St Paul's within the Walls

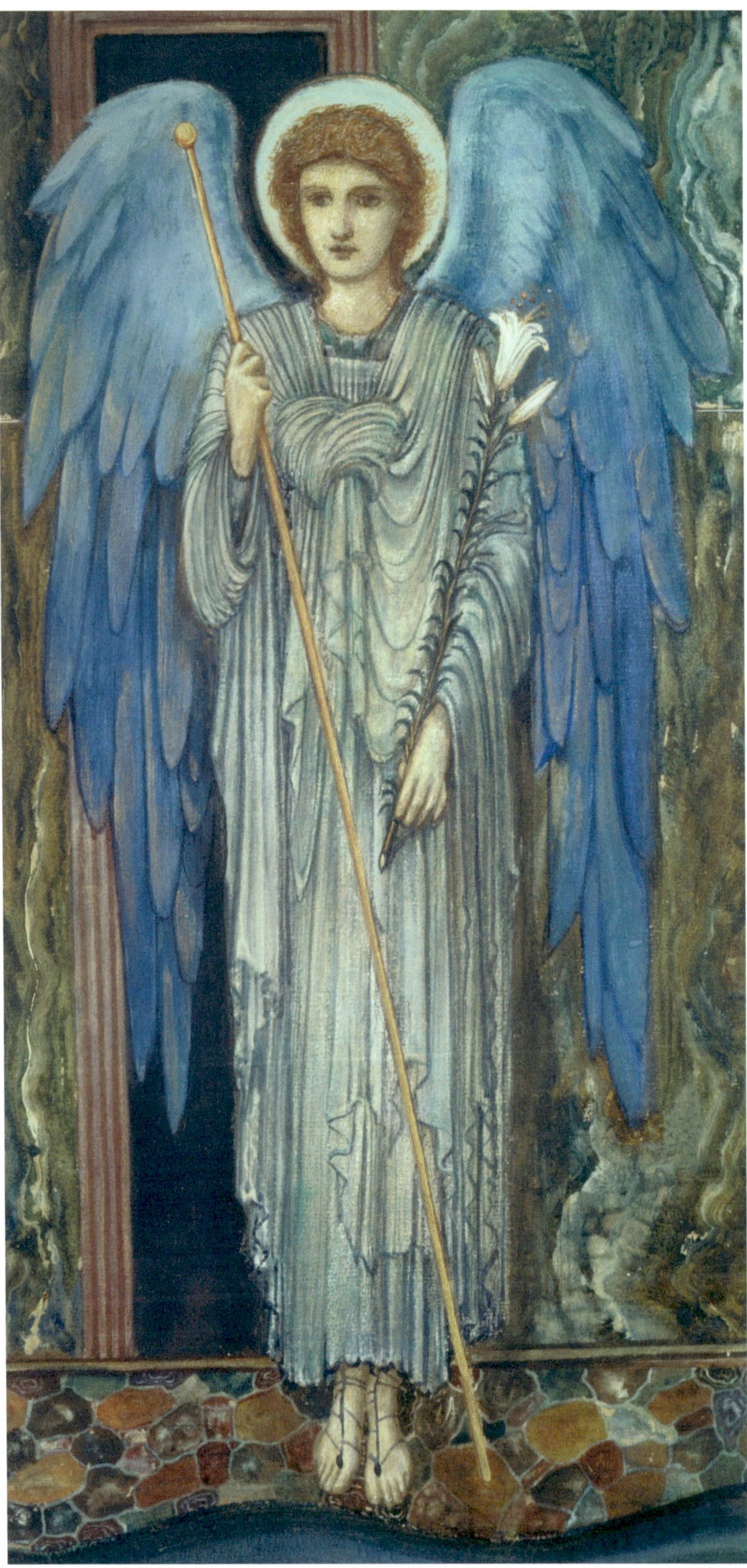

141
Sir Edward Burne-Jones
Gabriel, Angel of the Annunciation
Body colour on board, 50.8 x 25.5 cm
Board of Trustees of St Paul's within the Walls

142
Sir Edward Burne-Jones
The Tree of Life 1888
Watercolour and bodycolour on paper, 181 x 242 cm
Inscribed: *IN MUNDO PRESSURAM HABEBITIS SED CONFIDITE EGO VICI MUNDUM* ('In the world ye shall have tribulation: but be of good cheer; I have overcome the world' John 16.33)
Victoria and Albert Museum, London (584–1898)

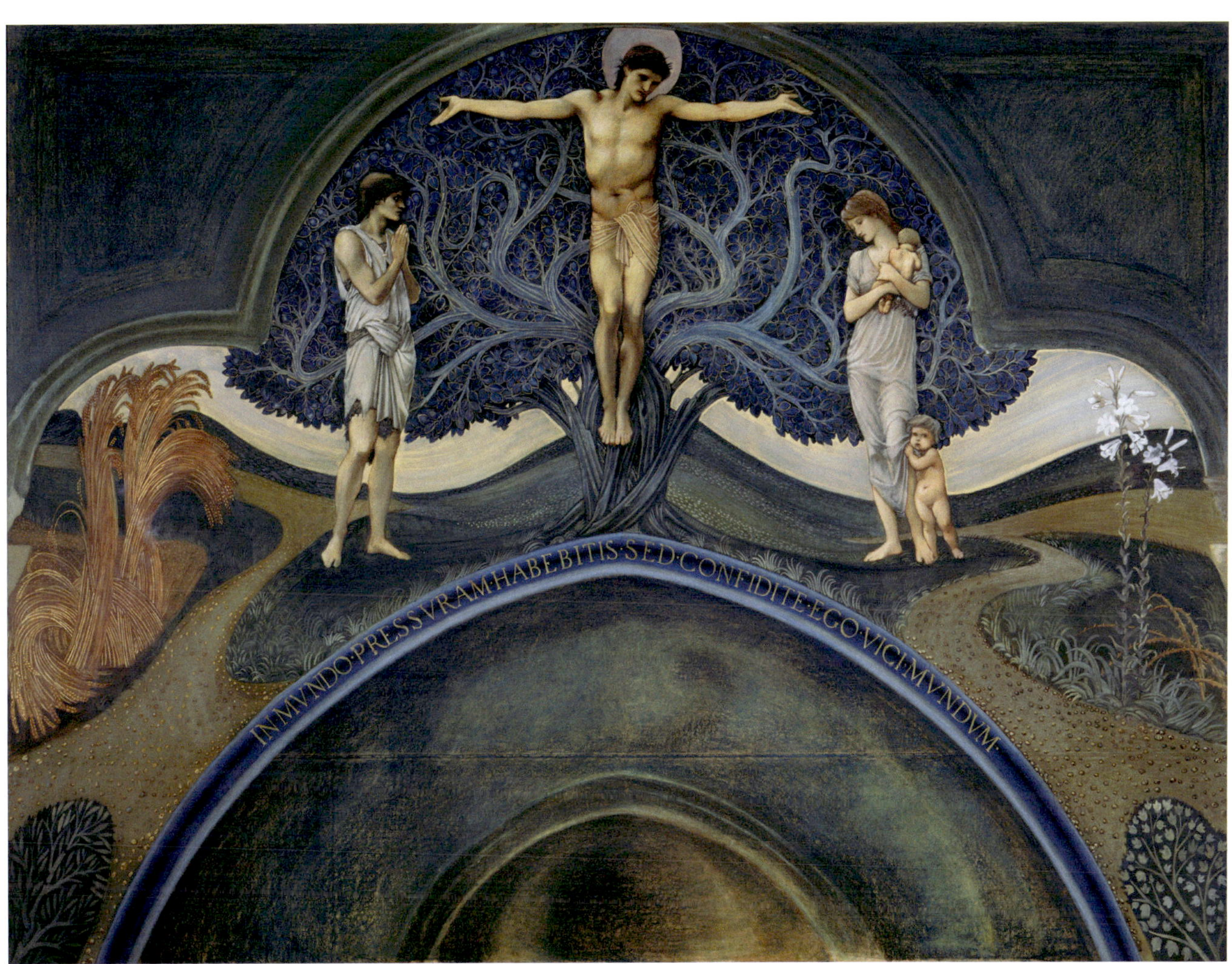

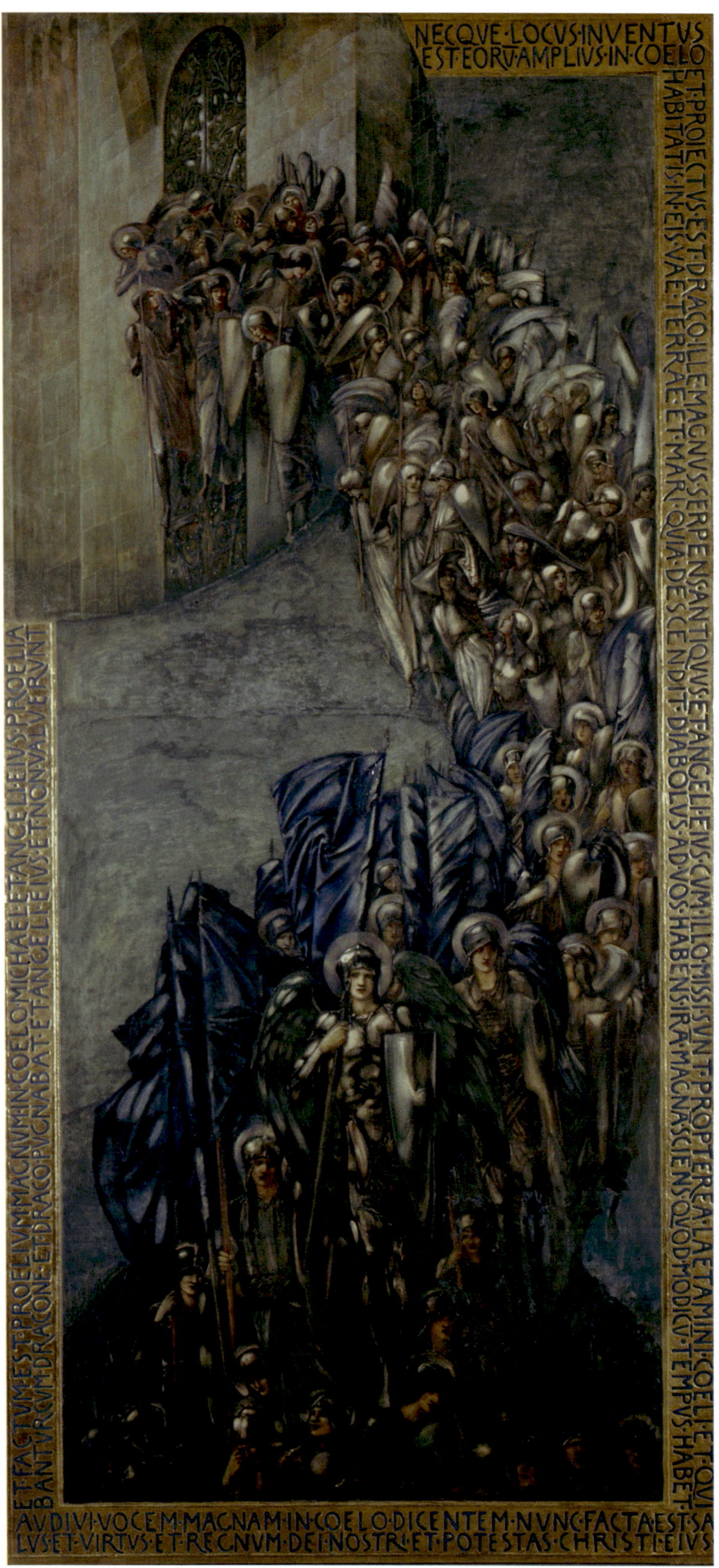

143
Sir Edward Burne-Jones
The Fall of Lucifer 1894
Body colour and gold paint on paper laid down on Canvas and stretched over board, 245 x 118 cm
Private collection of Lord Lloyd-Webber

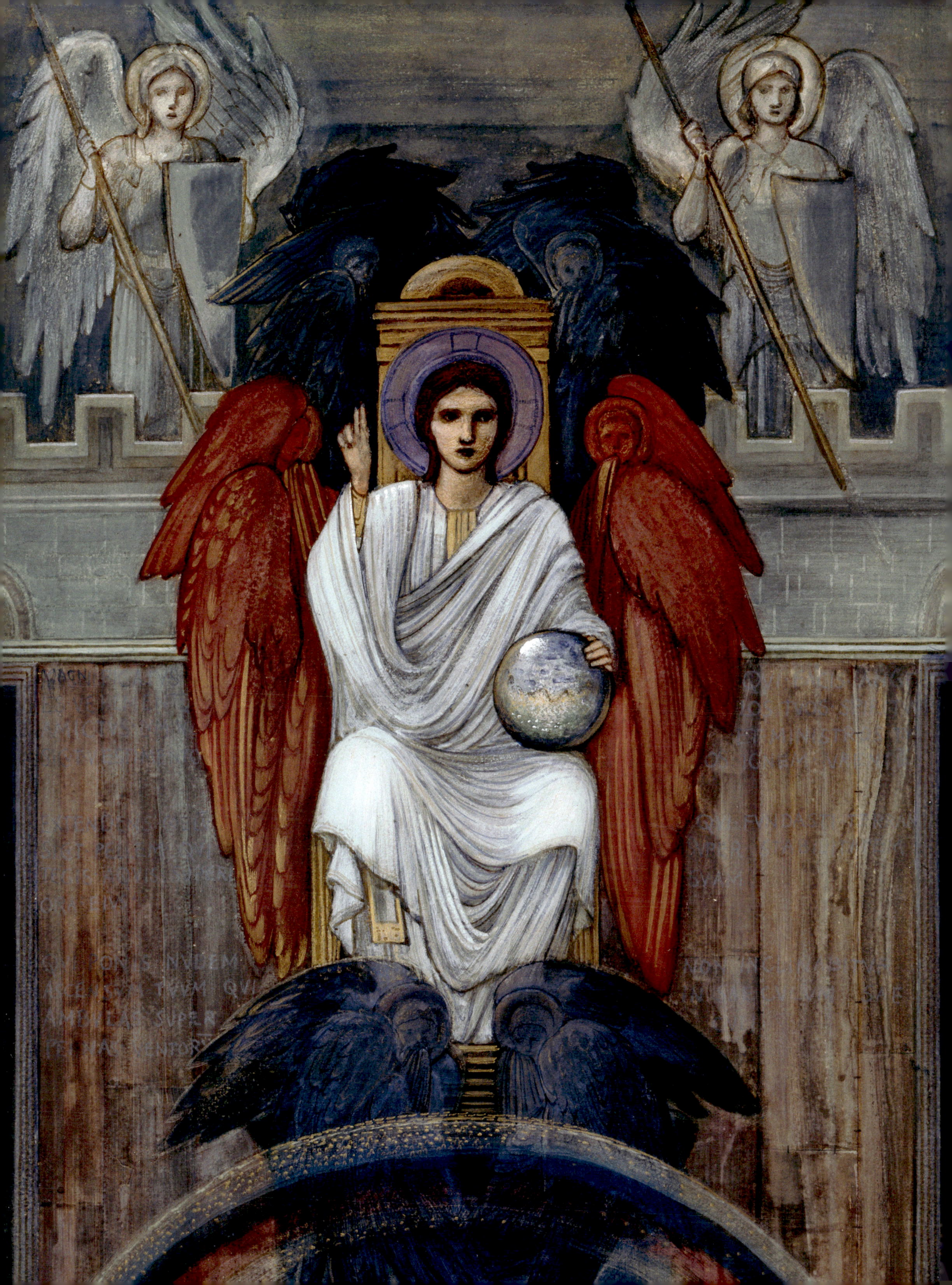

Bibliography

Manuscripts

Crane Journal
Journal of Mary Frances Crane (John Rylands University Library, Manchester; WCA/2/2/2/4)

Lear Diaries
Edward Lear Diaries (MS Eng 797.3). Houghton Library, Harvard University

Published Works

Agresti 1904
Olivia Rossetti Agresti, *Giovanni Costa: His Life, Work and Times* (London, 1904)

Babington 2006
Caroline Babington, *William Dyce and the Pre-Raphaelite Vision* (exh. cat., Aberdeen Art Gallery, 2006)

Baedeker 1867
K. Baedeker, *Handbook for Travellers Part Third: Southern Italy* (Coblenz, 1867)

Baker 1991
Malcolm Baker, '"Proper Ornaments for a Library or Grotto": London Sculptors and their Scottish Patrons in the Eighteenth Century', in *Virtue and Vision: Sculpture and Scotland 1540–1990*, ed. Fiona Pearson (exh. cat., National Gallery of Scotland, 1991), pp. 45–50

Barrington 1906
Mrs Russell Barrington, *Life, Letters & Work of Frederic Leighton*, 2 vols (London, 1906)

Benedetti 1978
Maria Teresa Benedetti, 'I mosaici di Burne-Jones nella chiesa di San Paolo entro le mura di Roma', *Paragone* 29–35 (1978), pp. 40–60

Benedetti and Piantoni 1986
Maria Teresa Benedetti and Gianna Piantoni, *Burne-Jones dal preraffaellismo al simbolismo* (exh. cat., Galleria nazionale d'arte moderna, Rome, 1986)

Boyce 1980
The Diaries of George Price Boyce, ed. Virginia Surtees (Norwich, 1980)

Bradley 1955
Ruskin's Letters from Venice 1851–1852, ed. John Lewis Bradley (New Haven, 1955)

Bronkhurst 1983
Judith Bronkhurst, 'Fruits of a Connoisseur's Friendship: Sir Thomas Fairbairn and William Holman Hunt', *Burlington Magazine* CXXV (1983), pp. 586–95

Bronkhurst 2006
Judith Bronkhurst, *William Holman Hunt: A Catalogue Raisonné*, 2 vols (New Haven and London, 2006)

Bryson and Troxell 1976
Dante Gabriel Rossetti and Jane Morris: Their Correspondence, ed. John Bryson and Janet Camp Troxell (Oxford, 1976)

Bunney 2007
Sarah Bunney, 'John W. Bunney's "Big Picture" of St Mark's, and the Ruskin-Bunney relationship', *Ruskin Review and Bulletin* 4 (2007) pp. 18–47

Burne-Jones 1904
Georgiana Burne-Jones, *Memorials of Edward Burne-Jones*, 2 vols (London, 1904)

Christian 1973
John Christian, 'Burne-Jones's Illustrations to the Story of Buondelmonte', *Master Drawings* 11 (1973), pp. 279–88

Christian 1975
John Christian 'Burne-Jones's Second Italian Journey', *Apollo* 102 (1975), pp.334–7

Clegg 1983
Jeanne Clegg, *John Ruskin* (exh. cat., Arts Council of Great Britain, London, 1983)

Clegg and Tucker 1993
Jeanne Clegg and Paul Tucker, *Ruskin and Tuscany* (exh. cat., Ruskin Gallery, Collection of the Guild of St George, Sheffield, 1993)

Costa 1927
Nino Costa, *Quel che vidi e quel che intesi* (Milan, 1927)

Costantini and Zannier 1986
Paolo Costantini and Italo Zannier, *I Dagherrotipi della collezione Ruskin* (Florence, 1986)

Cox and Ford 2003
Julian Cox and Colin Ford, *Julia Margaret Cameron: The Complete Photographs* (London, 2003)

Crane 1907
Walter Crane, *An Artist's Reminiscences* (London, 1907)

Cruise 2005
Colin Cruise, *Love Revealed: Simeon Solomon and the Pre-Raphaelites* (exh. cat., Birmingham Museum and Art Gallery, 2005)

Dini and Frezzotti 2009
Francesca Dini and Stefania Frezzotti, *Da Corot ai Macchiaioli al Simbolismo – Nino Costa e il Paesaggio dell'anima* (exh. cat., Centro per l'arte Diego Martelli, Castiglioncello, 2009)

Dorment 1978
Richard Dorment, 'Burne-Jones's Roman Mosaics', *Burlington Magazine* CXX (1978), pp. 73–82

Egerton and Newall 1987
Judy Egerton and Christopher Newall, *George Price Boyce* (exh. cat., Tate Gallery, London, 1987)

Fredeman 1975
The PRB Journal, ed. William E. Fredeman (Oxford, 1975)

Fredeman 2002–10
The Correspondence of Dante Gabriel Rossetti, ed. William E. Fredeman, 10 vols (Cambridge, 2002–10)

Garnett 2000
Oliver Garnett, 'The Letters and Collection of William Graham, Pre-Raphaelite Patron and Collector', *The Walpole Society* LXII (2000), pp. 145–343

Hewison 1996
Robert Hewison, *Ruskin and Education: The Art of Education* (exh. cat., Ashmolean Museum, University of Oxford and City Museum and Mappin Art Gallery, Sheffield, 1996)

Hewison 2000
Robert Hewison, Ian Warrell, and Stephen Wildman, *Ruskin, Turner, and the Pre-Raphaelites* (exh. cat., Tate Gallery, London, 2000)

Hunt 1905
William Holman Hunt, *Pre-Raphaelitism and the Pre-Raphaelite Brotherhood*, 2 vols (London, 1905)

Jacks 1917
Lawrence Pearsall Jacks, *Life and Letters of Stopford Brooke*, 2 vols (London, 1917)

Jones 1996
Stephen Jones et al., *Frederic Leighton, 1830–1896* (exh. cat., Royal Academy, London, 1996)

Leith 1996
Royal W. Leith, *A Quiet Devotion: The Life and Work of Henry Roderick Newman* (exh. cat., Jordan-Volpe Gallery, New York, 1996)

Liversidge and Edwards 1996
Michael Liversidge and Catherine Edwards, *Imagining Rome: British Artists and Rome in the Nineteenth Century* (exh. cat., Bristol City Museum and Art Gallery, 1996)

Levi 1995
Peter Levi, *Edward Lear, a Biography* (London, 1995)

London 2003
Pre-Raphaelite and other Masters: The Andrew Lloyd Webber Collection (exh. cat., Royal Academy, London, 2003)

McEvansoneya 1996
Philip McEvansoneya, 'The Cosmopolitan Club Exhibition of 1863: The British salon des refusés', *Re-framing the Pre-Raphaelites: Historical and Theoretical Essays*, ed. Ellen Harding (Aldershot, 1996)

Martineau 1924
Helen Martineau, 'A Pre-Raphaelite Painter', *The Studio* 87 (1924), pp. 207–8

Martineau 1942
Helen Martineau, 'Robert Braithwaite Martineau, a Follower of the Pre-Raphaelites', *The Connoisseur* 90 (1942) pp. 97–101

Millon 2001
Judith Millon, *St Paul's Within the Walls in Rome: A Building History and Guide, 1870–2000*, rev. edn (Rome, 2001)

Morley 1984
Catherine W. Morley, *John Ruskin: Late Work 1870–1890 – The Museum and Guild of St George: An Educational Experiment*, 2 vols in 1 (New York, 1984)

Newall 1989
Christopher Newall, *The Etruscans – Painters of the Italian Landscape 1850–1900* (exh. cat., Stoke on Trent Museum and Art Gallery, 1989)

Newall 1993
Christopher Newall, *John William Inchbold: Pre-Raphaelite Landscape Artist* (exh. cat., Leeds City Art Galleries, 1993)

Newall 2007
'"Val d'Aosta": John Brett and John Ruskin in the Alps, 1853', *Burlington Magazine*, CXLIX (2007), pp. 165–72

Nicholls 1982
Paul Nicholls and Sandra Berresford, *Nino Costa ed i suoi amici inglesi* (exh. cat., Circolo della Stampa, Milan, 1982)

Noel-Paton and Campbell 1990
M.H. Noel-Paton and J.P. Campbell, *Noel Paton, 1821–1901* (Edinburgh, 1990)

Parris 1984
The Pre-Raphaelites, ed. Leslie Parris (exh. cat., Tate Gallery, London, 1984)

Payne 2010
Christiana Payne, *John Brett, Pre-Raphaelite Landscape Painter* (New Haven and London, 2010)

Penny 1988
Nicholas Penny, *Ruskin's Drawings in the Ashmolean Museum* (Oxford, 1988)

Pitman 1988
Joanna Pitman, *Edward Lear's Tennyson* (Manchester, 1988)

Pointon 1975
Marcia Pointon 'W.E. Gladstone as an Art Patron and Collector', *Victorian Studies* XIX (1975), pp. 73–98

Pointon 1979
Marcia Pointon, *William Dyce, 1806–1864: A Critical Biography* (Oxford, 1979)

Read and Barnes 1991
Pre-Raphaelite sculpture: Nature and Imagination in British Sculpture 1848–1914, ed. Benedict Read and Joanna Barnes (London, 1991)

Reynolds 1995
Simon Reynolds, *William Blake Richmond: An Artist's Life 1842–1921* (London, 1995)

Riopelle 1999
Christopher Riopelle and Xavier Bray, *A Brush with Nature: The Gere Collection of Landscape Sketches* (exh. cat., National Gallery, London, 1999)

Roberts and Wildman 1997
Leonard Roberts and Stephen Wildman, *Arthur Hughes, His Life and Work* (Woodbridge, 1997)

Rooke 1981
Burne-Jones Talking: His Conversations 1895–1898 Preserved by his Studio Assistant Thomas Rooke, ed. Mary Lago (London, 1981)

Ruskin 1903–12
The Works of John Ruskin, ed. E.T. Cook and Alexander Wedderburn, 39 vols (London, 1903–12)

Ruskin 1956
The Diaries of John Ruskin, ed. Joan Evans and John Howard Whitehouse, 3 vols (Oxford, 1956)

Shapiro 1972
Ruskin in Italy: Letters to his Parents 1845, ed. Harold I. Shapiro, London, 1972

Smith and Hyde 1989
Greg Smith and Sarah Hyde, *Walter Crane 1845–1915: Artist, Designer, and Socialist* (exh. cat., Whitworth Art Gallery, Manchester, 1989)

Sponza 1988
Lucio Sponza, *Italian Immigrants in Nineteenth-Century Britain: Realities and Images* (Leicester 1988)

Staley and Newall 2004
Allen Staley and Christopher Newall, *Pre-Raphaelite Vision: Truth to Nature* (exh. cat., Tate Britain, 2004)

Stirling 1926
A.M.W. Stirling, *The Richmond Papers – From the Correspondence and Manuscripts of George Richmond, R.A., and his Son Sir William Richmond, R.A., K.C.B.* (London, 1926)

Strachey 1907
Letters of Edward Lear, ed. Lady Strachey (London, 1907)

Strachey 1911
Later Letters of Edward Lear, ed. Lady Strachey (London, 1911)

Surtees 1971
Virginia Surtees, *The Paintings and Drawings of Dante Gabriel Rossetti (1828–1882): A Catalogue Raisonné*, 2 vols (Oxford, 1971)

Taylor and Wakeling 2002
Roger Taylor and Edward Wakeling, *Lewis Carroll, Photographer: The Princeton University Library Albums* (Princeton, 2002)

Treuherz 2002
Julian Treuherz, 'Edward Lear in Syracuse', *Burlington Magazine* CXLIV (2002), pp. 532–8

Treuherz 2003
Julian Treuherz et al., *Dante Gabriel Rossetti* (exh. cat., Walker Art Gallery, Liverpool and Van Gogh Museum, Amsterdam, 2003–4)

Wildman 1995
Stephen Wildman, *Visions of Love and Life: Pre-Raphaelite Art from Birmingham Museums and Art Gallery* (exh. cat., 1995)

Wildman and Christian 1998
Stephen Wildman and John Christian, *Edward Burne-Jones, Victorian Artist-Dreamer* (exh. cat., Met. Mus. New York, Birmingham Museums and Art Gallery, Musée d'Orsay, Paris, 1998–9)

Wilton 1979
Andrew Wilton, *The Life and Work of J.M.W. Turner* (London, 1979)

Index of works

Bold figures indicate main illustrated catalogue entries; *italic* figures refer to other illustrations.

Boyce, George Price:

Near the Public Gardens, Venice **94–5**

St Mark's, Venice: South-west Angle 7, **93**

San Giorgio Maggiore from the Piazzetta, Venice - Moonlight **94–5**

Tomb of Mastino II della Scala **96**

Brett, John:

Capri in the Evening **108**

Florence from Bellosguardo **106–7**

Massa, Bay of Naples 108

Near Sorrento 108

A North-west Squall in the Mediterranean 108

The Ponte Vecchio, Florence **103**

Val d'Aosta 2, 7, *7*, **104–5**

Bunney, John Wharlton:

Castelbarco Tomb, Verona 5, 6, **110**

Ponte alle Grazie, Florence **109**

Burgess, Arthur:

Owl, Copied from a Photograph of Mantegna's Fresco of 'The Martyrdom of Saint James' in the Church of Eremitani, Padua **112**

Sculpted Moulding on Tomb of Mastino II della Scala 5, 6, **111**

Burne-Jones, Sir Edward:

The Annunciation *198*, 201–2, **204**

The Archangel Zophiel 199, **206**

Beatrice 33

Buondelmente's Wedding *32*, 33, **59–61**

Christ enthroned 199, **205**

Copies after Bernardino Luini's 'Saint Apollonia' and 'Saint Agatha' *17*, 18, **100–101**

Copy after the 'Allegory of the Battle of Lepanto' by Paolo Veronese *17*, 18, **97**

Copy after Tintoretto's 'The Circumcision' *17*, 18, **99**

A Dream of Nine Muses **102**

The Earthly Paradise 202

The Fall of Lucifer 201, **210**

Gabriel, Angel of the Annunciation 199, **208**

Gualdrada Donati presenting her Daughter to Buondelmonte *32*, **59–61**

Music **196**

Phyllis and Demophoön 18, 98, 194

Study for 'The Annunciation' 8, 199, **200**, 201, 202

Study for 'The Earthly Paradise' 202, **203**

Study for 'The Heavenly Jerusalem' 199, **201**

Study for 'The Meeting of Buondelmonte and Ciulla' 33, **59–61**

Study of Tintoretto's 'Saint Sebastian' in the Scuola Grande di San Rocco *17*, 18, **98**

The Tree of Life 201, 202, **209**

Troy Triptych 18, *18*, 194

Uriel, Archangel of the Sun 199, **207**

Venus Concordia **194–5**

Venus Discordia **194–5**

The Wine of Circe 98

Collingwood, William Gershom:

The Head of Ilaria del Carretto, from the Tomb Sculpture by Jacopo della Quercia **118**

Collins, Charles Alston:

Convent Thoughts 16, *16*

Corbet, Matthew Ridley:

From Volterra, Looking towards the Pisan Hills **179**

Montecelio from the Villa d'Este, Tivoli **171**

Costa, Giovanni:

After a Shower near Pisa **180**

The Faraglioni Rocks, Capri - An October Morning **167**

Porto d'Anzio **157**

Ruins in the Alban Hills **158–9**

The Salt-stealer 167

Scirocco Day 169

They Sleep by Day to Fish by Night **156**

A View of Monte Amiata, Tuscany **170**

Women Stealing Wood on the Shore near Ardea on an Evening when the Libeccio blows 156

Crane, Walter:

Cava dei Terreni **151**

The Grave of Keats **149**, 168

The Grave of Shelley **148**, 168

An Italian Villa **152–3**

The Renaissance of Venus 18

Vietri on the Gulf of Salerno, from Cava dei Terreni **150**

Dyce, William:

Francesca de Rimini 22, *23*, **44**

The Meeting of Jacob and Rachel **62**

Titian's First Essay in Colour 184

Harding, James Duffield:

View of San Giorgio from the Grand Canal *5*

Holiday, Henry:

Dante and Beatrice 33

Dante Meeting Beatrice as Children 33

Howard, George, 9th Earl of Carlisle:

The Baths of Caracalla, Rome **172–3**

Bocca d'Arno 177

The Fort at Bocca d'Arno **176–7**

Keats's Grave in the Protestant Cemetery, Rome **168**

The Maries at the Sepulchre **129**

Terraces near Amalfi with Rustics working in the Foreground **181**

A View within the Baths of Caracalla, Rome **174**

Hughes, Arthur:

That was a Piedmontese **63**

Hunt, William Holman:

Caught! **137**

A Converted British Family Sheltering a Christian Missionary from the Persecution of the Druids 14, *14*

Il Dolce far Niente *182*, **193**

A Festa at Fiesole **133**

Interior of the Cathedral at Salerno **134**

Isabella and the Pot of Basil 33, 132

An Italian Child **136–7**

Lorenzo at his Warehouse 33

Madeleine and Porphyro 13

May Morning on Magdalen Tower 20, *20*

Moonlight at Salerno 134

Past and Present **135**, 141

Il Ponte Vecchio, Florence **132**

Rienzi 13–14, *13*, 43, 131

Inchbold, John William:

The Green Horses of St Mark's 142

Inundation at St Mark's **144**

On the Lagoon, Venice 7, *7*, 77, **143**

The Redentore, Venice 143

Venice, Nocturne: San Giorgio Maggiore 144

Vesuvius and the Bay of Naples from Posilippo **145**

Vesuvius from Virgil's Tomb 145

Keene, Charles Samuel:

Portrait of Dante Gabriel Rossetti *4*

Lear, Edward:

Florence from the Villa San Firenze **138–9**

The Plains of Lombardy from Monte Generoso **140**

Leighton, Frederic:

A Byzantine Well-head **92**

Cimabue's Celebrated Madonna is Carried in Procession through the Streets of Florence 19, *19*, 184

Monte Croce 19, *19*

Staircase of a House at Capri **162–3**

A Street Scene at Capri 162, **164**

Study of a Lemon Tree 92, 162

View in Capri 162, **166**

The Villa Malta 9, **165**

Martineau, Robert Braithwaite:

The Knight's Guerdon 141

A Woman of San Germano *130*, 135, **141**

Mason, George Heming:

Italian Peasant Women in the Campagna Driving an Ox **161**

Ploughing in the Campagna 161

Villa Borghese 8, **160**

Millais, John Everett:

Christ in the House of his Parents 14

Cymon and Iphigeneia 33

The Death of Romeo and Juliet 13

Errant Knight 34

Isabella 13, *13*, 33

The Woodman's Daughter 58

Munro, Alexander:

Dante (attrib.) **47**

Paolo and Francesca 22, *23*, **46**, 52

Newman, Henry Roderick:

The Baptistery of San Giovanni, Florence **117**

The Façade of the Duomo, Lucca *90*, **126**, 128

Lagoon at Venice 114

San Martino, Lucca **128**

South Door of the Duomo, Florence **116**

The Three Arches of Santa Maria Novella, Florence **113–15**, 127

Paton, Sir Joseph Noel:

Dante Meditating the Episode of Francesca da Rimini ad Paulo Malatesta 22, *23*, **45**

The Dead Lady 45

The Death of Paolo and Francesca 13, 45

Paolo and Francesca - Inferno 43

Randal, Frank:

Angle of the Choir and Transept, Santa Maria Maggiore, Bergamo *41*, **123**

Mosaic Roundels of Sts Bartholomew and Matthew at San Vitale, Ravenna **120**

Mosaic of St Luke at San Vitale, Ravenna **120–21**

The North Porch of San Fermo Maggiore, Verona 5, *6*, **122**

The Passo del Fo, Lecco **125**

The Resegone of Lecco 6.30 p.m. **124**

Richmond, William Blake:

Near Viareggio, where Shelley's Body was Found **169**, 178

The Plains of Tuscany from Volterra *154*, **178**

The Sea, Bocca d'Arno **175**

Rooke, Thomas Matthews:

Drawing of Mosaics in the Vault of the Chancel of San Vitale, Ravenna **119**

Three Tombs beside Santa Maria Novella, Florence **127**

Rossetti, Dante Gabriel:

Aurelia (Fazio's Mistress) 30, *30*, **186**, 187

Beata Beatrix 25, *25*, **197**

Beatrice Meeting Dante at a Marriage Feast, Denies him her Salutation 24, *24*, **55**

The Boat of Love 28, *28*, **191**

Bocca Baciata 3, 29, *29*, 183, 186, 193, 197

The Borgia Family 29, *30*, **57**

Dante at Verona 28

Dante Drawing an Angel on the Anniversary of Beatrice's Death 16, *16*, 23, 26, *42*, **50**

Dante's Dream 56, 190

Dante's Dream at the Time of the Death of Beatrice 24, *25*, **56**

Dante's Vision of Matilda Gathering Flowers 27, *27*, 51, **54**

Dante's Vision of Rachel and Leah 26–7, *27*, **51**, 53

Dantis Amor 19, *20*, 25, **185**

La Donna della Fiamma 25, 26

La Donna della Finestra ii, 25, 31, **189**

Ecce Ancilla Domini 14

Elizabeth Siddal 24, *24*

Fazio's Mistress (Aurelia) 30, *30*, **186**, 187

Fra Angelico Painting 15, *15*, **49**, 184

Fra Pace 43

Giorgione Painting 15, *15*, **49**, 184

Giotto Painting the Portrait of Dante 23–4, 31

Lady Pietra degli Scrovigni 28–9

Lucrezia Borgia 29

Monna Vanna 35, **187**

Paolo and Francesca de Rimini 27, *27*, 52, **53**

Perlascura 25–6, *26*, **192**

La Pia de' Tolomei 26, *26*, 27–8, 188

Portrait of Fanny Cornforth 29, *29*

Portrait of John Ruskin 5

The Salutation of Beatrice 25

The Salutation of Beatrice on Earth 185

The Salutation of Beatrice in Eden 26

The Salutation of Beatrice in Heaven 185

Study of Dante for 'Dante's Dream' **190**

Study for 'Giotto Painting the Portrait of Dante' 15, *15*, **48**, 184

Study for 'Paolo and Francesca da Rimini' **52**

Study for 'La Pia de' Tolomei' 28, **188**

A Vision of Fiammetta 30

Ruskin, John:

The Baptistery, Florence: Study of the Upper Part of the Right-hand Compartment on the South-west Façade 64, **80–81**, 117

Copy after the Central Portion of Tintoretto's 'The Crucifixion' in the Scuola Grande di San Rocco, Venice **69**

Drawing of Abraham Parting from the Angels from Benozzo Gozzoli's 'Story of Abraham and Hagar' in the Camposanto, Pisa **66**

Drawing of Carpaccio's 'Dream of St Ursula' from 'The Legend of St Ursula' **86–7**

Drawing of Tintoretto's 'Circumcision' in the Scuola Grande di San Rocco, Venice **84**

The Duomo of San Martino, Lucca **86**, 128

The Gryphon bearing the North Shaft of the West Entrance of the Duomo, Verona **76**

Head of St Ursula, from Carpaccio's 'Dream of St Ursula' **88**

Part of the Façade of the Destroyed Church of San Michele in Foro, Lucca **68**

Pencil Outline of a Part of the Fresco of 'The Friends of Job' in the Camposanto, Pisa, Attributed to Taddeo Gaddi **67**

The South Side of the Basilica of St Mark's, Venice, from the Loggia of the Doge's Palace **72**, *79*, 93

Study of the Child in Tintoretto's 'The Circumcision' in the Scuola Grande di San Rocco, Venice **85**

Study for Detail of the Sarcophagus and Canopy of the Tomb of Mastino II della Scala at Verona **73**

Study for the General Chiaroscuro of the Sarcophagus and Canopy of the Tomb of Mastino II della Scala at Verona **74**

Study of a Panel of the Font, Baptistery, Pisa **78**

Study of Tomb of Can Grande della Scala at Verona **75**

Study of Verbena in Carpaccio's 'Dream of St Ursula' **89**

The Tomb of Frederick II in the Cathedral of Palermo **82**

Tomb of Ilaria del Carretto in the Duomo of San Martino, Lucca **83**, 86, 118

View from the Palazzo Bembo to the Palazzo Grimani, Venice **77**

Six daguerrotypes of architectural subjects **70–71**

Scott, William Bell:

Keats's Grave in the Old Protestant Cemetery at Rome **147**

Shelley's Grave in the New Protestant Cemetery at Rome **146**, 148

Upper Portion of the Façade of St Mark's, Venice vi, **142**

Solomon, Simeon:

Dante's First Meeting with Beatrice 33, *33*, **58**

The Painter's Pleasaunce **184**

Stillman, Marie Spartali:

Dante at Verona 33

Dante and Beatrice 33

The Enchanted Garden of Messer Ansaldo 34

Fiammetta Singing 33–4

First Meeting of Petrarch and Laura in the Church of Santa Chiara at Avignon 34

Madonna Pietra degli Scrovigni 33

May Feast at the House of Folco Portinari 33

A Rose from Armida's Garden 34

Waterhouse, John:

A Tale from the Decameron 34

Image credits

Aberdeen Art Gallery and Museums Collection

Archivio Araldo De Luca, Rome

Birmingham Museums and Art Gallery

Bradford Art Galleries and Museums

Bridgeman Art Library

The Trustees of the British Museum

Bury Art Gallery, Museums and Archives

The Castle Howard Collection

The Syndics of the Fitzwilliam Museum, Cambridge

The Mistress and Fellows of Girton College, Cambridge

Leeds Museums and Galleries

Manchester City Art Galleries

Museum of Fine Arts, Boston, Massachusetts

Museums Sheffield

National Gallery, London

The National Galleries of Scotland, Edinburgh

National Museums Liverpool

Nevill Keating Pictures

Pisa, Opera Primaziale Pisana

Royal Collection

Royal Institution of Cornwall, Royal Museum of Cornwall, Truro

Ruskin Foundation (Ruskin Library, University of Lancaster)

Spencer Museum of Art, University of Kansas

St Pauls within the Walls, Rome

Tate, London 2010

Todd White Art Photography

UK Government Art Collection

Victoria and Albert Museum, London

Whitworth Art Gallery, University of Manchester

W/S Fine Art